THE PHYSIOLOGY OF FAITH AND FEAR

OR

THE MIND IN HEALTH AND DISEASE

BY

WILLIAM S. SADLER, M. D.

PROFESSOR OF PHYSIOLOGIC THERAPEUTICS, THE POST-GRADUATE MEDICAL
SCHOOL OF CHICAGO; DIRECTOR OF THE CHICAGO INSTITUTE OF
PHYSIOLOGIC THERAPEUTICS; MEMBER OF THE ILLINOIS STATE
MEDICAL SOCIETY; THE AMERICAN MEDICAL ASSOCIA-
TION; THE AMERICAN ASSOCIATION FOR THE
ADVANCEMENT OF SCIENCE, ETC., ETC.

AUTHOR OF "THE SCIENCE OF LIVING, OR, THE ART OF KEEPING WELL,"
"THE CAUSE AND CURE OF COLDS," ETC.

ILLUSTRATED

ISBN: 979-8-89096-090-0

All Rights reserved. No part of this book maybe reproduced without written permission from the publishers, except by a reviewer who may quote brief passages in a review to be printed in a newspaper or magazine.

Printed: June 2023

Published and Distributed By:
Lushena Books
607 Country Club Drive, Unit E
Bensenville, IL 60106
www.lushenabks.com

ISBN: 979-8-89096-090-0

TO
ALL WHO WORRY;
TO THE VICTIMS OF FEAR,
MORAL DESPAIR, AND OTHER MENTAL MALADIES;
TO THOSE WHO ARE SEEKING TO KNOW THE TRUTH CONCERNING
THE POWER OF MIND OVER MATTER; AND ALSO TO
THOSE MENTAL SUFFERERS WHO HAVE BEEN
DECEIVED AND DELUDED BY FALSE
SYSTEMS OF MENTAL HEALING;
THIS BOOK IS AFFECTION-
ATELY DEDICATED.

PREFACE

IN recent years we have been literally deluged with literature on "Suggestion," "Mental Healing," "Hypnotism," "Psychotherapy," psychic fads, and various healing "isms," not to mention "New Thought," "Christian Science," and other systems of religious teaching. It would seem as if doctor, preacher, and layman were now vying with one another in an effort to atone for their past indifference to, and neglect of, the important subjects, Mental Healing and Moral Therapeutics.

We are now passing through a period of popular reaction against the scientific materialism of the last century. The common people are awaking to the fact that the mental state has much to do with bodily health and disease. The bookmakers, in their efforts to satisfy the universal demand for teaching on various phases of mental healing, have flooded us with literature, much of which is premature, unscientific, incomplete, and highly disastrous in its misleading influence upon the popular mind and morals.

It is to be deplored that practically every system of modern mental healing has declared as the secret of its success its association with some creed or cult — claiming that physical healing was dependent upon the acceptance of some particular moral teaching or system of religious belief. At the very outset we desire to *separate the study of mental healing from any and all particular brands of religion* — not from religion as a state of mind, but from any particular system, sect, or form of religious belief.

We approach the subject of mental healing from the standpoint of the physician — the physiologist. We examine all claims and apparent cures from the standpoint of actual experiments, clinical observations, and laboratory investigations which the author and numerous others have carried on for the purpose of discovering the real facts respecting the effect of the various mental states on the human body. In other words, how does the state of mind affect the bodily functions in health and disease? This story will be told in everyday English — divested of all scientific technicalities and laboratory terminology. The practical results of this highly technical work will be given in such simple language that a schoolboy may fully understand the narrative and comprehend the conclusions.

The author was long since convinced of the existence of certain universal laws of psychology and physiology which would serve fully to explain the vast majority of supposed mysterious and many of the so-called miraculous cases of recovery from disease. The application of the precise methods of modern science in the physiological and psychological laboratories has resulted in developing, step by step, the physiological basis which makes plain the working of this *universal law of mental healing.* This volume is devoted to telling the story of the laws of moral medicine and mental therapeutics — the Physiology of Faith and Fear.

Although it is found necessary in the discussion of this subject, frequently to refer to religion and so-called divine healing, we desire to make it plain that we are not here considering the validity or authenticity of so-called genuine miraculous acts, whether of Biblical or subsequent occurrence. We disclaim all intention to discuss the question of miracles from any possible standpoint. We only desire to discuss mental healing as effected by certain mental and physical laws, discoverable by clinical observation and laboratory experimentation. In no sense do we undertake the consideration of supernatural occurrences or so-called divine acts in connection with the restoration of health or the healing of disease.

In the preparation of this volume, the author has made careful research in the literature touching on every phase of the many subjects considered. For this purpose he has had recourse not only to his own library, but to the various libraries of Chicago and the great Congressional Library at Washington,

D. C. In a work of this kind, designed for laymen, and where brevity is so essential, direct quotations have been avoided, although the leading authorities in physiology and psychology have been drawn upon for material in the preparation of this work and the various lectures which preceded it.

We desire not only to call attention to the power of the mind over the body, but also to point out the equally neglected truth of the vast influence of the body over the mind; more particularly the influence of the diseased or disordered physical body on the mental state and the moral tendencies.

The practising physician is compelled to recognize that in many instances it is the disordered physical health which is to blame for the depressed mental state; and so the vicious circle widens — disorders of either mind or body react the one upon the other, each ever tending to make the other worse, until such a time as the body recovers its equilibrium of health, or the mind regains its lost mastery of the feelings and emotions.

This work is based largely upon the author's lectures on psychotherapy delivered in connection with his clinic at the Post-Graduate Medical School of Chicago, while much of the material is drawn from his Chautauqua lectures, "Worry and its Mental Cousins," "The Psychology of Faith and Fear," "The Physiology of Faith and Fear," "The Bible on Faith and Fear," "The Humbugs of Healing," and "The Moral Management of Mental Maladies."

It is evident that the common people are becoming terribly confused in their efforts to ascertain the truth about mental healing, and it was with the hope of providing a guide-book of reliable principles, trustworthy observations, and scientific conclusions, that we began the work of collecting and arranging the data; of classifying observations and experiences; and of further conducting the necessary experiments, which have resulted in the formation of the final conclusions herein expressed.

The author disclaims all pretensions of being a psychologist; but it was not possible to approach the physiological discussions of mental healing without some preliminary psychologic considerations. He has endeavored to remain within the field of physiological psychology, and this may explain the apparent incompleteness which may be observed in certain sections.

The author desires to acknowledge his indebtedness to Prof. Robert H. Gault, Ph. D., of Northwestern University, for his painstaking examination of those chapters dealing with the psychological phase of our subject, and for his many helpful suggestions and valuable criticisms. He is also greatly indebted to Prof. Winfield S. Hall, A. M., Ph. D., M. D., head of the Department of Physiology in the Northwestern University Medical School, for his careful review of the chapters dealing especially with the physiological aspects of faith and fear, and for numerous other valuable suggestions.

It should not be supposed that we recognize only mental causes for the many physical ailments dealt with. We freely grant that numerous influences outside of the psychic realm are capable of producing disease, but it is not possible herein fully to discuss *all* the manifold causes of disease, and this work is devoted to the consideration of the *mind* in health and disease. We also recognize that psychotherapy is not the only mode of treating human ailments. Psychic influences in the cause, cure, and prevention of disease are emphasized in this work because they have been neglected and belittled in the past, and not for the purpose of creating an exclusive system for their use.

Our one purpose is to tell the story of how the mind affects the body and its various functions in health and disease; how the fundamental mental states of *faith* and *fear* make for or against health. If we shall be able to convince the reader that fear is a generator of mental poisons, and worry a corroding canker — ever tending to destroy the mind and produce disease; if we have succeeded in glorifying *faith* and its moral attributes as the mental emancipator from the bondage of doubt and mind disease — this volume will have met fully the most sanguine expectations of the author.

WILLIAM S. SADLER.

32 N. STATE STREET, CHICAGO
January 1, 1912.

CONTENTS

PAGE

Introduction xvii

PART I — PSYCHOLOGIC SECTION

CHAPTER
I Mind and Matter 3
II Brain, Mind, and Personality 15
III How the Mind is Influenced by Bodily States 21
IV Psychology — How We Think . . . 35
V Key to Diagram of Psychology . . . 52
VI The Supreme Court of the Mind . . . 56
VII Phases of Consciousness 64
VIII Superstition as Related to Health and Disease 78
IX The Psychology of Faith and Fear . . 92
X Faith the Master Key to Mental Medicine . 106

PART II — PHYSIOLOGIC SECTION

XI How the Emotions Affect the Heart . . 113
XII Influence of the Mind upon the Circulatory System 122
XIII The Blood-Pressure as Modified by Psychic Influences 131
XIV Influence of the Mental State upon the Vital Resistance 143
XV The Mind as Concerned in the Action of the Secretory Glands 153
XVI The Mental Influences Concerned in Digestion 161
XVII The Psychic Factor in Nutrition and Metabolism 173
XVIII The Influence of the Mind on Respiration . 186

CONTENTS

XIX	How the Mental State Affects the Muscles .	198
XX	The Influence of the Mind on the Skin and the Heat-Regulating Mechanism . .	209
XXI	The Effect of the Mental State upon the Physical Brain	220
XXII	The Effect of the Mind and the Emotions on the Nervous System	229
XXIII	The Influence of the Mental State on the Behavior of the Special Senses . . .	241

PART III — THERAPEUTIC SECTION

XXIV	The Dawn of Scientific Healing . . .	253
XXV	Psycho-Prophylaxis, or Mental Hygiene .	266
XXVI	The Psychic Element in Heredity and Environment	276
XXVII	The Psychology of Disease	289
XXVIII	The Psychic Element in the Cause and Cure of Disease	300
XXIX	Mental Medicine and Moral Hygiene . .	311
XXX	The Bible on Faith and Fear . . .	321
XXXI	The Physiology and Psychology of Habit .	338
XXXII	The Nature and Cause of Worry . . .	349
XXXIII	The Cure of Worry	371
XXXIV	Nervousness and Relaxation	387
XXXV	The Principles of Modern Psychotherapy .	405
XXXVI	The Science of Suggestion	427
XXXVII	The Reëducation of the Will	443
XXXVIII	Psychic Fads and Fakes	457
XXXIX	Prayer the Master Mind Cure . . .	476
XL	The Emancipated Life	493
	Appendix A: Anatomy and Physiology of the Brain and Nervous System . . .	505
	Appendix B: A Case of Chronological Memory	518
	Appendix C: Multiple Personality . .	524
	Index	535

LIST OF PLATES

FIGURE		PAGE
1	Special Brain Centres	xviii
2	Diagram Showing Different Nerve Paths	xx
3	The Nervous System and the Nerves	4
4	Energy Granules of Nerve Cells	24
5	Diagram Showing the Fibrillar Network of the Nerve Cells	24
7	A Cretin Child	32
8	Diagrams Illustrating Optical Illusions	38
9	Diagram of Psychology, Illustrating the Action of the Mind in the Elaboration of Thought	50
10	Diagram Illustrating Phases of Consciousness	66
11	Diagram Illustrating the Central and the Marginal Consciousnesses	68
12	Diagram Illustrating the Three Planes of Consciousness — Conscience, Reason, and Instinct	70
13	Diagram Showing the Relation of the Physical Instincts and the Spiritual Emotions to the Intellectual Consciousness, Also a Comparison of the Central and the Marginal Consciousnesses	72
14	The Relation of the Parts of the Human Body to the Signs of the Zodiac	86
15	Diagram Showing Ancient and Modern Faith Generators and Fear Destroyers	100
16	Balancing Experiment: Subject Executing Problems in Mental Arithmetic	126
17	Balancing Experiment: Subject Thinking Intently and Continuously of the Feet	126
18	Normal Pulse of the "Faith Heart"	128
19	Pulse Tracing of the "Fear Heart"	128
20	The Heart and Circulation of the Blood	132

LIST OF PLATES

21	The Muscles Concerned in Swallowing and the Taste Buds	154
22	Diagram Illustrating the Pawlow Stomach . .	166
23	Graphic Tracing of the Respiratory Curve . .	196
24	A Modern Physiological Laboratory for Investigating Disease	260
25	A Modern Psychological Laboratory for the Study of the Mind	260
26	Diagrams Illustrating Right and Wrong Breathing	272
27	An Ancient Physician-Priest	312
30	Woman with a Spirit of Infirmity	326
28	Common Motor Obsessions	342
29	A Chronic Kicker	354
31	Vacations Destroy Worry	380
32	Right and Wrong Ways to Ride on the Train . .	400
33	The Work Cure for Neurasthenia	422
34	The Study Cure for Nervous Disorders . . .	422
35	Suggestive Panic	430
36	Will Power and Character	452
37	Charms, Relics, and Shrines	458
38	Astrology and Palmistry	458
39	A Phrenological Chart of Human Destiny . .	460
40	Crystal Gazing and Shell Hearing	462
41	Trance and Catalepsy	462
42	The Practice of Old-Fashioned Prayer . . .	478
43	Right and Wrong Social Tendencies . . .	494
6	The Sympathetic Nervous System	513

THE PHYSIOLOGY OF FAITH AND FEAR

INTRODUCTION

THE HUMAN BRAIN.— THE NERVOUS REFLEXES.— THE VOLUNTARY NERVOUS SYSTEM.— THE SYMPATHETIC NERVOUS SYSTEM. — THE PHYSICAL BASIS OF THOUGHT.

THE brain and nervous system represent the highest physical development of the material body. The nervous system is the instrumentality by which mind influences matter, and through which matter impresses mind. The brain is not only the citadel of the will, reason, judgment, and choice, but it is also the sanctuary of the soul — of the moral nature. It is the abiding place of conscience, and the home of the spiritual emotions.

THE HUMAN BRAIN

It is highly essential in the study of mental hygiene, that one should have a practical knowledge of the form and function of the brain and nervous system. The human brain consists of three parts: the *cerebrum* or fore brain, the *cerebellum* or hind brain, and the *medulla oblongata.* The brain substance consists of the cell bodies of untold thousands of little nerve cells with their numerous nerve processes or fibres.

The motor centres are found on the outside and superficial portions near the middle of the brain, while the intellectual centres are over to the front. There are well-defined special brain centres for writing, seeing, hearing, walking, talking, etc. (See Fig. 1.) The nerves passing to and from the brain are either sensory or motor.

The *basal ganglia* at the base of the brain have to do with the regulation of many special functions. They serve as sort of middlemen, or private secretaries, to the brain centres. When certain physical acts, such as walking or writing, are frequently performed, the basal ganglia acquire the ability to carry on these habitual movements without taxing the higher brain centres, it being only necessary to start the process by orders from the mind.

For a more complete and detailed consideration of the anatomy and physiology of the brain and nervous system, the reader is referred to Appendix A.

THE NERVOUS REFLEXES

The *spinal cord* is really a downward continuation of the medulla. It gives out thirty-one pairs of nerves, which contain both sensory and motor fibres. Each spinal nerve has two roots — the anterior or motor, and the posterior or sensory. The spinal ganglion is located on the posterior root, and is a sort of relay station.

The twelve cranial nerves are largely concerned with the special senses, except the tenth, or pneumogastric *(vagus),* which is the most widely distributed and most influential nerve in the body.

Reflex action is the short-cut passage of nerve impulses through the spine or the medulla, whereby sensations provoke motor responses without the action or knowledge of the higher conscious brain centres.

This explains how we can close the eye without thinking, and why we cough to remove mucus from the throat, sneeze to throw irritating substances out of the nose, and vomit to empty the stomach when nauseated.

Nerve impressions from the skin or other organs of special sensation (See diagram — Fig. 2.) may excite a muscle or group of muscles to action in different ways. The sensory impulses may pass up the spinal cord to the conscious sensory centres of the cerebrum over the long circuit, and excite to action the conscious motor centres of the upper brain.

The majority of common and habitual nerve impressions do not travel this long circuit, they go by the automatic or *short circuit* to the basal ganglia, where they are received, and set in motion the motor nerves going down from the brain to the muscles, just as effectually as if the impulses had been carried to the conscious brain centres.

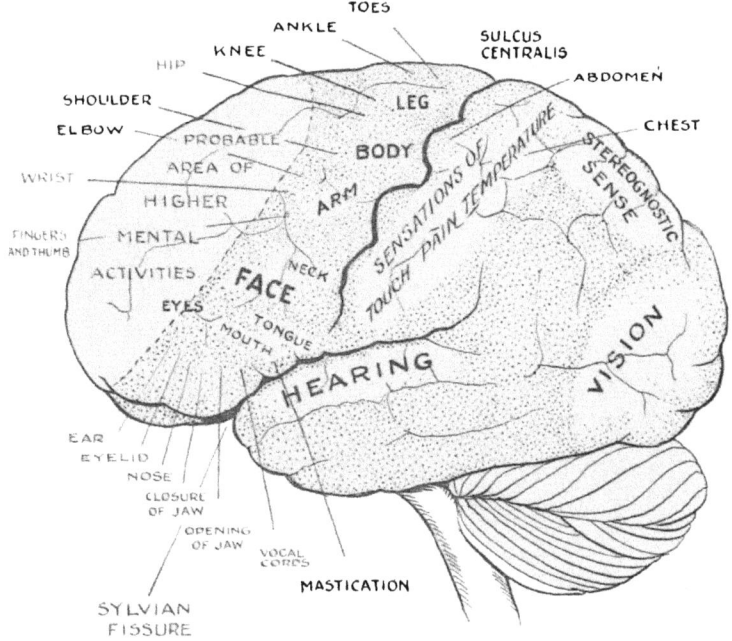

FIG. I.
SPECIAL BRAIN CENTRES

INTRODUCTION

Again, we possess certain *natural reflexes*, reflexes associated with breathing, the circulation, etc., whose sensory impulses are transferred to the motor nerves in the medulla. The cerebellum contains reflex centres which regulate posture and equilibrium.

Lastly, we have the *involuntary spinal reflex centres* previously mentioned. A study of the diagram (Fig. 2.) will make these various nerve paths perfectly plain. (A more complete consideration of this diagram will be found under the head "Reflex Action," in Appendix A.)

THE VOLUNTARY NERVOUS SYSTEM

The nervous system is in reality a continuation or extension of the brain and spinal cord, and is composed of individual units or neurons. The *neuron* consists of a cell body and its processes or branches. Every neuron possesses one branch for transmitting outgoing impulses. This branch is called the axone, neuraxone, or neurite. Most neurons possess one or more branches which bring afferent impulses toward the cell body. These afferent branches are called dendrites. Sensory impressions received by the sensory nerve-endings in the skin are transmitted over afferent fibres to the cells in the posterior root ganglion of the spinal cord; thence by way of the axonic branch into the spinal cord, where they may be transmitted either to a spinal motor neuron to form the reflex arc, or transmitted through sensory tracts to the sensory centres of the brain. (See Fig. 3.)

The nerves transmit impulses by means of neuricity — an energy resembling electricity. Nerves do not transmit messages as a dead wire does electricity. Time is required for the cell to receive and despatch impulses.

Energy granules appear in the rested neuron, but gradually disappear when the nerve is made to do work. These energy granules are thought by some to be chemical in nature, but they are probably electrical. (See Fig. 4.)

It would seem that the nerve cells during rest and sleep actually accumulate energy, and these little, sand-like granules might fittingly be compared to a minute storage battery or to a chemical powder, the explosion of which generates waves of nerve or electrical energy, which flash over its branches carrying the messages which the thinking part of the cell originates; for each little cell body must be regarded as a small brain.

The fibril network of the cell is thought to be the cell's nervous system. (See Fig. 5.) The larger brain of the skull, and the great solar plexus of the abdomen, are merely vast collections of untold millions of these tiny nerve cells or brain bodies. (Additional data regarding the physiology and anatomy of the nervous system will be found in Appendix A.)

THE SYMPATHETIC NERVOUS SYSTEM

While the nerves coming from the brain and spinal cord are more largely concerned with the body's sensations, muscular movements, and voluntary acts, all the vital processes of the body including breathing, the circulation of the blood, digestion, and elimination, are regulated very largely by the involuntary or sympathetic nervous system.

The sympathetic nervous system does not directly enter the skull, but controls all vital and involuntary functions. Special collections of sympathetic nerve matter — ganglia — are found throughout the body, the chief one being the solar plexus or abdominal brain.

The sympathetic system never sleeps; it is the never-tiring supervisor of all vital work, and the ever-present safeguard against brain-storm and mental panic. It directs the functions of the heart, the blood vessels, lungs, stomach, liver, spleen, kidneys, bowels, and other organs.

It is apparent that man has two brains — two nervous systems, two sources from which come orders of regulation and control. One can stop breathing for a few seconds, but as soon as enough carbonic acid gas (CO_2) collects in the blood, the respiratory centres are excited; imperative orders to breathe are sent to the lungs, and you can no longer hold your breath.

The *solar plexus* is the greatest collection of nerve matter to be found in the body outside of the skull. It consists of an extensive network of nerves and ganglia, and is found deep-seated in the abdomen in the region of the lower border of the stomach. It receives branches from the pneumogastric

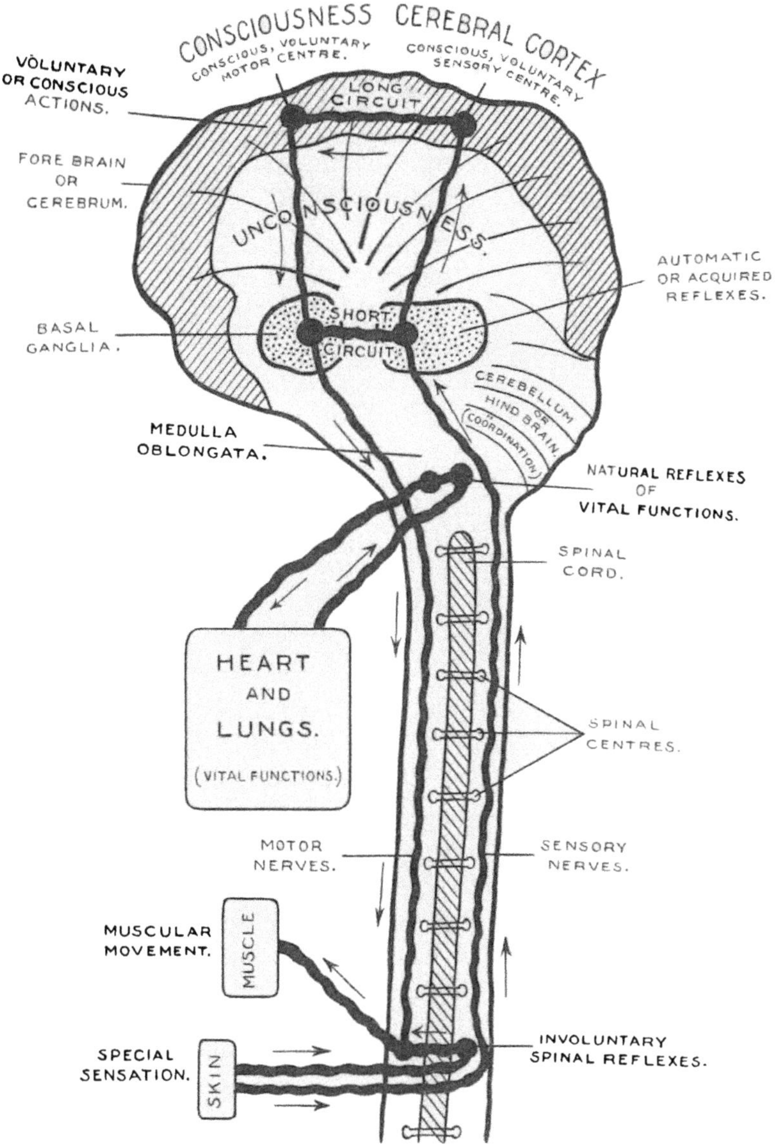

FIG. 2.

DIAGRAM SHOWING DIFFERENT NERVE PATHS.
(MODIFIED FROM SCHOFIELD)

nerve of the central nervous system in addition to numerous sympathetic nerves, and distributes many fibres to all the vital organs of the abdomen. (See Fig. 6.)

There are chains of sympathetic nerve ganglia extending down on either side of the spine into cavities of the chest and abdomen, which are connected by cross branches, while throughout the body, the two nervous systems make numerous contacts, often by means of certain special relay stations or ganglia. (The relation of the sympathetic nervous system to the general nervous system, together with further consideration of the functions of this wonderful mechanism, will be found in Appendix A, to which the reader is referred.)

THE PHYSICAL BASIS OF THOUGHT

The brain is the organ of thought just as the stomach is an organ of digestion. It handles thought just as the stomach handles food. The brain probably does not originate thought any more than the stomach originates food. The stomach digests the food we put into it. The brain digests the sensations, impressions, perceptions, and thoughts which are placed in it. Ideas are mysteriously hatched out in the mind. They appear sometimes to have come from without. We are almost startled with the suddenness with which we get a new idea. We sometimes describe such an experience by saying, "An idea has just come to me," or "A thought struck me."

While the origin of thought is enwrapped in more or less mystery, the process of thinking is perhaps better, although imperfectly, understood. It will be remembered that the nerve cells contain numerous branches, and that while no two nerve cells are actually connected, they are able to communicate freely with one another by means of their various branching "feelers" (dendrites and neurites). For instance, you try to recall the name of a friend, and you cannot. You are sure you know it; you were about to speak it, but it went from you. In the meantime, the various branches of numerous nerves are in vibration, feeling out anxiously to get in touch with, to complete the circuit, as it were, with the memory cell which holds the name you are trying to recall. Directly the cell is found, contact is made; the circuit is completed; and, like a flash, the name of your friend arises in your consciousness and you are able to speak it.

At night, when the energy granules are all used up in the nerve cell, and it is unable to continue the activity of its many processes, its little branches retract. The contact between the untold millions of cells in the brain is in this way more or less broken, so that it is very difficult to remain awake. The eyelids grow heavy, the centres of consciousness are dulled, the muscles relax, the head begins to nod, and you are all but asleep before you know it. Other theories concerning sleep attribute the drowsiness and unconsciousness to the accumulation of acid poisons in the blood stream, and to a lowering of the blood-pressure in the skull, thereby producing anæmia of the brain. While these various theories may all be more or less concerned in the production of sleep, the retraction of the nerve processes is probably the best explanation which can be given at present.

PART I
PSYCHOLOGIC SECTION

THE PHYSIOLOGY OF FAITH AND FEAR

PART I
PSYCHOLOGIC SECTION

CHAPTER I
MIND AND MATTER

WHAT IS MIND?—THE POWER OF MIND OVER MATTER.— ANCIENT ERROR AND SUPERSTITION.— THE BONDAGE OF IGNORANCE.— THE UNITY OF THE INDIVIDUAL.— CHEMICAL MESSAGES.— MENTAL MESSAGES.— THE VITAL MESSENGERS.— THE SUPREMACY OF MIND.— MIND, THE MONITOR OF HEALTH. — THE MENTAL SAFETY-BRAKE.— SUMMARY OF THE CHAPTER.

FOR ages the problem of mind and matter has engaged the thoughts and occupied the attention of physicians, philosophers, and physicists. The time-honored discussions respecting the "influence of mind over matter," etc., take on new meaning in the light of recent researches and experiments in psychology and physiology. It is doubtful if the average individual has a very clear idea as to either the real or relative meaning of the terms "mind" and "matter." Properly to define and explain these terms, then, is the first essential task in the study of their relationship.

WHAT IS MIND?

In all discussions concerning mind and matter, it is commonly understood that matter refers to the physical body and its various functions, such as muscular action, digestion, breathing, the circulation of the blood, etc., but the meaning of the terms "mind," "mental action," and "psychic influence," is by no means so clearly understood.

By mind, do we refer to the brain and nervous system? If so, it should be recalled that the brain and nerves are made up of certain little cells, in all essentials similar to those composing the stomach, the muscles, the liver, and other bodily organs. The brain and nervous systems are composed of living cells which are just as material and literal — just as truly matter — as are the cells which enter into the formation of any other part of the animal body. (See Fig. 3.)

What we commonly call the brain is merely the organ of the mind — the seat of intellect — and the nerves are simply the living telegraph wires over which the mind sends out its orders to the body and by which it is constantly receiving reports from various parts of the physical domain. Just as the stomach is the material organ in which takes place the chemical process of digestion, so the brain is the material organ where the mental process of thinking takes place — and it is this peculiar ability to think which gives origin to the term "mind." Thoughts are the offspring — the product — of mind, and mind operates from its seat in the brain, expressing itself through the nervous system by means of words, looks, and actions.

THE POWER OF MIND OVER MATTER

For centuries it has been known that mind could influence matter. It has long been recognized that the mental process carried on in the brain exerted more or less of an influence upon the physical functions carried on by the body; and so the brain has long been looked upon, more or less, as the body's supervisor. Full recognition has been given to the ability of the brain to direct the voluntary muscles in the performance of mechanical work, to direct the organs of speech as in talking, and to control numerous other voluntary and commonly performed actions; but not until recently was it fully understood just how far the mental attitude was responsible for or could directly influence the numerous complicated and delicate functions of the body which are involved in the maintenance of health and the prevention of disease.

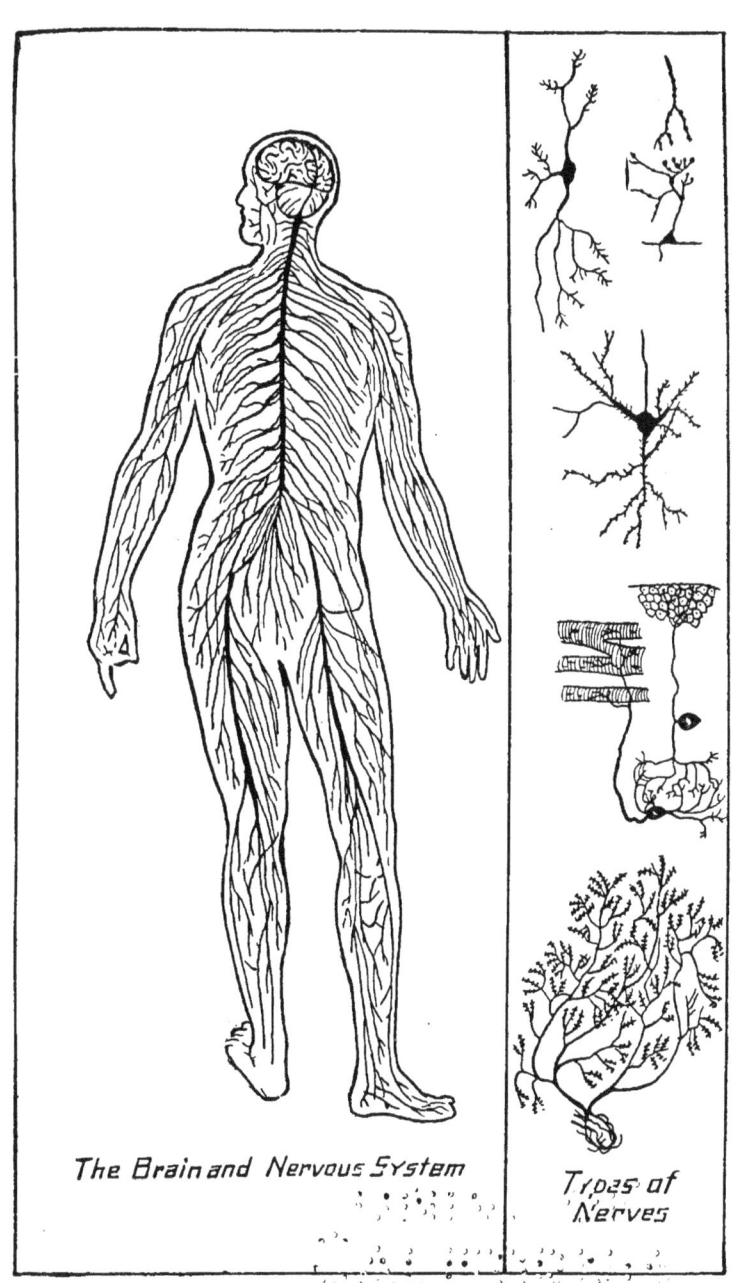

FIG. 3. The Nervous System and the Nerves.

MIND AND MATTER 5

Can the mind in and of itself actually bring disease upon the body? Do we really have imaginary diseases? Can a mental disorder produce a physical disease? Can the mind actually cure disease? Could the mind really remove a physical disorder? Likewise, questions on the other side of the issue. Can a physical disorder produce a mental disease? Can a sick body produce a sick mind? These, and many similar questions have engaged the attention of philosophers, physicians, and physiologists of the past, and will, undoubtedly, continue to engage their attention in the future.

ANCIENT ERROR AND SUPERSTITION

The study of the older literature abundantly proves that the ancients quite fully understood and recognized the fact that the mental state could favorably or unfavorably influence many physical functions. They certainly understood, at least in measure, that the state of the mind had much to do with the state of the health. In other words, they recognized the therapeutic value of the mind as a factor in preserving health and combating disease.

Past teaching, respecting the influence of the mind upon the body, has been clouded and distorted by the errors of superstition, the inaccuracies of ignorance, and the exaggerations of fanatical extremists, whose prejudiced observations and reports were more or less colored by commercial motives or sectarian enthusiasm. And so it was little wonder that teaching respecting mental healing grew into a mass of religious contradictions, unreliable observations, and groundless assertions. It has required much painstaking labor on the part of modern physiologists and psychologists to clear away this accumulation of rubbish and ignorance and lay a scientific foundation for a rational system of mental hygiene based upon the known laws of mind and matter.

THE BONDAGE OF IGNORANCE

The ignorance of past generations respecting the exact influence of the mind and its action, through the nervous system, upon the body, was responsible for a vast amount of superstition, mental deception, and moral delusion, and resulted in the production of unspeakable sorrow of mind and untold suffering of body, ranging from the ancient and inhuman treatment of the insane down through the dark ages to the ridiculous witchcraft procedures of the early history of our own country. We have long struggled under the bondage of ignorance — ignorance of the fundamental laws of mental hygiene, ignorance of the primary principles governing the interrelationship of mind and matter.

And even now, in our present state of advanced knowledge respecting the relations of mind and body, it is possible to lead but relatively few persons out of the bondage of the mysterious mysticism and superstition which have so long enshrouded the problems of mental health and physical disease. It seems almost impossible to convince many people that outside of certain hereditary tendencies, health and disease are largely matters of sowing and reaping, and that health or disease is determined by certain fixed mental and physical laws. The illuminating, scientific search-lights of the twentieth century have not yet fully penetrated the darkness of superstition and ignorance which so persistently enshroud the vital problems of mental happiness, moral peace, and physical health.

THE UNITY OF THE INDIVIDUAL

The scientific revelations of the last century have taught us that in the study of health and disease we must come to look upon man as a whole — as a unit — as an organized community of living cells. The human body is composed of some twenty-six trillions of little cells. Each little fellow is a distinct and separate being, with a life of its own to live, and with its special individual work to carry on as long as it lives. We are coming more and more to understand that the health and happiness or the disease and distress of any cell or group of cells, is in a measure shared by all the other cells composing the body's commonwealth. That is, disorder in any cell or organ of the body, be it brain, liver, or lung, must, in some measure, unfavorably affect every other cell of the body.

This intimate association, this close interrelationship of all the cells of the human body, is effected through two separate and distinct channels: the circulatory system and the nervous system.

MIND AND MATTER 7

1. *The circulatory system — chemical messages.* Every cell of the physical economy is constantly giving out from its own tiny body certain secretions and excretions formed within itself, which are gathered up by the lymph, and after being admixed with the blood stream, in a diluted form, are in time carried to every other cell of the body. This constant interchange of cellular products creates a channel by which any cell or group of cells is able to send *chemical messages* to any other cell or group of cells in the body; and in the aggregate, it turns the circulating fluids of the body into a great *chemical messenger,* carrying the messages from any cell to every and all other cells of the body.

Many important bodily functions, we now know, are carried on in coöperation and coördination by means of these chemical messages which are carried from one part of the body to another, by the body's circulating fluids. We now know that the pancreatic juice is secreted in obedience to just such a chemical message, which is sent out from the stomach and bowel. During the process of stomach digestion, from time to time, there is thrown out from the stomach a portion of its acid contents. The presence of this acid mass in the intestine causes the bowel immediately to produce a substance called "secretin," which substance, after it has been absorbed into the blood, proves to be the *chemical messenger* of the stomach, which is sent to the liver and pancreatic gland to tell them just how soon and in what quantity their secretions will be required to continue the digestion of the meal.

This "secretin" has been collected and when it is experimentally injected into the blood stream of an animal, it never fails to produce an immediate secretion and flow of both bile and pancreatic juice. There are a large number of these chemical messengers which are now known to be secreted in the body, and as a class, they are known as "hormones."

It must be evident then, that by means of numerous *chemical messengers,* various portions of the body are able profoundly to influence other parts of the body — that is, one organ of the body may directly exert an inhibiting or a stimulating influence upon another organ. In this way, disease in any one organ of the body results in producing more or less of a diseased state in some or all of the organs of the body; and so it is literally true, that disease in any part of the body does result in more or less derangement of the health of the entire organism.

Not only do we have *chemical messengers* which may be thrown out into the blood, and which are able to raise and lower blood-pressure, but we also have certain unnatural and abnormal chemical messengers, chemical toxins, which, when present in the blood, are able to produce painful irritation of the nerves, while others produce fatigue, mental laziness, and even despondency.

Many cases of mental depression owe their existence, primarily, to the circulation in the blood of certain poisons which have a tendency to raise the blood-pressure and at the same time lower the mental and moral courage of the individual. But powerful as are these means of chemical communication between the cells of the body, we have a still more important and intimate means of intercommunication between the various cells and organs of the body.

2. *The nervous system — mental messages.* Nearly all neurons or nerve cells possess two or more branches. (See Fig. 3.) One of these branches carries impulses from the nerve cell to other nerve cells or to special structures such as the muscles, while the other branch carries impressions to the nerve cell from the skin and other organs of sensation as well as from other nerve cells. Thus by means of two or more neurons and their incoming and outgoing branches, the various sensory impressions originating in the skin and in other organs of special sense are communicated to different nerve centres located in the brain and spinal cord.

It is estimated that there are over two billions of living nerve cells in the human brain and spinal cord, not to mention the untold millions of cells which are found in the sympathetic nervous system with its large central brain in the abdomen — the solar plexus.

It must be very clear that by means of these *living wires* — these relays of cables which run to and from the brain, and which branch and re-branch until practically every cell in the

MIND AND MATTER

human body is supplied with its tiny little nerve — it must be evident that through this channel of the nervous system, any one part of the body can almost instantaneously influence any or every other part of the body for weal or for woe. And it is exactly so. When one tastes or smells something disagreeable, the impression is immediately carried to the brain, the organ of the mind, from which there is instantly flashed out a mental message to the stomach. The taster becomes nauseated, and if the message is strong enough, he immediately vomits.

Let another person either smell or taste savory food — when quite hungry. These pleasant impressions of taste and smell are quickly carried to the nervous headquarters — the brain — from whence orders are immediately despatched to the stomach to secrete the necessary gastric juice to digest the meal about to be eaten, and in obedience to this *mental message* which the mind sends down from the brain, there begins to be poured out into the stomach in about four and a half minutes, an abundance of strong gastric juice, which, in both quantity and quality, is just adapted to the appetite and the digestion of the food which was instrumental in provoking its secretion.

THE VITAL MESSENGERS

Thus by means of chemical messengers carried by the blood, and mental messages flashed over the nerves, the most lowly of the body's cells are able to influence their fellow-cells favorably or unfavorably. In this way the overworked muscles produce nervous fatigue, bodily weariness, and mental drowsiness. The bile cells, as the penalty of their abuse, may jaundice the body, discolor the skin, and produce an attack of acute indigestion ("biliousness") accompanied by vomiting. The inactivity of the eliminating cells of the skin, bowels, and kidneys may result in throwing back poisons into the blood stream, which will, when carried to the brain, produce headache, mental despondency, sleeplessness, and even moral despair.

If a single group of body cells are thus able to influence so profoundly another group of cells, how much more powerful must be the influence of the mind which presides over the very centre and citadel of the nervous system, more or less controlling every mental message passing over the vast telegraph system of the body, and even indirectly controlling the secretions of the cells and the special secretory glands.

While it must be granted that the body constantly exerts more or less of an influence over the mind; and that disease, disorder, or pain, anywhere in the physical domain, contributes directly to the production of mind disturbance and mental panic; nevertheless, in view of these physiological facts respecting the circulatory and nervous systems, it must be evident — other things being equal — that the mind is enthroned in the place of power and intrenched in the position of controlling influence. The mental state must ofttimes prove to be the determining power and the deciding factor in the incessant battle — the ceaseless struggle — between health and disease, between man and the microbe.

THE SUPREMACY OF MIND

Does the mind have a body, or does the body have a mind? The physician and the physiologist, from the very nature of their studies, are frequently inclined to the position that the body has a mind — that man is essentially a material being, an animal organism; that the mind is simply the function of the brain and nervous system — a specialized development of the body designed to unite, control, and coördinate the organism. Until very recently, modern scientists largely looked upon man as controlled entirely by the laws of physics and chemistry. Physiologists are now coming to recognize other and stronger forces at work in the marvellous and mysterious vital activities of the living cell.

On the other hand, psychologists are quite apt to regard man as a "mind having a body." They take the position that man is "made in the image of God," that the human mind — creative power — is a distinguishing attribute of the race, that the body is merely the material instrument for expressing the will and carrying out the purpose and pleasure of the mind. It must be evident that these two views of man lead to entirely different conclusions respecting both moral beliefs and conduct.

A well-known lecturer in his recent challenge of the theory of evolution, raised the question, whether man was coming up from the monkey, or going down toward him, stating that he had seen men going both ways; and so it is with respect to the supremacy of mind over matter. Sensuous individuals with a low grade of intelligence and with a minimum amount of self-control — victims of every intemperate appetite and vicious passion — certainly appear to prove the contention that the body has a mind, and but little mind at that. On the other hand, and in contrast with such a picture, the rank and file of the civilized races stand out preëminently as intelligent beings. The glorious triumph of the mind, the superiority of intelligence, is abundantly shown in the case of the man with a great mind and an insufficient body; as well as in the case of the strong mind and the weak and diseased body. These common observations lead one strongly toward the viewpoint of the psychologist — that man is a "mind with a body."

And so it must be evident that any influence or power gaining control of the brain and nerve centres, will be able eventually to gain control of the entire body. Not only are the brain and its associated nerve centres the recipients of all the impulses coming in over the nervous system, but they are also the seats of authority from which the mind sends out all mental messages to the remotest cells of the body.

MIND — THE MONITOR OF HEALTH

Not only does the mind directly influence the life and health of every cell in the physical domain by means of these messages which it is able to send directly to the cell; but the mind is also able, indirectly, to influence the health and action of the entire body through the nervous regulation and control of the cellular and glandular secretions. That is, to a certain extent, the mind may be able to modify the chemical messages which every cell is sending to every other cell of the body; and so from whatever standpoint we examine the proposition, we are forced to admit the ultimate supremacy of mind over matter, at least in so far as mind and matter may be regarded as influencing and controlling the functions of the body in health and disease. We must recognize that the mental and moral powers having their seat in the brain are in position to wield a mighty influence for health and disease. We freely grant that all disease must have a definite cause; but may not long continued functional derangement resulting from abnormal and diseased mental control, directly contribute to predisposing the body to many acute disorders and chronic diseases?

It would thus seem that the mind, through the nervous system, and within certain limits, has considerable control over the functions of the body, with power to influence and modify these functions at will; and this would indeed be true, were it not for the fact that all the vital functions of the body are wholly or partially under the control of the involuntary or sympathetic nervous system — a nervous system which not only does not have its headquarters in the brain, but which does not so much as enter the brain by means of the smallest nerve fibre.

THE MENTAL SAFETY-BRAKE

The sympathetic nervous system is nature's great barrier against the whims of the mind; it is the physiological safety-brake against mental panic in the individual's brain; it is the everlasting safeguard against a demoralized mind — mental confusion, and suicidal tendencies.

The mind only indirectly dictates or controls the mental messages sent out over this sympathetic nervous system. The majority of the orders of the mind centres reach the vital organs only indirectly, by means of a system of cross connections between the voluntary and involuntary nervous systems; and even then, only after its messages are duly censored (in the sympathetic relay stations or ganglia) is the mind able to get its messages through to the various vital organs, upon whose faithful action life itself depends.

And this explains why, though fear or sudden fright may excite the heart to palpitation, one cannot entirely stop the beating of the heart or greatly modify its rate by the exertion of the will. Only for a short time can a person stop breathing by means of an effort of the will or an order from the mind.

And so our definition of mind must be enlarged to include that mysterious power seated upon the throne of the nerve centres, which so fascinatingly presides, not only over the realms of thought and intelligence, but also over those of function and physiology.

MIND AND MATTER 13

SUMMARY OF THE CHAPTER

1. The terms *brain* and *mind* must not be confused. The brain is matter — material; it is the organ of mind and sustains the same relation to the mental processes that the stomach does to digestion.

2. Throughout all time it has been recognized that mind could influence matter, but only recently have its scope and limitation been scientifically studied and defined.

3. Ignorance, superstition, and prejudice have ever stood in the way of light and truth respecting mental and moral hygiene — the relations of mind and matter.

4. Modern science regards man as a unit. The cells composing the animal body are all interrelated — there exists a community of interests.

5. The unification of the individual is effected by two distinct influences: (a) "chemical messages" which are carried to every cell by the circulation (hormones), and (b) "mental messages" which reach the cells by way of the nervous system (nerve impulses).

6. Chemical messengers or hormones are able to direct cellular secretion and influence the elaboration of important digestive secretions — as in the case of the pancreatic juice. Abnormal chemical agents may also circulate in the blood, as in the case of the bacterial toxins causing disease.

7. Practically every cell in the human body is in actual contact with a minute filament or branch from some nerve fibre which constantly carries to the cell impulses originating in other and remote parts of the organism.

8. The body is unified and coördinated by means of the combined action of these chemical and nervous forces, which, taken as a whole, may be looked upon as the vital messengers of the physical economy, enabling any single cell to influence any and all other cells.

9. Modern psychology and physiology testify that man is a mind with a body. Science concedes the supremacy of mind over matter — not absolute and unlimited, but according to laws which regulate the interrelationship of mind and matter.

10. Mind exerts an undoubted and far-reaching control over

all the physical functions. (The balance of power in health and disease not infrequently rests with the mental attitude.)

11. The sympathetic nervous system is the mental safety-brake. All mental messages from the higher brain centres reach the vital organs only after passing through the various ganglia or relay stations of the sympathetic system, where they are properly censored, or at least so modified as to be less injurious to the normal action of the organism.

12. The definition of mind must be enlarged so as to include the whole of that mysterious power which so marvellously presides, not only over the realm of thought and intelligence, but also over the vital physical functions.

CHAPTER II
BRAIN, MIND, AND PERSONALITY

SEAT OF THE INTELLECT.— THE TWO BRAINS.— THE BRAIN DOES NOT THINK.— BRAIN AND MIND.— THE IMPRESS OF MIND UPON MATTER.— SUMMARY OF THE CHAPTER.

IT is in the brain that mind and matter meet. Mind is close of kin to personality. The matter composing the human body is constantly changing. The average man eats an amount of food each month equivalent to his own weight. Notwithstanding this ever-changing character of the animal body, the mind continues to direct this new matter in the same old channels; and this expláins why a man's personality and identity remain unchanged.

The term *brain* is comparatively recent in its origin — especially as regards its association with the mind as a centre of the intellect. The word *brain* is not to be found in ancient literature. The ancients little suspected that the brain had anything to do with thought.

SEAT OF THE INTELLECT

The Babylonions and other ancient nations believed that the liver was the centre of the human intellect. The earliest attempts to connect the mind with some bodily organ, located it in the liver. Some among the ancients made an effort to locate the various intellectual processes in different physical organs, regarding the heart as the seat of the soul and the spiritual faculties, the kidneys as the abode of the mind or intellect proper, while all the tender and compassionate emotions were supposed to be located in the bowels.

While our modern thought regards the brain as the seat or headquarters of the intellectual and volitional processes, it does not by any means limit the scope and work of mind to this single physical organ. To say the least, the entire nervous system — both the central and sympathetic — must be regarded as the particular and immediate instrument and organ of mind.

The brain does not secrete thought as the liver secretes bile. That is, the thought does not originate in the brain, any more than food originates in the stomach, although the brain contributes to the elaboration of thought, even as the stomach does to the elaboration of food. The brain and nervous system sustain the same relation to mind and personality that a harp does to its player — as a telegrapher does to the wires, batteries, and instruments which he so wonderfully utilizes and marvellously manipulates.

THE TWO BRAINS

The brain itself cannot originate speech. The brain cannot create words. This is clearly shown by the fact that when the speech or word-memory centres, on the active side of the brain, are destroyed or diseased, the power of speech or word-utterance is lost, notwithstanding the other half of the brain is perfectly whole and healthy. It may be well in this connection to explain that while every man has two complete and perfect brains, he uses only one of them (one side or hemisphere) in his intellectual operations. Which side of the brain is destined to become the seat of our intellectual processes is early determined by such an apparently simple matter as which hand we begin first to make active use of. If we are right-handed — that determines that we shall be left-brained, and *vice versa.*

The question will no doubt come into the mind of the reader, What is the purpose of the other brain or hemisphere, which is not concerned in the intellectual processes of thought elaboration? That question is answered by explaining that, while only one side of the brain is directly concerned in ministering to the mind, both its halves are equally concerned in the work of ministering to the body; that is, both hemispheres of the brain are engaged in the work of receiving sensory impressions and despatching impulses of muscular control and contraction. Again, this other half of the brain — the intellectually inactive half — serves the splendid purpose of a second or emergency brain, which can be made, by a process

BRAIN, MIND, AND PERSONALITY

of reëducation, to take the place of the other half, in case of accident or disease.

Cases are on record, where certain brain centres, such as those of speech or word-memory, have suddenly been destroyed by accident; and by persistent training the other hemisphere of the brain was in time educated to take up the work of its destroyed counterpart. This work of developing and training new brain centres can usually be accomplished in the earlier years of life. (It is quite difficult to effect such changes after the age of twenty-five or thirty years.) Nature has very liberally provided us with two eyes and two ears, either one of which is quite able to do the work of both.

The brain, then, has come to be looked upon as the servant of the mind, while the mind is regarded as the designer, builder, and maintainer of the personality.

THE BRAIN DOES NOT THINK

That the brain is highly differentiated in its relation to the mental life of the individual is clearly shown by its behavior to various chemical poisons or drugs. For instance, opium stimulates the power of imagination, enabling its victims to be wholly absorbed and fully entertained by the never-ending procession of mental images and other creations which troop through the mind. On the other hand, alcohol stimulates an altogether different set of mental processes, exciting particularly the feelings and emotions, rendering its users sociable and communicative — the opposite of the opium users.

This one thing must be made plain: the brain, in and of its physical self, does not think, any more than a musical instrument can give forth melody without the touch of the musician's hand. The brain is indeed the instrument of thinking, but the mind is the skilful player that makes it give forth the beautiful harmony of thought. The eye, of its physical self, can no more see than can a telescope; it is only the sight centre of the brain that can translate visual impressions and re-create images for recognition by the mind.

BRAIN AND MIND

The size of the brain is of but little value in determining the dimensions of the intellect. A large mind may dwell in a small brain, and *vice versa*. The organization and training of the brain counts for far more than size.

Careful examination of the physical structure of the brain of man and of the monkey shows no essential difference; and yet a like examination of the mental phenomenon exhibited by the two presents abundant evidence that their minds are in every way unlike. The mind of the man not only eclipses that of the monkey in every phase of reason and every realm of thought, but presents the strange spectacle of possessing certain moral and spiritual attributes not to be found in the monkey's mind, even in the slightest degree. The brain of the man and that of the monkey resemble each other, but their minds are entirely different.

There is every evidence that mind uses certain portions of the brain as a sort of library. In the department of speech, the volumes of word-memory and word-speech are not only arranged in an orderly manner on the shelves, as it were, but facts and experiments go to show that on each shelf of this wonderful library the nouns and verbs are placed first, the pronouns next, then come the adjectives and prepositions, while the adverbs are last in order.

We have three distinct word-centres — one for hearing words, one for seeing words, and another for speaking words. As we shall see more fully later, education is not merely a process of mental training, it includes actual physical changes in the brain itself. All thought — all mental training — results in definite brain changes and the establishment of nerve habits which actually and literally render the man different from what he was before, and through the modification and transformation of the mental powers, the personality is ultimately influenced. And so we here come into contact with that wonderful and mysterious force which dominates even the intellect of man — that force or influence which we call *will*. It is the will which has power to direct the channels of thought; and thought actually changes and modifies the physical brain; and the modification of brain substance and nerve impulse literally changes our habits; and change of habit means a change of character; and character changed sig-

BRAIN, MIND, AND PERSONALITY 19

nifies a modification of personality. But more about the will later.

THE IMPRESS OF MIND UPON MATTER

Professor James says:

"The fact is that there is no sort of consciousness whatever, be it sensation, feeling, or idea, which does not directly and of itself tend to discharge into some motor effect. The motor effect need not always be an outer stroke of behavior. It may be only an alteration of the heart beats or breathing, or a modification in the distribution of blood, such as blushing, or turning pale, or what not. But, in any case, it is there in some shape when any consciousness is there; and a belief, as fundamental as any in modern psychology, is the belief at last attained, that conscious processes of any sort, conscious processes merely as such, pass over into motion open or concealed."

If every mental process, as James says, passes over into bodily action of some kind; and as one physiologist has said, that "each active cell is connected with a nerve," then this point becomes one of the highest importance. Herein lies the true basis of suggestive therapeutics. The theory is as follows:

"Nearly every cell in the body (except the epidermis and blood corpuscles) is supposedly connected with a sensory nerve, and, through it, is in touch with the central nerve cells. The cells are constantly sending impulses to the central nerve cells or to the brain, telling of their needs, such as of food or of rest. These common sensations of hunger, thirst, and fatigue are usually disposed of as the instincts; yet they are intelligences sent by the individual cells to the lower centres or to the higher consciousness. While thirst seems to be located in the mouth, it is not from there that the pressing call comes, but from the cells of the whole body. So it is with hunger. If the cells throughout the body could be nourished, the feeling of hunger would leave the stomach. There may be a feeling of hunger all the time — as in the case of persons suffering from indigestion — and yet the stomach be well supplied with food."

Mosso says:

"We are sometimes surprised by a sad or joyous piece of news. We all know what happens in a state of fear and distress. Physiological phenomena occur that cannot be described. But when we learn suddenly that the news which has troubled us is false, that our fear and distress had no foundation, the internal disturbance, does not cease, the physiological phenomena continue in the organism in spite of all efforts of the will to suppress them."

SUMMARY OF THE CHAPTER

1. The ancients variously located the mind in the liver, kidneys, bowels, and other organs. It is in the brain that mind and matter meet. While the brain is regarded as the seat of intellect, the scope of the mind is by no means limited to this single physical organ.

2. The brain does not secrete thought as the liver secretes bile. While both sides or hemispheres of the brain are concerned in motor activities, only one side — the left side in right-handed people — participates in the intellectual processes.

3. The brain does not think, it is merely the instrument of thought. The brain sustains the same relation to the mind that a musical instrument does to the musician.

4. Two brains — as the brain of man and monkey — may possess physical resemblance, while their respective presiding minds are wholly unlike or diametrically opposite. Two harps may be identical, while their players in no wise resemble each other.

5. The brain systematically stores its knowledge. In the word-memory centres, the elements of language are filed away in the following order: first nouns, then verbs, pronouns, adjectives, prepositions, and adverbs.

6. Mind never fails to impress itself upon matter. For every mental process there never fails to follow some physical response. Every thought of mind, every process of consciousness, is unfailingly translated into some form of material movement. This physical response to mental stimuli may be either conscious or unconscious, observed or unobserved, but none the less real.

7. The mind is not always able to stop or control the physiological phenomena which it may be able to initiate. Fear is able to set in operation many physical reactions which soon pass beyond the regulatory power of the mind.

CHAPTER III
HOW THE MIND IS INFLUENCED BY BODILY STATES

SUNLIGHT AND THE MIND.— FRESH AIR AND THE INTELLECT. — BREATHING AND BRAIN ACTION.—MUSCULAR EXERCISE AND MENTAL ACTIVITY.— MIND AS INFLUENCED BY THE STOMACH. — BILIOUSNESS AND THE BRAIN.— THE INFLUENCE OF EATING ON THINKING.— THE BLOOD AND THE BRAIN.— METABOLISM AND MIND.— ELIMINATION AND BRAIN ACTION.— REST AND RECREATION IN RELATION TO THE MIND.— BODY DISEASES AND BRAIN DISORDERS.— SUMMARY OF THE CHAPTER.

FOR more than a quarter of a century the thought of the scientific world drifted steadily toward materialism. The mind was accorded less and less prestige and power as a controlling influence in health and disease. At last the inevitable reaction occurred, and now in the midst of our mental revival and spiritual awakening, the pendulum of mind and matter threatens to swing disastrously to the other extreme. We are now threatened with a metaphysical deluge — a pantheistic flood.

In the preceding chapters, the physical facts pointing toward the supremacy of the mind over the body were pointed out. In this chapter we desire concisely to review the facts which portray and prove the tremendous influence exerted by the bodily states of health and disease upon the mind and morals.

We recognize that the mind holds the balance of power and control over many of the complicated physical processes which are concerned in health and disease; nevertheless, we give almost equal recognition to the powerful and dominating — sometimes tyrannical — control of the mind by a diseased, distressed, or abnormal body. (Even the healthy body exerts a very powerful influence over the mental operations.)

SUNLIGHT AND THE MIND

Numerous physical habits and practices, through their influence upon the health of the body, profoundly influence the mental state. There can be little doubt that lack of physical sunshine is often responsible for a lack of mental cheerfulness.

There is more than an accidental relationship between the sunshine of the body and the sunshine of the soul. Indoor living predisposes to mental despondency; and a sedentary life, in many cases, leads directly to moral depression. There is a direct relation between the physical darkness of the slum tenement and the spiritual darkness and moral perversity of those who dwell therein.

Sunshine is the fountain of physical energy and the wellspring of mental cheer, and it even contributes indirectly to strengthening the moral courage. Sunshine in the home favors sunshine in the heart. Sunny homes help to make sunny people — happy people.

Fogs depress the spirits, and, in measure, delay the mental activities. This is due to the fact that increase of moisture in the atmosphere decreases the evaporation of moisture from the surface of the body, and so decreases the elimination of poisonous matters through the sweat glands; and this reduction of skin elimination favors the accumulation of toxic substances in the blood, which poisonous substances depress the brain and greatly lessen mental action.

Even the cloudy day, but a passing incident in our lives, markedly influences the temper and disposition of most persons. It is doubtful if the best of people are as generous and philanthropic on a nasty, rainy day, as they are on a sunshiny afternoon of a beautiful summer's day.

FRESH AIR AND THE INTELLECT

Lack of food is not the only stunting influence which acts upon the mind of the growing child. The mental powers of the children of the slums are also retarded by lack of fresh air and sunshine. When the brain is stuffy, the mental action slow, and memory sluggish, the mind cannot be ventilated unless the lungs be ventilated; and the lungs cannot be veri-

HOW THE MIND IS INFLUENCED 23

tilated unless the living or working rooms also be ventilated. The proper lighting and ventilation of the schoolroom is directly concerned in the mental development and the intellectual training of the children in attendance. Many persons suffer all day from mental dulness and gain the reputation of possessing a mean disposition, as the result of breathing all night the foul and polluted atmosphere of an unventilated sleeping-room.

The breathing of impure air directly and powerfully influences the mind. It will be recalled how many a lecture or sermon, good in itself, was utterly spoiled because the hearers were breathing the foul air of an unventilated audience room. Scientific ventilation, especially during the winter, would add much to the success, happiness, and religious enjoyment of many persons who are morose, depressed, and even melancholic, as the result of their voluntary imprisonment in their miserably ventilated living-rooms.

Recent observations and experiments in France go a long way toward proving that the winter temperature of living-rooms has much to do with the physical health and mental buoyancy. Temperatures above 65 degrees F. are found to be more poisonous, hence, more deleterious to the health of both mind and body. At 65 degrees F., many of the respiratory poisons condense and so fall to the floor, where they are rendered perfectly harmless.

O_{xygen} feeds the vital fires which effectually burn up the poisons of the living machine. These poisons when not properly burned up (oxidized), prove equally powerful in the work of depressing both mind and body. The vast majority of the toxins of disordered metabolism and deranged nutrition prove to be mind poisons as well as body poisons. Insanity as well as paralysis frequently follows in the wake of raging fevers and prolonged infections.

Considered from every possible standpoint, mental vigor and moral health are greatly lessened by the indoor living of modern civilization; while the outdoor life, in every way, supplies conditions which favor the highest degree of mental strength and moral efficiency.

BREATHING AND BRAIN ACTION

The normal action of the lungs has much to do with the healthy action of the mind. Deep breathing favors deep thinking, while shallow breathers are condemned to inevitable shallow thinking. Healthy brain action is dependent upon the normal supply of good, red blood. Deep breathing purifies the blood and favors its circulation through the brain. If the brain is not properly nourished with pure blood, the mind is directly influenced and greatly crippled in its operation.

All victims of despondency, all downcast and crestfallen people, are shallow breathers. To convince oneself of the direct influence of breathing efficiency upon brain efficiency, try the following experiment: Sometime, when reading in a close and unventilated room, when the mind is wandering and it is exceedingly difficult to concentrate the attention — when it is almost impossible to keep from falling asleep — lay down the book for a moment; go directly out of doors, or stand before an open window; take twenty-five deep breaths of air, fully expanding the lungs each time. Now witness what a mental transformation has been so quickly wrought. The mind is all attention, the thoughts are quickly directed and easily controlled, while the brain is wide awake and highly active.

Deep breathing purifies the blood and sends it tingling through the blood vessels of the brain, where it washes away the poisonous excretions and nourishes the nerve cells with its life-giving stream. A ventilated and nourished brain cell is absolutely essential to normal and satisfactory mental action.

Insufficient breathing is directly related to "the blues." Systematic deep breathing will do much to prevent portal (abdominal) congestion, and we have long known that the mental state known as "the blues" was very largely due to congestion of blood in the large vessels associated with the liver. A flat chest too often means a frail mind, while a strong chest, as a rule, indicates relative strength and vigor of mind. Recent experiments go to show that physical endurance is increased thirty per cent by deep breathing.

There can be little doubt that bad breathing and worry go

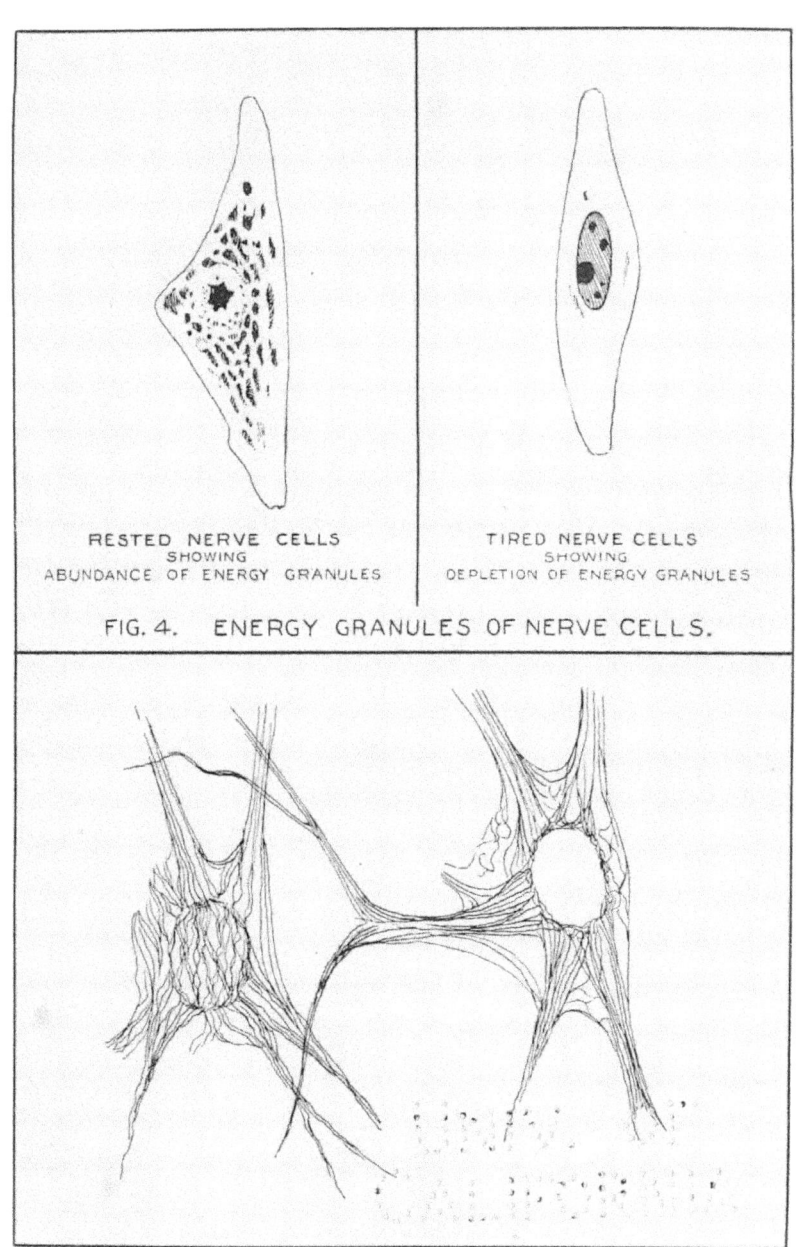

FIG. 4. ENERGY GRANULES OF NERVE CELLS.

FIG. 5. DIAGRAM SHOWING THE FIBRILLAR NET WORK OF THE NERVE CELLS.

Library.

together. Getting rid of one usually helps in overcoming the other. Shallow breathing beclouds the mind by favoring a retention of blood poisons, thereby placing heavy and unnecessary burdens upon the moral nature.

MUSCULAR EXERCISE AND MENTAL ACTIVITY

More or less body work is indispensable to first-class brain work. Physical exercise increases the circulation, favors digestion, promotes elimination, in fact, facilitates all those bodily processes, the proper performance of which are so essential to a healthy brain and a vigorous mind. Body work favors deep breathing and deep breathing promotes mental action.

Physical exercise greatly aids in the burning up of bodily poisons and thus relieves the mind from the depression which so surely results from the accumulation of these toxic substances in the blood stream. Systematic exercise will do much to help in the acquisition of a pleasant disposition and an agreeable temperament. Regular exercise — a daily sweat — will contribute much to mental peace and the enjoyment even of one's religion.

Just as truly as perfect physical development (when not carried to unnatural and pugilistic extremes) directly favors strong mental action, so must it be recognized that we cannot deform the body without in some measure deforming the mind. The physical body is the mind's only instrument of expression, and it stands forever true that perfect mental action demands a high degree of physical perfection in the working of the bodily functions.

Fashionable clothing, by its influence in crippling respiration and in lessening physical exercise, may be indirectly charged with crippling the mental powers and lessening mind action. Who can deny that careless clothing of the feet, which results in the production of corns and bunions, is directly responsible for producing a bad disposition, a quarrelsome temperament, and numerous other evidences of perverted and distorted mind action?

Overworking the body produces mental weariness, as well as physical fatigue. The industrial slave, toiling in the sweat shop, exhibits equal evidences of mental deterioration and physical disease. The abuse of the physical powers inevitably reacts in the lessening of the mental vigor.

THE MIND AS INFLUENCED BY THE STOMACH

The stomach probably exerts a greater influence over the mind than any other physical organ, except the brain. At certain times, when the mind is almost dethroned by a distracting pain in the cranium, the sufferer could truly be said to have a "stomach-ache" in the head. The stomach, as the portal of entry for all nourishment of the body, is able to contribute much either for or against the mental health and the moral happiness of the individual. The nerve which so abundantly supplies the stomach, liver, lungs, and heart — the pneumogastric nerve — also sends branches to the meninges — the covering membrane of the brain.

Many persons who are regarded as cross and crabbed, who are looked upon as possessing an unbearable disposition, whose minds are commonly regarded as altogether ignoble and cruel — are merely suffering from a chronic, dyspeptic grouch; and it will be a hard matter for orthodox religion or any of its twentieth century counterfeits, or any other genuine or fraudulent system of mental healing, to relieve such persons of their mental disorders until the stomach, liver, and bowels are set in order.

A sour stomach usually means a sour disposition. Intestinal fermentation commonly ends in intellectual fermentation. In order to sweeten up the mental process, we must sweeten up the digestive process.

Many failures in business, college, family life, and religion, if the facts were known, could be rightfully charged up to disordered nutrition — dyspepsia and constipation.

It is altogether impossible to have peace in the head and war in the stomach. Coarse eating and fine thinking are incompatible.

Sleep does not interfere with digestion, but it is a well-known physiological fact that digestion does interfere with sleep, and so midnight suppers do impoverish the mind and depreciate the mental powers, by robbing both mind and body of their natural rest and recuperation. Recent experiments go to show that sleep does interfere with the motility of the stomach — its muscular power upon which it is dependent for emptying itself.

BILIOUSNESS AND THE BRAIN

Biliousness is a disease by no means limited to the body. When one is bilious, the brain is bilious, the mind is forced to operate through a bilious brain and over a bilious nervous system, and that is exactly why one looks bilious, acts bilious, and talks bilious — the brain is jaundiced as well as the skin.

The liver is the body's poison-destroyer — the metabolic garbage crematory — and when it fails properly to do its work, when it is overworked, lazy, or torpid, the blood is literally flooded with toxins and poisons, and soon the brain becomes torpid, the mind lazy, and the thoughts sordid.

Even the powers of memory are directly influenced by indigestion, biliousness, and acidity of the blood. Many persons suffering from dyspepsia and indigestion, supposing their memory to be failing from old age, have found their mental energies restored and their thinking powers renewed, after the successful treatment of their distressing stomach difficulties and liver disorders.

THE INFLUENCE OF EATING ON THINKING

While we acknowledge as true the proverb, "As a man thinketh, so is he," we are compelled also to recognize the truthfulness of that old German saying, "As a man eateth, so is he."

Maximum mental efficiency demands that intelligent attention be given to the diet. Balanced thinking goes hand in hand with balanced eating. Pure food is a direct aid to pure thoughts.

Overeating, hasty eating, and the eating of indigestible foods, all detract from brain power and mental efficiency. The animal world — a cow, for instance — can spend all its nervous energy and vital strength in the work of digesting food. Animals are able to keep the stomach working all day long. They seldom suffer from indigestion or dyspepsia. The animal has only a physical life to lead; but man is a mental being, a moral creature, an intelligent animal — with a social career to carve out and industrial battles to fight; and, therefore, the human animal must plan to conserve its nervous energy and physical powers so as properly to support its intellectual activities in the arena of mind and morals — to enable the man to perform successfully in the theatre of society and commerce.

And these facts explain exactly why an animal can eat between meals or at any time of the day or night, and not incur dyspepsia; also, why men and women who have intellectual feats to perform, commercial battles to win, and moral problems to solve, cannot safely indulge in the careless and indifferent physical practices and dietetic digressions of the animal world, without incurring serious consequences in the way of stomach diseases, digestive disorders, and nervous breakdowns.

Bad food combinations — ignorant eating — are undoubtedly responsible for many bad mental decisions; and immoderate eating, especially of highly seasoned foods, must be recognized as indirectly leading to intemperance and immorality. As a rule, overeating is associated with under-thinking.

All food substances which are sufficiently irritating to produce headaches, like tea and coffee, must be looked upon as unfavorably influencing the mind through their irritating and narcotic effects upon the brain and nervous system. The effect of alcohol is not confined to the body; in the first stages of intoxication it is highly exciting to the mind, subsequently, it is narcotic and deadening in its influence and results in dulling, stupefying, and anæsthetizing the mental processes. Alcohol may excite the mind, but it does not nourish the brain.

Fiery foods — foods which are hot when they are cold — not only irritate and inflame the stomach, but when carried to the brain in the blood stream, favor the production of fiery thoughts.

THE BLOOD AND THE BRAIN

It is self-evident that brain action is dependent upon heart action. The mind is bound to be affected by circulatory disturbances, elevation of the blood-pressure, or congestion of the blood in any organ of the body. Diseases of the blood, such as anæmia, produce anæmia of the brain and emaciation of the mind. Elevation of the blood-pressure is often associated with depression of the thoughts,

An unusually low blood-pressure is usually associated with the mental states characterizing neurasthenia and brain-fag. The various drugs, such as tobacco and cocaine, which raise the blood-pressure, as well as the alcohol and morphine group, which lower the pressure, are all powerful in their deteriorating effect upon the mind. In fact, all states of systemic poisoning or auto-intoxication, result in more or less derangement of the mental action.

Deficient water-drinking may result in clouding the mind. The brain requires that its internal bath should be administered with clean blood, not dirty blood. That the brain appreciates its bath is shown by the fresh feeling of invigoration which results from washing the face in cold water. There probably exists no more powerful way of instantaneously arousing the brain and invigorating the mental powers than by dashing a little cold water into the face, and this is but one of the many evidences showing the direct and profound manner in which the body is able to influence the mind.

The myriads of microbes which inhabit the large intestine of man are often responsible for much of the mental sluggishness and moral depression from which many persons suffer. When these germs are too long retained in the bowel — when their number is greatly increased by gormandizing, constipation, or a too high protein diet — there is increased production and absorption of toxins, which are responsible for many disturbanecs of the mind and body, including sleeplessness, bad breath, brownish tint of the skin, headache, mental inaction, loss of memory, and moral despondency.

And so we must come to recognize that the quality of the blood has something to do with the quality of the thinking. There may be even some connection between the eating of adulterated foods and the thinking of adulterated thoughts.

METABOLISM AND MIND

Many strong minds, vigorous intellects, are held down and handicapped by the crippled assimilative powers of the physical body. Any practice which favors food assimilation — thorough mastication of the food and all other dietetic helps — in the end will prove of great value in strengthening the mind and increasing the health-seeker's self-control.

In chronic indigestion and stomach trouble, with their resultant starvation and anæmia, we have brain starvation — mental emaciation. Many a giant intellect has been effectually starved out and prematurely killed by the combined terrors of dyspepsia and the poisons absorbed as a result of chronic constipation.

Both physicians and criminologists are coming more and more to believe that there is a direct relation between decomposing food in the digestive apparatus and mental perversity; the results are variously exhibited and extend all the way from violent outbursts of temper down to criminal depredations and brutal tendencies. For, as previously pointed out, all secretions of the body, normal and abnormal, must indirectly influence the mind, through their action upon the brain and nervous system.

ELIMINATION AND BRAIN ACTION

Healthy, vigorous brain action is dependent upon normal elimination of body wastes; and normal elimination of wastes is dependent largely upon systematic water-drinking and regular bathing. Bathing is an antidote for the wearing of clothes and the sedentary life of modern civilized nations.

The proper action of the kidneys in the elimination of poisons, and the liver in their destruction, is essential to the healthy and normal action of the mind. A cloudy, dingy skin usually means cloudy thinking.

There is a direct relation between skin action and brain action. When the skin is pale and anæmic, the brain, as a rule, is congested and sluggish. The red glow of the skin is usually associated with mental vigor, while the pale skin is not infrequently accompanied by puny thinking.

There is an intellectual and social gulf of wide dimensions between regular bathers and non-bathers; and it is observed that cold bathing is conducive to clear thinking.

REST AND RECREATION IN RELATION TO THE MIND

The accumulation of energy granules in the neuron, the recuperation of the depleted vitality of the nervous system, the restoration of the brain's power to respond to the dictates of the mental powers, are all dependent upon regular rest and refreshing sleep. Loss of sleep quickly shows its reaction upon the mind, dulling the intellect, dimming the mental vision, and distorting even the moral concepts.

Regular recreation and an annual vacation are indispensable to first-class brain work. A regular rest-day, once a week, and even a half holiday in the middle of the week, are both of great value in producing strong and healthy mind control.

BODY DISEASES AND BRAIN DISORDERS

Last, but not least, attention should be called to the fact that all definite physical diseases result in more or less derangement of the mind. In all the *acute fevers* and *infectious diseases,* the mental powers are enfeebled, the mind is more or less distorted, the symptoms ranging from mild derangement up to raving delirium. The majority of poisonous disease toxins are alike disturbing to mind and body.

Typhoid fever and many other serious infections predispose to mental disturbances, and are occasionally followed by insanity. *Pellagra* has a terminal stage which closely borders on the insane state. *Malaria* not only racks the body, but also markedly affects the mental activities.

The social diseases constituting the great black plague, of which *syphilis* is chief, not only affect the body, but also react upon the mind, even to the point of producing tumors and softening of the brain.

Heart and *lung* diseases always affect the mind, the former producing unusual fear and depression, while the latter is characterized by a fatal optimism. The mental activity is also in measure influenced by most of the chronic diseases, such as rheumatism and gout, not only because of the pain associated with these afflictions, but also because of the toxins and poisons circulating in the blood, which are probably primarily responsible for these disorders.

That the mind is influenced by the body is shown by both *extremes of bodily weight.* There can be little question that obese, abnormally fat persons, as well as the thin, emaciated, and cadaverous, have their peace of mind and intellectual activity more or less interfered with, as the result of their bodily state.

When a child has *rickets* of the bones, his physical condition unfavorably affects the mental development. In other words, the child with rickets is rickety in mind as well as in body.

Recent investigations afford positive proof that *adenoids* in the child interfere with the development of the brain, and thus more or less permanently cripple the mentality of the child. Various other minor afflictions of childhood may similarly affect the mental development, such as chronic tonsilitis, chronic ear-ache, and many other maladies.

No one will seriously question the fact that *pain* invariably exerts a deleterious influence upon the mind. Intellectual activity and mental usefulness are restricted or well-nigh destroyed by severe or long continued pain in any part of the body, resulting from any cause whatsoever.

Minor disturbances or *bony growths in the nose* may result in persistent chronic headaches, which greatly interfere with peace of mind and mental usefulness. We have known of persons suffering from headache for years, who were immediately relieved by the removal of a bony growth from the nose, or by the straightening of a crooked nasal septum.

There can be no more marked illustration of the effect of the body upon the mind than in the case of *arteriosclerosis*, or hardening of the arteries. This harbinger of old age not only results in producing those familiar manifestations of physical decay which characterize senility, but they also result in producing a state of comparative brain starvation. The mind is under-nourished, all the mental powers are enfeebled, the memory is weakened, and we are brought face to face with that pathetic picture of increasing mental weakness commonly denominated "second childhood."

There can be little doubt that the various *internal secreting glands* such as the pituitary body, thymus gland, thyroid gland, suprarenal gland, the sexual glands, etc., are all concerned in powerfully influencing the mind, temperament, and disposition. Witness the mental inaction, the idiotic expression of the cretin — the child whose thyroid gland is not functionating normally. (See Fig. 7.) Observe the marked mental and temperamental changes which result from the disease or

FIG. 7.
A CRETIN CHILD.

UNIV. OF
CALIFORNIA

HOW THE MIND IS INFLUENCED 33

removal of the sexual glands, by depriving the brain of the influence of their internal secretions.

The effect of the various *nervous diseases* upon the mind is self-evident. Paralysis, various spinal diseases, neuritis and neuralgias all very directly and markedly affect the mind. Victims of paræsthesia — those who feel various pricking, burning, or itching sensations in different parts of the body — are sometimes driven almost to distraction by these abnormal manifestations.

Mental action is even interfered with by *eye-strain* and many other common disorders affecting some part of the nervous system.

In fact, every physical practice of the individual and the entire life conduct, react either favorably or unfavorably upon the mind. The young man may pass on gayly and heedlessly, sowing his wild oats in the seed-time of youth, but in the harvest time of after life, not only must the body pay a physical penalty for the follies of ignorance and sin, but the mind also is forced to share in the painful and sorrowful harvest.

Even worry is often caused by the bodily state, there being a whole group of worry causes which may properly be termed physical causes. These will be fully considered in the chapters devoted to worry.

SUMMARY OF THE CHAPTER

1. The mind is recognized as holding the balance of control over numerous physical processes; nevertheless, almost equal recognition must be accorded the power of the bodily state in its influence over the mental operations.

2. While sunshine and good weather elevate the emotions, fogs and cloudy weather universally depress the physical functions and decrease the mental activities.

3. Fresh air, ventilation, and breathing are all concerned in the development and operation of the intellectual powers. Oxygen is indispensable to the operation of mind and body.

4. Shallow breathers are nearly always despondent and easily discouraged. *D*eep breathing is conducive to deep thinking. "The blues" are due to superficial breathing and resultant portal (liver) congestion.

5. Regular body work is essential to first-class brain work. Physical idleness leads to mental indolence. Physical development — within physiological limits — favors mental development; on the other hand, overwork of the body leads to mental fatigue as well as physical weariness.

6. The stomach, digestion, and dyspepsia all exert a profound influence on the mental state. Sour stomach usually culminates in a sour disposition. It is impossible to have peace in the head and war in the stomach.

7. Biliousness invariably deteriorates brain action — the brain is jaundiced as well as the body. When the liver is torpid the mind soon follows suit.

8. Thinking is directly related to eating. Gluttony, intemperance, and dietetic ignorance, all react disastrously to the weakening of the mental powers. Table habits powerfully influence thinking habits.

9. The blood is the life — the life of mind as well as body. Mental action is immediately influenced by fluctuations in blood-pressure or alterations of blood quality. Bodily anæmia is usually accompanied by intellectual anæmia.

10. Self-poisoning or auto-intoxication is not infrequently mistaken for moral perversity and mental insubordination. Contamination of the circulating fluids of the body results in perverting the mental powers.

11. Many a giant intellect has been starved out or killed by the combined terrors of dyspepsia and constipation. There is a direct relation between putrefying food stuff in the digestive canal, and perversity of mental action in the brain.

12. Bathing is an antidote for clothes and sedentary living. Elimination is essential to healthy thinking. There is a direct relation between skin action and brain action.

13. All acute diseases and all chronic disorders operate to weaken, pervert, derange, or disease the mental action. There is not a single physical disease that does not react unfavorably upon the mind. There can be no disorder of body function without more or less derangement of mind action.

CHAPTER IV
PSYCHOLOGY — HOW WE THINK

MODERN PSYCHOLOGY.— THE ORIGIN OF THOUGHT.— INACCURACIES OF THINKING.— PERCEPTS, THE UNDIGESTED FOOD OF THE MIND.— CONSCIOUSNESS OR THE STATE OF ATTENTION.— IMAGES AND EMOTIONS.— IMAGINATION AND PHANTASY.— DANGERS OF DISEASED IMAGINATION.— THE PROCESS OF CONCEPTION.— MISCONCEPTIONS.— THE POWERS OF MEMORY.— RECOLLECTION.— RECOGNITION.— RETENTION.— IMPRESSION. —THE ASSOCIATION OF IDEAS.— INTUITION.—INTELLECTUAL HOUSE-CLEANING.— JUDGMENT AND REASON.— MAN A REASONING ANIMAL.— THE CROWNING ACT OF THOUGHT.

FOR centuries the nature and cause of disease, as well as the form and functions of the physical body, remained more or less of a mystery; and as a result of this ignorance of things physical, superstition and ignorance dominated medicine and controlled the treatment of disease. It was only the advent of the microscope, and the subsequent discovery that disease owes its origin to distortion of the form, or derangement of the function, of the living cell — and not to the wrath of the gods, to the flight of the stars, or to a mysterious dispensation of Providence — that changed our views of physical maladies; but even now, in the clear scientific light of the twentieth century, we find the remnants and relics of these ancient superstitions concerning disease, clinging tenaciously to the minds of the people.

MODERN PSYCHOLOGY

What the microscope with its discoveries did for disease, modern psychology with its scientific laboratory investigations is doing for the mind — dispelling the mists of ignorance and establishing a scientific foundation for the study of mind and the treatment of mental disturbances.

36   THE PHYSIOLOGY OF FAITH AND FEAR

It is little wonder that the functions of the brain and the operations of the mind have been enshrouded in mystery. The old psychology or mental philosophy consisted largely of fanciful theories, unproven assertions, and unscientific conclusions, and largely represented the personal opinions of certain text-book writers. The old psychology was dreamed out in the library, the psychology of to-day is wrought out in the laboratory and represents accurate observations, scientific experiments, and conclusions which are drawn from the systematic study of mental phenomena — conclusions which are based upon the known laws of mind and matter — laws deduced from actually experienced facts. Psychology is becoming an honorable and more or less definite science.

We do not intend to convey the idea that psychology has become such a definite science as mathematics, or as precise and well-understood as chemistry and other of the physical sciences. The laws of mind and their operation will probably never be so fully understood as the laws of matter; nevertheless, we possess sufficient information concerning the working of the mind to safeguard the common people effectually against the scores of cunningly devised and fraudulently perpetrated systems of mind cure and mental healing.

A proper understanding of the most elementary principles of psychology will serve to protect the average man from the delusions and deceptions of the modern humbugs of healing. While this volume is chiefly devoted to the consideration of the physiological aspects of mental healing, we regard it as highly essential to call attention to the fundamental principles of psychology, the knowledge of which will do much to remove the haze of mystery and the fog of ignorance which now surround *mind* and its operation.

The knowledge of physiology has been popularized to that point where the process of digestion is now quite generally understood. The mystery of physiology and anatomy passed with the last century; and it is the purpose of this chapter concisely to review — to present in outline, as it were — the mental processes, the physiology of the brain, to tell *how we think*.

THE ORIGIN OF THOUGHT

One of the fundamental facts connected with the study of the mind, as related to health and disease, is the *physical origin of thought*. All thoughts which are evolved in the brain and which finally find expression in various ways, are actually constructed out of literal physical impressions, transmitted over the nervous system from the organs of special sense to the brain.

No detailed description of the process of thinking will be here attempted. For those who are especially interested in giving more than passing attention to this phase of the subject, a diagram (Fig. 9.) accompanied by a key of concise definitions has been prepared and will be found in the next chapter. A brief study of this diagram and reference to the accompanying key, will afford a fairly accurate and practical knowledge of the general outlines of psychology.

Physical impressions are produced in various organs of the body by the action of certain stimuli. These impressions originate in the nerve terminals of the different organs of special sensation. Sensations of sight are aroused by the vibrations of light acting upon the optic nerve of the eye and its associated structures. Sensations of hearing are excited when soundwaves strike the ear, producing impressions which are conveyed by the auditory nerve to the hearing centres of the brain. Likewise, the sense of smell is stimulated by odoriferous fumes and vapors and other substances which find their way into the nose, thereby exciting the olfactory nerves which carry these impressions to the corresponding brain centre. Taste is excited by certain substances coming in contact with the taste buds on the surface of the tongue, from whence these impressions are immediately transmitted to the brain; and so sensations of temperature and weight, and even of pain, are originated in the various nerves found in the skin, and are carried up through the spinal cord to certain special centres in the brain.

The excitation of any or all of these special nerves and the carrying of their impulses to the brain, gives rise to *sensation;* and so we may define sensation as the conscious recognition by the mind of any and all impressions which are made upon one or more of the special sense organs of the body.

INACCURACIES OF THINKING

The accuracy of thinking, the reliability of thought, it will at once be seen, is entirely dependent upon the perfection of the nervous mechanism of the organs of special sensation, as well as upon the reliability of the nervous system in the transmission of its impressions, and still further upon the accuracy and correctness of the brain centres in their interpretation of these physical impressions, preliminary to their becoming a part of our thought — entering into our mental conclusions — and thus becoming a part of our final decisions.

That our physical senses do not always represent things just as they are will be shown by referring to the few simple illustrations of optical illusions shown in Fig. 8. Illustration *a* presents three lines having different terminal markings. Which line looks the longest? They are all three the same length.

Illustration *b* shows three differently constructed figures. Which one is square? Which the widest? Which the deepest? They are all three exactly square.

Illustration *c* shows two equal spaces. Which looks the longer? Illustration *d* shows a broken line, 1. Which line, 2 or 3, is the continuation of line 1? Line 2 appears to be, but line 3 is the continuation of line 1.

Illustration *e* shows two different arrangements of parallel lines. Do the horizontal lines look straight? They are all four perfectly straight and parallel with one another.

Illustration *f* exhibits another deceptive arrangement of four parallel lines. These simple illustrations for the eye only serve to show that our physical senses are not absolutely reliable in obtaining and reporting first impressions. Thus the eye reports that a man is only a foot high when he is a mile away. It is necessary to train our senses and to check up and correct many of our first impressions and the knowledge dependent thereon. Analogous illusions and sensory errors are found to exist in connection with all the other special senses.

It is evident that our mental conclusions are not necessarily right just because things *look* good, taste good, or sound all right. Liberal allowance must be made for errors and miscon-

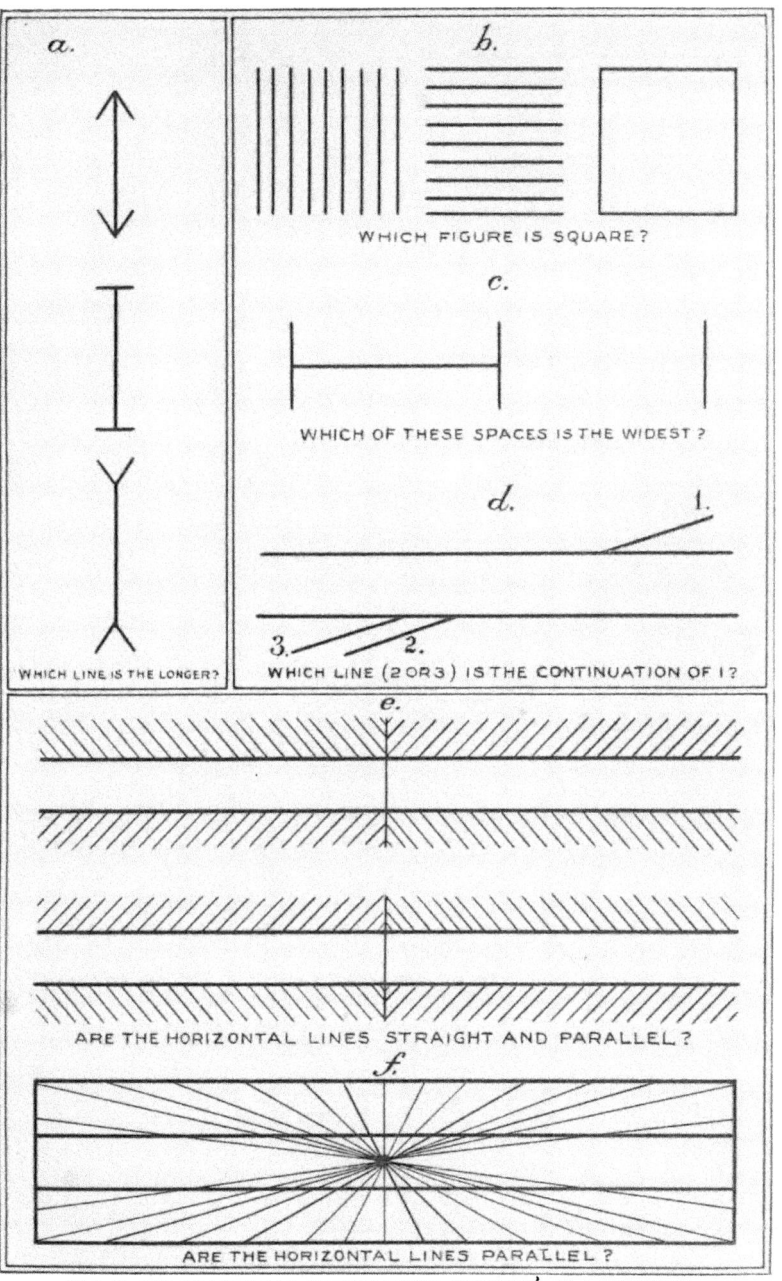

FIG. 8. DIAGRAMS ILLUSTRATING OPTICAL ILLUSIONS

UNIV. OF
CALIFORNIA

PSYCHOLOGY — HOW WE THINK

ceptions, in connection with our special senses; and if the physical senses are thus subject to mistakes and miscalculations, it is further evident that our thoughts and conclusions are bound to be more or less misformed and distorted as a result of these physical inaccuracies.

And so it is possible for the body to originate, and the mind to recognize, sensations which are not actually present; for instance, cancer of the foot can produce severe pain for months; cancer, foot, and all, may be amputated, and yet the patient may keep on recognizing pain as coming from the foot — recognizing it as in the foot, for weeks after the diseased member has been buried in some distant field.

And so various sensations of feeling — itching, pricking, burning — as well as sounds and voices, and sights and objects, may be aroused in the brain, while in reality they have no existence — they are merely illusions, sense delusions, or mental hallucinations. Sensations can produce ideas, and it should also be borne in mind that ideas can produce sensations.

"All our feelings possess a natural language or expression. The smile of joy, the puckered features in pain, the stare of astonishment, the quivering of fear, the tones and glance of tenderness, the frown of anger — are all united in seemingly inseparable association with the states of feeling which they indicate. If a feeling arises without its appropriate sign or accompaniment, we account for the failure either by voluntary suppression, or by the faintness of the excitement, there being a certain degree of intensity requisite visibly to affect the bodily organs"

The physical sense impressions become sensations and feelings in the brain; and feelings may be described as a translation of the more purely physical impressions into nervous sensations that can be recognized by the mind. And so the fundamental basis of thought is found to be wholly physical, and the first step in thinking, conscious sensation, has its foundation in the special organs of sense connected with the body.

PERCEPTS, THE UNDIGESTED FOOD OF THE MIND

Theoretically, sensation is the basis of thought, but it is highly probable that any person old enough to read these pages has long since ceased to experience simple sensations. All our sensations are almost instantaneously and automatically translated into percepts, and percepts represent the first step whereby sensations begin to take shape toward the formation of concepts, thoughts, and ideas. When our physical sense impressions have been recognized as sensations and feelings, the real process of conscious thinking has begun.

Percepts constitute the raw or undigested food which has been brought over the nerve tracts, from the sense organs to the conscious centres of the brain and into the mind; and *perception* may be said to be the process of forming percepts out of sensations and feelings. It constitutes the first step in the process of mental digestion — perception might be called intellectual mastication. Percepts, when once formed, are carried upward in the consciousness as images and emotions, entering into the imagination, phantasy, memory, association of ideas, and the process of conception.

CONSCIOUSNESS, OR THE STATE OF ATTENTION

Before proceeding further with the study of the process of thought, it will be well to define consciousness. Consciousness is not a separate mental power. It represents the action of the entire mind, it is the state of mental awareness — the power of attention and recognition. Consciousness is the recognition of all bodily sensations and mental operations in which all are bound together and unified.

The higher we ascend in the level of consciousness, the less sensation we have, and the more appreciation we have of the real meaning of things. Consciousness, then, represents the activity of the entire mind; it is the soul, the *I know* of the individual.

Attention may be regarded as the selective activity of consciousness, the ability of the mind to concentrate itself on an object or thought. Attention has two aspects: the outer, or sensory attention, which arouses the mental activity by means of physical sensory impressions; and the inner, or mental attention, in which the mind is aroused by the presence of an idea. This inner attention is the door of the real reflective powers. It is *the eye of the mind.*

IMAGES AND EMOTIONS

The influences which may act upon the body's senses may be divided into those which are true and those which are false.

PSYCHOLOGY — HOW WE THINK

Man himself is now commonly regarded as a threefold being, consisting of a body, mind (soul), and spirit. The body represents matter; the soul represents mind (and throughout this text will be used synonymously with mind); while the spirit represents the spiritual forces entering into the life of the individual. The nervous system is the channel by which both truth and error gain access to the mind The mind may be said to be dealing with and feeding upon truth, when it is engaged in receiving and contemplating principles or facts which are uncontradictory, when it is dealing with conclusions and teachings which are universal in their application. *Truth* constitutes the real food, the natural food of the mind *Error* is simply perverted truth — truth which is misstated, or otherwise distorted.

As the mind is fed upon truth or error, naturally its images and emotions will become true or false. As soon as percepts are formed in the lower levels of thinking, the mind at once chooses symbols to represent these percepts, which it forms out of sensations and feelings. These symbols or *images* may stand for thoughts or for objects, and they are true to life and facts only in so far as our sensations and perceptions have been truly formed and correctly interpreted. Images may be correct or incorrect, as the emotions may be genuine, porportionate, and in harmony with the perceptions; or through fear and sudden fright they may become exaggerated, distorted, and highly deceptive in their effect upon the mind.

The emotions are in reality the recognition of feelings which are going on in the various internal organs of the body in the presence of some unusual or extraordinary situation. The emotions all have their origin and basis in physical sensations and bodily states. The emotions are probably largely produced and influenced by the blood supply of the internal organs together with certain nervous conditions which may originate therein. Thoughts need words for their expression, but feelings and emotions require no words; in fact, we often vainly try to express our feelings in words, only to find that mere words **are** inadequate.

Here again, we discover abundant opportunity for **mental**

deception and other errors of interpretation. A diseased body, perverted sensations, and distorted perceptions, are bound to produce more or less deformity of our images and disparity of our emotions.

IMAGINATION AND PHANTASY

As our sensations are translated into perceptions, accompanied by the formation of images and the feeling of emotions, they may be said to pass upward in the level of thought by two routes, one leading to conception, the other to association of ideas; or we might say that our perceptions were made manifold, about seven copies being prepared, one designed for each of the departments of images, emotions, imagination, phantasy, memory, conception, and the association of ideas. Percepts, it will be remembered, constitute the raw, undigested food of the mind.

The imagination is in reality the creative power of the mind. It is ever at work forming new experiences out of our old ones. The powers of imagination take our ideas and fashion them into our ideals. This is the higher or creative imagination. Another function of this mental power, reproductive imagination, is very closely allied to memory, in fact, it is commonly regarded as a part of memory.

Closely associated with the imagination but entirely distinct from it, is the power of phantasy. Phantasy must not be confused with fancy. This peculiar power of phantasy represents what might be called the safety-valve of the mind. It is closely associated with memory, and may be regarded as its playhouse. Our powers of phantasy find expression in daydreams and day reveries. Phantasy represents the self adrift. It is the state of mind one finds himself in while resting in a hammock on a beautiful summer's afternoon, oblivious of all surroundings, wide awake, and yet letting the thoughts drift down the stream of mind without guidance, help, or interference.

As we ascend in the realms of thought, we reach more and greater possibilities of mental confusion and mind deception. It is quite impossible for the very young child to discriminate between imagination, memory, and images. The child of three years will vividly describe his meetings with lions and other wild beasts, and may tell these things as real experiences which have just happened. He is really recalling the pictures of lions from his books, or reviving the memory images of the beasts observed at the zoo.

No good is gained by scolding or punishing children for these mental inaccuracies, as if they were wilfully falsifying. Time and training will teach their young minds the distinction between these different departments of thought. But it is doubtful if even years and experience are able fully to separate these mental powers; and herein is the fruitful field for the birth of imaginary diseases, the production of unreal troubles, and the creation of false difficulties — fictitious lions and bears which await us in the highway of life, and which become just as real to the diseased adult mind as are the imaginary concepts and images of the nursery to the childish mind of the infant.

DANGERS OF DISEASED IMAGINATION

When the imagination becomes diseased, when the phantasy unduly influences and controls the mind, it is not difficult to conceive of a vicious combination of mental perversions in which the self drifts aimlessly over an imaginary ocean, beset with unreal dangers and threatened with false reefs; storm-tossed, battered, and beaten by imaginary winds; living in momentary danger of fictitious shipwreck and eternal doom — all of which is either wholly or in part imaginary.

What is to hinder the imagination from setting in operation false notions, resurrecting disagreeable impressions, and, by its well-known powers of reconstruction, creating new feelings and strange sensations? If you once had a disease of the stomach, what is there to prevent the uncontrolled imagination reporting that you now have a disease in the liver; or, if your neighbor across the street has a disease of the spine, what can hinder your imagination telling you that you also have a disease of the spine?

The imagination is the creative power of the mind, and it is not always exclusively exercised in creating labor-saving machinery and improved conditions of living, but it is also often engaged in creating mischief, fictitious difficulties, and even false diseases and unreal disorders of the body.

It is self-evident that victims of a diseased imagination need only to have the phantasy arrested and the current of imagination turned from a diseased into a healthy channel — and suddenly they find themselves well, completely cured. The tide of imagination was running against the health. Imagination is largely susceptible of control, and so when its powers become subject to a central thought, a religious conviction, or any other dominant idea, the imagination is directed into channels of health — and lo ! an apparent miracle has been wrought. Pain, weakness, sorrow, and a host of other afflictions apparently real in their physical basis, are put to flight — they instantly disappear; and so we here get a glimpse not only of how much sorrow and even sickness may be caused, but also how they are ofttimes cured.

THE PROCESS OF CONCEPTION

As we ascend upward in the levels of consciousness, our percepts — the raw, undigested food of the mind — reach the level of conception. Conception is that power of the mind which takes our percepts — the undigested food — and forms them into definite concepts; and it may also weave into the concepts our own ideas or mental conclusions. *Conception is the process of mental digestion,* in reality it is the preparation of our mental material for the review of the higher mental powers, such as judgment and reason. This act of analyzing the mental pictures consists of four parts, and comprises the fundamental process of thinking. The different phases of conception are: reflection, comparison, abstraction, and classification.

First, we *reflect,* and reflection is the first step in the digestive process of the mind. Then we *compare,* we recognize points that are alike and those that are unlike, we carefully identify the new and the old features of the mental picture. As we study, we *abstract,* we draw out the properties or qualities of our images, ascertain if they are large or small, sweet or bitter, good or bad; and then we *classify,* that is, we endeavor to arrange in an orderly fashion our newly formed concepts, according to certain fixed principles.

PSYCHOLOGY — HOW WE THINK

We now leave behind the percepts, which were originally formed out of our physical sensations. From now on we are dealing with *concepts,* and concepts may be defined as the symbols used to represent some mental image or material thing. The mental food may no longer be regarded as raw or undigested — it has now been subjected to mental mastication and digestion; at least it is certainly partially digested, and ready to pass upward into the higher levels of consciousness.

MISCONCEPTIONS

And again, we here discern many opportunities in this complicated process of mental digestion for errors and inaccuracies to creep in. What if we fail fully to reflect or properly to compare our percepts ? Will this not result in the formation of deformed and unhealthy concepts ? Suppose that unreasoning fear or unwarranted faith should dominate the mind at this particular time ! What if our classifications are faulty ? Is it not easy to conceive of the possibilities of intellectual indigestion — mental dyspepsia — and subsequent suffering and distress of mind ? Will not the ideas which are to be formed out of these faulty concepts be diseased and distorted by errors in the working of the mental machinery at this point ?

Suppose we but incompletely abstract the qualities of our percepts, or but partially and erroneously classify our experiences — will not these blunders lead directly to errors in judgment and mistakes in reason ? Will not such errors of thought give rise to illegitimate and unhealthy ideas ?

And so we begin to see more and more that an idea, an experience, a sensation, a pain, or even a disease, may be wholly unreal — that it does not follow that an experience is true and genuine just because the mind accepts it as true. The mind is capable of almost unlimited deception, monstrous imposition, and is subject to innumerable errors of internal working and inaccuracies of the thinking process.

THE POWERS OF MEMORY

But we must not proceed further without giving proper consideration to that wonderful and mysterious realm of the mind known as memory. Memory is the soul's power to recognize and hold images and ideas. It is the realm where the assimilated, intellectual food is stored for future use. Memory is thought by some to retain practically everything which passes through consciousness — percepts, concepts, and ideas. Undoubtedly, its capacity is well-nigh infinite. Like the process of conception, memory has four distinct departments. First, we have *recollection,* the door-keeper of memory — the active power of memory concerned in bringing knowledge, images, and facts back into the working consciousness. Recollection is a sort of librarian to the memory: when you wish to recall a fact or a name, recollection goes back into the storehouse of memory, and from its archives brings forth the fact or name desired.

Recognition — the second power of memory — is that well-known mental feeling of familiarity you experience when you meet something you have met before. It is to the memory a sort of bureau of identification, scrutinizing all new material and recalling whether or not it has ever before passed into or through memory.

Retention is the memory's faculty of holding facts and images, subject to future recall. This function is probably made possible by the fact that every impulse which passes over a nerve wears some sort of a track — creates some sort of a path — just as the frequent walking over the lawn creates a trodden path. Our mental impressions also undoubtedly make some actual physical impression upon the brain cells. And now we are beginning to recognize the physical basis of memory.

Impression, the fourth division of memory, represents the function of receiving memory-material and recording the intensity or degree of influence it exerts upon the mind. When the impression is strong, the memory, other things equal, is good; when the impression is weak, the memory is usually poor or faulty.

Memory, being the mental storehouse, receives the percepts directly from perception. It has knowledge of all concepts and images; in fact, it holds the transcripts of all the mental processes. All things are brought to it — sometimes direct, sometimes by the path which extends through the association of ideas.

And now again, in the study of memory, we are brought face to face with many possibilities for the birth of false impressions, the creation of unreal feelings, and, in conjunction with imagination, the actual construction of deceptive ideas and the formation of false ideals. It is impossible to conceive of the possibilities of mind deception, extending from mental delusions to fictitious physical disease, that would be made possible by a working conspiracy between imagination and memory, when both these mental powers are irritated and diseased by a poisonous blood stream. Untold mischief and almost unlimited torture could be imposed on a neurotic person already suffering from a worn-out and self-poisoned nervous system.

ASSOCIATION OF IDEAS

The product of the mental operations is now approaching the level of idea-formation. About this time in the mental operation, the mysterious process of *idea-association* takes place. This mental power is very early shown in the development of the child's mind. The process is usually an unconscious one, but may be highly conscious. The association of ideas may be regarded as the clearing-house of the mind, and the great majority of all our concepts and mental images pass this way *en route* to the higher activities.

Intuition is simply the spontaneous association of ideas. We commonly speak of the animal as having instinct, referring to its hereditary knowledge. In man, we call this hereditary or acquired knowledge which so strongly influences our concepts through the channels of idea-association and imagination, intuition.

What unlimited possibilities must exist for weal or for woe in the confines of this little-known realm of idea-association! A glance at the thought-diagram (Fig. 9) will suggest the tremendous possibilities of getting wires crossed, messages tangled, impulses twisted; in fact, it may not be out of the way to imagine thought-wrecks and other mental catastrophes and confusions, as a result of throwing wrong switches or misreading the signals in this important realm of the mind, or from failure on the part of some mental power to do its work in just the right way and at just the right time.

Imagine the possibilities for mischief when a good or healthy idea is seeking to reach the higher levels of thought and has to pass this way through a group of bad, diseased ideas. What is usually the effect of the association of one good person with a number of bad persons? Again, suppose we have a true idea which must struggle through this area of association against many false ideas, have we any assurance that truth will always triumph in this mental struggle? Or, suppose that the majority of the thoughts of the mind are about sickness and sorrow, disease and distress; will they not eventually succeed in polluting the whole train of thought?

INTELLECTUAL HOUSE-CLEANING

In such a case, it would require one of two things to afford deliverance from this bondage of diseased thought. Either persistent mental training carried to a point where a majority of our thoughts are healthy and wholesome; or the acceptance of a powerful and all-embracing idea which sweeps through the mind with absolute conviction and utterly vanquishes every opposing thought. This is exactly the sort of intellectual house-cleaning that takes place when one's mind is converted to a new way of thinking, a new mode of life, or to a new religion.

From now onward, as we ascend in the level of consciousness, we are dealing entirely with *ideas*. Our percepts having been acted upon by conception — mental digestion — are formed into concepts, and after receiving the contributions of imagination and memory, these newborn concepts are introduced to the idea-community of the mind, in the realm of the association of ideas; after which they ascend upward in consciousness to take their place in the intellectual struggle after the fashion of full-grown ideas. An idea, in this sense, may be defined as a mental picture or conclusion formulated by the combined action of the mental powers to be reviewed by judgment and reason.

Fully formed ideas now enter into the realm of *idea discrimination* — a higher centre of thought, preliminary to the action of judgment and reason; and now begins the intelligent scrutiny of the revised product of our mental operations, after having passed through the association of ideas.

JUDGMENT AND REASON

Judgment is the conscious verdict of the mind which is rendered, following the operation of conception and the other mental powers. The judgment may deal with any object of consciousness. It may concern itself with things or with ideas. The judgment is the formulator of facts, the constructor of conclusions, and is the one mental power to benefit especially by educational training. Systematic schooling does more to train and develop the judgment than any other mental power. The value of education consists not so much in the acquisition of facts as in the proper training of the powers of judgment and reason.

But suppose that the judgment is poorly trained! What if its conclusions are unreliable and its decrees untrustworthy? The higher we ascend in the level of consciousness, the more disastrous become the results of mistakes and errors in the working of the mental machinery. Regardless of whether sensations, perceptions, conceptions, and ideas are real or false, healthy or diseased, what must be the effect on the health of the mind and body if judgment blunders? If judgment is deceived and deluded, how can an imaginary disease which afflicts the mind and torments the body ever be cured? Is it not possible to see the effects of mistaken judgment upon the health of the body as well as upon the success of our financial enterprises'?

When judgment has rendered its decision, reason begins the work of analyzing and scrutinizing these judgment decrees; in fact, reason may be defined as the manipulation of judgments. It is 'a process of comparison and discrimination. Its business is the hatching of new judgments out of old judgments — a method of getting new truth from the truth already known.

MAN A REASONING ANIMAL

Reason is a mental power in which man stands preëminent above the brute creation. Recent experiments go a long way toward proving that animals do but little reasoning in connection with their mental operations, even in the performance of their apparently intelligent feats and wonderful tricks.

Man is the reasoning animal, but the trouble is that but few people fully use this wonderful power of the human mind. The majority of us do but little reasoning; and that is why the progress of civilization is so slow, why the causes of liberty and freedom are so backward. Men and women simply will not reason consistently. Again, when the process is started, it not infrequently works in the wrong direction. Many persons are just as likely to reason themselves into trouble as out of trouble. If the judgment is poor, and if the preceding mental work has been of an inferior quality, what can be expected of reason?

Reason is altogether too easily influenced by the judgments which are passed up to it. Now we come to the very citadel of the mind, to the very mental power which is so largely concerned in the moral cure of sickness and the mental cause of disease.

If you can captivate the reason with a single idea, paralyze it with erroneous religious teaching, anæsthetize it with some fascinating and deceptive cult, you have done much to prepare the way for the production of spectacular effects in mind cure — astonishing results in the line of recovery from disease. On the other hand, it must be easy to imagine how quickly one can reason himself into mental depression and imaginary physical disease, when he has lost perfect control of the reasoning powers, or when suffering from perverted imagination or distortion of the mind. Some of the causes of his troubles may have been wholly physical in their origin.

THE CROWNING ACT OF THOUGHT

Now we come to the final act of mental operation. Our thought had its origin in the body, passing up through the various levels of consciousness to judgment and reason; and, following the conclusions of reason, the mind takes the final step, that of choice. Choice or affirmation is the crowning act of thought. It really represents the final decree of combined judgment and reason, and when reduced to writing it constitutes our book knowledge.

This mental liberty — moral freedom — is the glory of man. The sensations which were the beginnings of thought are now

PSYCHOLOGY — HOW WE THINK 51

ripe for full translation into actions, the end of thought. Actions are the execution of the decrees of choice or affirmation by the order of the will. Our acts may be voluntary, as when we deliberately choose to do one thing in preference to another thing. They may be involuntary, as when we automatically do a thing from force of habit, just because we have repeatedly done that same thing in that same way; or our actions may be reflex, as in the case of quickly drawing the hand away from a hot stove. The mechanism involved in this act was fully explained in a former chapter.

By frequent repetition, physical acts result in the formation of habits, and habits constitute our mode of life. They represent the kind of thinking we have done, they stand for the thoughts which have ripened into actions; and these actions have been repeated until they have become automatic, reflex, unconscious, and sometimes uncontrollable. In a certain sense, habit may be regarded as physical memory. When conscious acts are performed thousands of times they become unconscious. In this way we are able to use, as it were, only the interest on our nerve energy and not the principal.

And so again, we see how the mind can influence the body. Perverted thinking, wicked living, may in time so pervert the nervous system and bring disease upon the brain, as to render the higher intelligence well-nigh helpless in the work of coping with intemperate habits and vicious passions. And so when habits of pain, of fear, of suffering, of vice, or of disease, are once formed, it is exceedingly difficult to break the binding fetters forged by the long-continued and daily repetition of physical impressions and sensations. In such cases, it actually seems as if a new mind of health and strength must be provided, which will prove sufficiently strong and powerful to take the place of the old mind of weakness and disease, before the patient can hope to find deliverance from the bondage of mental disease and the thraldom of physical vice.

(The will, conscience, and character are further considered in Chapter VI, which see. A summary of the matter contained in this chapter will be found in the next chapter.)

CHAPTER V

KEY TO *DIAGRAM OF PSYCHOLOGY*

The following key is in explanation of the diagram (Fig. 9) illustrating the action of the mind in the elaboration of thought, and is to be read with reference thereto.

1. *Man:* Body, Soul, and Spirit.
   "I pray God your whole spirit and soul and body may be preserved blameless."
2. *Truth:* Principles or facts which are uncontradictory; conclusions which are fundamental; teaching which is ultimate; and facts which are universal in application. Truth is the real food of the mind.
3. *Error:* Truth which is perverted, adulterated, misstated, or otherwise distorted.
4. *Sensation:* The conscious recognition by the mind of impressions made upon a sense organ.
5. *Feelings:* An attribute or universal accompaniment of sensation.
6. *Consciousness:* A state of awareness. The power of attention and recognition. The recognition of physical sensations and mental operations, in which all are bound together and unified.
7. *Attention:* The selective activity of consciousness or mind.

   a. The outer or sensory attention is the awakening of mental activity by means of sensory impressions.

   b. The inner or ideational attention is the awakening of mental activity by the presence of an idea or a combination of ideas.

   The inner attention is the threshold of the reflective powers. It is the door of real thinking — the eye of the mind.
8. *Perception:* The process of forming percepts out of sensations and feelings — intellectual mastication.
9. *Percepts:* Sensations are translated into percepts in consciousness. Percepts are the raw or undigested food of the mind.
10. *Images:* Symbols chosen to represent the perceptions which are formed out of sensations and feelings.

KEY TO DIAGRAM

11. *Emotions:* The feeling of bodily (visceral) changes going on in the presence of an unusual situation.
12. *Imagination:* The creative power of the mind. It works up our experiences into new forms; creates ideals out of ideas, etc. This is creative imagination. Another form — reproductive imagination — is a specialized function of memory.
13. *Phantasy* (not fancy): The safety-valve of the mind. The play-house of memory. ·Expressed in daydreams and day reveries. The self adrift.
14. *Conception:* The power of forming concepts out of percepts or from mental conclusions. The preparation of our mental material for the review of judgment and reason. This act of analyzing our mental pictures consists of four parts, and comprises the real process of thinking or mental digestion.
    a. Reflection — the first step in the digestive process of the mind.
    b. Comparison points out the like and the unlike. Identification of new and old.
    c. Abstraction — drawing out properties and qualities.
    d. Classification — orderly arrangement, according to fixed principles, of the abstracted qualities, ideas, or facts.
15. *Concepts:* Symbols used to represent some mental image or material thing. Conception is the process of forming these concepts. They originate within the mind, and represent the partially or wholly digested intellectual pabulum.
16. *Memory:* The soul's power to recognize and hold images and ideas. Probably it retains everything which has passed through consciousness — percepts, concepts, etc. Its capacity is well-nigh infinite. Memory is manifested through four different processes:
    a. Recollection — the door-keeper of memory. The active power of memory concerned in bringing knowledge and images back into consciousness.
    b. Recognition — the feeling of familiarity in meeting something you have met before.
    c. Retention — the holding of facts and images subject to future recall.
    d. Impression — the reception of memory-matter of varied intensity.
17. *Association of Ideas:* Usually an unconscious process, but may be highly conscious. The clearing-house of the mind. Nearly

all concepts and mental images pass this way *en route* to the higher activities.

Intuition is spontaneous association of ideas, hereditary or acquired knowledge influencing our concepts through the channel of idea-association and imagination.

18. *Ideas:* An idea is a mental picture or conclusion formulated by the combined action of the mental powers to be reviewed by judgment and reason.

19. *Idea-Discrimination:* A higher centre of thought — a complex process of thought-discrimination consisting of, or preliminary to, judgment and reason. The scrutiny of the revised product of our mental operations.

20. *Judgment:* The conscious verdict rendered following the operation of conception and other mental powers. This verdict may concern any object of consciousness — things or ideas. The formulator of facts. The great beneficiary of education.

21. *Reason:* The manipulation of judgments. The process of comparing, discriminating, and hatching new judgments out of old judgments. The method of getting new truth from the truth already known.

22. *Affirmation:* The crowning act of thought. The final decree of combined judgment and reason. Reduced to writing it constitutes our book knowledge.

23. *Actions:* The execution of the decrees of choice or affirmation, by order of the will. They may be:
    a. Voluntary.
    b. Involuntary.
        1. Automatic.
        2. Reflex.

24. *Habits:* The mode of life — actions repeated until they become automatic, reflex, unconscious, or uncontrollable.

25. *Character:* The real individual. The grand sum of sensations — ideas — memory — imagination — discrimination — affirmation — willing and doing — the finished material picture of the invisible mental painter.

26. *Conscience:* A guide to conduct and thought, having for its basis, our hereditary and acquired mental and moral attitudes. It is the voice of the spirit to the will. It is the essence or breath of the spirit — moral instinct. It imparts divine dignity to man and distinguishes him from the animal.

27. *Temptation:* The insinuations of evil. The acquired, hereditary,

KEY TO DIAGRAM 55

or suggested tendencies to depart from the way of right as dictated by the conscience.

28. *The Spirit:* The divine source of our higher emotions and affections. Judgment — ofttimes spontaneous — determines the right for the mind, and conscience prompts the will to order the execution of judgment's decrees.

29. *The Will:* Consists of several forms:
   a. Sensory-motor will.
   b. Idea-motor will.
   c. Inner-impulse will.
   d. Intelligent and deliberate will.

   The will is the supreme court of the mind. The final arbiter of choice. Has knowledge of and also includes all mental operations. It represents the combined spiritual, mental, and nervous forces brought to bear upon the mind or body to direct them in the channels of choice.

30. *Psychology:* The study of analyzable mental processes as influenced by the body, mental operations, or moral instincts. The study of the combined operation of the mind and spirit as influenced by the body. An examination of the operation of our mental powers. A classification of the laws of our mental life.

CHAPTER VI

THE SUPREME COURT OF THE MIND

THE SOVEREIGN WILL.— THE WILL AND THE MIND.— MAN A RESPONSIBLE BEING.— THE WILL AND THE BODY.— VITAL WORK AND THE WILL.— CHARACTER AND CONSCIENCE.—SUMMARY OF THE CHAPTER.

IN the two preceding chapters, the will has been given general consideration. The time has now come to study carefully the nature and operation of will-power. As already noted, the will is the supreme court of the human mind, and it is as such a tribunal of last resort that we shall proceed to examine this remarkable human attribute.

THE SOVEREIGN WILL

Reference to the thinking-diagram (Fig. 9.) will show at a glance that the will embraces the entire realm of our mental operations. While this is true, we must recognize that we really have four distinct forms or degrees of will-power. First, we have the sensory-motor will; that is the will-power which is aroused and acts as a result of having the sensations stimulated, and which then chooses a certain course of conduct as the result of the sensations experienced. Second, the idea-motor will, which causes the body to be set in operation as the result of an idea hatched out in the mind. Third, the will that is aroused by spontaneous impulses born within the mind; and, fourth, the will-action which accompanies the intelligent and deliberate making up of the mind to do a certain thing, and this probably represents the strongest action of the will-power — the complete action.

The will is the final arbiter of choice. It holds the balance of power in all mental operations. Its strength determines whether or not the body can be compelled to carry out the

SUPREME COURT OF THE MIND 57

orders of the mind. The man with the strong will has the body under the control of his own mind. The man with a weak will may have a mind controlled by the appetites and passions of the body; while one with a diseased will may find himself partially or wholly under the control of another mind. The will has knowledge of and also includes all mental operations.

The will represents the combined spiritual, mental, and nervous forces brought to bear upon mind and body to direct them in the channels of choice and conscientious conviction.

The will may be said to hear the voice of conscience and to receive the insinuations of evil. It is the clearing-house of the soul in the struggle between mind and matter. The will represents the supreme conclusions and the final effort of the mind, and it should be remembered that merely wishing is not willing. The will is the battle-ground of character formation.

The will is not a distinct mental power in the sense that judgment, reason, memory, etc., are powers of the mind. The will represents to the mind what the sum total does to a column of figures. It is the master-builder of character and the architect of eternal destiny.

THE WILL AND THE MIND

Man is not a mere machine, not even an intelligent machine. Machines can perform only the work for which they are constructed, they are not responsible. Man is in the highest sense responsible for his acts and habits; he has a will and possesses the power of choice. The majority of animals are quite dependent on their instincts and on the stimuli which reach their brains from the sensory nerves, but man is able to direct himself according to the choosing of his own will. While reason may be the highest act of the mind itself, practical experience goes to prove the reason, in fact the entire mind, is ever subservient to that mighty sovereign of the personality — the will.

We may rent our minds for a consideration, we may let out our intellects for hire, but no man ever leases his will to another. The will is inseparable from the personality. Reason is simply the attorney-general of the mind, appearing before the supreme court of the will. How frequently we see men who persistently hold on to certain opinions which are contrary to all reason. They will so to think, and you may be sure that such persons will see to it that their servile reasoning powers furnish them with abundant, and, to themselves, satisfactory reasons for their positions.

No man is responsible for the thoughts which enter the mind, but all men are responsible for the thoughts which are allowed to remain in the mind, for the will has complete and full jurisdiction over the entire intellect. The will can command the brain to think as it may direct, just as the mind possesses the power to direct the spinal cord to execute the physical movements which the brain may order. All, then, of the mental powers are coördinate and coöperative, while the will stands out as the ranking officer of the whole intellect, wielding the combined powers of direction, decision, and discipline.

MAN A RESPONSIBLE BEING

Because man has this splendid endowment of will, he at once becomes a creature of personal responsibility, and it is therefore incumbent upon him to exhibit a reasonable degree of self-possession, self-restraint, and self-control. Again, the will appears as the governor of the rate of mental activity. The mind with a weak will thinks rapidly and superficially. The strong will compels deep, deliberate, and logical thought. When the mind is not inhibited by the will, it roams about aimlessly from one end of the world to the other. It resembles a horse which has thrown its rider. Such a mind soon degenerates to the mere animal level — ever changing its course of thought with the constantly changing nerve impressions which are brought to the brain over the sensory nervous system. It requires downright hard work — constant effort — to keep the mind at work under the direction of the will. Without constant supervision by the will, the mind wanders aimlessly in the midst of the pleasant scenes of its own imagination. And it is just because we have so little will-thought that most of the mental energy of the world runs to waste, and all classes of society are overrun with idle dreamers. The divine gift of mental freedom carries the penalty of moral responsibility.

THE WILL AND THE BODY

The body, it would seem, has little objection to doing work at the request of the mind or sympathetic nervous system; but it seriously objects to the performance of special physical tasks by order of the will. To illustrate: there are numerous lines of physical work such as breathing, the beating of the heart, the muscular action of the stomach and intestines, all of which are cheerfully carried on from the cradle to the grave, with scarcely a murmur on the part of the body. In contrast with these incessant activities of the involuntary muscular mechanism of the body, let it be noted how quickly and profoundly the voluntary muscles are tired out and fatigued when the body is performing certain set tasks of work under the direction of the will.

The combined muscular work of breathing has been estimated as equivalent to raising several hundred pounds one inch, with each deep inspiration. The mind and body work together to effect the performance of this gigantic muscular task about twenty times a minute from infancy to old age, and yet we never get tired out or fatigued from breathing. This one illustration is amply sufficient to show that it requires something else besides physical work to exhaust the muscles. The muscles directed from the centres in the medulla are never allowed to slumber or sleep, they are in comparatively constant action; and so the nerve centres of the sympathetic nervous system are in unceasing action throughout life.

What, then, is it that causes the voluntary muscles and the central nervous system so quickly to wear out and break down? There seems but one answer to this question. The body seems able to perform almost unlimited and continuous service when such effort involves only natural and instinctive routine work; but the moment nerves and muscles are compelled to execute the mandates of the will — the moment the body is ordered into the harness for the performance of definite work, the moment the physical energies become subject to the direction and authority of the will — the whole organism begins to show evidence of being worked by some power external and foreign to itself, as exhibited by increasing weariness, fatigue, and, eventually, actual painful protest; and ultimately, if not allowed suitable rest, by exhaustion and death.

VITAL WORK AND THE WILL

As long as the body works only in response to the mandates of the medulla, it is simply doing *vital work,* and it cheerfully performs all such tasks without protest and without fatigue; but the instant the will orders arms and legs into action under its direction, that becomes work, *muscular labor,* and the body will not serve the will as it serves itself. It is not natural work that tires the body and exhausts the nerves, it is only *conscious effort* that wears and tears. Likewise, you daydream without a sense of mind effort or mental weariness, but the very moment you tighten the intellectual reins and begin to guide the mind into definite lines of thought and study, that very moment the brain begins to groan under the burdens imposed upon it and soon makes a definite outcry for rest and recreation.

The very fact that will-work so soon exhausts both mind and body, very strongly suggests that the will is not a mere mental power. It is conscious work and will-power that wearies us and renders sleep so essential to the restoration of our depleted energies.

CHARACTER AND CONSCIENCE

The character is the real individual. It is the grand sum of sensations, percepts, concepts, ideas, memory, imagination, discrimination, judgment, reason, affirmation, willing, and doing. It is the finished material picture of the invisible mental painter. The character is the combination of our physical habits and our mental operations. It determines the temperament, the morality, and the reliability of the individual. Our character is shown by our honesty, our spirituality, our self-control, our speech, and by our affections.

Character formation represents the grand and sublime purpose of life, and character formation is determined by our every thought, word, and action.

The formation of character is influenced not only by the process of thinking carried on within the mind, and its resultant physical acts, and the habits thereby formed, but also

SUPREME COURT OF THE MIND 61

by the spiritual powers — the higher moral influences to which the mind of man is subject, in contradistinction to the mind of the animal.

Man has a conscience. The conscience cannot be described as a separate mental power. It is the spiritual or moral guide to conduct and thought, having for its basis our hereditary and acquired mental attitudes and moral standards. It is the spiritual voice, speaking to the will. The conscience is man's moral instinct. It imparts divine dignity to the man, and forever distinguishes him from the animal.

The conscience is ever subject to education, and therefore it must never be looked upon as an infallible and unerring guide to conduct. The heathen is just as conscientious in praying to an idol as the Christian is in worshipping a personal God. The devout Hindoo mother is just as conscientious in throwing her innocent babe into the mouth of the crocodile as is the Christian missionary in his efforts to save her benighted soul.

The character is influenced in its formation not only by the heed we pay to conscience, but also by the insinuations of evil, commonly known as temptation; and these unfavorable influences represent our acquired, hereditary, and suggested tendencies to depart from the way of right as recognized by the mind and dictated by the conscience.

And so we must recognize that man is a spiritual being as well as an intelligent animal. The primitive man is always religious, he universally worships something. Absolute irreligion is only the product of artificial training and miseducation. The spirit which operates upon the mind of man constitutes the divine source of our higher emotions and affections. Judgment, ofttimes spontaneously, determines the right for the mind; and conscience prompts the will to order the execution of judgment's decrees.

THE SUMMARY OF THE CHAPTER

1. The will is the supreme court of the human mind — the "I DO" of the personality. The will consists of four distinct degrees: (a) *Sensory-motor* will. (b) *Idea-motor* will. (c) *Spontaneous-impulse* will. (d) *Deliberate-thought* will.

2. The will is the final arbiter of choice. It holds the balance of power in all mental operations. The will is not a distinct mental power. It represents to the mind what the sum total does to a column of figures.

3. The will represents the combined spiritual, mental, and nervous forces brought to bear upon mind and body to direct them in the channels of choice and conscientious conviction.

4. The will is the master-builder of character, and the architect of eternal destiny. It has knowledge of, and also includes, all mental operations.

5. Man is, in the biggest sense, a responsible being. Reason — the entire mind — is ever subservient to that mighty sovereign of the personality — the will.

6. Men rent their intellects for hire, but no man ever leases his will to another. The will is inseparable from the personality. Reason is the attorney-general arguing before the supreme court of the will.

7. The will can command and control the intellect, just as the mind has power to direct the spinal cord to execute the physical movements which the brain may order. The will is the ranking officer of the personality.

8. Weakness of will predisposes to superficial and rapid thinking. A strong will compels deep, deliberate, and logical thought. When the mind is not controlled by the will, it is comparable to a horse which has thrown its rider.

9. It is because we have so little will-thought that the mental energy of the world runs to waste, and society is overrun with idle and useless dreamers.

10. The physical body seems to be able to endure almost continuous exertion when its energies are employed in executing natural and necessary vital work, as in breathing or in heart action.

11. It is only conscious effort that tires and exhausts the body. The body wears out only when it is harnessed up and worked by the will.

12. Likewise, the mind will daydream forever without conscious weariness, but when forced to definite study by orders of the will, the brain soon groans under its burdens and clamors for rest or recreation.

13. Character is the real individual, it is the grand sum of intellectual operations, moral aspirations, and physical performances. It is the finished material picture of the invisible mental painter.

14. Character-formation represents the grand and sublime purpose of life. Character is determined by our every thought, word, and action.

15. Conscience is our moral guide to conduct, having for its basis our hereditary and acquired mental attitudes and moral standards. Conscience is subject to education. It is not an infallible guide.

CHAPTER VII

PHASES OF CONSCIOUSNESS

SUPRACONSCIOUSNESS, OR THE SPIRITUAL MIND.— THE CENTRAL CONSCIOUSNESS.— THE MARGINAL CONSCIOUSNESS, OR SUBCONSCIOUS MIND.— THE DUAL NATURE OF MIND.— THE MARGINAL CONSCIOUSNESS IN HEALTH AND IN DISEASE.— THE MARGINAL CONSCIOUSNESS AND THE BODY.— THE THREE PLANES OF CONSCIOUSNESS.— THE SPIRITUAL CONSCIOUSNESS. — THE INTELLECTUAL CONSCIOUSNESS.— THE PHYSICAL CONSCIOUSNESS.— THE THREEFOLD NATURE OF MAN.— THE DOUBLE FUNCTION OF ONE MIND.— COMPARISON OF THE CENTRAL AND MARGINAL CONSCIOUSNESSES.— SUMMARY OF THE CHAPTER.

IT is a well-known fact that the human mind is capable of various degrees of attention. It is possible to have all the mental powers directly focussed upon a single thought. It is also possible for the mind to wander, the attention may be more or less diffused, and the intellectual state may very closely approach the dreamy borderland of reverie and phantasy.

These different phases of consciousness are diagrammatically shown in Fig. 10. Both sound and light are taken as material illustrations of the different degrees of consciousness.

SUPRACONSCIOUSNESS, OR THE SPIRITUAL MIND

While it cannot be conclusively demonstrated by the laws of physiology and psychology, nevertheless, the evidence abundantly justifies the belief in a *spiritual consciousness*. The moral mind is a sort of spiritual intelligence; it might be regarded as the voice which speaks through conscience — the voice or influence speaking or acting through the conscientious element of the mind.

Reference to the diagram (Fig. 10) will show that when

PHASES OF CONSCIOUSNESS

sound vibrations are more than 41,000 per second, they are not recognized by the ear. We do not hear such rapid air vibrations, and these we have termed supra-auditory vibrations — vibrations which can be detected by certain instruments of precision although they are not recognized by the ear or by the hearing centres of the brain. Likewise, we have supra-visual oscillations of light — the ultra-violet rays. The actinic or chemical rays of sunlight belong to this class. They are unrecognized by the eye, yet they are real and are abundantly able to produce sunburns which are plainly visible the following day. And so it is clear that we have certain forms of light and sound which the eye and the ear fail to recognize. May it not be possible that we have to deal with spiritual influences which are not directly recognized by the so-called intellectual mind, but which are clearly understood and recognized by the spiritual or supraconscious mind?

THE CENTRAL CONSCIOUSNESS

By the central consciousness, we refer to the intellectual mind, the conscious mind, the voice of reason. Referring again to the diagram (Fig. 10), we observe that when air vibrations range from 16 to 41,000 per second, they are recognized by the ear and interpreted by the mind as sound. Likewise, with the oscillations of light, when they range from 699 billions per second down to about 477 billions, the sense of sight, through the eye, takes cognizance of the oscillations and they are recognized by the brain centres as light.

And so we have various mental processes going on in the mind which are entirely conscious and wholly intellectual. May we not also, as illustrated by the special senses of sight and hearing, have mental processes going on in the mind which are outside of the realm of the central consciousness, and which are therefore unconscious in the sense that they are not definitely recognized by the mind? Such processes might be regarded as supraconscious — above the usual intellectual activities — the voice of conscience or the spiritual perceptions; and as subconscious — below the level of the ordinary activities of the mind — the marginal consciousness — the voice of instinct or intuition.

THE MARGINAL CONSCIOUSNESS, OR SUBCONSCIOUS MIND

As we have a central consciousness, so we have also a marginal consciousness. When sound waves come down to sixteen per second or less, we have what might be called sub-auditory vibrations. We do not hear a sound, we recognize only separate beats. And so when the oscillations of light are less than those giving rise to redness, we have the so-called infra-red rays of light or heat. These might also be called sub-visual oscillations, as they are not discerned by the eye.

In the mind, when the consciousness becomes diffused to a certain point, when the concentration of the mental powers becomes scattered to a certain degree, when we get so far out from the centre of thinking that we fail properly to hold the various elements and factors of thought in the eye of the attention, or when we are merely acting from force of habit, we find that our actions arise largely from impulses originating in the unconscious areas of the mind. A person so doing may be said to be acting in obedience to the voice of instinct speaking through the subconscious or unconscious mind, the marginal consciousness.

This phase of consciousness has been variously called subconscious, unconscious, co-conscious, etc. We much prefer the term *marginal consciousness.*

THE DUAL NATURE OF MIND

It is a fact recognized by all physiologists and psychologists that the human mind presents phenomena of consciousness which can only be explained by the assumption of a dual mentality or other conditions analogous thereto. These two minds, so-called, are largely known by the terms "conscious mind" and "subconscious mind." We cannot help regarding it as exceedingly unfortunate that these terms ever came into general use. They carry the idea of the existence of two separate and distinct minds. Their use suggests even two separate brains or two distinct parts of one brain, but we believe this is all entirely wrong.

While it is true that the assumption of the existence of the so-called subconscious mind apparently explains the behavior

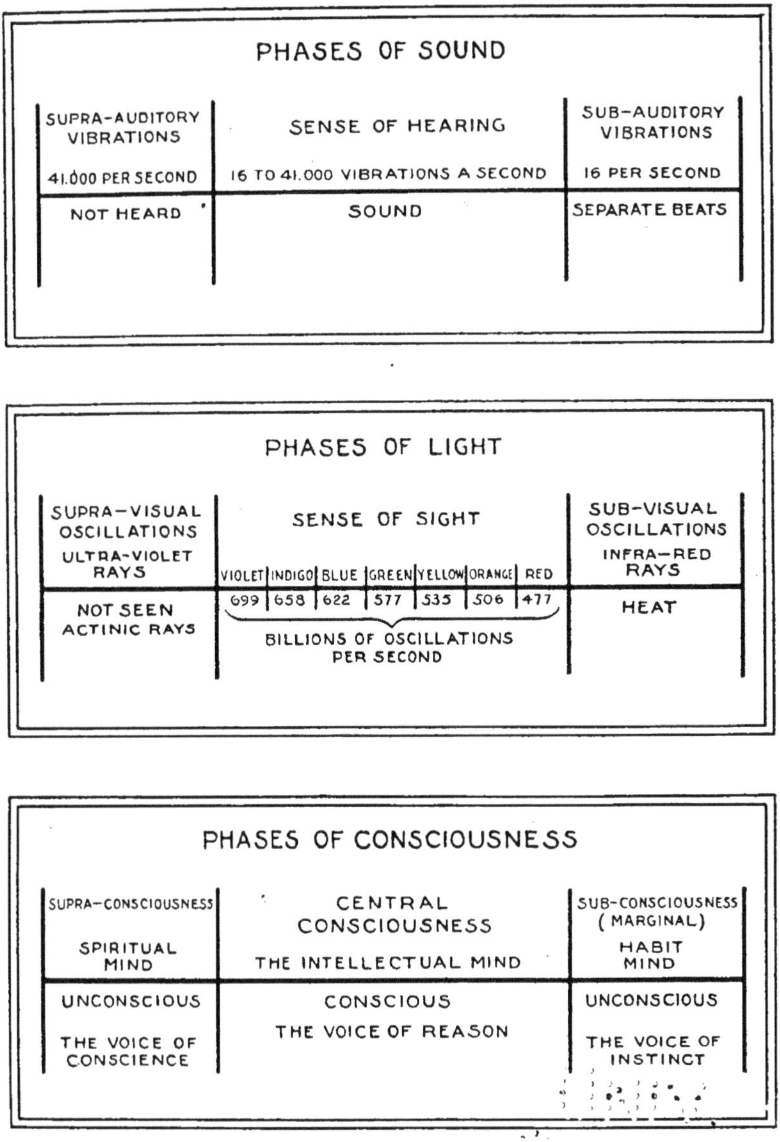

PHASES OF SOUND

SUPRA-AUDITORY VIBRATIONS	SENSE OF HEARING	SUB-AUDITORY VIBRATIONS
41,000 PER SECOND	16 TO 41,000 VIBRATIONS A SECOND	16 PER SECOND
NOT HEARD	SOUND	SEPARATE BEATS

PHASES OF LIGHT

SUPRA-VISUAL OSCILLATIONS	SENSE OF SIGHT							SUB-VISUAL OSCILLATIONS
ULTRA-VIOLET RAYS	VIOLET	INDIGO	BLUE	GREEN	YELLOW	ORANGE	RED	INFRA-RED RAYS
NOT SEEN ACTINIC RAYS	699	658	622	577	535	506	477	HEAT
	BILLIONS OF OSCILLATIONS PER SECOND							

PHASES OF CONSCIOUSNESS

SUPRA-CONSCIOUSNESS	CENTRAL CONSCIOUSNESS	SUB-CONSCIOUSNESS (MARGINAL)
SPIRITUAL MIND	THE INTELLECTUAL MIND	HABIT MIND
UNCONSCIOUS	CONSCIOUS	UNCONSCIOUS
THE VOICE OF CONSCIENCE	THE VOICE OF REASON	THE VOICE OF INSTINCT

FIG. 10.
DIAGRAM ILLUSTRATING PHASES OF CONSCIOUSNESS.

PHASES OF CONSCIOUSNESS 67

of the human intellect in many conditions of health and disease, nevertheless, we regard the term as altogether misleading and one which is wholly unnecessary.

In Fig. 11, we have endeavored to illustrate, diagrammatically, our view of the two states of consciousness, commonly called the conscious and the subconscious. We have represented the will as the centre or hub of the mind; and the area of consciousness immediately surrounding this, we have called the *central consciousness*. Radiating out from the will through the area of the central consciousness are all the various mental powers, such as reason, judgment, perception, memory, imagination, etc.

Now, following out any or all of these mental powers from the heart of the central consciousness, we sooner or later approach the borderland of the *marginal consciousness,* or the subconscious mind, indicated on the diagram by a wavy and irregular line. If we cross this line, we find ourselves in the realm of the subconscious mind, or, as we prefer to call it, the marginal consciousness. The various mental powers, as far as the elements of attention and consciousness are concerned, are diminished as we proceed outward from the centre of the central consciousness. This feature is shown by the diminished intensity of the various lines radiating outward through consciousness from the centre — the will.

The mental procedure of "making up our mind" is merely the process of groping around through the marginal consciousness for the purpose of finding the diverse ideas which are subsequently brought into focus and association in the realm of the central consciousness. After the mind is thus "made up" the will is able to order action.

THE MARGINAL CONSCIOUSNESS IN HEALTH AND IN DISEASE

We believe a careful study of the facts and phenomena connected with consciousness will prove to the satisfaction of all that the term *marginal consciousness* is to be preferred to *subconscious mind*. We are able to recognize a single mind only, but we recognize a dual consciousness in this single mind. This dual consciousness is never separated by hard and fast lines. The condition of the health of the nervous system, the degree of mental concentration, and the acuteness of the physical senses, are all concerned in constantly moving back and forth the lines of demarcation between the central and the marginal consciousnesses.

Under certain conditions a mental process may be taking place in the marginal consciousness; under other circumstances, this same process may occur in the central consciousness and the thinker be entirely conscious of his mental operations.

There can be little question of the fact that thoughts and ideas which may be born in the central consciousness may pass outward in the mind both during waking and sleeping — later to find themselves lodged in the marginal consciousness, where they will be able to influence the life and health of the individual for weal or for woe.

It is this element of the consciousness that is so largely appealed to in so-called suggestive or mental therapeutics. An idea is suggested to the patient with a view to its passing outward through the central consciousness to find permanent lodgment in the marginal consciousness, from which place it is supposed to influence unconsciously the mental state of the patient or the operations of the body. That is, wholesome, pure, and healthy thoughts influence the mind, body, and character favorably; while unwholesome and diseased thoughts exert a contrary influence.

But these matters will be dealt with more fully later. We desire here to make plain and establish 'the fact that man practically has a dual consciousness, but not a dual mind. We desire emphatically to express here the regret for this widespread and popular teaching which represents man as having two minds. We take the position that a human being has but one mind, but that there are two, possibly three, phases of that mind — central consciousness, marginal consciousness, and, if we may reason from the analogy of the recognition of light and sound, a supraconsciousness, or spiritual mind.

THE MARGINAL CONSCIOUSNESS AND THE BODY

The marginal consciousness has much to do with directing and influencing the physical functions of the body. Habits are largely directed by the marginal consciousness. A large ma-

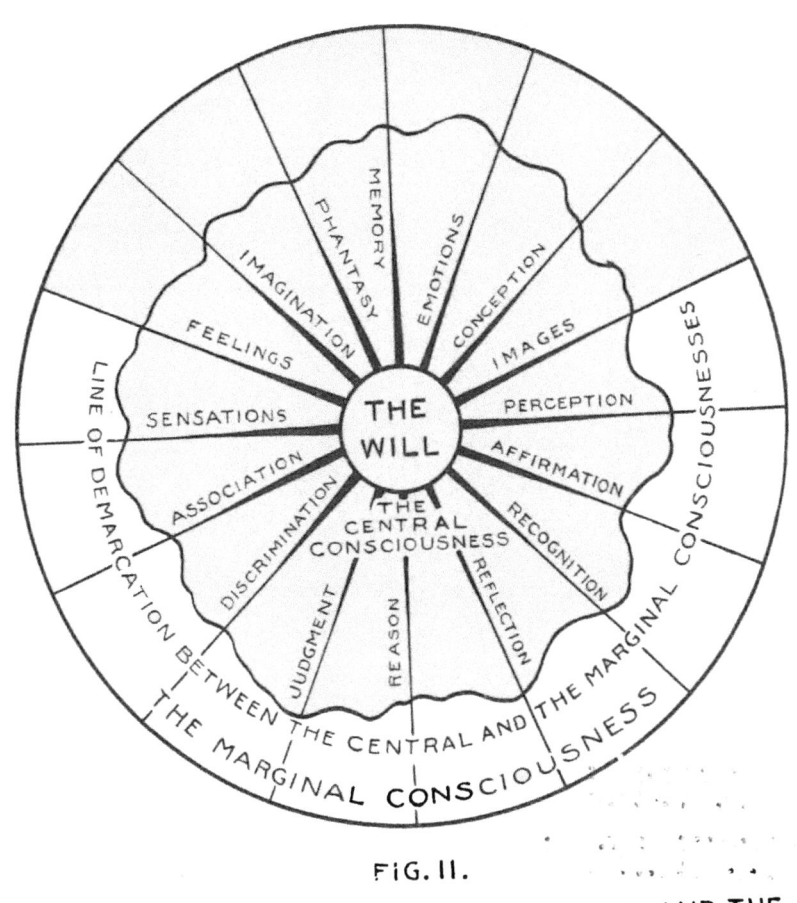

FIG. II.

DIAGRAM ILLUSTRATING THE CENTRAL AND THE MARGINAL CONSCIOUSNESS

jority of our physical actions and regular habits are wholly or partially unconscious processes. All of our reflex actions and many of our more complicated physical performances may take place by any one of three routes, all of which are unconscious; that is, pertaining to the marginal consciousness. (See Fig. 2.)

By strongly concentrating the attention upon a single thought, the mental powers can be so perfectly focussed as to bring the entire process of thinking almost within the central area of consciousness; that is, the area of consciousness is greatly decreased. On the other hand, when the attention is focussed upon a given thought and then is manipulated or misdirected, it is entirely possible so to control the channels of thought as practically to throw the whole mental process into the realm of the marginal consciousness; and this is exactly the feat which is performed in the practice of hypnotism, which will be more fully considered in a later chapter.

THE THREE PLANES OF CONSCIOUSNESS

Having demonstrated the twofold nature of the intellectual consciousness, we desire now to call attention to the threefold consciousness of the individual — the three planes of intelligence which have already been suggested by analogy from the comparative consideration of light and sound and consciousness. (See Fig. 10.)

Our aim thus far has been to show that the mind of man has two phases of consciousness. We now take up for further consideration the suggestion previously made that man practically has three phases of mind — three planes of consciousness. This threefold intelligence or consciousness is shown diagrammatically in Fig. 12, and these different planes of consciousness may be defined as follows:

1. *The spiritual consciousness — the voice of conscience — the moral plane.* By analogy, the existence of a spiritual mind has already been suggested. Man certainly possesses moral attributes, and manifests phenomena of consciousness which are far above the plane of the commonly accepted intellectual mind.

Man is distinctly a religious animal. Human beings all have some sort of moral perception — spiritual discernment — instinctive standards of relative right and wrong.

As the intellectual consciousness and the sensory centres of the brain are designed for, and engaged in, receiving physical impressions and translating them into sensations, percepts, and concepts, so the spiritual consciousness is occupied with the work of receiving spiritual impressions — wireless messages from the great spiritual intelligence of the universe — and translating them into religious sensations, spiritual percepts, moral concepts, and the lofty ideas and ideals of our inner and higher life.

Like as the intellectual consciousness was found to consist of two phases of activity — the central consciousness and the marginal consciousness — so we find an analogous condition of affairs in the action of the spiritual consciousness. The centre or hub of the spiritual plane of consciousness might be called the conscience, or the voice of conscience — the spiritual instinct. (See Fig. 12 A.) We must recognize the two phases of each of the three planes of consciousness or intelligence.

The central spiritual consciousness is found immediately associated with the voice of conscience, and represents man's definite moral convictions and his positive spiritual attitude — it stands for crystallized spiritual intelligence and moral instinct; while the marginal spiritual consciousness includes the vague spiritual longings, the uncrystallized religious instincts, the indefinite moral hunger, which all human beings more or less experience, and which, as before suggested, forever distinguish man from the animal.

And so, while all mankind are more or less religious — recognize more or less of the spirit impressions on the spiritual consciousness — when these moral sensations are translated into spiritual percepts and concepts, when definite religious ideas and moral ideals are built up in the spiritual mind; then a man's religious experience takes definite shape and he becomes identified with some particular religious organization and spiritual belief; or, at least in his own mind, he allies himself with some concrete code of morals, some definite standard of spiritual living.

2. *The intellectual consciousness — the voice of reason — the mental plane.* This is the plane of actual consciousness, and

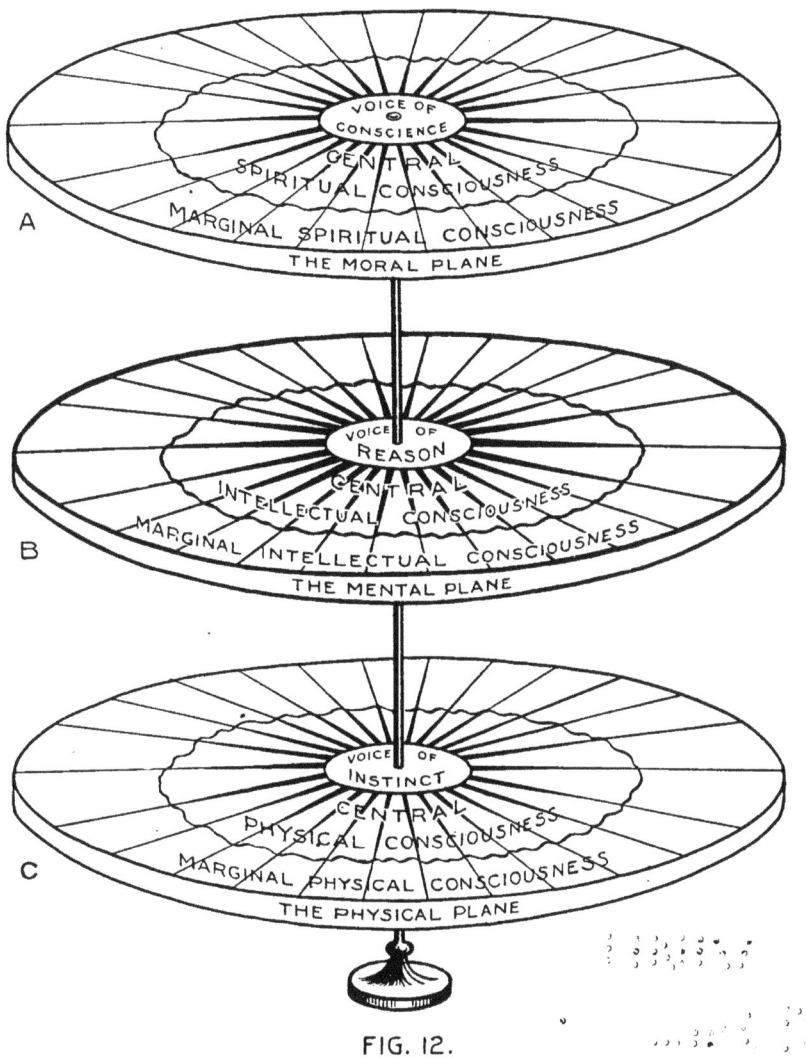

FIG. 12.

DIAGRAM ILLUSTRATING THE THREE PLANES OF CONSCIOUSNESS — CONSCIENCE, REASON AND INSTINCT.

UwU

accordingly is shown in heavier lines (Fig. 12 B) than either the spiritual consciousness above or the physical consciousness below. This plane of consciousness has already been quite fully considered and was also diagrammatically shown in Fig. 11. It is here again introduced merely to complete the scheme of the individual's consciousness as shown on three separate levels — the spiritual, the intellectual, and the physical.

3. *The physical consciousness — the voice of instinct — the physical plane.* There can be no longer any question as to the existence of some sort of intelligence which is ever guiding the individual cells of both the plant and the animal world in their selective activities in the realms of nutrition, secretion, excretion, reproduction, and other operations. The younger Darwin, the botanist, has even suggested that plants may feel and think, that they may have a rudimentary nervous system; and it is this instinctive intelligence — this cellular intuition — which we call the physical consciousness. It explains the extraordinary behavior and marvellous conduct of the tiny cells of the body as they so exquisitely and intelligently carry forward their diversified and complicated tasks associated with the metabolism and growth of the body, as well as in the apparent ingenuity they manifest in defending the body against disease.

When the physical appetites of the body are indefinite — when the hunger is general and not for any particular kind of food — the physical consciousness may be regarded as existing in the marginal state; but when the appetite crystallizes itself into definite form, and one experiences a hunger for some certain food, such as bread and butter, potatoes, or baked beans, then the physical consciousness or instinct may be regarded as operating in the central area of the physical consciousness. (See Fig. 12 C.)

THE THREEFOLD NATURE OF MAN

The attention of the reader is now directed to Fig. 13, where, by means of a diagram, an effort is made to show both the threefold nature of man — the three planes of consciousness — and the twofold nature of the intellectual consciousness. The *spiritual consciousness* is shown on the left-hand side of the diagram where are tabulated various acts and states pertaining to the spiritual mind or supraconsciousness, and which are designed largely to control or influence the central or intellectual consciousness. These special manifestations of the spiritual consciousness are such as the desire to worship, prayer, joy, patience, loyalty, humility, morality, charity, moral freedom; or perversions of these spiritual faculties, such as anger, jealousy, covetousness, revenge.

Now, on the right-hand side of Fig. 13, we have *physical consciousness*, which is designed to be controlled more particularly by the marginal consciousness, and only indirectly by the central consciousness.

The physical side of man naturally embraces the carnal nature, the appetites and passions. It represents the body, which receives the impulses despatched from the mind. It is the part which eats, drinks, breathes, works, rests, hungers. It is the part concerned in physical health and disease. Certain diseases result when the functions of the body are increased, others when they are decreased, and still others come from paralysis or cessation of function.

The organs of special sense are a part of the body. The body proves to be not only the instrument of the mind, the habitation of the spirit, but also the instrumentality of crime and intemperance, when controlled by a diseased mind or a disordered nervous system. The body is also a poison generator and therefore suffers from weariness, decay, and death. The body is also concerned directly in the phenomena of reproduction.

THE DOUBLE FUNCTION OF ONE MIND

The intellectual consciousness, the consciousness which presides over the brain and speaks through the nervous mechanism of the body, really controls two nervous systems as shown in Fig. 13. The voluntary or sensory nervous system, and the involuntary or sympathetic nervous system, are both connected with the intellect. This fact — the existence of two distinct nervous systems — is what probably led to the original assumption of the existence of two separate and distinct minds; but as we have previously shown, the sympathetic nervous system does not enter the skull, it is connected indirectly with the sensory

SPIRITUAL CONSCIOUSNESS	INTELLECTUAL CONSCIOUSNESS				PHYSICAL CONSCIOUSNESS
Acts and States Designed to Control the Central Consciousness (Conscience)	Voluntary Nervous System		Involuntary Nervous System		Controlled Directly by the Marginal Consciousness, Indirectly by the Central Consciousness
	Sensory Nerves	Central Consciousness	Marginal Consciousness	Sympathetic Nerves	
Spirituality	Controls All Voluntary Movements and Regulates All Involuntary Functions, by the Central Consciousness	Higher Thought	Habit Thought	Propels All Functions and Forms Habits, by the Marginal Consciousness and Abdominal Brain	Carnality
Worship		Memory— Partial	Memory— Complete		Originates Sensory Impressions
Prayer		Doubts	Trusts		
Morality		Fears	Believes		Receives Motor Impressions
Conviction		Worries	Indifferent		
Obedience		Sleeps	Never Sleeps		Instrument of Mind
Loyalty	**Functions**	Collects and Arranges Facts	Arranges Facts, Only	**Functions**	Spirit Habitation
Devotion	1. The Brain			Secretion	
Joy	Special Senses	Reasons— Inductive and Deductive	Reasons— Deductive (Largely)	Digestion	Appetites
Patience	Taste		Intuition	Assimilation	Passions
Humility	Smell	Intelligence (Volitional)	(Spontaneous Association of Ideas)	Oxidation	Eating
Meekness	Hearing			Circulation	Drinking
Self-Denial	Sight			Contraction	Breathing
Forgiveness	Feeling	Talent	Genius (Hereditary)	Vaso-Motor State	Working
Charity	Temperature	Suggestions—	Suggestions—	Elimination	Resting
Moral Freedom	Weight	Originates and Receives	Receives and Retains	Excretion	Locomotion
	Location			Respiration	Hunger
	Pain	Discretion	Impulsiveness	Peristalsis	Thirst
Perverted Spirit	Organic Sense	Actions	Habits	Skin Action	Health
Anger	2. Spinal Cord	Environment	Heredity	Visceral Action	Reproduction
Jealousy	Reflex Action	Judgment— Deliberate	Judgment— Instinctive	Internal Secretions	Disease
Revenge	Nerve Impulses Incoming Outgoing	Real World	Dream World	Growth	Increased Action
Covetousness		Acquired Knowledge	Inherited Knowledge (Music, etc.)	Repair	Decreased Action
Cowardice, etc.	Equilibrium			Healing	Paralysis
				Defence against Disease	Death
					Decay
	THE WILL The Combined Spiritual, Mental, and Nervous Forces, Brought to Bear upon Mind and Body to Direct Them in the Channel of Choice.				Return to Dust

FIG. 13. Diagram Showing the Relation of the Physical Instincts and the Spiritual Emotions to the Intellectual Consciousness, also a Comparison of the Central and the Marginal Consciousnesses.

PHASES OF CONSCIOUSNESS

nervous system; and thus in a sense both of these great systems of nerves are presided over by one mind — the intellectual consciousness — the central and marginal consciousnesses.

As shown in Diagram 13, the sensory nerves control the voluntary movements of the body, and to some extent influence and regulate the majority of the involuntary functions, operating more especially through the central consciousness. The function of this system is largely influenced by the taste, smell, hearing, sight, and feeling; and it operates largely by means of the impulses which it receives over, and sends out through, the spinal cord and its many branches.

The sympathetic nervous system is largely concerned in the formation of habits and the carrying on of the various vital functions of the body, and in general it may be said to be controlled largely by the marginal consciousness and the solar plexus — the abdominal brain. This involuntary nervous system regulates secretion, digestion, assimilation, oxidation, circulation of the blood, elimination of poisons, and the action of the skin and bowels. It is largely concerned in the healing of the body and in the process of defending it against disease.

The mind of man — the intellectual consciousness — bridges over the chasm between the spiritual and the material world — between spirit and body. The central consciousness makes contact with the spiritual mind and the moral realms above it, while the marginal consciousness makes contact with physical mind and the material realm below it. Mind is intended to control matter and in turn to be controlled by morals — and so we find three spheres in the scheme of mental regulation and physical control — mind, matter, and morals.

COMPARISON OF THE CENTRAL AND MARGINAL CONSCIOUSNESSES

In Fig. 13, a parallel comparison is made between the central consciousness, which is largely associated with the voluntary nervous system, and the marginal consciousness which, indirectly, is largely associated with the involuntary nervous system. We would not convey the idea that the comparisons shown in this parallel diagram are absolute and definite, they are only relative. The central consciousness and the marginal consciousness are but relative terms, nevertheless, there is a very clear-cut distinction between the typical activities of the central consciousness and those of the marginal consciousness, generally called the subconscious mind. The one is more largely concerned in the higher intellectual thoughts and mental activities; the other has more to do with habit-thought, the regulation of the natural bodily functions, and the direction of the instinctive acts of the body.

The central consciousness with its stronger powers of reason and judgment is the doubting power of the mind. The marginal consciousness is more trusting. It has less of reason and judgment and, therefore, is more likely to believe anything which it is told. In the case of the hypnotized individual, the central consciousness is diverted — practically obliterated; he is likely to believe anything which he is told, within certain well-known limits; and so while the central consciousness is more largely the abode of fears, the marginal consciousness trusts and believes.

From the very nature of this arrangement, the central consciousness worries as to the solutions of the problems of to-day and the avoidance of the dangers of to-morrow; while the marginal consciousness is more or less indifferent to these matters. The difficulties of life are not seriously regarded by this phase of the mind. The central consciousness sleeps at night, but the marginal consciousness never sleeps, and through the sympathetic nervous system it is able indirectly to influence the entire physical process even while the higher centres of thought are sound asleep at night.

The central consciousness, while it collects and arranges facts, is more largely engaged in the work of collection. The activities of the marginal consciousness are largely limited to arranging facts; and this explains why one may retire at night with the mind confused, the intellect greatly disturbed, the ideas all disarranged, but awake in the morning with ideas all collected and nicely rearranged — one half of his problems solved, while the troubles have largely vanished during the period of sleep and rest.

The central consciousness reasons inductively and deductively. It does not accept a thing merely as so because you tell it; while the marginal consciousness reasons very largely deductively, accepting as true almost everything told it, and acting accordingly. The hypnotized individual who is quite exclusively under the control of the marginal consciousness, when told he is a dog, only reasons deductively, and, therefore, immediately begins to bark. He does not use his higher powers of reason to examine himself carefully to see whether or not he is a dog. He acts largely upon the suggestions which are made from the outside.

The central consciousness is concerned in acts of volitional intelligence, while the marginal consciousness presides over our intuition, that is, our hereditary knowledge, and over those actions arising from a spontaneous association of ideas.

Talent, which is the result of training and thought, is the product of the centralized consciousness; while genius is largely an unconscious attribute, hereditary as to origin and pertaining to the marginal consciousness.

The centralized consciousness may originate a suggestion or may receive one. The marginal consciousness concerns itself largely with receiving and retaining suggestions; and it is this peculiar faculty of the marginal consciousness which renders it so susceptible of those suggestions which may favorably or unfavorably influence the health of the body.

The centralized consciousness is discreet in its control of actions, in the formation of habits; while the marginal consciousness is always impulsive, and when actions have been repeated a sufficient number of times to form habits, they are largely controlled by this phase of consciousness.

The central consciousness is largely influenced by our environment, while the marginal consciousness is more strongly influenced by heredity. The judgment and final conclusions of the central consciousness are deliberate and matured. Those of the marginal consciousness are usually instinctive, and often instantaneous.

The central consciousness has to do with our thoughts in connection with the real consciousness, with the acquirement of knowledge, with actual work and hard study; while the marginal consciousness may be more or less of a dreamy consciousness, and it is concerned more with our hereditary knowledge. It is the element of consciousness largely concerned in the case of the intellectual freaks, such as Blind Tom, the musician, and certain mathematical prodigies.

The will, as shown in Fig. 13, as previously considered, is the combined spiritual, mental, and nervous forces brought to bear upon mind and body, to direct them in the channel of choice.

SUMMARY OF THE CHAPTER

1. Every evidence points to the existence of a spiritual mind, a supraconsciousness. This constitutes the moral mind — the conscientious element of the intelligence.

2. The central consciousness is the highly conscious and purely intellectual process of the mind, while the marginal consciousness (the subconscious mind) represents that diffused and scattered mental action which occurs beyond the borders of so-called consciousness.

3. The will is the practical and potential centre of consciousness. The mental procedure of "making up our mind" consists in the assembling of the marginal data and arranging the same in systematic fashion in the central consciousness, preliminary to the action of the will.

4. Man presents the phenomenon of a dual consciousness in a single mind. The lines of demarcation between the marginal and the central consciousnesses are relative and ever changing. The marginal consciousness is highly concerned in all the problems of health and healing.

5. The marginal consciousness largely directs all habit-actions, reflex movements, and unconscious performances. Concentration of the attention can move back and forth the line of division between the central and the marginal consciousnesses.

6. Man exhibits three planes of consciousness: (a) the spiritual consciousness, the voice of conscience — the moral plane; (b) the intellectual consciousness, the voice of reason — the mental plane; and (c) the physical consciousness, the voice of instinct — the physical plane.

7. The study of man from every side presents the problem of his threefold nature — mind, morals, and matter.

PHASES OF CONSCIOUSNESS

8. The mind of man presides over two distinct and separate nervous systems. Both the cerebro-spinal and the sympathetic nervous system serve as the instruments of expression and operation for the mind, which is the master controller of all nervous mechanisms and mental machinery.

9. The mind bridges over the chasm separating the spiritual and the material world. The central consciousness touches the moral and spiritual realms above, while the marginal consciousness makes contact with the physical and material world below it.

10. At every point, a comparison of the central with the marginal consciousness discloses a striking parallel of differences. The practical operations of these two phases of consciousness are quite opposite. They occupy opposite extremes in the balancing scheme of mind — the one ever supplementing, reinforcing, and checking the other. They are dedicated to the performance of opposites.

CHAPTER VIII

SUPERSTITION AS RELATED TO HEALTH AND DISEASE

ANCIENT HEALTH DELUSIONS.— EXAMPLES OF ANCIENT MEDICAL SUPERSTITION.— DEMONOLOGY AND "TEMPLE SLEEP."— RELICS AS A HEALTH DELUSION.— MEDIÆVAL MEDICAL SCHOOLS.— THE PROVIDENTIAL IDEA OF DISEASE.— ASTROLOGY IN HEALTH AND DISEASE.— ANCIENT ALMANACS.— LATER HEALTH DELUSIONS.— SUPERSTITION AND INSANITY.— MEDICAL ERRORS AND SUPERSTITIONS.— MODERN MEDICAL SUPERSTITION.— SUMMARY OF THE CHAPTER

THE study of physiology and psychology discloses the vast possibilities existing in the human body and brain for the origin of inaccuracies, the birth of deceptions, the creation of delusions, and the production of a vast system of baseless fears, false conceptions, and erroneous conclusions. This systematized mental fear and moral cowardice may be summed up in the one word — *superstition.*

In all ages and at all times, there have existed health delusions and healing deceptions, and even the present age is no exception; but it is beyond the scope of this work, and foreign to its purpose, to dwell in detail upon these various systems of erroneous teaching, or even to expose the delusive philosophy, the cunning methods, and the deceptive inner workings of the many health and healing frauds which are perpetrated upon a long-suffering public. In this chapter we can but hope briefly to trace some of the ancient medical superstitions and connect them with modern health delusions — to show the influence of superstition upon the health teaching, medical practice, and the healing beliefs of the world.

ANCIENT HEALTH DELUSIONS

Superstition has ever paraded in the garments of faith, and so in the earliest records of ancient history, medical superstition is discovered travelling hand in hand with religious superstition. The earliest of these health delusions taught that disease was due to the ill-humor of the gods. When mankind suffered the blight of infectious disease and physical decay, some particular god was supposed to be in a state of anger, having taken offence at some sin of commission or omission on the part of the sufferer or his friends. This system of explaining the cause of disease progressed to that point where there appeared to be a different god for each disease; and following all this came the discovery of, and appeal to, Apollo, the god who was supposed to have invented the art of healing.

In their efforts to amuse these various gods of health and disease, to appease their wrath, and win their favor, the pagans were wont to engage in spectacular theatrical performances, elaborate banquets, and extraordinary dancing manœuvres; and, subsequently, professed Christians unfortunately incorporated much of this delusional teaching respecting health and disease into their systems of belief, and hence were led to endow the Creator — their personal God — with many of these health and disease practices which had been attributed to the numerous heathen gods. Almost every idea pertaining to physical health and bodily disease was steeped in ignorance, and saturated with superstition.

Later there arose a special class of the priesthood — the *magicians* — who claimed to work miracles by means of some supernatural endowment or some special influence with the gods. These ancient wonder-workers claimed to be able to relieve suffering and cure disease by the supernatural method. Alexander the Great is reported to have always had one of those medicine-men connected with his personal staff; and Nero was an ardent pupil of the magi. These religio-medical impostors, while they claimed to effect their wonderful cures by the direct working of the gods, nevertheless made use of all manner of drugs, bone powders, human fæces, urine, and various other unmentionable things, including the ropes that hung criminals. They instructed their victims to swallow these medicines while standing at the cross-roads at midnight, repeating prayers to the gods and saying over certain magic numbers such as three, seven, and nine.

EXAMPLES OF ANCIENT MEDICAL SUPERSTITION

As examples of some of these ancient health prescriptions, which superstitious practices are by no means altogether extinct at the present time, the following may be cited:

For warts and corns. Lie on your back along a boundary line on the twentieth day of the month, with the hands extended over the head. With whatever thing you grasp while so doing, rub the warts, and they will immediately disappear. After seeing a shooting star, immediately pour vinegar upon the hinge of a door. This is a sure cure for corns.

For headache. Tie a piece of a rope that hung a criminal tightly around the forehead. There is a physiological reason why this might have helped in stopping headaches. It is a well-known fact that pressure upon the aching head or the tying of a handkerchief about the head, frequently eases the headache by its pressure upon the nerves and its influence upon the circulation. Another illustration of how even superstition and ignorance sometimes unwittingly hit the nail on the head.

For stomach-ache. The one suffering from colicky pains must sit down on a chair and repeat to himself a prescribed formula of words (various formulæ adapted to different pains were used); or take the excreta of a wolf, together with small pieces of bone, bind them up together, and wear them on the right arm or hip. Another favorite prescription for colic was the heart taken from a living lark, to be worn on the left thigh.

For epilepsy. Gather peonies at night when the moon is on the wane; wrap up in linen and wear as an amulet. Or take a nail from a cross, and suspend it about the neck.

For gout. Take a gold leaf and write upon it certain formulæ when the moon is on the wane. This is then to be covered with a tendon of a crane, enclosed in a capsule, and worn by the patient about his heel.

For diseases of the eye. Rub the diseased eye with the eye of a wolf or the eye of some other animal having a cunning look.

These are but samples of ancient and foolish medical superstitions, but one can scarcely help recognizing numerous modern counterparts in the notion of planting potatoes in the light of the moon, wearing charms about the neck, carrying a rabbit's foot, and many other superstitious practices in vogue even at the present time.

DEMONOLOGY AND "TEMPLE SLEEP"

That diseases were caused by demons was a theory largely held in ancient times. Some devil, some bad spirit, or the influence of a bad god, was supposed to enter into a person and by its presence was supposed to produce various forms of disease. In the Middle Ages they believed in the so-called white and black magicians — those whose work was inspired by good and bad demons, respectively. When these superstitions crept into the early Christian churches, the good demon was dropped out of their philosophy and the production of disease was exclusively assigned to the bad demons, while health and healing influences were credited to the agents of heaven — the angels. And it is certain that this ancient idea of the cause of disease has not entirely departed from our modern philosophy of health and healing. The author is constantly meeting afflicted souls who believe themselves to be "under the power of the enemy" — to be subject to the "powers of darkness" — to be the "victims of doubt and unbelief," and who are ever praying for their release by messengers of light — the divine agents and dispensers of health and healing.

The "temple sleep" was a peculiar superstition of the Greeks. In carrying out this system of healing, the priests would fall asleep in the temple, and in their dreams would get prescriptions for disease from the gods. For many years this superstition which obtained among the Greeks was credited with remarkable cures. A little later, among the professed Christians, the same identical idea was practised under the name of "church sleep," and wonderful stories abound of how those who suffered from stone in the bladder would go to sleep in the church, where miraculous and mysterious surgical operations would be performed upon them, and they would awake entirely cured, often finding the stone by their side, or in the hands of the attending priests.

One interesting instance is related of how the ungrateful patient who had thus been miraculously operated upon failed to pay the priests for what the gods had done. He was again afflicted and it required considerable persuasion to induce the gods to perform the second operation.

While there were numerous saints in the later Christian superstition who ministered to the sick and performed surgical operations, St. Benedict was the saintly surgeon who acquired the greatest reputation for successfully operating upon patients during the "church sleep."

Later, this superstition was wonderfully developed and broadened, and there appeared the teaching that a certain celestial surgeon, one St. Martin, would perform operations and heal the sick, who would go to sleep in any place and under any circumstances; that if the sufferers would only call upon him, it was not necessary to sleep in a church; and thus the church, as a surgical hospital, was robbed of its peculiar healing influence and sacred climatic value.

And so it would appear that a whole faculty of medical and surgical saints was created. Ultimately there came into existence numerous specialists, some saints performing surgical operations of one kind, while other saints performed operations along other lines. In following out this superstitious system, they had these celestial practitioners grouped somewhat after the order of our present-day specialists. Some treated stomach troubles, some insanity, while other saints administered to the skin diseases.

RELICS AS A HEALTH DELUSION

From time immemorial, relics have been associated with health and disease. The bodies of either dead or living saints were supposed to be life-giving and healing to the touch — even to touch the tombs of some of the saints was reputed to cure one's disease.

A concoction made of a piece of the tombstone of a good man was supposed to cure malignant disease when everything else had failed. For some diseases, it was a sure cure to lick the tombstone of a saint. To kiss the temple floors whereon saints had trod was also supposed to confer extraordinary healing power.

The water with which the altars were washed at Easter time was supposed to be unusually efficacious in the cure of many obstinate diseases. Relic covers were boiled and the concoctions drunk by the sick and the afflicted. There was a white manna which was supposed to have come from the tomb of the Apostle John, and this was thought to possess extraordinary power in healing disease.

Many of these relic delusions were systematically practised right up to the seventeenth century, and to-day we frequently read of pilgrimages and excursions to the relics and shrines of the saints, where scores of people are reputed to have been instantly healed of their diseases. The relic superstition has not entirely disappeared.

MEDIÆVAL MEDICAL SCHOOLS

About the time of the height of the relic rage, the remnants of the early art of medicine took refuge in the mountain monasteries, where for years in the midst of a mystical and superstitious environment, the monks nursed the sick and practised medicine. Following this ministry of the monks, in connection with their church propaganda during the Middle Ages, there came forth that great horde of "miracle-workers" and disease-healers, whose activities were immediately followed by a revival of the teachings of demonology, and subsequently by witchcraft and its allied theories; and it is but a few years since witches were actually hanged on the shores of our much boasted free America.

It was not until the fourth century that the idea of exclusive and infallible healing by prayer became prominent; and immediately following this, it was taught that there were many material things which would prove of great help to prayer, such as placing one of the gospels on the affected part, or spreading over the patient the clothing which had been worn by a pious man.

THE PROVIDENTIAL IDEA OF DISEASE

Following the theory of prayer as a disease cure, came the teaching of Providence as a disease cause — the providential idea of human sickness and suffering — which came to be quite generally held by the professed Christian world. It was generally accepted that syphilis and the military fever which made their appearance in the fifteenth century throughout Europe were providential visitations. This idea that disease was a visitation of Providence naturally led back to those practices which were designed to appease the wrath of God and atone for the shortcomings of man; and it was in this connection that there arose the great army of *conjurors* and *mumblers,* as well as those who would chant hymns and hang charms about their necks.

In this connection there also arose a peculiar superstition in which little children were used as the unconscious mediums, great stress being placed upon their jargon or drollery. These words were many times repeated and certain of them were supposed to possess unusual healing power.

About the same time, there arose the teaching that some men had been taught by superior and cunning devils how to drive out the inferior or lesser devils, and, as previously explained, the saints and the heavenly angels later took the place of the so-called good and superior demons, in the Christian philosophy.

ASTROLOGY IN HEALTH AND DISEASE

It is indeed difficult to say just when medicine got mixed up with astronomy, so that the treatment of disease and the preservation of health came to be determined by the flight of the stars through space. There seems to be evidence that astrology existed back in the earliest Chaldean period. The idea of sun worship, the sun being the apparent source of energy and life, was probably at the root of this ancient astrology. The Assyrians and Babylonians developed a veritable system of astrological medicine. The following examples indicate how disease was treated by the astrologers:

If the wind comes up from the west, upon the appearance of the moon, disease will prevail during the month; while, if Venus approaches the constellation of Cancer, the sick in the land will recover.

If Mercury arises on the fifteenth day of the month, there will be many deaths. If Mercury comes in conjunction with Mars, there will be fatalities among horses.

If a planet becomes pale in opposition to the moon, many lions will die; while if Mars and Jupiter come in conjunction, many cattle will die.

If an eclipse of the moon occurs on the twenty-ninth day of the month, there will be many deaths on the first day of the next month; while an eclipse in the morning is sure to produce disease.

If a halo is observed surrounding the moon, it indicates that women will bear male children.

The ancient astrological medical teaching positively forbade the performance of surgical operations on certain days of the month, such as the seventh, fourteenth, nineteenth, and twenty-first.

Purging was supposed to be both difficult and dangerous during or just before the dog-days.

The appearance of comets, the heavenly mischief-makers, was regarded as a sure forerunner of world-wide pestilence and national calamity.

Acute diseases in general were supposed to be controlled by the moon, while the chronic affections were more largely influenced by the sun.

It was taught that each part or organ of the human body was subordinate to a distinct sign of the zodiac. For instance, the sun controlled the right eye, the moon the left eye; Saturn, hearing; Jupiter, the brain; Mars, the blood; Venus, taste and smell; Mercury, the tongue.

An emetic or a purge could be safely given only when the moon was in a certain relation to certain stars.

'The ancient astrologers prepared elaborate tables which indicated just how each physical function and mental faculty was subordinate to a certain star.

ANCIENT ALMANACS

During the Middle Ages, when the science of medicine had begun to take definite shape, the almanac was gotten out as a sort of compromise between the astrologer and the doctor.

This peculiar volume gave the signs of the zodiac so that the astrologer was able to know the fate of mankind rapidly and easily, and the doctor who had not yet found deliverance from the superstition of the day could also have recourse to its teachings in connection with the practice of his profession. And thus science has ever advanced with one hand upon the new truth ahead, and the other upon the errors and superstitions of past teachings — practices holy and hoary with age.

These tables based upon the signs of the zodiac (See Fig. 14) explained the proper times to have the hair cut, when it was safe to draw blood or to draw teeth. They also carefully indicated the days on which it was safe to take a bath; and even the best times to pray were indicated in the almanac, it being taught that when the moon was in conjunction with Jupiter, you were sure to receive an answer to your prayers. Prayers were especially sure of an answer when offered to the Virgin Mary on the first day of April at eight A.M.

And so the ancient almanac proves to be a monumental exhibition of the combined medical and religious superstitions of the Middle Ages, and it was not until the later Christian idea of a God of love in control of the universe became widespread, and the still later scientific teaching of the regulation of health and disease by the rulings of natural law, became generally accepted, that this blinding belief in the fate-ruling power of the stars was shaken. At one time, all the great courts of Europe had their astrologers; and even Melancthon, the reformer, was a believer in much of this astrology, believing that his own last sickness was incurable only because Mars and Saturn happened to be in conjunction.

We cannot yet regard ourselves as entirely free from the deceptions and delusions of astrology, as long as intelligent farmers continue to plant their potatoes by the light of the moon, and otherwise gauge their agricultural pursuits by the phases of the moon, or the flight of the stars. We sometimes regard ourselves as having wholly outlived a superstition, when, in so far as faith and fear are concerned, we continue to be victims of every principle of its erroneous teaching.

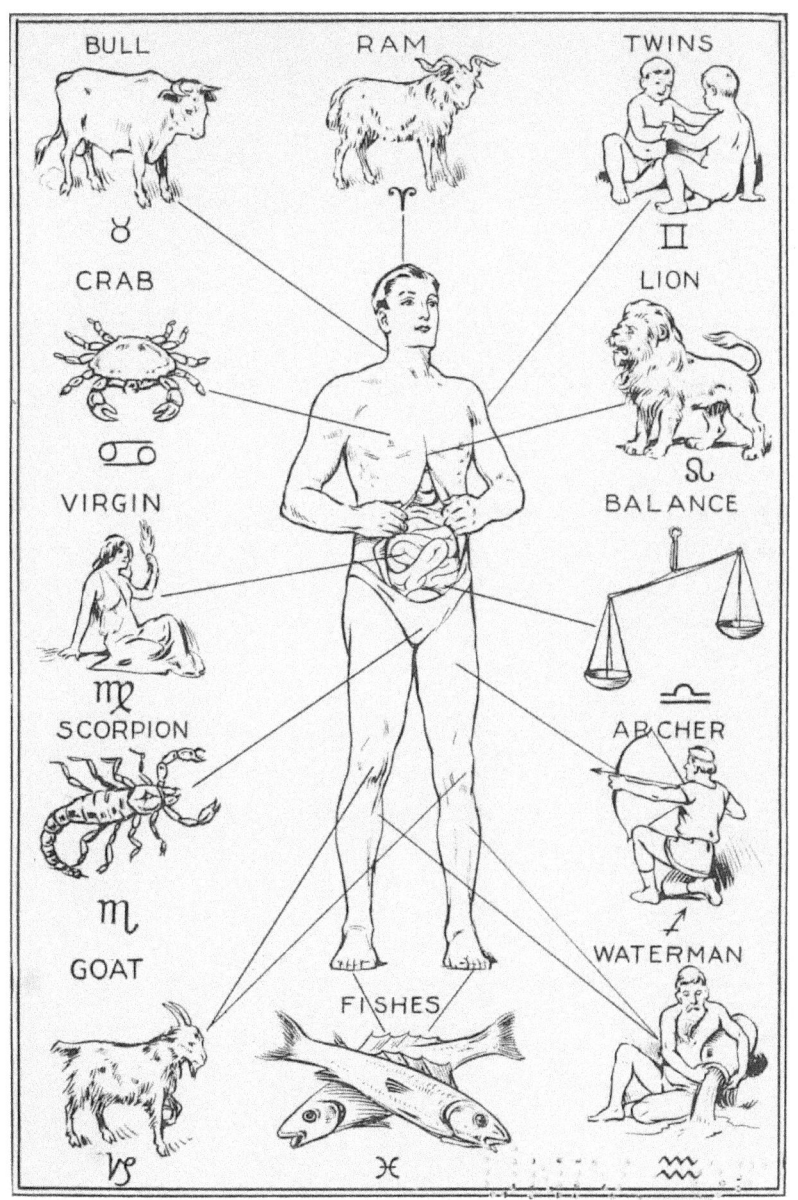

FIG. 14. THE RELATION OF THE PARTS OF THE HUMAN BODY TO THE SIGNS OF THE ZODIAC.

SUPERSTITION

LATER HEALTH DELUSIONS

Deliverance from the more ancient delusions of demonology and astrology did not come in a single generation. Numerous disease delusions sprang up on the heels of these departing sophistries. The following absurd medical practices are among the teachings found in a not very distant past:

A ring made from the wood of a coffin and slipped over a cramping limb, was supposed to be a sure cure for spasms.

Tumors and cancers could be effectually driven away by nine blows from the hand of a dead man.

To drive a new nail into an oak tree, was a sure cure for toothache.

"King's Evil" was a name given to scrofula, for it was supposed to be cured by His Majesty's touch; that is, the king, by laying hands on the sick and reciting a prayer, was supposed to cure thousands of scrofulous sufferers every year.

The "weapon ointment" cure was a remedy consisting of a large number of different things including human blood, pulverized mummy, and moss that had grown on the skull of a thief. The peculiar part of the procedure was that this ointment was to be rubbed on the weapon that had inflicted the wound, and this was supposed to cure the cut. Even Lord Bacon, in his day, would not presume to deny the efficacy of this treatment, but failing to account consistently for it, he said, "We must accept the facts, and leave them unexplained." He must have felt as the modern scientists feel when standing in the presence of the psychological frauds and deceptions of our own day. It is very difficult to refute superstition as long as it apparently cures disease and heals the sick. Even Hildanus, an eminent surgeon of that day, failing satisfactorily to explain the workings of the "weapon ointment," said, "The devil must have a hand in the business."

Following the widespread use of the weapon ointment, a so-called sympathetic powder came into general use. These powders could be applied to the blood-stained garments of a wounded person, thereby quickly and effectually healing the wound.

SUPERSTITION AND INSANITY

The superstition of the ancients respecting the insane led to the most unfortunate and inhuman treatment of these mental sufferers. The insane of past ages were the most maltreated of all the afflicted. The idea that mental diseases and insanity were directly attributable to demoniacal possession resulted in producing such a prejudice against the mentally unbalanced of olden times that they received but little or no sympathy and care from their fellow-men.

Another idea respecting insanity was that some forms of mental derangement came from allowing the moon to shine directly upon the face. Indeed, it was this belief that gave origin to the name *lunacy* — from *Luna*, the moon. In the good old days, mental patients would have some superstitious remedy tried on them, and if they made no immediate improvement, they were cast out from civilization as victims of lunacy, or else they were regarded as having become possessed of devils.

From the records of some of the ancient churches it would appear that the physician-priests regarded themselves as sometimes successful in their efforts to frighten the devils out of the insane by the employment of incantations, the use of long words, and the administration of certain malodorous and filthy drugs. In 1583, the Jesuit Fathers of Vienna boasted that they had by these means cast out 12,658 living devils.

At a later date, lunatics were sometimes confined in what were known as "fool towers," and still later they were incarcerated in the "witch towers." It is certainly a cause for universal rejoicing and gratitude that in the case of these mental sufferers, the superstitions of the dark ages no longer guide society in its treatment of the insane. Great progress has been made in the past fifty years by all civilized nations in the treatment of the insane and the mentally unbalanced. At the present time, in most parts of the United States, the mental patients confined in State institutions receive thorough-going, up-to-date, and scientific treatment for their mental maladies.

MEDICAL ERRORS AND SUPERSTITIONS

Even our orthodox schools of medicine, during the past century, were not altogether free from absurd and superstitious practices. Teachings which have been long accepted in the medical profession are indeed difficult to get away from. That this is true has been shown repeatedly during the past fifty years. The absurd and unreasonable practice of confining fever patients in close and unventilated rooms, denying the famishing sufferers all water — either for drinking or bathing purposes — at the same time drawing from their depleted systems large quantities of blood, and putting them through a "course of medicine" consisting largely of calomel, until sometimes the mouth and gums were horribly swollen and the teeth ready to fall out — such a method of treating fever patients represents the tenacity with which the practices of the past cling to the procedures of the present. The science of medicine has made tremendous progress during the past fifty years, having delivered itself from a vast amount of ancient superstition and medical delusion. In recent years, amazing progress has been made in the march away from superstition and empiricism in our modern methods of treating the sick and healing disease.

Among the last of the greater ancient delusions regarding the treatment of disease to pass out of our modern system of medicine, was the universal practice of blood-letting, a practice largely in vogue within the last hundred years. In England, the barbers were commissioned to perform this service. They were regarded as the surgeons of that day, and it is said that the present-day barbers' sign — a pole of red and white stripes — originated from this practice, the white representing the bandage and the red standing for the blood.

While physicians of to-day have largely delivered themselves from the bondage and errors of these ancient medical superstitions, the common people are still more or less tainted by these erroneous ideas of disease, as shown by the current use of such phrases as "disease striking in," "drawing out inflammation," "driving out pain," together with the notion that disease is a punishment for moral wrong-doing, or a providential visitation for spiritual misdeeds. Ancient notions die hard, and superstition is slow to release its victims; accordingly, the deliverance of the common people from the thraldom of medical superstition has been painfully slow.

MODERN MEDICAL SUPERSTITION

In recent years, medical superstition seems to have crystallized itself into numerous modern "mind cures" and "faith-healing" cults. By mind cure and faith healing we refer to those exclusive systems of treatment known by these terms; we shall not undertake to enumerate these faith-cure systems and "isms," for they are legion. They all operate on the same general lines.

There exists to-day the same willingness on the part of the people to be misled and deceived as was found in the minds and hearts of our forefathers; and the power of these modern humbugs of healing is found to consist in their ability apparently to cure disease. Having relieved physical pain and seemingly cured bodily disease, the teachers of these systems force their peculiar religious and ethical views upon their converts as the price of retaining healing and regaining health.

In a subsequent chapter, it will be shown that these various cults and isms all accomplish their healing work in accordance with certain definite laws. The fact that their devotees improve in health and find actual or pretended deliverance from disease, in no wise vouches for the truthfulness of their teachings or the trustworthiness of their claims to divine sanction and authority.

SUMMARY OF THE CHAPTER

1. Superstition has ever paraded in the garments of faith. Medical superstition has travelled hand in hand with religious superstition.

2. The ancients attributed disease to the anger of the gods, and went so far as to provide a different god for each disease.

3. The magicians were a special class of priests who claimed to work miracles by the aid of the gods. They employed medicine, charms, and prayers.

4. While the vast majority of these ancient health practices were utterly nonsensical, vast numbers of people were apparently helped or cured.

5. Demonology explained disease on the ground that the patient was possessed by an evil spirit, by the devil. This doctrine is still prevalent, many believing themselves to be "under the power of the enemy."

6. The early "temple sleep" and the later "church sleep" were procedures in which the patient went to sleep in the temple or the church, and while unconscious the saints were supposed to come down and treat the sick — even to perform surgical operations.

7. Relics have been looked upon as health restorers from a very early date. Pilgrimages to the holy shrines have restored thousands of sick ones to health.

8. The medical schools of the monks in **mediæval** times turned out a great army of "miracle-workers." Their teachings ranged from healing by prayer to subsequent witchcraft demonstrations.

9. Later, there appeared the providential idea of disease. This led to the practice of all sorts of methods calculated to appease the wrath of God. This idea is widespread to-day.

10. From the dawn of history, astrology, the forerunner of astronomy, has been connected with health and disease. This belief originated the ancient almanacs — forerunners of our modern combined calendars and patent medicine advertisements.

11. The latter-day health delusions are too numerous to mention, including "king's touch," "weapon ointment," and "sympathetic powders."

12. The barbarous treatment of the insane in past ages was due to the prevalence of the belief in demoniacal possession.

13. The practice of medicine in the last century was not entirely free from its empiric courses of medicine, atrocious blood-letting, and "driving out inflammations."

14. Modern medical superstition has crystallized itself into numerous cults, mind cures, and faith-healing procedures. The ability to cure disease is commonly regarded as proving that the healer is a special and accredited agent of God.

THE PSYCHOLOGY OF FAITH AND FEAR

THE INFLUENCE OF FAITH AND FEAR ON THE MIND.— SENSATIONS AS MODIFIED BY FAITH AND FEAR.— THE PSYCHIC ORIGIN AND NATURE OF SENSATION.— FAITH AND FEAR IN RELATION TO MENTAL MASTICATION.— ACTION OF FAITH AND FEAR ON THE IMAGINATION AND PHANTASY.— THE EFFECTS OF FAITH AND FEAR ON MENTAL DIGESTION.— FAITH AND FEAR IN THE REALM OF THE ASSOCIATION OF IDEAS.— THE EFFECT OF FAITH AND FEAR ON THE HIGHER MENTAL POWERS.— FAITH AND FEAR IN THE DEVELOPMENT OF CHARACTER.— FAITH AND FEAR IN HEALTH AND DISEASE.— IDOL-WORSHIP.— CHARMS.— ASTROLOGY.— SHRINE WORSHIP.— SACRIFICES.— MESMERISM.— FAITH HEALING.— CLAIRVOYANCE.— CHRISTIAN SCIENCE.— PATENT MEDICINES.— FETISHES.— SUMMARY OF THE CHAPTER.

IT now becomes necessary more fully to define the terms which enter into the title of this work — faith and fear. The term *faith* is used in this text as expressive of optimism, satisfaction, happiness, confidence, assurance, hopefulness, cheerfulness, courage, and determination; while the term *fear* is made to include pessimism, dissatisfaction, grief, anxiety, despondency, hatred, worry, moroseness, anger, and vacillation.

It will thus appear that faith represents a mode of life and thought — it represents the normal, the healthy, the natural state of civilized man; while fear stands for the opposite mode of life and thought — it represents the unnatural, the abnormal, the unhealthy mental and moral attitude.

In the next chapter the reader will find an exhaustive parallel arrangement of the numerous mental qualities and states which enter into the definitions of faith and fear. In the left-hand column there are shown the attributes and qualities of the

THE PSYCHOLOGY OF FAITH AND FEAR 93

faith life, ranging from optimism to determination. In the right-hand column will be found the qualifications and characteristics of the *fear life,* ranging from pessimism to vacillation. A study of this parallel arrangement of definitions will make perfectly clear just what the author intends to include under the terms *faith* and *fear,* which terms from now on will be frequently met with in this text.

THE INFLUENCE OF FAITH AND THAT OF FEAR ON THE MIND

When faith thoughts and optimistic ideas dominate the mind, the brain and nervous system seem to functionate in a normal, healthy, and vigorous manner. When fear thoughts and pessimistic ideas, or any of their numerous offspring, control the mind, the brain manifests abnormality in its action and disorder in its function, and the nervous system seems to be more or less demoralized.

A study of psychology in the light of faith and fear, abundantly proves that the faith life (the optimistic life) is the one which nature designed that man should lead. By nature the human mind and body are so constructed that the mental attitude of faith and optimism is absolutely essential to the normal and ideal working of every mental power and physical function.

SENSATIONS AS MODIFIED BY FAITH AND FEAR

The fundamental state of the mind has everything in the world to do with determining the kind, character, and intensity of all the sensations which we experience. The various special sensations, such as those of sight, hearing, and smell, are all capable of being greatly modified, and are often even prevented from coming into being, by the mental state of the patient. Observations and experiments which definitely prove this statement will be fully cited in a later chapter. Objects seen and sounds heard are differently recognized, according to whether the mind is in a state of rest, peace, and repose, or in a state of agitation, excitement, and panic.

Faith favors and facilitates a normal, healthy, and rational interpretation of the sensations which arise from the excitation of the organs of special sense. Every mental state included under the term *fear* directly favors a distorted and diseased interpretation of the sensations, producing an undervaluation of normal sensations together with an extraordinary exaggeration of abnormal sensations, accompanied by an aggravation of painful and unnatural impressions.

Pain and other disagreeable sensations are greatly increased in connection with the mental states of fear and worry; whereas, the optimistic and cheerful frame of mind tends greatly to lessen the inconvenience and suffering occasioned by these unnatural and otherwise painful sensations.

THE PSYCHIC ORIGIN AND NATURE OF SENSATION

In our previous study of the nervous system, it was made plain that the sensations of sight, sound, and pain are not located or experienced in the special sense organs. Here, to be sure, the first step is taken toward their arousal, but they finally depend, without exception, upon special activity in the cortex of the cerebrum — the outer portion of the upper brain.

These feelings, which we recognize and call sensations, result from the excitation of certain special nerves which end in the eye, the nose, the ear, the skin, and other organs, and which, when stimulated, cause waves of nervous energy to pass quickly over the nerves up to the brain; and it is only after these waves of nerve energy reach the brain, and are there received and responded to by the special centres, that the sensations of sight, sound, and pain are experienced.

Now, under certain diseased or unnatural conditions, what is there to hinder these nerves from automatically setting in operation waves of energy or reporting impressions on their own responsibility, entirely independent of the impressions made upon the organs of special sensation, with which they are connected; and, further, even if this did not occur, what is there to prevent the special brain centres, under certain abnormal conditions, from reporting to the consciousness of the individual that it has received certain impressions of sight, sound, or pain, when in reality it has received no such impressions? The special centre of sensation for some particular sense organ may automatically, independently, and spontaneously give origin to a false sensation — that is, a sensation which in that particular instance did not have a definite physical origin. In this way arise hallucinations, delusions, illusions, and various paræsthesias; for example, a bitter taste in the mouth.

This fact, no doubt, accounts for many of our so-called habit sensations, that is, pain and other physical sensations which have become habitual, so that even when the actual cause is removed, either the nerves continue to forward pain impressions to the brain, or the brain centres, having become habituated to reacting to such impressions, continue to awaken the consciousness of pain.

And so it will be seen, as our study progresses, that the mental state of fear, together with all its many phases and numerous psychic offspring, has a tendency to produce unnatural and abnormal sensations or to increase their intensity; and it may even torture the sufferer with sensations and feelings which have no objective source; that fear and worry demoralize the nervous mechanism of the body, and so greatly interfere with the normal and natural interpretation of physical impressions and the recognition of bodily sensations.

Faith, on the other hand, facilitates the production of natural sensations and normal feelings. Every mental state included under the term *faith* discourages the reception, recognition, and harboring of diseased physical impressions, unwholesome thoughts, and unnatural sensations.

FAITH AND FEAR IN RELATION TO MENTAL MASTICATION

Faith exerts the same salutary effect upon the process of mental digestion that it does upon the process of digestion in the stomach; while fear leads to the production of mental indigestion and other disorders of the mind, just as it does to the production of dyspepsia and indigestion in the stomach.

When the mind is confident and tranquil, our perceptions, images, and emotions are normally and healthfully formed. When the mind is alarmed and panicky, the perceptions, images, and emotions become unnatural, distorted, deformed, and diseased.

When the mind is actuated by faith and its attributes, the process of mental mastication is deliberate and healthy. The formation of the percepts is carried on in a natural and normal manner; but when the mind is dominated by fear, the sensations and feelings are rushed through the area of perception posthaste; they are not sufficiently masticated, and the result is the same as in physical digestion — sooner or later, diseased action of the mind, distortion of the intellect — mental dyspepsia.

It is impossible to form healthy percepts, correct images, and trustworthy emotions, when the mind is dominated by fear or any of its attributes.

ACTION OF FAITH AND FEAR ON THE IMAGINATION AND PHANTASY

The higher we ascend in the level of thought, the further we penetrate into the process of mental digestion, the more disastrous become the results of a lapse from faith to fear. The imagination and the higher processes of the mind have the same trouble in dealing with insufficiently masticated mental food, that the stomach does in dealing with bolted physical food. While sudden fright and fear directly influence the imagination, they disease the phantasy, and favor the generation of unwholesome mind poisons in the very beginning of mental digestion.

What is a diseased imagination? It is simply an imagination which is provided with unhealthful mental food — supplied with perceptions, images, and emotions which are abnormal, distorted, and diseased — mind food which is insufficiently masticated — mind food which is tainted with fear and poisoned with fright. When fear controls the mind, the imagination is doomed to functionate in a depressing and unnatural atmosphere, and its creations will usually be found so diseased and abnormal as only to add fuel to the fires of fear.

THE EFFECTS OF FAITH AND FEAR ON THE MENTAL DIGESTION

Still more terrible is the havoc wrought by fear when we come to the process of conception — mental digestion. When we come to classifying, abstracting, comparing, and reflecting upon our percepts (the process of the higher mental digestion), then it is that the terrible mischief wrought by fear becomes apparent. The images and emotions, the sensations and feelings, have now become concepts. They may be erroneously classified. They may be misinterpreted. Their qualities may be confused and wrongly abstracted; their comparison may be faulty and misleading; reflection is too often entirely absent.

The digestive process of the mind is incomplete, superficial; and right here the foundation is laid for mental malnutrition and intellectual anæmia. (The body cannot long remain well-nourished and healthy when the stomach fails properly to do its work.) Neither will the intellect long be found strong and vigorous if fear has thus paralyzed the mental digestion and demoralized the intellectual metabolism. Every mental power is destined to suffer as a result of this baleful influence of fear.

On the other hand, had faith and its associated qualifications dominated the mind, the products of mental mastication, and the internal productions of the imagination, would have brought to the process of conception, healthful, well-masticated, normal, natural material, which would have been promptly and satisfactorily classified, carefully compared, and otherwise fully and completely digested, to be subsequently passed upward in the stream of thought to nourish and sustain the entire mind, and especially to provide healthy material out of which the higher mental powers could elaborate healthy thoughts, wholesome ambitions, and noble aspirations.

Even the memory must fall an unwilling victim to these destructive and demoralizing influences of fear. Food which has not been properly masticated or fully digested, cannot be properly assimilated. Memory represents that power of the mind designed for the assimilation of impressions, the retention of images, the recognition and recollection of that which has been committed to it; but under the influence of fear the memory impressions become unreliable, unhealthy, and diseased. Objects and images are but imperfectly retained, and then only in distorted form. The recollection of impressions entering the mind when in a state of panic and fear are always unreliable, imperfect, and untrustworthy. Thus the memory may become an unconscious tool in the hands of fear and sudden fright, passing up to the higher mental powers, the diseased and unhealthy product of insufficient mental mastication, intellectual indigestion, and mental malassimilation.

98   THE PHYSIOLOGY OF FAITH AND FEAR

FAITH AND FEAR IN THE REALM OF THE ASSOCIATION OF IDEAS

By referring back to the diagram of psychology in Chapter V, it will at once become apparent that mind fear and mental panic are capable of producing untold harm and almost unlimited mischief at this point in the working of the mental machinery. Here, in this mysterious realm of the mind, insufficiently masticated and improperly digested perceptions result in mismated ideas, misformed conceptions, distorted imaginations, and deformed memories; and all these combined, produce that state of mental dyspepsia which gives rise to a vast horde of diseased ideas and unhealthy ideals which must seriously and unfavorably influence both the mental life and the physical health of the individual.

THE EFFECT OF FAITH AND FEAR ON THE HIGHER MENTAL POWERS

Bad as are the effects of fear on the mental powers considered thus far, it becomes even worse in its influence upon judgment, reason, and choice. Faith and the qualifications allied thereto are absolutely essential to the normal and healthy operation of the judgment. The judgment cannot functionate in a proper manner when the mind is dominated by fear. Not only are the ideas which the judgment must discriminate, distorted and deformed, but the action of this mental power is more or less paralyzed and directly distorted by the presence of fear thought in the mind.

But most disastrous of all is the effect of fear upon the reason. The individual whose mind is swayed by fear and harassed with worry, is unable to reason in a healthy and normal manner. The highest conclusions of the mind are apt to be of least value to the sufferer. Such a person is just as likely to reason himself into trouble as out of trouble. He is more likely to reason himself into disease than into health. From disuse, the reason soon grows weak and feeble, and this permits the diseased thoughts and imaginations to pass on unhindered, to find ultimate translation into words of discouragement, looks of despair, and habits of bondage and disease.

And thus we are forced to recognize fear as a mental blight, a moral mildew, and an intellectual poison.

THE PSYCHOLOGY OF FAITH AND FEAR

FAITH AND FEAR IN THE DEVELOPMENT OF CHARACTER

Inasmuch as faith and fear determine the character of our mental activity and the product of our minds, they powerfully influence the formation of character. Temperament, honesty, morality, the affections, and the entire conduct are moulded according as faith thought or fear thought is uppermost in the mind; especially is the influence of fear in character formation shown to be all-powerful when its effects upon the mind are studied in connection with its effects upon the body. The influence of fear on the body will fully be shown subsequently.

The child who is trained to fear his parents, to fear ghosts and hobgoblins, spooks and spirits, to fear both the real and fictitious dangers of life, and later to live in constant and unnatural fear of the Supreme Being, and in the end to fear an eternal hell-fire, certainly deserves the pity of all thinking creatures. A large percentage of grown-up people live in constant fear of something. Fear has become a well-nigh universal mental disease, and its constant entertainment is bound to result in swinging the character attributes of the people from the beautiful, noble, and happy characteristics of the faith life, over into the distressing and undesirable qualifications found under the fear life. (See parallel arrangement of the faith life and the fear life at the end of the next chapter.)

FAITH AND FEAR IN HEALTH AND DISEASE

We have now come to the place in our study for the practical application of faith and fear as they influence the mind and the body. As will be shown more fully later, all faith thoughts have a tendency to prevent disease and promote health; all fear thoughts have a tendency to produce disease and prevent health. Accordingly, any and *all influences which tend to destroy fear and generate faith are, in the last analysis, health-promoting agencies.*

At all times and in all ages the human race has ever sought after those agencies, influences, teachings, and religions which had power to generate faith and banish fear. All new religions have been invented with a view to producing faith within the human mind and destroying fear in the human heart. The latter they have not always succeeded in accomplishing: toward the former they have at least contributed something.

The accompanying diagram (Fig. 15) is intended graphically to illustrate how the religious beliefs, racial practices, and popular superstitions of both ancient and modern times have operated to destroy fear and generate faith. We desire in this connection to lay emphasis upon this important truth: *Any and all procedures, practices, superstitions, religious beliefs, or systems of healing, no matter how nonsensical or whimsical, if they succeed in generating faith and destroying fear, will, directly and indirectly, tend to improve the physical health of all who are influenced thereby.* In other words, there is positive curative power in any teaching, belief, or mental attitude which will cause the individual to exercise more faith and thus in some measure deliver himself from the mental bondage and the moral thraldom of the fear life. And fear, it should be remembered, is the handmaiden of disease, the one great cause of those mental attitudes and bodily states which in every way favor distress and disease.

The practices of the ancient tribal medicine-men were all designed to mystify the sufferer, to attract his attention, to inspire his faith, to create confidence; and just in proportion as the medicine-man was able to generate faith and destroy fear, with his harmless herbs and his innocent incantations, he was able to help his patients and relieve their mental tortures and physical sufferings.

The idol worship of the heathen and the relic worship of the later Christians, undoubtedly resulted in the cure of many sufferers, because it inspired honest souls to believe. They were able, in measure, to translate themselves from the realm of the fear life into that of the faith life, and, accordingly, they experienced improvement in their physical feelings, and in many instances recovery from bodily disease.

The working of charms and other forms of Oriental sophistry, undoubtedly operated along these same lines. The sick and suffering would hang something about their necks, pin their faith to it, and begin to feel better right away. The author well remembers wearing a little bag of asafœtida hung

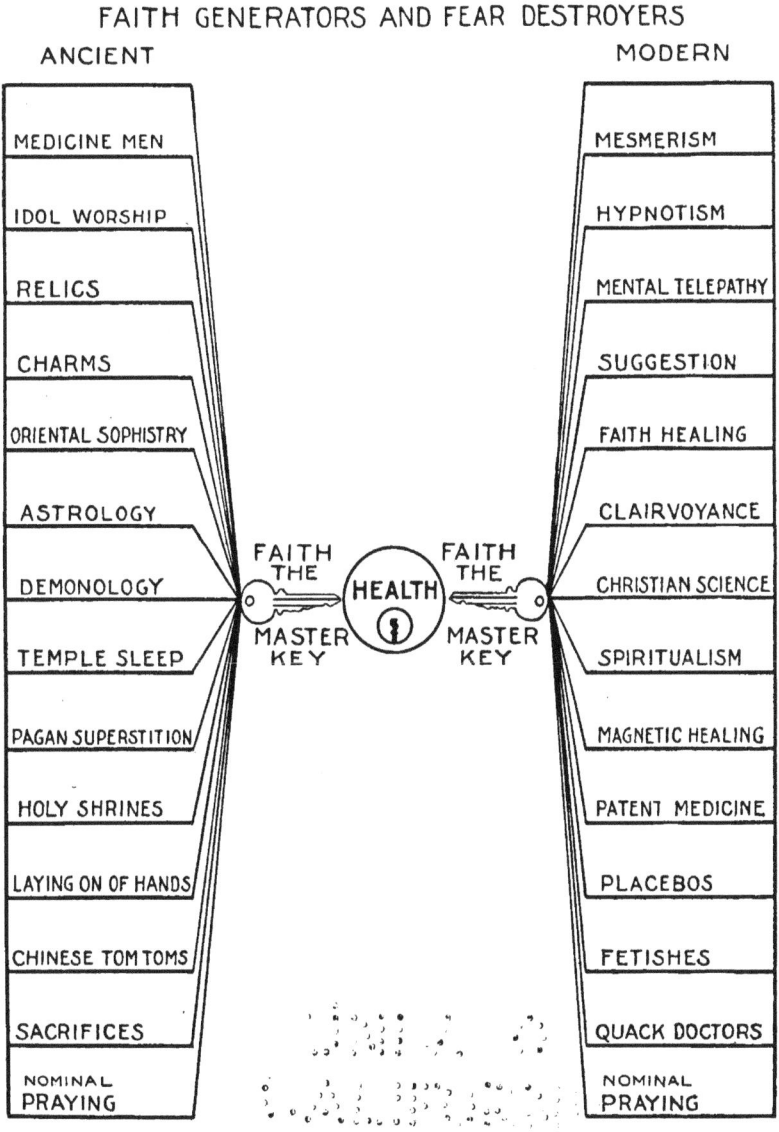

FIG. 15.

DIAGRAM SHOWING ANCIENT AND MODERN
FAITH GENERATORS AND FEAR DESTROYERS

around his neck, when a child, "to keep disease away." The practice was common at that time.

The old teachings of demonology and astrology operated along the same line. The sick and suffering were led to *believe* that doing certain things on certain days, when the stars were in certain positions, would lead to the recovery of health, and they believed it with sufficient ardor actually to influence the mind and body, and in many cases they no doubt did obtain some relief from their mental anguish or physical suffering.

The pagan superstitions of the "temple sleep" and the Christian nonsense of shrine worship, belong to the same category. The earnest and ignorant devotees of these ancient superstitions were helped mentally and physically to just the extent that their devotion was able to dispel fear and give birth to faith. Fear was responsible for much of their suffering and faith brought deliverance therefrom.

The beating of Chinese tom-toms or laying on of holy hands operated to inspire faith on the part of the sufferers and abolish fear, and, to just the extent that they were able to do this, they proved of value in aiding recovery from mental suffering and bodily disease.

The ancient practices of sacrifices, penance, and even of praying, all operated in accordance with this same great and universal law of mind healing — the exercise of faith and the suppression of fear.

Likewise, when we come to consider the modern methods of generating faith and removing fear, we are able to discover only a difference in technique. Science and civilization have made it necessary to revise and rearrange the methods whereby we seek to replace mental fear with moral faith. Accordingly, mesmerism and hypnotism have come largely to be practised as means of relieving sickness and lessening suffering, and it is a well-known fact that these practices are valueless if the sufferer does not have faith; in fact, they are quite impossible to use unless those whom they are designed to benefit, yield implicit faith and trust to the hypnotic operator. These modern practices, together with present-day superstitions such as mental telepathy, all operate in accordance with the same old law — the creation of faith and the abolition of fear.

Our modern methods of suggestive therapeutics are but a utilization of this same law of mental healing. To the victims of fright, to those who fear that they cannot get well, to those who worry because they do not get well, to those who are sure they never can get well, it is quietly suggested that they are getting well, and it makes no matter whether the suggestion is true or false, it is of no difference whether it comes from the patient's own mind, or from the mind of a friend or from his physician, as the new ideas of faith are allowed to displace those of fear, the individual begins to experience certain beneficial results in the way of mental improvement and physical recovery.

And so we come to faith healing — laying aside the discussion of everything that pertains to the operation of so-called miracles, or the miraculous acts of olden times — considering faith healing merely a restoration of health as the result of the beneficent action of faith on the mind, as the result of the influence of faith upon the body, and finally as the result of its banishment of the disease-producing fear thoughts which preceded it. There can be no question that faith is able to cure many diseases, to influence the body favorably in its struggles with affliction; while it is of undoubted value as an aid in the treatment of, and the recovery from, all diseases — even those organic and chronic diseases which it cannot directly cure, and for which fear thought was not wholly responsible.*

Clairvoyance and magnetic healing have been operated in recent times for the removal of mental distress, fear, and physical suffering, in harmony with these same principles. Even phrenology belongs more or less to this category. Men

---

*The author desires distinctly to emphasize that the "faith" herewith discussed, is psychologic faith, and not theologic or Christian faith — it is the state of mental hope and confidence common to all mankind, and not that sublime and supernatural faith which is the exclusive possession of the saints — of those who have, in accordance with the Master's words, been "born again."

and women have been told that such and such things would happen; that thus and so they would come to pass. They had faith in the clairvoyant, in the phrenologist, or in the magnetic healer; and as faith or fear was strengthened by these interviews, health or disease, happiness or distress, was promoted in the patient's experience.

Christian Science has accomplished its wonderful work along the lines of this same law of mental healing. This modern cult is so typical of how all ancient healing delusions and modern health deceptions have operated upon the human mind, it will be subsequently more fully dealt with in a later chapter, after we have completed our consideration of the influences of faith and fear upon both mind and body. Spiritualism and other spiritistic phenomena are also to be explained by this same universal law of mind healing, so far as regards their effects and influence upon the physical functions of the body.

And so patent medicines, placebos, and quack doctors have largely cured their patients because of the confidence they inspired, the faith they generated, the assurance they gave, their glowing promises, and their unqualified guarantee to cure. The sufferer who has swallowed a dose of patent medicine, after having read a score of glowing testimonials (their fraudulent and lying character in no way interferes with their power in this case) begins immediately to feel better, not only because of the alcohol or other stimulants contained in the medicine which was swallowed, but also because the patient has, for once, become possessed with the idea that *he is going to get well.* He has faith in the newly discovered medicine. It cured other people — he believes it will cure him; and to just the extent that fear moves out and faith takes possession of his mind, he begins actually to get better, the physical functions of the body take on a more natural, normal, and healthy movement.

Did not the quack doctor, in his newspaper advertisements, claim to possess extraordinary and unusual skill? Whereas the regular doctor had not arrived at a positive diagnosis and would not even promise definite improvement, did not the quack feel the pulse, look at the tongue, and instantly make a positive diagnosis? Did he not guarantee to cure the disease in six weeks? The positive manner, the absolute assurance, the apparent mastery and complete understanding of the case manifested by the quack, inspired faith on the part of the sufferer. Fear begins to flee. The patient becomes possessed with the idea that he is going to get well, that the quack can cure him, and this very fact explains why the inefficient, ignorant, and unscrupulous quack, by means of his commonplace medicines, is able to cure many patients who have found no relief at the hands of the most conscientious, skilful, and learned practitioners. The regular practitioner was not conversant with the practice of suggestive therapeutics. He did not know how honestly and scientifically to generate faith and destroy fear in the mind of his patient, and this the quack doctor unconsciously did by the very methods and deceptions of his ignorance and quackery; and so hundreds of sufferers have been relieved by the administration of placebos — sugar pills and bread pellets.

And so the fetishes of the ignorant heathen, and the charms and "lucky" objects of the civilized nations, all influence the minds of those who believe in them, by their power to increase faith or decrease fear. Some heathen tribes are literally fetish-ridden — they are unable to work, eat, or sleep, except under the protection of their favorite fetish.

SUMMARY OF THE CHAPTER

1. The term *fear* is made to include pessimism, dissatisfaction, grief, anxiety, despondency, hatred, worry, moroseness, anger, and vacillation; while *faith* represents the state of optimism, satisfaction, happiness, confidence, assurance, hopefulness, cheerfulness, courage, and determination.

2. Faith is essential to healthy mental action. Fear demoralizes the intellect. Every bodily sensation is capable of being perverted and distorted by fear.

3. Fear intensifies pain, misinterprets sensation, exaggerates abnormal feelings, and gives rise to false ideas regarding the bodily state.

4. Faith favors the normal working of the nervous mechan-

ism, while fear may give origin to false sensations, fraudulent feelings, and bogus impressions.

5. Fear destroys the power of the mind to reflect. It predisposes to panicky and premature mental action. It produces mental dyspepsia.

6. Faith steadies the imagination. Fear demoralizes the imagination and deranges the whole process of mental digestion. Even the power of memory is lessened by chronic fear or worry.

7. Fear interferes with the normal and healthy association of ideas — it relatively paralyzes the higher mental powers of judgment and reason.

8. Fear is a mental blight, a moral mildew, and an intellectual poison. It warps the temperament and stunts the character.

9. In both the child and the adult, fear — it matters not how generated — unfailingly makes for disease and distress; while faith is health-generating.

10. Any practice, religion, belief, or other system of healing, no matter how false or foolish, if it is able to destroy fear and give origin to faith, will prove itself able to cure disease and heal the sick in sufficient numbers to establish its claims as a new religion — perhaps as the only genuine belief.

11. The Indian medicine-man, the idol-worshippers, the relic devotees, the charm-wearers, and a score of other healers and practices have all been able to cure disease because they inspired faith on the part of the health-seeker. Faith makes for health, no matter by what name it is called.

12. Clairvoyance, magnetic healing, Christian Science, quackery, and other psychic and mental methods of healing, all utilize the same universal law of mental healing — mental rest, the generation of faith, and the destruction of doubts and fears.

CHAPTER X

FAITH THE MASTER KEY TO MENTAL MEDICINE

THE LAW OF MENTAL HEALING.— SUMMARY OF THE ELEMENTS, QUALITIES, AND FACTORS ENTERING INTO THE MEANING OF THE TERMS "FAITH" AND "FEAR" AS USED IN THIS TEXT.

AND *so it would appear that any practice, procedure, belief, medicine, cult, or ism which is able to generate faith and destroy fear, possesses definite curative powers in the treatment of mental and physical disease.* The fact that the sick and the suffering recover under such treatment in no way proves that the religion, ethics, or other ideas or ideals of those who treat them are either right or wrong. A wicked chemist can produce water by adding two atoms of hydrogen to one atom of oxygen, just as surely and unfailingly as can the most devout and prayerful, church-going, Christian chemist. It is not a matter of religion, character, or divinity; it is simply a proposition in chemistry; and the laws of chemistry, like those of gravitation, operate with unerring accuracy in the hands of the good, the bad, or the indifferent.

And so the law of mental healing — *faith is a health-producer; fear is a disease-producer* — operates when it is consciously or unconsciously utilized by any and all persons, at any and all times, and in any and all places. If John Alexander Dowie prayed for you and you got well, your recovery in no wise constitutes evidence that Dowie was a better man than the minister who prayed for you before, when you did not get well. It simply means that Dowie's means and methods — his dress and personal appearance, what you had heard about him, and what he said to you — resulted in making such a mental impression upon you that faith came into its own, took possession of your mind, routed fear, and banished doubt.

FAITH THE MASTER KEY

You threw your whole mind into the one grand conclusion that you were going to be healed, and many who did this were apparently healed, and, not understanding the laws of mind and matter underlying their healing, they immediately espoused the peculiar cause of the healer, adopted his beliefs as their beliefs, his religion as their religion, and his way of living as their way of living; and in this way vast churches, cults, and isms have been built up in both ancient and modern times. Practically every new cult in recent years has begun its career by claims and attempts to heal disease and relieve suffering.

The same patient who was thus apparently healed by repeating a form of prayer — nominal praying — would have been healed by any other method, agency, procedure, or practice, which would have generated an equivalent amount of faith. Had that transcendent psychic faith which possessed his soul at the moment of healing been generated by hypnotism, spiritualism, patent medicines, or by a visit to a holy shrine, he would have gotten well just as truly and just as quickly.

And so it becomes apparent that the healing of disease by means of faith, or by so-called prayer or by any other method, in no wise proves that the healer is a special agent of God, that his religion is the one true belief, or that his ethical teachings are right. Fear, then, is seen to be one great barrier to the recovery from sickness and the healing of disease. *Faith becomes the master key which unlocks many an ancient medical mystery and explains many apparent modern miracles.* Faith is the great key of mental healing. Mental rest is the keystone of the arch of health.

A SUMMARY OF THE ELEMENTS, QUALITIES, AND FACTORS ENTERING INTO THE MEANING OF THE TERMS "FAITH" AND "FEAR" AS USED IN THIS TEXT

THE FAITH LIFE	THE FEAR LIFE
1. *Optimism:* Sanguineness. Cheerfulness. Hopeful disposition. Light-heartedness. Belief that "all things work together for good."	1. *Pessimism:* Hopelessness. Dejection. Gloomy and despondent outlook. Magnification of evil and sorrow. Looking on the dark side.

108 THE PHYSIOLOGY OF FAITH AND FEAR

THE FAITH LIFE

2. *Satisfaction:* Contentedness. Resignation. Comfortableness.
3. *Happiness:* Pleasure. Felicity. Blessedness. Enjoyment. Smiling face.
4. *Confidence:* Faith. Deep-rooted belief. Firmness. Steadfastness. Security.
5. *Assurance:* Boldness. Making a declaration to oneself. Conviction. Freedom from doubt. Looking on the bright side.
6. *Trustfulness:* Implicit confidence. Faithfulness. Fully making up one's mind. Putting the mind at rest.
7. *Hopefulness:* Expectation. Confidence in the future. Good-humor. Self-confidence. Bright-facedness. Cheerful disposition.
8. *C e r t a i n t y:* Positiveness. Sureness. Indisputability. Unfailingness. Absoluteness. Solidity. Independence. Unquestionableness.
9. *Love:* Emotion. Sentiment. Kind-heartedness. Sympathy. Affection. Devotion. Attachment. Fondness. Admiration. Adoration. Brotherliness. Fellow-feeling.
10. *Cheerfulness:* Animation. Good spirits. Joyfulness. Mirthfulness. Gladness. Vivacity. Buoyancy. E a s y-mindedness. Trustfulness. Comfort. Perfect happiness.

THE FEAR LIFE

2. *Dissatisfaction:* Discontentedness. Uneasiness. Fretfulness. Disappointment.
3. *Grief:* Sorrow. Sadness. Heart-sickness. "Broken-hearted." Drooping spirits.
4. *Alarm:* Misgiving. Fright. Terror. Dread. Consternation. Insecurity. Apprehension. Panic.
5. *Timidity:* Dismayedness Diffidence. Faint-heartedness. Nervousness. "Bugaboos." Throbbing heart. Fear and trembling.
6. *Anxiety:* Care. Doubtfulness. Solicitude. Foreboding. Perplexity. Watchfulness. Disquietude. Suspense.
7. *Despondency:* Hopelessness. Discouragement. Despair. Down-heartedness. Melancholy. Gloom. Sadness. "The blues."
8. *Suspicion:* Mistrust. Conjecture. Jealousy. Uncertainty. Dubiousness. Questionableness. Hesitation. Scepticism. Ignorance. Vagueness.
9. *Hatred:* Antipathy. Aversion. Abhorrence. Detestation. Hostility. Animosity. Bitterness. Malice. Grudge. Contemptuousness. Lack of sympathy. "Bad blood."
10. *Worry:* Disquietude. Bad spirits. Heaviness. Trouble. Perplexity. Turmoil. Harassment. Irritation. Vexation. Annoyance. Hypochondria. Depression. Melancholy.

FAITH THE MASTER KEY

THE FAITH LIFE

11. *Courage:* Bravery. Power to face difficulties without depression of spirits. Valor. Intrepidity. Resolution. Fortitude. Firmness. Fearlessness. Spunk. "Bearding the lion in his den." "Taking the bull by the horns."
12. *Patience:* Endurance. Submission. Calmness. Forbearance. Perseverance. Resignation. Composure. Inexcitability. Serenity. Tranquillity. Coolness. Imperturbability. Repression of feeling.
13. *Enthusiasm:* Exhilaration. Ardent zeal. Sunniness. Zealousness. Heartiness. Jubilance. Brightness. Joyousness. Good-humor. High spirits. Enlivening the spirits.
14. *Conscientiousness:* Scrupulousness. *D*uteousness. Allegiance. Morality. Constancy. Fidelity. Honesty. Incorruptibility. Justice. Loyalty. Principle. Purity. Rectitude. Truth. Veracity. "Being true to one's colors."
15. *Determination:* Decision. The ability to make up one's mind. Firmness. Pluckiness. Tenacity. Steadiness. Fixedness. Immovableness. Self-control. Self-reliance. Strong-mindedness. Will-power. Readiness to "go through fire and water." Moral courage. Sturdiness.

THE FEAR LIFE

11. *Cowardice:* Pusillanimity. Unwillingness to face difficulties. Irresolution. Spiritlessness. Effeminacy. Skittishness. Softness. Losing one's nerve. "Showing the white feather." Chicken-heartedness.
12. *Anger:* Revengefulness. Indignation. Resentment. Wrathfulness. Fury. Rage. Ire. Fierceness. Exasperation. Fieriness. Irritability. Vehemence. Frenzy. Rant. Bombast. Impulsiveness.
13. *Moroseness:* Sullenness. Crabbedness. *D*umpishness. Peevishness. Crossness. Sourness. Surliness. Sulkiness. Cantankerousness. Glumness. Bad temper. Restlessness. Ill-humor.
14. *Remorse:* Anguish. Regret. Dishonor. Disgrace. Crookedness. Penitence. Sinfulness. Sorrow. Self-accusation. Self-reproach. Self-condemnation. Betrayal of trust. A burdened mind. Pangs of conscience.
15. *Vacillation:* Changeableness. Fluctuation of mind. Unsteadiness of character. Fickleness. Waveringness. Hesitancy. Half-heartedness. Inconstancy. Indecision. "Blowing hot and cold." Double-mindedness. *D*ubitancy. Mutability.

PART II
PHYSIOLOGIC SECTION

PART II
PHYSIOLOGIC SECTION

CHAPTER XI
HOW THE EMOTIONS AFFECT THE HEART

THE HEART'S STRENGTH.— THE CARDIAC RHYTHM.— THE HEART RATE.— THE HEART'S REST.— NUTRITION OF THE HEART.— THE CARDIAC ENDURANCE.— THE CARDIAC NERVE CENTRES.— THE HEART'S EMOTIONAL RESPONSE.— THE CARDIAC PSYCHIC RESPONSE.— SENSATIONS REFERRED TO THE HEART.— COMPARATIVE SUMMARY OF THE EFFECTS OF FAITH AND FEAR ON THE HEART ACTION.

THE study of preceding chapters will suffice to show the tremendons influence exerted by the emotional states of faith and fear upon both mind and body. Careful consideration has been given to the *psychology* of faith and fear, and it is now in order to consider more in detail the *physiology* of faith and fear.

For many years the author has painstakingly collected hundreds of authentic experiments and careful observations respecting the influence of the mind upon the body. Many of these experiments and observations he has verified in his own clinic and laboratory, while other and original inquiries have been carried forward for the purpose of accurately determining the exact range of the influence of the diversified mental states upon definite bodily functions.

While it would be out of place in a popular work of this sort to undertake to present detailed laboratory experiments, or to offer technical evidence of clinical observations touching these matters; we will, nevertheless, present a full and complete outline of the facts touching every phase of the subject of mind as related to matter, as determined by physiological and psychological experiments and observations.

And so, while avoiding the details and technicalities of our conclusions, we will outline in this and following chapters the fundamental facts touching the physiology of faith and fear, in such a manner as to give the reader a clear and definite idea as to just how far and in what manner the mental state is able, directly or indirectly, to influence and modify the physical functions of the human body. As a rule, fear operates to depress and retard the vital functions, and this is brought about by the inhibition of those vital functions whose controlling centres are located in the medulla.

THE HEART STRENGTH

Common everyday experience goes to show that the heart action is exceedingly sensitive and highly responsive to the most delicate shades of variation in the mental state. There is absolutely nothing mysterious about the manner in which the mind influences cardiac action, although, of course, the process of tracing out all the exact details of the *modus operandi* is only imperfectly understood.

Under the influence of faith and its associated optimistic state of mind, the strength of the heart-beat is strong, normal, and natural. Unusual mental buoyancy may even increase the heart strength. The vigor of the heart action increases hand in hand with the development of courage and the acquisition of confidence. On the other hand, fear and other phases of the mental state bordering on pessimism not infrequently tend actually to decrease the strength of the heart's action. Fear unfailingly demoralizes the cardiac functions and greatly weakens the power of the heart-beat.

Joy always increases the strength of the heart action, while terror never fails greatly to depress the heart, after a very brief initial period of excitability and rapid action.

We were once summoned to the bedside of a patient whose heart action was almost suspended as the result of a frightful hemorrhage. The pulse was not perceptible at the wrist and the heart had all but given up the struggle. While the attendants made ready to inject salt solution and administer restoratives, we spoke to the patient in very positive and assuring terms, in answer to her question as to whether or not she was dying, and immediately — almost instantly — before a single material thing

THE EMOTIONS AND THE HEART

had been done for her, she began to rally: the heart began to beat with increased vigor, in less than one minute the pulse could be distinctly felt at the wrist, and in but a few minutes she had almost completely rallied from a threatened collapse. This was very evidently a case of heart-rally in response to certain stimuli and nervous energy, originated and directed by that potent and powerful mental force, *faith*. It is easy to imagine what might have been the outcome of such a case had the priest been called, the candles lighted, and the last rites performed.

THE CARDIAC RHYTHM

The mental states of faith and assurance favor natural regularity of the heart action, thus enabling the heart muscle to do the greatest amount of work with the least expenditure of vital energy. Fear and anxiety usually produce more or less irregularity of the heart's action, while acute fright and unusual apprehension may result in producing actual palpitation of the heart. The normal, natural, galloping rhythm of the heart's action is more or less destroyed by every form of fear and worry.

It is doubtful if there are to be found many cases of intermittent pulse which are not largely or wholly due to some form of mental disturbance — worry, shock, fear, or sorrow.

The mind undoubtedly influences the rhythm of the heart by its indirect power upon the cardiac centres of the sympathetic system. The instances of complete heart failure from mental shock must be due to a paralysis of the sympathetic centres.

THE HEART RATE

In every way, faith and trust favor the normal rate of the heart's action. They prevent unduly rapid activity of the heart muscle, and thus postpone the evil day of partial or complete heart failure. Mental rest not only favors a rhythmic action of the heart, but also favors a more natural rate of heart-beat; that is, the contented mind allows the heart to beat just the right number of times per minute. Fear usually increases the heart action — greatly increases the number of heart-beats per minute. This abnormal activity leads to early breaking down of the heart's strength and to premature heart failure.

Many years ago attention was called to the fact that anxiety and apprehension contributed much to the causation and aggravation of Graves's disease, or exophthalmic goitre. The author recently had a case of this sort of goitre under treatment, and careful observation showed unquestionably that the mental states of faith and fear exerted a tremendous influence either to improve or to intensify the general nervous symptoms of the disease, especially the rate and rhythm of the heart-beat. In the treatment of all cases of exophthalmic goitre, care should be exercised to see that the mind is put to rest and filled with hopeful and pleasant thoughts, and that the bowels move regularly and freely.

The mind is able to influence the heart rate — causing it to beat rapidly under the influence of fear — by central impulses going to the heart over the accelerator nerve; while faith operates by way of the inhibitory nerve, holding the heart action down with a firm and steady hand, thus enabling the body to derive the greatest possible benefit from the least possible exertion and work on the part of the cardiac muscle.

THE HEART'S REST

The heart is a muscular organ. Like all other muscles it must have periods of rest between its periods of work, in order to recuperate its energy and rebuild its broken-down structures. The heart muscle secures this period of rest during what is known as its "diastolic pause" — the momentary rest between the heart-beats.

The mental state exerts considerable influence upon the heart's strength by determining the length of this pause between the heart-beats. Faith exerts a favorable influence upon the heart rate and rhythm by encouraging a natural and adequate rest between beats, thus enabling the heart to keep up its normal energy, and, in case of the weak heart, actually to gain in strength. On the other hand, the fearful and distrustful state of mind produces irregularity of rhythm and abnormal rapidity of the heart action, and so greatly shortens the time of the heart rest: the diastolic pause is inadequate; the heart fails to get its proper rest between beats.

We frequently have seen cases where the heart was rapidly

failing from overwork and overstimulation by the so-called heart tonics, which would show marvellous improvement in strength as a result of placing an ice bag directly over the heart for fifteen minutes every hour, coupled with rubbing the body to increase the skin circulation. This marked improvement in heart action is no doubt largely due to the slowing down of the cardiac activity, thus allowing the heart muscle more time for rest between beats; and since it has been shown that faith and hope actually slow down and steady the heart action, is it not entirely consistent to recognize the immense value of these natural and healthy mental states in the important work of securing proper heart rest; and as adequate heart rest promotes cardiac nutrition and recuperation, it is evident that faith is indirectly a contributor to heart strength.

NUTRITION OF THE HEART

The nutrition of the heart is favored by a peaceful and serene state of mind, while the opposite mental states of unrest and dissatisfaction, by their power to disturb the heart's regularity and decrease its periods of rest, greatly interfere with the nutrition of this important vital organ. Cardiac nutrition is invariably lessened by overwork and too little rest on the part of the heart muscle.

There is little doubt that certain cases of angina pectoris, that disease of indescribable pain in the region of the heart — at least the so-called pseudo angina — are indirectly caused by poor nutrition of the heart muscle; and we are coming more and more to recognize the important role played by the mental state and the nervous system as factors in overworking the heart and interfering with its natural and normal nutrition. A large number of experienced physicians believe that emotional excitement and mental anxiety figure very largely in the production of angina pectoris. A vast number of other and less serious pains in the region of the heart are largely the result of mental influences plus indigestion and gas on the stomach.

THE CARDIAC ENDURANCE

Faith actually increases the endurance of the heart under stress and strain. Determination and courage are even able to postpone heart failure when the patient is at the very point of death. It is not an uncommon occurrence to find an aged father or mother rapidly sinking into the grave, who, by sheer determination and will-power, are actually able to maintain the heart's action until the children, hastening to the bedside, arrive; then after a last farewell they willingly give up the struggle, to pass quickly and quietly away. That fright and fear may produce heart failure, and lead to immediate death, is a well-known and firmly established fact. Hundreds of people are literally frightened to death every year.

THE CARDIAC NERVE CENTRES

The nerve centres for heart action, found in the brain and elsewhere, are all favorably influenced by pleasant and agreeable mental states. That this is true is shown by the experience of numerous patients suffering from functional heart disease, due largely to fear and despondency, who, after going completely insane, in almost every instance, fully recover from heart disease. While this can hardly be offered as a suggestive remedy or cure for functional heart diseases, it does go a long way toward proving that mental worry and anxiety are sometimes able to produce functional heart disturbances. Colonel Townshend was able at will temporarily to stop the heart's action and thus simulate death. He did this once too often, and death actually took place.

On the other hand, direct experiments unquestionably establish the fact that the heart centres can be completely inhibited and absolutely paralyzed by fear. We have numerous cases on record where perfectly healthy persons have been actually frightened to death.

It is evident that faith and fear are able profoundly to influence the nerve centres which regulate and maintain heart action.

THE HEART'S EMOTIONAL RESPONSE

The action of the heart is most natural and regular when it is least thought of. The care-free mental state favors natural heart action. On the other hand, fear and every other form of mental anxiety interfere with the natural action of the heart, in common with the action of all the other vital organs. If you concentrate your mind on your heart you will immediately

THE EMOTIONS AND THE HEART 119

interfere with its normal action. To focus one's attention upon the heart is almost sure to result in altering its beat — its rate and rhythm. For one to imagine that he has some form of heart disease is enough, in itself, speedily to produce a cardiac functional disturbance of sufficient gravity to be sooner or later diagnosed by some physician as a heart disease.

The emotional response of the heart is probably due to sympathetic action. The sensations experienced in the heart are reflex and referred, as the heart itself does not originate either the pleasant or disagreeable sensations commonly referred to it. And so, while the heart action is greatly modified by the emotions acting through the sympathetic nervous system, it is quickened or slowed or even stopped by extraordinary mental shock, through the action of the tenth nerve, the pneumogastric. Such was the case with the condemned criminal, who, as he was about to be beheaded, was reprieved just before the axe fell, but after his head had been placed on the execution block. He died almost instantly from fright — heart failure.

THE CARDIAC PSYCHIC RESPONSE

The healthy heart beats quietly and regularly when the mind is at peace and free from fear. Faith is the ideal and natural mental state, so far as healthy heart action is concerned. Any agitation of the mind almost immediately produces a conscious thumping of the heart against the chest wall. The relation between the mental state and the heart muscle is direct, and the response of the heart muscle to mental disturbance is immediate, well defined, and clearly established.

An English physician has even reported a case of actual dilatation of the heart, which was thought to be due to a general disturbance of the mental state, with particular anxiety respecting the heart, and constant concentration of the mind on the cardiac muscle.

In order to understand the nervous mechanism whereby the emotions influence the heart, it should be borne in mind that the heart is directly regulated by two great sets of nerves: one, the accelerator, which hastens the action of the heart; the other, the inhibitor, which retards or checks the heart action.

The accelerator is constantly urging the heart forward — whipping it up, as it were; while the inhibitor nerve ever holds it back — putting on the brakes. It is like the case of the driver, who, while he urges his horse forward with the lash, holds a steady and firm rein lest the animal become uncontrollable and dash away. The inhibitor nerve serves as an ever-acting rein to hold the heart in, while the accelerator nerve incessantly prods the heart on.

Fear weakens the heart by means of a double mechanism: (1) By decreasing the impulses arising in the cardio-augmentor centres of the medulla the heart-beat is immediately weakened; (2) By greatly increasing the rapidity of the heart action. This is accomplished through the influence of the sympathetic system. The sympathetic influences whip up the heart action under conditions of fright and fear just as a panic-stricken driver sometimes lashes his frightened horse. In all this work the heart and lungs are more or less coördinate, because of the association of their respective centres in the medulla, an excess of carbon dioxid (CO_2) in the blood producing cardio-inhibition. And so, to refer again to the illustration of the driver, the reins, and the horse, we find there are two influences at work to quicken and weaken the heart action: first, the application of the whip — the sympathetic impulses; second, the dropping or looscuing of the reins — stopping the stimulating impulses coming from the augmentor centres of the medulla.

SENSATIONS REFERRED TO THE HEART

That the mental state directly influences the heart action, giving rise to cardiac sensations, must have been recognized in times of remote antiquity, as indicated by such familiar expressions as "my heart rejoices," and "heart-rending scenes." When one is in a pleasant frame of mind, there is such an exuberant and bounding heart action, as actually to lead the overjoyed soul to exclaim, "My heart rejoices." These are clearly referred sensations, nevertheless, they indicate the existence of a close nervous connection between the general mental state and the reflex or referred cardiac sensations. Unpleasant and disagreeable experiences are likewise referred to as "heart-breaking," "heart-grieving." We also speak of a

THE EMOTIONS AND THE HEART

"hearty welcome," "hearty sympathy," "kind-hearted people," and "hard-hearted people."

COMPARATIVE SUMMARY OF THE EFFECTS OF FAITH AND FEAR ON THE HEART ACTION

FAITH	FEAR
1. *Heart strength:* Increased. Normal and natural.	1. *Heart strength:* Decreased. Weakened.
2. *Rhythm:* Regularity — normal regulation.	2. *Rhythm:* Irregularity — palpitation.
3. *Rate:* Normal slowness.	3. *Rate:* Abnormal rapidity.
4. *Rest* (diastolic): Adequate; heart gains in strength.	4. *Rest* (diastolic): Inadequate; wearing on the heart.
5. *Nutrition:* Increased by rest and regularity.	5. *Nutrition:* Decreased by overwork and under-rest.
6. *Endurance:* Postpones heart failure at the time of death.	6. *Endurance:* Heart failure in case of profound fear.
7. *Cardiac centres:* Favorably influenced.	7. *Cardiac centres:* Depression and paralysis.
8. *Emotional response:* Action regular when not thought of.	8. *Emotional response:* Attention alters the beat.
9. *Psychic response:* Beats quietly and regularly when the mind is at peace and free from fear.	9. *Psychic response:* Conscious thumping against the chest when mind is agitated.
10. *Referred sensation:* Pleasant and agreeable — "My heart rejoices."	10. *Referred sensation:* Unpleasant and disagreeable — "Heart-rending scenes."

CHAPTER XII

INFLUENCE OF THE MIND UPON THE CIRCULATORY SYSTEM

THE BLOOD-PRESSURE.— ARTERIOSCLEROSIS, HARD ARTERIES.— CAPILLARY CONTRACTION.— CIRCULATORY SKIN REACTION.— THE BLOOD MOVEMENT.— LOCAL CONGESTIONS.— CIRCULATORY EQUILIBRIUM.— APOPLEXY.— THE PULSE.— COMPARATIVE SUMMARY OF THE EFFECTS OF FAITH AND FEAR ON THE CIRCULATION OF THE BLOOD.

IN a general way, we have long known that the state of the mind has much to do with the circulation of the blood; but not until the matter was put to actual experiment was it known in just what manner, and to what degree, the mind could influence and control the circulation, and thereby indirectly control the health and regulate the nutrition of the body.

THE BLOOD-PRESSURE

Careful experiments have demonstrated that faith and its allied mental states favor normal blood-pressure. Faith and trust actually possess some remedial power, in that they are able, in some instances, to lower the blood-pressure when it is abnormally high. The importance of maintaining normal blood-pressure the author has fully discussed elsewhere;* however, attention should be called to the fact that high blood-pressure is in a measure responsible for, as well as being a result of, such disorders as Bright's disease, heart failure, headaches, arteriosclerosis, and numerous other functional disorders, resulting from high tension within the blood vessels.

The mental factor in blood-pressure will be more fully considered in the next chapter.

*See "The Science of Living," Chap. XV.

THE MIND AND CIRCULATORY SYSTEM 123

ARTERIOSCLEROSIS — HARD ARTERIES

Arteriosclerosis, or hardening of the arteries, is commonly believed to be largely due to old age, but we now know that high blood-pressure greatly favors hardening of the arteries. As high blood-pressure may be produced by fear and worry, these mental states must be regarded as indirect factors in the production of hard arteries and consequent old age. The faith state of mind is able, therefore, to lessen in a measure the hardening of the arteries, by its salutary influence upon the blood-pressure; while it is evident that fear must tremendously aggravate this condition by its ability markedly to increase the arterial tension.

CAPILLARY CONTRACTION

Faith leads to natural, rhythmic, and regular action of the capillaries — the small arteries of the skin and of the various internal organs. When the mind is moving in a natural and normal channel, the small capillaries of the skin and internal organs execute a rhythmic, milking movement, which sends the blood moving along through its channels. This action of the capillaries is of great aid to the heart, in fact it is known in medical science as the "peripheral heart."

While there are numerous other influences besides mental fear that are able to produce harmful contraction of the capillaries, such as cocaine, tobacco, tea and coffee, and the poisons of indigestion and constipation; nevertheless, the mental factor is coming to be recognized more and more as one of the leading causes of chronic sluggish circulation, pallor of the skin, cold hands, and cold feet.

Anxiety, worry, and grief, by their influence through the nervous system, cause the small capillaries spasmodically to contract, thus forcing the blood into the internal organs of the chest, abdomen, and pelvis, thereby exposing the sufferer on the one hand to colds and catarrh, because of insufficient skin circulation, in connection with overcongestion of the mucous membranes; while on the other hand they predispose to passive congestion and chronic inflammations of the various internal organs, from bronchitis down through congestion of the liver, spleen, and bowels, to congestion of the special vital organs found in the pelvis of the female. And this is but a glimpse of the mischief which is wrought by a chronic state of worry, and its resultant effect upon the circulation.

It is a well-known fact that all victims of acute fright exbibit pallor; it is a common expression, "He was pale with fright." Chronic worriers likewise have more or less continuous disturbance of the skin circulation — pale face, cold hands, and cold feet.

In the treatment of many nervous and circulatory diseases by means of baths and electricity, it is not at all uncommon to observe the deleterious effect of the patient's mental state upon the reactive powers immediately following a short cold bath and other similar procedures. Those who fear cold baths do not react well when given cold applications. If a patient has a settled notion that a particular form of bath or a certain degree of temperature will chill or hurt him, experience has demonstrated that the treatment will almost invariably turn out exactly in accordance with his fear and forebodings.

CIRCULATORY SKIN REACTION

We once had a patient who positively refused to take an electric bath at a temperature below 104 or 105 degrees. He always insisted on having the bath thermometer in his hand or near by so that he could ascertain the temperature of the bath, and thus prevent his attendant gradually lowering the same. He averred that he would be seized with violent shivering and chills if he were compelled to take his bath at the prescribed temperature of 95 to 98 degrees, and every time the nurse lowered the temperature below his fear-established standard, he actually had a chill — a real chill. That this fear of chilling and aversion to baths below a certain temperature was a matter entirely of a mental nature, was conclusively proven by the following simple experiment: A bath thermometer was prepared which registered almost eight degrees too low. The patient was given his usual bath and allowed to test its temperature, the attendant permitting him to enter the water as hot as he could stand. As usual, the nurse began gradually to lower the temperature of the bath by admitting cold water. The patient watched the procedure without making complaint until the thermometer registered about 103 degrees, whereupon he began to exhibit signs of chilling. The temperature was held at about 103 and 104 degrees according to the tampered thermometer (really at 95 and 96 degrees) for twenty minutes. He enjoyed the bath and left it with a victorious smile on his face, saying, " You can't fool me, I've told the doctor I can't take his neutral baths at 95. I know I can't stand 'em, they chill me as sure as fate. Now I feel bully; I always do when you let me have the bath the way I want it."

And it was exactly so. He wanted the bath at a given temperature. He was possessed with a positive fear of a lower temperature, and when his fear was sufficiently excited it was able to produce such a powerful contraction of the small capillaries in the skin (by means of nervous impulses transmitted over the vasoconstrictor nerves) as actually to drive the blood into the internal organs, with the result of literally bringing on a *bona fide* chill. He could not and would not take his bath except as he wanted it, but you could have your way as long as the patient thought he was having his way; and he took his bath in comfort and without protest for two weeks at the literal temperature of 95 to 96 and the psychic temperature of about 103.

THE BLOOD MOVEMENT

The blood is the life; and any influence which is able to regulate blood movement is able, indirectly, to influence nutrition, metabolism, and the entire life. Next to hydrotherapy and massage, the mental state of the patient probably has more to do with controlling the circulation of the blood than any other single influence which can be brought to bear upon the human body.

When the mind is dominated by faith, the blood movement throughout the body is usually strong and exhilarated. Faith contributes in a measure to preventing stagnation of blood in any part of the body (congestion), and is therefore of undoubted value in relieving the chronic passive congestions, which so frequently accompany many chronic diseases and functional derangements. On the other hand, fear and its whole mental brood retard the circulation and interfere with the blood movement by causing capillary contraction, and thus in every way favor the production of chronic passive congestion in the internal organs of the body; and so worry and despondency must be regarded as powerful factors in the causation of chronic congestions in the internal organs, ranging from the bronchial congestions of the lungs down to the abdominal congestions, which figure so largely in the various derangements of the stomach, liver, intestines, bowels, and other special organs.

We have seen numerous cases of sordid, surly, and melancholic people with poor circulation, pale skin, and habitually cold hands and feet, wonderfully improve their circulation by simply cheering up. A pleasant frame of mind is of almost equal value to cold baths and good digestion, as a means of improving and promoting the circulation.

LOCAL CONGESTIONS

As far as the mental factor in the circulation is concerned, local congestions are prevented by taking care to keep the mind off the body. Care-free inattention to the body is one of the best ways to keep the circulation normal and active. On the other hand, fear, with a concentration of the mind upon any organ or part of the body, will almost immediately produce comparative local congestion. While general fear lessens the circulation of the blood through the skin as a whole, concentration of attention upon any part or organ of the body increases the local blood supply of that particular region.

Careful observations and experiments go to show that by continuously concentrating the mind on one arm, the surface temperature of that member can actually be raised considerably above that of the other arm. This rise in temperature signifies the increased accumulation of blood in the part — local congestion. Delicate measurements of the arm have also suggested an actual increase in size of the member upon which the mind had previously been vigorously concentrated.

Numerous cases are on record where fear and fright have apparently resulted in the production of a fatal attack of dropsy, through the tremendous power exerted by the mental state on the blood movement and the circulation of the body fluids. There can be little question that œdema and other minor swellings are

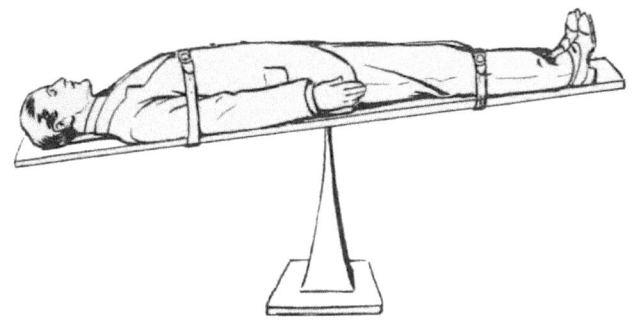

FIG. 16. BALANCING EXPERIMENT. SUBJECT EXECUTING PROBLEMS IN MENTAL ARITHMETIC.

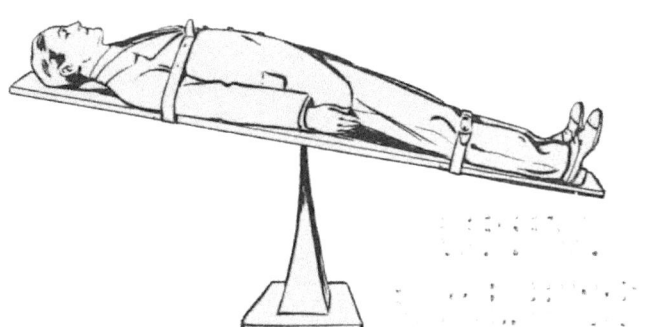

FIG. 17. BALANCING EXPERIMENT. SUBJECT THINKING INTENTLY AND CONTINUOUSLY OF THE FEET—

THE MIND AND CIRCULATORY SYSTEM 127

sometimes due to a circulatory disturbance, largely of mental or nervous origin.

CIRCULATORY EQUILIBRIUM

The power of the mind to regulate and control the circulation is beautifully and conclusively shown by the following experiment first made at an Eastern university, and afterwards repeated by the author: A young man aged twenty-two was placed on a board six feet long which was delicately balanced on an adjustable pivot. After obtaining equilibrium the limbs were all strapped down and the body adjusted to perfert balance. The subject of the experiment was now made to execute fairly difficult problems in mental arithmetic rapidly, with the result that in a very short time the head began to go down and the feet went up. The mental calculations caused the blood to accumulate in the head, thus producing a temporary congestion of that part of the body and effectually destroying the equilibrium of the circulation. (See Fig. 16.) Next, the conditions of the experiment were reversed. After placing the body once more in equilibrium, the subject was directed by a series of questions and commands to keep the mind centred upon his lower extremities. He was asked to think of his toes; commanded to imagine that he was running a hotly contested foot race; he was directed to think of moving the ankle joints, then the toe joints, and so forth. These mental manœuvres and imaginative exercises had been carried on but a little longer time than was occupied by the previous exercises in mental arithmetic, when the feet began slowly to descend and the head to rise. These experiments show conclusively that concentration of the mind on the feet will result in the production of comparative congestion in the lower extremities, just as surely as direct mental activity results in congesting the brain and head. (See Fig. 17.) The term *congestion* is used in this connection as a popular term indicating increased local blood supply, rather than in its pathological sense.

Angioneurotic œdema (periodic swelling) is the name given to a severe and sometimes fatal form of swelling or œdema, which is known to be due largely to the influence of the nerves controlling the blood vessels of the part attacked. Both the trophic (nutritional) and the vaso-motor nerves are involved. The best authorities in skin diseases now generally recognize that, in addition to toxic states of the blood, mental anxiety and chronic worry are directly concerned in the causation of this troublesome disorder. To say the least, this peculiar disease serves abundantly to demonstrate the fact that mental and nervous influences very materially and powerfully effect the movement of the circulating fluids of the body.

The author had a patient several years ago who possessed an unusual and unique control over his blood movement. His circulation was quite unstable, and as a result he was considerably troubled with cold hands and feet. By strongly concentrating the mind upon his cold feet, this man was actually able to cause a rush of blood to his frigid extremities. Sometimes it required more mental effort and a longer time to effect these circulatory changes than at other times. He was also peculiarly subject to periodical attacks of blushing and extreme pallor.

APOPLEXY

Apoplexy is caused by rupture of a blood vessel in the brain. Hardened arteries and high blood-pressure usually precede such attacks, but fear and anger, by their power greatly and quickly to elevate the blood-pressure, tremendously favor the conditions which predispose one to attacks of apoplexy and subsequent paralysis; while an even temperament and a quiet frame of mind are of real preventive value to all persons who are threatened with, or who have had, a stroke of apoplexy. But more about apoplexy in the next chapter.

We can no longer dispute the fact that the mind is able to influence the circulation both for weal and for woe. The common everyday phenomenon of blushing is a practical demonstration of the psychic power over blood movement. If the mind can thus produce the temporary and superficial inflammation or hyperæmia represented by blushing, who can deny that prolonged fear and chronic worry are able to produce more profound and protracted local inflammation or internal congestion.

French physicians have reported varicose veins cured or

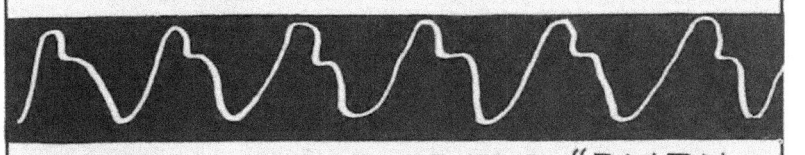

NORMAL PULSE OF THE "FAITH HEART"

FIG. 18.

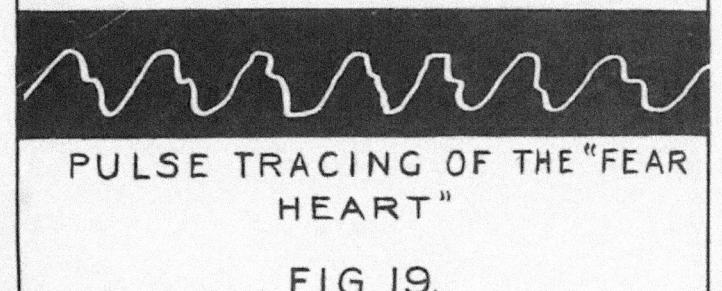

PULSE TRACING OF THE "FEAR HEART"

FIG. 19.

THE MIND AND CIRCULATORY SYSTEM 129

greatly improved by suggestion; and there are some physicians who believe that constant thinking of the appendix, coupled with the incessant fear of appendicitis, has had not a little to do with actually bringing about a nervous and circulatory condition which greatly favors infection and disease in this particularly predisposed locality.

THE PULSE

The pulse is regular, slow, and strong under the influence of optimistic faith; while it is weak and irregular when the mental powers are dominated by fear, pessimism, and anxiety. A careful examination of the pulse serves to disclose important facts respecting the mental and nervous states of the patient, as well as concerning the physical condition of the heart.

A medical student had his eyes bandaged while his fellow students pretended to open a vein in his arm for the purpose of bleeding him. A small stream of warm water was then caused to trickle over his arm and fall into a bowl. The student, supposing this water to be his own life-blood, grew deathly pale and fainted.

The effect of faith and fear on the pulse is graphically shown in Figs. 18 and 19, where may be seen tracings of the pulse under the natural influence of faith and trust, also under the influence of fear and anxiety. The examination of the pulse by no means discloses all that a physician should know about his patient, but it does reveal far more concerning both the physical and the mental status of the patient than the average doctor probably recognizes. The pulse is the barometer of the heart, and the heart is the one organ of the body most easily, quickly, and powerfully influenced by the psychic state.

COMPARATIVE SUMMARY OF THE EFFECTS OF FAITH AND FEAR
ON THE CIRCULATION OF THE BLOOD.

FAITH	FEAR
1. *Blood-pressure:* Normal. Lowers high pressure. (See cases cited in next chapter.)	1. *Blood-pressure:* Greatly raised. Pale face and cold extremities.
2. *Arteriosclerosis:* Lessened and prevented.	2. *Arteriosclerosis:* Increased and aggravated.

FAITH	FEAR
3. *Capillary contraction:* Natural, rhythmic, and regular.	3. *Capillary contraction:* Unnatural, spasmodic, and irregular.
4. *Skin reaction:* Increased reaction following cold bath.	4. *Skin reaction:* Decreased reaction following cold bath.
5. *Blood movement:* Accelerated. Prevents and relieves congestion.	5. *Blood movement:* Retarded. Favors and produces passive congestion.
6. *Local congestion:* Prevented by care-free inattention.	6. *Local congestion:* Produced by fear thought and concentration.
7. *Circulatory equilibrium:* Favors. Maintains an equalized and balanced circulation.	7. *Circulatory equilibrium:* Hinders. Favors œdema and local stagnation.
8. *Apoplexy:* Prevented by even temper.	8. *Apoplexy:* Favored by fear and anger.
9. *Pulse:* Regular, slow, and strong.	9. *Pulse:* Weak, irregular, and rapid.

CHAPTER XIII

THE BLOOD-PRESSURE AS MODIFIED BY PSYCHIC INFLUENCES

DETERMINATION OF BLOOD-PRESSURE.— SIGNIFICANCE OF HIGH PRESSURE.— A FEAR-RIDDEN EX-CONVICT.— SUDDEN EMOTIONAL CHANGES.— NERVOUS PROSTRATION AND LOW BLOOD-PRESSURE.— A CASE OF MISSIONARY WORRY.— BLOOD-PRESSURE AND THE AFFECTIONS.— DRINK AND DRUGS.— BLOOD-PRESSURE AND RELIGION.— SIGNIFICANCE AND SCOPE OF PSYCHIC REGULATION.— THE NERVOUS MECHANISM INVOLVED IN THE REGULATION OF BLOOD-PRESSURE.— APOPLEXY AND HEART FAILURE.— COMPARATIVE SUMMARY OF THE EFFECTS OF FAITH AND FEAR ON THE REGULATION OF THE BLOOD-PRESSURE.

FOR several years the author has endeavored to collect reliable data bearing on the mental factors concerned in the regulation of blood-pressure. While it is almost impossible, in making observations of this kind, always accurately to isolate the mental factors involved, we believe that the cases herein cited are sufficiently reliable to show the large part played by the mind in the work of altering and regulating the blood-pressure.

DETERMINATION OF BLOOD-PRESSURE

In this connection it may be well to offer a word of explanation as to the method of taking blood-pressure, and as to the standards of normal blood-pressure. There have been devised a number of instruments, one of which is shown in Fig. 20, having attachments which can be strapped around the arm, so that by means of pumping air into a little rubber bag underneath, pressure can be applied to the blood vessels of the arm. By means of a rubber tube, this air-pressure is communicated to a chamber containing mercury and surmounted by a glass tube marked with a millimetre scale, arranged somewhat after the plan of a barometer. The pressure is now gradually removed until the pulse at the wrist can just be felt, and then on the graduated glass is read off just how many millimetres of mercury are equivalent to the patient's blood-pressure.

An ordinary healthy adult under forty-five years of age has a blood-pressure varying from 110 to 130 millimetres of mercury (about 5 inches in English measurement). A series of five thousand apparently healthy adults, tested during the last seven years, showed a general average of 123 millimetres. The ages of this group ran from 20 to 45 years.

SIGNIFICANCE OF HIGH PRESSURE

The one thing characteristic of the present-day social and commercial world is its high tension. Everybody is keyed up to the last notch. People are living at a fierce pace, and the pressure-gauge of life registers all the while dangerously near the bursting point.

High blood-pressure, as noted in the chapter on the circulation, is directly and indirectly responsible for numerous bodily ailments and certain grave physical catastrophes. High arterial tension is intimately connected with such serious disorders as chronic headaches, arteriosclerosis or hardening of the arteries, apoplexy and its subsequent paralysis, heart failure, Bright's disease, insomnia, neurasthenia, chronic congestions, and even certain forms of insanity.

There are numerous substances which, when taken into the body, together with certain mental states, have power to influence the blood-pressure, some lowering it, while others cause it to rise. Now when the blood-pressure is raised, it will be seen at once that more blood will circulate through the brain as well as through other parts of the body; and therefore, when the blood-pressure is moderately high, since the blood is that which nourishes the body and gives it life, it will not be hard to imagine that the patient will feel exhilarated and buoyant, able to enter the arena of society and business more confident of success, with hopes and courage all at top-notch. On the other hand excessively and abnormally low blood-pressure produces such a sense of weakness, debility, and mental lethargy as to constitute

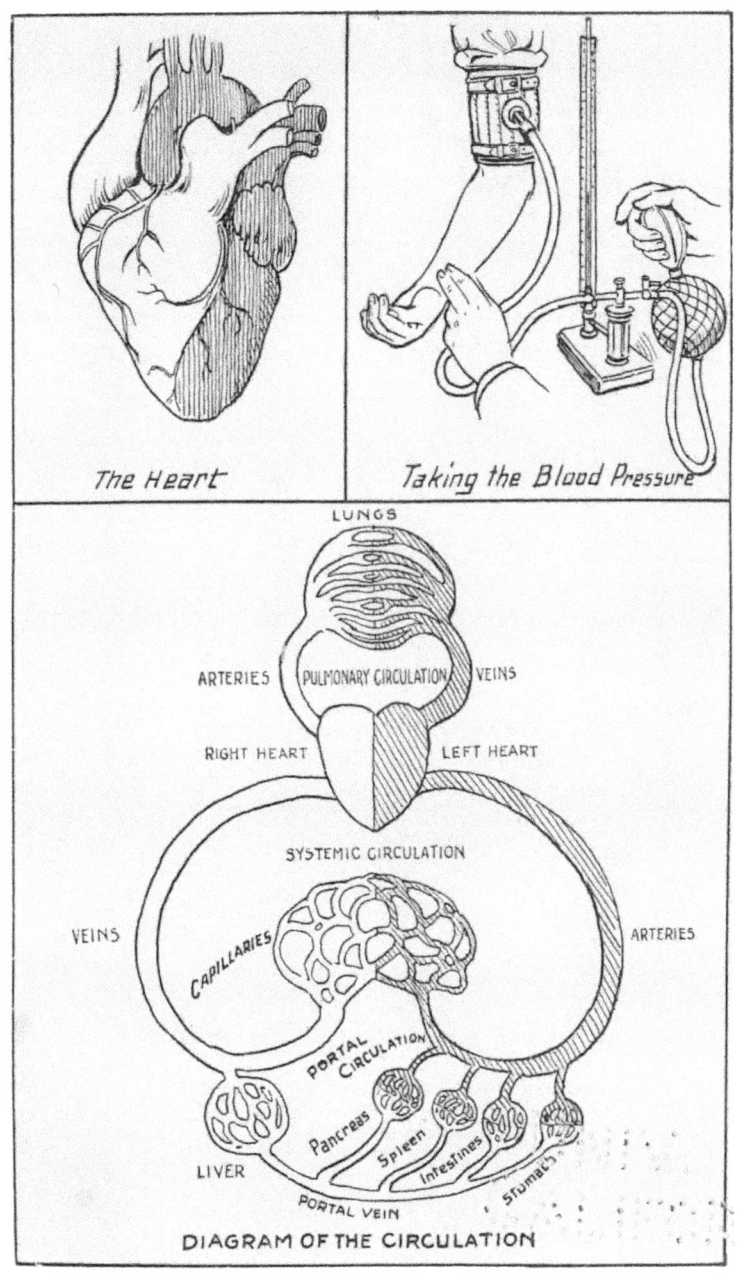

FIG. 20. *The Heart and Circulation of the Blood.*

LIBRARY OF
AMBROSIAS

a powerful temptation to resort to some convenient and artificial method of toning up the system — raising the blood-pressure.

In this chapter we are concerned chiefly with the important fact that fear and worry and all their psychic cousins are able actually to raise the blood-pressure to that point where real damage results to the health, and to such an extent as to create and confirm the demand for the use of certain drugs, highly injurious to the physical, mental, and moral welfare of the individual and the race. We refer to morphine, alcohol, the bromides, and a host of headache powders, quieting remedies, and pain relievers. While it is foreign to the purposes of this chapter to consider the right and proper methods of controlling high blood-pressure, other than the influence of the mental states, these questions have been fully treated in another work.

A FEAR-RIDDEN EX-CONVICT

There came to the clinic, one rainy morning, an ex-convict who wore a worried expression, complained of inability to sleep, and loss of appetite, and examination revealed a blood-pressure of 190 millimetres. Subsequent inquiry disclosed the fact that this man was living in constant dread of being arrested and returned to the penitentiary on the ground of "once a criminal always a criminal."

Physical examination, including the kidneys, blood vessels, and arteries, in no way accounted for his high blood-pressure. This condition of things continued for over two weeks, then on being assured that he would have thirty days immunity from arrest if he would faithfully perform the duties assigned him, he admitted that his chief trouble was incessant worry and perpetual anxiety. Within a very few minutes his blood-pressure actually began to drop, and within three hours it had fallen 20 mm., and by the following day had reached 155 mm., a total fall of 35 mm. This seems to be a reasonably clear case of high blood-pressure from fear and worry. It was largely relieved by setting the mind at rest. The arterial tension was lowered by the relief of the mental tension. Three months after these observations, several tests showed this man's blood-pressure to register uniformly in the neighborhood of 150.

SUDDEN EMOTIONAL CHANGES

A few years ago the author had an opportunity to observe a series of rapid and unusual fluctuations in blood-pressure on the part of a nervous and semi-hysterical young woman. Pressures taken just before and just after the receipt of a bit of bad news, exhibited a difference of over 50 mm. We were able to detect a difference of 20 to 30 mm. during a single observation, as a result of purely emotional disturbances. Such a high degree of vaso-motor instability as a result of mental influence is not at all common.

Sudden excitement, burning indignation, intense anger, and keen disappointment all serve instantly to alter the blood-pressure. It is not uncommon to observe an alteration of pressure varying from 10 to 25 per cent, and so it appears that the highly emotional person is constantly altering his blood-pressure, and, as a consequence, necessitating more or less of a complete rearrangement of the circulatory apparatus, and a readjustment of the whole process of nutrition and metabolism.

NERVOUS PROSTRATION AND LOW BLOOD-PRESSURE

Not only will ceasing to worry serve to reduce blood-pressure in cases where the high tension is wholly or partially due to psychic causes, but a change in the mental state is also sometimes able to *raise* the blood-pressure in certain cases of neurasthenia or so-called nervous prostration. Nervous prostration is one of nature's ways of preventing certain high-strung people from actually "blowing up." Nature removes the pendulum and allows them to run down, thus preventing the snapping of the constitutional mainspring. Neurasthenics complain of being "all run down," and that simply means that they were previously "all wound up."

We recently had a chronic neurasthenic with blood-pressure running from 85 to 90 mm. He finally got it into his head that he was going to get well. He went to work in earnest at his simple treatments and began to take an interest in the world; he actually forgot about his vague sensations and wandering pains, began to eat heartily and sleep well, and soon he was rapidly gaining in weight. In the meantime his blood-pressure had slowly and gradually climbed up to 120 mm. — practically

THE BLOOD-PRESSURE 135

normal, while his distressing morning headaches almost entirely disappeared.

Occasionally we meet with cases of abnormally low blood-pressure which are difficult to diagnose. There seems to be a constitutional tendency toward low tension, just as in other cases we observe a family tendency to high pressure.

A CASE OF MISSIONARY WORRY

A worried city missionary, troubled with sleeplessness, rapidly losing her appetite, also losing in weight, had been treated several weeks for stomach and nervous troubles, with electricity, and with baths. Blood-pressure remained about 165. Careful inquiry elicited the fact she had no family trouble, no church trouble, in fact she seemed to be free from everything that would lead up to the mental states of fear and worry. Further inquiry, however, disclosed the fact that she worried considerably over the subjects of her missionary endeavor. At first she resented our efforts to admonish her on this point; but one day she was told the story of the simple-minded boy, who insisted on carrying two bushels of chop-feed on his shoulders while riding horseback, and on being asked why he did so, replied: "Well, I reckon, if the horse can carry me I ought to be willing to carry the feed." She went home and began to think matters over, finally arriving at this conclusion: "If Christ's death on the cross can't save sinners, no amount of anxiety or worry on my part can effect their salvation."

She appeared at the office the following day, asserting that she had got a new brand of religion — a faith that could free her from useless worry and unnecessary anxiety. She affirmed that she had learned the meaning of such Scriptures as, "Casting all your care upon Him, for He careth for you," and, "Come unto Me all ye that labor and are heavy laden, and I will give you rest"; and strange to report, the taking of her blood-pressure showed that it had fallen to 140, and it subsequently went down to about 135.

Worry and anxiety always raise the blood-pressure until they result in bringing on nervous prostration, and then the unfortunate victim is found to be suffering from a depressive reaction — neurotic low blood-pressure. Disappointment, grief, and cankering care, all conspire together, gradually and surely to raise the blood-pressure. Likewise, anger, moral condemnation, and every cause of restlessness and mental dissatisfaction, all serve to increase arterial tension and raise the pressure.

The fact that one worries over a good cause — the fact that the objects of your anxious solicitude are wholly unselfish and altruistic — in no wise mitigates the inevitable consequences of the increased blood-pressure and other indescribable nervous complications which so surely follow in the wake of all protracted worry and long-sustained anxiety.

BLOOD-PRESSURE AND THE AFFECTIONS

A young man under observation exhibited a blood-pressure of 170. The usual procedures employed in high pressure did not give satisfactory results. Careful inquiry revealed that he had recently been disappointed in love, and while all medicinal means failed permanently to lower his blood-pressure, a reconciliation with the young lady at once dropped the pressure to 135, in which neighborhood it remained permanently. It probably would have gone even lower but that he was quite a heavy user of tobacco, and this, as is well known, tends to keep the blood-pressure up.

The author does not entertain the slightest doubt that a young woman under similar circumstances would have had her blood-pressure affected in like manner, both as to its rise in the face of disappointment, and its fall immediately after the reconciliation with the adored one.

DRINK AND DRUGS

Domestic infelicity and family jars all conspire to raise the blood-pressure, increase the nervous tension — and, indirectly, make for digestive disturbances and nervous breakdown. We commonly hear such statements as "Family trouble drove him to drink." In all such cases, in our opinion, the alcohol is taken largely for its immediate effect in lowering the blood-pressure and thus temporarily relieving the intense and wrought-up nervous state. While the continuous use of alcohol operates to raise the blood-pressure by its tendency to harden the arteries, the effect for the time being is to lower the pressure and thus relieve the oppressive tension.

Experience has taught us that high blood-pressure often leads its victims to drink and drugs. The very day of this writing there came to the office a lawyer begging for morphine. This man is a periodical drinker; and when we remonstrated with him he replied: " Well, doctor, if you don't give me morphine or something else to relieve this spell, it'll drive me to the saloon for whiskey." In this connection it should be explained that morphine does lower the blood-pressure — a discovery that this lawyer is not alone in having made. Indirectly, then, freedom·· from worry and anxiety proves to be a practical aid to temperance, in that faith — a peaceful frame of mind — operates to prevent high tension, with its accompanying tendency and temptation to resort to pressure-lowering drugs such as alcohol and morphine.

BLOOD-PRESSURE AND RELIGION

Religion, as a state of mind, seems to exert a salutary influence upon the blood-pressure. In all cases of nervous high tension where the sufferer seems to have heartily and sincerely embraced some form of religious belief or moral faith, the blood-pressure almost invariably begins to come down. On the other hand, in case the acceptance of some sort of religion leads to overscrupulous anxiety and overconscientious worry, the blood-pressure will certainly go up. It makes no apparent difference what particular brand of religion is embraced, as far as the blood-pressure mechanism is concerned, only one condition seems to be requisite, and that is that the religion must be accepted so fully and sincerely as absolutely to deliver the mind from the torments of doubt and the uncertainties of fear; actually to set the mind at rest and fill the thoughts with faith and trust.

Numerous cases in which religion apparently reduced the blood-pressure could be cited. A nervous man whom we had under treatment had a blood-pressure of 170. He became a devout Christian Scientist and the blood-pressure soon went down into the neighborhood of 145, and remained there permanently.

Another case, that of a somewhat disagreeable married woman, was greatly improved physically, still her blood-pressure was about 160. She claimed to have been converted in a gospel mission, and after that her blood-pressure was found to be in the neighborhood of 140.

An unfaithful husband who had a blood-pressure running from 170 to 180, after a professed conversion and after a reconciliation with his family, showed blood-pressure of 140 to 150.

The author would not for one moment suggest that he had discovered a method whereby it would be possible to determine by material tests as to whether or not a person was sincere in his profession of religion; but it is at least interesting to record, in this connection, the case of a certain politician suffering from a marked case of worry (high-tension) who confessedly joined a church for the purpose of furthering his political interests, but whose blood-pressure remained unmoved by his outward religious manœuvres.

SIGNIFICANCE AND SCOPE OF PSYCHIC REGULATION

A business man, in financial stress for three weeks, exhibited a blood-pressure of 180. After borrowing ten thousand dollars, and relieving this situation, his blood-pressure ran for seven weeks from 145 to 160.

A broken-hearted mother, grieving over a wayward daughter, exhibited blood-pressure of 175; after her daughter's return, during three weeks' observation, her blood-pressure ran in the neighborhood of 155.

As noted before, certain minor factors, other than the psychic state, may have entered into some of these observations, but as far as careful inquiry and physical examination were able to go, these particular cases belong to that class in which the chief agency of relief was mental. We have had under observation cases that showed even greater reduction of blood-pressure than those cited. These cases are presented as average illustrations of the amount of reduction in blood-pressure which can be brought about almost immediately by a thorough-going change in the mental state.

It is self-evident, if a change in the mental state can thus quickly and positively influence the blood-pressure, that the mind is able variably to influence almost a score of physical maladies that owe their existence and disagreeable symptoms more or less to high blood-pressure. It has been the author's observation that sincerity and religious devotion, unless they lead to hyperconscientiousness or an overscrupulous anxiety, always result in a reduction of high blood-pressure — at least in all cases where the high tension was largely psychic in origin — due to mental unrest and nervous excitability.

It has further been our observation that it is wholly immaterial what kind of religion the devotee embraces. As far as blood-pressure is concerned, the essential requirement is that the religion shall be whole-hearted, so as effectively to set the mind at rest. The nervous mechanism regulating blood-pressure is not a theological critic. Any belief or religion that is accepted without mental reservation suffices to set the mind at rest, and the blood-pressure immediately begins to be lowered.

The reader's attention is again called to the fact that the author is here considering the purely psychologic side of religion. We again disclaim any intention of discussing the spiritual and miraculous elements concerned in theological belief. While he recognizes the fact that any and all religions, when sincerely accepted and devoutly believed, are able profoundly to influence both mind and body; and while, as far as the body is concerned, it apparently makes no difference what brand of religion is accepted — certain physiological effects being the same, modified only by the intensity of the patient's faith — nevertheless, the author would by no means lead the reader to think that he regards the Christian religion as just one among equally good religions of the past and the present. In his personal belief he recognizes the sublime power of the true Christian religion not only to accomplish all the desirable physiological and psychological effects herein noted, but, in addition, to bring about a host of other and marvellous spiritual manifestations and mighty moral transformations; and so, while he continues to note the fact that all forms of religious belief exert a salutary effect upon certain bodily functions, the reader is cautioned not to form the conclusion that the author would in the least detract from the belief in Christianity as the supreme and genuine religion — as a supernatural influence designed to uplift humanity in a sense entirely different from and additional to, all the various psychic and physical benefits herein noted, and which apparently result from the nominal acceptance of any form of religious belief.

While he desires to make it plain to the reader that any sort of religious belief favorably influences the psychic state and the physical functions, he desires to make it equally emphatic and plain that the author, in his own belief, recognizes in the teachings of Jesus Christ something entirely above, and different from, the other great religions of the world. The author sincerely believes that there is a distinct and definite supernatural element in the Christian religion; but since such supernatural element does not lend itself to scientific investigation and laboratory inquiry, and since this work is devoted to the study of the psychology and physiology of faith and fear, it is entirely out of place further to discuss the matter in this connection. This paragraph has been added merely to prevent any Christian reader from gaining the impression that the author does not recognize Christianity as the supreme religious belief — as a spiritual energy and a supernatural force. Paul's statement is still true, that "The world by wisdom knew not God."

THE NERVOUS MECHANISM INVOLVED IN THE REGULATION OF BLOOD-PRESSURE

The physiologist offers the following explanation of the mechanism for manipulating blood volume and controlling blood-pressure:

"Another striking illustration of nervous regulation of the heart is that of *the depressor nerve*. Ever since Ludwig first discovered the function of this small nerve, physiologists have been greatly interested in its unique properties, one being, as demonstrated by its first discoverers, that it can quickly lower the pressure of the blood in the arteries all over the body from 30 to 50 per cent. To understand this it should be stated that in the medulla oblongata there is a centre governing the entire and most extensive system of special nerves which ramify on the coasts of the arteries, and whose business it is to regulate the calibre of the arteries so that their diameter becomes large or small according to whether the part which the arteries supply needs more or less blood. Thus, the stomach needs nine times more blood when actively digesting its contents than when it is empty; and the vaso-motor nerves, as they are called, of its arteries dilate the blood vessels so as to bring more blood, or contract them to shut it off, as the need may be. The function of these nerves, therefore, is of prime importance, for without their constricting action the vessels of the abdominal organs alone might relax enough to contain most of the blood of the body, as sometimes happens with quickly fatal results.

"But, on the other hand, during violent muscular exercise or under excitement, the blood may be driven to the heart so fast that its cavities become dangerously distended. Then it is that the depressor nerve instantly comes to the rescue. Ignoring its automatic nature, we may figuratively represent it addressing the medulla thus: 'Make haste! Emergency! Heart overfilling and distending so with blood that a valve may give way! Tell your vasoconstrictor centre instantly to order all its nerves to relax their grip on the arteries all over the body, to the degree which I direct. Order the accelerator centre to suspend operations; and the vagus centre to give an extra turn to its brakes!' The medulla obeys, and the overfull heart immediately relieves itself by a general widening of all the arterial channels. Thus we find this single regulatory nerve capable of inhibiting the action of the whole vast mechanism of the arterial constrictors. Unlike other nerves, it can not be fatigued or exhausted by prolonged stimulation, so that in every respect it is like a sleepless, tireless sentinel posted at the great gate of the heart's outflow."

It is also highly probable that the circulatory centres of the medulla are in turn more or less influenced by direct impulses from certain cortical centres in the cerebrum.

APOPLEXY AND HEART FAILURE

The practical conclusion of the blood-pressure matter is simply this: If the arterial tension is permitted to go on increasing from month to month and from year to year, eventually, the danger point will be reached (about 200 mm.), and then it is only a question of time when one of two things will happen — either the heart-pump will give out — the valves give way or the muscle dilate; or the arterial hose will burst at some weak point, usually in the brain, with the result of producing apoplexy and its accompanying paralysis. Apoplexy, paralysis, and heart failure are tremendously on the increase, and the strenuous living — the life of anxiety, overwork, and worry — is now generally recognized by the medical profession as being in a large measure responsible for the enormous fatality of these heart and circulatory disorders.

COMPARATIVE SUMMARY OF THE EFFECTS OF FAITH AND FEAR ON THE REGULATION OF THE BLOOD-PRESSURE.

(Average normal blood-pressure in adults, 123 mm.)

FEAR	FAITH
1. *Ex-convict:* Blood-pressure 190 when hunted by police.	1. *Ex-convict:* Blood-pressure 155 after promise of 30 days' immunity.
2. *Emotional state:* Blood-pressure may rise 30 to 50 mm.	2. *Emotional state:* Blood-pressure known to fall 50 mm. by emotional changes.
3. *Nervous prostration:* Pressure too low, 85 to 90.	3. *Nervous prostration:* Pressure favorably raised, 120.
4. *Missionary worry:* Christian worker had pressure of 165.	4. *Missionary worry:* Change of mental state reduced pressure to 135.
5. *Disappointment:* Jilted lover had a pressure of 170.	5. *Disappointment:* Reconciliation with his sweetheart lowered pressure to 135.
6. *Drink and drugs:* Raising pressure creates a demand for alcohol and morphine.	6. *Drink and drugs:* Lowering pressure materially assists in preventing and curing drug habits.
7. *Religion:* Case with pressure of 170 before becoming religious.	7. *Religion:* After becoming Christian Scientist pressure fell to 145.
8. *Business troubles:* Man in financial distress had pressure of 180.	8. *Business troubles:* After meeting his business obligations pressure fell to about 150.
9. *Nervous mechanism:* Fear excites the heart and contracts the small capillaries of the skin.	9. *Nervous mechanism:* Faith steadies and strengthens the heart, and promotes capillary circulation.
10. *Apoplexy and heart failure:* Greatly increased in frequency and severity by fear.	10. *Apoplexy and heart failure:* Lessened in frequency and severity by faith and calmness.

CHAPTER XIV

INFLUENCE OF THE MENTAL STATE UPON THE VITAL RESISTANCE

THE RED BLOOD CELLS.— THE WHITE BLOOD CELLS.— RELATIVE ANÆMIAS.— PSYCHIC BLOOD POISONS.— THE LYMPH STREAM.— ANTI-BODIES AND ANTITOXINS.— INFLUENCE OF THE MENTAL STATE UPON THE VITAL RESISTANCE.— FEAR AND INFECTION.— THE SOIL OF DISEASE.— THE HEALING POWER.— VITAL ENERGY. — SICKNESS IN GENERAL.— THE DEATH RATE.— COMPARATIVE SUMMARY OF THE EFFECTS OF FAITH AND FEAR UPON THE VITAL RESISTANCE.

WHILE it has long been recognized that the mental state is more or less able to affect the circulation of the blood, it has not until recently been known that the state of the mind is directly concerned in maintaining the quality of the blood, or that abnormal mental states can, in a certain measure, actually deteriorate the blood. This fact becomes more and more important as we continue to discover that the power of the organism to resist disease is very largely dependent on the quality of the circulating fluids of the body.

THE RED BLOOD CELLS

The mental state of courageous optimism is now known to favor an increase in the red blood cells, because of its valuable influence on the general health and the special blood-making organs. By contributing to the general health, faith actually protects the red blood cells from disease and destruction. In connection with the sluggish circulation coëxistent with mental depression, there is usually to be found a chronic portal stagnation. It is now generally believed that this portal congestion brings about the destruction of large numbers of red blood cells by their cousins, the white blood cells; for it is highly probable that the white blood cells, when irritated and intoxicated by the stagnant circulatory fluids of the portal (liver) circulation, turn traitors to the body commonwealth, and literally devour the red blood cells.

Ruddy cheeks and vigorous blood movement are the handmaidens of faith and courage. Viewed from every possible standpoint optimism favors the production and maintenance of a healthy blood stream, while pessimism works steadily and continuously for the deterioration of the blood-making and the blood-moving processes.

THE WHITE BLOOD CELLS

There can now be little question of the fact that a vigorous, happy mental state, by its influence on both the nervous and circulatory systems, tends to increase the defensive activity of the white blood cells. By favoring the healthy circulation of the blood, the white cells are protected from many influences which otherwise would depress and decrease their germ-destroying and life-saving activities. It is well known that any influence which causes a vigorous movement of the blood stream, enhances their action in the work of destroying the microbes of disease. Fear depresses the circulation and favors the accumulation of metabolic acid poisons in the body, which conditions not only decrease the activities of the white blood cells in their work of destroying germs, but actually tend to increase their pernicious activities in the direct destruction of the body cells.*

It is a singular and interesting fact that the macrophages, that is, the large white cells with a large nucleus, seem to evince a preference for an animal diet. They are the cells which eat up the dead tissue and debris that is scattered about a wound. And when under the influence of certain irritant poisons, absorbed from the intestine, they behave very strangely, especially if the body cells are weak, and there is evidence of senile decay. They have been observed to prey upon the body itself. Under the spell of these poisons, these former

---

*See "The Science of Living or the Art of Keeping Well." Chap. XIV.

defenders of the body turn insurgents, and devour brain cells, liver cells, and feed upon any part of the body that happens to be in a weakened state, showing great preference for the nerves, brain cells, and other of the more highly organized tissues. This affords a simple explanation of loss of memory and many other symptoms found in old age.

RELATIVE ANÆMIAS

Faith, by its favorable influence upon the circulation, has a tendency to prevent certain forms of relative anæmia. By both its influence upon the blood-making process and the circulation, a sunny disposition favors a healthy and normal blood stream; while worry, directly and indirectly, tends positively to deteriorate the quality of the circulating fluids.

Many a pale-faced woman would find speedy relief from her pallor, anæmia, and sluggish circulation by overcoming her downcast and despondent disposition — by simply "cheering up." We recently saw such a case with the hæmoglobin registering at 80. This young woman had been treated for anæmia for almost a full year, with but little improvement. She suddenly embraced some new psychic cult, ceased worrying, quit fretting; her digestion began immediately to improve, circulation grew better, and, in six weeks her anæmia had entirely disappeared; her hæmoglobin test showed about 100.

An English authority asserts that even that dreaded malady, pernicious anæmia, is frequently brought on by prolonged worry and chronic fretting. The blood count has been observed to increase and decrease all the way from five to twenty-five per cent in response to emotional changes in the mind. This apparent fluctuation in the blood count is due, as in the case of such changes following a cold bath, to the fluxion of the circulation and the resultant variation in the amount and quality of the blood at the point where the specimen was obtained for examination, and not to any actual and sudden creation of new blood cells on the part of the blood-making organs.

PSYCHIC BLOOD POISONS

The human body was defined by Bouchard as a "laboratory for the making of poisons." Faith, by its stimulating action upon the circulatory and eliminative processes, greatly lessens the danger of the body from the results of the accumulation of these pernicious poisons; while the depressing influence of fear not only favors their production and action, but, according to recent experiments, fear, worry, and anger, are in themselves directly responsible for the production of certain special, subtle poisons, which are exceedingly harmful to the human organism. It has long been recognized that animals which were worried or teased just before slaughter are very unhealthful — that their flesh is even dangerous to use for food.

It now seems altogether likely that an unwholesome mental state, by its direct influence over the nerves leading to the glands and cells, is actually able so to modify the natural and normal secretions, as to result in the production of substances which are positively poisonous to the other cells and organs of the body. Such a perversion of the secretory functions is not to be wondered at, in view of the physiological facts concerning the reflex chemical excitation and modification of glandular activity formerly noted in connection with the consideration of the "chemical messengers" or hormones in connection with the secretion of the pancreatic juice.

Several investigators have averred that fear and anger result in the production of extra body poisons, some of which are thrown out of the system through the lungs. These have been collected, and it is asserted that experimental tests made on animals prove these substances to be extraordinarily deleterious and highly poisonous. Other experimenters say that they have isolated such "emotional poisons" from the sweat and the urine. While the author is compelled to view some of these recent observations with considerable conservatism, nevertheless, he expects eventually to see these claims fully and scientifically established. Clinical observation on the nursing mother is entirely sufficient to indicate that changes in the emotional state actually effect changes in the bodily secretions, as a fit of anger on the part of the mother very commonly produces a fit of indigestion on the part of the sucking child.

THE LYMPH STREAM

The movement of the lymph through the lymphatic channels is favored by the joyous mental state, largely for the same

INFLUENCE OF THE MENTAL STATE 147

reasons that were shown to favor the circulation of the blood; and, of course, the circulation of the lymph would be likewise retarded by a gloomy and downcast state of mind. The author saw a case of dropsy a few years ago which appeared in one night, apparently as a result of acute fright; at least that was the only discoverable cause. The dropsy disappeared without medical treatment at the end of forty-eight hours, and did not recur.

The same influences which are able to retard the activities of the white blood cells are undoubtedly also able to decrease the action and influence of the lymphocytes — the sturdy white-cell soldiers of the lymphatic glands.

ANTI-BODIES AND ANTITOXINS

Faith and fear seem to be able to influence the elaboration of the various antitoxins which the body produces to neutralize and combat the toxins of the various microbic maladies. In all cases of infection it is highly important to maintain a perfect equilibrium of the nervous system and a well-balanced state of the circulation. Circulatory disturbances and nervous derangements of psychic origin indirectly react to retard the formation of anti-bodies and delay the production of antitoxin. Even if the body succeeds in producing a proper quantity of potent antitoxin, it is still very essential that the circulation should be uninterfered with in order that these protective substances should freely and uniformly circulate throughout the body.

Fear, by its paralyzing influence upon cell secretions, glandular action, circulatory power, and nervous impulses, constantly exerts itself against the maintenance of health and the prevention of disease; while faith fosters every process and function connected with the marvellous work of creating and disseminating these mysterious defensive anti-bodies and curative antitoxins.

INFLUENCE OF THE MENTAL STATE UPON THE VITAL RESISTANCE

The vital resistance of an individual signifies the sum total of his powers of defence against disease. It represents one's power to ward off disease and fight accidental infection. Habitual users of alcohol are exceedingly poor surgical risks, owing to the fact that alcohol lowers the vital resistance, and in case such patients are attacked by the germs of infection and blood poisoning, they are very likely quickly to succumb.

More recently we have come to recognize that a man's mental state also has largely to do with increasing or decreasing his vital resistance. The hair has been known to rapidly disappear as a result of worry; while diabetes and other serious diseases frequently follow on the heels of grief and prolonged anxiety.

Years ago Dr. Maudsley said:

"Emotion may undoubtedly favor, hinder, or pervert nutrition, and increase, lessen, or alter a secretion; in doing which there is reason to think that it acts, not only by dilating or contracting the vessels through the vaso-motor system, as we witness in the blush of shame and the pallor of fear, but also directly on the organic elements of the parts through the nerves, which, as the latest researches seem to show, end in them sometimes by continuity of substance. To me it seems not unreasonable to suppose that the mind may stamp its tone, if not its very features, on the individual elements of the body, inspiring them with hope and energy, or inflicting them with despair and feebleness."

FEAR AND INFECTION

Faith, no doubt, is a material aid in resisting most infectious diseases. Fear has long been recognized as a very powerful factor in diseases of this sort, predisposing its victims to infection and to contraction of the various contagious and infectious maladies. Those who fear a disease most are most likely to catch it. Those who fear it least are less likely to contract it. Doctors are seldom smitten with the contagious diseases they so frequently mingle with, not only because of the protective measures they use, but also because of the fact that they seldom fear these diseases; and therefore, their vital resistance is not seriously decreased by fear.

We recently saw a case where an unfortunate woman actually worried herself to death over the fear and dread of having cancer. Some physician had told her fourteen years previous that she had some symptoms of cancer, and ever since that time she had lived in constant terror of that disease. Post-mortem examination showed her to be absolutely free from cancer or any other organic disease, for that matter.

The fear of disease is often so intense and acute as really to cause one to fall a victim either to genuine infection or a deceptive and imaginative counterfeit, as is so frequently the case in cholera, hydrophobia, and lockjaw.

THE SOIL OF DISEASE

The fear life, by its unfavorable influence upon the nervous and circulatory systems, maintains a bodily state wholly unfavorable to health, while in every way favorable to the growth and development of disease germs. This is due to the fact that contagious diseases require for their propagation, not only the seed or the germs, but also a favorable soil in which these seeds may grow. Fear by its depressing influence upon the body cells, and by its retarding effect upon the nervous and circulatory systems, creates physical conditions which in every way favor the growth and multiplication of almost every kind of disease germs.

Resistance to all forms of disease, both acute and chronic, is favored by a cheerful and positive mental attitude; while despondency and despair greatly weaken and eventually tear down the body's powers of resistance to all ordinary diseases.

Acute functional disorders and various infectious maladies invariably follow in the wake of mental depression, moral defeat, business troubles, and domestic infelicity. The overthrow of faith and courage is accompanied by a downward tendency on the part of all the defensive forces and protective agencies concerned in maintaining the body's health and strength.

THE HEALING POWER

Since the blood is the chief agent concerned in healing, faith, for reasons already considered, necessarily facilitates the repair of bodily injuries, and favors recovery after surgical operations. Also, for reasons already noted, fear must inevitably interfere with the process of healing, and greatly delay the work of repair and recovery in all cases of accidental wounds and surgical operations.

Practical experience verifies and bears out this theoretic conclusion. Again and again have we observed two surgical patients who had passed through the same identical ordeal, the one with a cheerful and optimistic disposition, the other with a downcast and despondent temperament. The patient who exercised faith and practised courage would improve twice as fast as her companion sufferer. All things equal, surgical wounds heal more rapidly and satisfactorily in the case of patients who possess a sunny and cheerful mental habit. Faith and confidence are of actual aid to the surgeon in all his serious and important work.

VITAL ENERGY

By vital energy is meant that general feeling of functional and physical well-being which characterizes the well man, as compared to the depression and weakness experienced by the sick man. The generation and liberation of this vital energy and physical exuberance is most powerfully influenced and favored by the mental attitude of faith and, assurance, while fear vitiates the physical strength, dissipates the feelings, and demoralizes the manifestation of this so-called vital energy.

It is well known that faith lessens the liability to contract most contagious diseases, by favoring those physical states which facilitate the defence of the body against infection; while fear directly increases the liability of catching any and all diseases to which one may be exposed. Colds frequently follow funerals while they are almost unknown in connection with baptisms. At funerals the mind is depressed — filled with grief and fear; at baptisms the mind is dominated by faith.

SICKNESS IN GENERAL

All forms of sickness are decreased both in frequency and severity by hopefulness. A person with a sunshiny disposition is not only less likely to be stricken down with common diseases, but is also more likely to recover quickly when affliction does overtake him. It is a well-known fact that in any large body of men, such as an army in the field, sickness is lessened by success and victory. Armies are most healthy immediately after their great victories, notwithstanding the enormous hardships and the overtaxation of strength incident to military campaigns. On the other hand, defeat and failure of an army are followed by a tremendous increase in all forms of disease. And it is just so in the life of the citizen as well as the soldier.

INFLUENCE OF THE MENTAL STATE 151

Defeat in any of life's tasks is frequently followed by physical depression and actual illness.

Darwin says of protracted grief:
"The circulation becomes languid; the face pale; the muscles flaccid; the eyelids droop; the head hangs on the contracted chest; the lips, cheeks, and lower jaw all sink downward from their own weight. The whole expression of a man in good spirits is exactly the opposite of the one suffering from sorrow."

THE DEATH RATE

To sum up the influence of faith on the vital resistance, it must be evident in the case of both the individual and the community, that optimism lowers the death rate, while pessimism must be reckoned as one of the actual causes in raising it. If it were possible to isolate completely the mental factors concerned in health and longevity, it would no doubt surprise the most enthusiastic advocates of mental therapeutics to discover the vast influence exerted by the mind in all these matters of human health and happiness.

COMPARATIVE SUMMARY OF THE EFFECTS OF FAITH AND FEAR UPON THE VITAL RESISTANCE

FAITH	FEAR
1. *The red cells:* Increases and protects.	1. *The red cells:* Decreases and indirectly destroys.
2. *The white cells:* Increases activity in destroying microbes.	2. *The white cells:* Increases activity in destroying body cells.
3. *Relative anæmia:* Prevents. Favors normal blood. Increases hæmoglobin.	3. *Relative anæmia:* Favored by grief and worry. Decreases hæmoglobin.
4. *Psychic blood poisons:* Prevents their formation.	4. *Psychic blood poisons:* Favors their generation.
5. *The lymph stream:* Favors action of lymph cells and accelerates circulation.	5. *The lymph stream:* Hinders the action of lymph cells and retards circulation.
6. *Anti-bodies and antitoxins:* Assists in their formation and dissemination.	6. *Anti-bodies and antitoxins:* Delays their production and dissemination.
7. *The vital resistance:* Greatly increased.	7. *The vital resistance:* Markedly decreased.

8. *Infection:* An aid in resisting.	8. *Infection:* A predisposing cause.
9. *Disease-soil:* Creates soil unfavorable to germs.	9. *Disease-soil:* Creates soil favorable to germs.
10. *Healing power:* Hastens repair and recovery.	10. *Healing power:* Retarded. Delays recovery.
11. *Vital energy:* Generates and promotes.	11. *Vital energy:* Consumes and diminishes.
12. *Sickness:* Decreased by victory and success.	12. *Sickness:* Increased by defeat and failure.
13. *Death rate:* Lowered.	13. *Death rate:* Raised.

CHAPTER XV

THE MIND AS CONCERNED IN THE ACTION OF THE SECRETORY GLANDS

SECRETION IN GENERAL.— SALIVARY SECRETION.— QUANTITY AND QUALITY.— METABOLIC FACTOR.— THE SALIVARY FLOW. — GERMICIDAL POWER.— THE LIVER AND PANCREAS.— THE SECRETION.— QUALITY OF SECRETION.— THE SECRETORY MECHANISM.— THE MAMMARY SECRETION.— THE KIDNEY AND BLADDER.— COMPARATIVE SUMMARY OF THE EFFECTS OF FAITH AND FEAR ON THE ACTION OF THE SECRETORY GLANDS.

WHEN we come to the study of digestion, secretion, and assimilation, we find that the mind exerts no less an influence upon these important chemical functions than it does upon heart action and the circulation of the blood. We have long known that the mental state exerts considerable influence upon digestive secretory activities, but it remained for Pawlow, the Russian physiologist, to demonstrate this fact conclusively.

SECRETION IN GENERAL

Precise experimental inquiry and careful clinical observation have demonstrated beyond the shadow of a doubt that the physiology of secretion throughout the body is more or less influenced by the psychic state; while certain special instances, such as the stomach secretions, are almost wholly and completely under mental control and nervous direction.

Not only by its influence upon the glandular blood supply and circulation, but by direct nervous influence, the mind is found able directly and powerfully to modify and regulate the digestive juices and other important bodily secretions. The stomach represents the secretory function most easily and powerfully influenced by psychic stimuli, while the pancreas typifies the secretory gland which is least influenced by mental means — being almost exclusively under chemical control.

The mind is not only able to alter the character of the milk, but also to change and modify the nature of the sweat and the secretion of the kidneys (the urine), as will be more fully noted later. All the evidence goes to prove that the vast majority of the body's secretory functions are very largely dominated and modified by faith and fear. Even the lachrymal or tear gland is set in operation by the feelings and emotions.

SALIVARY SECRETION

The secretion of saliva and the behavior of the salivary glands, together with the quality or digestive power of the saliva itself, have long afforded experimental physiologists one of their best possible opportunities to observe and compare the relative influence and power of various physical, chemical, and mental stimuli, in their action upon secretory glands.

Nervous mechanism. The nervous mechanism involved in salivary secretion has been described by physiologists as consisting of the following:

1. Vaso-motor changes, causing alteration in the blood supply and blood flow through the glands.

2. Chemical and cellular changes in the gland itself connected with the elaboration of the organic and possibly of the inorganic constituents of the saliva.

3. Changes by which water is secreted, *i. e.*, passes through the basement membrane and gland cell, and the consequent movement of the fluid through the cells and along the ducts.

The reflex centres for the secretion of saliva lie in the medulla oblongata, at the origin of the seventh and ninth cranial nerves. The centre for the sympathetic fibres is also located there. This region is connected by nerve fibres with the cerebrum; hence the thought of a savory morsel, when one is hungry, often produces a copious secretion of a thin watery fluid — it "makes the mouth water." All these facts lead to the conclusion that the nerves must exercise a direct influence upon the secretory cells, apart from their action on the blood vessels.

The secretion of the saliva is not a simple matter of physics

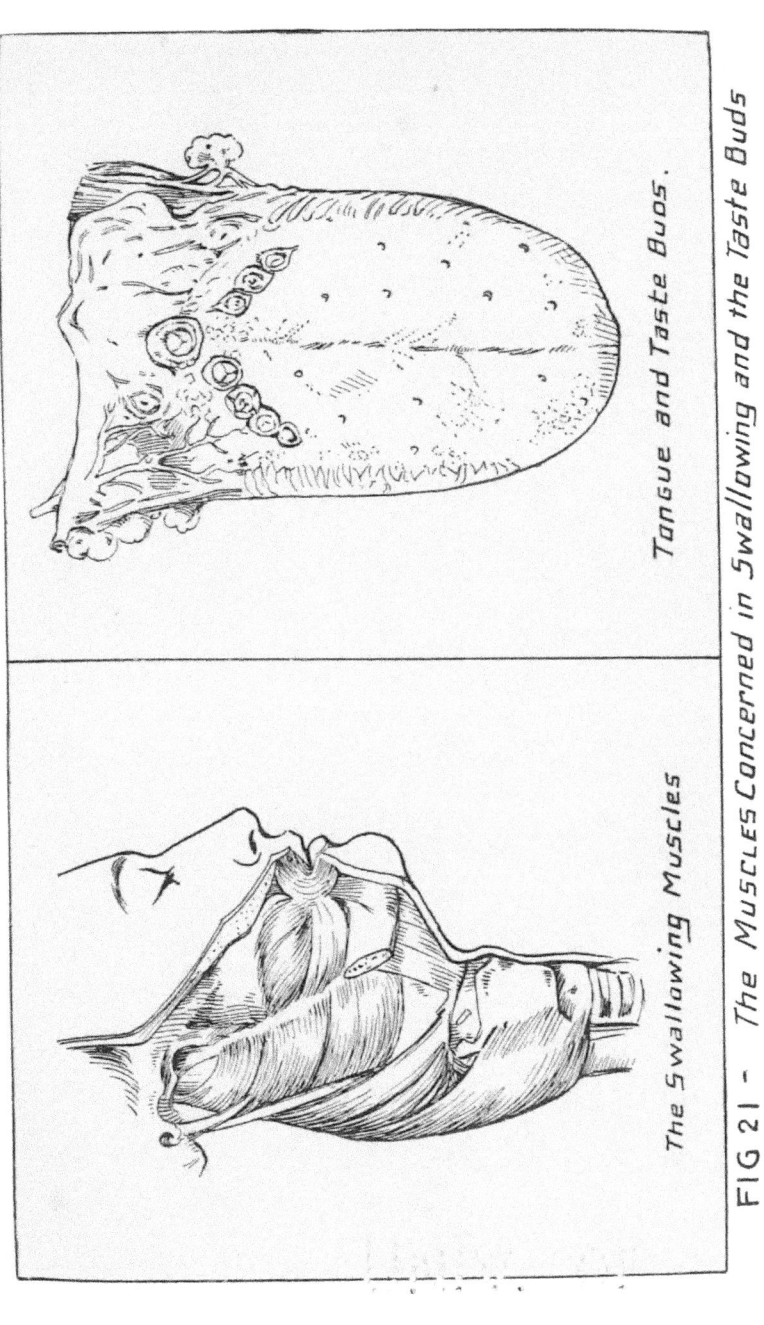

FIG 21 - The Muscles Concerned in Swallowing and the Taste Buds

THE MIND AND SECRETION

their internal pressure is vastly greater than that of the sur- and chemistry. Saliva is formed within the glands while rounding blood vessels, under which conditions, the saliva formed would naturally be secreted into the blood stream and not into the salivary ducts leading to the mouth, were its secretion a mere matter of osmosis and filtration.

Quantity and quality. Both the quantity and the quality of the saliva are increased by faith and decreased by fear. Faith and happiness encourage the production of a strong and active saliva — a secretion powerful in its ability to turn starch into sugar; while fear not only deteriorates the quality and digestive power of the saliva, but not infrequently results in the production of a secretion so modified as sometimes to become actually bitter.

The further action of the mind upon salivary secretion is shown on the one hand by the watering of the mouth when the mind is pleasantly disposed and anticipative of enjoying some favorite dish; and on the other hand, by the characteristic dry mouth resulting from the almost complete suppression of salivary secretion which so commonly accompanies so-called stage fright and other nervous and emotional states in which fear is the dominating element.

Metabolic factor. It does not appear just how far the influence of the mind goes in connection with its ability to regulate salivary secretion, until we pause to consider the great importance of salivary action and mouth digestion on the entire process of digestion and nutrition. The muscles of mastication and swallowing are the only voluntary muscles connected with the process of digestion. (See Fig. 21.) Mouth digestion is the only part of the digestive process which it is possible for a person voluntarily to direct and control. If salivary digestion is properly and completely carried forward, it constitutes a mighty assurance that the entire remaining portion of the digestive process will be satisfactorily and successfully completed.

When food is properly liquefied by mastication and admixture of saliva, it finds its way into the minute circular troughs which surround the taste buds at the base of the tongue. (See

Fig. 21.) Here the organs of taste are bathed with the various food flavors which are in solution, and in this way, through the nervous system, messages are sent to the stomach, in obedience to which that organ begins the outpouring of gastric juice in about four and a half minutes from the time the taste buds are excited. And since taste is the actual regulator of metabolism and the natural controller of appetite itself, the fact that the salivary digestion is more or less under the control of the mind becomes of more than passing importance.

The salivary flow. That fear is able markedly to decrease the flow of the saliva is shown by the ancient experimental test of the Chinese, who caused suspected criminals to be drawn up in line and then compelled quickly to chew and swallow a handful of dry rice. The guilty man would usually become so frightened that his salivary glands would refuse to work, his mouth and throat becoming so dry that he could not possibly swallow the rice in the time allotted.

Some one has suggested that an unwelcome and discordant street band can be successfully stopped by simply sucking a lemon in full view of the musicians, the suggestion being so effective that a profuse flow of saliva results, and at once puts the horn-blowers out of commission.

Digestive power. Fear, by depressing the activity of the salivary glands and thereby deteriorating the quality of the saliva as well as lessening its digestive power, no doubt greatly favors the growth of germs in the mouth. This abnormal growth of bacteria results in the production of an unusually bad taste in the mouth as well as a horribly coated tongue. Many a badly coated tongue has been attributed to an innocent and unoffending stomach, when the real trouble was to be found in a poor quality of saliva in connection with an utter neglect of the toilet of the mouth.

All melancholic persons are troubled by deficient salivary secretion. Fear and worry lessen the production of saliva and thereby predispose these unfortunate people to the temptation to drink unnecessary quantities of water or other liquids during the meal hour, so that by dilution, the digestive strength of the saliva is still further lessened.

THE MIND AND SECRETION

THE LIVER AND PANCREAS

The nervous control of the various digestive glands associated with the stomach in the work of digestion is not so profound as in the case of the salivary glands and the stomach, nevertheless, it will appear that the mind is far from lacking power and influence over these special functions.

The liver and pancreas will be considered together, as their secretory functions are somewhat related, in that their secretions are poured out into the bowel together, and the chemical stimuli which acts on one seems to act in like manner on the other.

The secretion. Faith and good cheer seem to favor the production of a normal amount of secretion by both the liver and the pancreas, while fear and grief tend to depress the action of these glands and thereby to lessen their secretions. On the other hand, acute fright and intense anxiety have been known actually to bring on an attack of jaundice. This is one of the well-known ways in which fear acts — always depressing in its ultimate effect, but sometimes highly stimulating in its first effect on the organism, especially in the case of acute, sudden, and overwhelming fright or shock.

Quality of secretion. The natural mental states permit the liver and pancreatic gland to carry forward their functions unmolested, while abnormal states of the mind react to the disturbance of their work. As previously noted, anger and fear may so disorganize the work of the liver as actually to bring on an attack of so-called biliousness accompanied by jaundice.

The pancreas seems to be especially subject to influence by faith and fear. It is a generally accepted belief that the pancreatic gland secretes a substance which is concerned in the oxidation or burning up of sugar in the system.

In diabetes, among other abnormal conditions there seems to be a derangement of this particular function of the pancreas. Now, it has been repeatedly observed that when diabetics are depressed — when they become violently angry or indulge in excessive worry and melancholic reflections — the percentage of sugar excreted in the urine is almost invariably increased. The degree of increase, at least in the majority of the cases, seems to be in a significant ratio to the intensity of the anger and the degree of the mental depression. In this connection it should be noted that several European authorities have reported that they have actually been able to reduce the amount of sugar in the urine by means of suggestive therapeutics — by promoting a healthy state of mind.

The secretory mechanism. In order to make perfectly clear just what part the nerves play in the secretions of the liver and pancreas, and in order not to give the impression that the mind wholly dominates these secretory functions as in the cases of the mouth and stomach, it will probably be best to explain more fully the chemical means whereby pancreatic secretory activity is excited.

During digestion, as the acid contents of the stomach are injected into the bowel, the action of the acid on the intestinal mucous membrane produces a sudden closure of the stomach. The stomach does not again open to empty itself until this acid has been neutralized by the bile and the alkaline pancreatic juice.

The presence of acid in the intestine causes the bowel to produce a substance called *secretin* — a sort of chemical messenger to the liver and the pancreas, telling them how soon their secretions will be needed. This substance has been collected, and, when injected into the blood stream of an animal, it never fails to produce an immediate secretion of both bile and pancreatic juice. There are a large number of these chemical messengers secreted by the body, and as a class they are known as *hormones.*

Notwithstanding the fact that chemical influences apparently dominate the pancreatic secretions, Pawlow conclusively demonstrated that the vagus nerve carried fibres, the stimulation of which excited a profuse flow of pancreatic juice in three minutes. The sympathetic system is also largely concerned in the work of both the liver and the pancreas.

THE MAMMARY SECRETION

Many a mother engaged in nursing her infant has had her milk dried up and has been compelled to wean the child as

THE MIND AND SECRETION

a result of chronic fear — worry. Fear cannot only diminish or stop the secretion of milk, but it is a well-known fact that anger and fretting, grief and despondency, are able actually to change the character of the secretion of the mammary gland, so that the milk may become highly injurious or positively poisonous to the sucking child.

Again, it has been observed that a mother whose breast contains but little or no milk, will, upon hearing her child cry continuously for food, actually begin to secrete an increased amount of milk in response to the nervous stimulation resulting from a knowledge and recognition of the babe's pressing needs. We know of several cases of young mothers who had but little milk and who did not desire to nurse their offspring, but who, upon having their minds changed and after choosing to suckle their children, began at once to have an increasingly copious secretion of breast milk. One observer reports a case in which the milk secretion was quadrupled in nine weeks, largely by suggestion and the production of a natural state of mind in the mother.

THE KIDNEY AND BLADDER

Laboratory studies of the urine serve to show that the mental habits of the individual have not a little to do with the secretory activities of the kidneys. While faith favors a normal quality of urine and a normal or increased quantity, fear almost invariably decreases the quantity and alters the quality. The urinary flow in certain nervous individuals is extremely susceptible to the emotional changes. This behavior of the urinary flow in response to the psychic state is no doubt largely due to the power of the mental state to influence and modify the flow of blood through the kidneys. Dr. Clifford Allbutt says it is an undoubted clinical fact that granular kidney is often produced by prolonged mental anxiety. Diabetes is undoubtedly caused by mental strain. Sir B. W. Richardson has known diabetes caused from pure mental strain. He also says: "Diabetes from sudden mental shock is a pure type of a physical malady of mental origin." He found that eleven parts of urine were secreted in repose, compared to thirteen when the brain was active.

The apparent influence of the mind and emotion over the bladder and urination is simply due to nervous reflexes and is a consequence of kidney circulatory disturbances. There is no question of the fact that fear can profoundly affect the muscular control of the bladder — leading to the sudden voiding of the urine, as in the case of children who are unusually frightened. The mind is also a prominent and powerful factor in the treatment of nocturnal enuresis in certain nervous children.

COMPARATIVE SUMMARY OF THE EFFECTS OF FAITH AND FEAR ON THE ACTION OF THE SECRETORY GLANDS

FAITH	FEAR
1. *Secretion in general:* Favors normal quantity and quality.	1. *Secretion in general:* Retards, modifies, and deranges. Lessens quantity.
2. *Saliva, quantity:* Increased.	2. *Saliva, quantity:* Decreased.
3. *Saliva, quality:* Produces an active juice.	3. *Saliva, quality:* Inferior. Sometimes bitter.
4. *Metabolic factor:* Promotes normal metabolism.	4. *Metabolic factor:* Deranges the nutrition.
5. *Salivary flow:* Abundant. "Mouth waters."	5. *Salivary flow:* Decreased. Mouth dry in stage fright.
6. *Digestive power:* Favored or increased.	6. *Digestive power:* Lessened.
7. *Liver and pancreas, secretion:* Normal amount.	7. *Liver and pancreas, secretion:* Decreased amount.
8. *Liver and pancreas, quality:* Normal and natural.	8. *Liver and pancreas, quality:* Altered.
9. *Mammary secretion:* Quantity increased. Quality improved or normal.	9. *Mammary secretion:* Quantity lessened. Quality altered or poisoned by anger.
10. *Kidney and bladder:* Quantity of urine increased. Quality normal.	10. *Kidney and bladder:* Quantity of urine decreased. Quality altered.

CHAPTER XVI

THE MENTAL INFLUENCES CONCERNED IN DIGESTION

THE GASTRIC JUICE.— QUALITY OF THE GASTRIC JUICE.— THE DIGESTIVE STRENGTH.— PSYCHIC DYSPEPSIA.— THE "APPETITE JUICE."— STOMACH MUSCULAR MOVEMENTS.— SLOW DIGESTION.— DIGESTION WORRY, NERVOUS DYSPEPSIA.— THE VOMITING CENTRE.— MENTAL INFLUENCE AND INTESTINAL ACTION. — QUANTITY AND QUALITY.— PERISTALSIS.— CONSTIPATION. — COMPARATIVE SUMMARY OF THE EFFECTS OF FAITH AND FEAR ON DIGESTION.

RECENT experiments and observation indicate that the activities of the various secretory glands are more largely influenced by the mental and nervous states than any other vital function of the body. Pawlow, among his other epoch-making investigations, showed that the appetite is the master regulator of gastric secretion and stomach digestion.

THE GASTRIC JUICE

Faith — expectant hunger — produces an abundant flow of gastric juice from the secreting glands located in the walls of the stomach; while fear, grief, worry, and fretting invariably decrease the secretion and lessen the flow of the gastric juice, as will be more fully noted later. Chronic worriers and despondent patients universally suffer from deficient gastric juice and slow digestion.

The pleasant emotions all favor the secretion of an increased quantity of gastric juice by their salutary influence upon a man's appetite and general good-humor; while the depressing and surly frame of mind unfailingly contributes to decreasing the amount of the stomach's secretions.

Let us hear some bad news or receive some shocking intelligence at meal time, and note how quickly the stomach suspends its activities, while the appetite positively refuses more food.

Pawlow in feeding one of his dogs by the so-called "sham feeding" procedure, reports that the dog ate greedily for six hours, the stomach glands secreting 700 cc. of gastric juice during this time, although not a morsel of food actually entered the dog's stomach — it all fell through the artificial opening in the gullet into a bucket on the floor. Nevertheless, as long as the dog enjoyed the taste of food and continued to eat, the gastric juice continued to be produced and flowed freely.

QUALITY OF THE GASTRIC JUICE

Faith and its allied mental states in every way favor the secretion of a natural and normally balanced digestive juice. On the other hand, the sordid and pessimistic emotions all contribute to demoralize the gastric secretion — to alter its proportions and decrease its strength. The author no longer doubts that many cases of so-called acid dyspepsia are due largely to mental and nervous causes.

The stomach is exceedingly susceptible to the slightest changes in the mental state. The stomach is probably the most suggestible organ in the whole body. The mere sight of a fly in the food is entirely sufficient to cause many persons to vomit forthwith. The thought of an emetic will produce nausea and even actual regurgitation in numerous sensitive and nervous individuals. The mind is able profoundly to control stomach digestion by means of the great pneumogastric nerves, and also indirectly through the vast sympathetic nerve supply going to the stomach from the solar plexus — the abdominal brain.

It is now known that the quality and constituents of the gastric secretion vary from meal to meal in perfect harmony with the change in food, the keenness of the appetite, and the sense of enjoyment connected with the sense of taste.

THE DIGESTIVE STRENGTH

When the nerve impulses are normal and the mental states healthy, the digestive power is usually excellent. Faith actually improves the digestion, while good cheer prevents dyspepsia. People are not only sour in disposition because they are suffering from indigestion, but many are suffering from dyspepsia because they were previously out of sorts. A sour disposition sooner or later leads to a sour stomach.

It is notorious that one's digestion is always good on a holiday. Vacation digestion is usually extra good. At such times you eat things with more or less impunity which would profoundly upset your digestion at other times. When the mind is carefree, when you are cheerful and happy — when the attributes of faith and hope dominate the mind and nervous system — the stomach glands do their best, they pour forth a copious and abundant juice, strong in digestive power. In contrast with this ideal digestive state, note the fact that most persons who habitually eat alone, sooner or later develop some form of dyspepsia.

Lack of sociability and good cheer at the table predisposes to indigestion. The mechanical, business-like methods of that unhygienic abomination, the quick-lunch counter, is responsible for a large portion of the rapidly increasing number of dyspepsia sufferers in this country. Mental courage and good cheer also favor a healthy nerve tone and strong muscular action on the part of the stomach itself.

PSYCHIC DYSPEPSIA

We recently had a woman patient who had had an attack of acute indigestion some eight years ago, and ever since had been a constant sufferer from a most obstinate and refractory form of indigestion, which had successfully withstood all efforts looking toward a cure. Her mind was ever on her stomach — it was the constant topic of her conversation. Strange to report, a careful chemical examination of the contents of her stomach, following the taking up of the usual test-meal which is given for the purpose of making a stomach diagnosis, revealed the curious fact that there was very little actually wrong with this patient's digestion; to say the least, not enough to account for her severe and long-continued suffering.

It would not have been the part of wisdom to present the full facts to her mind at once. She had nursed her complaint entirely too long and too lovingly ever to be persuaded that her indigestion actually and almost wholly existed primarily in her mind, and that her stomach disorder was but the reproduction of her own mental disorder. In other words, she was entirely too nervous to be convinced that her difficulty was of a nervous nature, largely psychic in origin — psychic dyspepsia.

The following plan was adopted: She was told that an exact diagnosis of her stomach trouble had been arrived at; that the laboratory findings were explicit and positive; that at last we knew the precise condition of her stomach, and that we were also able, as far as physicians ever are, to promise her that she would make a speedy and complete recovery under the proper treatment and diet, and that, in all probability, she would be entirely well within thirty days.

She was utterly dumbfounded at this promise and replied that it was too good to believe — too much to expect, after all the years she had suffered; whereupon, we replied that absolute trust — implicit faith — was required on the part of the patient in the treatment of all such forms of stomach disorder; and that if she continued to harbor distrust, it would give rise to such a nervous state as would effectively counteract the curative powers of our diet and other treatment. The latter consisted of the following: A general course of baths, massage, and electricity calculated to rest and soothe both mind and body, together with a graduated scheme of diet, arranged so as gradually to restore all the numerous wholesome foods which she had discarded on the supposition that they did not agree with her, or that they aggravated her indigestion.

Day by day she had restored to her diet these supposedly harmful articles of diet, while day by day we *assured* her that they would not disagree with her; and day by day she ate the prescribed diet, and it did not disagree with her. At the end of a week, she began to gain in weight and to gain in strength and courage. She actually got the notion into her head that she was going to get well. Her appetite began to improve; she began to smile and talk about her wonderful recovery; said she believed that the secret of her case had at last been

MENTAL INFLUENCES ON DIGESTION

discovered and that she was really going to get well. She did get well.

Within four weeks the battle was practically won, the long struggle with mental or nervous dyspepsia was over, and the patient has ever since been rejoicing in the blessing of good health and enjoying the inestimable boon of sound digestion.

THE "APPETITE JUICE"

In his remarkable experiments upon dogs, Pawlow, the Russian physiologist, demonstrated that the secretion of the gastric juice during the first half of digestion is entirely regulated by the sense of taste and the keenness of the appetite. The presence of food in the stomach, with the exception of milk and certain meat and vegetable juices, produces no secretion of gastric juice whatever; whereas, the thought of eating or the desire to eat, or even the agreeable smell of food, produces an abundant flow of strong gastric juice in about four and a half minutes. This initial juice — the only juice to be found in the stomach during the first half of digestion — has therefore been aptly called "appetitie juice," or "psychic juice." The quantity of this juice may be great or small, according as the appetite is strong or weak.

During the latter half of digestion, the appetite or psychic juice gradually disappears, its place being taken by a second form of secretion largely changed and called the "chemical juice," the nature and strength of which is entirely determined by the products of digestion formed in the stomach as the result of the action of its predecessor, the appetite juice. This chemical juice, which finishes the digestion of the meal, is probably secreted under the influence of the chemical stimulation of the half-digested food as it comes in contact with the walls of the stomach. It would therefore appear, if one had a good appetite and in consequence secreted a strong appetite juice during the first hour of digestion, that this would insure the subsequent secretion of a competent chemical juice to finish the digestion of the meal properly and satisfactorily.

Many of these facts concerning digestion were discovered by Pawlow by means of an ingenious surgical operation which he performed upon dogs for the purpose of creating a "sample stomach," separate and distinct from the main stomach and about one-eighth its size. (See Fig. 22.) This smaller stomach he created out of a portion of the wall of the stomach itself. Its opening was outside of the body, so that he was able at all times to collect from it a sample of the secretions formed in the larger stomach. He also made an opening into the gullets (œsophagi) of some of the dogs, so that when they were fed, the food would fall into a basin instead of entering the stomach. This process, already referred to, is called "sham feeding" and it was found to produce very strong gastric juice even when no food at all entered the stomach.

Pawlow, at the end of his very painstaking investigations, announced as his general conclusion that "appetite equals juice" and therefore, since good gastric juice means good digestion, we may very appropriately add, good appetite equals good digestion, all other things equal.

Fear, fright, worry, and disappointment cause an almost instantaneous suspension of the stomach's secretions. When the mind is in the least disturbed, the flow of gastric juice is altered. Anger, as a rule, absolutely suspends the secretory activities of the stomach.

STOMACH MUSCULAR MOVEMENT

Recent X-ray observations of the action of the stomach during the digestion of a meal, serve to demonstrate the wonderful influence of the mind over the muscular movements of the digestive apparatus. While faith — the natural and normal mental state — favors strong and regular action of the stomach muscle, fear and its psychic companions almost invariably weaken the muscular contractions of the stomach and retard its digestive activity. To pull a cat's tail during the process of digestion just following a meal, is sometimes sufficient to stop entirely — completely paralyze — the muscular contractions of the stomach and intestines. This inaction may persist from a few minutes to almost half an hour.

In view of these scientific experiments respecting the mental influences which are able to hasten and retard the digestive activity and muscular work of the stomach, it should cause little surprise that so many downcast, complaining, and sordid

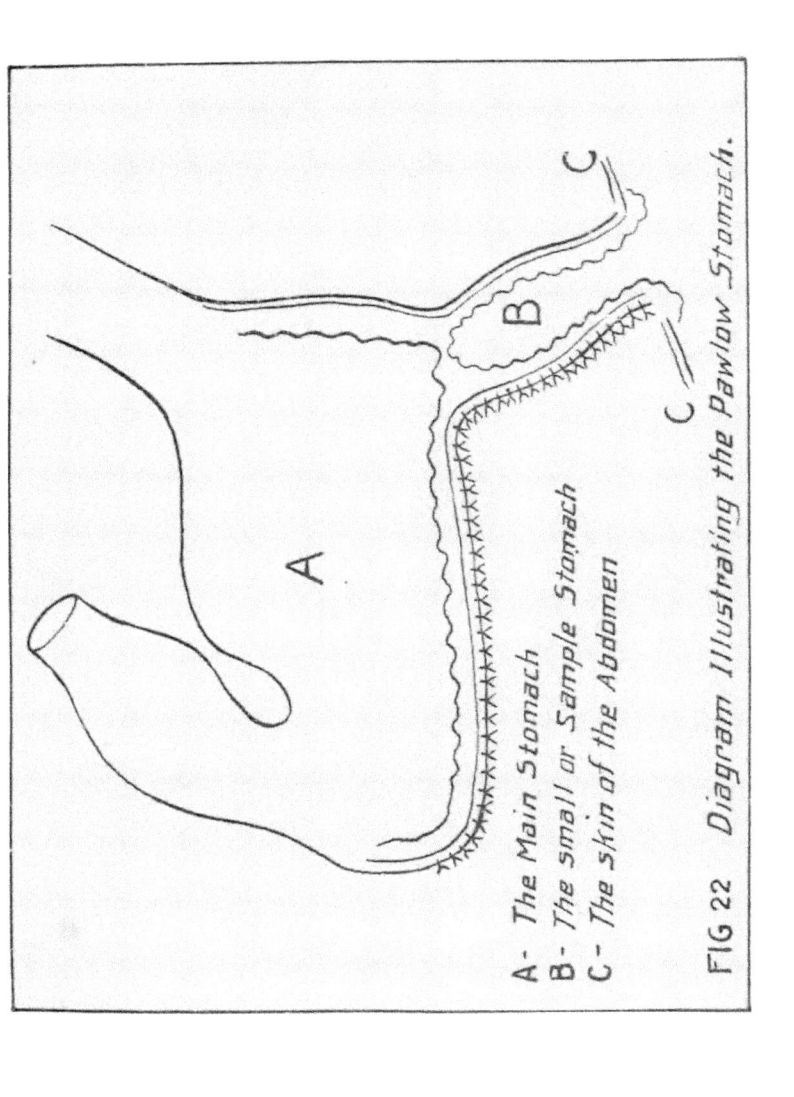

FIG 22 Diagram Illustrating the Pawlow Stomach.

A - The Main Stomach
B - The small or Sample Stomach
C - The skin of the Abdomen

MENTAL INFLUENCES ON DIGESTION 167

people are continuous sufferers from some form of digestive disturbance. Mental vigor and moral determination favor normal stomach action and digestive strength.

X-ray observations on animals that have had bismuth added to their food indicate that the muscular movements of digestion proceed in perfect harmony with the temperamental humor of the animal; strong and vigorous when the animal is in a good state of mind, weak or entirely suspended when the animal is in a bad humor.

SLOW DIGESTION

There can no longer be any doubt that many cases of slow digestion and sluggish stomach work are in some measure, at least, due to the unfortunate mental and nervous states of the sufferer. If the mind can be awakened and the spirits revived, such patients will immediately begin to show improvement, and many will pass on to full recovery.

One of Pawlow's dogs, when his temper was ruffled, produced absolutely no gastric juice, while the latest experiments of this extraordinary investigator go to show that even music is able to influence the digestive secretions. By means of diversified musical sounds it is said that Pawlow has actually been able to stimulate or retard the flow of the saliva.

There is one important thing connected with the action of the digestive ferments or enzymes that should not be overlooked. If the products of digestion are allowed to accumulate, the action of the enzyme (pepsin) is interfered with. If this failure to remove the products of digestion persists, the digestive enzyme begins what is known as its "reverse action," a process in which it actually undoes its previous work of digestion — takes the soluble products of its own action and literally builds them back into the insoluble substances of the food. This may afford some explanation of the poor nutrition of people who habitually suffer from dyspepsia, slow digestion, and weakness of the stomach muscle.

DIGESTION WORRY — NERVOUS DYSPEPSIA

Fear exercises an influence of general depression over the entire process of digestion, including stomach and bowels. Fear and fright are able, temporarily, to paralyze the secretory functions and muscular activities of both stomach and intestines.

We have known scores of patients who had been told they had a dilated stomach, straightway to contract a severe and troublesome case of dyspepsia; whereas, their stomachs had been doing fairly satisfactory work up to the time of the unfortunate blunder of telling them this organ was enormously overstretched.

The more some of these stomach cases think of their infirmity and the more they treat and coddle their supposed weak, dilated, and helpless stomachs, the worse their dyspepsia and indigestion become; whereas, a little sensible dieting, coupled with a period of absolute indifference and inattention to the whole process of digestion, would, in the vast majority of cases, be followed by a speedy and more or less permanent functional recovery. Why worry over your stomach, even if it is a trifle dilated, overstretched, or prolapsed, as long as it performs its functions properly and satisfactorily?

Years ago — owing purely to superstition and fear — watermelons were supposed to cause numerous digestive and bowel disorders. With the passing of such erroneous beliefs, the harmfulness of watermelon as an article of diet also passed. It is interesting to note that even when melons were in their worst repute they never made the small boys sick who hooked them under cover of darkness and gorged themselves to the limit on their stolen booty. The boys had faith in the melons — at least they did not fear them — they only feared getting caught, and so the melons never did them serious hurt. And so tomatoes, cucumbers, and various other articles of diet have been regarded as poisonous or injurious from time to time, and have disagreed with the people in perfect harmony with their beliefs.

The American people to-day not only suffer as a result of their *bona fide* dietetic sins, but they also languish because of the vast amount of indigestion and dyspepsia which has no existence outside of the minds of its victims. But as long as the dyspepsia remains in the mind just so long will the stomach continue to misbehave in sympathetic response to the mental state.

MENTAL INFLUENCES ON DIGESTION 169

THE VOMITING CENTRE

That the mental state can influence the vomiting centre and produce violent action of the stomach, has long been known. A physician gave one hundred patients in a certain hospital a little colored water and then rushed in and dramatically announced that he had given them a strong emetic by mistake. This suggestion was sufficient to cause eighty of them at once to sicken at the stomach and a large number actually to vomit. A young woman who was afflicted with obstinate and hysterical vomiting, and whose case the physician had not been able to relieve, was instantly and permanently cured on being told that her wedding-day must be postponed until she had recovered.

The author once gave sugar of milk and flour to five patients, who were led to believe that it was an emetic and that we were desirous of causing them to vomit. Within ten minutes two out of the five had vomited.

MENTAL INFLUENCE AND INTESTINAL ACTION

Next to the stomach, the mind is found to possess more regulatory control over the bowels than over any other of the organs of digestion.

Quantity. The buoyant and energetic mental state favors secretory activity of the intestinal glands by promoting the circulation and preventing congestion, as well as by nervous influences acting through the sympathetic system, which so largely control all intestinal work. The downcast and inactive mind is almost invariably accompanied by more or less inactivity of the bowel — constipation. There can be little doubt that mental constipation (sluggish and despondent action of the mind) in some way predisposes to intestinal inaction.

Quality. While the normal state of the nerves favors the production of a good quality of the intestinal digestive fluids, a deranged nervous system is sure to result in the production of an inferior and more or less inactive secretion.

The flow. The flow of the secretions formed in the intestinal glands is regular and natural when the mind is free from fear and worry. When the mind is occupied with distressing and oppressive thoughts, the flow of the intestinal fluids becomes spasmodic and may even be entirely suppressed.

Peristalsis. When the circulation of the bowel is normal and the mind is dominated by faith and good cheer, the muscular movements of the intestine are rhythmic, regular, and strong. When the feelings are ruffled or the temper aroused, the muscular action of the bowels becomes irregular and weak — it may even be entirely suspended for a considerable length of time by disturbed mental states.

Great and sudden fear may overstimulate intestinal peristalsis and actually produce diarrhœa. Unusual fright may also inhibit the voluntary control over the sphincter muscle of the rectum. This condition of affairs is brought about by the power of fear and terror to inhibit the nerve centres in the lumbar region of the spine which enable one to exercise voluntary control over the sphincter muscles of the bladder and the bowel.

A lady who received news of the death of a relative from cholera in a distant country was so frightened that she suffered for eight days from severe diarrhœa, and only recovered after being convinced that there was not a single case of cholera within hundreds of miles. Darwin mentions a similar case, that of a man who could so far increase the peristaltic action of his bowels by voluntary effort, that he could defecate at any time in half an hour. Many instances are on record of those who could by an act of will induce vomiting.

Constipation. Many despondent and discouraged persons suffer constantly from chronic constipation. This deficient functionating of the bowel is not alone due to circulatory disturbances — it is also the result of nervous derangement. There are found in the intestinal walls certain minute plexuses of nerves which have to do with peristalsis. These little nerve centres are directly connected with the great centres of the sympathetic system, and indirectly with the central nervous system, so that mental depression can react at once to the production of intestinal depression; and this is exactly what happens in nearly all cases where the mental state is continuously downcast and grieving.

Numerous cases are on record which abundantly demonstrate the large degree to which the mind is able to influence

MENTAL INFLUENCES ON DIGESTION

and control bowel action. In one case opium pills were given by mistake to a patient who was to have received a cathartic preparatory to a surgical operation. They produced a prompt and complete evacuation of the bowels. The patient believed she had swallowed a powerful cathartic and the bowels acted accordingly. We once had a patient whose bowels moved freely several hours after a cathartic was prescribed for her, although subsequent investigation revealed the fact that she had forgotten to take the medicine; but as she also forgot that she forgot, it worked just the same.

We have seen numerous cases of chronic constipation practically or wholly relieved by a change in mental attitude coupled with systematic or habit training of the bowel — going to stool at certain stated and regular intervals. Chronic fear never fails to produce sluggish and incomplete intestinal movements. In the case of a whining cat, X-ray observations showed that no intestinal action took place for over one hour.

The mind undoubtedly influences bowel action by cortical inhibition of the centres of the great splanchnic nerves, whose origin is located in the medulla. In the case of sudden looseness of the bowels following acute fright or profound anger, the diarrhœa is probably produced by the nervous inhibition of intestinal absorption; the bowel contents remain fluid and are thrown out in great quantities, for the simple reason that assimilation and absorption are temporarily suspended.

COMPARATIVE SUMMARY OF THE EFFECTS OF FAITH AND FEAR ON DIGESTION

FAITH	FEAR
1. *Gastric secretion:* Expectant hunger produces abundant flow.	1. *Gastric secretion:* Lessens or entirely suspends secretion.
2. *Quality:* Increased. Normally balanced juice.	2. *Quality:* Deteriorated. Alters proportion and strength.
3. *Digestive strength:* Excellent. "Holiday digestion" always good.	3. *Digestive strength:* Weak. "Quick lunch" dyspepsia common.
4. *Psychic dyspepsia:* Entirely cured.	4. *Psychic dyspepsia:* Produces and aggravates.

FAITH	FEAR
5. *"Appetite juice"*: Promotes generous flow in connection with hunger.	5. *"Appetite juice"*: Decreases and retards, as in "bad news" indigestion.
6. *Stomach movements:* Strong and regular. Normal digestion.	6. *Stomach movements:* Weak. Favors slow digestion.
7. *Digestion time:* Shortened.	7. *Digestion time:* Lengthened.
8. *Nervous dyspepsia:* Relieves and removes.	8. *Nervous dyspepsia:* Chief cause.
9. *Vomiting centre:* Quiets and controls.	9. *Vomiting centre:* Excites.
10. *Intestinal secretion:* Increases quantity. Copious.	10. *Intestinal secretion:* Decreases quantity. Scant.
11. *Quality:* Strong and active.	11. *Quality:* Weak and inactive.
12. *Flow:* Regular.	12. *Flow:* Spasmodic.
13. *Peristalsis:* Intestinal movements regular and normal.	13. *Peristalsis:* Intestinal movements irregular and sluggish.
14. *Constipation:* Decreased.	14. *Constipation:* Increased.

CHAPTER XVII

THE PSYCHIC FACTOR IN NUTRITION AND METABOLISM

THE NUTRITION OF THE CELL.— DIGESTION AND NUTRITION.— THE PROCESS OF ASSIMILATION.— OXIDATION IN THE CELL.— THE APPETITE IN NUTRITION.— THE BODILY WEIGHT.— THE PHYSICAL WELL-BEING.— THE DUCTLESS GLANDS.— THE THYROID GLAND.— THE SUPRARENAL BODIES.—THE PITUITARY BODY.— COMPARATIVE SUMMARY OF THE EFFECTS OF FAITH AND FEAR ON THE NUTRITION AND METABOLISM.

IT is not possible so precisely to trace the details of the mental factors in their influence on nutrition and metabolism, as in the case of the circulatory system and the digestive work of the stomach; nevertheless, the clinical evidence is so abundant, and striking illustrations are so frequent, that there is left but little question in the minds of careful observers respecting the profound influence exerted by the mind upon the nutritional processes of the human body.

THE NUTRITION OF THE CELL

Disease is now generally recognized to be either a derangement of the functions of the cell, or a degeneration of the substance of the cell. The health of every person is entirely dependent upon the health of one and all of the countless thousands of cells that compose the physical body. If the mind is indeed able to influence the nutrition of the cell, it must be evident that it is able to influence and more or less control the entire nutrition and metabolism of the whole body.

A study of the facts presented in Chapter II will suffice to show that the mind does in a large manner influence and regulate the nutrition of the cells. The individual cells of the body are influenced by the mind in two entirely different ways. First, by means of *chemical messengers* or *hormones* which circulate in the blood and lymph, and thus come in actual contact with the remotest cells of the body. The mind and nervous system have the power largely to control, regulate, and modify the cellular and glandular secretions of the entire body, and are thus able, indirectly, to control the nutrition, growth, and life-history of all the body cells. It is a recognized physiological fact that the numerous special secretions, which are so highly subject to nervous control, are all more or less concerned in the intricate work of regulating and modifying the nutrition of the individual cells.

In the second place, the mind is able to influence the nutrition and health of the body cells by the specific impulses — the *mental messages* — which are sent directly over the nerve tracts to the cell substance. All the cells of the body, with the possible exception of the blood cells and those of the outer layer of the skin or epidermis,* are in actual contact with some minute filament of some nerve process. It actually is true that practically every active cell, however remote from the great nerve centres, has an independent private line, a living telegraph wire, directly connected with one of the great nerve centres of the body, which centres are in turn connected, directly or indirectly, with that great telegraph centre of the organism, the brain. And the brain is the seat — the organ — of mind.

The cheerful, joyous livers of the faith life are bound to enjoy better nutrition than the downcast and despondent victims of the fear life. Worry not only debilitates the mind, but it also emaciates the body. Grief and cankering care invariably operate to bring about a condition of moral vacillation and physical weakness. Special worry, unusual sorrow, and protracted grief, never fail to pull down one's vitality. And so, by interfering with the nutrition of the cell, these depressive mental states interfere with the health and nutrition of the whole man.

Just at present we have under our care a patient who recently

---

*These cells — red blood corpuscles and epidermis cells — are strangely modified. They differ from all other cells of the body. The blood corpuscles have no nuclei, while the epidermis consists of dead cells. The fat cells, formed from modified connective tissue cells, also belong to that class of body cells which probably do not receive actual nerve filaments.

NUTRITION AND METABOLISM

lost her husband by means of a very unusual and unfortunate accident. Her grief, of course, is likewise very deep and unusual. This woman, before her bereavement, was the picture of health — strong, robust, and splendidly nourished. After the loss of her husband she began gradually to lose in flesh — her weight decreased to the point where her friends led her to seek medical advice. Her sorrow and her downcast mental state continue, and so far we have utterly failed to stay the march of that slow but sure wasting away which threatens her very life. No amount of special feeding or even forced feeding, suffices to produce a gain in weight. The most highly nutritious and specially prepared foods are not able to overcome the subtle influences which unceasingly operate to demoralize the nutrition and emaciate the patient. Medicine, baths, and scientific feeding have thus far failed to stay the devouring hand of incessant grief or to overcome the destroying power of corroding sorrow. This unfortunate sufferer is doomed to fill an untimely grave, unless some power, some religious consolation, some psychic influence, all of which she has thus far refused, comes in to change the mental outlook and thus relieve the physical organism from the nervous inhibition and chemical handicap under which the body is struggling on toward sure defeat and inevitable death. For it must be recognized that continual fear and grief — protracted sorrow — do positively interfere with, and otherwise prevent, the nutritional processes of the individual cells of the body. Cases such as the foregoing are of common occurrence; and the progressive loss in weight and decrease in strength are not alone due to poor appetite, deficient nourishment, and crippled assimilation.

DIGESTION AND NUTRITION

Faith encourages the entire digestive process, while fear deranges and retards the digestive functions at every point. One of the first steps in the great process of metabolism is digestion; and since the mind is able most markedly to control the digestion, it becomes very evident that the mental factor in metabolism must be large and powerful.

He that is despondent is sooner or later overtaken with constipation and indigestion; and one does not long endure the tortures and terrors of dyspepsia without discovering the fact that the nutrition of the entire body has become deranged. The vital resistance and physical strength are speedily deteriorated, and the patient passes into a state of general debility and disordered metabolism. In many cases this semi-invalidism is largely, if not wholly, the result of an abnormal nervous state, which owes its existence to the fact that the mind is dominated by fear. In all such cases the powers of assimilation seem to be more or less crippled.

Every year we observe several victims of malnutrition, chronic dyspepsia, and we may truthfully add, chronic fear, who take up some psychic fad, some newfangled religion, or perchance, adopt one of the old-fashioned creeds with a whole-souled enthusiasm; and, as a result of this change in mental habit, we behold an immediate and marvellous transformation. Not only are the mental and moral habits entirely changed, but this psychic, spiritual, or moral revolution — call it what you will — has actually extended to the physical domain, the health of the material body is positively improved. Of course, each of these special religions avers that this physical improvement is either providential or miraculous, and that it constitutes divine credentials, proving that this religion's adherents are the only genuine people of God on the earth.

We would not for one moment either question or deny the power of the Supreme Being to administer life and health, but we are compelled to recognize that any and all brands of religious faith and shades of ethical teaching are alike able to point to a long list of just such remarkable and undoubted cures. History reveals that in all ages men and women have been thus helped and healed, regardless of time, place, and the orthodoxy of their religious views. The only conclusion which a scientific and unprejudiced observer can draw is that the vast majority of these cases of diversified healing are due to the radical change of mind on the part of the afflicted soul. Faith comes in to depose fear, and instantly the recovery begins.

THE PROCESS OF ASSIMILATION

Digestion is but the first step in the preparation of the food for the nourishment of the body. Assimilation is the next

NUTRITION AND METABOLISM

important act in the conversion of the food into the living tissues. Fear is able, temporarily, almost to paralyze the process of assimilation, while chronic worry more or less permanently deranges the absorptive powers of the whole digestive system. By greatly delaying and interfering with the normal action of the digestive organs, the mental state may not only interfere with the assimilation of the food, but may indirectly bring about such a state of fermentation and putrefaction in the intestine, as actually to produce enormous quantities of poisonous toxins, which are, in time, absorbed along with the products of digestion and pass into the blood, subsequently to poison and derange the nutrition of countless thousands of faithful working cells of the body.

Both laboratory experiments and common, everyday observation, abundantly demonstrate the fact that faith encourages the assimilative powers of the body; while fear retards, delays, and even temporarily inhibits the process of assimilation.

We knew of a young woman who had long feared that she would fail to win the affection of a certain young man of whom she was passionately fond. She greatly feared that her ardent love would never be returned. She began progressively to lose flesh. Her nutrition rapidly failed. It was evident that her metabolism was badly out of order. The change in her countenance, and her loss of color, agility, and sociability testified to the fact that her mental attitude was disastrously affecting her physical health. Various physicians tried various remedies, while interested friends recommended everything from osteopathy to Christian Science. Nearly all of these the girl at one time or another tried, but all failed to restore her bloom of health and buoyancy of step.

At last the royal remedy for her mysterious wasting disease, which had so successfully resisted all scientific skill and baffled all medical knowledge, was unexpectedly found. The young swain of her choice began to reciprocate her affection, he professed actual love for her, and shortly he proposed. Enough said; the young patient ceased to pine away; she began rapidly to put on flesh; the bloom of health returned to her cheeks; she quickly returned to the happy, joyous, and vivacious life of former days: the mind had gained its coveted prize, the soul had satisfied its longing, and now the body was released from its terrible burden of fear and suspense; the mind was now filled with faith and hope, and their beneficent influence on the material body was manifested in a remarkable restoration of the physical health.

OXIDATION IN THE CELL

Even after food is properly digested and completely assimilated, it is absolutely useless to the body unless it is oxidized. The oxidation of food represents the last step in the process of digestion, and is effected by means of a digestive ferment or enzyme, called *oxidase*, which is secreted by the cells of the body, and by which the cells are able actually to burn up the digested food substances brought to them in the blood stream.

Faith and fear are able to influence the process of oxidation in a number of ways. As will be shown later, faith increases the depth of the breathing and thereby favors an abundant supply of oxygen, which can be taken up by the red blood cells in the lungs and carried to the remotest cell of the body. While the action of the lungs during fright and excitement proves that fear produces superficial and shallow breathing, faith, by favoring the respiration and the circulation, increases oxidation within the cells. Increased blood movement together with deep breathing increases the amount of digested food materials brought to the cell and also increases the number of red blood cells — the little fellows who carry the oxygen around to the individual cells — and thus oxidation is accelerated, the vital fires burn more brightly and evenly, for without oxygen, the living fires of the cell are soon smothered and extinguished. Thousands of people are but half alive, but half efficient, because they are but half breathers; their vital fires are half smothered all the time.

A disordered state of the mind seems actually to be able to interfere with the process of oxidation on the part of the cell. That this is true is convincingly shown by carefully observing diabetic patients. Diabetes is not primarily a disease of the kidneys. While the pancreatic gland is undoubtedly concerned in this disease, the chief difficulty seems to be a chronic inability

NUTRITION AND METABOLISM 179

on the part of the cells of the body to oxidize sugar — one of the important elements of cellular nutrition. Now, it is observed that fear, worry, and mental strain, in the vast majority of diabetics, serve greatly to increase the amount of sugar in the urine. By improving the mental state and allowing faith to dominate the mind, the percentage of sugar is more or less decreased in almost every case; and this interesting observation would suggest that the mental state does actually have some influence and control over the oxidizing process carried forward in the body cells.

It is not enough to suppose that oxidation is increased or decreased merely by increasing or decreasing the efficiency of the digestive and circulatory systems, in connection with improvement in the respiratory function. While these vital functions are all indirectly concerned in the regulation and modification of cellular oxidátion, the fact seems to be clearly demonstrated that the mind, by its direct action over and through the nervous system, is able, in a very large degree, to regulate and control the final step of digestion in the body — the process of cell-oxidation.

THE APPETITE IN NUTRITION

In the chapter on secretion, the facts were presented which go to show that the appetite is in a large measure the regulator of metabolism. The appetite controls and determines the strength of the digestive juices of the stomach; the appetite dictates the quantity and quality of the food eaten; and it is a well-known fact that the appetite is in a very large measure under psychic control. Who has not seen the invalid, void of appetite, brighten up and actually begin to eat and relish food on a daintily served tray? On the other hand, but in contrast with this salutary effect of faith upon the appetite, note the disastrous effect upon the patient's appetite when the food is improperly prepared or unacceptably served.

It only requires that one should review the vast influence exerted by the mind upon digestion, as previously noted, to be able to reach the conclusion that the mental factor is exceptionally strong in nutrition and metabolism. How can we satisfactorily explain the great benefit which dyspeptics and other metabolic invalids derive from a trip to the seashore, a sojourn in some sanitarium, or an ocean voyage ? We have seen a chronic sufferer from malnutrition and disordered metabolism of long standing permanently cured by a trip around the world. A certain wealthy, self-centred woman, who had endless trouble with her assimilation, lost her husband, fortune, and all, went to work in a store as a saleslady, forgot her troubles, abandoned her indolent life, and fully recovered from all her nutritional difficulties. She said: "I'd rather be poor, work hard, and be healthy, than be rich, idle, and sick."

Again, if we fail to take into account the mental factor in metabolism, how can we explain the sudden and immediate improvement in digestive power and general nutrition experienced by so many people while on their annual vacation, holidays, and excursions ? In many cases, the hygienic practices and sanitary surroundings of the pleasure-seeker are inferior to the health-promoting environment of the home life; but notwithstanding these numerous drawbacks, the health quickly improves, provided the change of scenery and surroundings is able to improve the mental state. The average man on vacation cheers up, forgets his troubles; and since the mind is dominated by faith, the body begins at once to perform all its functions more naturally, normally, and vigorously.

THE BODILY WEIGHT

Faith by its power to promote appetite, digestion, assimilation, and nutrition, encourages the natural and normal metabolism of the body, and in many cases, an improvement of the mental state results in actually increasing the bodily weight. On the other hand, fear is commonly observed to decrease a person's weight. How often we see grief and worry slowly but surely mar the physical beauty and decrease the bodily weight! The victims of grief and sorrow are sometimes reduced to the state of walking skeletons.

The author would not advocate fear and anxiety as anti-fat remedial specifics. The remedy in such a case bids fair to be worse than the disease; but we can heartily recommend cheerfulness as an aid in improving the personal appearance and promoting the nutrition of the physical body.

A few years ago a sullen, morose, and dyspeptic maiden lady frequently came to our clinic, complaining first of one difficulty, then of another. We were able to render her but little assistance in the direction of permanent help. We had not seen her for a couple of years, when one day she came back, bringing a friend suffering from a painful joint. Imagine our surprise and astonishment on seeing our former thin and cadaverous patient standing before us happy, smiling, and well nourished. When asked how it happened, she explained thus: "Well, doctor, I just got disgusted with myself; and my uncle who paid my doctor bills, he died, and I just made up my mind there was something wrong in my head or else in my heart, and so I began going around looking for some sort of mind cure. I tried hypnotism, Christian Science, and a lot of other fads and fakes. Several times I thought I was going to get well — but it didn't last. At last — it was on a nasty rainy day — I sat thinking how much better off I'd be if I was dead; when all at once it popped into my head what you told the doctors one day here in this clinic when you was talking about my case — how you thought that it would do a whole lot of good if I'd get married — get religion — or anything else that would *cheer me up.* And I just naturally got right down on my knees and asked God — just my mother's old-fashioned religion, you see — to help me cheer up; and maybe you won't believe it, but from that day I've been getting better — been improving in mind and body. Now I go around to the churches and such places, not looking for any special help for myself, but to tell all the rest of the foolish folks how to get out of the dumps; to tell them how thinking about yourself all the time — I call it cussed selfishness — is sure to make you sick and keep you ailing, while just cheering up will help make them well and happy. And so you see, doctor, I got some good here, after all, even if the baths and such like didn't seem to help me much, for it was here that I got my trolley on the right wire."

THE PHYSICAL WELL-BEING

Great grief paralyzes the body generally. Affairs of the heart usually affect the whole body — sometimes seriously involving the appetite, the digestion, and even the ability to sleep at night. The mental shock of breaking off an engagement invariably reacts on the physical organism, sometimes producing profound anæmia and other grave disorders of metabolism; not infrequently resulting in permanently deranging the nutrition or completely wrecking the health.

Eminent physicians have voiced their belief that prolonged anxiety and constant fear are actually concerned in predisposing certain susceptible persons to cancer. Our comparative ignorance of the actual cause of cancer renders it difficult to determine just how far the depressive influences of fear thought may be concerned in the terrible work of cancer-destruction. Cancer seems to be a disease following the disorganization and demoralization of the nutrition of the cell, and it may sometime be discovered that adverse mental influences, by their action upon the metabolism of the cell, are, after all, indirectly concerned in the production of cancer — the modern scourge.

When one is happy and contented, when one is able to believe fully and confidently in the present and the future, the circulation improves, the nutrition exchanges are accelerated, and the human machine works vigorously and harmoniously. On the other hand, when one doubts and fears, his strength and vital powers are all diminished. In many cases of insanity where the mind is so fully destroyed as to be no longer able to harass the body with fears and anxiety, the unfortunate creatures begin at once to put on flesh and to improve generally as regards their physical health.

THE DUCTLESS GLANDS

It is now generally known that the processes of bodily nutrition are largely influenced, and in many phases absolutely controlled, by the secretions of various so-called ductless glands, located in various parts of the body. These secretory glands are called ductless glands because there exists no visible duct whereby their secretions may be conveyed away from the gland. The secretions formed are absorbed indirectly into the blood through the cells of the gland and the walls of the blood vessels. It is highly probable that a man's varying and constantly changing mental states are able profoundly to influence the bodily nutrition by means of direct nervous influence

NUTRITION AND METABOLISM 183

upon some or all of these so-called ductless glands. There probably exist in the body many secreting glands belonging to this group which have not yet been discovered, the knowledge of which might shed still further light on the processes whereby mind is able to influence matter.

The thyroid gland. The thyroid gland, the enlargement of which is commonly known as *goitre,* seems to be influenced by both the mental state and an accumulation of certain poisons in the blood stream. The secretions of this important ductless gland exert a powerful influence on the regulation of the heartbeat and on the general nutrition of the body. In the case of infants, disorder in this gland may produce that well-known condition called *cretinism* — a species of idiocy. Administration of the thyroid gland of the sheep speedily relieves this otherwise incurable disease. Thus the body is profoundly affected by any influence which is able either to increase, decrease, or otherwise modify the secretion of this important gland.

There is now little doubt that the state of the mind and nervous system is able directly to influence the circulation and secretory behavior of this unique gland. Many forms of goitre are actually improved or partially relieved by a pleasant, hopeful, and optimistic mental state. In other cases fear, worry, and sorrow have been observed to increase the size of the gland — to enlarge the goitre. And so it would appear that if the mind can exert but the slightest influence, either directly or indirectly, over the function of these remarkable, ductless, secretory glands, the patient's mental state would be able most profoundly to influence the nutrition and metabolism of the body. That the mind does possess this power there now remains but little question.

The suprarenal bodies. The suprarenal bodies are situated just above the kidneys. Their internal secretion is called *adrenalin,* and possesses the power of raising the blood-pressure by its ability strongly to contract the small blood vessels. Rise and fall in blood-pressure, which so directly concerns the circulation of the blood, is in some measure at least, regulated by the secretion of these important ductless glands. Through the nervous connection, long-continued abnormal mental states are undoubtedly able unfavorably to influence these glands in common with the other secretory structures of the body; and in this way, the mind proves to be a potent factor in the indirect regulation of blood-pressure and the control of the circulation, as well as by its direct influence over the vaso-motor nerves.

Faith probably permits the suprarenal gland, in common with other glands of this class, to perform its work in a natural, normal manner, unhindered by any disturbing influence; while it is highly probable that fear and constant depression, result in an overproduction of secretion on the part of these glands. This increased secretion of adrenalin must result in raising the blood-pressure, thus contributing to the undesirable results of high tension and hard arteries.

The pituitary body. This small gland, about the size of a common pea, rests in a small bone depression at the base of the brain. It is known that when this little body is increased in size, the individual suffers from a peculiar over-development of bones and an overgrowth of the various bodily structures, including the thickening of the skin, etc. Enlargement of this peculiar little gland and a subsequent increased production of its secretion, leads to the condition just described and known in medicine as "giantism"; or it may lead to an overgrowth of certain portions of the body, such as the arms or the legs, known technically as "acromegaly."

An eminent investigator in this field has recently claimed to have found direct nervous connection between the pituitary body and the thyroid and suprarenal glands. It has long been known that the pituitary body was able to secrete a substance which could be so modified as either to raise or lower the blood-pressure. There is now no question that all these so-called ductless glands are more or less under nervous control. Their secretory functions are not altogether regulated by chemical stimuli; and the discoveries of the future may greatly illuminate this particular chapter of physiology, especially with respect to the part played by the various ductless glands in nutrition and metabolism.

COMPARATIVE SUMMARY OF THE EFFECTS OF FAITH AND FEAR
ON THE NUTRITION AND METABOLISM

FAITH	FEAR
1. *Cell nutrition:* Increases and promotes.	1. *Cell nutrition:* Decreases and retards.
2. *Digestion:* Encouraged.	2. *Digestion:* Deranged.
3. *Assimilation:* Increased.	3. *Assimilation:* Lessened.
4. *Oxidation:* Increased.	4. *Oxidation:* Decreased.
5. *Appetite:* Strengthened.	5. *Appetite:* Weakened.
6. *Bodily weight:* Favors increase.	6. *Bodily weight:* Favors decrease.
7. *Well-being:* Promoted.	7. *Well-being:* Decreased.
8. *Ductless glands:* Favors natural action.	8. *Ductless glands:* Deranges secretory action.
9. *Thyroid gland:* Decreases some forms of goitre.	9. *Thyroid gland:* Increases size of gland.
10. *Suprarenals:* Favors normal activity.	10. *Suprarenals:* Probably increases action.
11. *Pituitary body:* Normal action.	11. *Pituitary body:* May alter action (?).

CHAPTER XVIII

THE INFLUENCE OF THE MIND ON RESPIRATION

DEEP BREATHING AND SHALLOW BREATHING.— OXYGEN, THE VITAL FUEL.— THE CARBON DIOXID OUTPUT.— THE CHEST-DEVELOPMENT.— LUNG STRENGTH AND CAPACITY.— THE ACT OF BREATHING.— PSYCHIC COUGHING.— HABIT COUGH.— YAWNING AND HICCUPPING.— ASTHMA AND HAY-FEVER.— THE PLETHYSMOGRAPHIC CURVE.— THE NERVOUS MECHANISM OF BREATHING.— COMPARATIVE SUMMARY OF THE EFFECTS OF FAITH AND FEAR ON RESPIRATION.

NONE of the vital functions thus far considered are anything like subject to such a high degree of mental control as is the respiratory function. The ultimate control of the breathing function probably depends on the amount of carbon dioxid (CO_2) in the blood and the subsequent excitation of the respiratory centre of the medulla, nevertheless, the cortical or voluntary centres of the cerebrum possess the power, within certain limits, to override the involuntary respiratory centres of the medulla. In connection with all influences which are able to modify respiration, it should be remembered that the posture is greatly concerned. Breathing is more or less affected by stooping, standing, or reclining.

DEEP BREATHING AND SHALLOW BREATHING

Faith and courage induce deep breathing. The respiration of the optimist is usually regular, slow, and deep. The victims of fear and fright are always shallow breathers, the respiratory action being quick and irregular. Nearly all sufferers from the "blues" are observed to be superficial breathers, while the man who has a pleasant and hopeful disposition is almost invariably found to be a deep breather.

INFLUENCE OF MIND ON RESPIRATION

When we pause to consider the far-reaching effect of the breathing upon the nutrition and life of the body cells, we begin to appreciate the vast power of the mind, or any other influence which has the ability to influence the rate and depth of the respiratory function. The red blood corpuscles can not carry oxygen to the cells of the body unless the lungs draw in a sufficient amount of this vitalizing element from the atmosphere.

The successful man, who faces the world with courage and confidence, is usually a deep breather, and for this very reason he is more likely to develop into a deep thinker. On the other hand, when the mind becomes depressed and filled with foreboding thoughts of defeat and disaster, the respiratory function is greatly decreased, the breathing becomes shallow, while the lung action is quick and jerky. The amount of oxygen entering the lungs with each breath is decreased, digestion is interfered with, oxidation is crippled, the fires of life are literally smothered, and as a result the patient's vital efficiency is enormously decreased.

The author has seen the systematic practice of routine deep breathing exercises work wonders for certain despondent and downcast dyspeptics. There can be little doubt that mental peace and moral rest greatly help in increasing the efficiency of the respiratory function. Faith encourages the erect and physiological posture, which is indispensable to natural and normal breathing. It is utterly impossible for the bowed-over, stoop-shouldered victims of fear to indulge in deep breathing. Many such unfortunates are shallow breathers, as a result of both mental and material causes. The happy mind stimulates and favors deep breathing, and we could here describe the case of many a semi-invalid who has been restored to health by learning how to breathe properly.

OXYGEN, THE VITAL FUEL

Faith, by its power to increase the depth of breathing, greatly increases the oxygen-intake; while fear and its associated states of mental depression, greatly lessen the amount of oxygen entering the lungs with each inspiration. The oxygen-intake is vitally concerned in all the ultimate processes of metabolism. We are powerless to get the energy out of our digested and assimilated food stuffs unless we have present a requisite amount of oxygen to combine with the elements of nutrition and thus liberate the energy and heat contained in the products of digestion.

Since we are compelled to recognize the role of mind in the regulation of the depth and rate of respiration, and since the depth of respiration directly determines the oxygen-intake, it becomes evident that even the vital processes of oxidation in the individual cells of the body are, in a measure, subject to indirect psychic influence and control, through the avenue of the oxygen supply, as well as by the direct nervous and indirect secretory influences noted in the chapter on nutrition and metabolism.

THE CARBON DIOXID OUTPUT

The deep and natural breathing of the joyous livers of the faith life greatly increases the output of carbon dioxid (CO_2) in the expired air. In contrast with this desirable state of affairs, fear and depression never fail to decrease the amount of carbon dioxid in the air which comes from the lungs. It is evident that mental depression and its consequent deficient breathing, are directly responsible for the harmful accumulation of these poisonous and undesirable gases in the system.

Here again, we come in contact with that "vicious circle" of disease causes. The fear state of mind lessens breathing and thereby favors an undue accumulation of poisonous respiratory gases in the blood and tissues. These gaseous poisons circulating in the blood serve still further to depress the mind and discourage the superficial and shallow breather. This is a simple illustration of how a small and insignificant cause, primarily either mental or physical, can multiply and grow until the entire organism is profoundly affected.

THE CHEST-DEVELOPMENT

Good cheer and optimism help in the development of the chest. Men of courage and women of faith, as a rule, possess strong, robust, and well-developed chests. Their lung capacity is usually above the average. The unfortunate and melancholic victims of fear, grief, and worry almost invariably suffer from a depression of the chest as well as a depression of spirits.

There is a direct relationship between the mental state and the carriage and posture of the physical body. The soul that is constantly bowed down in mind is also frequently bowed down in body. The man who lacks mental and moral backbone is usually deficient in physical backbone. The one who so readily stoops down mentally before obstacles and difficulties, as a general rule, also stoops over physically as he moves along in the daily walks of life.

Watch the living stream of humanity as it surges along the crowded city thoroughfare. The physical courage, the gait, and the chest expansion, tell with almost unerring accuracy the story of success, courage, achievement, and the mental states of the various individuals composing the vast throng.

The well-developed chest of the man of faith constitutes a great safeguard against tuberculosis, while the shallow and hollow chest of the deficient breather and the downcast worrier constitutes an ever-present predisposition to consumption. There is now no doubt in the minds of physicians who make a specialty of tuberculosis, that a depressed mental state is not infrequently a leading factor in predisposing people of low vital resistance to tuberculosis and other infections. While it is proverbially true that those smitten with tuberculosis are optimistic and hopeful as to the outcome of their disease, it is an oft observed fact that many of these sufferers were aforetime victims of long-standing mental depression, grief, and worry.

LUNG STRENGTH AND CAPACITY

There are two important tests which may be applied to the lungs; one to ascertain the lung strength, the other to disclose the lung capacity. Faith and fear indirectly influence both the strength and capacity of the lungs, by their power to modify the depth of breathing, and consequently to control the development of the chest. We have long observed that when our patients are improving, as they become more cheerful and hopeful, their lung tests begin to show an increase in capacity. We have observed patients within one month's time, as a result of increased courage and an improved feeling of general well-being, increase their lung capacity from 15 to 20 per cent.

We have in mind a certain patient who had long believed herself to be suffering from an incurable disease. She was very much depressed and discouraged. The best lung capacity test we could get in her case was in the neighborhood of 150 cubic inches. Thirty days after she fully accepted the idea that she would get well — after she had become enthusiastic in the mental and physical cultivation of health — she registered a lung capacity of 215 cubic inches. This great gain in capacity was not equal, however, to her remarkable gain in lung strength. In her state of despair and discouragement, she was able to register but one pound of mercury in the test of her blowing power, whereas, after her mental rejuvenation, she registered a blowing strength equal to two pounds of mercury, an increase of 100 per cent in expiratory power.

It thus appears that hollow chest and stoop shoulders may result from mental discouragement as well as from physical depression; either of which seems to be able to bring about that state of physical indifference and muscular weakness observed in nearly all cases of shallow breathing and weak chests, whether observed in young or old.

THE ACT OF BREATHING

When the mind is serene and the attention is not fixed on the process of breathing, respiration is carried on in a normal, natural, and rhythmic fashion. When faith dominates the intellect the breathing is strong; all the muscles of respiration participate in the act, the abdominal muscles as well as those of the chest. The cringing and fearful devotees of grief and worry unfailingly exhibit an unnatural and abnormal mode of breathing. These fearful ones are prone to employ chest or thoracic breathing to the neglect or exclusion of the abdominal or diaphragmatic element of natural respiration.

When a person stands erect, with the chest well expanded and the abdominal muscles tense, the conditions are present for the execution of the natural and proper act of breathing. But we never find such ideal conditions present in the case of those who fret and worry. This is the picture of the indomitable and energetic apostles of the faith life, the courageous and determined optimists.

A study of groups of despondent and nervous individuals

INFLUENCE OF MIND ON RESPIRATION

before and after their entrance upon various new ethical and religious beliefs serves to show that in almost every case the respiration function deepened and improved in exact proportion to the improvement in the mental state of the patient.

PSYCHIC COUGHING

It is a well-known fact that the mind can immediately and strongly influence those modified and special respiratory manifestations known as coughing and sneezing. A very large percentage of common, chronic, hawking coughs are largely perpetuated by the mental state, coupled with the force of habit. Fear-attention is certainly able to generate and maintain a formidable cough. The author has made a careful study of the psychic element in various coughs, and there can remain no doubt of the powerful influence and ability of the mind both to cause and cure certain forms of coughing.

The following experimental observation the author carried out a few years ago, among a large number of similar inquiries, for the purpose of ascertaining the effect of suggestion on a company of students with regard to the tendency to cough. The number of students present was one hundred and fifty. All were perfectly ignorant of the experiment. The large class-room was divided into four equal parts while an assistant made record of all the students who audibly coughed, in their respective sections. The author proceeded to deliver his regular lecture, and during the first thirty minutes only three students in the entire class were heard to cough. During the second period of thirty minutes — the last half of the talk — the lecturer regularly coughed every three to five minutes. His cough was sometimes quite violent, at other times moderate, and sometimes very slight. The wonderful influence of this "suggestive coughing" on the class was clearly shown by the following summary of tabulations of the four watchers who recorded the number of coughs heard throughout the lecture. (It should be remembered that only three coughs were recorded for the first half of the lecture, covering a period of thirty minutes.)

First 5 minutes, 11 coughs were heard; second 5 minutes, 15 coughs were heard; third 5 minutes, 19 coughs were heard;

fourth 5 minutes, 17 coughs were heard; fifth 5 minutes, 27 coughs were heard; sixth 5 minutes, 16 coughs were heard.

The foregoing observation is quite typical of a large number of similar experiments which were made. Audiences differ greatly in their degree of suggestibility. This same audience was tried at another time, but the coughing became so suddenly and markedly increased that several students discovered the experiment and spoiled the same by setting up an immediate and incessant hawking and coughing. The maximum response in such experiments was secured sometimes immediately, but not usually until the end of ten or fifteen minutes. In the case just cited the greatest response did not develop until the end of twenty minutes.

In another experiment the class (200 in number) was observed for fifteen minutes and five coughs were recorded. The next fifteen minutes was occupied with describing and explaining the experiment on the class of 150, the one just described. Neither the lecturer nor any other person engaged in suggestive coughing. The only suggestion to cough consisted in the fact that the discussion was concentrated on coughing — all the details of the former experiment were very carefully and fully depicted before the class, their attention was focussed on coughing, and in spite of the fact that they were listening to the narration of an actual experiment in suggestive coughing, the following tabulation serves to indicate that even the story of suggestion has no less power to produce results. The number of coughs heard were as follows:

First 5 minutes, 9 coughs were heard; second 5 minutes, 21 coughs were heard; third 5 minutes, 18 coughs were heard.

HABIT COUGH

The author was once called to see a man who had been coughing continuously for three and one-half hours. He was almost prostrated with exhaustion. During our examination a neighbor's child was run over by a passing automobile, and in the excitement which immediately followed, the patient had his mind so distracted that he forgot to cough. It was over half an hour before he discovered that he had fully recovered; whereupon, he at once began frantically and violently to cough;

but this half hour of freedom from his affliction was sufficient to prove to the patient himself that his mind had figured largely in producing the cough; and so, by summoning all his will-power, he began to control and suppress his coughing impulse, and made a speedy recovery.

There can be little doubt that many persons have the cough habit. Others have acquired a very disagreeable and nervous habit of invariably clearing the throat — a sort of hawking — before they begin to speak in public. We know of a patient who had been coughing more or less for three years. She became a Christian Scientist, lost all belief in coughing and the necessity therefor, and immediately got over her coughing. This was a case of "mental cough," and faith cured it. This resembles the case of another patient the author recently heard of, who was effectually cured of a chronic cough and pain in the side by becoming some sort of Oriental sun-worshipper.

There is no doubt that whooping-cough can even be made worse by fear and concentration of the attention. We know of at least one case of prolonged whooping-cough, which was effectually cured by a good thrashing. Of course, we know that all coughs are not psychic in origin; but even in those cases where the cause is wholly physical, it is not unlikely that the mind sooner or later comes to play a not inconsiderable part in its severity and persistency.

Sneezing is not so largely regulated and so easily influenced by the psychic state. While suggestion may have some power in this direction, the influences which are far more important and powerful are the stimulation of the eye, as by brilliant light, or the irritation of the nasal mucous membrane by any cause whatsoever. By will-power we can produce a cough, but not a sneeze. The emotions can produce a feeling of suffocation, by causing the sensation of a ball rising in the throat; and so the short and regular breathing of joy is in great contrast with the long-drawn sigh of relief following a breathless suspense.

YAWNING AND HICCUPPING

The mental state is equal to, or greater than, fatigue in its power to produce yawning. The tendency to yawn is greatly increased by suggestion; but hiccupping is not so easily produced or cured by suggestion. It is a common experiment for one to yawn repeatedly and audibly, especially during the course of the evening when in the presence of a small company of people, and in five minutes from one-half to three-fourths of the entire number will have begun to yawn. Merely to speak of it is usually sufficient to start the majority of those present off into a series of yawns. Yawning is highly contagious.

Mental depression accompanying all forms of fear, affects the respiratory function in a very noticeable manner, by producing the act commonly spoken of as "sighing." When worried, one's respiration is likely to grow weaker and weaker, until eventually the deficient breathing is made up by one long-drawn inspiration often called a "sigh of relief."

These minor modifications of the respiratory function are all highly controllable by the mental state, and serve further to emphasize the fact that the mind exerts a minute control and a profound influence over the entire process of breathing.

An evening party consisting of eleven persons was carefully observed from eight-fifteen until eight-thirty, and not a single person was seen to yawn. At eight-thirty the author began to yawn every two to four minutes. Not a word was said — the periodical yawning was simply kept up. In the fifteen minutes between eight-thirty and eight-forty-five these eleven persons actually yawned forty-three times.

ASTHMA AND HAY-FEVER

The mind is able greatly to influence both asthma and hay-fever, yet it should not for one moment be supposed that these diseases are purely mind disorders; they usually represent a real physical disturbance or nervous derangement, nevertheless, numerous cases are on record where both of them have been entirely cured or greatly relieved by suggestion. On the other hand, numerous attacks of asthma and hay-fever have undoubtedly been precipitated by false fears.

That suggestion can bring on an attack of hay-fever is clearly shown by the well-known case of the patient who had a serious attack of hay-fever whenever in the presence of a rose. An artificial, wax rose was concealed in her room, and immediately

INFLUENCE OF MIND ON RESPIRATION 195

on recognizing the presence of the much-dreaded flower, she at once went into a terrific asthmatic attack of hay-fever. The influence of the mind over the breathing under such circumstances is further shown by the experience of the asthmatic patient who awakened in his hotel room in the middle of the night, attacked with a fit of suffocation. He made an urgent appeal to his nurse to open wide the windows. The nurse in the excitement and in the darkness, replied that he was unable to open the window, whereupon the patient exclaimed, " Break the glass! break it!" Immediately the nurse seized a chair and sent it crashing through the glass of the supposed window, and instantly the patient began to breathe more easily, and subsequently remarked that he thought he would have smothered to death had the nurse not promptly broken the window. All went well until by the light of the early dawn it was discovered that the windows were all securely and tightly fastened down; the nurse had only broken the glass door of a large book-case.

A certain patient, for ten years, had never failed to have her first attack of hay-fever on a certain day of the month each year. A week or two before this time she met with a bad accident — broke her leg and several ribs. She was, of course, confined to bed and allowed no newspapers and few visitors. The calendar near her bed was an old one — one of the previous year, and it is interesting to record the fact that the asthmatic attack did not appear until the calendar indicated the proper day of the month, although that day was actually a day later. This experience so aroused the disdain of the patient that she ceased to have her annual attacks of hay-fever.

Hiccupping can frequently be stopped instantly by suddenly speaking to the patient, or by any other procedure calculated to attract the attention By practice certain persons have developed almost perfect voluntary control over the hiccups. In other cases fear, coupled with other causes, has permitted hiccupping to go on unchecked to a fatal termination.

THE RESPIRATORY CURVE

Last but not least, the direct influence of faith and fear on respiration is shown by the examination of the respiratory (plethysmographic) curve, the graphic record of breathing taken by means of the plethysmograph — an instrument which is strapped about the chest, and, by a system of levers, is made to record graphically on a smoked drum, the latitude of the breathing movements, both as to frequency and depth. This is shown in Figure 23, which serves to indicate the vital difference between the deep, buoyant breathing of faith, and the depressed and deficient respiration of fear.

THE NERVOUS MECHANISM OF BREATHING

There are two nerve centres for respiration, the one strictly a natural reflex in the medulla; the other more or less voluntary, and located in the cortex of the cerebrum. The afferent stimulus, in the form of the sensation of the need of air, coming up by the afferent fibres of the vagus nerve, leads to the regular and rhythmic muscular movements of inspiration, and then of expiration. Now let the habit of interfering with the return swing of the pendulum during expiration be contracted, especially in childhood, by prolonged coughing, as in whooping-cough, and there is danger that this bad habit of breathing may last for years, or for life, in the form of asthma. The act of coughing always occurs in expiration, thus interrupting the regular rhythm of expiration which normally so quickly follows inspiration. In asthma, the air enters easily in inspiration, but is retarded in expiration, so that this latter instead of being equal to inspiration, as in health, may be five times as long. Once the normal habits of breathing become deranged, the respiratory centre may be at the mercy of a great variety of different stimuli. Thus one form of asthma is called "cat asthma," because the mere entrance of a cat into the room will start the patient wheezing.

Fear undoubtedly depresses the respiration by diminishing the impulses passing down over the phrenic nerves to the diaphragm and over the intercostals to the other muscles of respiration.

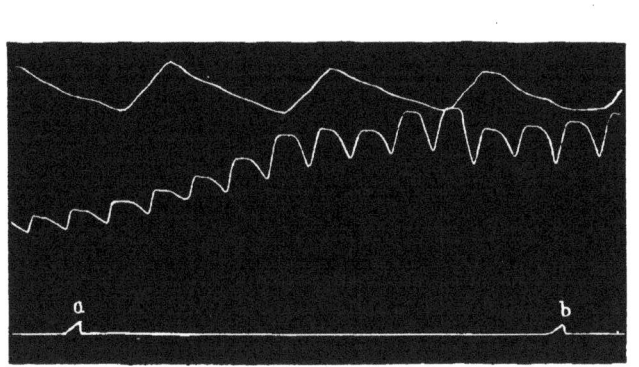

TRACING OF THE RESPIRATORY CURVE DURING AN
EXCITING HAPPY THOUGHT

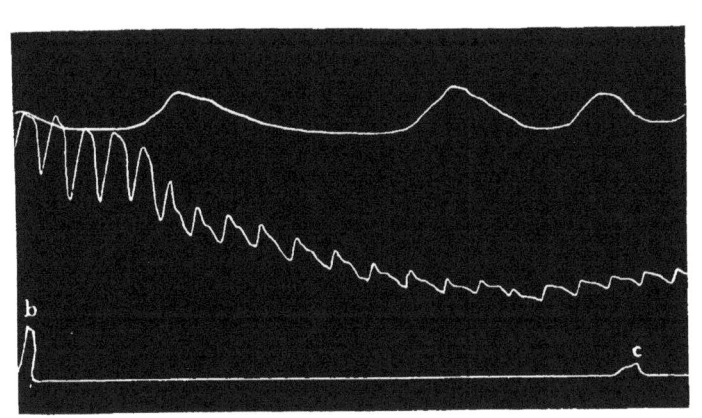

TRACING OF THE RESPIRATORY CURVE DURING A
SAD DEPRESSING THOUGHT

FIG. 23.   GRAPHIC TRACING OF THE
RESPIRATORY CURVE. (SCRIPTURE)

INFLUENCE OF MIND ON RESPIRATION 197

COMPARATIVE SUMMARY OF THE EFFECTS OF FAITH AND FEAR ON RESPIRATION

FAITH	FEAR
1. *Depth:* Breathing deep, regular, and slow.	1. *Depth:* Breathing shallow, quick, and irregular.
2. *Oxygen-intake:* Greatly increased.	2. *Oxygen-intake:* Greatly lessened.
3. *Carbon dioxid output:* Increased.	3. *Carbon dioxid output:* Decreased.
4. *The chest:* Well developed.	4. *The chest:* Flat and hollow.
5. *Strength:* Increased.	5. *Strength:* Decreased.
6. *Capacity:* Increased.	6. *Capacity:* Lessened.
7. *Breathing:* Normal, natural, and abdominal.	7. *Breathing:* Abnormal and unnatural. Thoracic.
8. *Coughing:* Relieved by inattention.	8. *Coughing:* Aggravated by suggestion.
9. *Yawning:* Can be produced by suggestion.	9. *Yawning:* The "sigh of relief" produced by depression.
10. *Hiccupping:* Relieved by attracting the attention.	10. *Hiccupping:* Rendered uncontrollable and even fatal.
11 *Respiratory curve:* Gradually increased.	11. *Respiratory curve:* Gradually decreased.
12. *Nerve control:* Strengthened.	12. *Nerve control:* Weakened.

CHAPTER XIX

HOW THE MENTAL STATE AFFECTS THE MUSCLES

MUSCULAR STRENGTH AND ENDURANCE.— MUSCULAR FATIGUE. — THE PHYSICAL GAIT AND CARRIAGE.— PSYCHIC MUSCULAR RESPONSE.— MUSCULAR SPASM.— MUSCULAR RELAXATION.— THE MUSCLES OF EXPRESSION.— CAPACITY FOR WORK.— MUSCULAR MOVEMENTS OF STOMACH AND INTESTINE.— MUSCULAR SENSATION.— ENTEROPTOSIS OR VISCERAL DISPLACEMENT.—COMPARATIVE SUMMARY OF THE EFFECTS OF FAITH AND FEAR ON THE MUSCLES.

THE human body is a vast and complicated system of muscular levers and bony fulcrums. All work is performed by means of muscular contraction, and all the muscles of both the voluntary and involuntary muscular systems are under the control of the mind — directly, through the cerebro-spinal system, and indirectly, through the sympathetic nervous system. The entire muscular system is absolutely dependent upon nerve impulse for the maintenance of its tone.

MUSCULAR STRENGTH AND ENDURANCE

Faith unfailingly increases the energy and endurance of the muscles. The courageous man can actually perform more work in a given time than can he whose mind is filled with doubts and despondency. Fear decreases the power of the muscular system to perform physical work; it diminishes muscular energy and lessens muscular endurance.

Confidence and courage are indispensable to the performance of gigantic muscular feats. Profound fear may even temporarily paralyze muscular action. Chronic fear or worry produces a relative paralysis of the entire muscular system. Fear and grief produce flabby, relaxed, and weakened muscles; while faith adds to the tone and strength of every muscle in the body.

MENTAL STATE AFFECTS THE MUSCLES 199

As a practical illustration of the enormous influence exercised by the mind on muscular strength, we will cite the following: A certain young man had long studied and worked to secure a position as private secretary to a prominent business man. After the receipt of two or three letters it began to look as if he would fail in securing the coveted position. He was downcast and depressed. During this period of discouragement he had his strength test taken — every group of muscles in the body was tested by means of a specially devised machine called the dynamometer. This test showed his total strength to be not quite 3,000 pounds. Three days after this test he received a telegram announcing his appointment as private secretary to the' gentleman in question. Of course, his joy knew no bounds, his delight was supreme, and another test of his muscular power gave a total strength of almost 5,000 pounds, an increase of considerably over 50 per cent in muscle strength — capacity for work. The first test was effected with considerable exertion and noticeable displeasure; while the second test was taken with keen pleasure and evident delight.

MUSCULAR FATIGUE

Careful laboratory tests respecting the psychic element in muscular fatigue go to show that the mental state has much to do in determining the degree of physical weariness which follows the performance of definite muscular tasks. Confidence and courage increase the "hand-squeeze" power; that is, when one squeezes with all his might on a little hand dynamometer, if the mind is dominated by faith one is able to register a strength test considerably higher than when one is controlled by doubts and depressive fears. Fear, both acute and chronic, is shown by repeated experiments, actually and definitely to decrease the "hand-squeeze" power.

Strength tests covering practically every group of muscles in the body have been made upon the same person when in different mental states. It is difficult to believe the results of some of these observations. A change in the mental state, as when receiving bad news or becoming suddenly frightened, is sufficient to decrease the showing of physical strength from 25 to 65 per cent. Single groups of muscles have, by fright, had their total strength decreased as much as 75 per cent.

It is a common experience for one to be able to tramp miles and miles over the country while out on a pleasure jaunt without experiencing a noticeable degree of muscular fatigue. This relative freedom from physical weariness is undoubtedly due to the fact that the mental state at such times is in perfect accord with the physical effort — such work partakes of the nature of play. If a corresponding amount of muscular work were performed under mental protest — without the complete and hearty coöperation of the mind, it would result in the production of not less than twice as much fatigue. Faith decreases the actual sense of fatigue following muscular effort; while fear directly increases the amount of fatigue following all physical work.

THE PHYSICAL GAIT AND CARRIAGE

The effect of mind on muscle is nowhere better shown than in the bodily carriage. The man of faith walks with a bold carriage and a confident step. The gait is elastic; the physical poise is energized; and the bodily movement indicates courage and self-confidence. This is the picture presented by a healthy person walking along the street, whose mind is in a natural and normal state — filled with faith and hope. In contrast with such a moving picture of muscular force and energy, let the reader recall the figure of some discouraged and disheartened man walking down the avenue. The carriage is weak and slovenly, the gait shuffling, and the step inelastic; the body is being fairly dragged along, every muscle weak and relaxed. The stamp of mental defeat has been transferred to the material body. The physical man reflects the picture of mental weakness, doubt, and defeat.

It is possible quite accurately to diagnose a man's mental state by merely observing his physical gait. Of course, it should be borne in mind that the physical condition or general feeling of well-being, also has much to do in determining the muscular tone and the gait. Many persons are addicted to a slovenly gait because they are run down physically — they are suffering from that ever-present "tired feeling." It is also true that such are usually suffering from mental discouragement and a general depression of spirits. Mental discour-

MENTAL STATE AFFECTS THE MUSCLES

agement, physical depression, and muscular weakness are the trio ever found associating themselves together in the same individual.

He who has a courageous mind exhibits a physical carriage that is both erect and vigorous, while the despondent and the despairing move through the world with a weak carriage, if they are not actually stoop-shouldered. One could almost judge of a man's success in life, at least, of his mental status, by the carriage and poise of his body. One of the essential elements in the treatment and cure of stoop shoulders and flat chest is to persuade their victims to cheer up and have confidence in their ability to achieve all-round success in life.

PSYCHIC MUSCULAR RESPONSE

The galvanometer used in the following experiment, is the mirror galvanometer of the D'Arsonval type. The mechanism is such that when an electric current of extremely slight intensity is passed through it, the mirror is deflected so as to reflect into the eyes of the observer successive marks on a scale which is in position before the mirror, and through an opening in which the observer can see the mirror.

The subject of the experiment was seated with his hands upon the poles of the galvanometer. The observer seated himself before the instrument. A third person suggested to the subject of the experiment words which were associated with pleasant situations and with unpleasant situations in turn, and also gave suggestions which were of a neutral order as far as pleasantness and unpleasantness were concerned. In every case in which the suggestions aroused feelings of pleasantness or unpleasantness, there was a deflection of the mirror in the galvanometer. The deflection was greater in proportion to the arousal of unpleasant feelings. In the case of the neutral words there was no deflection.

The same subject was tested furthermore with problems involving some intellectual activity of different degrees. In all those cases in which a considerable degree of intellectual activity was required, the deflection of the mirror was great. The less the intellectual activity required, the less the deflection. He was then tested with reference to the performance of muscular work. In those cases in which the muscular activity required a considerable effort and produced fatigue, as in the raising of the foot repeatedly from the floor to a height of five inches, the deflection of the mirror was great. In the case of less fatiguing exercises, the deflection was less. Habitual activities, whether muscular or mental, involve a less deflection of the mirror than do activities which are not habitual.

MUSCULAR SPASM

Fear, like certain poisonous toxins, is able to produce spasmodic contraction of the muscles — especially is the fear state of mind able to provoke spasm of the involuntary muscles of the blood vessels and the digestive system. These abnormal tendencies to involuntary muscular contraction are directly responsible for numerous cases of pale skins, cold feet, and other disagreeable functional disturbances.

Dubois tells of the case of two brothers who were bitten by a mad dog. One had to leave at once for America, and thought no more about it. Twenty years afterwards, when he returned to Europe he heard that his brother had died of hydrophobia, whereupon he was immediately taken sick, and died with all the symptoms of the same disease. False lockjaw and paralysis are induced in a similar manner.

MUSCULAR RELAXATION

While it is very desirable that the various groups of voluntary and involuntary muscles of the body should be energized during their periods of work, it is equally important that these muscles — particularly the voluntary muscles — should have proper periods of rest, seasons of perfect relaxation. Fear, worry, and other disturbances of the mental state are able to set in operation various influences which result in producing a condition of almost continuous muscular spasm. While all the muscles are influenced by emotional fear, only the voluntary muscles can be directly influenced by the will.

Such nervous and psychic high-strung individuals are constantly keyed up to the highest notch. They are strangers to the blessings and benefits of muscular and nervous relaxation. Such anxious intensity is disastrous to the general health; it results from fear and worry, and is effectually removed only by a restoration of the mental balance maintained by faith.

Faith, then, is able to tone up the muscles for work — to energize the machine for the successful performance of its physical tasks; and then to order and enforce that perfect and complete relaxation of the tired and worn-out muscle which is so essential to the restoration of muscular energy and the recuperation of physical strength.

An unfortunate woman who had suffered thirty-eight years with a hysterical contraction of the muscles of her hand, so tightly closing the fist that it could be opened only by employing great force, had her hand opened and her infirmity permanently cured, by an emotional and undoubting appeal before the shrine of a dead and departed saint.

THE MUSCLES OF EXPRESSION

All forms of fear and unhealthy emotion have a great influence on the muscles, especially of the face and hands. Expression, indeed, depends on contractions and relaxations of the facial muscles. Cheerfulness favorably excites all the museular system, and in its higher manifestations provokes laughter, dancing, jumping, and leaping; when more moderate, it causes the mouth and the eyes to become highly expressive of pleasure, the upper lips are elevated and the teeth are thus displayed. Joy brightens the eyes, expands the nostrils, raises the angles of the mouth, elevates the eyebrows, and energizes the vocal muscles, imparting a peculiar and characteristic expression to the voice — in fact, inspires the whole body to an expression of happiness and satisfaction. This salutary effect is no doubt partially due to an increased supply of blood to both the muscles and their controlling nerve centres. The heart is greatly accelerated, the oxygenation of the blood is increased, and the action of all the vital organs is stimulated.

Fear, when not sufficient absolutely to paralyze the muscles, generates a state of muscular panic, producing demoralized muscular action, as in the case of hasty flight. At other times the muscles are seized with spasm — fixed and contracted. The general effect of fear is that of crouching, caused by the contraction of the flexor muscles, in contradistinction to the effect of courage, which contracts the extensors, producing expansion and increased height. Trembling, palpitation, and pallor are experienced, sometimes equal to that which would accompany the actual evil feared.

CAPACITY FOR WORK

The state of the mind has a vast deal to do with the amount of muscular work which a person can perform in a given time. Faith increases the capacity for work, while fear greatly decreases the working capacity of the muscular system. The child engaged in joyful and gleeful play is able to perform an enormous amount of muscular work without complaining of a sense of fatigue. The same amount of muscular effort performed in the nature of routine work would have led the body to complain in no uncertain terms of weariness and fatigue. Good cheer increases the muscular efficiency.

A large percentage of our patients who habitually complain of great physical weariness following the slightest muscular exertion are victims of combined mental inertia and autointoxication, the latter resulting from chronic constipation. Let the mind become fired by some extraordinary exhibition — let the soul be swallowed up with some intense religious devotion, and see how quickly this old-time sense of muscular weakness and physical weariness entirely vanishes. Muscular strength is unfailingly increased in public and competitive exhibitions. It is also usually increased when the performance takes place in the presence of the opposite sex.

The author had a patient who had not done a good day's work for three and one-half years. He believed himself to be suffering from some insidious and incurable disease. He grew progressively weaker and finally took to his bed. No amount of medicine, treatment, or persuasion could induce him to shake off this lethargy and invalidism. Finally, there fell into his hands a book which contained the story of a case in many respects exactly like his own. The patient in the book cured himself by some method of practising deep breathing, focussing his mind on some object half a mile distant and repeating the words, "I can, I will, I am doing it now." It is needless to add that our patient got right up out of bed, dressed himself,

MENTAL STATE AFFECTS THE MUSCLES 205

walked around the block, went to work on the third day, and has ever since been an enthusiastic crank of this particular psychic fad or cult. But who can blame him? Both doctors and preachers failed to lead him out of his mental bondage, and it is little wonder that he seeks to make a cure-all system out of the thing that so wonderfully and marvellously led him out of the wilderness of depression and disease into the promised land of faith, health, and happiness.

MUSCULAR MOVEMENTS OF STOMACH AND INTESTINE

Faith favors a normal, strong, and continuous movement of the stomach muscle during digestion, while fear leads to weak and intermittent contractions of the stomach. X-ray observations upon animals that have had bismuth added to their food show that the mental state is very closely connected with the stomach and intestinal muscular movements. To worry a dog or pull a cat's tail immediately after it has eaten a meal is sufficient, temporarily, to paralyze the musculature of stomach and bowel — for the time being to stop all digestive muscular movements. In such cases it is from one-fourth to three-quarters of an hour before anything like normal muscular movements are resumed, unless special efforts are put forth to improve the mental state of the offended animal. We have previously noticed the mechanism whereby the mind is able to produce that peculiar and perverted action of the stomach concerned in vomiting.

As noted in the chapter on secretion, faith and the pleasant mental states increase and strengthen intestinal peristalsis. A healthy state of mind favors regular and rhythmic contractions of the intestinal muscles, while fear diminishes peristalsis and produces weak and irregular contractions. Thus we are reminded that constipation may often be caused by mental disturbance and nervous derangement. It is well-known that worry produces a sluggish bowel movement, while cheerfulness is an actual aid in the treatment of some forms of constipation. Of course, acute fright is able to stop absorption in the bowel and derange the circulation, and this may result in producing a transient diarrhœa. Acute fear is often exciting in its initial effects while subsequently depressing.

That the mental state is able greatly to influence the muscular action of the bowel is shown in the case of the patient who mistakingly took opium, supposing it to be a purgative. Notwithstanding the fact that opium· is an exceedingly constipating drug, in this particular case it produced the desired and expected laxative effect. The nervous system has power completely to reverse the muscular movement or peristalsis of the intestines. That this is possible, is shown in the case of the patient who had castor oil injected into the rectum, and then vomited it in fifteen minutes.

MUSCULAR SENSATION

It is well-known that concentration of the mind upon a muscle or a group of muscles is sometimes able to produce a muscular spasm, while mental relaxation has repeatedly proven itself able to cure muscular cramps and relieve muscular spasm. Pseudo-cholera has been induced by fright, due to sudden action of the intestinal muscles. Fear may excite one to a choking sensation as upon the receipt of bad news, while even false lockjaw is now known to come from fear and worry.

We knew of a patient, who, for years after seeing a baby choke to death was unable to swallow a mouthful of solid food owing to a spasmodic nervous muscular stricture of the gullet. By a process of psychic training this condition was finally removed and he was able once more to eat solid food.

The effect of the mind on the muscle is further shown by the common experiment of "muscle reading." One person conceals an object about the room, another is then led in from an adjoining room, blindfolded. The blindfolded one is allowed to place his hand upon that of the first person; and some are so expert in this experiment that they are able, in the majority of cases, to locate the hidden object. It is simply a matter of "muscle reading." As the object is neared, the person who concealed it unconsciously offers a slight muscular resistance, the pulse slightly quickens, and not infrequently the hand perspires a trifle; and in this way, by repeated manœuvres, the blindfolded one is able to reach the exact locality of the hidden object.

That the mental state still further influences the general

musculature is shown by the severity of the jar which one receives when he unexpectedly steps down an extra step. The mind and nervous system had not properly prepared the muscle for the jolt. The muscular control by the sympathetic system, and the marginal consciousness, in the case of the sleep-walker, are usually sufficient to prevent accident and bodily harm.

ENTEROPTOSIS, OR VISCERAL DISPLACEMENT

Mental debility invariably leads to muscular debility. The weakened mental attitude sooner or later produces weakness of the musculature. Thousands of people, especially women, are suffering from a prolapsus and general tumbling down of the internal organs of the abdomen and pelvis. In the vast majority of cases this is due to faulty clothing, deficient breathing, and weak abdominal muscles. Faith and fear, as' we have previously noted, are directly concerned in determining the type and depth of respiration. These mental attitudes are also greatly concerned in the maintenance of the normal and physiological attitude of the body, while walking, sitting, or resting.

Many chronic invalids suffering from misplacement of internal organs would be immensely benefited by acquiring a pleasant and vigorous mental state — a state of mind which would provoke deep breathing together with vigorous action and control of the abdominal muscles. It is almost impossible, by any scheme of exercises or massage, to improve these cases of abdominal prolapsus in the presence of a discouraged and despondent mental attitude. It is highly essential to have a nervous state which encourages the body to assume the physiological poise, and invigorates the muscles to natural and normal contraction.

COMPARATIVE SUMMARY OF THE EFFECTS OF FAITH AND FEAR ON THE MUSCLES

FAITH	FEAR
1. *Strength:* Energy and endurance increased.	1. *Strength:* Energy and endurance decreased.
2. *Fatigue:* Lessened.	2. *Fatigue:* Increased.
3. *"Hand-squeeze" power:* Greatly increased.	3. *"Hand-squeeze" power:* Greatly diminished.

FAITH	FEAR
4. *Gait:* Elastic step.	4. *Gait:* Dragging, slovenly.
5. *Carriage:* Erect and vigorous.	5. *Carriage:* Stooped and weak.
6. *Psychic response:* Galvanometer test shows slight deflection.	6. *Psychic response:* Galvanometer test shows great deflection.
7. *Spasm:* Lessens and prevents.	7. *Spasm:* Favors and increases.
8. *Relaxation:* Encourages.	8. *Relaxation:* Renders difficult.
9. *Expression:* Pleasant and agreeable.	9. *Expression:* Downcast and sorrowful.
10. *Work capacity:* Increased.	10. *Work capacity:* Decreased.
11. *Stomach movements:* Regular and continuous.	11. *Stomach movements:* Weak and intermittent.
12. *Intestinal movements:* Encourages peristalsis. Produces regular contractions.	12. *Intestinal movements:* Diminishes peristalsis. Contractions are irregular.
13. *Sensation:* Favors normal interpretation. Prevents cramps.	13. *Sensation:* Perverts and misinterprets.
14. *Enteroptosis:* Aids in preventing.	14. *Enteroptosis:* Assists in producing.

CHAPTER XX

THE INFLUENCE OF THE MIND ON THE SKIN AND THE HEAT-REGULATING MECHANISM

THE COMPLEXION.— THE SKIN CIRCULATION.— CUTANEOUS ACTIVITY.— LOCAL BLOOD SUPPLY.— THE SWEAT GLANDS.— ELECTRICAL-REACTION AREA.— NUTRITION OF THE SKIN.— CUTANEOUS SENSATION AND ERUPTIONS.— TEMPERATURE SENSE. — THE PROCESS OF HEAT-REGULATION.— SENSATION OF COLD. — CHILLS.— FEVER.— THERMO-ELECTRIC BODY TEMPERATURE. — COMPARATIVE SUMMARY OF THE EFFECTS OF FAITH AND FEAR ON THE SKIN AND THE HEAT-REGULATING MECHANISM.

A MAN of average size possesses about seventeen or eighteen square feet of skin, containing a vast network of small blood vessels which are capable of holding almost one-half of the total volume of blood circulating in the body. The activities of the skin, together with the circulation of the blood through its small vessels, are all under almost complete nervous control. The mind is able directly to influence practically all the functions and operations of the skin and the many glands, muscles, and blood vessels therein contained.

THE COMPLEXION

Faith, all other things equal, favors a normal, healthy, and ruddy complexion, while fear and worry predispose to a pale and anæmic appearance of the skin. The mental state, by its influence upon the nerves of nutrition and the circulation of the blood, is able very powerfully to influence the health and nutrition of the skin. Cheerfulness and happiness help much more toward beautifying the skin than the long-continued use of a multitude of cosmetics, skin foods, and complexion improvers. The bloom of health is seldom found on the cheek of the downcast and despondent. A beautiful complexion more frequently graces the joyous soul. There is a direct relation between the bloom of health and buoyancy of spirits.

A sound digestion, active bowels, good circulation, and cheerfulness are the secret and source of a fine complexion. Mental peace and moral satisfaction are reflected in the expression of the face — enhancing the personal beauty and indirectly improving the skin nutrition and the complexion. Again, faith is a great aid in promoting all those functional activities of stomach and bowel, upon which a good complexion is so dependent for its continued existence. "Cheer up and grow beautiful" is practical advice which contains more truth than poetry.

THE SKIN CIRCULATION

When the mental state is normal, provided the blood stream is not highly toxic, the circulation of the blood through the skin is usually normal and fairly vigorous. On examination, the natural skin is found to be supple, elastic, slightly oily, and warm. After fear has seized the mind and chronic worry has begun its deadly work, the cutaneous circulation begins gradually to diminish, the skin loses its natural elasticity, and soon becomes dry, leathery, and cold to the touch. The sufferer soon begins to experience chilly sensations and other abnormal skin feelings, due to deficient blood movement through the skin. Fear damages the health of the skin by its power to interfere with the nutritional nerves as well as by its power, spasmodically, to contract the small blood vessels, thereby greatly lessening the normal circulation of the blood through the cutaneous capillaries.

Thousands of pale-skinned and anæmic persons suffering from indigestion, headache, and habitually cold hands and feet, would be wonderfully and immediately helped if they could but discover the secret of happiness and the source of moral peace.

The skin circulation is a highly important item in the general health. When indigestion, bad temper, and a dozen other physical and temperamental disorders are laid at the door of "poor circulation," it should be remembered that many cases of so-called sluggish circulation are wholly or partially due to mental influences.

INFLUENCE OF MIND ON SKIN

CUTANEOUS ACTIVITY

When the mind and the nervous system are in that natural state characterized by good cheer and hopefulness, all the various functions of the skin are normal and active; the sense of touch or physical feeling, the action of the various glands, and, as will be noticed later, the heat-regulating mechanism of the skin, all carry on their work in a natural and normal manner. On the other hand, despondency and depression never fail to react unfavorably on the skin, lessening its healthy activities and rendering it more sluggish.

The skin is one of the important eliminative organs of the body. The psychic state, by its influence through the nerves and upon the circulation, is able very markedly to interfere with the normal process of elimination through the glands of the skin. Faith undoubtedly assists in skin elimination, while fear unquestionably hinders and hampers the process. As a result of deficient cutaneous elimination and its accompanying lack of circulation, it is proverbial that all anæmic and pale-skinned people are more or less prone to colds, headaches, and other minor maladies.

By interfering with the healthy activities of the skin, the fear mind is also able to lessen the prompt elimination of certain harmful poisons which are normally thrown out of the organism through the action of the pores of the external covering of the body. Deficient elimination of these special poisons results in their accumulation in the blood stream, thereby subjecting the brain to increased irritation as these harmful substances circulate through it. Thus we discover another of those " vicious circles " in which the mind deranges the body, and is in turn further disordered by the mischief of its own creating.

LOCAL BLOOD SUPPLY

In order to prevent internal congestion it is highly important that the skin should constantly be kept well supplied with blood. If the skin is allowed to become anæmic, some internal organ will certainly become proportionately congested. A tranquil mental state favors an even and equal distribution of blood throughout the skin and this results in producing warm hands and feet; while fear, by its power to produce spasmodic contraction of the blood vessels in the skin, greatly demoralizes the circulation, disturbing the equilibrium of the blood supply, and almost invariably producing cold hands and feet.

This peculiar power of the mind to disturb the local blood supply is most markedly illustrated by the common phenomenon of blushing. As the blood is moving through the capillaries imbedded in the skin of the face, the little arterioles are in a state of partial contraction, thus their muscular tone regulates and limits the amount of blood which they are able to hold at any given moment. Now, let the mind suddenly be overwhelmed with profound fear or surcharged with extreme anger; the nerves leading to the muscles in the walls of these small arteries (the vasoconstrictor nerves) are able to produce a sudden spasm of the capillaries, the blood flow is greatly lessened, and the sufferer is described as becoming "pale with fright," "white in the face," or "as white as a sheet." On the other hand, if instead of becoming unusually frightened, he is merely embarrassed or suddenly confused, another set of nerves is brought into play, which likewise are connected with the muscles of the small blood vessels, and known as the vasodilator nerves. They have power to interfere with — to inhibit — the contracting impulses of the vasoconstrictors, and their excitation accordingly results in a sudden relaxation and dilatation of the arterioles, which permits of a sudden inrush of the red blood, and this produces the phenomenon of blushing. Such embarrassed or baffled individuals are sometimes described as being "as red in the face as a beet."

The nerves and circulatory mechanism involved in blushing are further illustrated in the common phenomenon observed in gymnasiums when stripped athletes are engaged in strenuous competitive exercises. Just at the point of complete exhaustion, when the heart is under tremendous strain, the nervous system automatically opens the safety-valve, or floodgates, of the skin circulation, all the cutaneous blood vessels are immediately relaxed, and the entire skin surface is observed suddenly to blush, literally to glow with increased blood supply; and thus the heart is saved from over-dilatation as a result of this excessive muscular effort.

INFLUENCE OF MIND ON SKIN

THE SWEAT GLANDS

The cheerful mental state favors a healthy activity on the part of the sweat glands; the perspiration is normal, more or less unconscious, regularly and evenly poured out upon the skin surface. Mental disturbances of any sort interfere with the normal action of the perspiratory function. Sudden fear produces a spasmodic action of the sweat glands, cold sweat appearing almost instantly, sometimes standing out like beads on certain parts of the body. This perspiration is cold merely because the skin is pale and blanched, relatively bloodless; and this permits the sweat glands to produce perspiration that is much below the normal temperature. While sudden fear produces this phenomenon, chronic fear or worry has a tendency continuously to check the action of the sweat glands, to diminish the perspiration. Persons in a healthy mental state perspire much more easily than do the victims of despair and despondency. When one is worried it is much more difficult to sweat freely, and therefore much more dangerous to exert oneself during the heated season.

Some physiologists maintain that the secretion of sweat and the behavior of the sweat glands may occur quite independently of the cutaneous circulation. It is claimed that the perspiratory activities are under direct contral of certain nerves which are able either to increase or diminish the output of the sweat glands. This would account for the immediate effects of the emotions on the sweating process, and also afford some explanation of the well-known fact that those who are subject to worry are also much more subject to heat prostration and sunstroke. It is certain that cheerful persons stand hot weather better than do the dissatisfied and the despondent.

ELECTRICAL-REACTION AREA

In recent years certain delicate and precise electrical contrivances have been perfected which are able to recognize and register the very minute electrical changes which are constantly taking place on the surface of the human body. When the larger part of the skin surface is exposed, and the mental state rapidly and markedly changed, it is observed that the electrical reaction of the body also changes. Such changes in the electrical state of the body can be detected and measured quite a distance from the body — even as far as nine or ten feet.

Under conditions of faith, courage, and optimism, it has been found that such electrical measurements are usually positive, while fear and depression seldom fail to register negative. It would appear that the body itself is able to generate some force — some kind of electricity — which can thus be measured and studied. It also seems reasonably certain that the mental state is able to modify or entirely change the generation and manifestation of this force; the natural and normal mental state registering a positive reaction, while a depressed and abnormal state of mind registers a negative reaction.

NUTRITION OF THE SKIN

There are many influences connected with the nutrition of the skin besides those of a mental nature, nevertheless, the mind exerts a great influence over the health of the skin. Severe attacks of boils have been directly traced to worry. While faith increases the circulation of the skin and favors a natural growth of hair, fear is directly to blame for many cases of baldness following nervous strain and worry.

The hair may be turned gray or white in a few hours as a result of profound fear or great anxiety. Many such cases are on record. The possibility of the hair turning gray over night has been doubted by some writers. The following case is from the author's own clinic: The patient, a boy eleven years old, was subject to attacks of great fear — sometimes over trivial circumstances. His mother was suddenly taken sick, removed to the hospital, and kept there for about two weeks. When the mother went to the hospital the boy's hair was apparently perfectly normal and natural in color. Upon her return from the hospital, his hair was decidedly gray. Shortly after this, when the lad was brought to the author's clinic, his hair had completely turned — every hair was gray, some decidedly white. The neighbors with whom the boy was left reported that while he grieved and worried over the absence of his mother, the change in the color of his hair occurred during a single night, after he had been badly frightened by the burning out of a motor on a crowded trolley car on which he chanced to be a passenger. This is at least one case in which the author is fully satisfied the hair was turned gray by fright and fear. Careful investigation corroborated the mother's story at every point. There was no opportunity in this case to be fooled by supposing a sick man to be turning gray just because he had been forced to discontinue his secret practice of dyeing his prematurely white locks.

CUTANEOUS SENSATION AND ERUPTIONS

While faith heightens the sensibilities of the skin, it does not render them oversensitive. Fear greatly demoralizes the skin sensations, sometimes rendering them so abnormal as to exhibit false sensations of pricking, burning, or itching. Even actual pain has been produced by purely psychic stimuli.

Certain patients are able to produce actual blisters, due wholly to mental influences. That serious disease, angioneurotic œdema, which so markedly affects the skin, is now known to be largely a disorder resulting from anxiety and worry. Papules sometimes quickly make their appearance after nervous excitation and mental disturbance. Blisters have been raised on the skin of nervous patients by merely applying a wet cloth or an adhesive plaster; at least in one case, by merely sticking on a postage stamp. Numerous skin diseases are observed to grow worse under the influence of mental strain and worry.

Whatever may be the influence of the mind in causing warts, it seems probable that the mental state has, in some cases, had much to do with their removal. If the mind has no power over these peculiar growths, it remains exceedingly difficult to account for the success of numerous silly and foolish methods of curing them.

Suggestion has produced skin eruptions, papules, local congestion, and even actual nose-bleed. The author once saw a nervous hysterical patient who could cause her skin to be literally covered with small eruptions within a very short time, and in like manner, could effect their disappearance on short order — all of which was evidently the work of the nervous system and the mental state.

Sometime ago the author undertook an elaborate series of

experiments for the purpose of ascertaining to just what extent healthy persons could, by continuous concentration and autosuggestion, influence the sensations and feelings of different parts of the body. It was found that persons differ widely in their ability to modify the skin sensation, but practically all are able profoundly to change the normal sensation of any part of the body on which the mind may be stiongly concentrated. In some cases complete or relative anæsthesia was produced; in others burning, itching, tingling, pricking, numbness, coldness, together with various nondescript feelings, such as crawling and creeping sensations.

TEMPERATURE SENSE

The sensations of heat and cold are entirely based on the reports furnished by the temperature nerves resident in the skin. When faith dominates the mind, the temperature sense of the skin carries on its work after the natural, normal fashion. Fear never fails to derange this important part of the heat-regulating mechanism. Fear and fright are able to produce actual goose-flesh appearance of the skin. Mental disturbances have been shown to be able wholly or partially to abolish the sensations of heat and cold. The appearance of goose-flesh from psychic stimuli constitutes ample proof of the direct power of the mind over involuntary or unstriped muscle. (See thermo-electric experiments in Chap. XXIII, page 246.)

THE PROCESS OF HEAT REGULATION

The human body is able to maintain a constantly uniform temperature between 98 degrees and 99 degrees F., because of a most wonderful combination of nervous and circulatory influences, known in physiology as the heat-regulating mechanism. There are probably few vital functions of the body that are so highly subject to nervous influences as this process of heat regulation.

Sensation of cold — chills. Faith and courage are actually able to lessen the sense of cold. The same temperature appears colder when the mind is discouraged and the spirits are depressed. A pleasant frame of mind decreases not only common chilly sensations, but is also able to prevent certain chills, or to lessen their severity. On the other hand, it is a well-known

INFLUENCE OF MIND ON SKIN 217

fact that acute fright is able to produce *bona fide* chills. When seized by profound fear, many persons will shake from head to foot. They are seized with a veritable paroxysm. That the mind is able greatly to modify the sensations of heat and cold is shown by the experience which nearly all of us have passed through: that of going up to a stove in some public place on a cold day, and after warming ourselves to a comfortable degree, making the discovery that there was no fire in the stove. The author has had this experience two or three times in the last few years, and it is quite difficult to explain just how cheap one feels on making the discovery that he has been thus tricked by his own imagination.

Fever. Faith and courage possess the power within certain limits to prevent and lessen fever, while fear undoubtedly is able both to produce and increase fever. We have seen numerous cases where the temperature was actually raised by nervous fear. Fever is but an unnatural production and retention of heat in the body, and can sometimes be equally produced by decreased heat elimination on the part of the skin.

The mind is not able to produce an abnormally high temperature, but may also produce a more or less sub-normal temperature. That this can be done is shown in the case of the man who discovered an old woman stealing his wood one night. The wood thief on being detected proceeded to denounce the man in no uncertain terms, and at last, and in the most dramatic fashion declared: "You will never be warm again. You will never be warm. You will freeze up. You will never be warm again as long as you live." And it is a matter of record, that from that moment this man went into a state of chronic chilliness, and although he lived for twenty years, practically all this time he spent under blankets trying to keep warm.

Thermo-electric body temperature. This test is made by means of delicate electrical machinery which is very sensitive even to very slight changes in the temperature of the body. When the mind is free and easy it is found to be normal or negative. When the mind is filled with worry or fear, when even the attention is vigorously concentrated, this device shows a positive increase in temperature. When our courage is good and our spirits are high we feel the cold of exposure much less. Discouragement unfailingly increases the suffering and hardship of long-continued exposure to cold. One is much more likely to chill from exposure when he is out of sorts and worried. After a day of more or less mental activity all fever patients exhibit a decided rise of temperature. Visiting seldom fails to increase the fever in such patients.

Among the subjects employed for a series of experiments was a young woman who could voluntarily raise her temperature a degree or a degree and a half by simply making up her mind so to do and at the same time slightly stiffening her body. Her musculature became quite rigid, while her skin approached goose-flesh appearance — always pale and cool. It would thus appear that this woman was able to raise her temperature by increased heat production in the muscles, coupled with decreased heat elimination by way of the skin.

COMPARATIVE SUMMARY OF THE EFFECTS OF FAITH AND FEAR ON THE SKIN AND THE HEAT-REGULATING MECHANISM

FAITH	FEAR
1. *Complexion:* Ruddy, healthy, and natural.	1. *Complexion:* Pale and anæmic.
2. *Circulation:* Normal — warm.	2. *Circulation:* Poor — chilly.
3. *Activity:* Vigorous — normal.	3. *Activity:* Sluggish.
4. *Local blood supply:* Regular and even distribution. Warm hands and feet.	4. *Local blood supply:* Spasmodic and disturbed. Cold hands and feet.
5. *Perspiration:* Active and normal. Elimination increased.	5. *Perspiration:* Checked. Elimination decreased.
6. *Electrical-reaction area:* Positive at nine feet from the body.	6. *Electrical-reaction area:* Negative at nine feet from the body.
7. *Nutrition:* Increases. Promotes natural hair growth.	7. *Nutrition:* Lessens. Produces gray hair and baldness.
8. *Sensation:* Normal and acute. Prevents abnormal feeling.	8. *Sensation:* Abnormal. Produces itching and pain.
9. *Skin diseases:* Prevents, and aids in removing.	9. *Skin diseases:* Produces, and increases severity.

INFLUENCE OF MIND ON SKIN

FAITH	FEAR
10. *Temperature sense:* Natural and normal.	10. *Temperature sense:* Deranged. Goose-flesh.
11. *Sensation of cold:* Lessened.	11. *Sensation of cold:* Increased.
12. *Chills:* Lessened and prevented.	12. *Chills:* Produced by fright.
13. *Fever:* Prevented and lessened.	13. *Fever:* Produced and increased.
14. *Thermo-electric body temperature:* Negative (normal) when the mind is free and easy.	14. *Thermo-electric body temperature:* Shows increased temperature when the attention is concentrated.

CHAPTER XXI

THE EFFECT OF THE MENTAL STATE UPON THE PHYSICAL BRAIN

THE BRAIN CIRCULATION.— BRAIN ACTION.— BRAIN REST.— BRAIN FATIGUE.— BRAIN ENERGY.— BRAIN STRENGTH.— BRAIN ENDURANCE.— HYPOCHONDRIA.— APOPLEXY AND BRAIN DISEASES.— COMPARATIVE SUMMARY OF THE EFFECTS OF FAITH AND FEAR ON THE BRAIN.

THE brain is a physical organ — the special instrument of the mind — and, as would be expected, its physical condition is largely under the control of the mental state. Here again we meet another of those "vicious circles," so often encountered in the study of the interactions and reactions between psychology and physiology. The mind is able to disturb the physical state and functional behavior of the brain, and in turn the mind itself is disordered and diseased as the result of these various disturbances of brain function.

THE BRAIN CIRCULATION

The maintenance of a natural, tranquil mental state is the chief factor in promoting a normal flow of blood through the vessels of the brain. Faith favors a healthy and regular circulation throughout the entire brain. Fear, on the other hand, predisposes to cerebral congestions and headaches; while chronic worry may so congest the brain and so disorder its circulation as to lead to actual insomnia.

Too little blood in the brain may interfere with intellectual activity, while active congestion with its increased flow of blood through the vessels, as in the early stages of alcoholic intoxication, greatly excites certain brain centres, such as the talking centre. On the other hand, it should be remembered that chronic congestion — long-continued engorgement of the

EFFECT OF MENTAL STATE ON BRAIN

blood vessels of the brain — results in depressing the mental activities, disordering the mind, producing abnormal sensations ranging from a sense of "fulness" up to severe and distressing headaches.

The proper working of the intellect is largely dependent on the maintenance of a well-balanced circulation through the brain; and this in turn is dependent not only on certain physical conditions, but also on the state of the mind, which has been shown to exert such a tremendous influence over the circulation of the blood in other vital organs of the body. If the circulation is poor and sluggish and the hands and feet are cold, the brain is one of the first organs to be likely to suffer from congestion.

In case of chronic worry the blood-pressure is greatly raised and the increased force of the blood circulating through the small arteries of the brain exerts a powerful influence toward hardening these arteries, and in this way the foundation is laid for their rupture later in life — apoplexy and its consequent paralysis. On the other hand, mental influences which are able to diminish the cerebral blood supply by fluctuations in the brain circulation, are capable of working untold mischief. It should be remembered that one-fifth of the total blood volume goes to the brain. Cheerfulness dilates and flushes the blood vessels of the cortex of the brain and so stimulates mental action.

BRAIN ACTION

Faith promotes those physical conditions of the brain which lend themselves to clear and decisive mental action, while fear reacts on both brain and mind, to the disorder of one and the confusion of the other. Worry invariably beclouds the mental activities and renders the brain action more or less sluggish. The mental activities of the modern civilized races have become increasingly intense. To-day, men and women whose brains act promptly and decisively are at a premium. The care-free and the joyous are able to do a vast amount of taxing brain work, experiencing but little mental fatigue; whereas the victims of grief and worry find themselves on the verge of brain-fag after engaging in the most ordinary mental activities.

Common, everyday experience demonstrates that both the

general physical health and the general state of the mind are largely concerned in determining the amount of profitable brain work which a given person can safely and satisfactorily perform. The physical brain seems to be able to execute a phenomenal amount of work when its taskmaster, the mind, presides over it in the beneficent and optimistic moods of faith and joy; whereas it quickly rebels and is soon fatigued when its mental master rules it in the pessimistic role of fear, grief, and despondency.

We once had a patient whose mind had almost come to a standstill; brain action was far below par. This woman had worried and fretted for years; her memory was very poor, and she was rapidly losing interest in life. She came to the office one day thoroughly startled. Every remaining mental power was aroused — she had been seized with suicidal thoughts. At last she was aware of the ruin which worry had wrought, and she nobly rallied her every force of mental and moral resistance to fight and overthrow her mental enemies — worry, grief, and despondency. Within three months she had gained almost a complete victory. Her mental powers practically were restored to their old-time vigor, her memory was wonderfully strengthened, and her intellectual acumen marvellously improved.

BRAIN REST

In every way faith permits and favors sound and refreshing sleep, while fear and worry are responsible for that type of unnatural and disturbed rest which is almost invariably associated with mental depression. Grief and anxiety are able so greatly to disturb the circulation and other physical conditions in the brain as temporarily to drive away the ability to sleep. Not only is a disturbed state of the intellect responsible for insufficient brain rest at night, but it also prevents the proper rest and recuperation of the brain centres during the waking hours. Fear seems to dominate the mind with a tyrannical sway, overworking its every centre, and ultimately reducing the physical brain to a state of functional slavery, in which condition it is compelled to engage incessantly in useless and extravagant expenditure of energy, out of mere sympathy with the agitation and unrest of the worry-attitude of the mind.

Sleep is an antidote for work but not for worry. Both mind and body are able to work hard all day in legitimate physical and intellectual effort, and then one can retire at night confident of securing a period of natural, refreshing, and undisturbed rest, with the assurance of waking up in the morning completely refreshed in mind and body. It is not so with the victims of worry. They retire in the evening knowing that their night's rest will be more or less disturbed. The sleep is broken with dreams or nightmares. The body itself, during the night's rest, is more or less cramped and contracted. The sleep is in every way unnatural, unsound, and unrefreshing. They awake in the morning after having slept eight, nine, or even ten hours, with a feeling of utter bodily weakness and general physical lassitude. They actually feel as if they had been mentally tortured and physically suffocated throughout the whole night. Neither mind nor body feels fit to begin anew its work. And it is because of this common experience on the part of the victims of fear and worry that we reiterate: Sleep is an antidote for work but not for worry.

BRAIN FATIGUE

The physical brain centres are wearied with work just as the muscles may be tired out by physical effort. We have previously shown that the action of the nerve centres is dependent on the quantity and the quality of the energy granules which are found in the cell bodies of the neurons. Fear undoubtedly possesses the power of prematurely discharging and extravagantly using up the energy reposed in these so-called energy granules. It has been conclusively shown that the victims of fear are invariably visited with premature nervous exhaustion and untimely mental fatigue. On the other hand, faith seems to be able to conserve these vital energies of the nerve centres. Faith is conducive to that mental state which permits of the even, natural, and normal expenditure of the forces contained in these energy centres.

Optimism is a natural conservator of nervous energy. Happiness is the secret of mental and nervous economy. The joyous soul can perform twice the mind and body work with but one-half the expenditure of mental and physical energy. Faith is able to operate the mental powers and the bodily machinery on less than one-half the fuel and energy that fear requires to effect the performance of the same intellectual and physical tasks.

The run-down, neurasthenic victims of brain-fag have usually been transgressors of the laws of mind as well as guilty of breaking the laws of matter. Mental dissipation as well as hygienic transgression usually precedes the breaking down of the nervous powers and the weakening of the mental forces. While vice and intemperance contribute their terrible influence to the devitalizing of the nervous powers, at the same time it must be recognized that many of the victims of "brain-storm" and brain-fag have brought themselves into these undesirable states largely by allowing the mind to be dominated by prolonged fear — chronic worry.

BRAIN ENERGY

Faith begets mental courage and energized brain action. Fear lessens both the mental action and the vigor and force of the brain centres. Faith almost invariably inspires one to find a way out of his difficulties. It contributes to business success, to the preservation of health, even to the regaining of lost health. Every man who has achieved success by his own efforts is a man of faith. Optimism is the capital stock of the men and women who do things. At his best the pessimist is merely a barnacle on the ship of civilization, as it moves on through the ocean of time.

The energy with which a student can pursue his studies, a business man solve his problems, or a professional man discharge his duties, is determined by the nature of the thought which dominates the mind. Faith and fear hold the secret of power and success in all matters which depend upon brain energy and mental endurance.

Several years ago the author met a young man who had long suffered from chronic nervous prostration — brain-fag. Medicine, various baths, and other treatment, as well as hypnotism, had all failed to help him; at least they had afforded no permanent relief. About this time he accidentally drifted into a revival meeting, became interested, was peculiarly impressed, convicted, and professed conversion. The following day he attended a special meeting of the recent converts, where he was strongly urged to begin immediate work for his fellow men. He joined the ranks of the volunteer Christian workers, lost sight of himself, and began earnest work for his old acquaintances. This patient so forgot himself and his old infirmities that in ten days he had become another person; his countenance and entire personality had been changed. He became cheerful, hopeful, courageous, and happy. It is needless to add that he was cured of his neurasthenia, and that he rapidly gained in flesh, regained his former mental powers, and developed an extraordinary degree of brain energy.

Some would, no doubt, assign some of these improvements to supernatural influences, and that such was the case the author would not undertake to deny; but that the physical benefits were largely due to getting his mind off himself and engaging in unselfish work for others, is strongly suggested by the experience of another young man in a similar forlorn state. This youth about the same time became an ardent socialist — so devoted to his new cause that he delivered speeches on the street corners. It is interesting to record that he also quickly regained his mental energy, outgrew his nervous infirmities, and blossomed out into robust health.

BRAIN STRENGTH

Determination and perseverance are the watchwords of those who live the faith life. Vacillation and weakness characterize the victims of fear. Faith gives birth to that courage which enables one to surmount his obstacles and overcome his difficulties. Fear compels its victims to surrender in confusion and shamefacedly accept defeat.

Faith inspires the invalid to health cultivation, and cheers on the sufferer until the physical battles are won and health is regained. Fear increases the physical sufferings, prolongs bodily disease, and ultimately leads to health despair. Faith is a prophylactic against mental tension, nervous breakdown, and insanity; while fear is an actual cause of nervous collapse, mental insufficiency, and, in many instances, lunacy. Fear unfailingly leads the way to failure, defeat, and mental collapse, and ends in despair of overcoming obstacles or regaining the lost blessings of prosperity and health.

The cortex or outer portions of the brain, which are so largely concerned in originating the controlling impulses that are sent out over the nervous system, seem to possess the power actually to lessen or even inhibit pain and other sensations in various parts of the body. It has been fully demonstrated that the mind possesses the power to stop pain. Neuralgia has been cured by determined and persistent mental effort. A common illustration of the power of the mind to modify pain is shown in the case of the victim of a distressing toothache, who, as he approaches the dentist's office, suddenly discovers the toothache growing less; in fact, the ache has so nearly disappeared that he decides not to have the tooth pulled — at least not that day.

BRAIN ENDURANCE

The brain and nervous system are able to endure enormous stress and successfully stand tremendous strain, when the mind is dominated by faith. Joy strengthens the mind to the performance of unusual feats; on the other hand, fear demoralizes the brain powers, rendering them insufficient and incapable of standing continuous strain and performing extraordinary tasks. Fear is able so to disorganize the mental powers and brain centres as to result in the production of delusions, hallucinations, and other serious mental disturbances.

Strong-minded people are usually optimistic. Weak-minded people, as a rule, are pessimistic, and *vice versa*. Faith makes it possible to perform intellectual work with a maximum of mental endurance and a minimum amount of brain fatigue. Fear so shackles its victims that they are able to enjoy but a minimum of mental endurance, while they experience a maximum of nervous fatigue and brain-fag.

HYPOCHONDRIA

Hypochondria is a peculiar disease, or rather a state of mind and brain, which owes its existence largely to fear. Faith enables us to take a normal view of life and to have a natural outlook on the future. Fear is suspicious of the present and distrustful of the future. Its victims are unfailingly apprehensive of the future. Hypochondria is that disorder which the

EFFECT OF MENTAL STATE ON BRAIN

victims of worry have, when, not having any actual physical malady, they believe themselves to be suffering from some serious and insidious disease. In other words, hypochondria is a disease a man has when he is not actually physically sick, but mentally believes himself to be suffering from some grave, bodily disorder.

It is true, physical disturbances of the circulation or of the digestion are often contributory to hypochondria; in fact, most hypochondriacs are sick both in mind and body, but the mental state is usually the determining factor. Most hypochondriacs would speedily recover if they would but become confirmed optimists. Faith is the important remedy and the essential element in the cure of hypochondria. In this unfortunate and imaginary disease — none the less real and painful in its effects because it is imaginary — the entire brain seems to be disordered; and while every effort should be made toward the improvement of the bodily state, it is the author's experience that recovery seldom takes place until the fear life is abandoned for the joy and sunshine of the faith life.

APOPLEXY AND BRAIN DISEASES

As before noted, faith possesses an actual value in the line of preventing apoplexy and other brain disorders due to disturbances of the circulation and to high blood-pressure. Fear is an unvarying factor in producing or increasing the severity of nearly all brain diseases. From the common, everyday headache, which may result from the temporary disturbance of the cerebral circulation, to the production and growth of various brain tumors, the mental state must be recognized as a contributing factor in by far the majority of these disorders.

Fear is able not infrequently to counterfeit grave, physical diseases. It is now well-known that we may have fear hydrophobia. Nervous and hysterical persons who are bitten by dogs supposed to be mad are frequently attacked by false rabies. No doubt, in cases where the supposed mad dogs have been killed, many victims have died from this fictitious form of hydrophobia. Fear, by its distressing influence over the nervous system and the circulation, also exerts a powerful influence producing actual sunstroke.

Comparative Summary of the Effects of Faith and Fear on the Brain

FAITH	FEAR
1. *Circulation:* Normal and regular.	1. *Circulation:* Congestion, headache, and insomnia.
2. *Action:* Clear, decisive, and energetic.	2. *Action:* Confused and disordered.
3. *Rest:* Sleep sound and refreshing.	3. *Rest:* Sleep unnatural and disturbed.
4. *Fatigue:* Rests the mind.	4. *Fatigue:* Produces brain-fag.
5. *Energy:* Begets courage and action.	5. *Energy:* Lessens action and vigor.
6. *Strength:* Determination to regain and preserve health.	6. *Strength:* Ends in despondency and health despair.
7. *Endurance:* Strengthens the mind.	7. *Endurance:* Leads to deception and delusions.
8. *Hypochondria:* Prevents.	8. *Hypochondria:* Produces.
9. *Apoplexy:* Prevents.	9. *Apoplexy:* Favors.

CHAPTER XXII

THE EFFECT OF THE MIND AND THE EMOTIONS ON THE NERVOUS SYSTEM

NERVOUS CONTROL.— NERVOUS STRENGTH.— FAITH SUPERIOR TO VACATION.— NERVOUS ENERGY.— THE TROPHIC NERVES.— NERVOUS EQUILIBRIUM.— CONVULSIONS AND EPILEPSY.— NERVOUS PARALYSIS.— PSYCHIC CURES OF PARALYTICS.— THE SENSATION OF PAIN.— PAIN NOT WHOLLY SUBJECT TO MIND.— GENERAL NERVOUSNESS.— COMPARATIVE SUMMARY OF THE EFFECTS OF FAITH AND FEAR OF THE NERVOUS SYSTEM.

THE nervous system is the immediate servant of the mind, indeed, it is quite impossible to discuss mind and nervous system, the one separate and apart from the other. We cannot possibly present a picture of the influence of the mind over the nervous system as we have endeavored to detail the influence of the mind over the various other bodily organs and physical mechanisms. It was quite difficult clearly to show the effect of the mental state on the brain — the great centre and headquarters of the voluntary nervous system. It will be still more difficult to show the actual influence of the mind upon the physical mechanism of the nerves.

The rider and his horse as they dash by, present the spectacle of a single phenomenon, nevertheless, the rider is all the while controlling the action and directing the behavior of the horse; and so, while mind and nervous system in some respects present the picture of being a single influence or mechanism, they are, nevertheless, entirely separate and distinct. Mind and nerve sustain the same relation to each other that the rider does to his horse. The mind is the controlling power — the directing influence, presiding over the nervous system — using the nervous system as its messenger, as a means of directing, controlling, and influencing every part of the body, from the tiniest cell to the greatest vital organ, from the most minute secretory gland to the most magnificent and elaborate physical mechanism. It will therefore be the purpose of this chapter to point out how the respective states, faith and fear, are able to modify and influence the behavior of the nervous system in the performance of its customary work.

NERVOUS CONTROL

Faith increases the power of the mind to control the nervous system evenly and continuously. Self-possession steadies the nerves. Fear weakens the mind's control of the nervous system, unsteadies the nerves, and in some cases produces actual tremors. Many cases of so-called neurasthenia are entirely due to an unsettled and abnormal state of the intellect. If such patients could only focus their minds on something outside of themselves and busy their hands with some useful and agreeable work, they would almost immediately find themselves relieved of their distressing nervous affliction.

Embarrassment, mental frustration, and the teasing of children, all have a tendency to produce nervousness on the part of certain abnormal and neurotic persons. Chorea or St. Vitus's dance owes many of its nervous manifestations to the mental state; in fact, in the successful management of this distressing malady, it is usually necessary to remove the child from school and its social surroundings — to take it to the country where it will be free from mental embarrassment and nervous strain. On the other hand, there is observed a marked improvement in some choreic patients following an effort to strengthen their will-power and focus their control over muscular movements.

We recall the case of a young girl who, after remaining away from her friends one entire summer and autumn on a farm, showed but little improvement. The following spring she refused to return to the country. She said she was truly disgusted with herself; she wanted to try relaxation; and if that did not work, she would control her muscles even if she could n't relax. In three weeks' time this girl did more for herself by her own mental effort than had been done for her in six months of treatment and isolation. She was determined to control her

EFFECT OF MIND ON NERVOUS SYSTEM 231

muscles. She was possessed with the idea that she could do it, and she did do it. When we questioned her to ascertain whether she accomplished her purpose by relaxation or by concentration, she laughed and replied, "I am sure I don't know how I did it. I just did it, don't you see?"

It is not always necessary for us to know just how we do things. We are more or less ignorant of many common physiological functions and ordinary psychological processes which constantly take place in our bodies; but this one fact is well established, that faith and confidence steady the nerves — enable one more fully, completely, and accurately to direct all the voluntary functions and movements of the body.

NERVOUS STRENGTH

Sincere faith and optimistic trustfulness appear actually to strengthen the nerves. The mind probably exerts this favorable influence over the nerve centres by conserving the nervous energy and economizing the expenditure of the energy granules found in the neuron, as well as by lessening useless nerve impulses and decreasing unnecessary muscular movements. On the other hand, fear decreases the nervous strength. Anxiety and worry are among the leading causes of neurasthenia.

Humanity is afflicted with numerous nerve diseases and a host of nervous manifestations which are wholly and purely mental in origin. One would be quite safe in estimating that nine-tenths of our modern nervous disorders are either mental in nature or were psychic in origin. We should not make the mistake of thinking that these imaginary diseases are not real; they are unreal only in so far as they have no organic basis for their existence; they are very real in their ability to torture their victims and produce endless physical suffering and mental suspense.

When but a lad, the author knew of a neurasthenic neighbor who had for years carefully nursed his imaginary ailments to the point where he was scarcely able to walk about the yard; he could not carry five pounds of sugar three blocks — from the grocery to his own home. One day his house was discovered on fire. In the excitement which followed he entirely forgot himself, absolutely forgot that he was a weak and disabled neurasthenic. He ran upstairs. And after throwing several looking-glasses and the wash-bowl and pitcher out of the window, actually shouldered a monstrous black walnut clothes press, carried it downstairs single-handed and alone, and safely deposited the same in the middle of the street. In the next fifteen minutes he carried out more furniture than any three men. Of course, he was completely "done up" after the fire was over. It required three days for him to recuperate; but as he recalled his prodigious feats of muscular strength, and after the neighbors had laughed at him and joked about his marvellous performances, he was actually ashamed to return to his neurasthenic life. He got out of bed on the third day after the fire, and continued to improve from day to day, until within three months he was a well man, strong and hearty, without the slightest trace of neurasthenia.

Neurasthenia is a disease of manifold symptoms. The average text book on nervous diseases gives upward of fifty symptoms of neurasthenia. A careful analysis of these symptoms shows the majority to be purely functional, more than one-third are entirely psychical, while scarcely half a dozen symptoms are actually physical. The very manifestations of this disease are such as strongly to suggest that the disorder is largely psychic in origin.

FAITH SUPERIOR TO VACATION

But a few months ago I had a patient, a young man, whose nerves were all "going to pieces." Four weeks of treatment having helped him but little, he proposed to take a six months' vacation, and to this I agreed. All the while this young man was under treatment he was carrying some great burden on his mind. The last time he called at the office before starting on his vacation, as he was saying good-bye, I said, "There is just a word I want to say before you leave. I am impressed that you are carrying some extraordinary burden, something is worrying you. Now I want to be honest with you; I am fully satisfied that your vacation will do you little good unless you can change your state of mind. If there is anything you can do to help your mental state before going on the vacation, I beg of you to do it. If you are merely a victim of worry, cast it from you, otherwise I fear you will return to me at the end of your vacation in no way improved." My admonition brought a strange expression to his face; nevertheless, he bade me good-bye and disappeared, as I supposed, to go on his vacation.

Imagine our surprise the following day when he rushed into the office, all out of breath, exclaiming: "No vacation for me, I've found something better. I came to tell you I am a well man. That last talk of yours yesterday is what fixed me. That was worth a thousand dollars. You did me more good in two minutes than you have done by treating me for a month. I knew all the time a vacation would not do me any good, but just didn't have the nerve to straighten things up. After I left your office yesterday, I just went home and I began to clean everything up. I had five or six jobs to make right, but I did them all up square. Then I went up into the attic and I got right down on my knees and prayed like my mother used to pray; and I tell you, doctor, I am a well man, a new man. Look at my nerves this morning, aren't they steady? I tell you it is an awful thing to go around day after day with your conscience smiting you, and your mind all full of wrong-doing. Now the next time you get a chap like me, make a speech like that to begin with, and it will save you both a lot of trouble."

The young man continued to express his gratitude for the little part I had been able to play in his recovery, and I am glad to record that his mental rejuvenation was not transient, it resulted in permanent physical and psychic improvement. Of course, the patient saw no reason just then why this moral suggestion should not have been given to him the first time he consulted me, but it probably would not have worked at that time. The way had to be prepared, his confidence had to be gained, and it was also necessary to demonstrate to him that the best physical treatment was not able materially to help him, and then when the psychological moment came, it was possible to say the few words that resulted in his starting out on a campaign for his mental and moral deliverance.

NERVOUS ENERGY

Faith facilitates nervous recuperation and in a general way increases the nutrition of the nerves and nerve centres. When the mind is peaceful the nerve units are able to carry on their work with an expenditure of a minimum amount of energy. Fear is responsible for useless and wasteful nervous action; it squanders the nerve energy. Worry produces a sort of nerve starvation in consequence of the premature and extravagant expenditure of the energy granules contained in the body of the nerve cell.

The optimist, though he may be a veritable bundle of nerves, is able to carry on a vast amount of nervous activity without the slightest experience of a sense of fatigue. He is not constantly threatened with nervous prostration. The same amount of nerve work on the part of the pessimist would be almost sure to result in a nervous breakdown, more or less complete.

While fear and the other unhappy passions are able greatly to raise the blood-pressure, they invariably tend to decrease the nervous energy. Elevated pressure accompanies depression of spirits. High tension is the forerunner of low courage.

THE TROPHIC NERVES

The so-called trophic nerves are the nerves of nutrition. Their impulses have to do with cellular growth, nutrition, and reproduction. It is now generally accepted by physiologists that the mental states of fear and grief are able to inhibit and interfere with the nutritional impulses which normally pass over these nerves. On the other hand, it is believed that faith stimulates the trophic nerves of the body, and thereby contributes greatly to the improvement of nutrition and metabolism — to the strengthening of the body cells. It is thought that worry may contribute to the production of baldness by its influence on the trophic nerves. The mental state is no doubt at least a contributing factor in many cases of deficient hair. It has also been suggested that some cases of sudden grayness are due to the power of the mind to affect the trophic nerves. Metchnikoff has attributed sudden blanching of the hair to the general disorganization and irritation of the macrophages (the large white blood cells) which enter the hair at the roots and actually eat up the pigment — scrape off the paint and carry it away.

The profound influence of the mental state over the trophic nerves is further illustrated by the many authentic cases of

EFFECT OF MIND ON NERVOUS SYSTEM

religious fanatics who have long gazed on the crucifix at some renowned shrine, and, as a result, actual ulcers have appeared on the hands or feet at the very points pierced by the nails upon the crucifixion emblem.

NERVOUS EQUILIBRIUM

Faith and trust favor a maintenance of a well-balanced and perfectly coördinated nervous system, while fear tends to unbalance the nerves and not infrequently leads to hysteria. Confidence steadies the nerves, fear favors hysteria and nervous uncertainty. While joy may sometimes overexercise the nerves, when it occasionally mounts to ecstasy and psychic delirium, it can never accomplish the harm wrought by grief and sorrow in their terrible influence over the nervous equilibrium.

Hysteria, that protean malady which is able to impersonate wellnigh all diseases, serves to illustrate the direful consequences of disturbing the nervous equilibrium — the balance of power between the voluntary and involuntary nervous systems. The hysterical patient is able to simulate almost every known disease; skin eruptions may appear, phantom tumors may be present in the abdomen; serious disorders of heart and lungs may be manifested; the body may become rigid — cataleptic. Deformities may appear or the patient may have a fit varying in intensity from the slightest convulsion to a pseudo-epileptic attack. While insanity is a derangement of the central or intellectual consciousness, hysteria seems to be a disorder of the marginal consciousness — or rather a loss of coördination between the voluntary and involuntary nervous systems.

The tremendous influence of anxiety and suspense is well illustrated by the case of the nervous patient in a sanitarium. The management had endeavored to keep the rooms on either side vacant so as not to disturb him in the slightest manner. As the institution was filling up it became necessary to assign a new patient to one of the rooms adjoining this nervous individual. This patient was told that the one in the adjoining room was very irritable and nervous and was asked to be as quiet as possible. The new patient proceeded to undress and quite forgetting his uneasy neighbor, carelessly threw down one of his shoes on the floor; whereupon he remembered the nervous patient next door, so after removing the other shoe he very quietly laid it down. After he had finished undressing and had retired, he heard a vigorous pounding on the wall of the next room. Upon his acknowledging the rapping and asking what was wanted, his nervous neighbor shouted to him: "For God's sake, drop that other boot! I have been waiting ten minutes for it."

CONVULSIONS AND EPILEPSY

Fear, grief, and anger are sometimes able so to disturb the nervous system as to produce convulsions and other nervous attacks commonly called "fits." It is a well-known fact that faith and self-control are often able to prevent these attacks, and even to cure convulsions by their wonderful power to regulate nerve rhythm and maintain regular action of the nervous system. Fear demoralizes the flow of the nervous currents. Faith assists in maintaining a normal and natural movement of the neuricity currents throughout the nervous system.

There can be little question of the fact that fear is able to produce a form of epilepsy. There can be little doubt that worry and anxiety increase the frequency of epileptic attacks and that fear adds to the severity of many nervous disturbances. We once asked an epileptic patient at the clinic how long since he had his last attack. He started to reckon up the time when he suddenly remarked, "Doctor, I really don't like to think very much about when I had the last fit. Every time I get to thinking hard, tryin' to remember when I had the last one, I usually have another one." And true to his fear he did have another one right then and there. It is a common experience among epileptics that if they keep track of their seizures they are almost sure to have them with unerring accuracy, whereas, if they are heedless of the time they may go twice as long without having a fit.

NERVOUS PARALYSIS

Faith energizes and invigorates the nervous functions. Fear diminishes, retards, even paralyzes the nervous activities. Faith and determination have cured many a case of supposed genuine paralysis. Thousands of people are suffering from pseudo-paralysis; they were paralyzed at one time but have gotten well without knowing it. If such patients only would get it into their heads that they could walk, their paralysis would disappear on the spot. We knew of such a case several years ago, where an old lady who had lain in bed twelve years, supposedly paralyzed, announced one morning to her family she would like to be dressed. She thought she would get up and take a walk. They dressed her and then laughed and said, "Now, mother, let's see you get up and walk." Imagine their astonishment when she crawled right out of bed, walked across the room and to a chair in the adjoining room, and she has been able to walk ever since. Faith is able to cure these cases of pseudo-paralysis.

On the other hand, fear is responsible for numerous cases of paralysis and for perpetuating many others. Many of the physical functions of the body such as digestion, circulation, and breathing, are all the while partially paralyzed as the result of chronic fear — worry. If the mental powers could but effect their deliverance from the tyrant of pessimism, the vital functions would take on a new lease of life and would perform their work with that new energy and vigor which characterize the response of the body to the psychic touch of faith.

PSYCHIC CURES OF PARALYTICS

Paralysis of the legs has been cured by the terrorizing influence of thunder and lightning. An old lady who had been confined to her bed for fourteen years with supposed complete paralysis was one day left alone in the house. While all the family were absent the house caught fire. The building was at the edge of town and the flames did not attract attention. The paralytic patient shouted "Fire!" and called vociferously for help, but no help came. Finally, the flames broke through into her room, whereupon she simply crawled out of bed and made her exit through the window. Her paralysis was cured! From that day forward she walked with increasing strength and confidence. Prayer, suggestion, or any other faith-arousing procedure would have worked as well as the conflagration.

Paralysis has been cured by a patient sitting with a clinical thermometer in his mouth for one hour each day. The patient supposed it to be a new kind of treatment, and when it was discovered that he felt better after the application, he was required to come and hold the thermometer in his mouth daily for two weeks, and this treatment, unaided by any other method, resulted in rapidly curing his paralysis. Into my clinic, a few years ago, there came a colored man with some minor complaint; and, after placing a thermometer under his tongue, closing his lips with great care, asking him to breathe through his nose and keep his mouth closed, I left him seated in one corner of the room. In the meantime, I continued my lecture, and quite forgot about the patient. After some thirty minutes I chanced to glance about the room and discovered him sitting like a statue in the exact position I had left him. I immediately went over to him and, taking the thermometer out of his mouth, inquired, "Well, how are you feeling now?" Imagine my astonishment upon receiving this reply: "Well, professah, I did n't taste nothin' but I sho do feel better." This colored gentleman undoubtedly had never before seen a clinical thermometer, and, like the patient with the paralysis, supposed he had been receiving some new and mysterious mode of treatment. At any rate, after three applications of the thermometer on alternate days, he declared himself to be sufficiently improved to resume work at his old job.

THE SENSATION OF PAIN

Fear possesses the power of perverting, distorting, and even originating painful and other disagreeable sensations. Faith and joy are able to lessen, minimize, and, in many instances, actually to remove painful feelings and disagreeable sensations. The morbid mind is certainly able to originate pain. It should be remembered that the feeling or consciousness of pain takes place in the brain, while the physical sensation is referred out over the nerves to that portion of the body from which the nerves have reported those sensations which the mind recognized as painful. Thus pain is always referred to the origin of the nerve.

It is now a recognized fact in physiology and psychology that disorder of the brain and disturbances of the mind may set in operation impulses in the cortex of the brain which may be reflected outward over the nerves to some organ of the body giving rise to various abnormal and unnatural feelings, ranging

EFFECT OF MIND ON NERVOUS SYSTEM

from vague and indefinite sensations up to positive discomfort and actual pain.

That the mind is able to inhibit pain and thus relieve much suffering, is shown by repeated experiments in which plain distilled water, hypodermically injected into the arm of a suffering patient, has promptly relieved the pain. Some months ago I was called to see a patient who was suffering inordinately and who begged incessantly for morphine. On being warned by the patient's mother that she had been taking a considerable quantity of morphine of late, I decided that it was not best to administer this drug unless every other treatment failed to relieve her. Hot applications were used, but she acknowledged no relief; whereupon, I went into another room and prepared a hypodermic syringe, filling it with ordinary boiled water. This was injected into the patient's arm after the usual preparation, and she was assured that she would soon experience relief. In less than two minutes she had quieted down, ceased her moaning, and in less than fifteen minutes was sleeping peacefully. Such cases beyond the shadow of a doubt, demonstrate the power of psychic influences both to modify and obliterate pain.

PAIN NOT WHOLLY SUBJECT TO MIND

We would not infer that all pain can be relieved by the mind, but we would suggest that all pain can be made worse by mental influences. Human beings are compelled to endure a vast amount of pain which is in no wise psychic in origin. We have observed the most devout Christian Scientist writhing in agony. *Bona fide* pain is one of the greatest stumbling blocks in the way of the various new cults which deny the existence of matter and exalt mind. We cannot always remove pain by denying its existence; however, we can usually lessen its severity.

GENERAL NERVOUSNESS

Faith assists in the maintenance of temperamental calm. Fear generates constitutional panic. Unhappy people are generally nervous. The satisfied soul is usually composed and steady of nerve. The joyous soul sleeps soundly; the suspicious one is bothered with insomnia. Every nerve cell and nerve fibre are directly influenced by the state of one's mind. Those who fret and worry are always more or less nervous. The mind deranges first the voluntary nervous system and then the involuntary or sympathetic system. When the voluntary system is deranged we are rendered nervous during our waking moments, but when we disturb the sympathetic system we influence the vital functions both day and night; for it is this system that presides over all the activities of life.

It has been observed that the mental state is able to determine the amount of certain substances which are eliminated in the urine, and which are derived from the breaking down and wearing out of nervous tissues, such as the alkaline phosphates, lecithin, etc. Profound fear, great excitement, and unusual anxiety, always result in greatly increasing the quantity of these products of nervous activity in the urine.

COMPARATIVE SUMMARY OF THE EFFECTS OF FAITH AND FEAR ON THE NERVOUS SYSTEM

FAITH	FEAR
1. *Control:* Produces steady nerves.	1. *Control:* Causes nervousness and tremors.
2. *Strength:* Increases.	2. *Strength:* Decreased.
3. *Energy:* Recuperates and nourishes.	3. *Energy:* Produces nerve starvation.
4. *Nutrition:* Trophic nerves stimulated.	4. *Nutrition:* Trophic nerves inhibited.
5. *Equilibrium:* Keeps the nerves well balanced and co-ordinated.	5. *Equilibrium:* Leads to hysteria and unbalanced nerves.
6. *Convulsions:* Prevents. Favors regular action.	6. *Convulsions:* Favors. May produce "fits."
7. *Epilepsy:* Aids in preventing. Maintains healthy nerve current.	7. *Epilepsy:* May cause certain forms. Increases severity of others.
8. *Paralysis:* Cures pseudo-paralysis and similar conditions.	8. *Paralysis:* Causes partial paralysis and loss of function.
9. *Pain:* Lessens, relieves, and cures.	9. *Pain:* Causes, aggravates, and perpetuates.
10. *General nervousness:* Prevents.	10. *General nervousness:* Produces.

CHAPTER XXIII

THE INFLUENCE OF THE MENTAL STATE ON THE BEHAVIOR OF THE SPECIAL SENSES

THE SENSE OF TASTE.— THE SENSE OF SMELL.— THE SENSE OF HEARING.— THE SENSE OF SIGHT.— THE SENSE OF FEELING.— SPEECH AND EXPRESSION.— COMPARATIVE SUMMARY OF THE EFFECTS OF FAITH AND FEAR ON THE SPECIAL SENSES.— THE CONCLUSION OF THE WHOLE MATTER.

IN the previous chapter consideration was given to the influence of the mind upon the nervous system as a whole. This chapter is designed more particularly to discuss the influence of the emotions upon those highly differentiated mechanisms of the nervous system, commonly known as the "special senses." If psychic influence can largely determine the behavior of the special senses, it would appear that the mind possesses almost unlimited control over the ultimate formation of habits and the development of character. It must be recognized that both our moral temperament and our physical practices are formed out of the actions and reactions which are inaugurated by the stimulation of the various nervous processes included under the term, the "special senses."

THE SENSE OF TASTE

Faith and courage, confidence and calmness, never fail to increase one's hunger and sharpen the appetite. Good cheer creates a demand for food as well as satisfaction in partaking of the same. Fear, together with other morbid and sordid mental states, lessens the appetite, blunts the taste, depresses hunger, and sometimes completely abolishes the desire for food.

Taste is the monitor and appetite the regulator of metabolism. Bodily nutrition is largely under the control of the sense of taste. Whatever interferes with or destroys one's ability to appreciate keenly and enjoy highly the taste of his food, proportionately decreases the process of nutrition and demoralizes the metabolism of the body. Any influence which can increase one's ability to enjoy one's food and more highly to appreciate the pleasant flavors found therein, thereby promotes good digestion, encouraging assimilation and everything else connected with bodily nutrition.

When we think of a good dinner the mouth begins to water. Expectancy accentuates the sense of taste and increases one's ability to enjoy food. Faith actually adds to the gustatory capacity of the happy and healthy man. The sense of taste in the average person would be improved by good cheer, as well as by exercise and by discarding highly seasoned and unnatural foods.

Flaubert, the novelist, in describing how the creatures of his imagination came literally to possess him, said: "My imaginary people take hold of me and follow me, or rather, it is I who am in them. When I was writing the poisoning of Emma Bovary, I had so distinctly the taste of arsenic in my mouth, was so thoroughly poisoned myself, that I vomited my whole dinner." This experience of "fictitious taste" occurred while Flaubert was engaged in writing his famous novel, "Madam Bovary."

THE SENSE OF SMELL

A pleasant frame of mind undoubtedly enhances the sense of smell, while fear may so paralyze this special sense as greatly to decrease or entirely prevent one's ability to detect common odors. Not only does fear possess the power of crippling or inhibiting the sense of smell, but it is also actually able to create false odors; that is, to cause one to smell fictitious and imaginary odors.

We once had a patient whose cook accidentally allowed some kerosene to get into the food one day. This nervous and suspicious woman smelled and tasted the coal oil in the food; and for months thereafter, she seemed to detect the odor of kerosene in almost every article of food which was brought to the table; in fact, it required persistent and systematic training on her part to overcome this fear. She would often appeal to every member of the family to ascertain if any of them could not taste kerosene, and she would not eat the suspected food until all had assured her that they could detect not even the slightest odor of the coal oil.

Neurasthenic and hysteric patients not infrequently smell strange odors. These fictitious odors are sometimes pleasant and agreeable, but usually they are unpleasant. A patient, who had narrowly escaped losing her life in a burning building, continued for years afterwards to smell the odors of burning fabrics and wood. Others smell phosphorus, turpentine, various animal odors, etc.

An Eastern professor tested five hundred pupils in various schools with reference to the influence of suggestion upon the sense of smell. It was his plan first to discuss flowers and their characteristic perfumes. He would then ask the pupils if they thought they could detect the odor of a certain flower if it were in the schoolroom. He placed on the teacher's desk bottles bearing the labels of different perfumes and an atomizer filled with plain water. He next generously sprayed the water through the atomizer at several different places in the room. Each child was given a card upon which to write the name of the perfume which he thought he had smelled. Seventy-five per cent of these school children thought they had been able to smell some odor from the plain water that had been sprayed from the atomizer, and fifty-seven per cent were absolutely sure that they had detected some odor. In the first and second grades ninety per cent of the children were fooled in this manner, whereas, in the seventh and eighth grades only thirteen per cent were deceived.

THE SENSE OF HEARING

Self-confidence and moral peace never fail to render the hearing more acute. In fact, faith has cured many a case of hysteric deafness. It is 'a well-known fact that nervous people, whose minds are constantly in a state of agitation, are not able to appreciate good music as are those with a quiet and composed mental state.

Fear and worry, when long continued, are able to give origin to hallucinations. People so afflicted hear all sorts of strange sounds and hideous noises. Many of them are able to hear voices and receive commands. The early hallucinations of some forms of insanity serve indisputably to prove that the mind, under certain conditions, has power to originate auditory impressions which are referred outward to the organ of hearing. These abnormal impulses, the patient recognizes as literal sounds which have come to his ear from without. This goes to prove the fact that one's hearing a sound is not in itself evidence that the sound actually occurred; it merely signifies that the hearing centres of the brain have been aroused, and it is now known that these centres may be stimulated by influences arising within the brain and the mind, as well as by atmospheric vibrations which impinge upon the external apparatus of the ear.

Sounds of all sorts are heard as a result of irritation and disease of the auditory nerve, such as bands of music, the ringing of bells, and rushing water. This last is very likely due to the flow of blood in the arteries near-by. All these sounds would lead to erroneous conclusions were their causes not suspected and recognized by our reasoning powers. If we live near a boiler factory we soon cease to hear the noise, or if we reside in the city we soon fail to notice the cars and wagons in the street. The author used to lecture at a school near the elevated railroad, but after a few months he never heard the trains go by There appears to be in the mind some power of choice as to whether a hearing impulse shall be short-circuited or sent on up to the conscious centres of hearing.

THE SENSE OF SIGHT

Faith increases the ability to see and to see accurately. Fear distorts the vision and renders the sense of sight less reliable. Fear is also able to produce the well-known condition of hysteric blindness, while faith and determination are able to cure and entirely remove this troublesome ailment. Fear and its allied states are sometimes able to lead up to that point where delusions are developed. The sufferer sees things which have no real existence. He imagines strange people are dogging his steps, imaginary enemies are constantly on his trail. He thinks people on the street are making faces at him. Fictitious beings call to him and converse with him. The delusions of the insane are ample demonstration of the fact that the sense of sight, the power to create images, does not depend alone on the stim-

MENTAL STATE AND SPECIAL SENSES

ulation of the eye and the optic nerve. The ability to "see things" may also be set in operation by various influences resident in the mind or by some abnormal state of the seeing centre of the brain. On the other hand, faith and trust not infrequently prove themselves able to cure hysteric blindness and restore the patient to a state of normal vision. Faith is able to create new views of all nature — fully to restore the normal sense of sight.

We are indebted to Prof. Gault for the following experiments respecting the power of suggestion with reference to the sense of sight. The purpose of these experiments is to determine whether we can truthfully say that all persons are suggestible. In the first place, we have a series of experiments in which we determine the order of after images from white light. The subject is seated before a window covered with a black shade, in which there is an opening five inches square. Looking through this opening, he sees the clear sky beyond. After the eyes have been fixed upon the sky — impressed for twenty seconds by white light — they are covered with a heavy cushion of black velvet. Under such circumstances, normally, one should obtain after-images colored, first blue, second, green, third, red, fourth, violet, and then blue again, and so on until the images completely disappear. As soon as our subject has his eyes covered, the experimenter plies him with such questions as these: "Do you see the red?" "Is it red now?" "Have you got the red yet?" "Do you see orange?" "Tell me as soon as you see orange," and so on, the object being to find whether the subject will be made, by these suggestive questions, to reverse or alter in any way the normal course of after-images from white light. The subjects of the experiments had no experience in matters of this kind, and did not know the normal order. They did not know, therefore, what to expect in such tests. In every case the experimenter succeeded in altering more or less greatly the normal order. Thirty different subjects were tried.

THE SENSE OF FEELING

We have already considered the influence of the mind upon the temperature sense, and also, to some extent, the power of the mental state to influence and control pain. A pleasant frame of mind renders all the nervous sensations connected with the sense of feeling more normal and acute. Fear deranges the tactile sensibility, rendering the sensations unreliable, even to the point of creating false sensations of temperature or pain. While faith lessens the realization of pain, fear aggravates, increases, and promotes all painful sensations.

It is true that sudden fright — acute fear — may for a moment relieve pain. Unusual intellectual stress and strain may inhibit the sense of pain for the time being, but chronic fear usually renders all painful sensations more intense, and may in time prove itself able actually to originate painful impressions.

The same thirty subjects who were tested in the experiments for determining the power of the mind over the after-images of white light, were also experimented upon to determine their suggestibility in the face of thermal stimuli. An ordinary lighting current was passed through a bank of lamps and through a bare resistance coil. The operator was seated at one end of the table on which this apparatus rested. The subject of the experiment was seated at the side of the table facing the bank of lamps and the resistance coil, all of which were so close to him that when the lamps were lighted he could feel upon his face, the heat emanating therefrom. He was then asked to place the tips of his index and middle fingers of either hand upon the wire coil. The current was then introduced to the circuit. He was asked to let the operator know as soon as he felt a degree of warmth in the coil. Ten successive tests were made in which the current passed through the circuit as described above. A secret switch was inserted in the circuit by the operator's knee. By pressing it, the current could be shunted off from the wire coil, while it still passed through the bank of lamps, which were still able, therefore, to shed their warmth upon the face of the observer.

Now, in ten successive tests, the current was so shunted off while the observer had the tips of his fingers, as aforesaid, upon the wire coil, and he was asked again to let the operator know whether the coil in the successive tests was warm or not. Twenty-five out of thirty subjects reported warmth in the coil when there was actually no current present. Seven of the

MENTAL STATE AND SPECIAL SENSES 247

twenty-five reported warmth continuously, that is, in every one of the ten tests; the remainder reported warmth with greater or less unanimity.

Before these experiments began, the subjects were informed that the tests were to determine the lowest limit of the thermal sensation — this, merely to throw them off their guard. The results of these tests were compared with the tests of afterimages, and it was found that there was practically no relation between suggestibility in the one case and suggestibility in the other. That is to say, the subject who was highly suggestible to colored after-images from white light, might be or might not be highly suggestible when the stimulus is thermal on the basis of these experiments. Therefore, it seems probable that we cannot say broadly that one subject is suggestible and another is not. More accurately, we should say, perhaps, that one subject is suggestible to one kind of stimulus but not to another. There are specializations in suggestibility.

SPEECH AND EXPRESSION

Faith exerts a salutary influence upon the speech centres of the brain, very favorably influencing the ability to speak fluently; in fact, self-confidence, determination, and trust are essential parts of all systems of training designed to cure stuttering children or stammering adults. Fear cripples and paralyzes the talking-centres. Acute fright and chronic worry all contribute to stuttering, stammering, and backwardness of speech. Exalted faith has in many cases restored the speech when it has been lost from various causes.

After an attack of apoplexy the speech centres are often temporarily paralyzed. The ability to resume talking is not infrequently connected with some religious excitement or other experience when the entire mind is concentrated upon the one thought of regaining the speech. Faith dominates the mind and they are rewarded with a sudden and apparently miraculous restoration of their speech. On the other hand, fear possesses the power temporarily to destroy the ability to talk. It is a common experience to observe one who is dumb from acute fright.

In the chapter on the influence of the mind upon the muscles it was noted how the mental state influenced the muscles of expression. Faith makes for a youthful and healthful expression, while fear produces an unhappy and sordid look. Fear is a great beauty-destroyer. Faith creates a happy and optimistic countenance. A confident soul presents a joyful face and courageous features, while a fearing one shows a downcast and despondent countenance; its victims are always "down in the mouth." Some one has said: "Let no one aspire to make man beautiful without making him better."

COMPARATIVE SUMMARY OF THE EFFECTS OF FAITH AND FEAR ON THE SPECIAL SENSES

FAITH	FEAR
1. *Taste:* Increases, sharpens, and creates.	1. *Taste:* Prevents, blunts, and abolishes.
2. *Smell:* Increases normal function.	2. *Smell:* Decreases, prevents. May create false odors.
3. *Hearing:* Renders acute. May cure hysteric deafness.	3. *Hearing:* Produces hysteric deafness and hallucinations.
4. *Sight:* Enhances. Cures hysteric blindness and creates new views.	4. *Sight:* Distorts. Produces delusions and "fear blindness."
5. *Feeling:* Sensations and temperature normal. Rendered more acute.	5. *Feeling:* Renders sensations unreliable. Temperature-sensation false.
6. *Speech:* Makes fluent. Cures stuttering. Restores speech when lost.	6. *Speech:* Cripples and paralyzes. Produces stuttering and loss of speech.
7. *Expression:* Youthful and healthful.	7. *Expression:* Sordid and unhappy. A beauty-killer.
8. *The countenance:* Happy and optimistic, joyful and courageous.	8. *The countenance:* Downcast and despondent. "Down in the mouth."
9. *Pain:* Prevents, decreases, and relieves.	9. *Pain:* May originate painful sensations.

THE CONCLUSION OF THE WHOLE MATTER

We have now carefully traced the influence of faith and fear upon the heart, the blood vessels, circulation, respiration, secretions, digestion, muscles, skin, nervous system, brain, and the special senses. The entire matter can be briefly summarized as follows:

1. *All faith tendencies are toward mental happiness and physical health. All people, good or bad, get the physical rewards of faith, regardless of whether the objects of their faith and belief are true or false. Faith reacts favorably upon the body independent of the trueness of the object or the correctness of the thing believed. Faith is the natural, normal, and healthy state of mind for man. Faith is the state of mind that ever tends to make a man better, stronger, happier, and healthier.*

2. *Fear and all its tendencies are toward mental despair and physical disease. All people, good or bad, reap the physical rewards of fear, even though its basis may be entirely false. There is a reaction of despair and disease following all fear, doubt, and worry. The thing feared may be a hobgoblin or a phantom, but the effects of fear upon the body are, nevertheless, unfailingly deteriorating and disease-producing. Fear and worry are incompatible with mental peace and physical health. Deliverance from the thraldom of fear is essential to the mental, moral, and physical emancipation of the human race.*

PART III
THERAPEUTIC SECTION

PART III
THERAPEUTIC SECTION

CHAPTER XXIV

THE *DAWN* OF SCIENTIFIC HEALING

THE EMANCIPATION OF MEDICAL PRACTICE.— THERAPEUTIC EVOLUTION.— THE EVOLUTION OF MODERN PSYCHOLOGY.— THE SPIRITISTIC DELUGE.— THE SCOPE OF MODERN ▸ THERAPEUTICS.— MODERN METHODS OF INVESTIGATING DISEASE.— — THE NEW PSYCHIC TEACHING.— PSYCHOTHERAPY AND HYGIENE.— SUMMARY OF THE CHAPTER.

FOR ages the world has groped about in darkness and ignorance respecting the nature and cause of various physical diseases and numerous mental maladies. Not until the discovery of the microscope was the cause of many physical diseases revealed, and it is only recently that light has been shed upon the true nature of numerous psychic disturbances.

The dawn of the twentieth century witnessed the birth of modern medicine, the beginning of a new and scientific era in healing. The practice of medicine is undergoing a silent revolution. For centuries the treatment of disease was largely empiric, often thoroughly irrational. The therapeutic procedures of the present differ radically from those of the past. Future methods of treatment will undoubtedly become more and more simple, natural, precise, and scientific.

THE EMANCIPATION OF MEDICAL PRACTICE

The practice of medicine has long been shackled with superstition and handicapped with the ignorance and uncertainties of empiricism. In past ages the healing of disease was more of an art than a science. During the last century men of science began to apply precise tests and scientific methods to the practice of the healing art, and although medicine has not yet become a definite and exact science in all its departments, it is rapidly achieving this desired goal

The methods of medicine are rapidly changing, owing to the momentous scientific discoveries which succeed one another in rapid succession. Medical practice is at last breaking away from ancient delusions and sectarian prejudices. Physicians are dedicating their energies to the glorious work of preventing disease, while they put forth every effort to relieve sickness and mitigate suffering.

The present generation undoubtedly will witness the passing of the old medical authority — that absolute medical authority of the last generation, when the family physician was regarded with almost superstitious awe. His advice was looked upon as the acme of human wisdom. In many respects this loss of supreme confidence in the family medical adviser is to be deplored. But, on the other hand, this superstitious reverence of the doctor is incompatible with the modern increase in popular knowledge regarding scientific matters and hygienic practices. The minister has suffered the same decline in public prestige; and when the mills of justice are simplified and made more accessible to the people, the lawyer will no doubt undergo a similar depreciation. The decline of this old-time professional prestige means that the people have begun to deliver themselves from dogmatic influences, have begun to think for themselves, and this is bound to prove of great ultimate benefit to the race.

THERAPEUTIC EVOLUTION

The last century will probably go down in the history of the world as the era of promiscuous drugging. The doctors prescribed drugs in enormous quantities; the common people took the cue and liberally patronized the drug stores, annually swallowing thousands of gallons of patent medicines and other secret nostrums which undoubtedly contributed much toward undermining the health of the individual and deteriorating the civilized races.

When the drug mania was at its height, there arose a school of medicine known as homeopathy, whose doctrine demanded the giving of infinitesimal doses with almost infinite dilution, and strange to record, people seemed to get well just as quickly (some thought more quickly) under the influence of homeopathic medication, as they did under the regular allopathic drugging. This, of course, led the medical profession to examine more carefully into the effects of medicines and dosage, and pointed the way toward a universal reduction in the use and dose of drugs. The use of medicines by modern physicians is becoming more and more restricted and more and more precise. Drugs are now generally used only in certain diseases. They are administered to accomplish specific purposes, or to relieve certain well-defined symptoms.

What the homeopaths did in limiting the use of drugs, the hydropaths did in calling the attention of doctors to the wonderful possibilities connected with the intelligent and scientific use of hot and cold water. The electropaths came forward with the therapeutic uses of electricity. And again, more recently, the osteopaths, notwithstanding their extravagant and unwarranted claims, have performed a valuable missionary service, not at present fully recognized or appreciated, but nevertheless, valuable, by calling the attention of medical practitioners to the curative value of manipulation, massage, and vibration. And so all these sectarian faddists and therapeutic specialists have contributed to the evolution and expansion of modern medical practice.

During the transition stage of therapeutic procedures, it is not to be wondered at that extreme positions have been assumed. We must not expect to escape this transition fanaticism in passing from one regime to another. Let us hope that the practice of medicine has largely passed through this unsettled period, and that the practitioner of the future will be a broad-minded, wide-awake, and non-sectarian physician, using every known agency and method which science has demonstrated will prevent disease or aid in effecting its cure.

THE EVOLUTION OF MODERN PSYCHOLOGY

Until recently the medical profession has paid but little attention to the treatment of psychic disorders, unless they assumed the gravity of insanity or approached near-lunacy. Mental disturbances have been either ignored, relegated to quacks, psychic incompetents, and clairvoyants, or turned over to the ministrations of the theologians. But as the homeopath, the hydropath, and the osteopath, by the establishment of their special schools of therapeutics, were able so successfully to demonstrate the value of their methods as materially to change the practices of the so-called old school of medicine; so in the last generation there have arisen numerous psychic cults and healing "isms," chief of which is Christian Science, whose phenomenal success in relieving psychic distress and apparently curing many physical disorders, has compelled the medical profession to stop and consider — to recognize the colossal blunder of medicine, its continued ignoring of the tremendous possibilities centred in the mind as a preventive agent and a therapeutic power in the physician's work of dealing with the sufferings and afflictions of the human race.

And so we are now in the midst of the fanatical transition period in which psychotherapy and psychic "isms" are passing from the stage of superstition and empiricism, from the hands of the ignorant and the incompetent, into full recognition and appreciation on the part of men of science, to be successfully and scientifically applied by men of medicine.

The early hydropath made such unwarranted and extravagant claims for his water-cure that his methods were soon brought into disrepute in medical circles. Likewise the present-day psychopath makes unscientific and absurd claims for his new school of treatment. The physiological and psychological laboratories are slowly pointing out the false and establishing the true; and so, while psychotherapy may never become such an exact science as materia medica or hydrotherapy, the present generation undoubtedly will witness the further evolution of psychic teaching to that point where it will be rescued from the limbo of religious fanaticism and be permanently established upon a sound basis of scientific physiology and approved psychology

THE SPIRITISTIC DELUGE

Humanity in its philosophical teaching forever surges in generation cycles from one great extreme to another. The last century grew increasingly materialistic until, near its close, the world passed through an era of great scientific progress, accompanied by a very general reaction against the superstitious

THE DAWN OF SCIENTIFIC HEALING

theology and the empiric therapeutics of preceding generations. But the materialistic revolt was carried too far; rationalism was run to the ground, so that the close of the last century and the dawn of the present witnessed a new revolt against the materialistic teaching of medicine and the rationalistic dogmas of science.

The common people were suffering from moral starvation and spiritual inanition, and, when Mrs. Eddy and her kin unfurled their spiritistic banner and raised the battle cry of "All spirit and no matter," the famished people rallied to the standard of her teaching by tens of thousands, finding it more satisfying and cheering to believe the new doctrine of "all soul and no body" than to feed further upon the scientific husks and erroneous teaching of "all body and no soul."

The time has come for sensible men and women to look this proposition squarely in the face. Nothing is to be gained by scientists and men of medicine ridiculing and poking fun at Christian Science. As a profession, we are largely to blame for bringing this flood of spiritism upon the world. The more earnestly and actively we wage scientific warfare on these various healing "isms" and psychic deceptions, the more certainly and strongly will they become enthroned as a religion in the hearts of their advocates and devotees.

The physician and the minister can ridicule Christian Science and show its utter fallacy, but this will have but little influence on the patient whom they failed to help or cure, and who subsequently was cured under its influence and teaching. Let science and theology learn the lesson which Christian Science is designed to teach, that is, the power of mind over matter. Let rational psychotherapy become a part of the practice of medicine in the life of every physician; let moral therapeutics come into its own. Let every physician and surgeon recognize that he is ministering not only to a physical organism, but that he is also dealing with a marvellous mind. Let men of medicine come to recognize that man is a moral and spiritual being.

THE SCOPE OF MODERN THERAPEUTICS

We are now in the midst of a great revolution in therapeutics. The practice of medicine has gradually evolved until the physician of the present is coming to appreciate the importance of preventing disease, and, in case his efforts fail, of *treating the patient, and not simply the disease.* To-day, the doctor combats the causes of disease instead of merely suppressing its symptoms. The highest present conception of the work of the physician in his relation to the people may be summarized as follows:

1. *Prophylaxis, the prevention of disease.* The chief purpose and aim of all physicians, excepting those possibly who may be purely commercial, is to prevent disease — so effectually to inoculate the race with the principles of hygiene that the great world-plagues eventually will be driven from the face of the earth, while the host of chronic diseases due to erroneous mental habits and unwholesome physical practices will be gradually eliminated.

2. *Psychic therapy.* The proper treatment of mental disturbances ranging from fear and worry up to insanity, must become a part of the physician's work. The prevention of physical disorders by means of psychic control and the treatment of functional disturbances by the aid of the mental powers in coöperation with all other known methods of preventing and combating disease.

3. *Moral therapy.* The time has come for the physician not only to recognize the value of psychotherapy, not merely to accept "mind cure" in its ordinarily accepted meaning, but to espouse the cause of moral therapy, to recognize the moral nature of man, to accept the self-evident teaching that man is by nature a religious animal, and that the highest health of mind and body can hardly be attained without giving due and proper attention to the nutrition of the moral and spiritual natures.

4. *Physical therapy.* It is a cause for rejoicing to the author to witness the almost universal acceptance on the part of the medical world of those methods of treating disease commonly included under the term "physiologic therapeutics"; by which is meant the use of water, electricity, exercise, massage, vibration, diet, rest, light, heat, and fresh air. After all, the utilization of this group of natural agencies constitutes the most

THE DAWN OF SCIENTIFIC HEALING 259

useful and most powerful procedure known to modern therapeutics.

5. *Medicinal therapy.* Future generations will undoubtedly come to regard drugs as least in value of all the known methods of preventing and curing disease; nevertheless, there will always be a useful field for medicine. First, in preventing disease, the employment of antiseptics is of inestimable value in killing microbes, as illustrated in the use of ordinary gargles to destroy the microbes in incipient sore throat, as well as the germicidal substances employed to disinfect the stools of the typhoid patient. Second, in cases of specific medication, such as the use of quinine to destroy the parasites of malaria. No doubt, in the future, many other specific causes of disease will be discovered, in which the internal use of proper medicinal substances or appropriate serums will prove of great value, as in the case of antitoxin in diphtheria.

It is certainly unbecoming our good judgment to swing so radically from one great extreme to the other. Having detected the materialistic errors of the last century and having recognized the folly of exclusive and excessive drug medication, let us carefully study our principles and stay our judgment, and not make the absurd mistake of swinging over to such extremes that we deny, on the one hand, the existence of the material body, with its possibilities of disease and deformity; while, on the other hand, we repudiate the moral and spiritual nature of man. Let us not now swing the therapeutic pendulum so far to the other extreme that we shall become so fearful of medicine as to refuse to use soap on our hands because we discover it is a drug — sodium oleate — or discard common table salt because it, too, is a medicinal substance — sodium chloride.

MODERN METHODS OF INVESTIGATING DISEASE

We are warranted in entertaining the hope that we have largely passed through the day of empiric therapeutics and the irrational treatment of disease. Considerable forbearance should be shown toward the therapeutic blunders of the last century, owing to the fact that the doctors of that day were not in possession of so complete a knowledge of the nature and cause of disease as we are blessed with at present. While there are numerous diseases, notably cancer, which still baffle our profession and have so far withstood all efforts to discover their cause, nevertheless, one by one the important diseases which afflict the human race are yielding up their secrets to the persistent researches of the laboratory and the careful observations of the clinic. (See Fig. 24.) Each new discovery of the cause of disease points the way to the possible discovery of a cure.

In the development of the new methods of investigating and diagnosing disease, it was only natural that the physical or material disorders should receive first attention; and so, beginning with the discovery of the microscope, the study of the cells of the body, and the pathologic changes found in certain diseases has progressed steadily, until at the present time nearly all the serious chronic diseases which afflict the race can be diagnosed by the appearance of the diseased cells when viewed under the microscope.

And so, while it was but natural that the physical changes connected with the phenomena of disease should receive first attention, we are now in the midst of a great awakening respecting the importance of carefully studying and classifying the mental or psychic causes of disease. To-day, we stand on the brink of a new era — the dawn of modern scientific psychotherapy. And it is the author's purpose in the preparation of this volume to present the facts, the fundamental principles, to state our present knowledge concerning the development of this new science of mental healing.

THE NEW PSYCHIC TEACHING

Every new method of treating disease has been largely empirical in its early history, and not infrequently accompanied by much superstition and fanaticism. Almost without exception every new therapeutic discovery is heralded to the world as a cure-all. And this is not strange. If some disease that has heretofore resisted all efforts at treatment is partially or wholly relieved, it is not surprising that the newly discovered remedy should have its initial use enthusiastically published abroad.

And so it was with psychotherapy. Tens of thousands of

FIG. 24. A MODERN PHYSIOLOGICAL LABORATORY FOR INVESTIGATING DISEASE

FIG. 25. A MODERN PSYCHOLOGICAL LABORATORY FOR THE STUDY OF THE MIND

THE DAWN OF SCIENTIFIC HEALING 261

honest people were weighed down under a burden of sorrow and held in bondage by shackles of fear. They had patiently sought the aid of the doctor and his medicines on the one hand, they penitently attended the preacher and his theology on the other, all without avail. It is little wonder then when such an army of downcast, despondent, and heart-broken captives confined in the prison-house of fear, suddenly discovered the possibility of escaping from their prison, that they immediately and enthusiastically entered into the joys and privileges of their new-found mental freedom and moral peace; it is little wonder that they availed themselves of the opportunity and welcomed deliverance from their psychic sorrows and physical distress, in the teachings and consolations of the various mental cults and healing "isms," which have thrived and are now thriving in our midst.

How can we consistently blame our fellows for this landslide to the psychic teachers, when we gave them no relief or consolation? They repeatedly sought our help, but in vain. Should we chide them for clinging to the idol which has wrought their temporary deliverance, even though we know that idol to be a false god? Let us rather renovate the halls of science and rejuvenate the temples of religion; let us dig deep for the facts and search carefully for the gems of truth; let the true scientists of this century erect an altar to the *God of Truth;* let the philosophy of modern psychotherapy become so free from error and delusion as to beckon the materialist to come forward and accept the teaching which portrays the true relation between mind and matter; while, on the other hand, it beckons the spiritist to descend from the delusional clouds of mysticism and accept a gospel of mental healing which is amenable to scientific proof and acceptable to human reason.

And so the psychology of to-day, the psychotherapy of the present, is being investigated by methods of precision; it is being tested out in the laboratory and the clinic (See Fig. 25.), and the next few years will witness the formulation of a system of psychic teaching which will unite the intelligent minds of the world on all the essential features of the mental factor in medical practice.

No doubt, theological buccaneers will continue to seize upon the psychic factor in therapeutics and endeavor further to mystify it as a means of advancing sectarian religious propaganda. Homeopathy and osteopathy have certainly become a sort of religion with some people, for the same reasons, and in still a larger measure, psychic philosophy, better known by the names of Christian Science, Divine Healing, and New Thought, will undoubtedly continue to be vested with religious authority and dignified with theological sanctity for years to come; but notwithstanding all this, modern psychotherapy is destined to command the respect of thinking people, and eventually to stand separate and apart from all sectarian connections and fanatical religious teachings. Not that psychic teaching should not be associated with religious work — it should; but that sectarian religions, as such, shall not be confounded and confused with the natural psychic powers which exist independent of any and all sects, cults, "isms," and other special propaganda.

PSYCHOTHERAPY AND HYGIENE

In this volume, the author has endeavored to tell the truth about psychic influences and their relation to the body, but while we are thus seeking to present the facts in the case and do justice to a long-neglected subject, we would much regret it if our efforts should be misunderstood and misconstrued into meaning that psychotherapy or mind cure was regarded as an exclusive system of treating disease, as the sovereign remedy for all the ills to which human flesh is heir. In order to make this matter perfectly clear, it should be here stated that we regard psychotherapy as but a part of the great system of preventing, treating, and healing disease, and that its most successful employment is in connection with moral suggestion and in association with various forms of physical therapy.

It has been the author's experience that but few patients stand in need of exclusive psychotherapeutic treatment. Patients requiring psychic procedures are usually in need of moral encouragement on the one hand, and physical help on the other. We regard the following remedial procedures as highly useful, and most usually essential to the success of psychotherapeutic practice.

THE DAWN OF SCIENTIFIC HEALING

1. *Hydrotherapy.* The scientific application of hot and cold water — various baths, both hygienic and medical, by their power to influence the circulation, digestion, assimilation, and oxidation, are of marvellous healing value; while their use in numerous acute diseases is very gratifying, as in the control of fever. Baths may be administered so as to act as a stimulant in certain chronic diseases, while they may be so modified as to act as a sedative in numerous nervous conditions. The skilful use of water constitutes one of the most powerful remedial agencies which may be used to preserve health and combat disease.

2. *Thermotherapy.* Heat and cold in various forms, such as hot air baths, are exceedingly useful in many forms of acute and chronic disease.

3. *Phototherapy.* The use of sun baths or the employment of the electric light, more particularly the rays of the electric arclight, constitutes one of the most valuable and helpful methods of treating many common diseases.

4. *Electrotherapy.* Much that is connected with electrotherapeutic practice is largely psychotherapy in disguise, nevertheless, there are numerous applications of electricity which are of definite and positive value in the treatment of various diseases.

5. *Massotherapy.* Massage, embracing special and general manipulations and manual Swedish movements (so-called osteopathy) are all of value in treating certain diseases.

6. *Vibrotherapy.* All forms of mechanical vibration, oscillation, and treatment by mechanical devices, are of great value when suitably employed.

7. *Dietetics.* One of the chief factors in the treatment of disease consists in the regulation of the diet. No physical treatment or psychic influence can take the place of scientifically feeding the body and properly adapting the diet to the needs of the patient, his work, and his disease.

8. *Climate.* With some special diseases, climate is of great value, and must be taken into consideration in all plans for the preservation or restoration of health.

9. *Special therapy.* Radium, X-ray, serums, and other ap-

pliances all have their place in the twentieth century therapeutics.

10. *Sanitation.* All phases of sanitation are of importance in the preservation of health, including ventilation, exercise, quarantine, disinfection, and sewage disposal.

11. *Materia Medica.* In many cases medicines are of actual value in combating disease; they are of great service in temporarily relieving pain, and otherwise preventing human suffering. The most rabid enemy of drugs will recognize the value of an anæsthetic when a major surgical operation is necessary, and even the devotees of the extreme psychic cults will seldom hesitate to use laxatives and cathartics to move the bowels.

SUMMARY OF THE CHAPTER

1. The twentieth century witnessed the birth of a new era in the art of healing. The practice of medicine is undergoing a silent revolution. Future methods of treatment will become more simple, natural, precise, and scientific.

2. The healing of disease has been more of an art than a science. The practice of medicine has been shackled with superstition and handicapped with ignorance. Therapeutics is rapidly breaking away from ancient delusions and sectarian prejudices.

3. The passing of the old-time authority of the family physician is due to a world-wide scientific awakening — the universal diffusion of hygienic knowledge. The minister has likewise declined in public prestige.

4. The last century will go down in history as the era of promiscuous drugging. Patent medicines have contributed to undermining the national health. Homeopathy was a contributing influence in lessening the professional and popular use of drugs.

5. Hydropaths and osteopaths have emphasized valuable therapeutic procedures which are destined to become generally recognized and employed by regular physicians. Therapeutic specialism, while often extreme and unscientific, serves the important purpose of arousing the people and awakening the doctor.

6. As homeopathy emphasized the harmfulness of over-medication, Christian Science and allied cults are calling the attention

of the medical profession to their utter neglect of psychotherapy and moral therapy. We are now in the midst of the fanatical transition stage of psychic teaching. This is the formative period of a new psychology.

7. The last generation witnessed a materialistic reaction against theological superstition and medical empiricism. The twentieth century was ushered in with a spiritistic revolt against materialism and rationalism.

8. The teaching of "all spirit and no matter " is more acceptable to the people than the dogma of "all matter and no spirit." Instead of ridiculing the psychic cults, let scientists raise the standard of true psychotherapy and moral suggestion.

9. The physician of to-day aims at the prevention of disease. Modern therapeutics treats the man, not merely the disease. Science works to detect and remove the causes of disease, not simply to suppress the symptoms.

10. The physician's work in behalf of the patient and the community may be summarized under five heads: (1) Prophylaxis. (2) Psychotherapy. (3) Moral therapy. (4) Physical therapy. (5) Medicinal therapy.

11. Each new discovery of the cause of disease points the way to a possible discovery of the remedy. While the physical causes of disease were the first to be discovered, the psychic influences concerned in disease are now being scientifically studied.

12. Every new therapeutic agent has been empiric in its early use, and was usually heralded to the world as a cure-all. The beneficiaries of psychotherapy are all too enthusiastic in its glorification. Physicians of to-day should rescue psychotherapy from the limbo of empiricism and fanaticism, and establish it upon a sound basis of physiological psychology. It is to be deplored that psychotherapy should be converted into a religion.

13. Scientific mind cure (psychotherapy) is not an exclusive system of treating disease, it is merely a factor in the modern system of preventive and curative medicine. Psychotherapy should be associated with moral suggestion and various phases of physical therapy, such as hydrotherapy, electrotherapy, light therapy, massage, dietetics, sanitation, and all other useful remedial agencies.

CHAPTER XXV

PSYCHO-PROPHYLAXIS, OR MENTAL HYGIENE

FEARFUL EMOTIONS.— THE PSYCHIC ELEMENT IN THE CIRCULATION.— HIGH-PRESSURE LIVING.— THE MENTAL FACTOR IN VITAL RESISTANCE.— HOW THE MIND CAN PREVENT INDIGESTION.— THE MENTAL INFLUENCE OVER SECRETION.— NUTRITION AS RELATED TO THE MENTAL STATE.— THE PSYCHIC SIDE OF DEEP BREATHING.— THE MIND AND THE MUSCULAR SYSTEM.— HOW THE MIND INFLUENCES ANIMAL HEAT.— THE BRAIN AND THE NERVOUS SYSTEM.— SUMMARY OF THE CHAPTER.

THAT old saying, "Prevention is better than cure," is as true of mental hygiene as it is of physical hygiene. Probably the greatest service which the mind can render the body is along the lines of preventing disease and maintaining health. A healthy and natural state of mind possesses curative value in various diseases, and the abnormal mind is known to be an actual cause of certain maladies; nevertheless, it is in the realm of prophylaxis (the prevention of disease) that the healing influences of the psychic powers figure most conspicuously.

Man can live at the equator, or exist at the poles; he can eat almost anything and everything — but he cannot long stand self-contemplation. The human mind can accomplish wonders in the line of work, but it is soon wrecked when directed in the channels of worry. The practice of bodily hygiene cannot be carried on successfully without the coöperation of the mental powers, and this psychic assistance we term psycho-prophylaxis, or mental hygiene.

Throughout this chapter and elsewhere, the author makes free use of such expressions as "mental control prevents high blood-pressure"; "worry emaciates its victims"; "faith prevents fatigue." I freely use such expressions without throwing my-

PSYCHO-PROPHYLAXIS

self liable to the charge of pedantry; for I might consistently employ, as indeed I sometimes do, what may seem to the general reader a much stronger type of expression, such as: " mental control is *equivalent* to the prevention of high blood-pressure "; " worry *is* the emaciation of its victims "; " faith *is equal* to the prevention of fatigue." In adopting such language I should be in strict conformity with the usage of reputable specialists in the study of problems of the mind. If, in most instances, the popular mode of expression is employed, the author does so merely as a matter of convenience.

FEARFUL EMOTIONS

Most functional and chronic diseases result from derangements of the nervous system, due in many cases to depression of the nerve centres. This depression or fatigue of the nerve centres is largely due to two great causes, toxicity — the presence of poisons in the circulation; and fear — chronic worry and despondency.

Drugs and other agencies possess the power of greatly stimulating and marvellously arousing certain debilitated and weakened nerve centres. It is now known that the mind — the will — possesses similar power. Drugs and other material means do not possess curative power, except in cases of specific medication, as quinine in malaria, and antitoxin in diphtheria. It is the reaction of the body to medicine or treatment that effects the cure. It is the arousal of the natural and inherent powers of the living organism that heals and restores.

It not infrequently develops that psychic influences can invigorate and arouse the sleeping and lethargic nerve centres just as acceptably as can chemical and physical agents. At least, the psychic factor in preventing and treating disease must be recognized as one of the chief factors in speedy recovery and permanent health.

We must admit that the jurisdiction of the mind over the physical body has its limits, but these limitations have as yet not been accurately defined or definitely ascertained. While the psychic powers concerned in health and disease are by no means unlimited, while they are more or less unknown, they constitute a force for health which is far greater than the average man imagines.

THE PSYCHIC ELEMENT IN THE CIRCULATION

A tranquil state of mind exerts a great influence toward preventing numerous disturbances of the heart action. Faith tends to preserve the natural rate and rhythm of the heart-beat. Courage and confidence are undoubtedly able to improve the cardiac nutrition and to increase the strength of the heart-beat, through their favorable influence in regulating the heart action, thereby increasing the amount of rest obtained between beats. The mental state of determination is even able to postpone the hour of inevitable heart failure in the face of approaching death. We have previously shown that faith exerts a wonderful influence over the nervous centres of the heart.

A well-balanced mental state prevents some common but injurious emotional disturbances of the heart's action, as well as certain fictitious sensations and mock pains which appear to have their existence in the cardiac region. Cheerfulness, by favoring low blood-pressure, actually tends to prevent and lessen arteriosclerosis or hardening of the arteries. A good state of mind also favors a good circulation through the skin, preventing vascular spasm which is so often responsible for inactive skin and chronic cold hands and feet.

The mental state has a large part to play toward the prevention of local congestions, because of its power to increase and facilitate the general blood movement throughout the body. The mind is, in a certain measure, able to contribute toward the prevention of heart failure as well as of apoplexy and its consequent paralysis.

HIGH-PRESSURE LIVING

The psychic resources constitute the one great influence which can be exerted toward the prevention of nervous high-tension. The high-pressure life of our present civilization is partially due to the psychic state as well as to certain physical practices. A well-balanced mental control prevents worry and eliminates grief, which, in a large measure, are responsible for the universal high nervous tension and elevated blood-pressure.

Mental serenity and moral peace directly contribute to the prevention of nervousness and the maintenance of normal blood-pressure. Moral self-condemnation unfailingly raises the arterial tension.

The control of the imagination, together with the maintenance of a healthy mental state, is equivalent to the prevention of the creation of countless imaginary diseases and to the dissipation of those vague and uncertain sensations which otherwise might come to be recognized as actual pain.

THE MENTAL FACTOR IN VITAL RESISTANCE

Psychic influences are greatly concerned in maintaining and strengthening the vital resistance. The ability to resist numerous diseases is in exact ratio to mental courage and moral confidence. A healthy state of mind conserves the red blood cells, and is a valuable influence in preventing and combating anæmia. There is every evidence that the maintenance of a strong and natural mental attitude is an actual aid in the body's efforts to resist infection through the medium of the white blood cells, which possess the extraordinary power of catching and destroying the microbes of disease.

It is interesting in this connection to quote Goethe on the power of the mind to resist disease. He says: "I was once inevitably exposed to the infection of a malignant fever, and warded off the disease only by means of determined volition. It is almost incredible how much, in such cases, the moral will can effect! It seems to permeate one's whole being and to render the condition of the body active enough to repel all harmful influences. Fear is a condition of sloth in which any enemy may take possession of us."

Concerning the hygienic influence of a tranquil mind, Schiller wrote: "Who can fail to understand that a constitution able to draw pleasure from every event and to sink every personal sorrow in the perfection of the universe must also be most profitable to this bodily machine?"

Cheerfulness contributes to the prevention of weariness and fatigue by its power to decrease the production of those subtle poisons which are generated by fear and worry, and which, when thrown into the blood stream, are able tremendously to depress the sufferer.

Psychic influences are undoubtedly able to hasten the process of repair and encourage the work of healing, following both accidental wounds and surgical operations. The mental and moral powers seem to be able to exert themselves in such a manner as greatly to augment the vital energies of the physical body, thereby adding greatly to its power to resist disease; and therefore, in the last analysis, psychic influences are found to exert themselves toward lowering the death rate and increasing the average length of human life.

"Where are you going?" asked an Oriental pilgrim of the Plague one day. "I am going to Bagdad to kill five thousand people," was the reply. A few weeks later the pilgrim met the Plague returning. "You told me you were going to Bagdad to kill five thousand people," said the pilgrim, "but instead you killed fifty thousand." "No," said the Plague, "I killed only five thousand, as I said I would. The others all died of fright."

HOW THE MIND CAN PREVENT INDIGESTION

The hygienic value of the mental state is nowhere better demonstrated than in the study of secretion and digestion. Psychic influences are the chief factors in the furtherance of good digestion and the prevention of dyspepsia. Mental influences are able to increase or decrease both the quality and the quantity of nearly all the digestive secretions, particularly those of the mouth and stomach. The quality of the saliva can be improved and the digestive power of the gastric juice increased by pleasant thoughts and a healthy mental state.

The mind possesses almost unlimited power which can be exercised toward the prevention of dyspepsia and the improvement of digestion. The courageous and vigorous mental states may contribute much toward the prevention of slow digestion and inactivity of the stomach muscle, which conditions are so largely responsible for dyspepsia and indigestion.

The mental state can contribute much toward the prevention of sour stomach. The dyspeptic who is confident that a certain food will disagree with him — sour on his stomach — is almost sure to experience indigestion and sour stomach if he eats that particular food. On the other hand, faith and trust encourage the formation and secretion of the powerful "psychic juice," which so vigorously and promptly attacks the food on entering the stomach, that the meal is so quickly carried forward in the process of digestion that souring is effectively prevented. The healthy mental state further favors the elaboration of a well-balanced gastric juice, contributing to the lessening of acid over-production.

Faith increases the activity of all muscles, including those of the stomach and bowel, as well as encouraging the work of the liver and pancreatic gland in the formation of their normal secretions. The mental and nervous states are also concerned in influencing the quality and quantity of the intestinal secretions, as well as favoring strong intestinal muscular movements.

THE MENTAL INFLUENCE OVER SECRETION

Psychic influences are very powerful in regulating the secretion of the mammary gland. The quality of the milk is immediately improved by improving the mental state. Fear and anger are able immediately to deteriorate and poison the secretions of this important gland. Recent investigations are beginning to shed a flood of light on the power of the mind to influence and control the secretions of the numerous ductless glands — the pituitary body, the thyroid and suprarenal glands — which are such powerful factors in the regulation of nutrition and growth.

NUTRITION AS RELATED TO THE MENTAL STATE

Psychic influences are exceedingly powerful in the realm of nutrition and metabolism. Worry can quickly emaciate its victims, while faith and courage assist in quickly building up and strengthening the body. Fear lessens nutrition, secretion, and metabolism. Faith increases oxidation in the cell. Good courage strengthens the appetite, while confidence and cheerfulness improve the general feeling of physical well-being.

The proper control of the mind prevents all harboring of fear, which is able so profoundly to pervert and destroy every function connected with health and nutrition. Happy people are usually healthy. Cheerfulness is an aid to preventing numerous constitutional disorders. Faith fortifies the system against decay and disease — it materially assists in postponing your funeral.

THE PSYCHIC SIDE OF DEEP BREATHING

Faith encourages deep and natural breathing, while fear is equivalent to rendering respiration superficial and unnatural.

Cheerfulness actually possesses the power of increasing respiratory depth, thereby increasing the oxygen intake. (See Fig. 26.) The assimilated food is useless to the body without oxygen to burn it up. The courageous man, other things being equal, is the deep breather, and so faith is able to expand the chest, increase the respiratory function, and promote oxidation changes.

The mental state is also able to exert a great influence toward the prevention of various abnormalities connected with breathing, such as coughing, and asthmatic attacks. More than one-half of chronic coughs are purely nervous in origin and can be largely controlled or completely cured by psychic influence.

Dr. Bernheim was about to treat with electricity a young woman who was afflicted with aphonia (loss of voice). Before doing so he put his hand over the larynx and moved it up and down and said to her, "Now you can speak aloud." He told her to say "Ah." She said it, and the aphonia disappeared.

THE MIND AND THE MUSCULAR SYSTEM

Mental courage augments muscular strength. Faith prevents fatigue, while fear generates weariness. When the mental state is healthy, the physical carriage and the walking-gait are greatly improved. Cheerfulness contributes to the prevention of stoop-shoulders and spinal curvature.

A good state of mind undoubtedly increases the working capacity; that is, a man can do more work when in a cheerful state of mind than he can when depressed and discouraged. Faith gives one those powers of physical exertion which are characteristic of the play state of mind — a state in which one is able to perform a maximum of physical work with a minimum of fatigue and physical weariness. The maintenance of the strong psychic state favors that high degree of muscular tone throughout the body which prevents weakening of the supports of the internal organs, and this prevents the tumbling down of the viscera, a condition so prevalent in those patients with relaxed and flabby abdomens.

It is related that "during the naval fight off Santiago, while the *Oregon* was pushing after the *Cristobal Colon* under forced draught, the stokers were nearly overcome by their labor, and

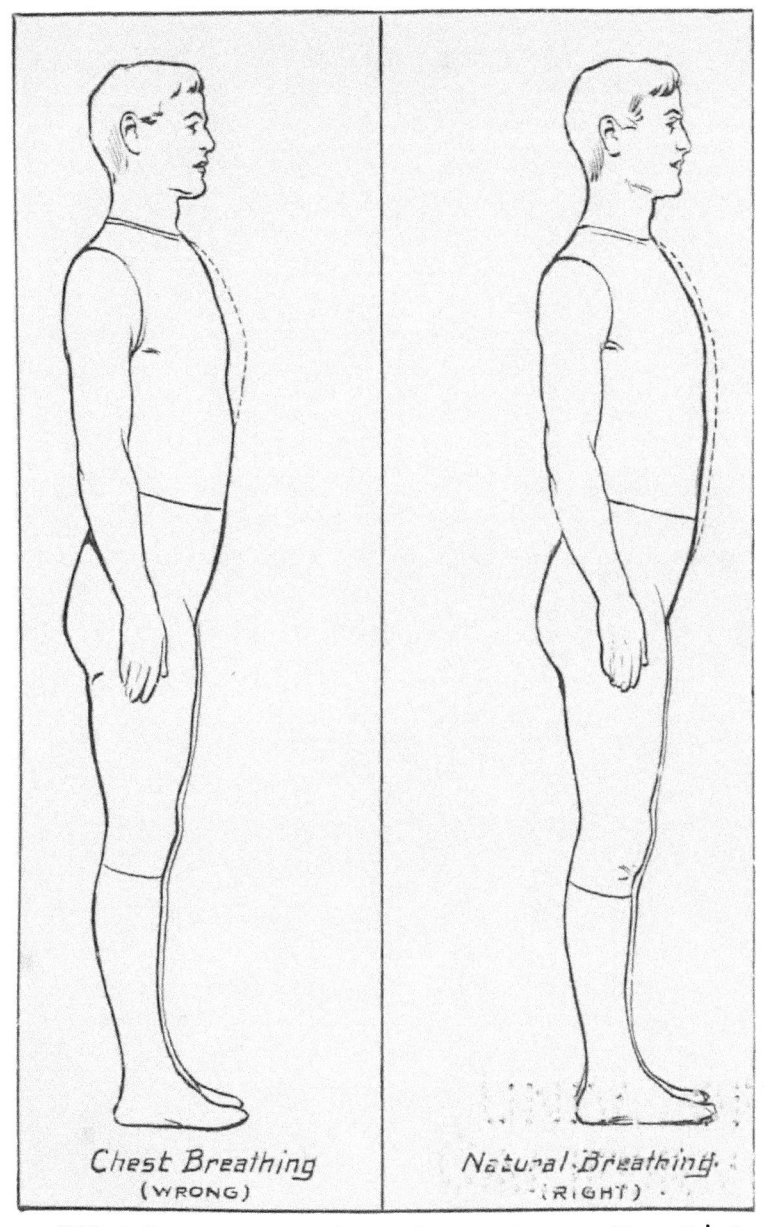

FIG. 26.— *Illustrating Right and Wrong Breathing.*

DIARY OF
A HYPOCHONDRIAC

the tremendous heat of the hold. As yet she had not partaken in the fight. The chief engineer, noticing the condition of his men, signalled up to Captain Clark, 'Give them a gun.' The gun was given — and exhaustion passed away in the excitement of the belief that the battle had begun."

HOW THE MIND INFLUENCES ANIMAL HEAT

From the study of the chapter on the physiological action of the mind on the skin and the heat-regulating mechanism, it is apparent that psychic influences are very powerful in this realm. The mind can do much to increase the circulation of blood in the skin and to prevent cutaneous inactivity and lethargy. In this way, a good mental state favors normal heat elimination, promotes local blood supply, and even contributes something to the prevention of common colds. Cheerfulness promotes healthy physical feelings and favors a normal recognition of the sensations of heat and cold, while fear demoralizes the temperature sense and is able to produce shivering and actual chills. Even fever is, in a measure, under the influence of the mental state. Fear and anxiety may raise the temperature, while intellectual composure exerts a favorable influence upon the fever patient.

THE BRAIN AND THE NERVOUS SYSTEM

When we come to the consideration of the psychic control of the nervous system, we are face to face with the chief problem in the study of mind and matter. The nervous system is the immediate instrument of mind and is almost entirely under the control, and subject to the domination, of the psychic state. Faith and good cheer favor mental endurance and seem to be actually equivalent to an increase of brain energy. The state of one's mind has much to do with the quality of the brain work. The psychic state has the ability to increase fatigue, or to enhance rest. The mind may either cause or prevent all forms of worry and anxiety, and even hypochondria. Mental composure increases the efficiency and rate of the transmission of nervous impulses; that is, we can think faster and act more rapidly when the mind is dominated by faith. Fear demoralizes the entire nervous mechanism. Good temperament economizes the energy of the nerve centres, giving the greatest possible return with the least expenditure of the nervous forces. The psychic state has everything to do with the preservation of nervous equilibrium. The mind can prevent various nervous diseases, ranging from hysteria to convulsions, as well as be a direct aid in preventing nervous loss of muscular function, and overcoming actual paralysis.

Mental control can do much to lessen pain and to prevent or mitigate other abnormal sensations arising in the body. There is a tremendous psychic element concerned in the enjoyment of all the special senses, such as taste, smell, and hearing. The mental state of faith renders more acute and accurate both hearing and sight. Good cheer and confidence are highly influential in promoting fluency of speech; in fact, they render all the physical feelings more natural and reliable, while the countenance and expression are almost wholly dependent on the psychic state.

SUMMARY OF THE CHAPTER

1. It is in the realm of prophylaxis that psychic healing power figures most conspicuously. Psycho-prophylaxis represents the greatest field for the employment of mental medicine.

2. Fatigue of the nerve centres is largely due to toxic poisons and chronic worry. Psychic influences can invigorate and arouse the nerve centres much the same as chemical and physical agents.

3. Courage and confidence sustain the heart, improve the circulation, and prevent numerous minor disturbances in the cardio-vascular system. A tranquil state of mind encourages general blood-movement and prevents local congestions.

4. Well-balanced mental control prevents high blood-pressure and nervous high-tension. Worry unfailingly elevates the arterial pressure.

5. The ability to resist numerous diseases is in exact ratio to mental courage and moral confidence. Cheerfulness combats anæmia and increases the vital resistance. Faith hastens healing and tissue-repair.

6. Faith tends to prevent dyspepsia. Good cheer improves the quality of the digestive secretions. Courage prevents slow digestion and inactivity of the bowels. A good state of mind encourages the formation of an abundant " appetite juice."

PSYCHO-PROPHYLAXIS 275

7. Psychic influences are very powerful in regulating the secretion of the mammary gland. Fear and anger are able to poison the milk. The mental state is probably able to influence and modify the secretions of the numerous ductless glands.

8. Worry can rapidly emaciate its victims, while faith and courage assist in quickly building up the body. Faith promotes the nutrition. Happy people are usually healthy. Faith fortifies the system against decay and disease.

9. Faith encourages deep breathing, while fear renders the respiration superficial and unnatural. Cheerfulness increases the oxygen intake. The mind is often able to control nervous coughing.

10. Mental courage augments muscular strength. Faith prevents fatigue, while fear generates weariness. Cheerfulness prevents stoop-shoulders and spinal curvature. A good mental state strengthens the muscles and assists in keeping the internal organs in proper place.

11. The state of the mind contributes to the regulation and elimination of animal heat. Fever is made worse by fear. Faith is even of some value in preventing common colds.

12. Faith favors mental endurance. Good cheer appears to increase brain energy. Mental composure increases the rate of thinking and acting. Good temperament economizes the expenditure of nervous energy. Mental control can lessen pain, accentuate the special senses, facilitate the speech, and determine the countenance and facial expression.

CHAPTER XXVI

THE PSYCHIC ELEMENT IN HEREDITY AND ENVIRONMENT

THE PSYCHOLOGY OF CHILD-CULTURE.— MENTAL INFLUENCES IN RELATION TO HEREDITY.— SUGGESTION IN THE EARLY SOCIAL LIFE.— THE MIND AS CONCERNED IN CHARACTER-DEVELOPMENT. — THE PSYCHIC FACTOR IN INTEMPERANCE AND DRUG HABITS. — PSYCHOLOGY OF THE FAMILY LIFE.— TEMPERAMENTAL SHORTCOMINGS.— DISSATISFACTION *versus* DISCONTENT.— THE PSYCHOLOGY OF THE CROWD.— SUMMARY OF THE CHAPTER.

IN recent years we are coming more and more to recognize that psychic influences are largely concerned in all the social problems of heredity and the economic questions of environment. Psychology will receive more and more consideration in the future study of the life problems of both the individual and the nation.

THE PSYCHOLOGY OF CHILD-CULTURE

Every successful method of child-training must take into cognizance the powerful influence of mind over matter. We must recognize the vast power of suggestion when properly made by parents and teachers, in the work of character-culture and intellectual development.

One of the greatest of modern crimes is the common practice of early teaching the child to fear. Unfortunately, and with most disastrous consequences, the child is taught to fear the dark, to fear strange noices, to fear its parents, to live in constant dread of being caught by hobgoblins or the bogy-man; and the little ones are even taught an unnatural and unhealthy fear of devils and demons, as well as to live in constant dread and unwholesome fear of the Supreme Being — the Heavenly Father. The result of this early life of fear is to distort the emotions and deform the conceptions; in fact, thoroughly to demoralize the psychic life of the growing child. This sort of training is bound to react most disastrously in depressing the physical functions of the body, dwarfing the growth, and deforming the psychic powers.

Children can be quickly and easily trained to exercise faith instead of fear. When between two and three years of age, one of the author's children began to manifest great fear of the dark. Within a few weeks this fear was entirely removed by merely saying to the child on entering a dark room, "The dark is nice; we are not afraid of the dark, are we?" The child listened in silence to these statements for a few days and then began to join in the declaration with more and more courage and confidence, until within a few weeks, it became habitual with him to say on entering a dark room, "Nice dark, we're not afraid of the dark, are we? — No."

The same policy was pursued with reference to strange noises and various other things commonly feared by children, until the last apparent trace of fear was banished from his mind. It is needless to add that such training acted favorably on the child's disposition and temperament, and that his physical health was everything to be desired. The author is coming more and more to believe that proper psychic training in the life of the child has much to do with its subsequent growth and development along mental, moral, and physical lines.

The time to prevent fear and to instil the courageous instincts into the character of a child is while he is in the cradle. If the coming generation is to be delivered from fear, the emancipation will have to be inaugurated during prenatal times and persistently carried on from birth up through infancy and childhood to adolescence. Those who are thus favorably born and bred will not, unless the intellectual powers are undermined by physical disease, become victims of fear, grief, and melancholia, later in life.

MENTAL INFLUENCES IN RELATION TO HEREDITY

The question has recently been raised just how far the mind of the mother could influence the growth and development of the mind and nervous system of the child *in utero*. While there exists direct physical connection between the mother and the child, through which the blood is able freely to circulate, there exists no direct connection between the nervous systems of the two. The reader is referred to the discussions in Chapter I, where attention is called to the power of the mind and the nervous system to influence the secretions of the body, and, in all probability, to modify even the formation of the internal secretions of the ductless glands.

If the glandular secretions of the body are subject even to the slightest control by the psychic state, it would seem highly probable that the mother's state of mind would, in this indirect way, be able enormously to influence the nervous system of the embryonic child by her power to regulate the elaboration of these wonderful secretions of her own body, which would be immediately carried to that of the child, where these internal secretions would undoubtedly exert their wonderful power to influence the body of the unborn child.

Whether viewed from the standpoint of heredity as based on the original parental cells concerned in reproduction, or on the subsequent nourishment of the embryo by the mother's nutrient fluids, it is coming to be regarded as more and more likely that the psychic state of the parents, more particularly that of the mother, is able to exert a direct influence toward controlling and modifying heredity — toward the formation and development of both the brain and the body of the child. As these likely facts are demonstrated more and more to be true, it will certainly emphasize the duty of all mothers to put forth extraordinary efforts to maintain a cheerful and happy mental state during the period of maternity.

That the psychic state of the mother is able actually to influence the physical development, has long been believed. It is popularly believed that a severe fright, sudden surprise, or some extraordinary shock, may result in producing a birthmark upon the child. If mental impressions on the part of the mother are thus able to interfere with the physical development of the child *in utero*, it seems not altogether unlikely that these same psychic changes in the mother could also influence the growth and development of the child's nervous system, and thereby, in the end, influence the child's mentality and character.

PSYCHIC ELEMENT IN HEREDITY 279

Even those who believe in birthmarks admit that the most shocking experiences on the part of the mother, which would be supposed to result in the deformity of the child, do not produce disfigurement when the mother makes a definite and successful effort to overcome the shock — when she persistently believes that it will not result in marking her offspring. On the other hand, the vast majority of supposed birthmarks following fear and fright seem to occur after the mother has, for months, been possessed by the fear that her child would be marked, confidently expecting it to be disfigured at birth as the result of her unfortunate and shocking experience.

Certainly, every child has the right to be well born, mentally, morally, and physically; and that it should receive this splendid legacy it is absolutely necessary that the mother should maintain a healthy mental state, and carefully look after the nourishment and health of her own body.

SUGGESTION IN THE EARLY SOCIAL LIFE

The early social life of a child — the time of its early play and romping — constitutes the golden opportunity for parents and teachers, by proper suggestion, to bend the twig in the way of desirable growth. The most successful training of a child is by suggestion and not by offers of reward or threats of punishment. From the earliest dawn of mind, the human baby is recognized to be the most imitative animal on earth. Its earliest endeavors are to imitate every action, word, and expression which it observes on the part of its elders, especially its parents.

This is the formative period in character development, and the positive suggestions, the good suggestions, the cheerful, hopeful, and happy suggestions, given at this period, will exert a great influence on the child's character throughout life. On the other hand, if fear and depression, unhappiness and discontent, are allowed to spring up in the child's mind during these earlier years, they are quite likely to cripple and dwarf its entire life-career.

Much as we would like further to discuss the psychology of child-training, space will not permit; suffice it to say, that if the child is trained up in the way it should go, when it is young, it will hardly depart from it when it is old; in fact, it cannot depart from it; for habit is master of us all, and habits are formed by the constant repetition of acts, and acts are psychic in origin. The habits of the child are primarily and entirely due to suggestion — to its teaching by precept and by example.

THE MIND AS CONCERNED IN CHARACTER-DEVELOPMENT

Character is simply the finished product, the final harvest, which reflects and portrays our psychic life — our mental habits. "As a man thinketh, so is he." We can never become anything except what we desire and expect to become; and it is equally true, that we actually do become what we expect and desire to be. Character is not mightily influenced by wishing, but it is wholly and absolutely controlled by *willing*. If the patient complains that he has not the moral strength to direct his will, then we advise that he place himself in some situation that forces exertion and compels action. If he has no definite occupation, find one. Bind him by definite plans and promises to engage in some effort or work where the demands of honor will force the will to assert itself. The physical character is determined not only by the hereditary start, but also by the suggestive environment from earliest infancy to old age.

While certain dominant strains of the character are acquired by heredity, environment exerts by far the greatest influence upon its evolution. Environment is able even to modify and practically change numerous hereditary traits. To a certain extent, the laws of heredity are inexorable, and it will remain forever true that "the fathers have eaten sour grapes, and the children's teeth are set on edge"; nevertheless, there is another Scripture which is equally true, and which portrays the operation of the laws of environment and personal obedience, which declares that when men's thoughts and hearts are changed it shall no longer be said of them, "The fathers have eaten a sour grape, and the children's teeth are set on edge"; but, "every man that eateth the sour grape, his teeth shall be set on edge."

The upbuilding of a strong character or the rebuilding of the misformed character, is largely a matter of controlling the environment, mastering the realm of thought and placing it under proper psychic influences. The overthrow of fear and the crowning of faith upon the psychic throne of one's inner life will result in such a transformation of thought as eventually to change one's whole habit, life, and character. Fear and doubts represent that stagnation of the soul which eventually ends in more or less complete mental and moral paralysis.

If such marvellous transformations of character are possible by the exercise of purely psychic 'influences, what limitations can be placed upon the possibilities of character-transformation when the mental forces, in addition to their own marvellous influence upon the body, are reinforced and directed by the limitless resources of the spiritual powers and the moral agencies resident within the soul? Who dares to doubt the truth and possibility of the so-called new-birth of theology? When the human mind is focussed, concentrated, and strongly directed by a positive will, and this is all backed up and reinforced by the infinite power of the indwelling spiritual forces and the mighty will of the *Divine Mind*, who can limit the power and possibilities vested in the intellectual and moral forces of the human mind? And so we see that faith tends to lift up and deliver one from hereditary taints and depressing bondage, while fear casts down and condemns one to repeated defeat and life-long hereditary bondage.

THE PSYCHIC FACTOR IN INTEMPERANCE AND DRUG HABITS

Fear thought is most dangerous because it not infrequently comes to be disguised in the role of forethought. Worry frequently robs us of our happiness, while it masquerades in the name of discretion, carefulness, and conservatism. The common practice of repressing fear, doubt, suspicion, and worry will never lead to their overthrow. These passions and emotions will accumulate until the nervous tension is greatly increased and the blood-pressure is enormously raised. All this is predisposing to violent outbursts of anger and the use of pressure-lowering drugs, such as alcohol and morphine. The proper method of removing these mental states is to surrender the mind to their opposite; to displace fear by faith; to dispel doubts by trust; to replace worry with confidence, cheerfulness, and happiness.

Much of our intemperance is due to high blood-pressure and

fear. Worry, as has been previously shown, raises the blood-pressure. (See Chap. XIII.) Alcohol and morphine immediately lower the blood-pressure. And this explains why family troubles and business worries apparently drive so many men to drink. They take the alcohol not only to secure mental peace, but also to lower the blood-pressure and relieve its accompanying nervous tension. Faith is an aid to temperance, while fear directly and indirectly predisposes to intemperance and tends always further to enslave and to confirm its helpless victims.

The mind is more powerful in overcoming drug habits than any other single agency. It is the inability to endure pain, or the unwillingness to withstand trouble and adversity, that usually leads to the use of drink and drugs. The psychic powers are able to sustain a person both in times of affliction and adversity, and in this way the mind is able largely to prevent the use of these habit-forming drugs.

Psychic determination, moral faith, and spiritual energy are all necessary to effect permanent deliverance from these drug habits. The one grand essential in the treatment of alcoholism is that *the victim shall make up his mind to quit.* While we have seen a few men who were successful in overcoming the drink habit by sheer mental power, by far the majority are unsuccessful, unless their mental resolution is backed up by, and reinforced with, moral resolve and spiritual strength.

PSYCHOLOGY OF THE FAMILY LIFE

It is in the family life that psychic influences are unusually powerful for good or for evil. The happy family life under existing modern conditions of high tension is quite impossible, unless the psychic states of parents and children are dominated by faith and trust. Many a family has been wrecked, and thousands to-day exist in misery and unhappiness, because the mind of husband or wife succumbs to fear, surrenders to jealousy, or becomes permeated with distrust.

Many divorces have no other ground than suspicion and distrust. A little auto-suggestion, or a little of the charity of the Christian religion would bring thousands of estranged husbands and wives together and literally fill their souls with joy and rejoicing. Fear is the destroyer of family happiness as well as individual peace of mind. No family can long stand where fear thought dominates one or more of its members. Faith promotes undisturbed happiness, while fear sooner or later generates family distrust and jealousy.

The business man who is diffident and fearful is quite certainly doomed to meet with ultimate failure. Courage and confidence are essential even to business success. The industrial world of to-day with its vast and intricate financial machinery is all built upon confidence. Look what happens to the industrial world in times of panic! And what is panic? Merely a disturbance in general business confidence and commercial faith. The psychology of panics would be an interesting study if space would permit. When men, or a group of men, have deliberately and wilfully inaugurated a panic, they have done it by frightening the public, producing raids upon banks, and scaring people into simultaneously unloading their securities. Fear is the father of panic — mental, moral, psychic, physical, and commercial.

TEMPERAMENTAL SHORTCOMINGS

A great many good people are constantly worrying over their faults, their temperamental shortcomings. It would take only about fifteen minutes of real mental determination or moral resolve to bring most of these trifling matters to an end. Some persons are continuously defeated by their shortcomings because they live in constant fear of their faults. They exist in perpetual dread of making these very mistakes.

Faith actually aids in making you what you ought to be and what you want to be. Fear confirms your weaknesses of character — increasingly enslaving you to your petty temperamental shortcomings.

Some may resent such methods of cure as belonging to the realm of the imagination, but that would be a great mistake. The psychic nature of your cure in no sense robs it of any dignity. Just because you are cured by the imagination, it does not follow that your cure was an imaginary one.

When you desire to abandon some habitual practice, to abolish some temperamental fault, or to overthrow some idol of character, make up your mind to do it: abandon the intellect to faith; throw open every psychic channel to courage and confidence; in fact, begin to rejoice in the victory you are about to gain, just as though you had already gained it. Banish doubt, refuse to entertain the least suggestion of the possibility of failure. But is this not the very essence, the very secret, of success as outlined in the militant Christian religion? Does not the Apostle Paul himself define faith as "The substance of things hoped for, the evidence of things not seen"? And so it would appear that the findings and teachings of modern psychology are close akin to the philosophy and time-honored teachings of the Christian religion.

The psychology of faith and fear contains nothing new; the physiology of faith and fear is as old as the hills. The discussion of them at this time is merely to emphasize the necessity of our thorough coöperation with the moral energies and the spiritual forces ever at our command, which render it possible for us to effect well-nigh any desirable transformation of character and achieve the victory over every removable besetting sin.

In every effort looking toward the conquest of self, it must be borne in mind that thought produces action, action produces habit, and habits form character. When we take a certain thought into our minds without reserve, when it is literally fused on to the intellect by the white heat of emotion, it becomes a part of our psychic character, shortly to work its way out into the habit life; soon it is crystallized and becomes a part of our moral character, a part of our psychic life.

On the other hand, we all possess certain temperamental peculiarities which we shall probably carry to our graves. Perhaps they are what the Apostle Paul defined as "thorns in the flesh," concerning which he prayed three times for deliverance, but was compelled to rest content with merely the grace to bear his infirmity. Perhaps if we banished all our little shortcomings and overcame the little peculiarities which so annoy our friends and associates, we might unwittingly emasculate our characters and greatly cripple our usefulness.

All great men have had their little peculiarities and infirmities. Socrates had fits; Tolstoi nearly killed himself trying to fly when a boy; Balzac had a walking mania; Schopenhauer was so afraid of a razor that he singed his beard; Schiller used to put his feet on ice and gaze upon rotten apples to get an inspiration. There are those who have affirmed that both Milton and Richard Wagner were crazy. Mohammed had convulsions; Annie Lee, spasms; Mozart believed that certain people were trying to poison him; and even Abraham Lincoln was subject to fits of melancholia; while Samuel Johnson could not pass a post without touching it. We should not despair of succeeding in life because we have some little temperamental shortcoming, even though it be so severe as to become an obsession. Experience proves that the vast majority of these psychic infirmities are due to some form of fear, and that they are in large measure removable by the exercise of strong faith.

DISSATISFACTION *versus* DISCONTENT

Dissatisfaction is divine; discontent is diabolical. All the world's progress is due to dissatisfaction with existing conditions, and the putting forth of courageous efforts to improve the same. All the sorrow of the world is born of discontent with our present circumstances and surroundings after we have done our best to improve them. Again, we find the Apostle Paul a good psychologist, for it was he who wrote, after he had done what he could to improve conditions in the world: "I have learned in whatsoever state I am therewith to be content." Happiness has its origin and existence only in the mind. The psychic conception of joy and happiness is quite independent of the conditions which characterize our environment.

Psychic contentment and moral peace are not incompatible with the highest possible degree of social dissatisfaction and economic discontent. It is the condition of one's mind that determines the possibilities of personal contentment — an experience which may be enjoyed in the face of extraordinary physical difficulties, industrial strain, social revolution, and any amount of economic upheaval. The imagination is the real climate of the soul. It is possible to live in a world of supreme unrest and yet keep the mind in perfect peace, even that supreme peacefulness; for is it not written, "Thou wilt keep him in perfect peace whose mind is stayed on Thee"? While it is true that we all have our unpleasant moods, nevertheless, the real trouble does not begin until our varying moods come to have us — come to possess and control our mental life.

THE PSYCHOLOGY OF THE CROWD

It must be true that the psychology of the individual is the psychology of the crowd, only it would seem that numbers multiply the intensity and power of suggestions. The psychology of faith as applied to the crowd gives birth to the courageous abandon and victorious confidence of the army as it sweeps on to conquest, unmindful of difficulties and blind to obstacles. On the other hand, fear as applied to the nation spreads with the rapidity of a contagious disease, alarm is communicated with increasing intensity from man to man until the disquietude becomes universal, and a whole nation of sane and intelligent people are quickly plunged into unreasoning panic and economic upheaval.

It is because of the disastrous results of fear thought, not only on the individual but on the nation, that it becomes the duty of every sane man and woman to establish quarantine against fear. Fear is a psychic disease which is highly contagious and extraordinarily infectious. And we speak advisedly when we say that fear is one of the chief factors in the contraction of physical contagious diseases. The only antitoxin we know of for this highly contagious and exceedingly dangerous psychic disease, is faith thought. Faith is the antitoxin for fear.

Practise the overthrow of fear in its infancy, nip worry in the bud. For it must be remembered that fear thought can become a habit, and then it may attach itself to any department of thought or practice of life, and thus permeate the character with its destructive influence. We may become chronically afraid of sleeplessness, or live in everlasting dread of pain. Others fear they may fall victims to consumption or to constipation. We become fearful that we shall have cancer, paralysis, or a score of other diseases, and, in this way, the entire life is lived in the terrible bondage of fear.

SUMMARY OF THE CHAPTER

1. One of the greatest of modern crimes is the common practice of teaching the child to fear. Proper psychic training of

the child has much to do with its subsequent growth and development along mental, moral, and physical lines.

2. The emancipation of the race from fear will have to be inaugurated during prenatal times, and persistently carried on from birth up through infancy and childhood to adolescence.

3. The mother's psychic state is probably able, through the power of the mind over glandular secretions, indirectly to influence the formation and development of both the mind (brain and nerves) and the body of the child.

4. Birthmarks do not usually follow sudden shocks when the mother makes a definite and successful effort to overcome her fear. On the other hand, it is well-known that in most cases where birthmarks do appear, the mother was possessed by the fear that her child would be born disfigured.

5. The most successful training of a child is by suggestion and not by offers of reward or threats of punishment. The human baby is the most imitative creature on earth.

6. Fill the child's mind with good suggestions during the formative period of character development. As a general proposition, the way in which the child is trained when it is young, it cannot depart from when it is old.

7. "As a man thinketh, so is he." We seldom become anything except what we desire to become; and it is equally true, that we usually do become all that we confidently expect to be.

8. To a certain extent the laws of heredity are inexorable; nevertheless, the laws of environment and personal obedience are able, by psychic power, greatly to modify hereditary influences and even effectually to transform the entire character.

9. If psychic agencies alone can so wonderfully change thought and character, what limitations can be placed upon the possibilities of character-transformation, when the mental forces are effectually backed up by moral energy and spiritual power?

10. Fear thought is most dangerous when it parades as forethought. Combat fear by replacing it with faith. Resist worry with confidence.

11. Violent outburts of anger, fear, and worry operate to raise the blood-pressure, and thereby predispose their victims to the use of alcohol, morphine, and other drugs which possess

the power of lowering the blood-pressure and lessening nervous tension. Faith is an indirect aid to temperance.

12. Many families are wrecked by fear, jealousy, and distrust. Divorces are born of distrust and suspicion. The family life cannot long survive fear thought. Fear is the father of panics — mental, physical, and financial.

13. Faith actually aids in making you what you ought to be and what you want to be. Fear confirms your character weaknesses and enslaves you to your temperamental shortcomings. The psychology of faith and fear is highly akin to the philosophy of the Christian religion.

14. Psychic contentment and moral peace are not incompatible with the highest possible degree of social dissatisfaction and economic upheaval. It is possible to live in a world of supreme unrest and yet keep the mind in perfect peace. *D*issatisfaction is divine, but discontent is diabolical.

15. Numbers multiply the intensity and power of suggestions. Fear is a highly contagious psychic disease — we should establish quarantine against it. **The only known antitoxin for fear thought is faith thought.**

CHAPTER XXVII

THE PSYCHOLOGY OF DISEASE

FUNCTIONAL AND ORGANIC DISEASE.— THE SPECIAL FIELD OF PSYCHIC INFLUENCE.— COMPARATIVE TABLE OF FUNCTIONAL AND ORGANIC DISEASES.— ACUTE AND CHRONIC DISEASE.— THE MISSION OF PAIN AND THE LANGUAGE OF DISEASE.— THE EVOLUTION OF PSYCHIC DISTURBANCES INTO PHYSICAL DISORDERS.— FEAR A PSYCHIC CONTAGION.— THE FATIGUE OF FEAR.— THE CASTING-OUT OF FEAR.— SUMMARY OF THE CHAPTER.

HAVING considered the psychic element in prophylaxis — mental hygiene — and the influence of the mental state as related to heredity and environment, it is now in order to consider the influence of the mind with reference to the causation and treatment of disease.

FUNCTIONAL AND ORGANIC DISEASE

In a general way, all the diseases affecting the human race are classified as functional and organic. When the functional behavior of the cells of the body is abnormal or in any way disturbed, it may result in deranging the action of some vital organ or in disturbing the circulatory and nervous systems in such a manner as to result in disease. Such diseases are termed functional, owing to the fact that they consist in a perversion or disturbance of the body's functions — no actual anatomical changes being found in the cells and tissues of the body.

On the other hand, organic disease represents a bodily state in which the cells and tissues of the body are actually changed. In most organic diseases these changes are so definite that they may be identified under the microscope; that is, in many organic diseases, the actual changes in the cell are so literal and characteristic as to permit of a diagnosis being made when these cells or tissues are viewed under the microscope. To illustrate the difference between functional and organic disease, it might be stated that acid dyspepsia (sour stomach) is a functional disease of the stomach, while gastric ulcer is an organic disease.

THE SPECIAL FIELD OF PSYCHIC INFLUENCE

Psychic influences are especially powerful for good in the prevention and treatment of functional diseases. The functional disorders represent the realm of human suffering in which psychotherapy is of special value. The mind is unquestionably able to prevent numerous functional disturbances. Unhealthy mental states are likewise also able, sooner or later, to produce a large number of common functional disorders. The mental powers are also able directly or indirectly, partially or completely, to cure a large percentage of these so-called functional diseases, provided other exciting and aggravating causes are not present in too great a degree.

On the other hand, in the field of organic disease, the influence of the mind as a preventive and curative agent is greatly curtailed. It is very seldom that mental influences are directly responsible for organic disorders. The mind contributes to organic disease, by first setting up functional disturbances, which, when long continued, may predispose to actual derangement of the cells and organs of the body, and thereby, indirectly, contribute to the production of actual organic disease.

Only in this indirect manner, by preventing preceding functional disturbances, can the mind exert any great influence toward the prevention of organic diseases. With respect to the cure of organic disease, the mind does not possess that direct and powerful influence which it is able to exercise in the relief of functional disorders. In the treatment of organic diseases, the mind acts merely as a contributing factor because of its profound influence over the nervous and circulatory systems. It is able either to hasten or delay the recovery of organic disease. The mind may either increase or decrease the numerous functional symptoms and transitory disturbances which accompany organic disease, but it is never able instantaneously and apparently miraculously to cure organic disease as it is sometimes able to banish functional disorders.

It should be borne in mind that while many diseases may be

THE PSYCHOLOGY OF DISEASE

purely functional when acute, they usually become organic on becoming chronic or sub-acute. In this way, the mind indirectly becomes a factor in the causation of chronic and organic disease. The dividing line between functional and organic disease is not always easy to follow. It is sometimes exceedingly difficult to say whether certain diseases are functional or organic.

In order that the reader may more clearly understand and more fully comprehend the difference and distinction between functional and organic disease, there is herewith given a classification of the more common diseases, arranged in parallel columns, the functional disorders on the left and the organic diseases on the right.

COMPARATIVE TABLE OF COMMON FUNCTIONAL AND ORGANIC DISEASES

FUNCTIONAL DISEASES	ORGANIC DISEASES
Heart Diseases:	*Heart Diseases:*
Palpitation.	Pericarditis.
Rapid Heart.	Myocarditis.
Intermittent Pulse	Endocarditis.
Angina Pectoris (?)	Senile Heart Failure.
Fainting and Collapse	Cardiac Hypertrophy.
Nervous Heart Failure	Dilatation of the Heart.
Irregularity of the Heart.	Valvular Heart Diseases.
Heart Sensations and Pain.	Fatty Degeneration of the Heart.
Circulatory Disorders:	*Circulatory Disorders:*
Local Hyperæmia.	Aneurisms.
Anæmia — Relative.	Hemorrhoids.
Congestion — Active.	Varicose Veins.
Vaso-motor Instability.	Arteriosclerosis.
Angioneurotic Oedema.	Anæmia — Positive.
Capillary Spasm — Pale Skin.	Rupture of Blood Vessels.
Blood-pressure, High and Low.	Chronic Passive Congestion.
Digestive and Secretory Disturbances:	*Digestive and Secretory Disturbances:*
Constipation.	Hernia.
Enteroptosis (?)	Gall Stones.

FUNCTIONAL DISEASES
Urinary Variations.
Gastralgia and Colic.
Diarrhœa and Colitis.
Vomiting and Nausea.
Jaundice — Biliousness.
Nervous or Acid Dyspepsia.
Slow Digestion — Dilatation.
Acute Gastritis — Flatulence.
Variations in Secretion of Milk.

Mental and Nervous Disorders:
Brain-fag.
Hypochondria.
Trophic Disorders.
Insanity — Delirium.
Paralysis — Hysteric.
Migraine — Headache.
Epilepsy and Convulsions.
Neuralgia — Various Pains.
Neurasthenia — Nervousness.
St. Vitus's Dance — Tremors.
Hysteria — Abnormal Sensations.
Eye-strain, Hysteric Blindness.
Loss of Speech, Illusions, Delusions, Hallucinations.

Nutrition and Metabolism:
Emaciation.
Malnutrition.
Diabetes (?)
Deficient Elimination.

Respiratory Disorders:
Shallow Breathing.
Asthma and Hay-fèver.
Coughing and Hiccupping.
Derangements of Breathing.
Acute Catarrh — Colds.

ORGANIC DISEASES
Peritonitis.
Appendicitis.
Gastric Ulcer.
Chronic Gastritis.
Ulcerative Colitis.
Cancer of the Stomach.
Cirrhosis of the Liver.
Obstruction of Stomach Outlet
Permanent Dilatation and Atony.

Mental and Nervous Disorders:
Apoplexy.
Blindness.
Brain Tumors.
Spinal Sclerosis.
Facial Paralysis.
Locomotor Ataxia.
Infantile Paralysis.
Paralysis — Actual.
Neuritis — Chronic.
Insanity — Organic.
Raynaud's Disease — Ulcers.
Paresis — Softening of the Brain.
Organic Diseases of the Eye, Ear, and Nose.

Nutrition and Metabolism:
Bright's Disease.
Obesity — Goitre.
Arthritis Deformans.
Chronic Rheumatism — Gout.

Respiratory Disorders:
Pleurisy.
Tonsilitis.
Bronchitis.
Chronic Catarrh.
Thrush — Sore Mouth.

THE PSYCHOLOGY OF DISEASE

FUNCTIONAL DISEASES	ORGANIC DISEASES
Miscellaneous Diseases:	*Miscellaneous Diseases:*
Fever.	Rickets.
Lumbago.	Cancers.
Functional Pain.	Adenoids.
Muscular Spasm.	Gangrene.
Writer's Cramps.	Abscesses.
Shock — Nervous.	Deformities.
Muscular Fatigue.	Various Tumors.
Chills — Shivering.	Spinal Curvature.
Abnormal Sweating.	Warts and Moles.
Insomnia — Sleeplessness.	Various Bone Diseases.
Stammering and Stuttering.	Cataract, Decayed Teeth.
Skin Diseases — Functional.	Skin Diseases — Organic.
Enuresis — Wetting the Bed.	Pain in Organic Diseases.
Nervous and Skin Sensations.	Stone in Bladder or Kidney.

In this classification of diseases no mention is made of the acute infectious and contagious disorders; they will be discussed in the next chapter.

ACUTE AND CHRONIC DISEASE

In this connection it will be well to emphasize the distinction between acute and chronic disease. Acute disease is ordinarily an effort on the part of nature to overcome infection, eliminate poison, or repel some other invasion of the body by germs or other agents destructive of health. On the other hand, chronic disease represents a condition present very often after a change has taken place in the structures of the body, or after its functions have been more or less permanently deranged. Chronic disease is usually organic. The picture of chronic disease is not that of an active battle. It rather represents a state of compromise or partial surrender — a condition of more or less complete defeat sustained as the result of the unsuccessful struggles of acute disease — repeated attacks. Continued transgression, or the persistent operation of original exciting causes has overcome the body's defences. The acute disorder, the functional derangement, has become chronic or organic.

' In reality, disease is but an extraordinary struggle for life under conditions wholly unfavorable to health. Acute disease is simply nature fighting a brave battle for the sufferer's existence. The health-battle may be provoked by some acute infection or by the continued transgression of the laws governing the physical being. Disease is not an entity, but a condition; it is not a thing, but a relation. Health is nature at work in man under conditions of obedience — natural conditions; disease is the same force and power at work in man under conditions of disobedience — unnatural conditions.

Owing to erroneous ideas of the source of affliction and the nature of disease, many sincere souls have gone down to the grave in despondency and despair, because of physical afflictions supposed to be due to "the power of the enemy." These misguided sufferers question their Christian experience and doubt the genuineness of a faith which is unable to lift them above their physical infirmities, which they have been taught were solely due to the "power of Satan over their bodies."

THE MISSION OF PAIN AND THE LANGUAGE OF DISEASE

Pain is the outcry of the physical conscience against all bodily abuse and physical danger The language of suffering, when interpreted, tells of wrong habits and practices, unwholesome and unsanitary surroundings, and warns the afflicted one to reform and make speedy amends, to cease to do evil and learn to do well

Disease has been spoken of as both a corrective and curative process. This is not true of chronic disease: it is only acute disease that is curative. While disease is in its earlier stages, it is, in general, an effort on the part of nature to cure; but if the habits of life are not corrected, and if unfavorable surroundings are not removed, then, in the later states, it becomes a process of degeneration and destruction.

In the acute stage, nature ordinarily cures disease when the cause is removed; in chronic disease, even after the original causes have been removed, health is usually secured only by a process of persistent cultivation; or the disease may have taken on the form of an incurable malady.

Not only are most functional diseases acute while the organic disorders are usually chronic, but there exists a vast group of acute infections and contagious diseases not listed in the comparative summary of functional and organic diseases just cited. Being largely contagious and infectious, the mind, of course, exerts but a minimum of influence in their cause or cure, although mental influence may contribute much to lessening the severity of their numerous symptoms and complications.

THE EVOLUTION OF PSYCHIC DISTURBANCES INTO PHYSICAL DISORDERS

One of the most important facts in the relation of the mind to health and disease has been largely overlooked in the past; that is, the power of the mind to produce functional disturbances, which, when kept up from day to day, are able ultimately to produce such perversion of function and irritation of structure as eventually to result in the production of chronic disorders, or to lay the foundation for ultimate organic disease.

And this is what renders it so difficult — well-nigh impossible — to prepare a list of diseases which may or may not be wholly psychic in origin, or which may be amenable to psychic treatment. The foregoing classification of common diseases is intended to be merely suggestive, it cannot possibly be anything more. It is out of the question, in our present understanding of the case, accurately to classify diseases in any such a manner. The author has ventured to give these lists in this connection merely to suggest a working division of common diseases into those which are largely amenable to psychic treatment, and those which are either uninfluenced by the mental state, or else but doubtfully.

FEAR A PSYCHIC CONTAGION

In this connection, it may be well to notice some of the dangers connected with the well-meaning efforts of the physician and the sanitarian to enlighten the public; in fact, the same dangers attend the efforts of the medical practitioner as he seeks to teach his patients the care of the body. It is this: if the public are to be left in hygienic ignorance, disease is bound to spread and the death rate be greatly increased; on the other hand, owing to the peculiar tendency of most people to think unduly of themselves, and owing to the powerful influence of the mind to disturb the functions and disorder the body when allowed inordinately to dwell on things physical, the health-teacher is confronted with this great danger: Hygienic enlightenment not infrequently carries along with it almost certain danger of dyspepsia and neurasthenia.

There is no question that the spread of hygienic information and the diffusion of sanitary knowledge has done much to lessen disease, and to increase the average length of life; nevertheless, there can be but little doubt that thousands of nervous and self-centred people, experiencing but a fair degree of health, are actually made sick by reading health books and health magazines, especially that health literature belonging to the old-fashioned alarming and gloomy doctor-book class. Auto-suggestion does much to give them the diseases about which they read. The almanac thrown on the porch has made an invalid of many an unfortunate woman who has read it.

The psychology of the world plagues and epidemics would indeed be an interesting bit of history if it were fully known. There can be no doubt that large numbers of people die in connection with great epidemics, whose disease and departure must largely be charged up to the panic of fear prevailing at the time. There is no doubt that yellow fever, smallpox, and diphtheria, when they obtain an epidemic foothold in the community, scare hundreds and even thousands of people so badly that they fall ready victims to the disease. Hundreds die as a result of this unhealthy mental condition which lowers the vital resistance and invites a fatal attack of the prevailing malady.

Fear itself is a contagious disease, and swiftly sweeps from one mind to another when large numbers of people are gathered together. A single excited soul can render a vast crowd panic-stricken in less than sixty seconds.

THE FATIGUE OF FEAR

Dr. Hodge of Clark University some time ago made a very extraordinary and interesting series of observations respecting the relation of fatigue and exhaustion to certain nerve centres. He first made use of honey-bees, and later other small animals. A careful microscopic examination disclosed great visible differences between the nerve cells when in a state of fatigue, and their appearance when in a rested state. For instance, it is possible accurately to tell upon microscopic examination of a nerve cell taken from a bee, whether the bee was killed on leaving the hive in the morning, or captured on returning at night after a day's work. (See Fig. 4.) It is highly probable that the psychic state is able to contribute much toward the prevention of these fatigue conditions in the nerve cell. This explains exactly why one can do such a great amount of work when the mind is happy and the heart is in the labor performed.

The power to sustain the lagging steps of a tired army, the influence of expected reward, and an effectual appeal to the emotions are all sufficient partially to overcome fatigue and energize the exhausted muscles. These psychic influences are able to give the body what might be called its "second wind."

Some people possess the power of carrying forward their life's work from day to day quite independent of the stress and strain experienced by those who lack this intellectual balance and nervous control. They are able to perform a tremendous amount of work with a minimum amount of fatigue. The fatigue of extraordinary muscular effort is easy to recover from, while the fatigue of mental strain and long-continued worry not infrequently persists to that point where it becomes well-nigh continuous, and this results, sooner or later, in producing a chronic state of neurasthenia.

It is well-known that when one greatly fears exhaustion, muscular weariness soon follows. To doubt one's ability to perform a task, either mental or physical, is a sufficient guarantee of early exhaustion and severe fatigue symptoms.

THE CASTING-OUT OF FEAR

From the cradle to the grave the barbarian, the semi-civilized, and even the modern civilized races, all live under the debilitating blight of fear. In childhood, fears are early entertained lest the little ones shall be stricken with the numerous diseases common to that period of life. In advancing years, physical, mental, and moral dangers are incessantly feared; and at last, on-coming old age and inevitable death constitute an ever-present fear during the declining years of life. Some fear the weather and the winds, catching cold and hay-fever, drought and floods; while a thousand and one other pessimistic and morbid unrealities harass others at various periods of life.

In addition to the common fears of life, certain persons suffer from fear of accident, calamity, fire, pestilence, and other disasters. The life is constantly tortured with ghosts, and tormented with hobgoblins. Men and women fear to live, and fear worse to die.

The only hope of deliverance from this perpetual bondage of fear is so fully to surrender the mind to natural faith and normal trust, that there shall take place a sweeping intellectual housecleaning, after which the psychic forces shall be allied on the side of faith and health, and fear shall finally and forever be cast down and forced out of its dominant role in our thoughts and meditations. If we are not always able to thus overpower and eject our fear thoughts by the power and influence of positive faith thoughts, then let us temporarily assume the belief in certain dogmatic truths — pretend that faith is the victor — and proceed to think and act in perfect harmony with this assumption. If we persist in the mental declaration that hate can be mastered by love, if we daily insist that love is conquering hate in our lives, eventually it will appear that our thoughts have triumphed — love will indeed be found to have ascended the throne and assumed command.

SUMMARY OF THE CHAPTER

1. In general, all diseases may be classified as functional and organic. The functional disorders constitute the special field of operation for psychic influences.

2. In the field of organic diseases, the influence of the mind as a preventive and curative agent is greatly curtailed. The mind contributes to the causation of organic disease by producing preceding functional disturbances.

3. With respect to the cure of organic disease, the mind does not possess that direct and powerful influence which it is able to exercise in the relief of functional disorders.

4. In chronic disease, the mind may hasten or delay recovery; it may increase or decrease the numerous functional symptoms and transitory disturbances which usually accompany organic disorders.

5. Many disorders are functional when acute, but become organic when chronic. Acute disease is ordinarily an effort

THE PSYCHOLOGY OF DISEASE

on the part of nature to cure — it is an active battle to overcome infection and preserve life.

6. On the other hand, chronic disease represents a physical attitude of more or less complete surrender to the forces of disease. Ordinarily, acute disease will recover of itself, provided the exciting causes are removed; not so with chronic disease, it yields only to persistent treatment, and not infrequently is found to be incurable.

7. Disease is not an entity, but a condition; it is not a thing, but a relation. Health is nature at work in man under natural conditions; disease is the same power at work under unnatural conditions.

8. Pain is the outcry of the physical conscience against physical danger. The language of disease constitutes a solemn warning against wrong habits, unwholesome practices, and unsanitary surroundings.

9. Acute disease is both curative and corrective; chronic disease, in its later stages, becomes a process of degeneration and destruction.

10. It is entirely possible for one-time psychical disturbances to evolve into later physical disorders.

11. Fear is a psychic contagion. It is even dangerous for some susceptible persons to read health-literature — they are so liable to acquire the disease about which they read. The almanac has manufactured many an invalid.

12. Fear undoubtedly adds greatly to the mortality of all great epidemics. Worry weakens the resistance of the body to all infectious and contagious diseases.

13. The nerve cell of a honey-bee looks different at night after a day's work from what it does in the morning. Fear and worry exhaust the energies of the nerve centres much sooner than physical work.

14. Neurasthenia is a state of the nervous system where fatigue has become continuous — chronic. Fear and worry are the chief factors in producing nervous prostration.

15. Cast out fear. Surrender the mind to natural faith and normal trust. Let the psychic forces be allied with faith and health, let fear be finally and forever cast down and banished from the mental domain.

CHAPTER XXVIII

THE PSYCHIC ELEMENT IN THE CAUSE AND CURE OF DISEASE

THE AFFIRMATION OF HEALTH AND THE DENIAL OF DISEASE.— DISEASES WHICH MAY BE DIRECTLY AND IMMEDIATELY CURED BY PSYCHIC INFLUENCES.— DISORDERS OF THE HEART AND THE CIRCULATION.— DISEASES OF THE DIGESTIVE SYSTEM AND DISTURBANCES OF SECRETION.— MENTAL AND NERVOUS DISORDERS. — DISORDERS OF RESPIRATION, NUTRITION, AND METABOLISM. —MISCELLANEOUS DISEASES.— THE RELATION OF THE MIND TO ACUTE CONTAGIOUS AND INFECTIOUS DISEASES.— ACCIDENTS, POISONING, AND INTOXICATIONS.— SUMMARY OF THE CHAPTER.

IT is generally believed by experienced physicians that at least two-thirds of the ordinary cases of sickness which doctors are called upon to treat would, if left entirely alone, recover without the aid of the doctor or his medicine. In the majority of cases, the recovery would occur almost as quickly and completely as under medical treatment, provided the patients could have good hygienic care and proper nursing; together with influences tending to produce a positive expectation of recovery.

THE AFFIRMATION OF HEALTH AND THE DENIAL OF DISEASE

There are preventive possibilities and curative powers in the positive affirmation of health on the part of the mind. There is genuine ability to resist sickness in the positive denial of disease. This fact probably constitutes one of the great secrets of success in the spread of so-called Christian Science. By means of the fallacious denial of all human diseases, the Christian Scientist is able at least to escape those disturbances which are purely psychic in origin.

Human health and happiness cannot be greatly promoted if

the civilized races do not bear in mind two great truths: first, the influence of the mind in the prevention of disease; second, the marvellous power of nature to heal. The mind exerts its wonderful influences over the body largely through the avenue of three special sets of nerves, the sensory nerves, the vasomotor nerves, and the trophic nerves.

Concerning the influence of the mind on health, the noted Dr. Osler says:

"The psychical method has always played an important, though largely unrecognized, part in therapeutics. It is from faith, which buoys up the spirits, sets the blood flowing more freely, and the nerves playing their part without disturbance, that a large part of the cure arises. Despondency or lack of faith will often sink the stoutest constitution almost to death's door. Faith will enable a spoonful of water or a bread pill to do almost miracles of healing when the best medicines have been given up in despair. The basis of the entire profession of medicine is faith in the doctor, his drugs, and his methods."

The author does not place so much faith in the negative side of psychotherapy; that is, the denial of disease. The positive affirmation of health is the important thing, and this is nothing more or less than hygienic auto-suggestion.

DISEASES WHICH MAY BE DIRECTLY AND IMMEDIATELY CURED BY PSYCHIC INFLUENCES

Having quite fully considered the difference between functional and organic diseases and the distinction between acute and chronic disorders, in the preceding chapter, it will now be in place more specifically to discuss the exact relation of the mind to the cause and cure of various common physical maladies.

It should be recalled that a great many diseases can be wholly produced and completely cured by mental influences alone. Such diseases, of course, are purely functional. Other chronic and organic diseases, as such, cannot be produced by exclusive mental influences, neither can they be fully cured by unaided psychic power. It is true that many such chronic organic diseases are but the results of preceding acute and functional disorders, and it must be recognized that very often these functional diseases, which prove to be the forerunners of chronic and organic disorders, were not infrequently wholly or partially due to psychic influences.

We are forced to recognize two great classes of physical disorders: one in which the mind is a powerful factor in both the cause and the cure; the other — the organic diseases — in which the mind exerts but a minimum influence. In addition to these two great classes of diseases there may be recognized a third class of physical disorders, in which the mind exerts a varying and uncertain influence, both as to causation and cure.

There exists a great class of human diseases which the mind cannot cause and which it cannot cure, and yet it can contribute much toward increasing or diminishing the intensity of the disease and the severity of its symptoms. Psychic influences often can do much to control symptoms as well as to lessen the progress of the disease and mitigate the suffering. We will now take up briefly various groups of common diseases and note more specifically the influence of the mind in connection therewith.

In all our study of the psychic cause and treatment of disease, there is one important fact which should constantly be borne in mind: *The majority of the diseases which can be mentally produced and psychically cured, can also be produced by other (material) influences, and likewise they may be cured by the employment of physical agencies — material treatment.* Psychic influences are able to cause many physical disorders, which, when they have long existed, the mind is by no means able to cure by its own unaided efforts.

I. DISORDERS OF THE HEART AND CIRCULATION

A. Diseases which can be caused and partially or wholly cured by psychic influences:

Intermittent Pulse.
Fainting and Collapse.
Nervous Heart-failure.
Palpitation of the Heart.
Abnormally Rapid Heart.
Pain in the Cardiac Region.
Capillary Spasm — Pale Skin.
Irregularity of Heart Action.
Local Hyperæmia — Mild Forms of Congestion.

Low Blood-pressure, as in Nervous Prostration.
High Blood-pressure with its Attendant Disorders.
Sluggish Circulation — Chronically Cold Hands and Feet.
Vaso-motor Instability — Loss of Circulatory Equilibrium.
Abnormal and Unpleasant Sensations in the Region of the Heart.

CAUSE AND CURE OF DISEASE

B. Diseases in which the mind may be only indirectly concerned in the causation, and which the mind alone cannot possibly cure, although the psychic state may mitigate symptoms and assist in relieving the suffering:

Aneurisms.
Hemorrhoids.
Varicose Veins.
Anæmia — Positive.
Senile Heart Failure.
Valvular Heart Diseases.
Permanent Dilation of the Heart.
Fatty Degeneration of the Heart.
Cardiac Hypertrophy — Enlargement.
Myocarditis — Inflammation of the Heart Muscle.
Arteriosclerosis or Hardening of the Arteries.
Endocarditis — Inflammation of the Heart Lining.
Pericarditis — Inflammation of the Heart Coverings.

C. Diseases in which the mind exerts a varying and uncertain influence, sometimes being more or less responsible for the causation, and more or less concerned in the cure:

Arteriosclerosis.
Angina Pectoris.
Relative Anæmia.
Angioneurotic Oedema.
Rupture of Blood Vessels.
Chronic Passive Congestion.
Local Congestion and Inflammation.

II. DISEASES OF THE DIGESTIVE SYSTEM AND DISTURBANCES OF SECRETION

A. Diseases which can be caused and partially or wholly cured by psychic influences:

Diarrhœa.
Constipation.
Acute Gastritis.
Slow Digestion.
Nervous Dyspepsia.
Nausea and Vomiting.
Gastralgia — Stomach Neuralgia.
Flatulency — Eructations of Gas.
Variations of the Urinary Secretion.
Secretions of the Mammary Gland — Milk.
Acid Dyspepsia — Souring of the Stomach.

B. Diseases in which the mind may be only indirectly concerned in the causation, and which the mind alone cannot possibly cure, although the psychic state may mitigate symptoms and assist in relieving the suffering:

Hernia.
Gall Stones.
Appendicitis.
Gastric Ulcer.
Ulcerative Colitis — Ulcer of the Bowel.
Peritonitis — Inflammation of the Bowels.

Cancer of the Stomach.
Permanent Dilatation of the Stomach.
Cirrhosis of the Liver — Hobnail Liver.

Chronic. Gastritis — Catarrh of the Stomach.
Pyloric Obstruction — Obstruction of the Stomach Outlet.

C. Diseases in which the mind exerts a varying and uncertain influence, sometimes being more or less responsible for the causation, and more or less concerned in the cure:

Acute Colitis.
Jaundice — Biliousness.
Dilatation of the Stomach.
Gastric Atony — Muscular Weakness.

Certain Forms of Cramps and Colic.
Enteroptosis — Falling down of Abdominal Organs.

III. MENTAL AND NERVOUS DISORDERS

A. Diseases which can be caused and partially or wholly cured by psychic influences:

Delirium.
Brain-fag.
Headaches.
Hypochondria.
Nervous Tremors.
Hysteric Blindness.
General Nervousness.
Paralysis — Hysterical.
Pain — Pseudo-neuralgia.
Spasm and Convulsions.
Epilepsy — Certain Forms.
Insanity — Certain Forms.

Hysteria — In Certain Cases.
Neurasthenia — Nervous Exhaustion.
St. Vitus's Dance — In Some Cases.
Trophic Disorders — Disturbances of the General or Local Nutrition.
Temporary Loss of Speech, Illusions, Delusions, Hallucinations.

B. Diseases in which the mind may be only indirectly concerned in the causation, and which the mind alone cannot possibly cure, although the psychic state may mitigate symptoms and assist in relieving the suffering:

Brain Tumors.
Facial Paralysis.
Spinal Sclerosis.
Chronic Neuritis.
Locomotor Ataxia.
Paralysis — Actual.
Blindness — Actual.

Infantile Paralysis.
Raynaud's Disease — Ulcers.
Paresis — Softening of the Brain.
Insanity — Organic Brain Disorders.
Organic Diseases of the Eye, Ear, or Nose.

C. Diseases in which the mind exerts a varying and uncertain influence, sometimes being more or less responsible for the causation, and more or less concerned in the cure:

Apoplexy.	Epilepsy — Certain Forms.
Neuralgia.	Migraine — Nervous Sick Head-
General Hysteria.	ache.
St. Vitus's Dance.	Eye Strain and Other Eye Weak-
Paralysis Agitans.	nesses.
Insanity — Certain Forms.	

IV. DISORDERS OF RESPIRATION, NUTRITION, AND METABOLISM

A. Diseases which can be caused and partially or wholly cured by psychic influences:

Malnutrition.	Coughing and Hiccupping.
Chronic Emaciation.	Derangements of Breathing.
Hay-fever — Certain Forms.	

B. Diseases in which the mind may be only indirectly concerned in the causation, and which the mind alone cannot possibly cure, although the psychic state may mitigate symptoms and assist in relieving the suffering:

Gout.	Chronic Catarrh.
Goitre.	Bright's Disease.
Obesity.	Arthritis Deformans.
Pleurisy.	Chronic Rheumatism.
Tonsilitis.	Thrush — Sore Mouth.
Bronchitis.	

C. Diseases in which the mind exerts a varying and uncertain influence, sometimes being more or less responsible for the causation, and more or less concerned in the cure:

Asthma.	Colds — Acute Catarrh.
Diabetes.	

V. MISCELLANEOUS DISEASES

A. Diseases which can be caused and partially or wholly cured by psychic influences:

Functional Pain.	Insomnia — Sleeplessness.
Shock — Nervous.	Stammering and Stuttering.
Muscular Spasms.	Skin Diseases — Functional.
Muscular Fatigue.	Abnormal Sensations Arising in
Abnormal Sweating.	the Skin and the Nerves.
Chills and Shivering.	

B. Diseases in which the mind may be only indirectly concerned in the causation, and which the mind alone cannot possibly cure, although the psychic state may mitigate symptoms and assist in relieving the sufferings:

Rickets.	Organic Skin Diseases.
Cancers.	Various Bone Diseases.
Adenoids.	Stone in Bladder or Kidney.
Gangrene.	Pain Attending Organic Diseases.
Abscesses.	
Deformities.	Spinal Curvature — Long Standing.
Decayed Teeth.	
Various Tumors.	Cataract and Other Defects of the Eye.
Warts and Moles.	

C. Diseases in which the mind exerts a varying and uncertain influence, sometimes being more or less responsible for the causation, and more or less concerned in the cure:

Fever.	Writer's Cramps.
Lumbago.	Enuresis — Wetting the Bed.

THE RELATION OF THE MIND TO ACUTE CONTAGIOUS AND INFECTIOUS DISEASES

The reader has no doubt noticed that in the study of functional and organic, as well as acute and chronic disorders, no mention has been made of the numerous acute infectious and contagious diseases. The mental state is but little concerned in these diseases, as before noted, except in so far as the psychic state may contribute to the weakening of the vital resistance, by means of fear and worry disturbances, thus predisposing the sufferer to "catching disease." Only in this indirect way is the psychic state concerned in the causation of these common contagious and infectious disorders. A possible exception is the case of the venereal infections, where the individual directly and knowingly exposes himself to infection; but this can hardly be included under the head of psychic influences, as it is a case of deliberate exposure to known danger.

The following list of diseases comprises the more common infections, and are those which are particularly dangerous to the race, when the idea is entertained that all diseases are mental in origin and wholly subject to psychic cure. This list of contagious diseases includes the maladies which are rendered more dangerous by all those systems of belief which deny the existence of disease, and which are therefore liable to resist all efforts of quarantine or to ignore the isolation imposed by the health authorities.

TABLE OF ACUTE INFECTIOUS AND CONTAGIOUS DISEASES

Boils.	Mumps.	Leprosy.
Erysipelas.	Measles.	Anthrax.
Inflammation.	Smallpox.	Cholera.
Typhus Fever.	Diphtheria.	Glanders.
Yellow Fever.	Meningitis.	Influenza.
Typhoid Fever.	Hydrophobia.	Pneumonia.
Malarial Fever.	Chickenpox.	Dysentery.
Relapsing Fever.	Scarlet Fever.	The Plague.
Rheumatic Fever.	Whooping-cough.	Tuberculosis.
Septicemia — Blood Poisoning.	Tetanus — Lockjaw.	Syphilis and Gonorrhea.

ACCIDENTS, POISONING, AND INTOXICATIONS

There remains but one more miscellaneous group of human afflictions to be considered. It is quite difficult, in a general way, to explain the relation of the psychic state to these disorders. Accidents, intoxications, and poisoning may be summarized as follows:

Poisoning	*Accidents*	*Parasites*
Alcoholism.	Burns.	Worms.
Heat Stroke.	Scalds.	Itches.
Drug Habits.	Fractures.	Trichina.
Food Poisoning.	Hemorrhages.	Tape Worms.
Auto-intoxication.	Dislocations.	
Mineral Poisoning.	Surgical Disorders.	

In the case of alcoholism (drunkenness) the mind certainly plays an important part in the acute or early stage. Later, the disease becomes one of general degeneration both in mind and body, and it is very seldom that a cure is effected by the mind alone, unaided by other influences and treatments. The same state of affairs exists in morphinism. The mind as concerned in treating these drug habits was quite fully considered in a previous chapter.

Cases of food poisoning and mineral poisoning are usually accidental, while auto-intoxication or chronic self-poisoning, is a condition usually associated with errors in diet and deficient elimination. Heat stroke usually results from an accumulation of metabolic poisons in the body, and is directly due to the demoralization of the heat-regulating mechanism.

With reference to accidents, the mind is only concerned in the capacity of negligence or unawareness, and it is self-evident that the mind cannot of itself effect a cure of fractures, dislocations, or hemorrhages, though the mental state may directly contribute toward relieving the suffering, as well as toward encouraging the patient bearing of the subsequent inconvenience and embarrassment. There is a vast group of so-called surgical diseases which demand mechanical interference for their relief, and the mind can be regarded only as a contributing factor in either the cause or the cure of disorders belonging to this class.

With reference to the parasites which may infest the skin or infect the body, the mind certainly is but little concerned. The psychic state may control functional itching of the skin, but it would be difficult for the mind to overcome the sensations attending the burrowing of the itch-mite underneath the skin. Worms, tape worms, and trichinæ, likewise invariably demand appropriate treatment.

SUMMARY OF THE CHAPTER

1. There are preventive possibilities and curative powers in the positive affirmation of health and the firm denial of sickness.

2. There are two great health truths which should not be forgotten: first, the power of the mind to prevent disease; and, second, the marvellous power of nature to heal.

3. Faith will enable a spoonful of water or a bread pill to accomplish almost miracles of healing when the best medicines have been given up in despair.

4. Many functional diseases can be wholly produced and completely cured by mental influences alone. Other chronic and organic disorders, as such, cannot be produced or cured by exclusively psychic influences.

5. Functional diseases, wholly or partially due to psychic influences, not infrequently prove to be the forerunners of chronic and organic disorders — diseases but little subject to the psychic curative powers.

CAUSE AND CURE OF DISEASE

6. Even when mental influences cannot remove disease, the state of the mind is able to accomplish much toward the controlling of symptoms, as well as to lessen the progress of the disease and mitigate suffering.

7. The majority of diseases which can be mentally produced and psychically cured can also be produced and cured by material influences — physical agencies. The mind is able to cause physical disorders, which, when they have long existed, the psychic powers are unable to cure by their own unaided efforts.

8. Numerous heart diseases and disorders of the circulation can be caused and partially or wholly cured by the mind, such as fainting, heart failure, palpitation, high blood-pressure. Other disorders in which the mind is but little concerned are, valvular heart diseases, arteriosclerosis, and fatty degeneration of the heart. In numerous other disorders, the mind is only indirectly concerned.

9. Many disturbances of secretion and disorders of indigestion are almost wholly due to the mental state, such as acid dyspepsia, nausea and vomiting, diarrhœa, and constipation. while such disorders as gastric ulcer and gall stones are but little related to the psychic state.

10. Numerous mental and nervous diseases — brain-fag, neurasthenia, hysteria, and headaches — may be directly caused by the state of the mind. Other nervous disorders, such as infantile paralysis, locomotor ataxia, and brain tumors, are quite independent of the psychic state.

11. While coughing, hay-fever, and malnutrition may spring from purely psychic influences, tonsilitis, gout, and Bright's disease are neither caused nor cured by exclusively mental power.

12. Fatigue, stammering, and insomnia may result from fear and worry; but cancers, tumors, and stone in the bladder are physical disorders over which the mind wields but little direct power in either their causation or cure.

13. The mind is concerned in the production of acute infectious and contagious diseases, only in so far as fear is able to weaken the vital resistance of the body and predispose a person

to infection. Faith contributes to hastening the recovery from all these disorders, such as typhoid fever, pneumonia, and influenza.

14. The mind is a powerful factor in the cause and cure of alcoholism and other drug habits, but it usually requires that the mental powers should be reinforced by moral strength and physical treatment.

15. Only in so far as carelessness is concerned, the mind is unable either to prevent or cure accidents and their consequences; although the mental state of sufferers from accidents has much to do with determining the degree of inconvenience and embarrassment which may attend fractures and other surgical accidents.

CHAPTER XXIX

MENTAL MEDICINE AND MORAL HYGIENE

THE ANCIENT PHYSICIAN-PRIESTS.— THE DIVORCEMENT OF THEOLOGY AND THERAPEUTICS.— THE EMMANUEL MOVEMENT.— FAITH A VITAL ENERGY.— THE RELIGIOUS LIFE.— SIN AND SICKNESS.— THE MORAL MASTERY.— SUMMARY OF THE CHAPTER.

IN recent years, we are coming more and more to look upon man as a whole — to recognize that every human being represents a community of diversified interests, embracing problems of mind, morals, and matter. Nowadays, we seldom treat a sick man by administering medicine designed merely to relieve his immediate symptoms; we rarely exclusively direct our therapeutic efforts simply at the ailing vital organ or the offending physical member. In most diseases, we find it advisable to treat the whole physical man — not merely to combat his local symptoms.

And so, having advanced in modern therapeutics to that point where we recognize the necessity of treating the whole physical body in most cases of common disorders, the time is certainly ripe for a further forward movement in the scientific and sensible treatment of human disease. The next great advance in modern therapeutics consists in a greater recognition of the importance of treating not merely the whole *body*, but of administering therapeutically to the whole *man* — to the mental man and the moral as well as to the material man; to the psychic man as well as to the physical man.

THE ANCIENT PHYSICIAN-PRIESTS

In ancient times (the pre-Christian era) the professions of physician and priest were often combined in the same individual. The ancient ministers of religion were also the custodians of the physical happiness and sanitary welfare of the people.

The Hebrew priests gave the same careful attention to the dietetic practices and the sanitary regulations affecting the physical health of the Jews, that they gave to ceremonial rituals and the theological teaching concerned in their mental and moral instruction. The priest of that day and age represented the highest knowledge and skill in medicine as well as in theology. (Fig. 27.)

In the Mosaic laws there may be found most careful and minute instructions relating to diagnosis, sanitation, quarantine, and dietetics, and many of these sanitary laws would do great credit even to our modern sanitarians.

Since the physicians of the ancient peoples were often their own priests, it is highly probable that the sick and afflicted among them were in receipt of abundant religious consolation. To call a priest of that day to the bedside of the sick and suffering, was equivalent to calling a doctor, a minister, and a psychologist. The old-time priest practised to the best of his light and knowledge; and there were none in his day who understood these things better than he — all the principles of medicine, the physical treatment of disease; and religion, the moral treatment of disease. While through his forms and ceremonies, in a most wonderful and effective manner he appealed to the faith of his subjects, he was also a successful practitioner of mental medicine — psychotherapy.

Mediæval medicine was closely allied to priest-craft, and was necessarily permeated with the superstitions of that credulous age. All down through history, the practice of the healing art has been closely related to the religious thought of the times; and it was not until the last century that a purely materialistic medical philosophy came fully to bud and blossom.

THE DIVORCEMENT OF THEOLOGY AND THERAPEUTICS

The real foundation for the divorcement and separation of theology and therapeutics was laid in the dark ages, when there sprang into prominence the doctrine of physical penance and bodily humiliation, which culminated in the teaching that "the healthiest souls dwelt in the sickliest bodies." From that day forward, while religion continued to grope its way in the uncertain realms of superstition and speculation, medicine began

FIG. 27. AN ANCIENT PHYSICIAN - PRIEST

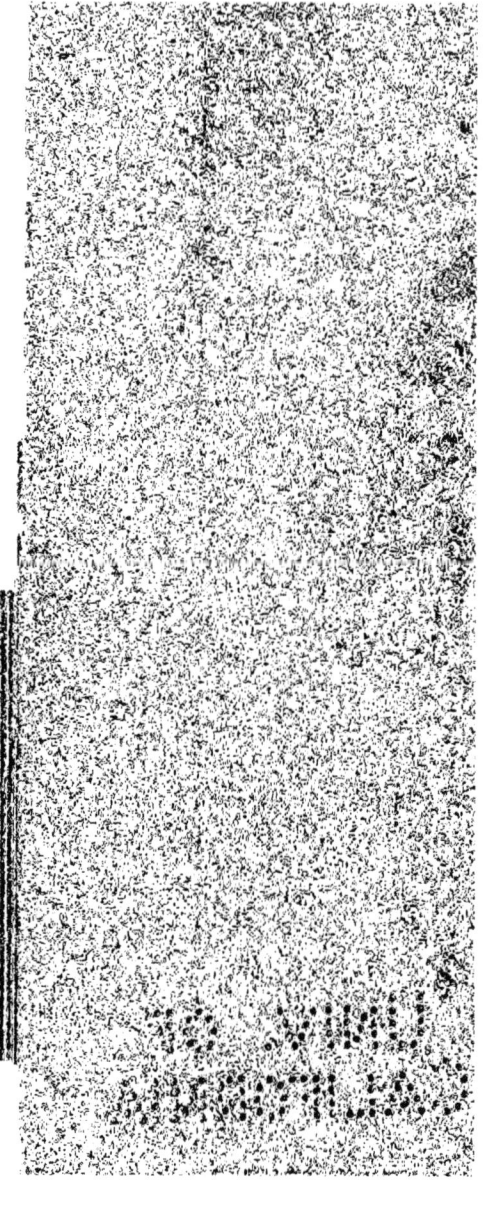

MENTAL MEDICINE AND MORAL HYGIENE 313

its long and laborious march on a new and materialistic pathway, toward its ultimate goal of scientific accuracy — freedom from empiricism and superstition. From decade to decade, from century to century, the breach widened until the last generation witnessed the absolute and final separation of theology and therapeutics. The preacher developed exclusively into a moral teacher; the physician came to be occupied alone with physical disease and its treatment.

In the olden time, the afflicted soul could summon the priest, and this one man represented the highest knowledge and attainment in mental medicine, material medicine, and spiritual succor. But times have changed. The last generation has established a new order of dealing with human sickness and sorrow; now the afflicted one must summon a doctor for physical help, a preacher for spiritual help, and, unless doctor and preacher, singly or together, understand and appreciate mental therapeutics, he may, in the end, be forced to summon a third party to give him needed help along the lines of mental medicine.

And so the modern priest has come to deal only with religion, while the work of his old-time predecessor in the line of treating physical disease has been wholly taken over by a carefully trained and highly specialized medical profession. Both the preacher and the doctor have made a fatal mistake in utterly ignoring the principles and practice of mental medicine; so that, while the doctor may treat the body and the preacher minister to the soul, the people have been turned largely over to quacks and charlatans to secure their needed help in ministrations to the burdened mind and the sorrowful heart.

The separation of theology and medicine was inevitable. The ancient theologians directed therapeutics into superstitious channels, and in many other ways stifled scientific investigation and therapeutic progress; on the other hand, the leading spirits in medicine were becoming more and more materialistic and were gradually undermining the spiritual foundations of religious hope. For the time being, it was to the interest of both professions that they should be completely divorced; and the two have grown steadily apart, until in very recent years we are beginning to observe a disposition in some quarters to effect a more cordial working relation between the doctor and the minister.

THE EMMANUEL MOVEMENT

We have only kind words to say for the Emmanuel Movement or any other movement capable of uplifting humanity and bringing together ministers and doctors for the purpose of helping forward the great movement to popularize psychotherapy. Until the minister has given more attention to the questions of health and disease, we believe that all successful efforts and permanent movements for the practice of mental medicine will have to be largely carried forward by the medical profession, with the coöperation of minister and layman, of all who have a mind to help in the glorious work of emancipating the people from the bondage of fear.

We cannot but doubt the efficiency and permanency of such movements organized by ministers, with physicians merely coöperating. Not only so, but we seriously doubt the wisdom of the physician who for an hour would resign a difficult case, though it were known or thought to be merely functional, to the care of one whose training has been that of the psychotherapist alone. This we urge on the ground of what has been previously said with regard to the behavior of functional disorders. We cannot draw a sharp and indisputable line between functional and organic diseases. The medical practitioner cannot foretell the time when the apparently functional disturbance which he turned over to the mental healer may become organic, and so pass entirely out of the reach of the psychic practitioner. Let the two coöperate as the leaders of the Emmanuel Movement suggest, but good sense will insist that the coöperation shall be of the closest kind, and that it shall be only a makeshift, pending the day when medical men may be equipped to undertake both methods of treating disease.

It is a great mistake on the part of the medical profession that physicians of the present generation have not led out in all this work, for certainly the medical man is the proper person to assume the grave responsibility of the practice of mental medicine. Perhaps physicians of the next generation, who have had more training in physiological psychology, will assume the burden and leadership of this new work of mental healing. It is certainly to be hoped that medical psychology will soon become a part of the regular curriculum of all first-class medical schools.

Until physicians, as a profession, are able and willing to blaze the way for the advance of scientific psychic teaching and practice, we should certainly be very sparing of our criticism of those well-meaning ministers who have had the courage to move out along these new lines. Let us be exceedingly charitable toward the blunders they may make, until such a time as we are prepared to direct them into more successful and scientific methods of work.

The people are hungry for sympathy, for encouragement, for advice and guidance; and, in the light of modern psychology, we are forced to recognize that all systems of religious belief, more or less afford this psychic help. Every phase of religious teaching which specializes on divine healing, is moving forward in the world with great rapidity. The Roman Catholic Church undoubtedly holds many of its members because of the peculiar mental relief afforded by the confessional. Troubled souls unbosom their sorrows and go away consoled, and, of course, physically and psychically helped in proportion.

FAITH A VITAL ENERGY

Faith, as used in this text, means decidedly more than mere belief. Living faith is not merely a theological adjunct to a theoretical religion. Faith is a vitalizing attribute of the human mind — it possesses tremendous physical possibilities and extraordinary therapeutic powers. Tolstoi once called faith "the force of life."

"After all," says Dr. Osler, "faith is a great leveller of life. Without it, man can do nothing; with it, even with a fragment, as a grain of mustard seed, all things are possible to him. Faith in us, faith in our drugs and methods, is the great stock in trade of the profession. . . . It is the *aurum potabile*, the touchstone of success in medicine. As Galen says, 'Confidence and hope do more good than physic.' He cures most in whom most are confident."

Faith means more than belief. To believe a thing is merely to accept it by our reason: to realize that no facts or logical considerations of any kind exist which can prevail against it. Faith implies such acceptance even in the face of considerations of fact or of logic; their reality may be recognized, but they are consistently ignored when they appear in relation to the object of our faith. Faith calls for a complete and unconditional surrender of one's whole body, soul, and spirit, to the idea or thing which is believed in. Faith, of necessity, must further include the idea of obedience to that which it accepts.

Belief only requires the coöperation of the intellectual powers, and an impartial distribution of the affections, over the whole field of those mental processes by the activity of which belief is attained. Faith demands the consecration of the whole mind, the concentration of the affections upon a given idea or upon a preconceived object. Faith demands and implies a thorough control of the emotions; the coöperation of the spiritual forces on the one hand, and the physical forces on the other. The highest known development of faith is to be found in the faith of Christianity, which represents the most all-inclusive, the most powerful and transcendent mental action, moral exercise, and spiritual force known to man. The "Faith of Jesus" is a supernatural power — a divine attribute, and must not be confused with our discussions of faith in the psychologic sense.

The religions of modern times have been in imminent danger of becoming weak and effeminate. The world to-day needs more of the militant but wisely directed spirit of the early Christian religion. We must come to exercise more faith and manifest more determination in the pursuit of the higher and nobler aims of life. Faith is a tremendous motive power and when it once dominates the soul, it is able to harness the mind and control the body; it is able to combat disease and relieve suffering; yes, it is able to vanquish sorrow and establish peace.

THE RELIGIOUS LIFE

Why is the religious experience of so many thousands of church members so unsatisfactory? Why are professed Christians so downcast and discouraged? Why is it so few people get happiness and joy out of their religion? They apparently accept religion with a whole heart, join the church, and, instead of growing more and more joyful, they not infrequently become more and more sorrowful, and a small number subsequently land in the asylum, leaving behind them the stigma of having "gone crazy over religion."

While the author would not undertake fully to account for this condition among professed Christians, he suspects that many of these people have embraced theology instead of accepting Christianity. Many of these unfortunate devotees of religion are trying to duplicate in their lives the religious experience of some other human being with whom they are acquainted or about whom they have read. Had they become like little children, simply accepting the teachings of the Christ, they would have found an abundant entrance into the three glorious kingdoms: the kingdom of Heaven, the kingdom of happiness, and the kingdom of health. Fear unfailingly leads its victims on the pathway to moral defeat, physical suffering, and sanctified sorrow.

There can be no doubt that religious suggestion is far more powerful with the average individual than secular suggestion. Religious suggestions probably carry a greater force because of their power to appeal to a far greater group of psychic powers and spiritual energies. The feelings and emotions are usually considerably aroused in connection with religious suggestion, and it is well-known that suggestions are frequently welded on to the mind in exact proportion to the height of the feelings and the intensity of the emotions. Not that one cannot secure new ideas without feeling or emotion, but rather that feeling and emotion quickly cause the new idea to become a permanent part of the old mind.

Of course, this very power of religious emotion, quickly and completely to control the mind, can be used for evil as well as for good; as for instance, the cat-mewing mania that ran through France, and the devil-chasing fanaticism connected with the early history of Kentucky, not to mention the witchcraft disgraces of Massachusetts. We cannot expect unusual opportunity for good in religious suggestion without facing the possibilities and probabilities of superstitious belief and fanatical conduct.

SIN AND SICKNESS

Wrongdoing is at the bottom of a large percentage of human sickness and suffering. Immorality is the real cause of a tremendous amount of modern disease. A guilty conscience predisposes to invalidism. Fear is a handmaiden of sin. The transgressor lives in momentary dread lest his sin shall find him out. Such a state of moral uncertainty and mental disquietude is incompatible with the continued enjoyment of a high degree of physical health. Until the condemning conscience reaches that point where it ceases to protest against wrongdoing, it is bound to derange the circulation, disorder the digestion, and disease the nerves.

One of the most powerful health-promoting agencies it is possible for one to utilize, is nothing more or less than "a conscience void of offence toward God and toward men." There are two great disturbers of the mental peace and moral happiness: worry and sin.

It is true that sickness is often the cause of sin, while physical derangement and nervous degeneracy may even be the cause of crime; nevertheless, in a far greater number of cases, it is the sin that is indirectly responsible for the sickness. Physicians are compelled to spend much of their time in repeatedly helping men and women out of physical difficulties which are wholly preventable, and it is sometimes exceedingly discouraging, this work of constantly helping people out of the pit of their own digging; lifting them out of the mire of their own choosing.

THE MORAL MASTERY

The so-called moral powers are capable of exerting a tremendous influence in the control of both mind and body. When the moral mandates are reinforced with a positive will, there is absolutely no limit to their far-reaching influence and their great power for good in the regulation of mental habits and physical practices.

The moral mastery of the individual is the one safeguard against all those mental tortures and physical sufferings, which so certainly come from conscious sin and moral depravity. The moral mastery gives birth to an invincible and determined spirit. The spiritual sovereignty creates a sense of conscious superi-

MENTAL MEDICINE AND MORAL HYGIENE 319

ority, which contributes much to the mental peace and physical health. Spiritual peace and moral satisfaction carry with them the ability to ignore trifling worries and the power to rise above our common everyday harassments.

No stronger illustration of the efficacy of the moral mastery in the psychic and physical realms can be cited than the case of the habitual drunkard, the dipsomaniac. The author has seen many a case who had in no way been helped by treatment in various sanitariums — to say nothing of fraudulent liquor cures and various other fakes — who was sobered up by religious enthusiasm and kept sober year after year by the moral mastery of constant faith. In fact, in the opinion of the author, about the only sure cure to be recommended for dipsomania is religion-mania.

SUMMARY OF THE CHAPTER

1. In most diseases, it is advisable to treat the whole physical man — not merely to combat local symptoms. We should also recognize the necessity of treating the *whole man* — the psychic man as well as the physical.

2. The ancient priests of religion were also the custodians of the physical and sanitary welfare of the people. The priest often represented the highest knowledge and skill in medicine as well as theology.

3. The early history of medicine is bound up in the history of religion. Moral and material medicine travelled together. Theology and therapeutics were finally divorced during the dark ages.

4. The last century witnessed the absolute separation of science and religion, and both preacher and doctor made the fatal mistake of turning away from the principles and practice of mental medicine.

5. The separation of medicine and theology was inevitable; the theologians directed therapeutics into superstition, while the leading spirits in medicine became so materialistic as to threaten the foundations of religion.

6. The Emmanuel Movement represents a modern effort to reunite medicine and religion. Criticisms should be withheld. The experiment should be given a fair trial. Meanwhile, let the preachers study hygiene, and the doctors study psychology.

7. It is a great mistake that medical men have not assumed the leadership in this great movement looking towards the revival of mental medicine and the development of moral therapeutics.

8. The people are hungry for sympathy, encouragement, and guidance. They welcome the psychic help that is brought in the guise of various cults and religions.

9. Faith is a vital energy. It is "the force of life." Confidence is the touchstone of medicine. Faith demands unconditional surrender, complete consecration, and implicit obedience, to the thing believed.

10. The highest known development and exercise of faith is found in Christianity, which represents the most all-inclusive, powerful, and transcendent mental action and moral exercise known to man.

11. The religious life of so many is unsatisfactory because they are trying to experience theology instead of Christianity; trying to duplicate in their lives the religious experiences depicted in books.

12. Religious suggestions are more powerful than secular ones, because of their ability to appeal to a more extensive group of psychic powers and spiritual energies.

13. Immorality is indirectly responsible for a tremendous amount of human disease. Sin and sickness often sustain the relation to each other of cause and effect.

14. When the moral mastery of the mind is backed up by a positive will, there is absolutely no limit to its far-reaching influence and power for good in the regulation of mental habits and physical practices.

CHAPTER XXX

THE BIBLE ON FAITH AND FEAR

HEALTH AND DISEASE.— THE BONDAGE OF FEAR.— THE LIBERTY OF FAITH.— CHEERFULNESS AS A THERAPEUTIC AGENT.— THE CURSE OF ANGER.— THE FUTILITY OF ANXIETY.— THE FOLLY OF WORRY.— THE POWER OF SUGGESTION.— THE ASSURANCE OF FAITH.— THE MERRY HEART.— THE REWARD OF FAITH AND THE REWARD OF FEAR.— THE TORMENT OF FEAR.— FAITH ESSENTIAL TO HEALING.— MATERIAL AIDS TO MENTAL BELIEF. — DIVINE SUSTENANCE.— THE SPIRIT OF FEAR.— THE DAMNATION OF DOUBT.— THE SWORD OF FEAR.— " HE HATH BORNE OUR GRIEFS." — THE BLIGHT OF FEAR.— COMPARATIVE SUMMARY OF THE BIBLE ON FAITH AND FEAR.

K NOWING the Bible to be the most reliable ancient authority on hygiene and sanitation, after long experimentation and research along the lines of physiological psychology as herein presented, it occurred to the author to institute a systematic examination of the English Bible to ascertain what it might contain relative to mental medicine, faith and fear, and psychotherapy. Imagine our surprise, when this examination of the Scriptures was completed, to find that practically every fundamental and essential principle respecting the physiology and psychology of faith and fear was to be found in this wonderful Book.

The mass of psychologic material gathered from this examination of the Scriptures would fill a volume of itself, so that in this chapter we are able to give but an outline — a glimpse — of the surprising teachings of the Old Book concerning faith and fear.

HEALTH AND DISEASE

Throughout the Scriptures, God is pictured as a Health Giver, Joy Giver, and as an Everpresent Healer. The psalmist says,

"God . . . is the health of my countenance." (Ps. XLII: 11.) Again, the psalm-writer asks that the divine face might shine upon us to the end "that Thy way may be known upon the earth, Thy saving health among all nations." (Ps. LXVII: 2.) We should not so quickly surrender our moral courage and mental happiness to every passing influence of wind and weather, when God himself is the very health of our countenance and the source of our life and strength.

As Christ stood in the midst of the people teaching, the Scriptures declare that "the power of the Lord was present to heal them." (Luke V:17.) The Old Testament carries the same teaching, for in speaking of instructing the children of Ephraim and taking them in His arms, it further says, "But they knew not that I healed them." (Hosea XI:3.) The wonderful and mysterious arrangement whereby mental health and bodily vigor are momentarily maintained, and the physical powers constantly renewed, is nothing less than the continuous ministry of the healing power of God.

The Apostle John in writing to Gaius says: "Beloved, I wish above all things that thou mayest prosper and be in health, even as thy soul prospereth." (III John 2.) The prophet Isaiah fully recognized the value of unselfishness as a medical remedy in the promotion and restoration of health, for he writes in condemnation of fasting, affliction of soul, going around bowed down like a bulrush, and the use of sackcloth and ashes; while he bears this testimony to the health-giving efficacy of whole-hearted and unselfish ministry to our needy fellows: "Is not this the fast that I have chosen? to loose the bands of wickedness, to undo the heavy burdens, and to let the oppressed go free, and that ye break every yoke? Is it not to deal thy bread to the hungry, and that thou bring the poor that are cast out to thy house? when thou seest the naked, that thou cover him; and that thou hide not thyself from thine own flesh? Then shall thy light break forth as the morning, and thine health shall spring forth speedily." (Isa. LVIII:6-8.)

Concerning the cause of disease and the source of affliction, the Scriptures certainly do not recognize human suffering as a visitation of the wrath of God. The Bible does not recognize disease as a "mysterious dispensation of Providence." Even so far back as Job's time, his friend in discussing his sufferings said: "Affliction cometh not forth of the dust, neither doth trouble spring out of the ground." (Job V:6.) The wise man gave utterance to the same philosophy respecting the cause of disease when he wrote: "The curse causeless shall not come." (Prov. XXVI:2.)

Elihu, one of Job's wise friends, said: "Touching the Almighty, we cannot find Him out: He is excellent in power and in judgment, and in plenty of justice: He will not afflict." (Job XXXVII:23.) Even when we bring the penalty of transgression down on our own heads, even when natural law administers the harvest of affliction, and apparently the Lawgiver is engaged in the process of punishing and chastening the sinner, Jeremiah writes: "He doth not afflict willingly nor grieve the children of men." (Lam. III:33.)

THE BONDAGE OF FEAR

Fear is everywhere throughout the Scriptures recognized as a state of bondage. The prophet Isaiah speaks of fear and sorrow thus: "The Lord shall give thee rest from thy sorrow, and from thy fear, and from the hard bondage wherein thou wast made to serve." (Isa. XIV:3.)

The psalmist looked upon fear as a destroying force, for he prayed, "Hear my voice, O God, in my prayer: preserve my life from fear." (Ps. LXIV:1.) David, in the shepherd psalm, voiced his deliverance from the bondage of fear, when he sang, "Though I walk through the valley of the shadow of death, I will fear no evil." (Ps. XXIII:4.)

"Fear not," is the perpetual injunction of the Scriptures from Genesis to Revelation. As regards the service of Jehovah, there is a gradual and progressive growth from the fear of early Old Testament times to the sublime faith and trust of the times of Jesus — New Testament times. Even Solomon exhorted the people to "be not afraid of sudden fear." (Prov. III:25.)

Even in Old Testament times it was recognized that the fear of a calamity had power in and of itself to assist in bringing the dreaded disaster upon those who feared it, for did not the wise man say: "The fear of the wicked, it shall come upon him." (Prov. X:24.)

The New Testament abounds with joy and hope. Christ, in discussing the daily need of food and raiment, said: "Fear ye not therefore, ye are of more value than many sparrows." (Matt. X:31.) At another time He reproved His disciples, asking, "Why are ye fearful, O ye of little faith?" (Matt. VIII:26.)

THE LIBERTY OF FAITH

The teachings of the man Christ are everywhere permeated by faith; faith is the keynote and the burden of His message of good cheer and happiness. It was the Master who said, "If ye have faith as a grain of mustard seed, . . . nothing shall be impossible unto you." (Matt. XVII:20.)

The Apostle Paul declared that "the just shall live by faith." (Rom. I:17.) It is interesting to note that this expression did not originate with the apostle. This truth had been uttered six hundred years previous to Paul's time by an Old Testament prophet, who rendered it all the more personal when he expressed it thus: "The just shall live by his faith." (Hab. II:4.)

Christ, throughout his ministry of healing and restoration, seldom failed to acknowledge the saving power of the patient's faith. After restoring the sight of the blind beggar, Jesus said unto him, "Thy faith hath saved thee." (Luke XVIII:42.) To the woman who was healed by touching the hem of the Saviour's garment, Jesus turned and said, "Daughter, be of good comfort; they faith hath made thee whole." (Matt. IX:22.)

Paul taught that "without faith it is impossible to please God." (Heb. XI:6.) He exhorted his young convert Timothy to "fight the good fight of faith" (I Tim. VI:12), while the apostle in speaking of his temporal sojourn on earth wrote: "The life which I now live in the flesh I live by the faith of the Son of God." (Gal. II:20.)

The Apostle James, after admonishing the man who lacks wisdom to ask of God, adds: "Let him ask in faith, nothing wavering." (Jas. I:6.) It was this same writer who declared that "the prayer of faith shall save the sick." (Jas. V:15.)

John, the beloved disciple, gave expression to the greatest and grandest truth concerning the triumph of faith over fear,

THE BIBLE ON FAITH AND FEAR 325

when he wrote, "This is the victory that overcometh the world, even our faith." (I John V:4.)

The Bible, especially the New Testament, clearly teaches the same fundamental principles respecting the harmfulness of fear and the helpfulness of faith, that we have discovered in all our psychological and physiological inquiries. The mental, moral, and material natures of man seem to be governed by the same essential and underlying principles. Faith invigorates and strengthens mind, soul, and body; while fear depresses, diseases, and ultimately destroys mind, soul, and body. This is the conclusion of psychology, physiology, and theology.

CHEERFULNESS AS A THERAPEUTIC AGENT

From the earliest times, cheerfulness — a merry heart — has been recognized as possessing positive therapeutic power. Solomon must have understood the psychology and physiology of faith and fear, when he indited the following passages:

FAITH	FEAR
"A merry heart maketh a cheerful countenance: but by sorrow of the heart the spirit is broken." (Prov. XV:13.)	"The spirit of a man will sustain his infirmity; but a wounded spirit, who can bear?" (Prov. XVIII:14.)
"He that is of a merry heart hath a continual feast." (Prov. XV:15.)	"Be not hasty in thy spirit to be angry: for anger resteth in the bosom of fools." (Eccl. VII:9.)

These Scriptures teach the same important truths which the study of physiological psychology emphasizes. The countenance is dependent on the mental state, while sorrow of heart — worry — breaks the spirit — destroys courage and initiative. That the mind can uphold the body in the presence of actual disease and physical infirmity is clearly taught — "The spirit of a man will sustain his infirmity." Cheerfulness is represented as the psychic source of "a continual feast"; while the anger of the hasty spirit is condemned as fit for a lodgment only in "the bosom of fools."

THE CURSE OF ANGER

FAITH	FEAR
"He that is slow to anger is better than the mighty; and he that ruleth his spirit than he that taketh a city." (Prov. XVI:32.)	"He that is slow to wrath is of great understanding; but he that is hasty of spirit exalteth folly." (Prov. XIV:29.)

In these passages we have depicted the weakness and folly of giving vent to temper. The psychic power which will enable one to control anger is praised as better than physical might; while the ability to rule one's own spirit is placed above the power to lead men in the storm of battle on to the victorious capture of a city. The wise are slow to wrath, while every time one loses one's temper, every time one is "hasty of spirit," one is simply making a public exhibition of his weakness of character and lack of self-control, simply exalting his folly.

THE FUTILITY OF ANXIETY

At every step, the writers of the Bible have warned humanity concerning the waste and worry of useless and needless anxiety. In both the Old and New Testaments, we are repeatedly admonished to cast "all your care upon Him; for he careth for you." (I Peter V:7.) Jesus taught His disciples, saying: "Take no thought for your life, what ye shall eat, or what ye shall drink; nor yet for your body, what ye shall put on. Is not the life more than meat, and the body than raiment?" (Matt. VI:25.) The teachings of Christ concerning the futility of anxiety can, perhaps, best be shown by a parallel comparison of the following two passages:

FAITH AND TRUST	FEAR AND ANXIETY
"Which of you by taking thought can add one cubit unto his stature? . . . Therefore, take no thought, saying, What shall we eat? or, What shall we drink? or, Wherewithal shall we be clothed? . . . for your Heavenly Father knoweth that ye have need of all these things. . . . Take therefore no thought	"But Martha was cumbered about much serving, and came to Him and said, Lord, dost thou not care that my sister hath left me to serve alone? Bid her therefore, that she help me. And Jesus answered and said unto her, Martha, Martha, thou art careful and troubled about many things: but one thing is need-

FIG. 30. Woman with a spirit of Infirmity.

Univ. of
CALIFORNIA

THE BIBLE ON FAITH AND FEAR 327

FAITH AND TRUST	FEAR AND ANXIETY
for the morrow: for the morrow shall take thought for the things of itself. Sufficient unto the day is the evil thereof." (Matt. VI :27, 31, 32, 34.)	ful; and Mary hath chosen that good part, which shall not be taken away from her." (Luke X :40-42.)

THE FOLLY OF WORRY

The theology of past ages, with its burdens, its sorrows, and its gloom, was certainly not the religion of the Christ, who declared: "Come unto me, all ye that labor and are heavy laden, and I will give you rest. Take my yoke upon you, and learn of me; for I am meek and lowly in heart; and ye shall find rest unto your souls." (Matt. XI :28, 29.)

Professed Christians going around all bowed down like a bulrush are a libel on the teachings of Christ. If modern Christians in their own lives had done more to recommend Christianity to the people, there would never have arisen the opportunity for shrewd and designing adventurers to steal the very heart and essense of the psychology of Christ's teachings and herald it to the world as a newly discovered religion — New Thought, and whatnot.

The Christian philosophy concerning worry is very well represented in the two following texts:

CONFIDENCE	WORRY
"Be careful for nothing; but in everything by prayer and supplication with thanksgiving let your requests be made known unto God." (Phil. IV :6.)	"But Jesus said unto him, Follow me; and let the dead bury their dead." (Matt. VIII :22.)

THE POWER OF SUGGESTION

Both the Old and the New Testaments abound in passages which recognize the power and possibilities of positive thought. The writers of those books clearly recognized the force of suggestion. Note the two following passages, one from the Old, one from the New Testament:

MORAL SUGGESTION	MATERIAL SUGGESTION
"Finally, brethren, whatsoever things are true, whatsoever things are honest, what-	"And Jacob took him rods of green poplar, and of hazel and chestnut tree; and pilled white

soever things are just, whatsoever things are pure, whatsoever things are lovely, whatsoever things are of good report; if there be any virtue, and if there be any praise, think on these things." (Phil. IV:8.)

strakes in them. . . . And he set the rods which he had pilled before the flocks in the gutters in the watering-troughs when the flocks came to drink. . . . and the flocks conceived before the rods, and brought forth cattle ring-straked, speckled, and spotted." (Gen. XXX:37-39.)

Paul in his exhortation to the Philippians certainly outlined very effectively the power of good suggestion — auto-suggestion; while this passage from Genesis is a striking illustration of the antiquity of the knowledge of suggestion in the realm of prenatal influence. Jacob had been promised all the cattle which should be born ring-streaked, spotted, and speckled, and he resorted to the principle of suggestion, to enrich his flocks. It is further recorded that he only subjected the strong and robust cattle of the flocks to this experiment, and when it proved successful, it appears that Jacob not only had the larger, but also the stronger herd.

THE ASSURANCE OF FAITH

FAITH

"Now faith is the assurance of things hoped for, the proving of things not seen." (Heb. XI:1, Rev. Ver.)

"But godliness with contentment is great gain." (I Tim. VI:6.)

FEAR

"And deliver them who through fear of death were all their lifetime subject to bondage." (Heb. II:15.)

"Heaviness in the heart of man maketh it stoop; but a good word maketh it glad." (Prov. XII:25.)

Faith imparts assurance and contentment to all who are exercised thereby. Many are the fears which torment humanity, but the greatest of these fears is probably the fear of death — a fear that renders life itself one long and wearisome bondage. No experiment or observation in psychology will ever more fully define the province of faith and the punishments of fear than these Biblical passages. Thus, the oldest of literature affords us an exceptional glimpse into the thorough-going and practical understanding which the ancients had of faith and fear.

THE MERRY HEART

All through the Bible there runs the recognition of the great fact that a happy frame of mind reacts favorably upon the physical body. Almost every sacred writer has touched upon this vital psychological fact. Sorrow of heart is set down as the cause of a sad countenance, while the cares of life are represented as effectually smothering the spiritual life. The therapeutic value of merriness is clearly set forth in the following passages:

MERRINESS	HEAVINESS
"A merry heart doeth good like a medicine; but a broken spirit drieth the bones." (Prov. XVII:22.)	"Wherefore the king said unto me, Why is thy countenance sad, seeing thou art not sick? This is nothing else but sorrow of heart." (Neh. II:2.)
"Casting all your care upon Him; for He careth for you." (I Peter V:7.)	"Say to them that are of a fearful heart, Be strong, fear not." (Isa. XXXV:4.)
"And He said unto her, Daughter, be of good comfort: thy faith hath made thee whole; go in peace." (Luke VIII:48.)	"The care of this world, and the deceitfulness of riches, choke the word." (Matt. XIII:22.)

There is an interesting physiological hint in the statement that "a broken spirit drieth the bones." It should be recalled that the marrow of the long bones is probably concerned in the blood-making process; and it is certainly and emphatically true that sorrow and sadness literally dry up the fountains of blood-making, and sooner or later result in deteriorating the blood stream.

THE REWARD OF FAITH AND THE REWARD OF FEAR

FAITH	FEAR
"And He said unto her, Daughter, thy faith hath made thee whole; go in peace, and be whole of thy plague." (Mark V:34.)	"For the thing which I greatly feared is come upon me, and that which I was afraid of is come unto me." (Job III:25.)

It matters not whether we are dealing with a miraculous occurrence or an ordinary case of recovery from disease by so-called natural processes, faith is the one grand essential to wholeness — to health and happiness. To-day, the Great Spirit of life and health hovers over humanity with healing in His wings for all who will believe, all who will exercise that marvellous power of the mind — faith.

This passage from Job is certainly of more than passing import. Job, in his extraordinary affliction, says that he had long feared that just such a thing was going to happen unto him. He had even "greatly feared" that such calamities would overtake him. This is a clear case of definite mental fear which long preceded the occurrence of the physical disease, and strongly suggests that Job either had a premonition of his afflictions, or that his constant worry and fear might have contributed something toward the causation of the particular and peculiar maladies which encompassed him. The people of olden times undoubtedly recognized the power of adverse suggestion as a cause of disease — as a forerunner of disaster and calamity.

THE TORMENT OF FEAR

"There is no fear in love; but perfect love casteth out fear: because *fear hath torment*. He that feareth is not made perfect in love." (I John IV:18.) This contains a strong hint to all victims of fear and worry that they might derive great benefit by falling in love with something — say, humanity — and find deliverance from the torment of fear in the loving ministry of cheerfulness and helpfulness to our less fortunate fellows. Unselfishness is unquestionably the essential link in the perfection of fearlessness, for "he that feareth is not made perfect in love."

"But the wicked are like the troubled sea, when it cannot rest, whose waters cast up mire and dirt. There is no peace, saith my God, to the wicked." (Isa. LVII:20, 21.)

FAITH ESSENTIAL TO HEALING

"And Jesus said unto him, Go thy way; they faith hath made thee whole. And immediately he received his sight." (Mark X:52.) "And He could there do no mighty work, save that He laid His hands upon a few sick folk, and healed them. And He marvelled because of their unbelief." (Mark VI:5, 6.)

It seems that Christ was limited in His work of healing by the degree of faith which the people exercised. When the faith of the people was strong, His works of healing were great and marvellous; but when the people were filled with unbelief, it is recorded that "He could there do no mighty work." In all His work, Christ seemed to operate upon the oft-repeated plan of "according to your faith, be it unto you."

MATERIAL AIDS TO MENTAL BELIEF

The fanatical followers of numerous healing cults are often very careful that no material ministration shall be given to the subjects who are under mental treatment. It is evident that Jesus did not take this view of the matter, for in His miraculous restoration of sight to the blind man, He made use of material means to appeal to the sightless sufferer, and further to strengthen his faith We read: "When He had thus spoken, He spat on the ground, and made clay of the spittle, and He anointed the eyes of the blind man with the clay." (John IX:6.) The prophet Isaiah, after he had prayed for the healing of King Hezekiah, instructed that a fig poultice should be put on his abscess. (See Isa. XXXVIII:21.)

If anything can improve the quality of one's faith, it would seem that the Scriptures sanction its use. The degree of faith, plus the intelligent choice of means, seems to be the only limitation placed upon the wonderful things which sincere belief can accomplish. We read further: "Jesus said unto him, If thou canst believe, all things are possible to him that believeth. And straightway the father of the child cried out, and said with tears, Lord, I believe; help thou mine unbelief." (Mark IX:23, 24.)

DIVINE SUSTENANCE

"Cast thy burden upon the Lord, and He shall sustain thee." (Ps. LV:22.) Thousands of unfortunate downcast and grief-ridden souls could instantly find relief and deliverance from their life-long bondage of burden-bearing, by simply unloading their life-sorrows — casting their burdens upon the Lord. It should be remembered that the Everlasting Arms are underneath us, and that it is no greater task for the Almighty to sustain His children while they rest on top of their burdens than it is to support them while they groan underneath this weight of fear and sorrow. The Lord has to carry it anyway, so why not rejoice and be happy in the liberty which comes from the knowledge that our burdens are all underneath and not overhead?

Again, the psalmist says: "Commit thy way unto the Lord;

trust also in Him; and He shall bring it to pass." (Ps. XXXVII:5.)

THE SPIRIT OF FEAR

"For God hath not given us the spirit of fear; but of power, and of love, and of a sound mind." (II Tim. I:7.) What a change would come over the professed Christian world if this text were really believed and received into the hearts of so-called Christians! The vast majority of Christians who are sincere and earnest in their religious experience are more or less dominated by fear and cursed with worry. They are filled with fear and devoid of power — the very power which Paul declares God has given His children, along with love and a sound mind.

In writing to the Romans, the apostle again emphasizes this great truth of mental liberty, saying: "For ye have not received the spirit of bondage again to fear; but ye have received the spirit of adoption." (Rom. VIII:15.)

The psalmist further suggests the value of religion as a deliverer from fear, saying: "I sought the Lord, and He heard me, and delivered me from all my fears." (Ps. XXXIV:4.)

There can be little doubt that in the battle against fear, religious faith is the master weapon, even as Paul wrote: "Above all, taking the shield of faith, wherewith ye shall be able to quench all the fiery darts of the wicked." (Eph. VI:16.)

THE DAMNATION OF DOUBT

It is in every sense true that all is eventually lost, if we doubt. Faith is essential to success in every avenue of experience and every department of life. Paul, in writing of both the sacramental service and the common, everyday table service, recognizes the necessity of faith, the value of a clear conscience and gladness of heart; he says: "If any of them that believe not bid you to a feast, and ye be disposed to go; whatsoever is set before you, eat, asking no questions for conscience' sake." (I Cor. X:27.) It may be added that Paul did not say that we might not ask some questions for the stomach's sake.

Again, the apostle writes: "And he that doubteth is damned if he eat, because he eateth not of faith: for whatsoever is not of faith is sin." (Rom. XIV:23.) And this is just as true in a physical sense as it is in its spiritual application. In previous

THE BIBLE ON FAITH AND FEAR

chapters, we have clearly shown that doubts and fears culminate in dyspepsia. Faith in the food and the digestion is absolutely essential to nutrition and good health.

THE SWORD OF FEAR

"Then it shall come to pass that the sword, which ye feared, shall overtake you there in the land of Egypt; and the famine, whereof ye were afraid, shall follow close after you." (Jer. XLII:16.) From the remotest times, it has been the accepted belief that mankind usually reaped a harvest of their materialized fears — that sooner or later the sword of fear strikes down its victims.

The debilitating dangers of fear were so well known and so generally recognized that faint-hearted warriors were not allowed to enter into battle engagements. We read: "What man is there that is fearful and faint-hearted? Let him go and return unto his house, lest his brethren's heart faint as well." (Deut. XX:8.)

"Fear thou not; for I am with thee: be not dismayed; for I am thy God: I will strengthen thee; yea I will help thee; yea I will uphold thee." (Isa. XLI:10.)

"HE HATH BORNE OUR GRIEFS"

The psalmist in describing the natural course of life in this world says that it is spent in grieving and sighing; while the prophet pictures the world's Saviour as One who bears our griefs and carries our sorrows. Compare and contrast the following passages with reference to faith and fear.

FAITH	FEAR
"Surely He hath borne our griefs, and carried our sorrows." (Isa. LIII:4.)	"For my life is spent with grief, and my years with sighing; my strength faileth." (Ps. XXXI:10.)

THE BLIGHT OF FEAR

"Our flesh had no rest, but we were troubled on every side; without were fightings, within were fears." (II Cor. VII:5.) Fear is able continuously to harass both soul and body; neither mind nor flesh can gain rest. Fear is an everlasting tormentor and troubler.

The psalmist offers good advice to all who fret and fume, when he admonishes us to "Cease from anger, and forsake wrath; fret not thyself in any wise to do evil." (Ps. XXXVII:8.)

The only deliverance from fear thought is faith thought. At every turn Christ gave expression to this great truth. He constantly exalted faith as the great deliverer from physical bondage and mental torture. "And He said to the woman, thy faith hath saved thee; go in peace." (Luke VII:50.) "Then touched He their eyes, saying, According to your faith be it unto you." (Matt. IX:29.)

The Christian philosophy throughout is built upon *faith* — upon the principle that by beholding we become changed. (II Cor. III:18.) Accordingly, the believer is admonished ever to look "unto Jesus the Author and Finisher of our faith." (Heb. XII:2.)

The Christian religion is based upon a process of *reckoning* yourself to be something you are not — but something you desire to be — and by faith in Christ, eventually you will actually grow into the likeness of the thing you reckoned and believed yourself to be — a child of God.

And so we come to recognize that the physiological facts and psychological principles herein set forth are far from being new and novel — they are as old as the experience of the human race. The Gospel of faith is the very power and essence of the Great Religion.

COMPARATIVE SUMMARY OF THE BIBLE ON FAITH AND FEAR

FAITH	FEAR
1. "A merry heart maketh a cheerful countenance: but by sorrow of the heart the spirit is broken." (Prov. XV:13.)	1. "The spirit of a man will sustain his infirmity; but a wounded spirit who can bear?" (Prov. XVIII:14.)
2. "He that is slow to anger is better than the mighty: and he that ruleth his spirit than he that taketh a city." (Prov. XVI:32.)	2. "He that is slow to wrath is of great understanding; but he that is hasty of spirit exalteth folly." (Prov. XIV:29.)
3. "He that is of a merry heart hath a continual feast." (Prov. XV:15.)	3. "Be not hasty in thy spirit to be angry: for anger resteth in the bosom of fools." (Eccl. VII:9.)

FAITH

4. "Which of you by taking thought can add one cubit unto his stature? . . . Therefore take no thought, saying, What shall we eat? or, What shall we drink? or, Wherewithal shall we be clothed? . . . For your Heavenly Father knoweth that ye have need of all these things. . . . Take, therefore, no thought for the morrow: for the morrow shall take thought for the things of itself. Sufficient unto the day is the evil thereof." (Matt. VI:27, 31, 32, 34.)

5. "Be careful for nothing: but in everything by prayer and supplication with thanksgiving let your requests be made known unto God." (Phil. IV:6.)

6. "Finally, brethren, whatsoever things are true, whatsoever things are honest, whatsoever things are just, whatsoever things are pure, whatsoever things are lovely, whatsoever things are of good report; if there be any virtue, and if there be any praise, think on these things." (Phil. IV:8.)

7. "Now faith is the assurance of things hoped for, the proving of things not seen." (Heb. XI:1, Rev. Ver.)

8. "But godliness with contentment is great gain." (I Tim. VI:6.)

FEAR

4. "But Martha was cumbered about much serving, and came to Him and said, Lord, dost thou not care that my sister hath left me to serve alone? Bid her, therefore, that she help me. And Jesus answered and said unto her, Martha, Martha, thou art careful and troubled about many things: but one thing is needful; and Mary hath chosen that good part, which shall not be taken away from her." (Luke X:40-42.)

5. "But Jesus said unto him, Follow me; and let the dead bury their dead." (Matt. VIII:22.)

6. "And Jacob took him rods of green poplar, and of the hazel and chestnut tree; and pilled white strakes in them. . . . And he set the rods which he had pilled before the flocks in the gutters in the watering-troughs when the flocks came to drink. . . . And the flocks conceived before the rods, and brought forth cattle ring-straked, speckled, and spotted." (Gen. XXX:37-39.)

7. "And deliver them who through fear of death were all their lifetime subject to bondage." (Heb. II:15.)

8. "Heaviness in the heart of man maketh it stoop: but a good word maketh it glad." (Prov. XII:25.)

FAITH	FEAR
9. "A merry heart doeth good like a medicine: but a broken spirit drieth the bones." (Prov. XVII :22.)	9. "Wherefore the king said unto me, Why is thy countenance sad, seeing thou are not sick? this is nothing else but sorrow of heart." (Neh. II :2.)
10. "Casting all your care upon Him; for He careth for you." (I Peter V :7.)	10. "Say to them that are of a fearful heart, Be strong, fear not." (Isa. XXXV :4.)
11. "And He said unto her, Daughter, be of good comfort: thy faith hath made thee whole; go in peace." (Luke VIII :48.)	11. "The care of this world, and the deceitfulness of riches, choke the word, and he becometh unfruitful." (Matt. XIII :22.)
12. "And He said unto her, Daughter, thy faith hath made thee whole; go in peace, and be whole of thy plague." (Mark V :34.)	12. "For the thing which I greatly feared is come upon me, and that which I was afraid of is come unto me." (Job III :25.)
13. "There is no fear in love; but perfect love casteth out fear: because fear hath torment. He that feareth is not made perfect in love." (I John IV :18.)	13. "But the wicked are like the troubled sea, when it cannot rest, whose waters cast up mire and dirt. There is no peace, saith my God, to the wicked." (Isa. LVII :20, 21.)
14. "And Jesus said unto him, Go thy way; thy faith hath made thee whole. And immediately he received his sight." (Mark X :52.)	14. "And He could there do no mighty work, save that He laid His hands upon a few sick folk, and healed them. And He marvelled because of their unbelief." (Mark VI : 5, 6.)
15. "Jesus said unto him, If thou canst believe, all things are possible to him that believeth. And straightway the father of the child cried out, and said with tears, Lord I believe; help thou mine unbelief." (Mark IX :23, 24.)	15. "When He had thus spoken, He spat on the ground, and made clay of the spittle, and he anointed the eyes of the blind man with the clay.' (John IX :6.)
16. "Commit thy way unto the Lord; trust also in Him; and He shall bring it to pass." (Ps. XXXVII ·ϵ)	16. "Cast thy burden upon the Lord, and He shall sustain thee." (Ps. LV :22.)

FAITH	FEAR
17. "For God hath not given us the spirit of fear; but of power, and of love, and of a sound mind." (II Tim. I:7.)	17. "For ye have not received the spirit of bondage again to fear; but ye have received the spirit of adoption." (Rom. VIII:15.)
18. "Above all, taking the shield of faith, wherewith ye shall be able to quench all the fiery darts of the wicked." (Eph. VI:16.)	18. "I sought the Lord, and He heard me, and delivered me from all my fears." (Ps. XXXIV:4.)
19. "If any of them that believe not bid you to a feast, and ye be disposed to go; whatsoever is set before you, eat, asking no questions for conscience' sake." (I Cor. X:27.)	19. "And he that doubteth is damned if he eat, because he eateth not of faith: for whatsoever is not of faith is sin." (Rom. XIV:23.)
20. "The same heard Paul speak; who steadfastly beholding him, and perceiving that he had faith to be healed, said with a loud voice, Stand upright on thy feet. And he leaped and walked." (Acts XIV:9, 10.)	20. "Then it shall come to pass that the sword, which ye feared, shall overtake you there in the land of Egypt; and the famine, whereof ye were afraid, shall follow close after you." (Jer. XLII:16.)
21. "Fear thou not; for I am with thee: be not dismayed; for I am thy God: I will strengthen thee; yea, I will help thee; yea, I will uphold thee." (Isa. XLI:10.)	21. "What man is there that is fearful and faint-hearted? Let him go and return unto his house, lest his brethren's heart faint as well." (Deut. XX:8.)
22. "Surely He hath borne our griefs, and carried our sorrows." (Isa. LIII:4.)	22. "For my life is spent with grief, and my years with sighing; my strength faileth." (Ps. XXXI:10.)
23. "And He said to the woman, Thy faith hath saved thee; go in peace." (Luke VII:50.)	23. "Cease from anger, and forsake wrath; fret not thyself in any wise to do evil." (Ps. XXXVII:8.)
24. "Then touched He their eyes, saying, According to your faith be it unto you." (Matt. IX:29.)	24. "Our flesh had no rest, but we were troubled on every side; without were fightings, within were fears." (II Cor. VII:5.)

CHAPTER XXXI
THE PHYSIOLOGY AND PSYCHOLOGY OF HABIT

THE PHYSIOLOGY OF HABIT.— THE PSYCHOLOGY OF HABIT.— THE ECONOMY AND TYRANNY OF HABIT.— THE SLAVERY OF OBSESSION.— PSYCHIC OBSESSIONS.— MOTOR OBSESSIONS.— VITAL SEEPAGE.— ENERGY LEAKAGE.— SYSTEM AND ORDER.— COOL-HEADEDNESS.— THE NERVOUS RHYTHM OF HABIT.— CAN THE HABITS BE CHANGED? — SUMMARY OF THE CHAPTER.

HABIT represents the methodical way in which mind and body come to act as a result of the frequent repetition of a certain definite set of nervous impulses and muscular responses thereto.

Some habits are instinctive; that is, they are set in motion at or immediately after birth; for instance, the newborn child is possessed of the sucking instinct; if this is not immediately exercised, it is soon partially or wholly lost, whereas the immediate performance of the act of sucking fixes the instinct.

THE PHYSIOLOGY OF HABIT

The physiology of habit is explained by reference to the nervous reflex arc, by which means certain sensory nervous impressions are carried to the various nerve centres, where, after a time, they come spontaneously and automatically to produce certain definite motor responses. (See Fig. 2.) Nerve paths, as it were, are worn deeper and deeper, and this causes a given habit to become more and more deeply rooted. Frequent repetition of nervous impulses passing over the same path serves to wear the nervous groove deeper and deeper, just as the frequent walking over the lawn will soon wear a deep path down through the sod.

The period of infancy is the special time for starting or initiating mental and physical habits. The longer the infancy

PHYSIOLOGY AND PSYCHOLOGY OF HABIT 339

of any animal, the greater the range and possibility for the formation of numerous habits — good or bad — which will prove either of great help or hindrance in after life. It is evident that not all our habits are formed in infancy. Habits may be formed in after life; but the older the learner, the more difficult it is either to form or reform a habit.

All our established habits form actual and literal pathways through the nervous mechanism of the body. Habits have a material foundation, and no habit when once thoroughly established can be changed without effecting a change in these nerve paths through the body, as a result of placing the nerve centres concerned under the absolute domination of an ever-watchful and all-powerful new idea.

When we yield willingly and readily to the impulse to do a certain thing, the next time that same impulse is experienced, the responsive action of the body will be just a little more quickly and easily performed. This frequent repetition establishes what the physiologists call the "path of motor discharge"; and when a nervous path becomes well established, we have laid the foundation for a new habit. This constitutes the physiological explanation of habit.

It is highly probable that in the early formation of habits, the discharge of motor impulses excited by sensory impressions follows the path of least resistance. Just as the small streamlets from a cake of melting ice make their way toward lower levels in obedience to the law of liquids, wearing a larger and larger groove as the volume of water increases, converting obstructions and obstacles into high retaining walls; so, eventually, the stream of nervous energy is compelled to flow in the deep and permanent grooves formed by its own long-continued action.

THE PSYCHOLOGY OF HABIT

Just as various groups of nerve cells in the spinal column and the lower nerve centres get into the way of working together (form habits of coöperation, in other words), so in the case of the nerve cells in the higher brain centres. Various sensory and conscious nerve impressions come to be definitely associated, sooner or later, with the activity of certain definite groups of motor brain cells. Certain associated feelings and ideas are aroused by a given impulse, and by the repetition of this connection a mental habit is formed, which gradually wears down for itself definite material grooves in the paths of the brain.

The machinery of thought rapidly settles into the ruts and grooves of its own formation. These psychic channels are formed in the early periods of life, and it is quite likely that they are largely established by the time a man reaches thirty years of age. Not that new channels of thought cannot be formed, and new associations of ideas effected, but, after this age, the mind forms new methods of thought and action with great difficulty, and only in response to definite mental training and continuous intellectual activity.

Our psychic habits are formed also by the care or attention we pay to the constant stream of sensations which have their origin in all parts of the body, in sense impressions which never cease to recur as long as life lasts. Ordinarily, the vast majority of these impressions do not arouse sensations at all. Normally, furthermore, the majority of sensations so awakened have at most but a fleeting or momentary claim upon our attention. Those unfortunates who develop the habit of recognizing all these sensory reports from the outlying physical domains of the body, soon degenerate into confirmed neurasthenics. The old lady was not far from right when she advised the nervous young girl to keep her mind off her thoughts.

THE ECONOMY AND TYRANNY OF HABIT

It must be evident that the formation of habits is a source of great economy to both mind and body. It should also be recognized that when habits are misformed, when mind and body are trained in unfortunate and unhealthy modes of thought and action, that the results upon the health, happiness, and character may be highly disastrous.

Habit is a sort of partnership arrangement entered into between the mind and the body for the purpose of accomplishing a maximum amount of work with a minimum expenditure of mental energy and physical force. If habits are well formed,

PHYSIOLOGY AND PSYCHOLOGY OF HABIT

intelligently shaped, and properly controlled, they become the great secret of mental conservation and a source of great physical economy; on the other hand, if habits are misformed — if they are injurious to mind and body — after they once become thoroughly established, they may enslave and rule their subject with an absolute tyranny.

When we recognize that it is just as easy to form a good habit as a bad habit, just as easy to acquire helpful habits as those which are injurious, it becomes apparent that a great responsibility rests upon parents and teachers to see to it that the children under their care early form correct and proper habits of thinking and acting.

THE SLAVERY OF OBSESSION

By obsession we refer to those constantly recurring ideas, feelings, or emotions which present themselves so insistently and automatically in our consciousness, and which always lead to the performance of certain useless actions or the thinking of certain foolish thoughts. These needless acts and thoughts are ofttimes injurious to peace of mind and health of body. Our obsessions are not useful, and they are otherwise inharmonious with our useful mental experience and modes of acting; they are troublesome interlopers which have chosen our minds and bodies as their regular playground; their conduct results in constantly interfering with the normal work of both mind and body. Mental obsessions are probably due to a mild form of dissociation of ideas, while bodily obsessions are established after the usual methods of habit formation.

Psychic obsessions. The inconsistent notion that one must always be right has spoiled the health and ruined the happiness of thousands of people. This desire is born of an unhealthful tendency to want our way, to become the pattern, after which all others must shape their conduct. This leads to an everlasting wrangle with one's associates, in which the victim of this obsession is ever contending that he is right and all the world is wrong. It would add much to the happiness and health of some of these obstinate contenders for their own personal infallibility if they would come down from their perch of perfection — confess their humanity — admit their blunders

— actually "to acknowledge the corn" now and then. The world is filled with unhappy and irritable people who have never been known to confess to having made a mistake or done wrong in all their lives.

Others live in constant slavery to fashion, to the fear of man and the conventional way of doing things. The author has a dear friend who is simply killing himself with the obsession that he must carry through everything that he undertakes — at any cost. His life is devoted to "carrying things through" — to patching up his evident blunders and trying to make successful his repeated failures.

Others are obsessed with the insane notion that they must set other people right — the notion of reforming the world. These people live in a constant state of worry and irritation because their petty hobbies do not gain the recognition which they think their schemes deserve.

Certain sensitive and self-centred nervous people get the notion into their heads that they are being terribly persecuted; they fancy themselves living a life of perpetual martyrdom. They are victims of constant imaginary sufferings and fictitious slights. It would seem that some of them really learn to love this life of the false martyr.

We are acquainted with a man who has made life unbearable for himself and family because of his ever-present obsessing ideas that he must accept no favors, allow no one to assist him, be under obligations to nobody; and these ideas have brought him almost to the verge of a form of insanity, so that he is a *persona non grata* in all circles.

Motor obsessions. This form of slavish worry has succeeded in fastening itself on the nervous system and the daily behavior of most of us in some form or other. It is shown in the case of the small boy, who, while going downtown on an errand for his mother, easily forgets what he was sent to the store for, but in no wise forgets to kick every hitching-post he meets on the way downtown. (See Fig. 28.) It is likewise shown in the case of the man who tries to keep from stepping on the cracks or seams of the sidewalk on his way down street. The awkward, uneven steps of such an indi-

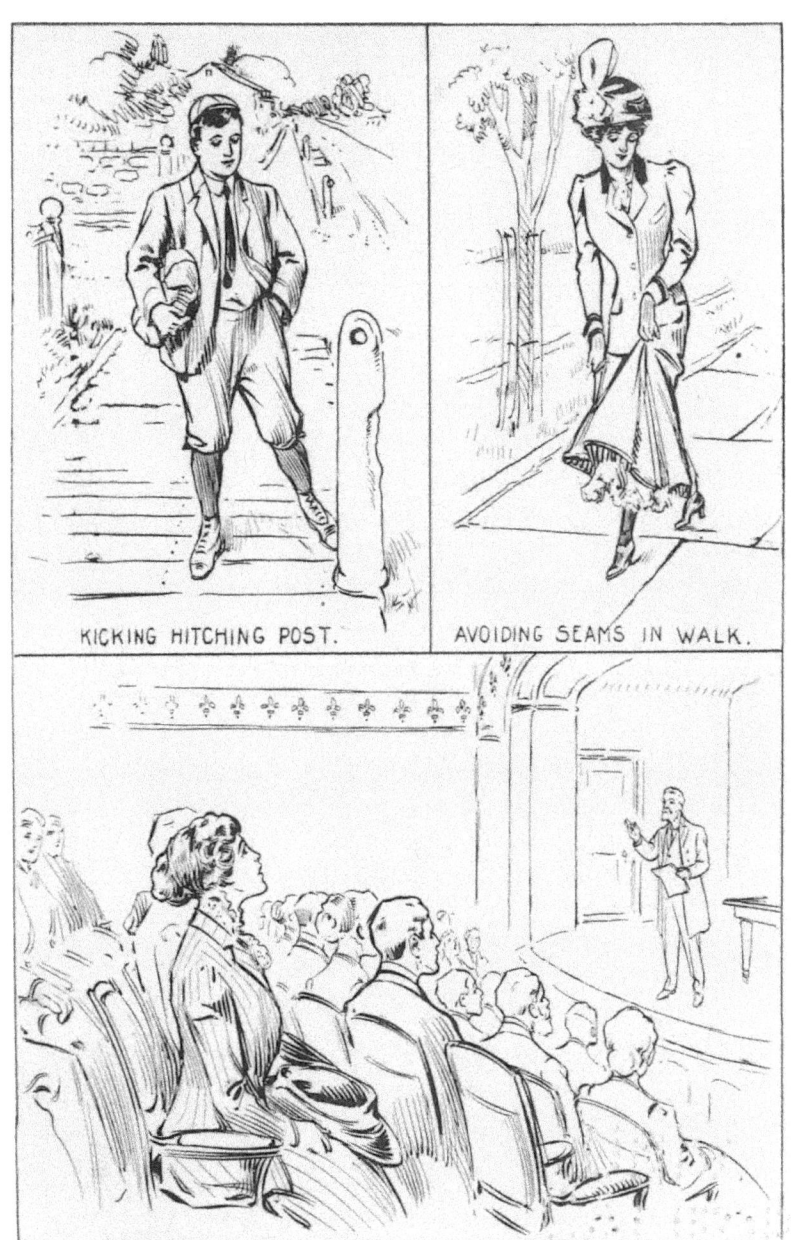

FIG. 28. COMMON MOTOR OBSESSIONS.

UNIV. OF CALIFORNIA

vidual sometimes are sufficient to attract the attention of the passer-by. The author once followed a young lady for fourteen blocks and observed that this obsessed soul did not once permit her shoes to fall upon a seam in the cement walk. (See Fig. 28.)

Have you not known the man who could not put his hand in his pocket without continuously counting the pieces of money contained therein? A patient recently told the author that he could not enjoy a stroll unless he had a bunch of money to count in his right-hand trousers pocket; that if he did not have any loose change when he went out for a walk, he would have to go and get some; that he knew just how many pieces of money the pocket contained, and, if on any single count, he failed to find the right number, he would often have to stop dead still and carefully recount the coins to make sure that none had been lost; after which he could resume his walk.

Another case of obsession is that of the person who cannot sit in a public auditorium or church without counting the number of rings, roses, or stripes on the wall-paper, usually trying to settle on the centre one and then to watch it with an eagle eye. (See Fig. 28.) If for any reason the attention is distracted from this centre figure and it is momentarily lost to view, the whole number of designs must be counted over again and the centre carefully located.

After speaking of this matter in a Chautauqua lecture one afternoon, an intelligent looking lady told us she had counted every seam in the tent, knew the middle seams, and likewise had counted the stripes of all the other tents on the grounds. She said this was her favorite pastime — to count the stripes, figures, and other objects: if nothing else presented itself, she would count the pickets on the fence.

We once had a patient, a young man, who, when not otherwise employed, would hie himself to the railroad and watch for the numbers on the freight-cars, taking great delight when he would see a number which he could recall having seen sometime previous.

A woman school-teacher of middle age once consulted the author to see what help she could get for her obsession — of everlastingly counting her steps. She said it was 19 steps from her front porch to the gate; that it was 555 steps from her house to the grocery; that the court-house had 21 steps going up the first flight, etc., etc. She said she made the trip from the house to the gate one day in one step short of the usual count, and was so disturbed that she had to go back to the house and walk the distance over again, that she might walk it in the usual number of steps. Others are possessed of obsessions born of their physical appearance, or determined by their undue tendency toward being too fat or too lean. Another very common obsession is the habitual twirling of the thumbs while the fingers are interlocked.

VITAL SEEPAGE — ENERGY LEAKAGE

The world is filled with nervous, fidgety persons who, while they are probably not victims of definite mental or motor obsessions, are constantly engaged in numerous physical activities which are wholly useless and unnecessary.

Such slaves of habit cannot sit down without crossing their legs and tossing the foot, or tapping the foot on the floor. Some part of their anatomy must be in rhythmical and incessant action. Others will twist their moustaches, or play with their hair. We are acquainted with a professional man who cannot sit down a moment without starting up a drumming with his feet on the floor, or else he will beat an incessant tattoo with his hands on the chair. Others are everlastingly fixing their clothes or adjusting the necktie; they seem never to be able to complete their toilet. All these needless and useless manœuvrings constitute a tremendous nervous and vital drain on the victim's constitution. It is a sort of vital seepage — there is a constant leakage of nervous force and muscular energy.

We know a young business man who is constantly clearing his throat. We have a patient who engages in incessant coughing — purely nervous coughing. Numerous cases of nervous breakdown from worry are due to just this sort of nervous extravagance plus incessant brooding and perpetual worry. No constitution can long stand to be drained by worry, other vital leakage, and obsessions. Sooner or later, the strongest nervous system will be undermined, the vitality of the sufferer effectively sapped, and the resultant catastrophe strikes: there occurs either a blow-up or a breakdown.

"Sidetrackability" is the name which some one has given to the condition of those nervous, erratic people whose energies are being diverted from a legitimate and natural source into abnormal and harmful channels.

SYSTEM AND ORDER

Many persons would improve their peace of mind and health of body if they would learn to be systematic and orderly in the details of their everyday life. To look at the desks of some business men; to look into the study rooms of some professional men; to go through the homes of some housewives; is enough to explain why so many of these people work so hard and accomplish so little. Everything is in disorder — no system prevails.

It is highly essential that intelligent methods and automatic habits should be formed for carrying on one's regular, daily work; on the other hand, it is altogether possible to make a veritable obsession out of law and order. We are acquainted with a young man who accomplishes but little in life except to keep his study in order. So, while we recommend system and order as a means of economizing time and energy, we do not mean that they should be carried to the point of unbounded fussiness and unbearable neatness.

Nevertheless, it is a fact, that by making as much of our work as possible automatic, we relieve the higher controlling centres of the brain from the necessity of attending to these details, and in this way, we vastly increase the opportunity and power of the mind for the performance of additional useful and original work.

COOL-HEADEDNESS

One of the things most needed in our modern civilization is cool-headedness, the power to think more than once while in the same spot. Thoughtlessness is responsible for many of our difficulties. Some unfortunate souls have got into a chronic habit of "being constantly rushed." It makes no difference where or when you meet them, they are "simply rushed to death"; "have n't time to think"; "so glad to see you, but have n't time to talk it over now"; etc., etc. Why, it really makes you nervous simply to meet them on the street. They seem to have a sort of psychic St. Vitus's dance.

These restless people are like a steam-engine with the governor off; they are making a great fuss, a big noise, but they are accomplishing but little in the line of real, useful work. These chronically rushed folks keep both mind and body working under a terrible strain, until by and by this state of strain becomes habitual; they become chronically keyed up; they cannot let go; they cannot relax. Even when they go to bed at night, they are still so rushed that they are often unable to find time to go to sleep, and consequently they lie awake half the night.

This unnecessary and abnormal rushing through life is probably due to exaggerated ideas of one's importance, or else it must be due to an overestimation of the importance of the work one is doing. Most of us need to learn to take ourselves less seriously, and some ought to learn to take even their work less seriously. It was a wise mother who said to her nervous daughter, "My child, you cannot possibly exaggerate the unimportance of things."

THE NERVOUS RHYTHM OF HABIT

We should constantly bear in mind that habits usually establish themselves in harmony with certain laws of periodicity. There is a tendency toward regularity in the motor discharge of our established habits, whether it be the drumming of the fingers on the arms of a chair or the regular sprees of the periodical drunkard.

We get the habit of having periodic stimulation — that is, periodically whipping our nerves; some are addicted to the use of alcohol and other drugs, still others make use of tea and coffee. The use of these nerve excitants and depressants is a confession of weakness of character on the part of those who depend on these various unnatural and harmful methods of exercising the nervous system. This rhythmic tendency of nervous impulses is an important factor in overcoming bad habits — the reëducation of the nervous system. It is neces-

PHYSIOLOGY AND PSYCHOLOGY OF HABIT 347

sary that all formative and reformatory efforts should be systematic and regular; every effort to retrain the body and form new habits should faithfully be carried out in accordance with this law of nervous periodicity.

CAN HABITS BE CHANGED?

Since habits possess a real physical foundation and an actual psychologic basis, can they be modified, reshaped, or otherwise changed after their slave has reached maturity? The answer to this question embraces a number of factors. The eradication of the old habit or the formation of the new, first demands the absolute coöperation of the will, the complete. making up of one's mind tc do the thing in question. It next requires that the body itself shall be set in operation in the desired direction of forming the new habit. New thoughts must be formulated and actually placed in command of the mind. The new actions must be executed with decision and regularity. The new habit must repeatedly and persistently be wrought out through the physical body.

Persistent, intelligent, regular, systematic, and determined effort on the part of the mind will prove successful in uprooting almost any and every habit which can fasten itself upon the human mind or body.

SUMMARY OF THE CHAPTER

1. The period of infancy is the special time for initiating habits. The longer the infancy of an animal, the greater the range and possibility for the formation of habits.

2. Habits are due to actual pathways through the nervous mechanism of the body. Habits have a material foundation as well as a mental basis.

3. Every time an act is repeated its performance becomes easier and easier; the "path of motor discharge" becomes increasingly automatic and established.

4. Colonies of brain cells and groups of ideas (psychic centres) come also to form definite and habitual associations. In this way, mental habits are formed, habits of thought.

5. The thinking machinery readily settles into the ruts and grooves of its own formation. After thirty years of age, new habits are formed only as a result of persistent psychic training.

6. Habit is a sort of partnership arrangement between the mind and the body for the purpose of accomplishing a maximum of work with a minimum expenditure of energy.

7. It is just as easy to form a good habit as a bad one. When bad habits become established, they rule their slave with absolute tyranny.

8. An obsession is a constantly recurring idea, feeling, or emotion, which presents itself incessantly and automatically in our experience, and which leads to the thinking of certain foolish thoughts and the performance of certain useless acts.

9. Mental obsessions are probably due to a mild form of idea-dissociation, while motor obsessions are simply habitual acts resulting from automatic and uncontrolled motor discharges.

10. Common obsessions are such as insistent ideas, counting, kicking posts, wiggling the toes, twirling the thumbs, twisting the moustache, drumming on the chair, or tossing the foot when the legs are crossed.

11. These obsessions and near-obsessions constitute a tremendous vital drain upon the constitution. These useless manœuvres represent a species of vital seepage — a leakage of nervous force and muscular energy.

12. System and order in doing one's daily work are highly economical and helpful. Automatic action conserves the time and energy of the higher brain centres. It is possible to convert law and order into an obsession, so that instead of proving a help in the daily affairs of life, it becomes a veritable bondage.

13. The habit of "being rushed" is chronic with some persons. It is an extravagant practice — wasteful of vital energy. Coolheadedness would help numerous people out of many of their troubles.

14. Habits are usually formed in accordance with the nervous laws of periodicity. Motor discharge usually follows a law of regularity when it becomes habitual, as in the case of the periodical drinker.

15. Persistent, intelligent, systematic, and determined effort on the part of the mind will usually prove successful in uprooting any undesirable habit which may have fastened itself on mind or body.

CHAPTER XXXII

THE NATURE AND CAUSE OF WORRY

WORRY DEFINED.— THE PSYCHOLOGY OF WORRY.— THE GENERAL CAUSES OF WORRY.— HAPPINESS-HUNGER.— TEMPERAMENTAL PECULIARITIES.— WEATHER-WORRY.— THE MAGNIFICATION OF TRIFLES.— THE CHRONIC " KICKING " HABIT.— PERVERTED PROVERBS.— THE WORRY CIRCLE.— EXCESSIVE SELF-CONSCIOUSNESS. — MENTAL WORK AND REST.— SPECIAL FEARS AND HOODOOS.— THE SPIRIT OF INFIRMITY.— FICTITIOUS WORRIES.— MORAL CAUSES OF WORRY.— RELIGIOUS FANATICISM.— PHYSICAL CAUSES OF WORRY.— WORRY DEPENDENT ON AGE.— PERNICIOUS HEALTH FADS.— SOCIAL SOURCES OF WORRY.— INDUSTRIAL CAUSES OF WORRY.— SUMMARY OF THE CHAPTER.

IN every age, the human race has suffered from the disastrous consequences of fear and worry, but it has fallen to the lot of our present-day civilization, with its intensity and complexity, to suffer in an unusual degree, the direful consequences of mental strain and social anxiety.

WORRY DEFINED

It is exceedingly difficult to frame an acceptable definition for worry. A patient once described her mental state to the author by saying that her ".mind took tight hold of an idea, and just would not let go." It would seem that worry might truthfully be called "a spasm of the attention," or a continued fit of mental concentration. Concentration of the mental energies is highly essential to the performance of first-class brain work, and it would seem that the danger of worry is ever associated with a high degree of mental concentration. It is very necessary that the mind should take fast hold upon a group of ideas in order to perform efficient mental work; on the other hand, if this intellectual concentration is too long continued; if the mind fails to release its grasp; if the psychic focus becomes continuous, then we have reached the borderlands of anxiety, fear, and worry.

And so we find worry to be a sort of "one-sided mental action." Worry may be defined as fear thought in contradistinction to forethought. Forethought is highly necessary to the smooth running of our daily affairs, while fear thought is wholly unnecessary and even highly injurious; indeed, worry has been called "chronic fear." It is a well-known fact that any single fear or group of fears, when long entertained in the mind, tend to crystallize themselves into definite worry, which incessantly harasses the soul and everlastingly dissipates the mental energies.

Forethought is a wise general of the intellectual forces, making an intelligent comparison between the past and the present, while discriminatingly planning for the future. Forethought is never unmindful of our present difficulties, neither is it blind to those which may be encountered in the future. Fear thought is nothing more or less than a process of borrowing trouble from the future for the purpose of augmenting our present sorrows. Worry, while ever posing as solicitous for our welfare, is a false friend — a dangerous traitor to the natural laws governing the realm of mind and morals.

THE PSYCHOLOGY OF WORRY

Man is the only animal that makes himself ridiculous by worry. The biologists teach us that intelligence (the liability to worry) exists only in those animals high enough up in the biologic scale to possess associative memories. Man possesses a high degree of memory association; as Shakespeare says, Man is made "with such large discourse, looking before and after." Numerous experiments made upon lower animals serve to prove that much of their apparently intelligent action is purely instinctive — hereditary. They do not reason intelligently. The lower forms of life seem utterly unable to profit by experience — they have no associative memories, and, of course, they are not addicted to worry. In ascending the scale of animal life, interesting problems are encountered when we reach the ant tribes; and it seems highly probable that wasps do actually possess certain powers of associative memory.

THE NATURE AND CAUSE OF WORRY

And so the higher we ascend in the scale of animal life, the greater the tendency to worry — to look with fear and misgiving upon that which the future holds in store, or to be unduly apprehensive concerning the difficulties and problems of the present.

THE GENERAL CAUSES OF WORRY

The uncertainties and vicissitudes of life upon our planet are such as to render more or less worry inevitable. A certain degree of mild worry, a certain amount of mental anxiety, it would seem, is ever attached to the living state. Life is the one great source of worry. Death alone affords perfect and permanent relief from the liability to fear and worry.

The fact that man is the only animal that worries is but a demonstration of the superiority of the human mind over that of the lower animals. Animals are not given to looking backward, and, as a rule, they do not look very far into the future; on the other hand, the mind of man sweeps back over past ages, and, from the page of history, as well as from the perplexing incidents of the present, forms those conclusions which cause him to look with fear and trembling into the future.

The causes of human worry are indeed varied, but in the last analysis, they are usually found to consist in some form of irritation, anxiety, or fear. It not infrequently develops that numerous habits of life and physical practices are contributory to the worry habit. The use of alcohol, and other forms of psychic and physical transgression, are often discovered to be the handmaidens of worry and sorrow. Lack of self-control is another great cause of worry. A strong will would cure nine-tenths of this unnecessary form of grief. Even the proverbial "wet hen" could undoubtedly overcome her anger if she would but become indifferent to the matter of always keeping dry. We stand other people's troubles, and, by vigorously making up our minds, we ought to be able to stand our own.

HAPPINESS-HUNGER

Whatever the immediate cause of worry, a solicitude for our own general welfare, material prosperity, and mental happiness, or that of our loved ones, must be recognized as the real cause of all our worry. We worry lest we may lose or fail to obtain those material blessings which will make us and our friends happy.

The desire for happiness, then, is found to be the real, fundamental cause of worry, but it should ever be borne in mind that under no circumstances can worry ever contribute to our happiness; on the other hand, it should be remembered that worry and anxiety never fail to detract from the enjoyment of life, to destroy mental peace, and not infrequently they store up for the future that which will everlastingly destroy the very happiness for the love of which we are wont to worry.

Many good people entertain the false notion that the possession of material riches can bestow happiness upon the soul. They are fully possessed of the idea that riches are essential to the joy of living. Accordingly, they toil in anxiety, endure hardships, and experience much mental torture, in their efforts to provide themselves with these supposed essentials to life and happiness; but all this is a mistake. True happiness is rather derived from the blessings of sound, physical health, mental peace, and spiritual rest.

TEMPERAMENTAL PECULIARITIES

Some good people constantly worry because they are "criticised" either justly or unjustly. Some folks are veritable human sensitive-plants; they are always being "neglected" or "slighted," even by their best friends. Other good people are depressed and dejected because they are sure that their great worth is not fully appreciated by their associates or employers. Still others fret and fume and worry because they feel it is their duty to resent some supposed or real injury or injustice which has been done them.

This temperamental sort of worry frequently gives rise to violent outbursts of temper and extraordinary manifestations of anger, all of which are exceedingly injurious to the health of the nervous, digestive, and circulatory systems, while they are highly destructive to every form of happiness and spiritual peace.

Other people worry because they are inordinately timid— backward. Many earnest souls constantly fear imaginary difficulties, fear they will make some awful blunder, or that they will utterly fail to "make good" with the task they have in hand. Some persons always feel that after they have done their best they will still be unable to meet the demands which their position makes upon them. This abnormal timidity necessarily results in producing an unnatural state of discouragement, brooding, and despondency.

Still others worry over their grave responsibilities. As a rule, these anxious individuals are found to be altogether too anxious about certain minute details and other matters for which they are not at all personally responsible, and over which they exercise little or no control; and yet they constantly worry over these things to the point where they lose both appetite and sleep.

WEATHER-WORRY

Every time you meet some people you will find that they are worrying over the weather. They are not quite satisfied with what nature provides: the sun shines too much, or else it rains too much. They are something like the grumbling farmer whose fault-finding and complaining were proverbial for miles around. In the midst of one ideal summer (so far as weather conditions and crops were concerned) a delegation of neighbors called on him one afternoon and expressed the thought that he must for once be satisfied with the fine weather and the excellent crops. The old farmer knitted his brow, scratched his head for a moment, and then replied: "Yes, neighbors, the crops are good, and the weather is fine, but I want to tell you it is mighty hard on the land."

Some men and women are literally human barometers. As the result of their rheumatic tendency, coupled with constant thought of the weather, they are able to detect a storm long before the weather bureau is aware that it has appeared on the horizon. Such unfortunates are able to keep themselves on the border of nervous prostration by their constant worry over the weather, and from fear that all their plans will be upset by rain, storm, or drouth.

Another class of mental sufferers might be classified as "science worriers." They are more or less bothered over the great problems of the universe. Some are afraid the sun will sometime burn out, and that our old world will gradually freeze up. Others live in constant fear lest our planet will collide with some stray comet. Several frightened people committed suicide during the recent visit of Halley's comet to the neighborhood of our world. Still others are possessed with the constant fear of being struck by lightning; they are always terror-stricken by loud thunder.

THE MAGNIFICATION OF TRIFLES

It is something terrible the way intelligent human beings will make a mountain out of a molehill, how they persist in magnifying trifles beyond all measure and reason. A discouraged and downcast fellow, struggling with obstacles and fighting with failures, will often deliberately attribute all his misfortunes and difficulties to some trifling mistake in his youth, or to some insignificant blunder or transgression of later life.

There recently came to our clinic a young man whose life was a perfect failure; he had contemplated suicide, but a friend urged him to come and see us. This patient had made a certain mistake in his youth, which he later greatly magnified, and so led himself to believe that he could not succeed in life, that he was doomed to certain failure. For seven years he had lived in this slough of despond, and now he seriously thought of taking his life. He had been looking through the glass of life from the wrong end, and it was only necessary to reverse his telescope, as it were, to give him a new viewpoint in life. After an hour's talk he was ready to go to work and he has continued to make rapid and satisfactory improvement.

We are all subject to the little ills of life. Other people are not free from these vexing trifles; why should we expect to be? In times of trouble and harassment let us swell out our chests, breathe deeply, and face these trifling difficulties like men. Let obstacles breed the spirit of conquest, the determination to conquer, instead of causing us to wilt and surrender.

THE CHRONIC "KICKING" HABIT

Another great cause of worry and kindred mental dissatisfaction is to be found in the disposition of some grouchy dyspeptics to find fault with everything and everybody. They

FIG. 29. A CHRONIC KICKER.

THE NATURE AND CAUSE OF WORRY 355

have literally acquired the "kicking" habit. (See Fig. 29.) Such unfortunate creatures seem utterly unable to see good in anybody or to be satisfied with anything.

It should be remembered that worry grows by what it feeds on. When we nurse and nourish this spirit of dissatisfaction, it acts and reacts upon ourselves until the very soul is filled with discontent, and the mind is permeated with complaining. However small and trifling the matter over which we begin to worry, the insignificant cause of our mental dissatisfaction will be found entirely sufficient to feed and nourish the spirit of uneasiness to the point where it gains possession of our minds, threatens to wreck our career, and constantly harasses the soul to the point where life is unbearable.

But after all that can be said of the causes of worry, we cannot overlook the fact that some people have come to the place where they enjoy poor health. They would not be happy if they could not complain of headache, backache, stomach-ache, or something of the kind; their complaints have become chronic; they enjoy enlisting the sympathy of their fellows, having delight in describing their sufferings and explaining their miseries; they are constantly consulting the almanac and the patent medicine advertisements to find some new cause for physical complaint, and they usually find what they are looking for.

PERVERTED PROVERBS

Many a good old saying, proverbial for its truthfulness when properly understood, has destroyed the peace and happiness of those who have come to worry over its too literal fulfilment. Take such a proverb as "Look before you leap." This old saying certainly contains good advice; but we have known a number of earnest men and women who have long remained stationary in their life plans, looking with such care and scrutiny over the present and the future, that they have failed to take advance steps; they have been altogether too fearful to leap; they would not dare take a chance, they were afraid of the risk. Old age is creeping upon them, and their careers have been ruined by a too literal interpretation and over-regard for such a good proverb as "Look before you leap."

Another of the old proverbs, responsible for causing much

worry, is the oft-repeated saying, "What is worth doing at all is worth doing well." While this proverb contains sound and wholesome advice for every young man and woman, it must also be remembered that every day of our lives we are called upon to perform a large number of wholly unessential tasks, tasks which are but temporary scaffolding, as it were, compared to the more important character-structure we are building. It is true that these minor tasks must be done with sufficient care so as not to endanger the real structure we are erecting, nevertheless, it would be a great waste of energy to try carefully to square, polish, and paint the scaffolding which stands but to-day, and to-morrow is torn away.

And this is true of much of our common work. Each day's efforts should be wisely divided up into the *essential* and the *unessential;* and as we review the events of the day in its closing hours, it should be no occasion for worry and self-reproach that some trifle has had to be slighted or altogether neglected. If the brick and mortar you have put into the real character-structure are sound and good, if your wall has been raised up true to the plumb, let not the miscarriage of some detail either distress or worry you.

Many conscientious young people have worried altogether too much over such teaching as, "Be sure you are right, then go ahead." Owing to their peculiar mental make-up, their naturally diffident and hesitating disposition, they could never be quite sure that they were absolutely right; and so they never went ahead. For years they remain stationary in their life plans, first contemplating one thing, then another, and then pretty soon they begin seriously to worry because they have not gone ahead.

"Haste makes waste" is usually found to be true; but there are times in life when it is absolutely necessary that one should make haste; when decisions must be quickly formed and speedily executed; delay would be fatal. Now, if in the sober after moments it should develop that the highest wisdom had not characterized the formation of these hasty conclusions, it should be no cause for life-long worry and everlasting regret. Perhaps no one else could have done better under the circum-

THE NATURE AND CAUSE OF WORRY 357

stances; after all, you did the best you could. If there is anything to learn from your apparent mistakes, learn it cheerfully, and then let the matter forever rest.

And so we see that the misunderstanding and misinterpretation of even good and true teaching may lead to such a one-sided and extreme regard for truth and duty as to create a condition of mental uneasiness and dissatisfaction, eventually leading to chronic worry, with all its evil effects upon mind, soul, and body.

THE WORRY CIRCLE

When the attention is directly concentrated upon any part of the body, there is a definite tendency to magnify the sensations arising in that part. Special, peculiar, or unusual physical sensations always have a tendency to engender more or less fear; and it is a well-known and generally recognized fact of psychology that fear unfailingly increases and focalizes the attention.

Sensation, fear, and attention constitute the elements which enter into the formation of that wicked and destructive mischief-maker, the "vicious worry circle." It will be recalled that one of the definitions of worry was, "a spasm of the attention." This health-destroying and mind-ruining "circle of worry" starts with some extraordinary conscious impression, upon which the attention is forthwith focussed. The vividness of the impression is thereby greatly increased and fear is aroused, perhaps worry is born. Then all this fear and worry reacts by increasing and focalizing the attention anew upon those impressions which were the original source and cause of all this mischief. In this manner, concentration of the thoughts upon any organ of the body or upon any local pain therein, is usually found to make matters worse or indefinitely to perpetuate the ailment.

It would thus appear that worry is seldom likely to cure itself by being allowed to run its natural course. It soon wears for itself definite grooves in the brain and nervous system, and ever tends to perpetuate itself after the manner of this "vicious circle," and in almost every case slowly but surely increases its intensity, thereby becoming more and more destructive to mental peace and physical health.

We would not dispute the fact that the meek and humble, soul-eyed, hollow-cheeked woman may be on the certain road to heaven, but we are quite certain that she must have a "stop-over ticket for some sanitarium" or hospital where she will have to be long treated for the mental and material results of her constant worry, as well as for the indigestion, dyspepsia, and nervous prostration, that are so surely produced by this unnatural, unhealthful, and downcast mental state. And so, the "vicious worry circle" is found to consist of the following factors — attention magnifies sensation; sensation produces fear and worry; and worry further increases and focalizes the attention.

EXCESSIVE SELF-CONSCIOUSNESS

Among the everyday mental causes of fear and worry should be mentioned the exaggerated self-consciousness found especially in the case of certain young people. Stage-fright is an acute exhibition of this form of mental uneasiness and physical discomfort Many sensitive persons find it almost impossible to get away from these insistent feelings of self-consciousness. Their minds are peculiarly concentrated on the thought that other people are thinking about them, and it is certainly a demonstration of the fact that our thoughts are a real part of ourselves.

We well remember hearing some one say, "An imaginary worry may be unreal, but a worried imagination is very real"; and this is true. The basis of our worry may be entirely false and unreal, but the final results of the worry upon the mind, soul, and health are in every sense real and highly injurious.

MENTAL WORK AND REST

We must learn to strike an intelligent balance between the dangers which threaten us on the one hand from too much work and the friction attendant thereon; and, on the other hand, from too much rest and the rust of character which is sure to follow. We do not want either to "worry out" or "rust out," but to possess that wisdom which will enable us to lead the normal, rational life which promises deliverance from the threatened dangers of both these unnecessary extremes. We must be able to strike a practical balance between friction and rust.

THE NATURE AND CAUSE OF WORRY 359

Both mental idleness and physical inactivity predispose people to worry. Those who would cease from worry must constantly guard against intellectual inactivity; for, if it is true that Satan finds mischief for idle hands, it is even more true that he is sure to find worry for idle minds; and worry obscures our outlook on life, both for this world and the next; it throttles the higher powers of the mind; it beclouds our view of life and distorts our appreciation of the duties thereof. Worry is the smoke on the field-glass of life, and quite effectively it paralyzes all the creative faculties of the intellect.

Mental work never kills. Mental work plus worry is highly destructive to strength of brain and health of body; while heavy and taxing mental work coupled with unusual worry and its resultant insomnia, presents conditions which will more quickly destroy the physical health and break down the mind than any other possible combination of mental vices and physical sins.

SPECIAL FEARS AND HOODOOS

Among the more grave mental causes of worry should be mentioned the various "phobias" or specialized fears. Men and women, otherwise intelligent and sound of mind, are frequently found to be horribly afraid of certain foods or the drinking-water of certain localities; still others are possessed with a great fear of such numbers as thirteen, twenty-three, etc. Of course, much of this popular fear passes under the name of common, everyday superstition. Others live in constant fear of some particular disease; they live through a long life constantly nursing the fear that they will eventually die from cancer or some other malignant disorder.

We have all along heard the old proverb, "Nothing kills so sure as care"; and it is literally true. Constant fretting and worrying over our special fears are bound to do more harm to mind and body than physical fatigue and muscular weariness. The health of mind or body is greatly hindered by all this uncertainty, indecision, anxiety, hesitancy, and doubt; and any of these abnormal and indefinite mental states when long continued, when unduly entertained, are sure to give birth to fear and chronic worry.

Intelligent people live all their lives in everlasting dread of some great disaster, some terrible catastrophe. They are positive they will eventually be killed in an earthquake, struck by lightning, or be swept off the earth by a cyclone. Still other people are possessed with an unnatural gravity fear: they fear great heights, and will not even go up in a high office-building, if they can possibly avoid it. Others fear animals during the summer season, carefully avoiding all dogs for fear of being bitten by a mad dog, not knowing that mad dogs are just as plentiful during the winter season as during the so-called dog days. There seems to be no end of these special fears, and when long continued they often crystallize themselves into definite obsessions.

THE SPIRIT OF INFIRMITY

"And, behold, there was a woman which had a spirit of infirmity eighteen years, and was bowed together, and could in no wise lift up herself. And when Jesus saw her, He called her to Him, and said unto her, Woman, thou art loosed from thine infirmity. And He laid His hands on her: and immediately she was made straight, and glorified God." (Luke XIII:11-13.) (See Fig. 30.) Here was an unfortunate sufferer who had been held in bondage by an imaginary spirit of infirmity for almost a score of years. The Master broke light into her darkened mind by announcing that she was free from her infirmity. She had never really been bound. She was bowed together as a result of her long worry and sorrow. So long had she assumed this physical attitude that her body had become permanently deformed — another illustration of a physical disorder resulting from purely mental causes.

Thousands of suffering souls are held to-day by the chains of imaginary bondage. They have no real physical disease. Their ailment is in reality a spiritual infirmity. They might go free at any time, but they do not know it; they will not believe it. These prisoners of despair are held securely in their prison-house of doubt, by force of habit. They are very much like the elephant in Central Park, New York City, which had stood in one spot for many years, shackled with heavy chains. He had never left his tracks except when he had been unfastened and led away by his keepers. One day it occurred to them to remove the fetters from his legs and see if he would leave his place. After the beast was free from his shackles, he steadfastly refused to move; even after he was allowed to become exceedingly hungry, and when food was placed within a few inches of his reach, he stood in his tracks swaying from side to side and trumpeting loudly, but not a step did the huge beast take toward the food.

The elephant was free, but he did not know it; therefore, he stood there in his old place just as securely bound by the chains of his own mind as if the steel bands were about him as of old. And so it is with humanity; altogether too many of us are like unto the elephant. We are absolutely free to-day, but not realizing or not believing the glorious fact — not having faith and courage enough to step out into our mental freedom and begin to enjoy our spiritual liberty — like the elephant, we stand in the place of habit-bondage and bitterly mourn our terrible fate. We are not surprised when an elephant behaves in this way; but it ought to be a cause for great astonishment that intelligent men and women, sons and daughters of God, will allow themselves to be held down by fictitious bondage and bound down by a mere " spirit of infirmity."

FICTITIOUS WORRIES

We recently saw a picture which greatly impressed us concerning the uselessness of worry. It was a picture of an old man, bent in form, sad of expression, suggestive of a life filled with perplexities and anxiety; and underneath the picture was this statement: " I am an old man and have had many troubles — most of which never happened."

A recent writer, in discussing the question of worry and the weakened condition of the mind which permits the " worry circle " to go on forever revolving, getting worse and worse, put it very aptly as follows: " You say you cannot; your friends say you will not; the truth is, you cannot will." There is need of a determined effort to strengthen the will, to control the mind. The methods for the accomplishment of this will be discussed in connection with the treatment of worry.

Certain nervous diseases are caused by worry. Most important among these is the condition known as neurasthenia, commonly called "nervous prostration." Patients suffering from this condition are usually spoken of as "all run down." The truth is that they are patients who have been "all wound up," and, as a result of high tension, coupled with mental anxiety, they have broken down, collapsed.

Hypochondria is another disease which owes its origin and perpetuation largely to worry. Hypochondria is simply a condition in which one worries about having other diseases. Whenever the most intelligent of men begin to examine their mental or physical life, they usually discover themselves to be sick. Some one has truthfully said: "We are all afflicted with a disease called life." This is a form of hypochondria which it is entirely possible to cure by mental means. There is another kind of hypochondria which usually requires the coöperation of the physician for its permanent removal. A third form of nervous complaint largely due to worry and anxiety is hysteria; and hysteria, it should be remembered, is the impersonator of almost every known disease.

MORAL CAUSES OF WORRY

The moral habits and spiritual state of the individual not infrequently contribute much toward the production of worry. Sin is not only a cause of physical sickness, but it also lies at the bottom of many a mental malady. Immorality, dishonesty, and infidelity, all operate to destroy the peace of mind and give rise to that prick of conscience which is altogether incompatible with a tranquil mental state.

Religion may be either a cause of worry, or it may play the role of a cure. We speak of "religion" in the sense of some particular form of theological belief.

Worry is frequently generated by false ideas and arbitrary views of the Supreme Being. Doctrinal and interpretative errors of religious beliefs are responsible for much of the downcast, sad, and despondent experience of many professed Christians, as well as for the unsatisfactory and miserable experience of thousands who do not profess to be followers of Christ. Many earnest and honest souls have such constant wrestlings with the doubt of the forgiveness of their sins, or they live in such incessant fear of death and eternal damnation, that the mind is held in constant bondage to these insistent and oppressive thoughts, and all this must inevitably result in the production of a chronic state of worry.

RELIGIOUS FANATICISM

Religious devotion and faith, while they may prove the quick and certain cure for worry, may also be perverted — carried to such fanatical extremes as to produce serious mental worry and even spiritual despondency. Every now and then, we hear of some one "going crazy over religion." Such a one usually belongs to that class of morbidly conscientious and over-scrupulous people who possess a nervous system already greatly weakened; or perhaps they have a strain of insanity in their family, and probably some of their ancestors were alcoholic or syphilitic. The combination of such physical soil, taken together with the unusual mental strain or excitement, connected with extraordinary religious enthusiasm, is frequently able suddenly to overturn the mind or else to produce such an unnatural condition of anxiety and worry as gradually to undermine the mental vigor and result in producing some form of insanity. Religious fanaticism is one-sided moral reasoning, simply the extreme over-emphasis of one aspect of religious or moral life. It sometimes results from an apparent exhaustion of the mental energies and overwork of the spiritual faculties.

Still other sincere persons are suffering from the results of their own misguided zeal. They voluntarily possess themselves of such extraordinary burdens for the salvation of the souls of their fellow men, that they, in a measure, actually assume the worry and responsibility of the world's Saviour; and, as a result, their brains are overburdened, and their souls are crushed beneath the weight of this constant worry and anxiety for the welfare of their fellows.

Religious hope of the right sort, when sincerely cherished, undoubtedly exercises a positive power toward the prevention of worry. It is an important observation which the author is not alone in making, that, as the so-called old-fashioned religion declines, worry increases. As men and women depart from the simple faith and trust in the fundamental principles of the

Christian religion, there is a growing tendency to worry. We sincerely believe that the religion of the soul should be as a bright light shining in a dark place, our guiding star, instead of being perverted into a source of worry, grief, and despondency.

PHYSICAL CAUSES OF WORRY

Many sensitive souls are caused more or less worry throughout life by the legacies handed down by father and mother in the shape of physical weaknesses and bodily deformities. Still others, owing to a weakened nervous system and overstrain, have fallen into a condition of nervous irritability that renders them very liable to anxiety and worry upon the least provocation. Such persons — in fact all of us — are greatly predisposed to worry by sleeplessness. Sound sleep is a great preventive of the mental state that borders on worry.

The state of the physical health is not an infrequent occasion for worry. Many worry because of lingering illness or unusual affliction, while others grieve because of the sickness and suffering of their loved ones.

There is little doubt that nine-tenths of all the ordinary diseases of the body originate in the mind, and it is worry that produces the soil from which these infant diseases spring. The seeds of mental disease and physical affliction may fall upon us thick and fast, but if they fail to find the soil of worry and depression in which to develop and grow, we are not likely to be seriously affected by their presence. It requires not only a germ to produce disease, but also a favorable soil in which it may grow. Worry produces just that condition of mind and body most favorable to the growth and development of all the vicious diseases which prey upon the mind and destroy the body.

WORRY DEPENDENT ON AGE

Many of the worries which afflict the human mind are incident to some particular time of life — they are more or less dependent on age. For example, we have certain worries belonging to the period of childhood, others to adolescence. Certain difficulties are more likely to harass the soul during the adult period of life, whereas other troubles are more likely to give birth to worry and anxiety during old age.

The worries of childhood are just as real as those of later life. The little girl who is made to wear short dresses which come considerably above her knees, when she has long outgrown them; or the small boy who is compelled to wear clothes which he regards as suited only to infants — both have their worries; and it should be remembered that their childish grievances are to them very real. They take these little troubles of childhood very seriously. Likewise their griefs and sorrows resulting from ridicule and teasing tend to induce unhealthy mental activity, and seriously to warp the nervous system in its early development.

Another form of worry which may be very properly classified among this group, is the fear and worry of old age. As the years pass over us, the arteries begin to harden, the memory gradually fails, the skin becomes visibly wrinkled and leathery, and old age brings its peculiar worries to the majority of people. There is a tendency to undue anxiety on the part of the aged that is born both of the retrospective view of life and anticipation as to what the future holds in store. Especially is this true in the case of those who do not have sufficient means laid up properly and comfortably to care for them to a good old age.

PERNICIOUS HEALTH FADS

Some new-fangled health fad may set the whole country worrying about indigestion and dietetics. Newspaper articles and health literature are able so to alarm the people as markedly to upset the nerves and digestion of thousands of susceptible persons. Some editorial novice, who cannot earn his living in a better way, sends out an article to the newspaper syndicate proclaiming that some scientist has discovered that strawberries are poisonous; and forthwith ten thousand people begin to have stomach trouble from eating strawberries, or begin seriously to worry over their liability to disagree with them. Some persons cannot read a book on health and hygiene without immediately acquiring a new disease. It is proverbial that medical students are prone to have, or at least to think they have, the numerous diseases which they study from time to time.

The author would not have it understood that he in any

way decries the good that has been and is being accomplished by the great hygienic awakening which is making its way over the land; we believe that human beings should be capable of studying about themselves for the purpose of gaining needed instruction without allowing their minds to become morbid, faddish, and filled with worry concerning their physical health.

Not only are numerous physical conditions responsible for worry, but it should be remembered that numerous physical disorders may directly result from chronic worry. Among the common physical ailments which may directly result from long continued worry may be mentioned, insomnia, loss of weight, anæmia, rise of blood-pressure, hardening of the arteries, premature old age, apoplexy, headaches, dyspepsia, constipation, pale skin, poor circulation, and predisposition to catching all contagious diseases and colds.

SOCIAL SOURCES OF WORRY

Among the social causes of worry, family trouble, either real or false, probably comes first. Divorces, desertions, and social dissipations result in a vast amount of human worry, sorrow, and sickness.

Household problems are another cause of worry. The proper rearing of the boy, the successful training of the girl, the usual petty cares of the home, to which all women are subject, together with the modern servant problem — all serve to create anxiety and worry, together with the useless and unnecessary toil connected with the family life. Housewives are constantly worried over the proper performance of little things that would in no way affect the family happiness if they were left undone.

Many a mother, when she wakes up in the morning, begins the day in a state of anxious and nervous agitation; she feels herself already crushed under the weight of all the burdens she will have to bear. The little household cares and domestic trials which every mother experiences are not to her simple annoyances; they are actual catastrophes, and she suffers every one of these calamities a score of times before it comes. By noon her life is swarming with apprehensions, difficulties, and troubles, worry reigns supreme on the throne of her mind, and distraction has come to possess the soul. At the close of the day this unhappy mother has borne a hundred sorrows which were wholly imaginary, produced entirely by abnormal emotion. Among social causes of worry are those of jealousy and distrust, the social rivalry and ambition found among the "smart sets" of our metropolitan centres. Undue sympathy for friends may be set down as another cause of mental uneasiness.

Social and family friction may cause worry to the point of producing such high blood-pressure as to lead its victims to the use of alcohol, in an effort to secure relief from mental nervous tension. Intemperance may be set down as both a cause and a result of worry.

INDUSTRIAL CAUSES OF WORRY

Every product of modern inventive genius which tends to decrease the physical work of the body is bound to increase the tendency toward worry. The less we use the body, the more likely we are to over-use (abuse) the mind by worrying.

An inordinate worldly ambition may generate worry on the one hand, while there can be no denying the fact that poverty is a provoker of worry on the other hand. Financial difficulties and business reverses must be set down as among the industrial causes of an uneasy mind.

Industrial disputes and labor difficulties, the constant friction between combinations of money and those of muscle, produce conditions which are ever provocative of industrial uncertainty, and therefore result in generating mental anxiety and worry.

Accidents incident to our modern industrial life produce worry both in those who fear them and those who are compelled to suffer because of them; in fact, the complexity of the demands of our modern social and industrial organization is such as constantly to entoil us in the meshes of anxiety and worry.

SUMMARY OF THE CHAPTER

1. Worry may be defined as "a spasm of the attention" — too long continued concentration of the mental powers. Worry is fear thought in contradistinction to forethought. It is chronic fear, one-sided thinking. Worry is a process of borrowing trouble from the future to augment our present sorrows.

2. The liability to worry exists only in those animals high enough up in the biologic scale to possess associative memories. Man possesses a high degree of the power of memory association, and, therefore, is most liable of all animals to worry.

3. The general cause of worry is the universal desire for happiness, and the quest for those things and conditions which are generally supposed to confer happiness on their possessor.

4. In the last analysis, much worry has its origin in some form of irritation, anxiety, or fear. The use of alcohol, and other forms of physical transgression, are not infrequently the handmaidens of worry and sorrow.

5. Many people constantly worry because of their temperamental peculiarities. They feel that they are always being "neglected," "slighted," or "criticised." Others are inordinately timid, fearful, and backward.

6. Some people are literally human barometers. They can detect a storm almost before the weather bureau knows of its existence. They constantly worry over the weather, lest their plans be upset by rain, storm, or drouth.

7. Some men persist in magnifying trifles beyond all measure and reason. They insist on making mountains out of molehills. Other people are not free from the little vexing trifles of life; why should we expect to be?

8. Some people have acquired the chronic "kicking" habit; they are utterly unable to see good in anybody or to be satisfied with anything. Some folks have come to the place where they actually enjoy poor health, taking great delight in recounting their numerous complaints.

9. "Look before you leap," and numerous other good proverbs may be so perverted as to lead to much worry and inaction. Other proverbs commonly perverted are, "What is worth doing at all is worth doing well"; and "Be sure you are right, then go ahead."

10. Each day's efforts should be wisely divided into the essential and the unessential; and it should be no occasion for worry if some trifle has been slighted or neglected, as we review the events of the day.

11. Sensation, fear, and focalized attention are the elements

THE NATURE AND CURE OF WORRY

entering into the formation of the wicked and destructive "worry circle," by which means anxiety is perpetuated and chronic worry tends ever to grow worse and worse, fed by the very elements of its own creation.

12. Exaggerated self-consciousness is a common cause of worry. An imaginary worry may be unreal, but a worried imagination is very real.

13. We must strike an intelligent balance between too much work on one hand, and friction attendant thereon; and on the other hand, too much rest and the rust of character which is sure to follow.

14. Mental work never kills. Mental work plus worry is highly injurious, while mental work plus worry plus insomnia represents a combination which will quickly destroy the health of mind and body.

15. "Nothing kills so sure as care." Thousands are made miserable by special fears, "phobias," and hoodoos. Intelligent people live all their lives in everlasting dread of some great disaster, some terrible catastrophe.

16. Thousands of souls are held in perpetual bondage by imaginary fetters. They are victims of a "spirit of infirmity." A discouraged and downcast mental attitude may so habitually bow down the body as to produce permanent physical deformity.

17. When tempted to borrow trouble, when harassed by fictitious worries, remember the old man who had passed through "many troubles — most of which never happened."

18. The moral habits and spiritual state not infrequently contribute much toward the production of worry. Religion may be either a cause or a cure of worry. As the old-fashioned religion declines, worry increases.

19. Physical weakness, bodily deformity, and numerous diseases all figure as causes of worry. Nine-tenths of ordinary diseases originate in the mind as a result of worry. Every age has its peculiar worries; there are childhood worries, as well as old age worries.

20. Some new-fangled health fad may set the whole country worrying about indigestion and dyspepsia. Magazine articles

and health books are often able to give their nervous readers a set of new diseases.

21. Common physical ailments which may be traced to worry are insomnia, loss of weight, anæmia, rise of blood-pressure, hardening of the arteries, premature old age, apoplexy, headaches, dyspepsia, constipation, poor circulation, and predisposition to catching disease.

22. Among the social causes of worry may be mentioned divorces, family cares, household problems, and servant difficulties, as well as business difficulties, industrial disputes, and labor troubles.

CHAPTER XXXIII

THE CURE OF WORRY

MENTAL THERAPEUTICS, OR SO-CALLED SUGGESTION.— AUTO-SUGGESTION, OR POSITIVE THINKING.— THE PRACTICE OF SELF-CONTROL.— DISCOUNTING FEAR AND SENSATION.— MINIMIZING DIFFICULTIES.— REAL WORRY AND FICTITIOUS WORRY.— LEARNING TO TRUST NATURE.— COMBAT SELFISHNESS.— THE ART OF LIVING EASY.— THE MORAL NUTRITION.— THE DELUSION OF DRUGS.— CULTIVATE THE PHYSICAL HEALTH.— THE LIFE OF THE GOLDEN RULE.— SUMMARY OF THE CHAPTER.

THE fundamental requirement for the successful treatment of worry is the restoration of legitimate confidence in yourself and the development of faith in your friends and associates. It is also of great assistance if the victims of worry can acquire simple faith and trust in the Supreme Being. After the analysis of the causes of worry in the preceding chapter, it seems useless to add that those who would begin its treatment must first put forth every effort and make every provision for the removal of all the causes, both remote and direct. We cannot, by any process of treatment, expect to be successful in our escape from worry so long as we permit its causes to remain in operation in our lives.

MENTAL THERAPEUTICS, OR SO-CALLED SUGGESTION

It must be remembered in dealing with our fellows who are victims of worrying over mental delusions and physical diseases, that, so far as the mind is concerned, we are called upon to treat these conditions largely by mental and moral means, not necessarily by material means, although it will often be found that the body is in such an abnormal condition as the result of chronic worry, as to require treatment by natural remedial agencies such as water, air, exercise, and diet.

In our efforts to help the individual over his worries and other mental difficulties, we should ever recognize that there are true and false suggestions. True suggestions appeal to the reason, deal with facts, point out causes, and offer a cure which is rational and right. False suggestions (and the world is deluged with systems of mental healing based upon falsity and untruth) appeal to the imagination. They aim to give immediate relief although temporary; they aim to "heal the hurt of the daughter of my people slightly"; they seek to produce immediate effects, no matter at what future expense of pain to the body, disappointment to the mind, or destruction of the soul. *All methods of sympathy, suggestion, and advice to mental sufferers should be based upon truth,* free from falsity and deception.

Suggestion, either true or false, is the key that unlocks many a medical mystery, and explains the cure of mental diseases in all times and by a thousand different methods. The systems of the ancient medicine-man and the modern bogus healer are all based on the destruction of fear and the generation of faith. Trust and confidence are the mental states prerequisite to the banishment of worry, and, for the time being, it matters not whether the suggestions responsible for the change in the mental state are true or false — the *physical effects* are just about the same. Please bear in mind that we are not referring to the after effects upon mind, the subsequent results upon the soul; these are wholly deleterious and disastrous, and will be dealt with later.

AUTO-SUGGESTION, OR POSITIVE THINKING

Train the mind to think *positive thoughts.* For instance: Instead of saying to yourself all the time, " The noise of those children will drive me crazy," seek to calm your nerves and control your mind by thinking like this: " The innocent noise of these little ones will not drive me crazy; it won't hurt me at all." A patient once remarked that he had greatly helped himself in overcoming insomnia, when, after retiring, the thought kept running through his mind, " I cannot sleep, I cannot sleep," by simply changing it around and saying, " I can sleep, I can sleep, I will sleep."

THE CURE OF WORRY 373

If these therapeutic suggestions are to be made to us, it is altogether proper that we should make them to ourselves. If they are to be made to the patient by a second party, let them be made in accordance with reason and while the patient is awake and conscious. This is not the place to consider hypnotism; but the author desires, in this connection, to emphasize the uselessness of this practice in the permanent relief and help of these mental sufferers.

No amount of mental resolution and moral determination, in and of themselves, will be able to overthrow and cast out worry. Positive thinking is not only required in the battle against worry, but it is essential that our positive thinking shall also be *opposite* thinking. We must overcome worry with its opposite mental states; we must cultivate faith and trust. This is the one vital factor in the permanent cure of worry: *Replace the worry thought with an opposite thought which will occupy the mind and inspire the soul.* Drive out fear thought by exercising faith thought This is the substitute cure for worry; and when backed up by the strong resolution of a determined will, this method will always be found effective. Even in the moral and spiritual treatment of worry it is the substitution principle that works best. Replace the doubting, restless, and fretting attitude toward God, by a calm, confident and trustful belief in the wisdom of the Great Mind which is directing the affairs of this universe.

Have the moral courage to enforce your own anti-worry mandates. When you have commanded the mind to cease worrying, keep right after it and see that it does. In all these little things that harass one's soul, as some one has said, " Don't forget to remember the probability that *you have not,* as well as the possibility that you have, made a mistake."

THE PRACTICE OF SELF-CONTROL

In these days, we hear a great deal about suggestive therapeutics. Suggestions to a disobedient mind are best, when they come straight from the higher mental sources — the divinely taught faculties of the mind itself. *The secret of the treatment of worry is the acquirement and cultivation of self-control.* Purpose to be a brave captain of your own mind. Summon to your aid all possible spiritual help, moral resolution, and mental decision. Dictate positive commands to the faculties which direct the physical sensations that influence the bodily state. Learn to be a master of your moods. Do not permit yourself to drift along like a helpless, rudderless bark, tossed to and fro by every sensation of pain and every wind of mental distress.

Keep the mind filled with faith thoughts. Fear thought is the ancestor of all worry, and do not forget that fear thoughts cannot be successfully driven out of the mind except by faith thoughts. Persistently cultivate cheerfulness, confidence, restfulness, and trustfulness.

Some persons can be reasoned out of much of their worry, others are best helped by judicious ridicule. You can sometimes help a woman to overcome her absurd fear of a tiny mouse by reasoning with her along the line of showing that the mouse is far more afraid of her than she is (or should be) of the mouse. If reason does not effect a cure, try ridicule in such cases as these unreasonable fears. Point out the absurdity of a woman over five feet high and weighing one hundred and fifty pounds, shrieking hysterically at the sight of a badly frightened and fleeing mouse hardly two inches long!

It is so necessary thoroughly to eradicate this unnatural element of fear, that if it is found that fear of the lifeless human body cannot be cured otherwise, it would be advisable to pay a visit to some dissecting-room, repeatedly touch the dead bodies if necessary, and once and for all time be rid of this unreasonable fear of the dead. Act likewise with reference to the abnormal fear and dread of insects and snakes which so many people experience. If you have cured the fear of one dreaded beast, you have done much to remove the fear of all others.

The author had a friend who would almost have a spasm on seeing a reptile. We induced this fear-ridden person to go with us one day to a certain drug store in San Francisco where some ten or fifteen living snakes were on exhibition in the front window. It was a difficult ordeal for our friend; but the watching of these reptiles for three-quarters of an hour was sufficient effectually to cure that horrible dread of creeping and crawling things, and ever since this person has been able to look at snakes without experiencing the least sensation of fear or feeling of terror.

DISCOUNTING FEAR AND SENSATION

It is a good habit to form, systematically and persistently to practise sensation-neglect, if the causes of your worry are certain physical conditions. If your worries are of a moral or a family nature, make your peace with God and your fellowmen, and then practise a little common sense. The employment of a great and good motive will do a great deal to drive worry out of your experience.

The majority of our fears and many of our sensations should be liberally discounted. We should not form the habit of taking our emotions and feelings too seriously. They are very liable to impose upon us, unduly to alarm and frighten us. Even if we find it exceedingly difficult to exercise control over our own fears and worries, let us at least succeed in meeting the fears and anxieties of our associates without appropriating them to ourselves or otherwise echoing them.

Never resist worry as such. It is increased many times by all effort to overcome it in this manner. The strain of the effort makes it increasingly difficult to drop the strain of the worry. Do not dignify every little petty fear with so much attention. Learn liberally to discount all your fears, emotions, sensations, and worries. In all the realms of human experience there are to be found no greater deceivers than these imps of false fear and sham feeling. Even much that passes for religious experience is nothing more or less than sham emotion, psychological deception.

Another illustration of how easy it is to overestimate the value of our fears and apprehensions is shown in the excitement and consternation which prevail in some homes when a thunderstorm is approaching, especially if the lightning is severe. The mother becomes panic-stricken, her face assumes a frightened expression, and she begins to gather the children around her in one corner of the room — or may be in a closet — where they pass the time in fear and trembling, momentarily expecting to be hurled into eternity by a malicious bolt from the skies. And so from infancy, most children are led to look upon the elemental forces of nature with fear and terror, when they might have been taught the beauties and grandeur of nature's powers.

MINIMIZING DIFFICULTIES

Most of us need to practise the art of minimizing our difficulties. Do not look at your obstacles with a magnifying glass. Make up your mind that in many instances you will be able to rise triumphant over apparent defeat and to move right on in the even tenor of your way. Do not become greatly disturbed by the little ripples of life which pass through your experience from day to day. Practise taking your own good advice and all the suggestions you give to other people about not worrying. Don't forget to use them yourself.

"You may learn," says Dr. William Osler, "to consume your own smoke. The atmosphere is darkened by the murmurings and whimperings of men and women over the nonessentials, the trifles that are inevitably incident to the hurly-burly of the day's routine." Let us learn to live only one day at a time. You need not live your past life over every day. It is not necessary for you to borrow trouble from the future. Lincoln used to say of his troubles, "And this too, will pass." There is a good deal of common sense in that saying of the street: "Never trouble trouble, till trouble troubles you."

Begin to pin your worries down to definite facts. Most of our difficulties are vague and indefinite. Many of our fears and worries are wholly imaginary. Make a practice of writing down in black and white the objects of your worry. The process of writing them down will usually disclose their absurdity and assist in the work of overcoming them.

REAL WORRY AND FICTITIOUS WORRY

If one is suffering from fictitious worry, all that is necessary is to make a declaration of emancipation. Formally publish to your own soul that you are free from these vexing delusions and destructive imaginations. Recognize that your worry is usually about unreal situations; that even if they were real, further worry would only be useless — it would only make a bad matter worse; resolve to cease worrying and follow up your resolution so carefully as really to do it.

Now, we might just as well differentiate here between the honest man who is trying to overcome worry and yet conscientiously perform his duties to the world, and the common ne'er-do-well, who neither worries nor thinks. A happy-go-lucky sort of creature is he, caring neither for his own progress nor for the progress and betterment of the world. He drifts with the stream of time, taking everything just as it comes. We do not make a plea for the development of such as he. We recognize the necessity for thought, deliberation, meditation, for carefully weighing one's problems and difficulties. We believe in the considerate attention that belongs to every worthy problem. It is the "spasm of the attention," that chronic mental state resulting from long-continued fret and distrust, doubt and despair, for which we are seeking relief.

If we can't get rid of these fictitious worries by any other method, we might try the old plan of selecting one hundred beans, and as the beans are dropped one by one into a bag, repeat the following: "The worry is in the bean and the bean is in the bag."

LEARNING TO TRUST NATURE

How long will it take humanity to learn to trust Mother Nature? Having done our part in the scheme of life, how long will it be before we can quietly and confidently depend on Nature to do the rest? Think health thoughts instead of disease thoughts. Take your mind off your diseases, your aches and pains. Have the mind dwell upon the wonderful provisions which Nature affords for regaining health. Think of the fresh air, pure water, good food, and engage in exercise of the body. Come close to Nature herself and replace the thoughts of disease with a mental current bearing messages of health and strength. Exercise good emotions, even if you have to put them on for the time being, and you will joyfully discover that ere long you have actually become what you at one time had to pretend to be.

Let the servants of worry and the victims of grief turn their efforts toward the cultivation of health. Let the mind be occupied with health efforts in the place of anxiety and evil foreboding. Give attention to the cultivation of health, and little time will be left for sorrow and sadness.

For instance, take those nervous beings who do not sleep well. All day long they fear they will not be able to sleep. As night approaches, they become more and more convinced they will not be able to sleep. They go to bed with the settled conviction that they will not go to sleep. Now, such persons, in addition to baths and other proper physical treatment, will do well to go to bed with the idea uppermost in their minds that *they will sleep,* and not care at all if they do not sleep. This will relieve the mental tension, partially remove the anxiety, effectually destroy the state of worry, and help a great deal in producing natural sleep.

In your efforts to overcome worry and regain a natural mental equilibrium, suggest to yourself thoughts of health and peace at the retiring time — just before you go to sleep — and let these thoughts rest in the mind as a part of yourself while you sleep. This self-suggestion to the mind is of great value, as evidenced by the experience of many persons who can resolve, just before falling to sleep, to wake up at a certain time, and in the vast majority of instances, they are able to wake up at just the time settled upon in their suggestion.

COMBAT SELFISHNESS

The mind must be taken off self-interests if we would strengthen it and prepare it for deliverance from worry. There are three things essential to the ideal mental state:

1. Do everything possible to lessen self-consciousness and direct thought of yourself.

2. Make a positive effort to externalize your thoughts; that is, think of others and the great creation of God — everything possible outside of yourself and your own interests.

3. Widen your field of vision, and broaden the sphere of your interests; take up new lines of study; take an interest in new people; spread out the scope of your mental action.

We know a great many people who have cured themselves of chronic worry and despondency by simply enlisting in "the cheering-up business," going about systématically and persistently cheering other people up. A constant effort to help other people to cease worrying is sure to react favorably upon ourselves and prove of great assistance in our battle to banish fear thought and worry.

Laughter and light-heartedness seem to be of real value in the treatment of these melancholic subjects of chronic fear. They seem to serve the purpose of relieving the "attention spasm"; they get the mind off itself for a moment, and contribute greatly to one's ability to take up a new line of thought.

THE ART OF LIVING EASY

The unfortunate victims of worry are much influenced by the society in which they move. They should make up their minds to get along the best they can with their friends and associates. *Cultivate the art of living with yourself as you are, and with the world as it is.* Train yourself to pay more attention to the value of what you are doing and how you are doing it, than to how you are feeling or what you have done in the past. Make every reasonable effort to live within your income. Avoid debts; they always generate worry. The mortgage is bound to harass the mind and reflexly lower the vital resistance of the body. Do not borrow unless for business necessity or safe investment.

The nation once had a strenuous president, who explained his good health in the face of hard work, by saying, "I like my job." Make up your mind that you will either like your present job or else immediately abandon it and get one you can or will like. Contentment with daily toil, satisfaction with one's regular employment, is a great aid in dispelling worry.

Cultivate the society of children and cheerful adults. There is many a chronic worrier about the home who would be cured by the advent or the adoption of a bright-faced baby. Their light-hearted freedom from care and worry is contagious, and the men and women who live with them find it easier to live the faith life in the place of the fear life.

It is a good thing to cultivate the ability to forget some things as well as the ability to remember others. It is this temporary forgetfulness of the burdensome routine of life that gives one such happiness of mind and health of body during a holiday or the time spent on a vacation. At such times the mind is comparatively free from worry, and this undoubtedly contributes much to the sum of physical benefits received. (See Fig. 31.)

It is also a good plan to practise sleeping over things before you take them too seriously. Many difficulties will be found to adjust themselves more hopefully if left alone over night, and then after all, even when things seem to be at their worst, when, as you say, "It never rains but it pours," even then you can console yourself with the old lady's philosophy, that, after all, "maybe it ain't so."

THE MORAL NUTRITION

Some one has suggested that worry should be treated by dogma and not by drugs, and this is good advice so far as it goes. *The author regards the Christian religion as the ideal system of mind treatment* — a real and efficient system of psychotherapy. *Prayer is the most powerful and effectual worry-remover with which we are acquainted.* That man or woman who has learned to pray with childlike sincerity, literally talking to and communing with, the Heavenly Father, is in possession of the great secret whereby he or she can cast all their care upon God, knowing that He careth for us. A clear conscience is a great step toward barricading the mind against the entrance of worry. A moral taint of whatever sort is bound to breed mental uneasiness and result in destroying perfect balance and poise of mind.

We believe many are victims of fear and worry because they fail properly to maintain their spiritual nutrition. As our perceptions, memories, emotions, and thoughts control our bodies, so our unthought aspirations, our unsatisfied spiritual yearnings for those things that are, but for us, perhaps, not yet — those indefinable experiences within us, which, taken all together, we commonly call the soul — these in turn contribute balance, direction, and inspiration to our intellectual powers. The majority of people liberally feed their bodies, and many make generous provision for their mental nourishment; but the vast majority leave the soul to starve, paying very little attention to their spiritual nutrition, and as a result the spiritual

FIG. 31. VACATIONS DESTROY WORRY.

nature is so weakened that it is unable to exercise that restraining influence over the mind which would enable it to surmount its difficulties and live in an atmosphere above despair and despondency.

We believe that perfect trust in a Supreme Being is one of the essential steps in the successful treatment and effectual deliverance from the bondage of worry. If your religion does not help you in these matters, if it does not change you, then it would be better to change your religion and get one that does.

Gladstone was once asked what kept him so serene and composed in the midst of his busy life; he replied: "At the foot of my bed, where I can see it on retiring and on arising in the morning, are the words, 'Thou wilt keep him in perfect peace whose mind is stayed on Thee, because he trusteth in Thee.'" There is good mental therapeutics in that old method, called the "practice of the presence of God."

THE DELUSION OF DRUGS

We are aware that there are many drugs the use of which affords temporary relief from worry, but it must be remembered that when worry is cast out by drugs, like the demon of old it is sure to return ere long, with seven devils more wicked than itself. We should be slow to employ drugs to help us over our mental harassments or physical sufferings. A settled state of mind will aid much in helping us to endure either suffering of mind or pain in body.

The numerous false methods of mind cure (fraudulent psychotherapy, including the common employment of hypnotism for the cure of worry) may very correctly be looked upon as constituting a class of mental drugs, psychic deceivers, procedures calculated to relieve mental symptoms and allay psychic suffering temporarily, without in any way removing the causes of worry, or curing the real mental malady. Hypnotism will be fully considered in another chapter; but we would here emphasize the uselessness of this practice as a permanent cure for worry and its mental cousins.

Every new religion has been invented directly or indirectly to cure worry and its consequences; and every self-respecting man should see to it that he preserves his own intellectual freedom and chastity in the effort to overcome worry. Do not resort to these deceptions and delusions. In reality they are mental drugs and will debilitate the mind just as literal poisons will deteriorate the body. *Remember that while false faith will bring a physical reward, it is bound to bring moral disappointment and spiritual disaster.* It should be remembered that hypnotism is only symptomatic treatment; it does not remove the cause, and all efforts of mind healing which involve mental surrender to any but the Supreme Being, are fundamentally wrong and cannot afford true and permanent relief. Fraudulent suggestion or mental deception is just the same, no matter by what name it is called.

Just as morphine immediately relieves physical pain, so all these cures are temporary, superficial, and ungenuine.

CULTIVATE THE PHYSICAL HEALTH

Careful observation has taught us that the less attention we pay to the function of any organ in the body, the more regular and healthful it becomes in its action. That is why dyspeptics should never engage in the discussion of diet at meal-time. If you want the stomach to do regular work and good work, keep your mind off it when it has food in it. *Do* all your study of diet between meals, and at the table never think of your stomach.

There is one cause for worry which might be considered in this connection, and that is the conscious violation of the laws of life. This is a rightful and sufficient cause for worrying. A man should not expect peace if he lives in deliberate sin. Both the mental and physical consciences will torment him, and they ought to. The transgressor will have a hard time overcoming worry and finding happiness. The pleasures of sin contain the sting of remorse.

In the battle against worry, every effort should be made to promote good digestion, and it is imperative that chronic constipation be removed. Combat portal congestion or stagnation of blood in the liver by making frequent pressure over the abdomen or wearing a moist abdominal bandage at night, covered with waterproof and with dry flannel on the outside.

Engage in exercises for the strengthening of the abdominal muscles. Years ago, Doctor Abrams called attention to the fact that the "blues" were due to congestion of blood in the abdominal vessels associated with the liver.

An effort should be made, by proper bathing, to keep the blood circulating in the skin. Drink two quarts of water a day (not at meal-time) and obtain suitable medical treatment and advice for any real disease you may have. Cold baths and rubbing of the body are also of great value because of their influence upon the general nervous system, and more particularly because they flush the brain and increase the circulation of the blood about the worried nerve cells. Deep-breathing exercises accomplish the same purpose. It is a crime for those who are victims of worry and despondency to sleep in close, stuffy bedrooms. They should come as near sleeping outdoors as possible.

Games and other competitive exercises are all good in their place, but we have seen cases where they have generated what some one has termed "mock worries"; that is, there is constant excitement and worry over the fear of being beaten in the contest, which produces much annoyance and harmful anxiety.

THE LIFE OF THE GOLDEN RULE

If you would be successful in completely and finally overcoming worry, do something helpful for your neighbor now and then. Remember the Golden Rule. Do not allow your own artificial needs to accumulate unnecessarily and demand all your time. Reserve a little energy for Good-Samaritan work, and you will finish the day's tasks refreshed and satisfied instead of hungry, thirsty, and dissatisfied.

To sum up: All chronic worriers should see to it that they have the following:

1. Active mental and physical employment; in other words, a good job.

2. They should have regular and healthful recreation; in other words, a good fad.

3. They should have suitable and regular spiritual nourishment; in other words, a good religion.

Professor James says: "The sovereign cure for worry is

religious faith. The turbulent billows of the fretful surface leave the deep parts of the ocean undisturbed; and to him who has a hold of vaster and more permanent realities, the hourly vicissitudes of his personal destiny seem relatively insignificant things."

Of all things, do not make the mistake of worrying now because you have worried in the past. Do not be so shortsighted as to worry over your worries. Watch your habitual expression and cultivate one that is cheerful and happy. It will react on the mind and greatly help you in the battle against worry.

SUMMARY OF THE CHAPTER

1. The fundamental requirement for the successful treatment of worry is the restoration of legitimate confidence in yourself, and the development of faith in your friends and associates.

2. Suggestion is of great value in combating worry. All methods of sympathy, suggestion, and advice to mental sufferers should be based on truth, free from falsity and deception.

3. Suggestion is the key that unlocks many a medical mystery and explains the cure of mental diseases in all ages and by a thousand different methods. The physical effects of suggestion are the same, regardless of their truth or falsity.

4. Train the mind to think positive thoughts. Replace worry thought with an opposite thought which will occupy the mind and enthuse the soul. Drive out fear thought by exercising faith thought.

5. The secret of the treatment of worry is the practice of self-control. Purpose to be a brave captain of your own mind. Summon all possible spiritual help, moral resolution, and mental decision.

6. Fear thought is the ancestor of worry. Some people can be reasoned out of their fears, others can be cured by ridicule. Still others are only cured of certain fears by directly challenging their fear and fighting it out to a finish in one grand struggle.

7. The majority of our fears and many of our worries should be liberally discounted. The strain of effort employed in resisting worry makes it increasingly difficult to drop the strain

THE CURE OF WORRY

of our fears. Do not dignify petty fears with so much attention.

8. Learn to minimize your difficulties. Don't look at obstacles with a magnifying glass. "Learn to consume your own smoke." "Never trouble trouble, till trouble troubles you."

9. Make a "declaration of emancipation" in your own soul against fictitious worry. We fight fear thought, not forethought. Exercise good emotions — after a while you will actually become what you now pretend to be.

10. Learn to trust Nature. Sow the seeds of health, then let the harvest rest with Mother Nature. Go to bed expecting to sleep, but not caring if you don't. This indifference is often successful in producing sleep.

11. Combat selfishness. Lessen self-consciousness, externalize the thoughts, and broaden your interests. Enlist actively in "the cheering-up business."

12. Cultivate the art of living with yourself as you are, and with the world as it is. Learn the art of living easily. Learn to "like your job." Associate with children and learn how to forget the vexing trifles of everyday life.

13. It is a good plan to practise sleeping over things before taking them too seriously. Worry should be treated with dogma and not by drugs.

14. The Christian religion is an ideal system of mind treatment for chronic worry. Prayer is the most powerful and effectual worry-remover with which we are acquainted.

15. Much worry is due to a failure to feed the spiritual man. Perfect trust in the Supreme Being is one of the essential factors in the prevention and cure of worry.

16. When worry is cast out by drugs, like the demon of old, it is sure to return with seven devils worse than itself. Hypnotism and other false methods of curing worry may be regarded as a species of mental drugs — psychic morphine. Every new religion has been invented to cure worry and its consequences.

17. The less attention we pay to the functions of any organ in the body, the more regular and healthful it becomes in its action. Keep the mind off the stomach when it has food in it.

18. In the battle against worry don't forget to cultivate the physical health. Give attention to digestion, constipation, diet, water-drinking, deep-breathing exercises, and regular bathing. The "blues" result from congestion of the liver.

19. Live according to the Golden Rule — reserve a little energy for Good-Samaritan work. Don't work all the time for yourself. Have these three things: A good job, a good fad, and a good religion.

20. Lastly, don't make the mistake of worrying because you have worried. Cultivate a cheerful habitual expression.

CHAPTER XXXIV

NERVOUSNESS AND RELAXATION

WHAT IS NERVOUSNESS?— THE NEURASTHENIC.— THE PSY-CHASTHENIC.— THE HYSTERIC.— THE HYPOCHONDRIAC.— THE INSOMNIAC.— THE FIDGETY STATE.— NERVOUS TEMPER. —THE FATIGUE STATE.— EXTRAVAGANT TENSION.— " GETTING ON THE NERVES."— FALSE SYMPATHY AND SELFISHNESS.— NEEDLESS HURRY AND USELESS RUSH.— THE PRACTICE OF NERVOUS CONTROL.— THE GOSPEL OF RELAXATION.— RELAXATION *versus* RESISTANCE.— HARMONIZING WITH ENVIRONMENT. — THE HAPPINESS HABIT.— METHODS OF TREATMENT.— SUMMARY OF THE CHAPTER.

THE civilized nations are becoming more and more afflicted with nervousness, nervous tension, neurasthenia, and nervous prostration. During the last twenty-five years these various nervous disorders have multiplied enormously. It must be recognized that certain physical transgressions are indirectly concerned in this tremendous increase of nervous diseases, nevertheless, a careful study of these nerve disorders serves to demonstrate that the psychic state is, in all probability, the chief contributing agency concerned in the production and perpetuation of these manifold nervous disturbances and mental maladies included in the general term of nervousness.

WHAT IS NERVOUSNESS?

That physical and mental condition commonly known as nervousness can hardly be called a disease. It is rather a condition — a state of mind and body due to a combination of over-stimulation and under-control of the nervous system. Many conditions of so-called nervousness are primarily due to indigestion and auto-intoxication, which result in greatly irritating the nerves and the nerve centres. These poisoned and irritated nerves are in turn subjected to overstrain; and this high tension is responsible for that complex and troublesome disorder called nervousness.

The majority of healthy people are more or less nervous from time to time, but, as a rule, a night's sleep is able fully to remove the difficulty. In the case of certain high-strung persons this nervous condition becomes highly acute, they become wrought up to the last degree, and when this nervous state is long continued, we may have a general collapse, a constitutional breakdown, resulting in that condition commonly known as nervous exhaustion, nervous prostration, neurasthenia. The two great sins of our modern civilization are our atrocious dietetic practices and the increasing tendency to live "on our nerves."

Nervousness is by no means limited, as some seem to think, to the rich and the well-to-do. Our clinics are thronged with day laborers, factory hands, and servant girls, to say nothing of sedentary workers such as stenographers and teachers, all of whom are suffering from nervousness. This condition is common to all classes of society, and we are forced to look upon it as consisting of two factors: first, the excessive excitability of the nervous system, due, in many cases, to a toxic condition of the blood stream, resulting from insufficient exercise, and constipation; and, in the second place, the imperfect control of the nervous system on the part of the brain and higher nervous centres. Either of these conditions can produce nervousness; in a majority of cases, they are found combined in varying proportions.

The majority of this nervousness is, therefore, founded on nervous irritation, overstrain, and lack of control. The immediate or exciting cause may be nothing more or less than a monotonous or tedious mode of life, chronic worry, a disposition to magnify small difficulties and exaggerate trivial bodily sensations, or it may be an undue tendency to give way to the emotions, to indulge in outbursts of anger. When a group of any of these influences have long acted upon the nervous system, they are bound so to change both the habits of mind

NERVOUSNESS AND RELAXATION

and body as to result in the production of nervousness of varying intensity and severity.

This general state of nervousness may be more specifically defined or made to include the following forms of common nervous disturbances which are more or less familiar to all:

1. *The neurasthenic.* Neurasthenia is an exhaustion of nervous energy giving rise to a chronic sense of fatigue, fleeting pains, abnormal sensations, mental instability, and moral vacillation. Sooner or later, there is developed the well-known "habit fatigue" — a fictitious weariness which is in no sense relieved by rest and sleep. The one uniform and unchanging symptom is chronic worry.

2. *The psychasthenic.* This word has been coined recently to describe certain cases of nervous exhaustion which are largely, if not wholly, due to psychic disturbances, the physical state of the patient having but little to do with the prevailing nervous weakness and melancholic tendencies. The patient is filled with fears, dreads, and obsessions.

3. *The hysteric.* As a result of disease or from birth, hysterical patients are highly suggestible; any transient idea, emotion, or sensation may gain an overpowering mastery of the nervous system, producing adept imitations of various bodily diseases and numerous physical disorders.

4. *The hypochondriac.* Sufferers from hypochondria have become personifications of their long-entertained fears; worry has become second nature to them. They live in everlasting fear of disease, and are usually exceedingly melancholic.

5. *The insomniac.* The victim of insomnia exists in constant fear of sleeplessness. In his own mind, he lives "without hope and without sleep." He spends every waking moment in doubting his ability to sleep when he goes to bed at night.

THE FIDGETY STATE

Most of these nervous people live in a state of constant agitation. It seems impossible for them to keep still for even a short time. The entire body seems to be working under a continual nervous lash. The vital powers are driven at a ruinous pace, while the energies of mind and body are dissipated with a lavish and extravagant hand; the energy granules of the nerve centres are being used up to no useful purpose. There is a tremendous waste of fuel and energy in these various useless movements on the part of the human machine.

It must be admitted that many nervous persons, especially nervous women, reach that place where they actually seem to enjoy this continual state of nervous agitation. They are never happy except when they are excited and fidgety. To make them keep still would be equivalent to compelling them to serve a prison sentence in solitary confinement. It is almost impossible for some victims of the fidgety state to concentrate the mind for five minutes without straining every nerve and muscle in their bodies, without clinching their fists and making their muscles rigid. In this way, a vast quantity of nervous and muscular energy is dissipated at a hundred points where it might be saved. Such persons are the most extravagant thinkers and workers in the world. A minimum of mental and nervous work is bound to result in a maximum of mental weariness and physical fatigue.

The human body, when functionating normally, is the most economical engine in the world; that is, the same amount of fuel will produce more heat and energy in the bodily engine than in any other engine; but it is not so in the case of nervousness; here the body becomes an exceedingly extravagant and wasteful mechanism.

NERVOUS TEMPER

The culmination of nervous irritation and lack of nervous control is seen in the case of acute anger. Both the circulatory and nervous systems are concerned in these manifestations of nervous temper. Not only are the nerves irritated and under loose control, but we know that these angry emotions are largely determined by certain changes in the visceral circulation. In the initial state of anger or passion the face is pale, while the small blood vessels of the brain are greatly dilated, enormously congested. The internal pressure is greatly raised; in fact, sudden death from apoplexy, due to the rupture of a blood vessel, is not an uncommon result of a fit of anger.

Immediately following this pale-faced stage of anger, there takes place a reaction similar to that following an application of cold water to the face; then we have the characteristic red appearance and flushing of the skin of the face, accompanied by burning sensations and even swelling.

Anger represents the culmination, the climax of nervousness. During a fit of temper, every function of the body is run at an extravagant pace, and all its work is carried on in a wasteful fashion. Tears may flow and saliva run, while all the muscles of the organism are in a state of intensity and contraction. This tenseness is also found to pervade the sympathetic nervous system, and, as a result, all the smaller blood-vessels are caused to contract down in a sort of spasm. The blood-pressure is enormously raised, the patient executes a host of useless movements, which may consist in biting the finger nails, clinching the fists, stamping the floor, throwing objects, and giving other exhibitions of demoralized and inefficient nervous control.

In all conditions of nervousness, ranging from the common fidgety state up to acute anger, the heart is overworked; the circulation, the digestion, and the elimination are interfered with, while the breathing is superficial; the entire physical mechanism is disorganized.

Such a state of affairs might be looked upon as a short-circuit at some point in the brain, whereby certain sensations or ideas are allowed to throw the body into this state of useless agitation by means of some sort of short cut to the motor nerves, instead of passing over the customary route to the higher centres of reason and judgment; in fact, this state of nervous agitation represents a condition in which the body is acting without the moderation and control of its customary governor — the willpower. The will is the seat and source of control for the prevention and cure of these conditions, and will be dealt with more fully in a subsequent chapter.

It must be admitted that the enormous amount of work performed by brain and body when in a state of anger, represents just so much mental and physical energy which has run to waste. Not only is this work lost, but it results in actual harm to both mind and body. Regular and systematic body and brain work constitute a great safeguard against these harmful, useless, and unwholesome upheavals.

THE FATIGUE STATE

We cannot have long-continued over-functioning of the nervous system without having a subsequent and corresponding stage of under-functioning; and so, the fidgety state is sooner or later followed by the fatigue state. The sufferer who is all "keyed up," high strung, nervous, fidgety, and overactive to-day, must necessarily to-morrow or next day begin to experience unusual mental weariness and unnatural physical fatigue. Such a patient will then describe himself as feeling "all run down." Exactly so; which only goes to show that he was previously all wound up. Nature allows this nervous exhaustion to overtake them for the express purpose of keeping the nerves from "snapping," to prevent the "boilers from bursting." This sense of nervous prostration and physical fatigue which supervenes in the case of these excited and agitated creatures is a great and wise safety device — it is an efficient life-saver.

And so, these nervous ones begin to complain of being tired, tired all the time, tired in the morning and tired at night. They are constantly telling people they are tired and worn out, and they are everlastingly telling this same thing to themselves, little dreaming that this very contemplation and reiteration of their tired feelings is directly adding to the sum of their fatigue. Suggestion is, itself, a powerful fatiguer of both mind and body. A little economy in nervous and muscular movement, a little less nervousness, coupled with more mental control (counter-suggestion), would cure many people of at least one-half of their habitual fatigue.

We should not resist our fatigue and tired feelings. Having done your best to economize muscular and nervous expenditure, if at night you find yourself tired and weary, simply reason like this: "Yes, I am fairly tired out to-night, but that is only natural. I will go to bed and get rested. I shall be all right in the morning." And this very acceptance of your fatigue will rest you, more or less, immediately. We must learn to cast from us the magnification of our weariness and the emphasis of our fatigue. Especially is it desirable that these things should be cast out of the mind during the meal hours and at bedtime.

EXTRAVAGANT TENSION

Some women wear themselves all out by talking fifteen or twenty minutes; the tongue and throat become exhausted; in fact, the nerves and muscles connected with expression are in a constant state of extraordinary tension, and, of course, they are bound to become prematurely wearied. We see this same unnecessary and fatiguing concentration manifested by people who are reading, attending a lecture, shopping, and in a score of other ways. They wear themselves out prematurely and unnecessarily because of this unnatural tension. In fact, someone has said that most people at church listen with their spines and not with their ears.

The author recently rode in a passenger coach behind a lady who was in a state of high muscular and nervous tension throughout the journey. She would not give her body to the train to be carried, but insisted on sitting up in her seat and helping push the train on to its destination. At the conclusion of the journey, as she alighted from the train, we overheard her say: "Oh, Mary, I am simply worn out, I am tired to death."

And so we find people whose eyes tire out from reading, due not alone to eye strain, but also to nerve strain. Others cannot visit without becoming unnecessarily exhausted. Some women are unable to sew for half a day without having a tired, aching feeling between the shoulders, largely due to unnecessary nervous and muscular strain. In our everyday work we employ not only those nerves and muscles which are necessary to the performance of our task, but we also allow the entire nervous mechanism to exert itself in needless tension sympathy with the working groups of muscles.

"GETTING ON THE NERVES"

There is something decidedly wrong with one's nerves, when everybody is constantly "getting on them." They are either highly diseased or abnormally sensitive. This unnatural sensitiveness has been compared to the psychology of a shying horse. When a horse shies at some new object, it is customary to drive it repeatedly up to that object and let it get used to the situation, let it become accustomed to the experience; and we think it would be an excellent plan for some nervous people to back right up to those things which "get on their nerves"—brush up and take a square look at them.

Make up your mind no longer to submit to such tyranny on the part of your uncontrolled and unbalanced nerves. If you are doomed to have a fit because Mrs. Brown eats sugar on her tomatoes instead of salt, it would be well for you to hire some one to sit down before you and eat sugar on tomatoes until you have actually habituated and reconciled your nerves to the idea of letting other folks do as they please. Some one has said that "every woman is a slave of every other woman that annoys her." Every woman should declare herself free from this peculiar nervous bondage. What do you care if Mrs. Brown rocks incessantly, or if Mrs. Jones tosses her foot while visiting you? There is no good reason why these things should "get on your nerves." If your friends want to rock, let them rock; develop immunity against these petty harassments and insignificant sources of worry.

We really believe some mothers drive their children into difficulties and harmful practices because of their constant fretting and everlasting worry about these things. We can do a great deal to encourage people to become strong by showing that we are strong enough to trust them.

FALSE SYMPATHY AND SELFISHNESS

False sympathy does much to confirm certain people in their chronic nervousness. We find women who are cheerful and charming in all their intercourse with strangers and when away from home, but who are extraordinarily disagreeable, selfish, and quarrelsome when at home. They expect and demand much of their loved ones, and these people are made exceedingly selfish by having received too much sympathy, false sympathy, from the various members of their family. Occasionally, we run across a patient who literally takes sympathy out of every one with whom she comes in contact. Such persons are really professional invalids, and they depress, weaken, and impose upon everybody they meet.

People of all religions and no religion are affected with this semi-invalidism, commonly called nervousness. In all probability, there was a time when devotion to their religion would have saved them from passing through these unnecessary troubles. But, when things have gone thus far it usually requires something more than a mere theoretical theological belief to rescue them from the ruts of their own complaining and morbid introspection.

Sometimes the doctor unconsciously contributes much to confirming these invalids in their chronic nervousness, by his false professional sympathy. It is very important that the medical adviser should steer these nervous patients away from their thoughts of self and direct them into channels of thought which are unselfish and altruistic. This appetite for sympathy grows so inordinately that very soon the patient actually begins to manufacture fictitious symptoms in order to gain the sympathy of friends and professional attendants.

NEEDLESS HURRY AND USELESS RUSH

A great deal of the excitement, hurly-burly, and rush of everyday life is to no purpose whatever. Even when it is necessary to make haste, let us make it calmly, without excitement and needless exertion. The unnatural and needless strain of this hurry and rush so contracts the muscles that they cannot engage in rapid locomotion without undue exertion, and consequently premature and unnecessary fatigue. In fact, some people are so hurried, chronically rushed, that they cannot take time to eat, to breathe, or to sleep, in a natural and normal manner. A little systematic planning would enable most of them to do a great deal more work each day, and to do it with one-half the expenditure of vital energy.

We know of people who have the hurry habit so thoroughly established in their character that they will actually race up and downstairs, rush from one room to another, and go through all sorts of uncalled-for and unnecessary exertion simply because they have "got such a terrible day's work to do"; they have "got so much work to do that they are driven to death."

Some day, we shall pay more attention to muscular and nervous coördination; that is, to the science of using one's nerves in doing the work in hand, and to employing only those muscles which are essential to the task before us. We may progress to the point where we shall learn how to rest the unused portions of the body, while the active groups of nerves and muscles are engaged in their necessary work.

THE PRACTICE OF NERVOUS CONTROL

Nature would do very well for most of us if we would learn to keep our hands off, if we would simply leave her unmolested. We are constantly and unnecessarily adding to her stress and strain. We are incessantly overworking certain organs and underworking others. Everlastingly, we are injecting unhealthy impulses into the nervous regulation of our physical forces. In fact, thousands of semi-invalids, if they would but learn to relax, to effect a nervous surrender, and then practise the simple laws of hygiene with respect to eating, drinking, and sleeping, would experience a speedy and more or less complete recovery.

But some persons will systematically have to practise nerve-control. It would be an excellent idea for some nervous women to begin this discipline on their talking propensity. Some women talk too much and so intensely that they keep themselves on the verge of nervous prostration, independent of the excitement and tension that may pertain to the topic of their gossip.

It is a good plan to begin practising on some of the smaller nerve strains, and, as you acquire the ability to relax while resting, you will soon acquire the power of working without this unnecessary nerve strain and vital leakage.

It would be a good idea to sit down for an hour or two, go over your experience and isolate those things which are responsible for nerve strain, seek to locate your nervous weaknesses, the source of your lack of nerve-control. Ascertain if it is due to congestion of the liver, constipation, overeating, under drinking, or superficial breathing. See if you are unnecessarily resisting something in your life; or are you the victim of some chronic worry? If not exactly sure as to why you are so hurried and rushed, write down in black and white the apparent cause of your nervous strain, and then begin the persistent and systematic practice of nerve-control at the point where you most need it, beginning with the smaller deliuquencies first, and attacking the greater weaknesses later.

We need to acquire more of the play spirit of the child who

can run about and romp all day without getting unnaturally tired in either mind or body. We need to practise relaxation. The author had a patient call him up on the telephone one day, who was so excited that he could hardly understand what she said. After a moment, he interrupted and advised her to talk lower, to be calm, so he could understand her better; whereupon she began calmly and quietly to describe her case, and this relaxation of the nervous tension produced such immediate and favorable results that before discontinuing the telephone conversation, she actually decided that she would not need to see a physician. There are thousands and thousands of invalids who, if they would cool off and quiet down, would begin to experience immediate improvement both in mind and body.

A great many women have had their minds burdened for years with the idea that they will get sick or go crazy, when they reach the time of the change of life; and, true to their long-cherished opinions, some of them do manage to have quite a hard time of it during this period. It is the author's humble belief that the majority of these mental and nervous difficulties, which are experienced by ordinarily healthy women during the period of the change of life, are entirely due to suggestion and to imagination. Their trouble is in reality nothing more or less than a specialized form of neurasthenia, the neurasthenia of the change of life.

In this practice of nerve-control, it must be recognized by these nervous people that it is themselves that are out of order; that nervousness is not a disease like other diseases; that is, it is not a condition in which something is really wrong in the physical body. It is a condition of the mind and body and is in no more need of a physician to effect its cure, than one needs a doctor to tell him when to get up in the morning or when to go to bed at night; it is simply a matter of self-control.

THE GOSPEL OF RELAXATION

Having considered nervousness from the standpoint of its nature and cure, we shall now lay a special emphasis upon the value of relaxation. It seems especially necessary in this generation, that men and women should remember to relax. Nervous patients should practise perfect relaxation from fifteen minutes to half an hour in the middle of the day.

Most patients will find it best to begin the practice of the gospel of relaxation in connection with their regular rest and sleep at night. Learn to give yourself entirely over to the bed whereon you sleep; do not try to hold yourself in the bed or on the bed. If the reader will observe himself to-night (unless he is fortunately one who has already learned how to relax), he will be surprised in noticing how continuously and strenuously he holds himself in a certain position on the bed. He will find most of his muscles cramped, his head held rigidly in a certain position, the whole spinal column more or less rigid; in fact, he has taken up his customary job of engaging in hard muscular work in an effort to go to sleep. In some cases, the knees will be found all drawn up, the fists clinched, the chin flexed, and the jaws set. The entire physical picture is one of downright hard labor.

Now, it will not be an easy matter to change this picture. The gospel of relaxation is very easy to preach, but exceedingly hard to practise. Not only do we have this harmful physical tension on going to bed, but it is on retiring that some people begin to do their most strenuous mental work. The thoughts troop through the mind in a regular procession. If you cannot otherwise stop thinking on retiring, success may be achieved by allowing the train of thought to march on with all its energy, while you begin to concentrate the mind on relaxing the body; and it will usually be found that your train of thought slows down just in proportion as the muscles are relaxed. There is a great deal of reciprocal action between mind and body.

We have witnessed excellent results in insomnia, when the patient's whole mind was concentrated on relaxation. The body has been released from its nervous tension, and the mind has been occupied with helpful work, instead of being engaged in harmful, sleep-destroying, and useless worry.

In all the animal world, man is the only animal that maintains such incessant rigidity of the muscles, and such constant nervous tension. It is only necessary to lift a sleeping cat or a slumbering babe to see how completely relaxed they are; they give over entirely their weight to your supporting arms. And still, we would not assert that relaxation alone is the secret of health. It is highly necessary that we should have muscular and nervous work. Nerves and muscles must work together; but what we are concerned about is the unnecessary strain, the wasteful and extravagant tension which accompanies otherwise useful work, and which so successfully invades even our periods of rest and sleep.

RELAXATION *versus* RESISTANCE

In overcoming most abnormal states of mind and nervous conditions of the body, it will be found, as a rule, that more good can be accomplished by relaxation, by surrender, than by resistance, by fighting. A large percentage of those things which harass and vex us would be robbed of their power further to torture the soul, if we could but become thoroughly reconciled to their presence. It is our perpetual resistance of these annoying trifles of life that gives them such great power to harass and disturb us.

Many a chronic pain is made worse by complaining about it and resisting it. Had we calmly accepted the pain, as a matter of fact, it would have been immediately robbed of one-half its torture. Now, we do not make a plea for over-relaxation, for that passive submission which shall rob us of the power to resist wrong, and the disposition to combat evil; we are simply here registering a plea for nervous equilibrium, for regular periods of relaxation, for periods of rest following periods of work, and, further, to lessen the useless expenditure of energy in needless stress and strain, while engaged in our daily work.

Sometime ago, a writer suggested that pain would be much better borne by calmly relaxing while sitting in a dentist's chair, instead of contracting the muscles, clinching the fists, and thus exhausting the nerves and the muscles before a pang of pain has been experienced. And there can be little doubt as to the truthfulness of this teaching. Our pain is made a great deal more tense and acute by our tremendous resistance, whereas, calmly and quietly surrendering to the inevitable, would have reduced the intensity of the pain to an enormous degree. The fatigue which results from this nervous tension, while sitting two hours in a dentist's chair, is ten times more than the weariness which could result from the suffering of actual pain.

It would, therefore, appear that in many cases, the victory over either mental difficulties or nervous tension can best be secured, not by fighting and resisting, but by unconditional surrender.

HARMONIZING WITH ENVIRONMENT

It is a great gift to know how to get along with one's surroundings; how to react to the changes and experiences in one's environment; how calmly to accept those changes which cannot be made different; how to be a successful reformer, and yet how to keep from worrying over those things which cannot be changed. It requires strong character to live with one's associates and yet not to resent their incivilities or to be chafed and exasperated by their shortcomings. It is a good plan, "when in Rome, to do as Rome does." The chameleon is a fortunate animal: it has power to change its own color to harmonize with the color of its environment.

A certain degree of muscular rigidity is required, when one is standing, but this is wholly unnecessary when resting in a chair. How many of us hold ourselves just as tight in the chair as if we were holding the body upright, while walking! Why should a carriage ride completely exhaust a healthy man? Simply because he did not adjust himself harmoniously to the environment of the drive, he did not fully relax and enjoy the ride. All the while, he was in constant fear of the horse running away, or else by his anxiety and tension he endeavored to assist the horse in pulling the carriage, instead of entering into the joys and pleasures of the drive.

When riding on the train, we should become as one with the coach and be carried along without resistance, by the engine, stopping, starting, and otherwise moving in perfect harmony and attune with the train; this is what we mean by *harmonizing with one's environment;* it is a process of moving through life with the least possible friction consistent with the greatest possible mental and physical action. (See Fig. 32.) It is a scheme for improving and changing every remediable and objectionable factor in our environment, without in the least fretting or fuming over those conditions which we cannot change or remove.

RESISTING ENVIRONMENT.

HARMONIZING WITH ENVIRONMENT.

FIG. 32. RIGHT AND WRONG WAY TO RIDE ON THE TRAIN.

THE HAPPINESS HABIT

The victims of nervousness need to form and cultivate the happiness habit — strong and positive methods of thinking. Weak habits of thought condemn one to life-long bondage to heredity and environment; while strong habits of thinking will enable us largely to rise above our hereditary tendencies and master our environment.

Modern religious teaching largely consists in the proclamation of the gospel of love; religion has thereby become a great source of mental stimulation and moral illumination. The theologians have performed a great work of deliverance by this preaching of love, but they have failed in the presentation of the new religion of faith and love, fully to expose and denounce the old religion of fear. Perhaps, this is due to the old teaching that human progress was built on faith, hope, and fear. It must be admitted that fear enters largely into human progress — it is a powerful motive in uncivilized man, even as it is in the life-career of all animals. Whatever might have been the service of fear in times past, it is certain that the children of Christian civilization have nothing to gain from the cultivation and indulgence of fear and its offspring — nervousness, worry, and anger.

Let us cultivate the happiness habit as our mode of life. Trouble does not actually exist; in this respect, the philosophy of our Christian Science friends is right. Trouble exists only in the fear thought of our own minds. The moment we cease to fear trouble, it vanishes, it becomes a passing event in life, which we react to while it passes, and hold only in our memory after it has gone.

The royal remedy for nervousness, then, is the acquirement of that happy frame of mind which results from the constant exercise of faith and the repression of fear — it is the normal, healthy mode of life.

METHODS OF TREATMENT

In the treatment of nervousness, numerous methods and fads have been suggested from time to time. The thing of first importance is to teach self-control, to reëducate the will, to teach the minimizing of difficulties, and to stop the magnification of trifles. There is absolutely no reason, except a failure of nervous control, why a woman should go to bed for six months with nervous prostration, simply because her child breaks a looking-glass. Hypnotism was tried in the treatment of these cases several years ago, but it proved a failure; in fact, its results have been disappointing, and in some cases, highly disastrous.

Outside of the proper psychic treatment of nervousness, the physical treatment consists in liberal feeding with nutritious food easy of digestion, regulation of the bowels, abundant water-drinking, out-of-door life, and useful work which is suitable to the strength. In many cases, a uniform, graduated system of exercises, in connection with baths, will be found very helpful. It should be remembered that of far more importance than all of this physical treatment, is the reëducation of the patient's will, the inauguration of the patient's personal control over the nervous centres.

In dealing with nervous people, never meet their resistance by resistance on your part. Practise the gospel of nonresistance by the very way in which you refuse to resist them. There is an actual therapeutic value to be attached to the old words of the wise man: " A soft answer turneth away wrath; but grievous words stir up anger."

SUMMARY OF THE CHAPTER

1. Nervousness is not a real disease. It is merely a state of mind and body. It is usually due to combined irritation, overstimulation, and lack of control. No class of society is exempt from nervous disorders.

2. Nervousness commonly leads to some form of nervous exhaustion or nervous prostration, but may result in producing certain types or forms of nervous disturbance such as the neurasthenic, the psychasthenic, the hysteric, the hypochondriac, and the insomniac.

3. Constant nervous agitation constitutes a tremendous drain on the vital energies of mind and body. Nervous people are the most extravagant thinkers and workers in the world.

4. Acute anger is the culmination of this lack of nervous control. During a fit of temper, the functions of the body are run at an extravagant pace, while all mental and physical work is carried on at a great disadvantage. Anger represents a short-

circuit in the nervous impulses — cutting out the higher controlling centres.

5. We cannot have long continued over-functioning of the nervous system, without a subsequent stage of under-functioning, and so all high strung and nervous persons sooner or later " run down," experience unnatural mental weariness and unusual physical fatigue. This is nervous exhaustion, nervous prostration, neurasthenia.

6. A great deal of nervous energy is lost in useless tension, both nervous and muscular. A nervous woman instead of resting while riding on the train, actually insists on sitting up rigidly in her seat, doing her utmost to help the engine pull the train to its destination.

7. There is something decidedly wrong with one's nerves when everybody is constantly "getting on them." They are either highly diseased or abnormally sensitive. Every man is a slave to every other that annoys him. Let us become reconciled to the idea of letting other folks do as they please.

8. False sympathy does much to confirm certain people in their chronic nervousness. Some of these professional invalids demand sympathy from everybody they meet. They create fictitious symptoms to secure the sympathy they so crave.

9. A great deal of the excitement, huly-burly, and rush of everyday life is to no purpose whatever. Even when haste is necessary, let us make it calmly. Let us rst unused portions of the body, while the active groups of neres and muscles are doing their work.

10. Practise the art of nerve control. Vrite down in black and white what it is that excites, agitates, an' worries you. Let us acquire more of the free play spirit of thechild. Many people are not really sick — they only need to lern self-control to get well.

11. Most people have lost the power of nervus and muscular relaxation. They are intense and contracted ven on retiring at night. Learn first to relax during sleep, ad then during other phases of the daily life.

12. In overcoming many forms of nervousnes and worry, it will be found that relaxation is more useful tan resistance.

We do not advocate over-relaxation to the point of nonresistance to wrong, but rather the nonresistance of those conditions in life which we cannot possibly change.

13. "When in Rome, do as Rome does." The successful reformer is the one who can keep from fretting and fuming over the things he cannot remedy or remove.

14. Cultivate the happiness habit. Embrace a religion of faith and love; get away from the ancient teachings of fear. Trouble is really non-existent. It exists only in our fear thought for it, and our memory thought of it.

15. Hypnotism is useless in the treatment of nervousness. It is cured only by self-control and will-power in connection with the practice of hygiene—diet, water-drinking, physical exercise, and regulation of the bowels.

CHAPTER XXXV

THE PRINCIPLES OF MODERN PSYCHOTHERAPY

FICTITIOUS SENSATIONS AND FALSE IDEAS.— DISLOCATION OF IDEAS.— SUGGESTIVE IMAGINATIONS AND DREAMS.— ASSOCIATIVE MEMORIES.— "COMPLEX FORMATION."— DISSOCIATION OF IDEAS.— PSYCHIC INSURRECTION.— EMOTIONAL ENERGY.— PSYCHO-ANALYSIS, OR MENTAL DIAGNOSIS.— SUGGESTION AND REËDUCATION.— THE TREATMENT OF THE FATIGUE STATES.— HYPNOTISM.— THE WORK AND STUDY CURES.— RELIGIOUS EMOTIONS AND MORAL THERAPEUTICS.— SUMMARY OF THE CHAPTER.

PSYCHOTHERAPY is a term which includes the modern methods of treating mental disorders and disturbances by means of suggestion, diversion, reëducation, and persuasion, including moral therapeutics. Psychotherapy should not be confused with so-called mind cure. The old-fashioned mind cures utilized the identical psychological and physiological laws which are employed in modern psychotherapy; nevertheless, psychotherapy stands for the systematic, scientific, and rational treatment of psychic disturbances; while so-called mind cure consists in desultory, empiric, and ofttimes deceptive efforts at relieving mental disturbances; and, although sometimes highly successful, it must be looked upon as representing the quackish element in psychotherapeutics.

In considering psychotherapy, the author presumes that the reader is more or less familiar with the fundamental principles of psychology and physiology as outlined in Parts I and II of this book. This chapter must further be read in the light of the studies on habit, worry, and nervousness, which precede it, as well as in the light of the discussion of suggestion, reëducation of the will, and moral therapeutics, which follows in subsequent chapters. It will therefore be unnecessary to reiterate in full those conditions of mind and body which constitute the necessity for the practice of psychotherapy. Suffice it to say, that psychotherapy plays an important part in the treatment of all patients who are misguided in mind, misadapted to their environment, as well as those who are suffering from perverted feelings, disruptive sensations, the worry habit, and also those who fear disease or who have fixed beliefs in fictitious physical disorders; in short, all who suffer from anxiety, morbid introspection, self-consciousness, or the abnormal fixation of the mind upon some special mental state or some particular physical function.

Before giving attention to the diverse methods of psychic treatment, it will be well briefly to review the psychologic principles which underlie the successful and scientific employment of psychotherapy.

FICTITIOUS SENSATIONS AND FALSE IDEAS

Attention has been previously called to the fact that fictitious sensations may be produced by stimulation of the sense organs, or more directly by immediate excitation of the central areas in the brain, the sense organ performing no function in the case whatever. Furthermore, it has been observed that, however these sensations are occasioned, they are interpreted (unless the patient corrects himself by reflection) as if they arose through the usual stimulation of the peripheral terminals of the nervous mechanism. On the other hand, false and deceptive thoughts, ideas untrue to the facts, may assemble in the mind and palm themselves off in the sufferer's reason and judgment as being the real and legitimate offspring of *bona-fide* experience and mature reflection. In this way, it is possible for a man to form ideas which are highly deceptive, and conclusions which are directly false, and, in the end, lead to misdirection of action and misadaptation to one's health, habits, and environment.

A very good illustration of the unreality of some sensations is the common experience of "seeing stars" when we receive a powerful blow between the eyes. Of course, every one knows that he does not see real stars under such circumstances. These false ones are brought to view as a result of irritating the optic nerve, which, in turn, arouses special sensations of light, which are referred outward into space — where we commonly observe the stars. Patients who have had the eye removed without an anæsthetic have described their experience at the moment the optic nerve was severed, as that of the sensation produced by a sudden flash of light.

DISLOCATION OF IDEAS

By referring back to the diagrammatic representation of mental processes (Fig. 9.), the reader will observe how easy it must be to get our thoughts and ideas sidetracked in that complicated mind-centre known as the association of ideas. Not infrequently it happens that whole groups of thoughts, ideas, and memories become detached, lost from their fellows, and in this way our thinking becomes more or less fragmentary, our conclusions incomplete and immature; and the resultant actions and habits are wholly unadapted to the circumstances. Unbalanced and onesided thinking always results in perverting and destroying the reliability of the mental action and the resultant physical behavior.

The tendency toward the formation of groups of associated memory images, of whatever sort, is the means of their conservation; that is, of their retention in such a form that they may be recovered when occasion demands; and this, on the whole, is a happy economy of nature. In some cases, however, we would welcome an exception to such economy. When the memory of a fear or an alarm has become the hub of an associated group of ideas, it often occurs that the arousal of any idea in the group may have the effect of arousing that central fear in all its original intensity and with all the agitation and other physical symptoms, which, in the original instance, accompanied the emotion. For example, a person who was in a runaway ten years ago and was greatly frightened thereby may to-day, while quietly riding in a carriage, again experience the memory image of the runaway. Thereupon his heart begins to palpitate, and his hands to shake; a feeling of great muscular weakness arises; he displays all the physical symptoms of the emotion; in fact, he is again stricken with profound fear. And so it is in general; fear or other emotional disturbances of long ago, in the meantime apparently buried or effaced by the accumulation of the experiences of the years, may to-day be brought to the light through the influence of a happy — or unhappy — associated experience. This fact has an important bearing in both the diagnosis and the treatment of many psycho-physiological phenomena.

SUGGESTIVE IMAGINATIONS AND DREAMS

A great deal of nervousness, fear, worry, and even obsession, is found sometimes to have originated in connection with dreams. Certain susceptible persons, when not sleeping soundly, become terribly frightened in connection with some dream; and on awaking suddenly, this fear is carried over into the waking state, accompanied by the physiological perturbations which usually accompany fright. Thus this idea becomes associated in the mind as the centre of that group of fear thoughts and ideas, so that in the future, if this morbid state of mind is not resisted and overcome, the memory of that dream or of experiences similar to those which have been imaged in the dream, will be sufficient to arouse all these feelings of fear and to reproduce the physical exhibitions of fright; and if this matter is allowed to go on and increase, in time it may give rise to a veritable obsession.

There are numerous cases on record in which some psychic shock, afterwards entirely forgotten, has given rise to mental aberration and even insanity; as some one has said, hallucinations are merely waking dreams, while dreams were merely sleeping hallucinations. Dreams unconsciously influence the mind. Although not remembered in the waking moments, they may, nevertheless, as indefinable mental traces, or predispositions, determine the association of ideas. Thus they may, in a perfectly normal way, affect behavior, and even the logical sequence of our judgments.

What has been said of the effect of dreams may also be said of the imaginations of our waking hours. They, too, may influence and direct both mind and body; and they may guide us in the way toward depression and disease, or into channels of happiness and health.

ASSOCIATIVE MEMORIES

As formerly noted, only animals possessing associative memories are addicted to worry. The associations formed by ideas before they are finally deposited in the memory, have much to do with our future habits of thought and consequent modes of action. The author some years ago had under observation a patient suffering from Jacksonian epilepsy, who frequently had attacks of post-epileptic insanity covering periods of several days. During this time, it was observed that certain ideas or emotions would almost always result in convulsive paroxysms and would usually be followed by an indefinite chronological recital of his life-experience, beginning at some certain point and continuing progressively until the next fit, thus demonstrating conclusively that certain ideas and actions were so associated in his mind and memory as invariably to result in the production of convulsive attacks when the patient was in this peculiar state of temporary mental aberration. For a more complete account of this remarkable case, the reader is referred to Appendix B.

"COMPLEX FORMATION"

It is one of the fundamental laws of psychology that our sensations, feelings, ideas, movements, and visceral functions — of any and all kinds — when frequently repeated or when accompanied by unusual emotion, become bound together — associated or grouped together in such a way that the excitation of any one member of the group, sets in action all the others. This binding up together of ideas and emotions, actions and memories, is known in psychology as "complex formation." It is dependent upon the ability of the mind to associate ideas and memories, and is one of the links in the chain which explains habit formation. "Good complexes" result in the formation of good habits of thought and action, while "bad complexes" result in bad habits of thinking and acting — worry, obsessions, or even fixed delusions.

In the normal man, the majority of these complex formations are healthful and useful. Illustrations of such complexes, which consist both of memory of mental processes and of muscular activity, are found in those exceedingly intricate complexes involved in writing, piano playing, and other delicate muscular movements involving an intimate association of ideas and physical processes.

And so in neurasthenia, certain ideas and thoughts may become illegitimately attached to or associated with certain physical conditions, so that the thinking of these thoughts may result in the production of dizziness, trembling, or palpitation of the heart. This whole proposition is one of education — repetition of our methods of thought and modes of action. These unhealthy complexes may be formed as the result of persistent and long-continued misthought and wrong action. On the other hand, they may be formed wholly unintentionally or purely accidentally, certain nervous persons associating certain ideas and certain acts without the least intention of so doing.

Therapeutic methods of complex formation, together with other procedures which can be utilized in the reëducation of nervous patients, will be noted later. It might be well to note in passing that abnormal complexes are the explanation of many so-called functional diseases, while they certainly demonstrate the fallacy of all teaching which denies the existence of purely functional disorders.

Complex formation further explains the peculiar and sometimes rapidly changing moods which some persons exhibit. When the mind falls under the control and domination of a set of abnormal complexes, the disposition and temperament are so largely and suddenly modified as almost to amount to a change in personality. Indeed, these changing moods might very properly be looked upon as a mild form of multiple personality.

The physiological memory becomes bound up in these numerous memory complexes, as shown in Pawlow's dogs. It was necessary only to show the dogs sand, bread, or meat, when they began immediately to secrete a saliva which corresponded to the food or other substances seen. That is, the sight, the memory, of an article of food resulted in producing the same quality of saliva that would be secreted if that food were actually in the mouth. This same memory association is shown in the common tendency of the bladder to empty itself when a person hears the sound of running water. This may also explain why the sight of a rose (even a wax rose) is sufficient to give some persons an attack of hay-fever.

- DISSOCIATION OF IDEAS

It is entirely possible for a group or a number of groups of ideas to become so associated, established, and isolated, as to set themselves up in some corner of the mental domain as a new personality; that is, when the mental functions are not harmoniously and uniformly bound up and held together in the state of consciousness, or when as a result of disease, the continuity of contact, or the power of intercommunication is in some way interfered with or destroyed — we may then have exhibitions of that remarkable phenomenon, multiple personality. This, at any rate, is one of the well-known explanations of multiple personality.

It often happens that a man is called upon not only to experience the common warfare between the so-called carnal and spiritual natures, but he may also have within himself, apparently, two distinct personalities or minds — personalities which may be diametrically opposite to each other, and which may alternate in the control of his life. These conditions explain the difficulty some people have in controlling certain ideas or groups of ideas, which have taken fast hold of their minds. The methods of dealing with these conditions as well as the most interesting account of the remarkable case of Miss Beauchamp — who had four distinct personalities — will be found quite fully described in Appendix C.

Complete or partial dissociation of ideas coupled with irritation and undue activity of the sympathetic nervous system constitutes the explanation of hysteria, while common, everyday forgetfulness and absent-mindedness are illustrations and demonstrations of a mild degree and temporary phase of dissociation. Some form of dissociation is, usually present in most cases of marked neurasthenia, while such a condition is usually to be found even in mild hysteria. Certain ideas, emotions, and conclusions may become detached from the mental stream of consciousness in the dream state. These dissociated complexes either as minds different from the old, or as distortions of the old mind, may obtain such control as to produce what in the dream state would be called nightmares, but in the waking state, hysterical seizures or delusions. Such a psychic state might be described as a case of "subconscious nightmare," or as a condition of mind in which the patient may be said to be suffering from "fixed dreams." This is probably the state of the mind which prevails when certain nervous persons are said to have "brain storms."

Dissociation is the explanation of those interesting and remarkable cases where long periods of time are literally blotted out of the mind — at least out of the conscious memory. In those cases where the patient is unable to remember anything that occurred in his experience for a certain period, it is known that the memories of those experiences are really retained, for they can be recovered in hypnosis, but as they are dissociated from the memory images which are a part of his everyday conscious life, they are apparently lost.

That the deformities and paralyses of hysteria are purely functional and due to dissociation is shown by the fact that we can both produce and remove these symptoms by suggestion. And right here is the secret of the successful treatment of such cases: they can be cured by building up new associations of ideas, new complexes, which shall be able to overpower and eject the old and abnormal association of ideas.

It should be remembered that in discussing and dealing with the phenomenon of dissociation we are considering a perfectly normal process. Dissociation becomes harmful only when perverted or misused. Normal sleep is probably due to dissociation, resultant from the loosening of the physical contact between the processes of the nerve cells in the brain.

PSYCHIC INSURRECTION

Psychic insurrection, or automatism, is the explanation of how a group of mental habits may become so strong and individualized as to be able to control the behavior of mind and body, and thus to dominate a man and influence the formation of his character. When our mental habits become thus organized and employed they may be fittingly compared to a provincial rebellion in an empire. They represent certain groups of ideas which seek not only to free themselves from the sovereignty of the will — not only to be free and independent of all other mental processes, but ultimately to eliminate them, and so of themselves to exercise complete control. Thus it is that our habits first lead us astray, then assert their independence of our control, and subsequently establish a tyrannical mastery over us, over both mind and body.

And so in the establishment of fixed habits of thought, and in the formation of deep-rooted beliefs and vivid ideas, we are unconsciously forming those complexes which in time, if not carefully controlled, may secede from the commonwealth of consciousness and establish themselves in the role of psychic rebels — become capable of more or less independent thought and uncontrolled habit.

Again, we are dealing with a condition which is normal to the healthy mind. Automatism is simply a scheme of economy in expression, an association of thoughts and actions into groups ready for immediate expression. Certain explosive phrases and appropriate gestures always accompany the indulgence of emotional states of mind. Accordingly, when these same groups of associated ideas become more or less dissociated from the main stream of consciousness, they become capable of independent and mischievous action. The reassociation, the subjugation, of these belligerent complexes or groups of ideas is the aim of all modern methods of psychotherapy.

EMOTIONAL ENERGY

Excess of emotion stimulates the physiological functions to undue activity, while depressive emotions produce opposite effects. It is now generally recognized that every thought, every idea, is attached to what psychologists call "a feeling tone"; that is, a given idea is always accompanied by a certain emotional phase.

Sometimes the intensity of our emotions is disproportionate to the importance of the idea; sometimes the emotion itself may be inappropriate to the content of the idea or the character of the external situation. For instance, one may abnormally derive distinct pleasure from self-mutilation; the emotion is then inappropriate to the situation. The repetition of such a connection creates a predisposition thereto, and it becomes established as a habit. In time, the emotions came to wear for themselves certain definite psychological ruts. With the increasing distinctness of the situation, or vividness of the idea, as the case may be, the emotional element may become exaggerated and enormously disproportioned, as seen in hysteria and insanity.

On the other hand — and here is a great opportunity for treating both psychic disorders and physical diseases — if the emotions of health and happiness, of joy and pleasure, can be associated with certain ideas, and those ideas are persistently expressed, it will readily appear that the establishment of these new habits of thinking will result in the establishment of more intensified emotions of happiness and health. These new complexes are able to arouse feelings of courage, energy, well-being, and capacity for work; whereas the old and depressive complexes never failed to originate feelings of fatigue, despondency, and indisposition for work. Exalting emotions exert an organizing and rallying influence upon the mind and body, while the depressive emotions operate to disintegrate and disorganize the mind, producing the so-called "emotional trauma" of the psychologists.

The field of emotional energy promises great things to the future of psychotherapy. Herein is the explanation of the almost unlimited power of religious emotion — which, as previously noted — is able to appeal to the largest possible group of mental units, and exerts the greatest possible influence over the mental and emotional states. Thus again, we are dealing with purely normal and natural psychological tendencies, the perversion or misuse of which constitutes functional disease.

It is the purpose of modern psychotherapy to utilize systematically and scientifically the natural mechanisms of the mind in an effort to restore the psychic elements to their normal relationship to one another and to the mind as a whole, and thus contribute to the development of a strong mind and a healthy body, that is, to happiness.

PSYCHO-ANALYSIS, OR MENTAL DIAGNOSIS

It not infrequently happens that some group or groups of ideas which become formulated in the mind, for some reason or other, are unacceptable to the mind as a whole. The personality — the mind — fails properly to assimilate this particular group of ideas. The mind is active to subjugate these ideas and emotions — it tries to submerge and suppress. But it often appears that this temporarily suppressed and rejected complex has acquired the power and dignity of a separate and automatic existence; and thus it continues to act the role of a mischief-making intruder in the commonwealth of the mind, just as some foreign body would produce troubles in the physical organization. And thus it would appear that many forms of psycho-neurosis, such as worry or obsession, are indirectly due to this incomplete digestion, this crippled mental assimilation.

Professor Freud years ago called attention to the fact that a great number of the common psycho-neuroses owe their origin to a protracted conflict or disagreement between two groups of ideas or two inharmonious modes of thinking. To illustrate this theory of the origin and nature of many of our mental difficulties, let us suppose that a highly conscientious and religious person should passingly conceive the idea of committing some shocking crime. The thought of this wickedness arises in his consciousness, but it so shocks and horrifies his moral sensibilities that he immediately represses and disowns the idea. Every time this group of ideas arises in his mind he again promptly denies his responsibility therefor. He resists, combats, represses, denies, and fights the idea, and all the while his very mental warfare constitutes an ever-present source of autosuggestion which tends to grow stronger and stronger, impelling him to do the very thing he is fighting to keep from doing.

The methods of psycho-analysis would suggest that the tempted and tortured soul promptly recognize this wicked group of ideas as a dangerous intruder into an otherwise peaceful, well-disposed intellect, and that its existence be fully acknowledged. Further, instead of making incessant resistance, he should begin the process of full acceptance and immediate digestion and assimilation of the idea, and then promptly and effectively eliminate the whole wicked thing from the psychic domain, leaving behind only the memory of having effected its overthrow and banishment.

The actual process of accepting, digesting, assimilating, and eliminating an undesirable idea is carried out somewhat as follows: First, confess, acknowledge the existence of the idea; face it like a man; do not shun, disown, or deny the thing. Second, instead of continually resisting the offending idea, cultivate, strengthen, and multiply the *opposite* groups of ideas — think opposite thoughts — until its psychic fellows, as it were, become sufficiently strong to swallow up the bad idea with their superabundance of good ideas. This is what is meant by the psychological term of "digestion and assimilation"; and then the bad idea becomes lost to our psychic view; it is eliminated. And is not this the very essence of that old philosophy of "overcoming evil with good"?

If these disturbing ideas be not thus permanently cast down and destroyed, they may linger for years in the marginal consciousness (the subconscious mind), from which point they are able to haunt, tempt, and torture their victims indirectly through dreams and by their continuous unconscious activities.

One of the factors in the successful practice of modern psychotherapy is the process of definitely locating these mischief-making, foreign groups of ideas which have not been taken up and properly assimilated by the whole mind; and it is this process of isolating and recognizing the precise and definite idea which is making trouble in the mind, that is known as psychoanalysis. It represents to the realm of mental disorders what definite physical examination and precise diagnosis does in the world of physical diseases. We cannot successfully treat mental disturbances without securing exact knowledge respecting their cause.

While hypnotism may apparently remove many of these psychic symptoms for the time being, it is unable to effect a real cure. Almost invariably they speedily return. The only value of hypnotism in these cases (and even here it is of doubtful value) is that it sometimes assists in locating the group of ideas concerned in the process of mental diagnosis. When the sufferers are of themselves unable definitely to locate the psychic origin of their trouble, it is sometimes found that in a state of hypnosis it is very easy to secure from them an exact idea as to the nature and extent of these psychic disturbers.

As far as the author has been able to observe, this is about the only useful purpose hypnotism can be put to in the treatment of psychic disturbances, and then its usefulness is strictly limited to the process of diagnosing the condition. Hypnotism will be more fully dealt with in another place. This method of psychoanalysis is destined to become the great field of future expert work in psychotherapy; and it bids fair actually to accomplish the brilliant results which were expected of hypnotism alone, but which have not ensued. Of far more value than hypnotism in this work of mental diagnosis is the method known as " free association of ideas." This consists in suggesting a central idea and then allowing it to call up its associated memories, in this way seeking to uncover the real psychic source of the difficulty. Much can also be learned by a study of the patient's mannerisms, conversation, and other personal traits, not to mention his dreams. For a further consideration of the subject of mental diagnosis by the reaction method, the reader is referred to Appendix D.

In conclusion, attention should be called to the fact that psycho-analysis and reëducation are not founded on the great laws of suggestive therapeutics — they are purely educational; and while these methods have much that is in common with suggestion, they must be regarded as a distinct and separate phase of psychotherapy. There can be little doubt that the great psychic upheavals which accompany religious "conversions" and similar mental revolutions do actually rearrange and realign many of these groups of ideas to such an extent that the sufferer not only becomes possessed of a "new mind," in a spiritual sense, but that he literally has a new mind in the psychologic sense also.

SUGGESTION AND REËDUCATION

The power of suggestion and the principles of reëducation constitute the fundamental laws underlying all the various successful methods of treating psychic disorders. That this is true is evidenced from the entire philosophy and experience of mental healing. It is certainly true that man, in the highest sense, is a suggestible animal, a creature highly susceptible of education and reëducation.

The suggestion may often be hidden, even as it is in the case of the regular practice of medicine, for it is undoubtedly true that the more faith the patient has in the drugs he takes, the more good he gets from them. We have to recognize the psychic element even in the use of electricity, baths, and massage, and, of course, it becomes the exclusive element operating in the various cults of mental healing, including Christian Science.

Suggestion-education is what led the common people into their disastrous patent-medicine habits. They soon discovered that the doctor had a drug for every symptom, for every disease. They observed that the final result of his numerous well-charged-for visits was usually a row of empty medicine bottles setting on the table; and so instinctively seeking to obviate this expensive middleman, they went direct to the drug store for their medicines, and, after reading the literature and the rosy testimonials accompanying their patent remedies, they came to acquire great faith in the new medicine, took it, and usually got well.

But it is the reëducation of the will with which we are most concerned in modern psychotherapy. As the result of psychoanalysis, we are able quite accurately to locate the cause of the mental disorder. Suggestion represents the general method of our treatment, while the reëducation of the will is the goal toward which we are steadily aiming, to enable the patient to become the master of himself, to reinstate the will in its place of sovereign ruler over mind and body. But more about both of these methods in succeeding chapters.

THE TREATMENT OF THE FATIGUE STATES

Physiological fatigue is explained by the fact that physical work actually destroys muscular substance; and by the further fact that bodily activity results in the production of certain metabolic poisons of an acid nature, which circulate in the blood and tend to depress both mind and body. Psychic fatigue is explained on the ground of the exhaustion of the energy granules found in the cell bodies of the neurons; but independent of the combined physical and psychic fatigue which overtakes one as the result of a hard day's work, we are

MODERN PSYCHOTHERAPY 419

frequently brought face to face with cases of psycho-pathological fatigue — fatigue which is out of all proportion to the preceding mental and physical exertion, and which is quite unrelieved by prolonged rest. That these forms of nervous fatigue are artificial — really fictitious — is further indicated by the fact that they can often be entirely relieved by suggestion.

It is evident that the fatigue of nervous prostration, neurasthenia, or brain-fag is due to changes which are wholly psychic. In the case of the neurasthenic, it is certainly due to the fact that the sufferer has formed certain adverse idea associations or complexes, to whose depressing influence this chronic state of fatigue must be charged. It is simply a case where the central idea in numerous groups has become an idea of fatigue; and as long as these convictions of weariness dominate the personality, both mind and body are doomed to suffer the tortures and handicaps of this continued feeling of weariness.

What takes place in the mind in the case of the sudden and complete exhaustion which overtakes the patient, as a result of nervous shock or extraordinary fright? In this case, the fatigue is probably best explained by assuming that the shock produces a state of comparative dissociation, more or less resembling the psychic and nervous states which precede sleep, a more or less complete breaking of contact between the neurons of the central nervous system, as well as a dissociation of idea complexes.

The author has had the greatest success in treating these fatigue cases by the direct and honest conversational method, first recommended by Dubois. This consists in systematically and judiciously laying the real facts before the patient, and while physical treatment, such as baths, etc., is administered to alleviate his symptoms, the real dependence to effect a cure is placed upon this suggestion and reëducation.

The so-called rest-cure is of use in some of these cases, but the majority of neurasthenics are better helped by the work-cure, which will be presently considered. If the confidence and coöperation of the neurasthenic can be fully secured, the progress he will make under a few weeks of treatment by these simple methods is sometimes phenomenal, provided the physician is wise and positive in his procedure. Much depends on the wise planning of the patient's regime, so as not to overwork him, all the while providing him with a reasonable amount of good and nutritious food.

We recently had under treatment an attorney who had suffered three distinct attacks of nervous prostration. He was scarcely able to leave his bed, had distressing headaches, and all the other symptoms of neurasthenia. Three months of treatment in a well-equipped sanitarium had helped him but little. He came to us for the purpose of continuing his baths and massage. After several weeks of this treatment, with but little apparent improvement, we devoted fifteen minutes, two times a week, to a straight but graduated conversation-method of laying before him the real cause of his fatigue, and enlisting his mental and moral coöperation in its mastery. In less than two weeks he began to gain in weight and to recuperate his strength; and at the end of four weeks he stopped all treatment, resumed his practice, and to all practical purposes was fully cured.

HYPNOTISM

The employment of hypnotism in psychotherapeutic procedure is with the idea of increasing the suggestibility of the patient and facilitating the formation of new and healthy complexes in his psychic life. While it must be admitted that hypnotism does greatly increase suggestibility, it has been found that this state is transient and the desired effects are not permanent. It further appears that, when skilfully made, suggestions are just as acceptable and influential to the waking mind as to the sleeping; while the newer processes of reëducation and psycho-analysis can in no possible way be assisted by the employment of hypnosis. Hypnotism has been enthusiastically tried — and been found woefully wanting. Its value is demonstrated only in certain rare cases, and in connection with perfecting the mental diagnosis in certain difficult and obscure psychic disorders.

The author has come to recognize hypnotism as having but little or no value in the practice of psychotherapy, neverthe-

MODERN PSYCHOTHERAPY

less, there are certain misconceptions of this practice which should be set right in the public mind. These wrong ideas of the nature and practice of hypnotism may be summarized as follows:

1. Hypnotism is in no way related to spiritism and kindred cults. Hypnotism is a phenomenon pertaining to natural law, and unconnected with spiritism; it is not the work of either bad spirits or good spirits.

2. It is generally supposed that a person to be hypnotized must lose consciousness, but this is a mistake; many practitioners of hypnosis seldom place their patients beyond that drowsy stage known as the hypnoidal state, in which the subject is really awake and conscious.

3. It is commonly believed that weak-minded people form the best subjects for hypnotism, but this also is a mistake. Strong-minded and well-educated persons, when willing, are most readily hypnotized.

4. While most people can be hypnotized if they are willing, no person can be put into a hypnotic sleep against his will.

5. Hypnotism cannot be used to compel persons to commit crime. Hypnotized subjects will never do things which are contrary to the standards and practices of their moral nature.

THE WORK AND STUDY CURES

In these days we hear a great deal about the work-cure for neurasthenia and other phases of psychic disability. Great good is often accomplished by means of regular, systematic, and suitable physical employment for sufferers from these ailments. The work must be one in which the patient takes pleasure, and must not be too severe or too long continued. (See Fig. 33.) The ancient rule of dividing the day into eight hours for work, eight hours for play, and eight hours for sleep is difficult to improve upon. Pleasure-seeking as such will not help these patients to any great extent. Theatre-going and all such unnatural forms of recreation will not yield the desirable results. It is the pleasure which naturally arises from having done useful work, or having accomplished some actual achievement, that strengthens and comforts the neurasthenic. The wise man must have understood this when he wrote:

"Wherefore I perceive there is nothing better than that a man should rejoice in his own works; for that is his portion." It is certainly a great consolation to these sufferers to come to know that God has given every man his work to do. This spiritual foundation for our life-work is a great and helpful incentive to many neurasthenics; numbers of them have been entirely cured by taking up some special line of study in which they are interested, and which will not overtax their minds, such as botany or zoölogy. (See Fig. 34.)

RELIGIOUS EMOTIONS AND MORAL THERAPEUTICS

As noted in the chapter on mental medicine and moral hygiene, religious suggestions are the most powerful in most cases. It will not be necessary to repeat here the reasons, as they were fully discussed in the chapter referred to. We will, however, call attention to the psychic value of music; for it must be recognized that most of the suggestive influence connected with great religious movements is to be found in the music.

The author has carried forward many experiments for the purpose of ascertaining the psychological and physiological effects of music. These are largely dependent on its associations, the general environment, the individual's appreciation of music, and also upon his personal associations with the particular piece of music under consideration. While the personal element is largely concerned in determining the physiological effects of music, there are certain tunes and forms of rhythm which always stimulate the physical functions, increasing the blood-pressure, the force of the heart-beat, and the depth of respiration, as well as heightening the mental activities.

We find that a certain piece of music will produce stimulating and exciting effects in one patient, while it produces sedative and relaxing effects in another.

Even in ancient times the psychotherapeutic value of music must have been recognized, for David was employed to play before Saul when the latter found himself in bad humor.

From experiments made by the author and others who have worked in this field, it has been found that the general effects of certain well-known musical selections upon the average listener are as follows:

FIG. 33. THE WORK CURE FOR NEURASTHENIA

FIG. 34. THE STUDY CURE FOR NERVOUS DISORDERS.

Library of
California

MODERN PSYCHOTHERAPY

MUSIC WHICH IS GENERALLY STRENGTHENING AND STIMULATING.	MUSIC WHICH IS GENERALLY WEAKENING AND DEPRESSING.
Dixie.	Ben Bolt.
America.	Old Black Joe.
My Maryland.	Old Cabin Home.
Rock of Ages.	Stand up for Jesus.
Yankee-Doodle.	Home, Sweet Home.
The Old Oaken Bucket.	John Brown's Body.
The Old Folks at Home.	My Jesus, I Love Thee.
My Old Kentucky Home.	Jesus, Saviour, Pilot Me.
Jesus, Lover of My Soul.	I would not Live Alway.
Nearer, My God, to Thee.	We are Tenting To-night.
Listen to the Mocking-Bird.	The Star Spangled Banner.
Onward, Christian Soldiers.	*Depths of Mercy can Ever Be.*
Blest be the Tie that Binds.	
All Hail the Power of Jesus' Name.	*Do They Think of Me at Home?*
The Mighty Fortress of Our God.	Jesus, I My Cross have Taken.
	Behold, a Stranger at the *Door.*

SUMMARY OF THE CHAPTER

1. Psychotherapy should not be confused with so-called mind cure. Psychotherapy stands for the systematic, scientific, and rational treatment of psychic disturbances in accordance with the laws of psychology and physiology.

2. False and deceptive thoughts may assemble in the mind and palm themselves off on a person's reason and judgment as being the real and legitimate offspring of *bona-fide* experience and mature reflection.

3. Not infrequently whole groups of thoughts, ideas, and memories become detached, lost from their fellows, and this results in unbalanced, one-sided, unhealthy, and perverted thinking.

4. The associative grouping of our memory images is a means of conserving them; and it often happens that the recalling of any single idea in a group will serve to arouse all

the ideas, fears, and other emotions which were originally associated with that idea or experience.

5. The basis for much of our nervousness, fear, worry, and even obsession, is sometimes found to have originated in connection with dreams. Dreams are also able unconsciously to influence the mind although the dream may not be remembered during the waking hours. Likewise, conscious and unconscious products of the imagination are able to exert a powerful influence over the mind.

6. Associative memory may be not only the basis for worry, but it may also be an explanation of the rearousal of passions, such as anger, by the recall of certain ideas; and it may explain even the reproduction of those gestures which are characteristic of the passion.

7. This grouping or binding together of ideas and memories is known as "complex formation"; and it should be remembered that "complexes" may be either good and healthy, or bad and diseased. The latter leading to worry, obsessions, and even fixed delusions.

8. Illustrations of good complexes are the exceedingly intricate combined mental and muscular movements involved in writing and piano-playing; while a common illustration of unhealthy complexes is the fatigue, dizziness, and palpitation of the heart, so commonly associated with neurasthenia.

9. It is possible for a group or a number of groups of ideas to become dissociated in the mind, producing the common phenomenon of absent-mindedness; or, carried out on a grand scale, that extraordinary and unusual phenomenon, multiple personality. Forgetfulness on the one hand and hysteria on the other, are also practical demonstrations of transient dissociation.

10. In the mental realm we may have psychic insurrection or automatism — a group of ideas assuming an existence independent of the psychic life as a whole — tyrannizing over the mind with obsessions, and dominating the body by fixed and uncontrollable habits.

11. Every thought, every idea, is attached to what psychologists call a "feeling tone"; that is, a given idea is always

MODERN PSYCHOTHERAPY 425

accompanied by a certain feeling or emotion. These emotions may become disproportionate, misadapted, and so overdeveloped as to result in neurasthenia, hysteria, and even insanity.

12. The process of emotion-training is one of the great and promising fields in modern psychotherapy. Herein lies the almost unlimited power of religious emotion-suggestion.

13. Psycho-analysis is the process of locating the exact mental cause of psychic disturbances; it is precise mental diagnosis, and further embraces the therapeutic methods of subjugating independent and troublesome ideas — the digestion and assimilation of rebellious and unabsorbed complexes. Its object is to facilitate the ultimate elimination of these mental mischief-makers.

14. An unacceptable or unacknowledged group of ideas in the mind sustains the same relation to the mentality that a foreign body does to the physical organism. Such disturbing ideas are seldom overcome by mere resistance. They are usually mastered by the methods of mental assimilation, after psycho-analysis.

15. Psycho-analysis and reëducation are not founded directly on the principle of suggestive therapeutics; they are purely educational. They are distinct and separate phases of psychotherapy.

16. The power of suggestion and the principle of reëducation constitute the fundamental laws underlying all the various successful methods of treating mental disturbances, as well as the psychic treatment of functional physical disorders.

17. The fatigue accompanying neurasthenia and following nervous shock, is neither a true psychic nor a real physical weariness; it is a psycho-pathological fatigue, a fatigue out of all proportion to preceding mental and physical exertion, and is properly and successfully treated by suggestion and reëducation.

18. Probably the best method of treating the fatigue states of the neurasthenic is the direct conversational method of candidly laying all the facts before the patient; depending upon suitable physical treatment, suggestion, persuasion, and moral therapeutics, to effect a cure.

19. But little place is assigned to hypnotism in modern psychotherapy. Its chief value is as a means of diagnosis in certain obscure psychic disorders. Hypnotism cannot be employed as a means of inducing innocent persons to commit crime or other immoral acts.

20. While some cases of nervousness and neurasthenia are greatly helped by the rest-cure, a larger number are benefited by the work-cure, and still others are greatly improved by systematic nature study.

21. One of the most powerful factors in psychotherapy is religious emotion — moral therapeutics. Religious emotions exercise a maximum influence on the average mind. Music exerts a varying influence on different individuals. Some tunes are quite generally stimulating, while others are usually depressing.

CHAPTER XXXVI
THE SCIENCE OF SUGGESTION

THE PSYCHOLOGY OF SUGGESTION.— THE UNIVERSALITY OF SUGGESTION.— SUGGESTION IN RELATION TO HEALTH AND STRENGTH.— SUGGESTION IN THE TREATMENT OF PAIN.— NERVOUS DISORDERS AND SUGGESTION.— SUGGESTION AND SLEEP.— SUGGESTION AND THE SPECIAL SENSES.— SUGGESTION IN OBSCURE DISEASES.— METHODS OF NON-DRUG HEALING.— SUMMARY OF THE CHAPTER.

BY suggestion, from the point of view of the operator, is meant the systematic use of any means which will bring about the arousal of an idea or any other process or state in the mind of a subject or patient. The spoken word is usually the means that is employed, though any other means whatever by which any sense organ can be stimulated may be used. The immediate purpose of the suggestion is, of course, to awaken the desired mental activity; to impress, influence, strengthen, or modify the mental state of the patient. But the operator is invariably interested, finally, in the expression of the mental activity either in overt conduct or in some internal physiological changes, or both. The suggestion may be direct, as when one commands another to close a door, for instance; or indirect, as when one says, 'The room is chilly on account of the open door,' in order to occasion in the mind of the person addressed the judgment, 'The door must be closed,' and to bring about the expression of that judgment in the act of closing the door.

Children are the most teachable, the most suggestible of all people, for the simple reason that they are unsophisticated; it is easy for them to exercise faith. Where faith abounds the science of suggestion is productive of far-reaching results. At the holy shrines of Europe and at the great gatherings of the healing cults, in every country and through every creed, faith and suggestion have wrought their marvellous and ofttimes apparently miraculous cures.

THE PSYCHOLOGY OF SUGGESTION

When an idea becomes uppermost in the human intellect, when a certain notion becomes set in the mind, there are only two ways of removing it. One is by suggestion, and the other is by the development of the opposite ideas, by a process of reëducation. Suggestion becomes then one of the greatest known methods for changing, improving, cleansing, and strengthening the human mind. People sometimes get the notion that they are going to die, and it is almost impossible to remove this idea from the mind. Not long ago, while the author was waiting for a train in a Southern city, he chanced to visit a large tombstone factory. While there he observed an old gentleman drive up, come into the office, and proceed to order his tombstone. He gave his name and other data for the stone; stated that he was born in 1841 and died in 1910 (this was in the month of August, 1910). Here the clerk interrupted him saying, "You are not yet dead, sir, and this is already the last half of 1910." Whereupon the old gentleman in a most emphatic and decisive manner replied, "No, young man, of course I am not dead, but I will be dead before this year is over"; and the probabilities are that he did die during 1910. When a man is thoroughly possessed with the idea that he is going to die, we doubt if there can be found any power that can long keep him alive.

The marginal consciousness, by which I mean the consciousness of all ideas and emotions that are not at a given moment in the centre of the field of attention, while it is normally a beneficent servant, may, nevertheless, in a sense, tyrannize in our lives. This marginal consciousness is described by many as the 'subconscious mind.' Normally, I say, it is a beneficent servant, because in the marginal or dim consciousness are conserved all those ideas and other mental complexes which are not required to meet our present needs. They are conserved in such a systematic order that when, in the course of suggestion, any mental process comes into attention it brings out from the dim marginal

THE SCIENCE OF SUGGESTION 429

area its appropriate supplement; and it is when this supplementary image discharges into activity that the course of suggestion becomes complete. This marginal consciousness is a tyrant when its contents over-freely and without system attach themselves to the contents of clear consciousness, and so disturb the balance of the mind and render unreliable the course of our judgments. Continuously, even without our apprehension, this marginal consciousness influences the character and the ebb of processes in our vivid consciousness. It is not something different and apart from our usual conscious life, but an integral part of it.

Thus the marginal consciousness, commonly called the subconscious mind, becomes an excellent servant to the mind of man when it is properly trained; but it becomes a tyrannical master when it is left to do as it pleases. The marginal consciousness is that great force of the mind which receives the suggestions of health and disease, of happiness and despair, and in turn is able to energize or weaken the body, in accordance with the suggestions it habitually receives. Sometimes a patient can be waked up by a direct suggestion-challenge. For example, you tell him you doubt his ability to stop worrying or to control his mind, and not infrequently this challenge is sufficient to arouse him to that point where he will arise and take command of his thoughts.

The art of scientific suggestion consists in placing an idea in the mind in such a way and under such circumstances that it shall become dominant; that is, so that the mind is caused to be possessed by that one idea. This dominant idea plays the role of a liberator — it breaks up harmful associations of ideas, and so creates an opportunity for the establishment of new and healthy groups of ideas. It brings about a dissociation between certain powerful ideas and physical actions, and often dissolves those physio-mental associations which are responsible for obsessions and bad habits.

THE UNIVERSALITY OF SUGGESTION

In the author's opinion, the science of suggestion is best carried out by making these suitable impressions upon the mind during the waking state. This is the normal state in which reformative ideas must take root and be developed. Hypnotism is an unnatural and unnecessary process of carrying on this work. Of course, this same method of suggestion has been used in all medical and religious work from time immemorial; but in modern psychotherapy an effort has been made to reduce this mode of teaching to a system of scientific healing.

What is it, when a child has fallen down and bumped his head, that causes him to run to mother and beg to have it kissed? Mother promptly kisses the head, saying, "Now, never mind, it is well." The child acts on the suggestion, tears are stopped, and the smiles return; and soon he is back to his play as if nothing had happened. And so minister, lawyer, doctor, and salesman, if they are successful, all use this very principle in the carrying on of their business. Many of the great false revivals are apparently built upon this psychology of suggestion. This power of successfully persuading one's fellows to accept an idea, has in the past often been attributed to personal magnetism.

The author insists upon the importance of making all suggestions true. In our dealings with the sick we should make only those suggestions which are based upon good physiological and psychological law; thus the work can be built upon a sure foundation; it can then be carried forward with confidence and sincerity.

No more powerful testimony to the value of suggestion can be found than the very fact that there exist to-day scores of different methods of treating disease, some diametrically opposite, all of which are more or less successful. Various schools of medicine and the numerous therapeutic specialists are all more or less successful in treating and apparently curing disease. John Alexander *Dowie* comes along teaching the existence of a physical body afflicted with disease because the devil controls it. He also taught that God heals disease in answer to prayer, thus destroying the devil's power. *Dowie* cured thousands. Mrs. Eddy and Christian Science teach that there is no physical body, no sickness; that these things exist only in the mind; and likewise they are able to cure other thousands. Both of these teachings cannot be true, yet both can cure disease. *It is simply a problem in suggestive therapeutics, and the element of cure*

FIG. 35. SUGGESTIVE PANIC.

Diary of a Nymphomaniac

THE SCIENCE OF SUGGESTION 431

is not the correctness of either their physiological or their theological teaching, but rather the intensity and sincerity of the faith which the sick one exercises respecting the idea upon which he depends for healing.

Suggestion is, figuratively, a form of mental contagion; in fact, it becomes epidemic in the presence of large numbers. This is splendidly shown by the following observation which some one has suggested: It is thirty minutes before train-time. The travelling men are sitting about the hotel, the 'bus and its driver are waiting in front, numerous passengers are walking leisurely on their way to the station, when a certain travelling man, desiring to play a joke on the public, suddenly looks at his watch, quickly grabs his hat, coat, and grip, and starts on the run for the station. The 'bus driver catches the spirit and shouts, " All aboard "; and this is followed by a rush of the other travelling men for the 'bus, and the driver begins to lash his horses. On the way to the station, fat women with babies, and lean women without babies, catch the spirit of panic: there is one grand rush all along the line to get to the station as soon as possible, and everybody arrives fifteen minutes before the train is due. It is simply the panic of suggestion — the psychology of the crowd. (See Fig. 35.)

The author has experimentally demonstrated that the healing power of electric belts and similar means of treatment is purely suggestive. In the use of therapeutic magnets, wooden magnets are often found to accomplish just as much for the relief of the patient as the real ones.

People become possessed by some foolish notion and it becomes a habit, a religion, or a mania. Some lunatics in the asylum spend their time collecting pebbles and gathering twigs, even to the extent of wagon loads; on the other hand, many unbalanced business men spend their entire lives collecting dollars; and while they escape the asylum, they are none the less abnormal and unhealthy in mind — they are slaves to money-making.

Some people keep their minds so constantly on the disease they have, that they not infrequently know more about it than the doctor. They become like the old neurasthenic who remonstrated with his young physician, saying, "You are but a young doctor; I am an old invalid. I know more about my disease than you do"; or like the locomotor ataxia patient in the hospital, who, when the interne of his ward was changed at the first of the year, and he found himself being examined by a new doctor, said, "You need n't bother about me, I can tell you all what's the matter of me"; whereupon the new doctor inquired, "Well, sir, what is the matter with you?" To this question the self-confident patient replied, "I have got locomotive attachments" — meaning, of course, that he had locomotor ataxia.

Young children are very suggestible, both when awake and when partially asleep. You can speak to the sleeping child, it will respond and obey, and the following morning be wholly unconscious of what has taken place.

We should remember that there probably exists far more energy in brain and body than we ever use. We have two lungs, two eyes, two kidneys, etc., either one of which is capable of doing the work of both. In the marginal consciousness of the mind we have vast realms of psychic energy which are ordinarily not in use. And it is by means of suggestion that this vast source of energy can be tapped and made available in the work of the daily life of every man. It should further be remembered that there is no sensation or emotion commonly excited by influences from without, which cannot also be set in action by the nerve centres within the body, and then be so referred outward over the nerves that it will really seem that these sensations actually were originated by outside or external stimulation. On the other hand, an intense physical impression may be vaguely apprehended, while the reception and interpretation of a weak sensory impression may be exceedingly vivid and exhaustive.

SUGGESTION IN RELATION TO HEALTH AND STRENGTH

Every case of physical disease which has been improved by a change in the mental state, as cited in Part II of this text, is a direct illustration of the powerful influence of suggestion in influencing the various functions of the body. The most serious functional disorders are sometimes immediately relieved by suggestion. The regulation of digestion, secretion, and even of the temperature of the body, are all more or less, as we

THE SCIENCE OF SUGGESTION　　　433

have previously shown, under the influence and control of the mind.

The influence of the mind over the temperature sense is illustrated in the case of the chilly patient whose friends were told by the doctor to "surround her with hot-water bottles." The patient was immediately relieved, but the next day on calling at the house, the doctor discovered that his prescription to "surround the patient with hot-water bottles" had been carried out by filling with hot water a score of empty bottles and glass fruit-jars, and putting them around the patient's bed on the floor.

Professor Mosso is very positive in his belief that fear is capable of so disarranging the circulation as to permit or favor the production of inflammation, fever, and other circulatory disturbances of the body, which predispose the patient to attacks of various diseases, even those caused by microbes.

A Southern physician has reported an interesting case showing the power of fright profoundly to prostrate the individual. The case was that of a big burly negro, who supposed he had been shot — fatally shot. Fear had seized him with tremendous power; he shook like an aspen leaf; he bordered on a state of collapse, and death seemed imminent. Not finding any blood, the examining physician ordered all his clothes removed, and while he was being undressed, a flattened bullet fell upon the floor. The doctor exhibited the bullet to the frightened patient, explaining that he had had a miraculous escape; whereupon his circulation was immediately restored; his countenance improved; temperature became normal; and the look of life returned to the eyes, which had been almost fixed with the gaze of death, while a broad grin crept over his face. The negro got down from the operating table and dressed; apologized for the fuss he had caused, and walked home.

A simple illustration of the power of the nerves apparently to strengthen or weaken the body is shown in the common experience of eating. While it requires food several hours ordinarily to pass from the stomach into the intestines, where it is absorbed into the blood and subsequently assimilated by the body cells; nevertheless, in just a few minutes after food has been received into the stomach, the eater usually feels greatly strengthened and ready for work. This feeling of physical strength immediately following the meal must be attributed largely to nervous impressions of strength which the nerve centres are able to transmit to the body.

It is an old and true observation that care-free travellers and happy bridal couples are quite immune to disease and death.

SUGGESTION IN THE TREATMENT OF PAIN

A physician — a prominent medical teacher — recently told the author of his personal experience with a nervous headache. He had been bothered with headaches since his youth. While a medical student, one of his teachers advised him to take antipyrin — that it was a certain cure. He took antipyrin and it cured him almost instantly. As years went by and his experience ripened, he observed that apparently even the taste of antipyrin was able to cure his headache; that as soon as he would place a tablet in his mouth, his pain would disappear. It suggested itself to his mind that perhaps his headaches might be caused by a nervous habit, and he decided to discontinue both the headaches and the antipyrin, and he was successful in both. A year had gone by at the time of this conversation, and no headache had made its appearance. Thus it appears that not only the unlearned and unscientific are victims of the pranks of mind and the whims of nerves, but the skilful and learned suffer as well. No class of society can pride itself on being free from the influence of these mental mischief-makers.

Major General O. O. Howard recently related an incident from his own life which illustrates the possibility of forgetting pain by means of mental diversion. He lost an arm during the Civil War, and in the process of recovery some of the nerve-ends were not properly cared for, so that ever since the wound healed, the General has not been free from a sensation of pain, whenever his mind reverts to it, and yet he is able at any time to forget it by diverting his thoughts or distracting his attention.

The heroism and endurance of mothers during child-birth is well-known, but there is a great difference between the suffering and discomfort attending the process in different cases, which is no doubt largely due to the mental attitude of the mother toward the new arrival.

The following incident is taken from the Memoirs of General Grant: The night before General Lee's surrender, General Grant was suffering so acutely from a headache that he could not sleep. It was a splitting headache; and no wonder, with the gallant Lee to contend with. He spent the night vainly trying to alleviate the pain; "but," he says, "the instant I saw the contents of the note of surrender, I was cured."

A concrete illustration of what psycho-prophylaxis can do is afforded by a recent medical communication, which shows that fifteen per cent of attacks of migraine are preceded for several days by psychic symptoms either of an excitable or a depressant type.

The reputation of a certain liniment was so great that the British Government bought the recipe for a large amount of money, intending to give it to the public, so that all chronic rheumatic sufferers might be cured. It was subsequently analyzed and found to consist of turpentine and the white of an egg. The liniment's efficacy was destroyed. This would be true also of many modern medicines and prescriptions, if the real ingredients were known.

Sometime ago there came one morning into the author's clinic a large negro wearing an anxious expression, limping painfully, and holding his hand low down on the left side of his abdomen. As he entered the room he began talking: "Yas, sah, I done got it; they done fixed mah brother, and now I got it." Upon being asked what he had, he replied: "Certainly, I got the 'pendigitis. I had an awful pain ever since last night after supper. I sho' got it." After being carefully examined and having his constipated bowels washed out with a copious enema, the pain entirely disappeared; and on being assured that he did not have appendicitis, that appendicitis usually comes on the right side and not on the left, where he complained of his pain, he climbed down off the examining table, arranged his clothes, and walked out, saying, "Mah Lordy, what a fright I had!"

NERVOUS DISORDERS AND SUGGESTION

The author has seen some remarkable cures of discouraged and despondent patients who imagined themselves the victims of many and varied diseases, by merely having their energies enlisted in some simple altruistic work — carrying food to some poor family, or engaging in other simple works of mercy. By this their minds were so taken off themselves that they rapidly recovered their normal strength and vigor.

Many imaginary sufferers are completely wrapped up in themselves, they think of their own comfort only. They constantly brood over their many supposed afflictions, and they can never be cured until, by the grace of God, they are delivered from self-service, and become enlisted body, soul, and spirit in the glorious ministry of disinterested service for the race.

Several years ago the author had a patient, a broker by profession, who gradually became despondent. He became possessed by the fixed fear that he would some day die in the poor house; he seemed rapidly going into melancholia. All the medicine, baths, and other treatment seemed to help him but little. At last we arranged with his wife to try a plan of getting him interested in some one else. The author, through one of his nurses, selected a family in the stockyards district in Chicago, a deserted mother with five children, the youngest ten months, the oldest ten years. It was arranged that the patient was to come to our office just as we were leaving, one afternoon, and we would request him to go out to see this family, as one of the children was very sick. After remaining in the house but a few minutes, we came out to the automobile and asked him if he would n't like to come in and see the poverty and suffering that could exist in a great city abounding in churches and luxury. He readily consented, and as we began to give the history of the case, exhibiting the barefooted children — one little fellow so devoid of clothing that his picture could not be exhibited in public — a new expression crept over this patient's face. After I had left written directions regarding the treatment for the visiting nurse, he took me by the arm and asked the way to the nearest grocery store.

To make a long story short, he purchased twenty-five dollars' worth of groceries, coal, and other necessaries of life for this needy family. He returned with his wife the following morning and saw that the children were all well clothed. He called me up by telephone and asked if a trained nurse could be of service, and volunteered to pay for a nurse for two weeks, or until the sick child should fully recover. And what was the result of all this? He became a Good Samaritan; he sought out other families; and instead of expending thousands of dollars for doctor bills, he was soon out from under the care of all physicians, while spending his money in helping his fellows. In six months he became a new man; he was back at his desk, and we did not know until months later that he was aware that a therapeutic trick had been played upon him, if trick it may be called. Some time after he called us up over the telephone, saying, "I am sending you a patient, Mr. —; he has the same mental disease coming on him that I used to have. You look him over and see if there is anything wrong with his body; leave this job of fixing up his mind to me. I will have Jim, that's my chauffeur, take him down into the stockyards district. I have another family down there that needs help badly. I have tried your scheme on two or three different self-centred fellows, and it never fails to work. You know, a lot of these fellows are going crazy over getting a few more dollars; he is one of them, all right, but just as soon as you give me the word, I'll put him through; and I will guarantee that turning Good Samaritan will cure any poor devil who is headed for the lunatic asylum. What about me? Don't you worry about me; once is enough of that kind of trouble for me; I will keep my trolley on the right wire, and you can be sure of it."

Numerous fake operations have been performed upon nervous patients in an effort to cure them of their imaginary troubles. One woman was sure she had a live lizard in her stomach; and not until she was taken to the operating room, a slight cut made on her abdomen, a few stitches taken, removed to her room and shown a lizard in a bottle, did she get over the notion she had a lizard in her stomach. It had been repeatedly explained to her that animals could not live in the stomach — that the gastric juice would eat them up alive, but no scientific explanation would satisfy her. Again, a nervous woman was so thoroughly convinced that she had a foreign substance in her arm that a sham operation was performed on her, and afterwards she was shown a piece of beef gristle, which set her mind completely at rest.

SUGGESTION AND SLEEP

To illustrate what a prominent factor suggestion is in the treatment of insomnia, the following case may be cited: The patient, a nervous woman thirty years of age, had been long troubled with insomnia, but had at last been greatly helped by daily treatment with high frequency electricity. After several weeks of this treatment a "doctored" wire was substituted for one of the connections — an electric cord, which, although it looked perfect to the eye, had some six inches of the inner wire removed. The method of procedure in this case was to begin the treatment with a real wire, and demonstrate, by means of the vacuum tube placed on the forehead, that the patient was really getting the electric current, then, before leaving the patient to rest on a couch while receiving the current, a switch was turned and the current was diverted from the real circuit to the false. The patient would lie there very quietly for twelve minutes, supposing she was receiving high frequency electrical treatment (this particular mode of treatment produces no sensations in the bodies of patients unless some one touches them during the treatment), while, in reality, she was not getting a particle of electricity. It is interesting to record that she slept just as well after this procedure as she did when she had the genuine electric treatment. This is no proof that electricity does not possess power favorably to influence the body, it is simply another proof of the tremendous power of suggestion.

SUGGESTION AND THE SPECIAL SENSES

A few months ago the author tried the following experiment on an audience of some three hundred and fifty people. At the beginning of our lecture we stated that we desired to make some tests relating to the purity of the atmosphere and the individual acuteness of the sense of smell on the part of the people in the audience. We exhibited a small bottle containing a clear liquid, and said that after we had sprinkled it on the platform, we desired each individual in the audience to raise the right hand the moment he discovered an odor resembling that of steaming vinegar. We suggested that those on the front seats would naturally detect the odor first, but any one having an acute sense of smell, even if seated in the middle or back part of the room, might discover the odor first. We discussed this matter some fifteen or twenty minutes, then emptied our liquid, sprinkling it very carefully all over the rostrum. We then plunged into our lecture, having previously intimated that it might be five or ten minutes before the odor would be sufficiently diffused throughout the atmosphere to be detected. In twelve minutes after this, the first hand went up on the front row. This was immediately followed by a number of hands on the other side of the room. Within twenty minutes twenty-two hands had been raised. Within twenty-five minutes hands had been raised even at the back of the room. Within thirty-five minutes, the time the lecture had to be concluded, over one hundred hands had been raised; and then we acknowledged to the audience that what we had poured out over the rostrum was only six ounces of Lake Michigan water drawn from the faucet downstairs. Even this did not satisfy some. They thought it was a part of the experiment — that we were trying to fool them again in some way. A score of people persisted in the belief that they had smelled odors resembling those arising from an open vessel containing steaming vinegar.

All nervous people are so influenced by systematic suggestion, that in the treatment of certain patients suffering from paralysis or locomotor ataxia, we employ a regular and gradnated systematic series of exercises, known in medicine as a process of reëducating the nerves and retraining the muscles.

SUGGESTION IN OBSCURE DISEASES

A devout woman went to a physician to consult with him about her illness. He suspected that she had an incurable malady and told her so. She turned away with a sigh. "Ah," she said, "if I only had some of the water of Lourdes, then I should be cured." It so happened that a friend had brought the doctor a bottle of genuine Lourdes Water, that he might chemically analyze it to ascertain its medicinal properties. He told her that he had some of that water and promised to give her some of it, provided she would first try a more potent remedy, Aqua Crotonis — ordinary drinking water brought to the city through the Croton Aqueduct. She expressed doubt that it could help her case. The doctor now gave her a small bottle of the real Lourdes Water, but labelled it Aqua Crotonis. She returned to his office in a few days no better, whereupon he gave her a little vial of the ordinary drinking water and labelled it "Water of Lourdes." She was completely and permanently cured.

METHODS OF NON-DRUG HEALING

So-called Christian Science is but one of numerous methods of non-drug treatment which are slowly but surely making headway among the people. These "systems" are all more or less of an aid to the national health, in that the majority of them serve the purpose of removing numerous "brakes" which handicap and constantly interfere with the health and happiness of the people. The majority of these cults enjoin abstinence from tobacco and alcohol; being drugless systems of healing, they do away with the habit of taking patent medicines. Many persons keep the physical and psychic "brakes" constantly set; they are greatly handicapped by their wrong habits of living. Their methods resemble those of the new brakeman on the freight train. The engineer had just succeeded in pulling his train over the crest of a steep grade, when the brakeman climbed up over the tender into the cab. The engineer said: "Whew! that was a hard pull. I was afraid I wasn't going to make it." Imagine his surprise when the brakeman replied: "Yes, I was afraid we wouldn't make it too, so on the way up I set the brakes so we wouldn't run back down-hill."

We recently made an effort to find out about how many people in the United States are devoted to some drugless system of healing. We are satisfied that there are at least ten million people in this country who never employ regular physicians; while we believe that the numerous psychic and non-drug systems of healing such as Suggestive Therapeutics, Mental Science, Christian Science, Naturopathy, Osteopathy, Magnetic Healing, Physical Culture, Chiropratic and Faith Healing, support no less than ten thousand professional practitioners and healers, who are engaged in the work of trying to heal the

THE SCIENCE OF SUGGESTION 441

sick. Of the sixteen million families in the United States, there are probably three million who do not take drugs or employ regular physicians; at least only in exceptional cases, for example, fractures and other surgical emergencies.

And so it is a question which the medical profession must take seriously. We have a moral responsibility in the matter. The doctor, after all, is the man who has the greatest knowledge, and, therefore, carries the greatest moral responsibility; we cannot dodge it. In the end we shall have to face it, even as in the case of the man in the story, who, after dying, walked up the golden stairway and applied to St. Peter for admission through the pearly gates to glory; whereupon St. Peter informed him that his name was not on the list. But the man protested he had lived a sincere life, and that he had been led to believe that he would surely go to heaven when he died; he requested St. Peter to look over the list again. St. Peter carefully went over the list again and said: "Why, certainly, brother, your name is on the list. Come right in; but say, you are not due up here for twenty years! Who was your doctor?"

SUMMARY OF THE CHAPTER

1. Suggestion is the systematic and scientific employment of various methods designed to bring about a process or state of mind and thereby to determine the physical reaction.

2. There are only two ways of removing a set idea from the mind — one way, by suggestion; the other, by a process of reeducation — the persistent cultivation of "opposite ideas."

3. The marginal consciousness (subconscious mind) is our beneficent servant in so far as it conserves our mental processes when they are not in the focus of attention, in such a manner that they may be recalled by the process of appropriate suggestion. It tyrannizes over us whenever its contents disarrange the sequence of our ideas and judgments.

4. The art of suggestion is the placing of good ideas in the mind so that they shall become dominant ideas, psychic liberators. In this way helpful groups of ideas are formed, while harmful groups are dissociated.

5. Suggestions should be made to the mind during the wak-

ing state. Hypnotism is both unnatural and unnecessary to the practice of suggestive therapeutics.

6. Suggestion has been consciously or unconsciously practised from time immemorial; it is one of the secrets of success in the work of doctor, preacher, lawyer, and tradesman.

7. There are scores of different methods of treating disease — all more or less successful, notwithstanding their opposite and contradictory teachings. The chief element of efficiency in nearly all healing procedures is simple suggestion — faith.

8. Suggestion is, figuratively, a form of mental contagion; in fact, it often becomes epidemic when large numbers are involved. A fixed idea may eventually become a mania, leading to such foolishness as collecting pebbles, twigs, or — dollars.

9. Both mind and body are always in possession of vast stores of reserve energy. The marginal consciousness is in control of these reserve powers, and they are largely available through suggestion and concentration.

10. Fear is capable of so disarranging the circulation as to permit or favor the production of inflammation, fever, and other circulatory disturbances.

11. Many chronic and periodical headaches are "habit" pains, and can be readily cured by systematic suggestion. Pain is often relieved by forgetting it, by having the attention distracted.

12. Many a marvellous remedy has had its power destroyed by the discovery that it consisted of some simple and commonplace ingredients. Secrecy is essential to the success of all false and ignorant methods of practising suggestion.

13. Many imaginary sufferers are completely wrapped up in themselves; they constantly brood over their supposed afflictions, and they can never be cured until they are delivered from this self-service.

14. Suggestion may effectually deceive the special senses. Taste, smell, and touch are by no means infallible.

15. All methods of non-drug healing are on the increase in this country. We probably have ten million people who do not take drugs or employ regular doctors — this is equal to about three million families out of sixteen million.

CHAPTER XXXVII

THE RE-EDUCATION OF THE WILL

ORGANIZATION OF THE MIND.— IDEAS AND EMOTIONS.— THE CONTROL OF EMOTION.— HOW NEUROSES ORIGINATE.— METHOD OF PRACTISING REËDUCATION.— THE RANGE OF REËDUCATION. — REFLECTION AND ACTION.— SELF-MASTERY.— SYSTEM IN THOUGHT AND WORK.— SUMMARY OF THE CHAPTER.

IN the practice of psychotherapy, reëducation must be recognized as a distinct process of mental training. While it may include the valuable and powerful elements of suggestion, it is, nevertheless, dependent for its success upon intelligent, methodical, and persistent educational processes; it is a method of reforming the patient's habit of thought respecting himself, his nervous difficulties, and his other disorders.

The will-power of most people is comparatively weak; that is, there exists a tremendous disproportion between the high degree of modern intellectual culture and the humiliating weakness of the will in the average man. Self-mastery is not the crowning virtue of the age. Self-control is the crying need of the hour. Two men accidentally bumped into each other while walking along a busy street. One of them, a high-strung nervous sort of fellow, turned around and began to abuse his brother with all sorts of cursing and swearing, while the other stood there calmly listening, and when the abuse had stopped, he said: "Now, brother, you have told me all about what you think of me, but I have the satisfaction of knowing that you do not know what I think of you." It was such a jolt to the nervous fellow that he shook hands and apologized for his lack of self-control.

ORGANIZATION OF THE MIND

It will be well in this connection to call attention to the plan upon which the human intellect seems to be organized for work. It is now generally agreed among physiologists and psychologists that the nerve cells, especially those in the cortex of the brain, are individual and relatively independent units. These nerve cells, called neurons, form associations and combinations of increasing complexity. The associated groups of neurons form systems and communities, and these in turn are organized into clusters and constellations. This organization, in fact, is that of the mind and not of the brain; it is purely mental, functional, and not in any sense material or anatomical; so that the organization of the human mind may be looked upon as a complex system of specialized and coördinated powers of consciousness, presided over by the supreme power and authority of the will. The human intellect may be looked upon as being a complex system of many minds. As in other phases of life, the stability of these psychic coördinations decreases as their complexity increases. This fact, I may say in passing, may be of assistance in accounting for the phenomenon of multiple personality, which has been discussed in another place.

In the practice of psychotherapy, reëducation is nothing more or less than a process of mental re-formation — new groups of ideas are created, and by persistent repetition are forced into positions of power and influence in the scheme of mental organization. The false conclusions, the harmful and unhealthy ideas and groups of ideas, are forced into the background, while the new idea becomes enthroned in a position of power and authority.

While the intensity of mental action is greatest in the central consciousness, it should be remembered that the contents of the mind — the number of association groups, etc.,— is greatly increased as we go out toward the periphery, the marginal consciousness. The central consciousness is concerned with a small number of clear and vivid thoughts, while the marginal consciousness is occupied with an almost infinite host of thoughts and ideas, all of which are more or less hazy and indefinite, and even unconscious.

It is interesting to observe, in this connection, that the use of certain drugs is able to light up, or make connection with, the marginal consciousness, so that long-forgotten experiences may be called up into the central consciousness. Thus De Quincey, in his "Confessions of an English Opium-eater," says:

"The minutest incidents of childhood or forgotten scenes of later years were often revived by the use of opium. I could not be said to recollect them, for if I had been told of them when waking, I should not have been able to acknowledge them as my past experience. But placed as they were before me in dream-like intuitions, and clothed in all their evanescent circumstances, and accompanying feeling, I recognized them instantaneously."

IDEAS AND EMOTIONS

A great many of our psychic difficulties arise from a failure properly to control our ideas and regulate our emotions. Others fail to distinguish between their ideas and their emotions. They experience emotions, and then in their confusion, are led to believe that they had really formulated an idea, when they had only experienced a passing emotion, due partially to transient disturbances in the circulation.

It frequently develops that the mind becomes concentrated upon our failures, focussed upon our weaknesses, and there is no hope of success until this matter is controlled or overcome. As Dr. Barker says:

"The patient afflicted with a so-called 'functional' nervous disorder must, it is true, believe in his physician; but the physician's task is to reëducate the patient to believe in himself. More than half the ills of one class of nervous patients depend upon a loss of confidence in their own ability, upon a sense of past failure and of future impotency. They have tried to do things outside their powers, and, having failed, have become convinced that they cannot in any way be efficient. Their minds are concentrated upon their failures and their disabilities, instead of upon their successes. It is necessary to teach them how again to become confident and self-reliant, by assigning to them small tasks, well within their powers, and proving to them that they are capable of overcoming difficulty after difficulty. Many may soon be taught to count victories where formerly every effort spelled defeat."

The power of emotions for good is not to be ignored, but

they become a dangerous psychic influence when allowed to wield the balance of power in the mind. It is very easy for an overpowering emotion, in the presence of an unusual situation, entirely to override the will, to displace reason and judgment, literally to sweep the sufferer off his feet. Strong emotions interfere with the correct interpretation of sensations, and otherwise have a tendency to disorganize the reasoning power of the mind as well as to stampede the judgment and the will. Emotional people may hear all sorts of strange noises during the night and grossly misinterpret the most commonplace disturbances.

There is an unfortunate class of people who have become "conventionally emotional"; they are socially trained to experience only those emotions which are proper and decorous; and while they seem to possess well-controlled and beautifully ordered minds, they have lost their individuality and originality; they have become merely social automatons, mechanically following the fashion; they have but the one standard for the regulation of their thought and conduct — "What will people say?"

THE CONTROL OF EMOTION

If the mind is not carefully organized, and the thinking conducted in a systematic and orderly fashion, the emotions, when running riot, may even go into the realm of memory and there pervert, distort, and destroy our very recollections of things. Emotions excite the heart to increased action, and in a variety of ways produce an extravagant expenditure of vital energy. This is probably due to the fact that when strong emotions are experienced, the higher nervous centres, so to speak, take it for granted that the body will be thrown into more or less violent sympathetic action; thus they anticipate the need of increased circulation, and at once start the machinery to going at increased speed.

Why should intelligent human beings be so agitated and thrown into extraordinary panic by hearing a piece of gossip, or by discovering that some one has told a falsehood about them? Just the other day we saw a splendid woman almost go into a fit of hysteria upon learning a bit of gossip about her-

THE RE-EDUCATION OF THE WILL

self which had been peddled about the neighborhood. She had palpitation of the heart, twitching of the muscles, pain in her right side, and a violent headache, which lasted for two days. She was first white in the face, then flushed. And this picture represents the common experience of those who suffer from deficient emotional control. It is nothing more or less than an animal outburst of passion, although it may be called "rightcous indignation," and by sundry other dignified and civilized names.

Emotion represents a very intimate interassociation between the mind and the body. The man who would acquire a high degree of self-control must begin on the emotions. Never suppress or annihilate them — rather control and coördinate them. Those who have chronic congestion in any one organ of the body; those who suffer chronically from cold hands and feet and pale skins, are much more likely than others to become victims of violent emotional outbreaks. To balance the circulation and purify the blood will greatly aid in securing control of the emotions. If the emotions are not controlled, they will eventually evolve into veritable psychic desperadoes, charging around through the mind in disorderly fashion, utterly destroying the finer sensibilities, building themselves up into tyrannical masters, swaying the mind at will, and utterly supplanting reason and judgment.

It is a common experience that anger is augmented by indulging in muscular gesticulations and physical demonstrations. To suppress the physiological reaction of temper does much to control the anger at its seat — in the mind. A common illustration of this is shown in the case of children, who often begin their pranks with a playful scuffle and end up with a dead-in-earnest, hand-to-hand slugging match.

HOW NEUROSES ORIGINATE

The larger part of our nervous disturbances and psychic disorders have their origin in wrong methods of thinking — false conclusions and uncontrolled emotions. For example, a woman begins to lose her memory, so she thinks. She at once begins to reason that a loss of memory means loss of mind, and that loss of mind eventually spells insanity; so she at once begins to plan on going crazy. She thinks about it, worries about it, and talks about it until her mind is so unsettled that she consults a physician. Unless she is rescued by the skilful employment of reëducation, it is even probable that she may effect a temporary derangement of her mind.

ſ Another illustration of the origin of nervous disorders is found in the attitude that many persons take toward loss of sleep and its consequences. It is a universal belief that one will soon get sick or go crazy if he does not have regular sleep. It is not generally known that ordinary rest in bed, or even being comfortably seated in a chair, will very largely take the place of sleep. The layman does not understand that he can go without sleep for weeks, and have comparatively little sleep for months, without in any way permanently or seriously harming the mental or physical health, provided he is able quietly to lie in bed and rest. We frequently find persons who have reasoned and worried themselves into a state of chronic neurasthenia because they do not sleep soundly for eight or nine hours every night. They talk about their disturbed sleep, their lack of sleep, their inability to sleep — it has become a hobby with them; they think about it and talk about it all the time. A great many of these persons, if they would become thoroughly indifferent to sleep, would probably be able to secure an abundance of refreshing rest in short order.

These are but common illustrations of false methods of reasoning which make nervous wrecks out of many people. A nervous dyspeptic will render himself miserable over what his dyspepsia might grow into, when the truth is, his stomach troubles would largely disappear if he would quit thinking about them. So, in many other ways, nervous and emotional people reason themselves into a maze of difficulties, and worry themselves into a tangle of fictitious troubles and imaginary obstacles.

METHOD OF PRACTISING REËDUCATION

More or less psycho-analysis must precede the successful practice of psychic reëducation. It will not be necessary here to repeat the principles underlying psycho-analysis or mental diagnosis, which were discussed in the chapter on psychothe-

THE RE-EDUCATION OF THE WILL

rapy. After having carefully examined the mind of the patient and having arrived at a diagnosis of the underlying causes of his nervous disorders and psychic difficulties, the method to be pursued in the process of reëducating the patient's mind and strengthening the will may be summarized as follows:

1. Make sure that you have not overlooked any physical condition or bodily disease which may be acting as a contributing cause in the mental disturbances or nervous disorders. See that digestion, circulation, metabolism, and elimination are proceeding normally.

2. One of the best methods of arriving quickly at a mental diagnosis is to allow the patient to tell his story — talk it all out. It is the author's practice, after getting pleasantly settled in the office and becoming fairly well acquainted with the patient, to start him on his story and never to interrupt, never to ask a single question, until he has finished talking. We knew of a nervous woman who talked of herself this way for an hour and a half; made up her mind she was the "biggest fool in town"; analyzed the cause of her difficulty, and within six weeks had practised reëducation and auto-suggestion on herself to the point where she was completely restored. It was one of the most successful and remarkable cases the author has ever met.

3. After the patient's story is told, arrive at just as accurate a diagnosis as possible respecting the false methods of reasoning and the erroneous conclusions which have led him into this neurotic condition. It is absolutely necessary that the definite ideas, emotions, and false conclusions shall be isolated, preparatory to the successful employment of reëducation.

4. Now that the examination and diagnosis are completed, the time has come for reëducational therapeutics. Begin at once to point out to the patient the exact error in the working of the mental machinery. Explain simply, fully, and specifically, wherein the trouble lies. Be methodic and positive as far as you are conversant with the case. Explain things to the patient honestly, frankly, and fully, just as they appear to you. Lay aside all this nonsense about laymen not being able to understand their diseases. If explained in plain English, it is

the author's experience that most patients are able to understand their difficulties just about as well as a physician. Endeavor to make a logical, full, and rational presentation of the whole thing to the patient's mind, just as it appears to you.

5. The next essential step, having laid matters before these ervous patients, is to secure their full confidence and hearty coöperation; and then day by day and week by week continue that persistent, systematic, and methodical work of repeating this story, building it up, developing it and adding to it from time to time, until the new teaching comes to occupy the centre of the stage and effectually drive the old and false ideas into the background.

6. It is highly important that these nervous patients should specifically recognize wherein their former mental habits (their old ways of looking at things) were wrong. It is highly essential that they should individually recognize their mistakes and acknowledge them, for in these cases confession is good for the soul. See to it that their false ideas of disease are cast out of the mind. Make them definitely promise to work with you toward the development of the new and right ideas.

THE RANGE OF REËDUCATION

It will readily appear that the practice of this method of psychotherapy requires no unusual skill, no extraordinary knowledge, not even special knowledge respecting psychology on the part of the practitioner. It is entirely possible for certain people who have awakened to a recognition of their psychic condition to practise this method upon themselves; in which case it would, of course, partake largely of the nature of auto-suggestion. Any physician can practise this method upon his patients; any intelligent parent can utilize it in child culture; any wide-awake teacher can use it in the work of teaching. And herein lies its greatest power; that is, it is practical and entirely free from deception, sophistry, and delusion. This method is certainly the most simple, and at the same time the most successful, of all the procedures of modern psychotherapy.

It is a great mistake to shock nervous patients by telling them they are abnormally neurotic, neurasthenic, or psychasthenic. It is our practice to tell such patients that they are in difficulty as the result of ignorance, or from long-continued misinterpretation of their emotions, or as a result of false reasoning and the formation of unsound conclusions. We often explain to such patients that they have reasoned entirely right, that they are not to be blamed for the conclusions they formed, but that their mistake consisted in the fact that they began to reason from a false premise; and then we seek to make clear to them the falsity of their premises, substituting therefor a true basis. Almost immediately they begin the process of reasoning themselves out of trouble, just as formerly they so disastrously reasoned themselves into trouble. It is not so debilitating and humiliating to be told that we are ignorant as it is to be told we are neurotic or neurasthenic.

This method of reëducation may be used on a large range of worried, nervous, so-called neurotic patients. It demands neither hypnosis nor suggestion, as that term is ordinarily understood. It occupies the greatest possible field of psychic endeavor; and while it is useful and successful in a large number of cases, and results in greatly strengthening the mind, in the end it is found to be nothing more or less than a process of reëducating the will. It must be remembered that it is probably inadequate in marked cases of hysteria, in disorders of personality, and in extreme cases of obsession.

REFLECTION AND ACTION

The strong mind acts slowly; the weak mind acts quickly, on the spur of the moment. Daydreaming is good for the imagination, and is a pleasant and profitable exercise for the mind; nevertheless, we should never allow the creations of our daydreaming to assume control of the intellectual reins. We need to cultivate the habit of reflection — that is, of thinking before we act. The acquirement of the reflection habit would save us a great deal of unnecessary suffering and sorrow. By reflection we do not mean study, or mere thinking. Study leads to knowledge, but reflection is manifested in *action*. The highest degree of reflection is possible only in the presence of a high degree of will-power. As we strengthen the will by reëducation, the mind will have a better opportunity to reflect, and then our actions will become better ordered and controlled. (See Fig. 36.) Payot has very fittingly described the processes which take place when the mind is held composed and under the influence of a dominant idea. He says:

"In chemistry we learn that if one plunges a crystal into a solution in which several substances are held in saturation, the molecules of the same nature as the crystal, drawn together from the depths of the solution by some mysterious attraction, will begin to group themselves slowly around it. The crystal grows little by little, and if it is kept perfectly quiet for weeks or months, it will form those wonderful crystals whose size and beauty are the joy and pride of the laboratory. But if the solution be constantly jarred or disturbed, the deposit will be formed irregularly, the crystal will be imperfect and will remain small. The same thing is true in psychology. If one keeps any psychological state whatever in the foreground of consciousness, it will insensibly, by an affinity no less mysterious than the other, gradually attract to itself other intellectual states of the same nature. If this condition is kept up for a long time, it will gather around it an organized group of forces of considerable power, and will acquire a decisive and almost absolute control of consciousness, silencing every other idea that is opposed to it.

"If this 'crystallization' goes on slowly without disturbance or interruption, it will acquire a remarkably strong character. The group of feelings thus formed will be sharply defined, powerful, and calm. And here we may note that there is perhaps no idea which cannot, if we so wish, create within us such a group or clan of associated ideas. Religious ideas, maternal feeling, and even such low, despicable sentiments as love of money for its own sake, may rise up in us and gain this powerful ascendency. But few are the men and still fewer are the young men who possess the calmness necessary to carry on this work of slow 'crystallization.'

SELF-MASTERY

"The most efficacious way of attaining this mastery of self is to arouse vigorous likes or vehement dislikes in the soul. We must, therefore, try to keep in mind certain reflections which will help us to make ourselves love work and detest an easy, useless, stupid, idle life.

"Our words frequently follow one another so quickly and call up such a multitude of pictures, that none of them achieve any distinctness. As a result this superficial thinking merely fatigues the mind

FIG. 36.   WILL POWER AND CHARACTER.

uselessly. A sort of stupefaction is produced by this jumble of images which comes to nothing. The remedy for this evil is to see things clearly and in great detail. For example, do not say: 'My parents will be pleased'; but call up a picture of your father, imagine that you are seeing the manifestation of his joy at each of your successes; picture him receiving the congratulations of his friends and his family. Try to imagine your mother's pride, and her pleasure during the vacation, when she strolls up and down on the arm of the son of whom she is so proud; imagine yourself invisibly present at the evening meal where they are talking of you.

"Meditative reflection is an indispensable element in the education of the will, but by itself it is powerless. It gathers the scattered forces of the mind together for united action and gives enthusiasm and incentive; but, just as the strongest winds of heaven pass uselessly by if they meet no sail to swell and drive forward, so even the most powerful emotions lie sterile if they do not, each time that they arise, contribute some of their energy to our activity, in the same way that some of the work a student does is registered in his memory. Nothing is lost in our psychological life; nature is a most scrupulous accountant. Those actions which appear the most insignificant, if only they are constantly repeated, will form for us in the course of weeks or months or years an enormous total which is inscribed in the organic memory in the form of ineradicable habits. This crystallization of our energy into habits cannot be accomplished by meditative reflection alone; it requires action.

"Unmethodical, scattered work is very wearying, and what often is imputed to the work itself, comes from work which is merely badly directed. The thing that wearies one is the multiplicity of occupations which bring with them none of the joy of an accomplished task. When the mind is drawn in several different directions, it always has a sense of dull uneasiness during its work. It is the undertakings which are left in a rough, unfinished state that give rise to such wearisome mental worry."

SYSTEM IN THOUGHT AND WORK

As a part of the therapeutics of reëducation, the author has found it very desirable to insist upon the reorganization of the patient's life upon a systematic basis, to make provision for the regular and periodic performance of certain tasks, so that when established in healthy channels, these acts shall become automatic; in other words, to lay the foundation for good habits, to whose power we trust for the final overthrow and vanquishing of the bad habits. Further, the systematic method of doing big things assists in overcoming the tendency to worry over the difficulties represented by a host of inconsequential trifles in the daily life. Now, it is necessary to watch some nervous patients. It is very important that you do not too soon over-emphasize the necessity for system, or else the patient may merely throw his mental switches and suddenly acquire a veritable craze for orderliness, and thus defeat the real purpose of your therapeutic procedures. It is necessary to study one's strength, and then to arrange for a proper amount of physical and mental work, and not be too easily frightened by apparent weariness of mind and body; for what some patients call "nervous collapse" is nothing more or less than a common, everyday tired feeling — normal and natural fatigue.

Systematic, natural, and honest ways of thinking about things and looking at things will do much to deliver nervous people from their bondage. We must learn to call things by their right names and to look upon them in their true relationship. There is nothing to be gained by allowing jealous, high-tempered, gossiping women to call their troubles "sensitive nerves," while one doctor calls it neurasthenia and another hysteria. The best way is to put your finger directly on the devilment, and then work intelligently for its removal.

Too many people are nervous cowards. Their souls are literally filled with fear, but it should be recognized that courage and cowardice are mere states of mind, and that they are susceptible of control by the will-power. Thousands of people are constantly bemoaning their shortcomings and recounting their obstacles. Of just such people it has very fittingly been said, "Better play the game than bewail the handicap."

SUMMARY OF THE CHAPTER

1. Reëducation, as a procedure in psychotherapy, is dependent for its success on intelligent, methodical, and persistent educational processes — it is a reforming of the habits of thought respecting oneself.

2. The human mind is organized on the basis of associated groups of ideas which are in turn formed into systems, commun-

ities, clusters, and constellations, with increasing complexity. This organization is functional, not anatomical.

3. The central consciousness is active with a small number of clear and vivid thoughts, while the marginal consciousness is occupied with an indefinite host of hazy and even unconscious thoughts and ideas.

4. Many psychic disorders arise from a failure to control ideas and regulate emotions. Nervous disturbances frequently result from the continuous contemplation of one's failures and blunders.

5. It is entirely possible for an overpowering emotion absolutely to override the will, to displace reason and judgment, to sweep the sufferer off his feet.

6. Uncontrolled emotions disorganize the circulation, agitate the nerves, and diminish strength. On the other hand, a well-balanced circulation assists in gaining control of the emotions.

7. If the emotions are not properly controlled, they may evolve into psychic desperadoes, demoralizing the intellect, tyrannizing over the will, and utterly supplanting all judgment and reason.

8. Anger is usually augmented by gesticulations and other physical demonstrations. To suppress the physiological reaction of temper does much toward controlling anger.

9. Many nervous disorders owe their origin to false fears — fear of losing the memory, fear of going crazy, fear of losing one's mind from lack of sleep. Such sufferers are cured by demonstrating the falsity of their fears.

10. Following psycho-analysis and mental diagnosis, therapeutic reëducation is practised by repeatedly, frankly, and fully explaining the real cause of the patient's nervous disorder, pointing out specifically wherein his reasoning and conclusions are false.

11. Reëducation is adapted to the treatment of all sorts of neurotic and neurasthenic patients. It requires neither hypnotism nor suggestion. It is inadequate for the cure of profound hysteria, persistent obsessions, and disorders of personality.

12. Strong minds act slowly; weak minds act on the spur of the moment. Study leads to knowledge, but reflection leads to

action. "Crystallization" of thought goes on slowly in the mind — calmness is essential.

13. "This crystallization of our energy into habits cannot be accomplished by meditative reflection alone; it requires action."

14. An essential part of reëducation is the reorganization of the life conduct upon a systematic basis. The systematic method of doing big things assists in overcoming the worry about small things.

15. Some nervous persons make a craze out of orderliness. They have "nervous collapse" on experiencing the least mental weariness or physical fatigue. We have too many nervous cowards. "Better play the game than bewail the handicap."

CHAPTER XXXVIII

PSYCHIC FADS AND FAKES

CHARMS, RELICS, AND SHRINES.— QUACKERY AND PATENT MEDICINES.— ASTROLOGY AND PALMISTRY.— PHRENOLOG*Y* AND PHYSIOGNOMY.— CLAIRVOYANCE AND FORTUNE-TELLING.— CRYSTAL-GAZING AND SHELL-HEARING.— TRANCES AND CATALEPSY.— AUTOMATIC WRITING AND TALKING.— TELEPATHY AND MAGNETIC HEALING.— SPIRITUALISM.— *DOWIEISM* AND DEMONOLOGY.— NEW THOUGHT AND MENTAL SCIENCE.— HYPNOTISM AND MESMERISM.— CHRISTIAN SCIENCE.— REASON *vs.* SOPHISTRY.— SUMMARY OF THE CHAPTER.

ALL through the ages sharp and unscrupulous persons have deceived and imposed upon the credulous and unsuspecting. Many and varied have been the means of their deception, trickery, and imposition. The world's greatest frauds, fakers, and impostors have operated largely along psychic lines, and in the field of so-called divine healing. In every age the common people have been deceived not only by these out and out frauds and fakes, but also by various other psychic fads — teaching more or less true, but which has been perverted by exaggeration and distortion. After the authorities have been able to do something toward the proper regulation of patent medicines and food adulterations, let us hope that some legal means will be devised for putting these psychic sharks and healing impostors permanently out of business.

CHARMS, RELICS, AND SHRINES

It is to be deplored that in the twentieth century of our civilization people can still be found flocking to various noted shrines, depending upon charms for the protection of life and the maintenance of health, as well as looking to relics for the healing of disease. To this class of psychic deceptions belongs the whole category of Indian magic and Oriental psychic sophistry. (See Fig. 37.) It is all nothing more or less than a gigantic system of trickery and humbuggery, which, whenever it works, is successful through the efficacy of that same suggestion which we have so much discussed. While a Hindoo magician was causing snakes to crawl up a rope, an enterprising Yankee took a snap-shot of the performance, and on developing his negative discovered only the picture of a rope — there was no snake.

These various forms of occult teaching all depend upon their mysticism to hold the attention and reverence of the people. And it must be recognized that mysticism still possesses great power over the average citizen.

QUACKERY AND PATENT MEDICINES

In former chapters we have called attention to the fact that quack doctors and famous patent medicines owe their reputation to the power of suggestion. There can be little doubt that the majority of the prominent patent medicines on the market to-day, that do not owe their power to alcohol or some other deceptive habit-producing drug, owe their popularity and success to ingenious advertising and carefully prepared testimonials, all of which possess a high degree of suggestive therapeutic power. The author has investigated the methods of prominent quacks and charlatans, and knows that their great success is due almost entirely to the methods of suggestion as hereinbefore described.

ASTROLOGY AND PALMISTRY

In connection with the consideration of ancient medical deceptions, the reader's attention was called to the fact that the movements of the stars (astrology) has absolutely nothing to do with health and disease; and yet there are to be found to-day intelligent men and women who still believe that the march of the heavenly hosts through space is connected with the cause and cure of disease.

Palmistry is more or less believed by a large number of people. A well-known professional palmist some time ago told the author that the only thing she could tell from looking at a person's hand was whether or not he did hard work. She

FIG. 37. CHARMS, RELICS AND SHRINES.

FIG. 38. ASTROLOGY AND PALMISTRY.

UNIV. OF
CALIFORNIA

PSYCHIC FADS AND FAKES 459

further explained that she made her delineations of character by looking at the face, talking with the person, and from her general impressions; that the practice of palmistry was merely a ruse for securing the attention of the people and getting their money. Certainly the study of the palms will not reveal the outcome of disease or the likelihood and character of future maladies. Palmistry, as it is professionally practised, is a fraud from first to last. (See Fig. 38.)

PHRENOLOGY AND PHYSIOGNOMY

Phrenology was never a science excepting in name. The term suggests a multitude of frauds. The author has a friend who used to be a professional phrenologist, who says he depends more upon the facial expression and the countenance than on the cranial bumps, when he tries to delineate character. Like palmistry, phrenology has been the means of separating many curious persons from their money. We know of a young man who was studying medicine, when a phrenologist told him he would make a better lawyer. He gave up the study of medicine, and commenced to study law, but made a complete failure of it. There ought to be a way of preventing these phrenological scalawags from misleading the unsophisticated and ignorant. The bumps on one's head might indicate something of what he had been and what he had done, but they are of little value in determining what he can be or what he can do. It is true that when the brain has long been exercised and greatly developed at one particular point, the skull will protrude outward to accommodate this increased formation of brain substance, but it requires years to make these noticeable changes. The bumps on one's head can hardly be said to be definitely indicative of anything in the way of character or of specific mental powers. It is true only in the rough that a man can be judged by the form of his head. (See Fig. 39.)

CLAIRVOYANCE AND FORTUNE TELLING

Clairvoyance and fortune-telling are ingenious psychic fakes. Clairvoyants are those persons who have elected to commercialize their natural gift, the gift of discernment, the ability to read human character. Most successful clairvoyants are women who possess a keen sense of discrimination and discernment of character — psychic gifts which are certainly worthy of better employment than in the ways and means commonly followed by professional clairvoyants.

The clairvoyants' advice cannot be true in the whole. Their claim of ability to predict events, to locate valuable mines, to settle domestic difficulties, to consummate love affairs, as well as to direct business policies, are all mere fraudulent pretensions. Sorrow of heart and pecuniary disaster have rewarded many an unsuspecting and trusting soul who attempted to follow their advice.

Fortune-telling and the use of dream books are other methods of confusing and confounding the minds of honest people. This whole nefarious scheme of keeping alive superstition is to be deplored. The time has certainly come when intelligent men and women should strike off these ancient fetters of psychic bondage.

CRYSTAL-GAZING AND SHELL-HEARING

Among the psychic delusions of the recent past which persist even to the present hour are to be found the practices of crystal-gazing and shell-hearing. (See Fig. 40.) Certain persons with unstable nervous systems, when they have long gazed intently into a crystal, become, in a measure, auto-hypnotized. In such a state, groups of thoughts may be transmitted from the marginal consciousness to the central consciousness, with such a suddenness and vividness as to impress the crystal-gazer with the idea that they originated in the external world. These thoughts are suddenly projected outward from the consciousness, and take hold of the semi-hypnotized inquirer after the fashion of an ordinary hallucination. That is, the crystal-gazer has his subconscious images apparently projected into the crystal, so that he sees images, pictures, and other things, which, in his ignorance, he believes originate and actually exist in the crystal.

The old practice of shell-hearing is an instance of this same sort of reversion of psychic behavior. In this case voices originate in the marginal consciousness (the subconscious mind) and are projected outward into the shell, and thus the listener experiences auditory hallucinations. Crystal-gazing

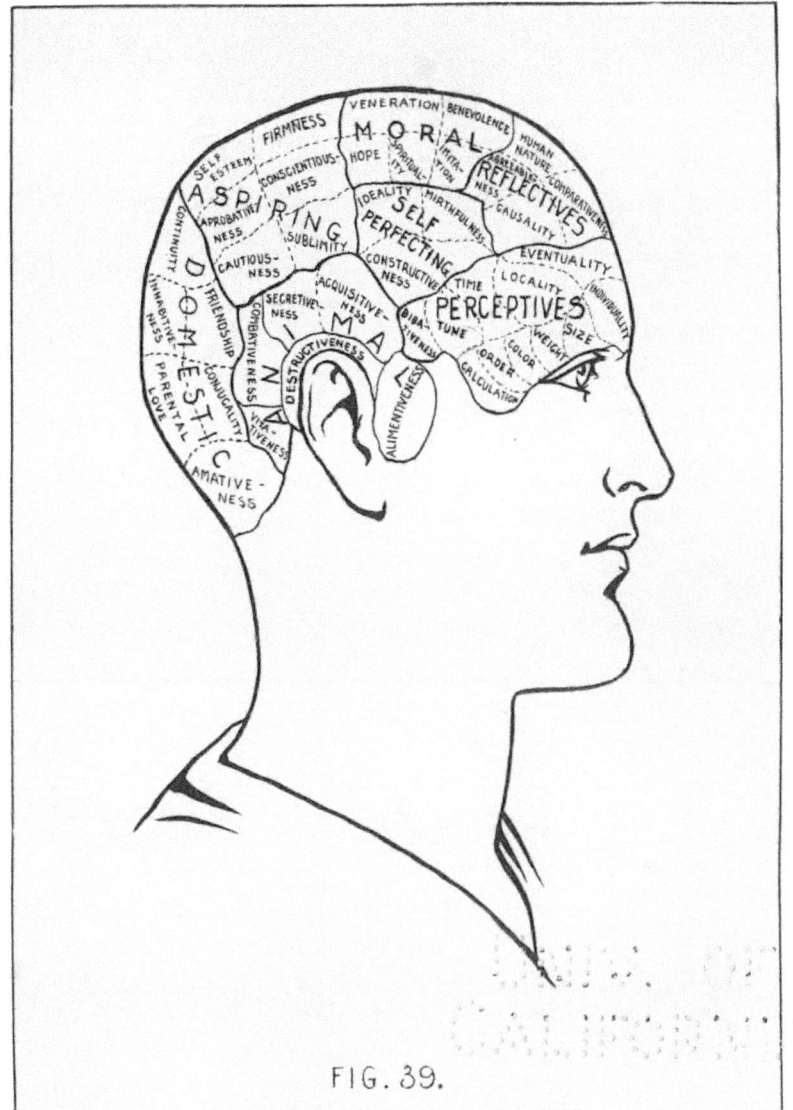

FIG. 39.
A PHRENOLOGICAL CHART
OF HUMAN DESTINY

and shell-hearing are analogous to automatic writing and speaking, which will be considered presently.

TRANCES AND CATALEPSY

In the cataleptic state consciousness is diffused — seems to be pushed far out toward the periphery. It is at a dead level of intensity. The mental life is largely in the dim marginal state. The physiological processes of the body are slowed down; in fact, they come to assume conditions very much like those which prevail in the hibernating animal. The body may become stiff and extraordinarily rigid. It is in this condition that the great trance mediums of history and of the present time usually are found when they receive their wonderful revelations and visions. (See Fig. 41.)

It is not uncommon for persons in a cataleptic trance to imagine themselves taking trips to other worlds. In fact, the wonderful accounts of their experiences, which they write out after these cataleptic attacks are over, are so unique and marvellous as to serve as the basis for founding new sects, cults, and religions. Many strange and unique religious movements have thus been founded and built up. It is an interesting study in psychology to note that these trance mediums always see visions in harmony with their own theological beliefs. For instance, a medium who believed in the natural immortality of the soul, was always led around on her celestial travels by some of her dead and departed friends. One day she changed her religious views — became a soul sleeper, and ever after that, when having trances, she was piloted about from world to world on her numerous heavenly trips by the angels; no dead or departed friends ever made their appearance in any of her visions after this change in her belief.

Nearly all these victims of trances and nervous catalepsy, sooner or later come to believe themselves to be messengers of God and prophets of Heaven; and no doubt most of them are sincere in this belief. Not understanding the physiology and psychology of their afflictions, they sincerely come to look upon their peculiar mental experiences as something supernatural, while their followers blindly believe anything they teach because of the supposed divine character of these so-called revelations.

AUTOMATIC WRITING AND TALKING

As close of kin to trances and so-called visions should be mentioned the practices of automatic writing and speaking. The study of multiple personality has shed much light on the psychology of automatic writing. When practising it the patient may appear to be in his usual state; in fact, he may be conversing with some one in a perfectly normal and natural manner, when, if a pencil is placed in his hand, he will begin to write continuously, writing long essays which are carefully composed, logically arranged, and sometimes extraordinarily fine in rhetorical expression; and all this is accomplished while the central consciousness is entirely ignorant and unconscious of everything that is going on.

This automatic writing is in no essential different from the experiences of crystal-gazing, shell-hearing, and hypnosis. In automatic writing the activities of the marginal consciousness are projected outward along the motor line of writing. In this case the subconscious activities are not sensory; the primary cause rests neither in auditory nor visual sensation, as in shell-hearing and crystal vision, but in sensations of touch and movement — they are entirely motor. The central consciousness does not become aware of what is going on in the marginal consciousness until it sees the thoughts expressed by means of the words automatically written. It will be apparent that to the central consciousness these messages would indeed appear as coming from another world; and so many a psychically unbalanced person, who has been exercised by automatic writing, has been led in this way verily to suppose that these written messages were from the dead, or from the spirits inhabitating other planets.

The phenomenon of automatic speaking occurs in the same way. It is another case of a motor expression of psychic projection. This time the subject is concerned with spoken words, instead of written words. The speaking may take the form of meaningless syllables, which may sound like a new tongue, or the language may be entirely intelligible and logical. These cases, several of which the author had the opportunity of fully examining a few years ago, are illustrations of those peculiar

FIG. 40. CRYSTAL GAZING AND SHELL HEARING

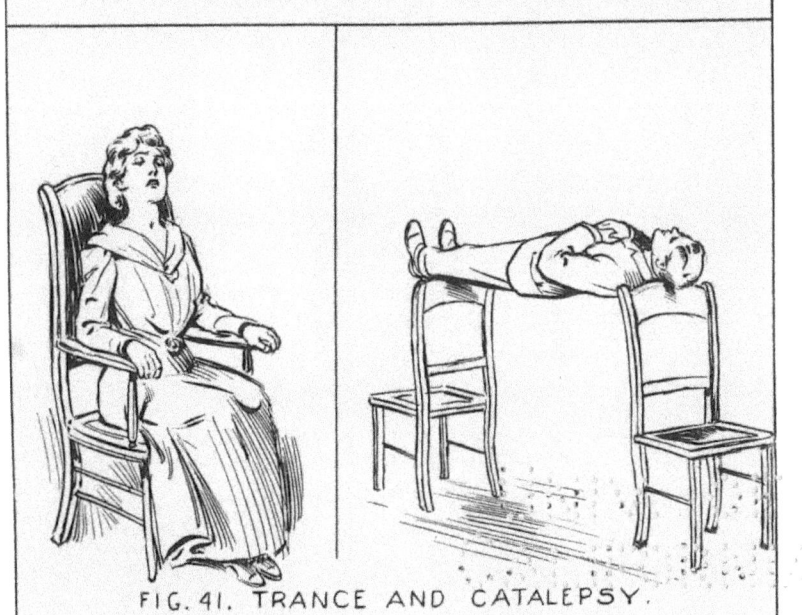

FIG. 41. TRANCE AND CATALEPSY.

and unusual automatic talking performances which come to be regarded as the miraculous gift of tongues; and every syllable of their jargon is reverently listened to by their followers, who regard these mysterious utterances with awe, as messages from another world.

TELEPATHY AND MAGNETIC HEALING

Telepathy is supposed to be the psychic ability to send and to receive messages independent of the ordinary organs of sense. That is, one is supposed to think a thought and then telepath it across a room or across a city to another person, who is supposed to be in harmony — *en rapport* — with the mind of the sender. Telepathy is based upon certain assumed laws of intercommunication between human minds, and serves to keep alive the witchcraft delusions of former times. It also serves as the basis for the present-day belief in absent treatments and malicious animal magnetism. We may emphatically state that there exists no scientific proof of mental telepathy. Its existence is an unfounded assumption. What in many cases seems to be telepathy is due to physical means of communication which escape the attention of the ordinary observer.

There are cases on record in which the same thoughts have been thought at the same time by two individuals in different parts of the world. Numerous tests have been made in which one person has been able correctly to describe the thoughts and words of another person on the opposite side of a room, and of a large city. But why is it necessary to resort to the hypothesis of mental telepathy to explain such phenomena? The investigation of a few cases of so-called telepathy suggests an illuminating, clear-cut, explanatory hypothesis. Two Danish investigators, Hanses and Lehmann, while experimenting with two men who apparently possessed the power to communicate thought across a room without the use of words or other signs, discovered that when the "thinker" and the "guesser" were placed at the foci of two sound mirrors, the latter decidedly increased the number of right guesses as to the thought of the former. This obviously means that there was a physical communication between the two men, otherwise the sound shields could not have effected the result at all. It must have been through waves of air — the very means by which our ears are ordinarily stimulated. As the "thinker" kept his mind on his part of the performance he was unconsciously in the act of saying the words under his breath, just as many an auditor in a concert does — and then goes home with a tired throat, because he has been incipiently singing all the evening. These fine *under the breath* movements set the air in motion and another may actually hear, as did the man in the experiment just referred to. This is not impossible, especially in view of the fact that many — for instance, some who are of hysterical disposition — have remarkably sensitive ears. On such a ground as this, many cases of so-called telepathy may be explained, and it affords a hypothesis on which many more cases may, in the future, be accounted for.

No doubt many illustrations of so-called telepathy are merely coincidences. It would be very remarkable, indeed, if no such coincidences should ever occur. I am far from believing, however, that this offers anything like a general principle which can clear up the whole problem. One must remember, too, that the fallibility of memory may lead to the description of coincidences which never actually occurred. Likewise it may lead to a judgment of agreement between the thought of the "receiver" and that of the "transmitter," when no such agreement, as a matter of fact, exists.

All intelligent beings recognize the existence of gravitation — that universal law of cohesion which holds all things together. If a new world should be created in the universe, untold billions of miles away — so far that hundreds of years would pass before its light would reach our earth — the moment such a new planet was born, our world would feel its pull of gravity. Gravitation is an omnipresent force acting independent of time and space; and even if we were not confronted with the universal religious teaching of a Great Spirit, we would suspect that there existed an all-pervading and universal spiritual intelligence, by the suggestion of analogy from the well-known force of gravitation.

This plausible hypothesis of a Universal Mind completely does away with the assumption of the transfer of thought from one finite mind to another. There is a Universal Intelligence whose emanations radiate to all who are in harmony with the *Divine Mind*. Every soul who is "in tune with the Infinite" enjoys the possibility of receiving messages and inspirations from the Holy Spirit. If this is true, it is not difficult to see that two minds may have the same thought at the same time, just as two wireless telegraph stations which are attuned alike may receive, at the same time, the same message, which has been flashed from a vessel many miles from each station. Many good people adhere to this view and derive comfort therefrom. Their own intimate experiences, they affirm, supply testimony in its favor.

Even the American Indian had in his religion the "Great Spirit." All modern religions recognize the presence of a universal spirit. It is a cardinal thought of Christianity that God should pour out His "Spirit upon all flesh." Jesus told His followers before His death — before He departed, that He would send them the "Comforter," the "Holy Ghost," who would teach and guide them "into all truth."

The author is not disposed to follow the deceptive and illogical reasoning of the telepathist in order to find an explanation of these common experiences of thought harmony and identity. We are rather disposed to accept the equivalent of the Christian doctrine of the omnipresent Spiritual Mind, the doctrine of the Great Spiritual Teacher, as a basis for the phenomena described under the title of telepathy.

If such phenomena find their explanation either in the doctrine of the Universal Mind or in any other doctrine which assumes the activity of spiritual forces in their production, they, of course, lie outside the realm of physical science and in that of personal religious belief; they are problems in spiritual science.

Magnetic healing is largely a matter of mental suggestion. Persons who are supposed to be magnetic healers are found upon experimental test to possess no stronger electrical reaction than common, ordinary people. Magnetic healing is like palmistry and clairvoyance; it is simply a name and a scheme to secure patients and their money.

SPIRITUALISM

Like mental telepathy, spiritualism is not a matter which can be adjudged in the experimental laboratory. Recent investigations have convinced the author that nine-tenths of all so-called spiritualistic phenomena are purely fraudulent, sheer chicanery and trickery; but we are equally willing to admit that in certain rare cases real phenomena are produced in the name of spiritualism, which are not of a fraudulent nature. These spiritualistic manifestations we regard as beyond the pale of scientific investigation. They are problems in theology and spiritual science. They are problems whose solutions lie beyond the borders of empirical science. Our discussions of physiological psychology do not refer to them. There can be no doubt that many of these spiritualistic mediums are deluded, and more or less unable to understand their own performances. They are often greatly influenced by suggestion; as in the case of a person who asks for communication with a dead brother, when he has no dead brother, and yet he receives from the medium long messages, supposed to come from the imaginary brother.

There can be no doubt that the minds of many so-called mediums are striking illustrations of that dissociation among groups of conscious processes which was previously discussed in connection with double personality, and hysteria in general. In as far as this is the case, one must in fairness admit that such a medium is not fundamentally (I mean morally) a fraud, but rather the subject of an elusive functional nervous disorder, and at the same time, clever enough to capitalize the disorder and make it provide the necessaries of life. In whatever instances this is the case, the so-called messages from the dead are made up of the more or less coherent trains of ideas that troop in from the marginal consciousness in response to those suggested ideas which come into the medium's attention when he or she is in a state of semi or complete trance. To whatever extent this represents the nature of mediumship, it, together with so-called spirit messages, admits of scientific psychologic investigation.

It must be said at this juncture, however, that there are many men of science in good repute who believe that the whole problem of spiritualistic phenomena cannot be fought out on this line; that there is a residue that cannot be approached by means of scientific experiment. It seems highly probable that the ultimate problems involved in the solution of the phenomena of spiritualism will have to be referred to the theological courts.

The readers of this book are no doubt familiar with the Biblical standard by which these phenomena are measured. According thereto, they are disreputable, owing to their source in and connection with evil spirits. Consequently, we have the scriptural denunciation of the practice of seeking information from the dead and the exhortation to make our appeal to the Living God.

The author of this book is personally inclined to accept the Biblical diagnosis, and urges again, as he repeatedly does in this volume, that his readers adopt the attitude of faith in their own better selves and in the Supreme Being. This, he believes, is the key which, together with a rational use of material means, will unlock the mysteries of the present and the future. From his personal experiences with spiritualistic mediums, he thinks that we have in them themselves about the strongest imaginable empirical evidence pointing to the existence of those spiritual powers which are by nature liars and deceivers. We feel confident that the phenomena of spiritualism will never be settled by so-called scientific investigation and laboratory experimentation.

DOWIEISM AND DEMONOLOGY

Of all modern healing cults which confuse and confound sickness and sin, and claim to heal all disease by means of prayer, Dowieism stands out as the most recent and best known. Its basic error consists in regarding sickness and sin as analogous, and, therefore, if God will forgive sin in answer to prayer, why will He not also cure sickness in answer to prayer? But sin and sickness are not analogous. You can be forgiven for sowing thorns and thistles in your backyard, but that does not remove the thorns and thistles after you have allowed them to grow up It will take hard work in addition to prayer, to clear the thorns and briers out of the backyard.

The secret of the success of these bogus systems of divine healing, as noted in former chapters, is the power of suggestion — nothing more, and nothing less. The future will no doubt witness the birth of many new systems of so-called faith healing. They are all based upon the psychology and physiology of faith and fear, as well as upon the error that when one is sick, his body is possessed of a devil, and if the devil could only be cast out, the sick one would immediately be restored to health.

NEW THOUGHT AND MENTAL SCIENCE

It is difficult to ascertain exactly what New Thought or the new so-called Mental Science embraces. But the author is decidedly averse to taking an old truth, burnishing it up, clothing it with the garb of modern thought and language, and then presenting it to the world as a new thought, a new religion, or a new cult. We have shown throughout this text that all the fundamental principles of modern psychotherapy, respecting suggestion, etc., were in some measure known and practised by the ancients; in fact, they are found throughout the Bible. What right, what justice, is there, in taking the comforting and reassuring truths of Christianity, and seeking to make a new religion out of them? What business have professed Christians to disfigure and discount their Gospel in order to facilitate the establishment of these psychic creeds and cults? Why should we have healing movements organized within the Christian Church, when the whole Church, if the author understands anything of the Master's commission, was instituted to go out into the world with a healing message for spirit, soul, and body?

It seems to us that scientists have largely forgotten their psychology and psychotherapy; while religionists are comparatively blind to the healing power and comforting possibilities of the Christian message. In the presence of this combined weakness and impotency of both science and religion, the common people have become the helpless prey of a score of mental-science cults and "isms," which have borrowed the thunder of science, and stolen the chariots of Christianity, in which to aggrandize themselves and establish their new religions. The time has come to call a halt. In the author's opinion, the plain, everyday science of physiological psychology, such as we have endeavored to outline in this text, constitutes a sufficient scientific and material foundation; while the simple and time-honored teachings of Jesus Christ furnish the moral background and spiritual foundation for all that is needed to construct the most efficient, helpful, and simple psychotherapeutic procedures for the relief of human sorrow and suffering.

It is not New Thought that the world stands in need of, as far as the moral philosophy of healing is concerned. It is rather *old thought,* thought at least two thousand years old; the thought of the Great Physician — the Son of Man, called also the Son of God — that is most needed to-day. To see that this is so, the reader needs only to peruse again the chapter, " The Bible on Faith and Fear."

HYPNOTISM AND MESMERISM

From time to time mention has been made of hypnotism. Its position in the psychotherapeutic system has been discussed, but it will now be in place briefly to inquire into the philosophy underlying this practice. Hypnotism may consist of the hypnoidal state, in which the patient is really awake but in a passive state of mind, ready to receive the suggestion and teachings of the healer; on down through increasing passivity to a profound state of hypnosis, in which the patient is oblivious of his surroundings and under comparatively full control of the hypnotizer. It will be evident from the study of preceding chapters that the author sees very little place in the practice of psychotherapy for hypnotism. There is no good to be accomplished at all by hypnotism which cannot be better accomplished by other efficient procedures.

Hypnotism is basically wrong, as a method of strengthening the intellect and educating the will, in that it leads its victims to depend more and more upon the hypnotic operator. Hypnosis is certainly not a natural state of mind; it is highly artificial and unnatural. Some authorities have endeavored to show that hypnotic sleep was analogous to natural sleep, but this is certainly a mistake. The hypnotic state may in some respects resemble the somnambulistic state, but somnambulism is not a state of natural and normal sleep.

We believe that human beings are free moral agents, kings

and queens in their own domains, and that the Creator never intended that our minds should submit to be dominated by, be dictated to, or be controlled by any mind in the universe except that of man's Maker. Hypnotism necessitates the surrender of the mind and will in a peculiar way to the influence of another personality; and we regard these procedures as unscientific and un-Christian, and in the highest degree subversive of individual strength and stamina of character.

The Almighty who gave existence to the human mind, never compels man to surrender or submit to anything against his own individual will, not even to the influence of the *Divine Mind*. God seems to possess such a respect for the will of man that He is more willing that man should do wrong (sin and have his own way), than do right (God's way) by coercion or compulsion.

Hypnotism possesses that peculiar fascination that is found in connection with all the procedures of mystical occult teaching. These psychical superstitions are very much like a set of powerful cog-wheels in action: when the fingers are caught in the wheels, they never stop until they have drawn the whole body in.

Hypnotism operates to produce a dissociation between the higher reasoning centres of the mind (the central consciousness) and the lower and automatic centres (the marginal consciousness).

Mesmerism is the old-fashioned method of inducing hypnosis, by making physical contact with the patient. Modern hypnotism is usually practised without this physical contact. All leading physicians throughout the world now recognize hypnotism as an exceedingly dangerous two-edged therapeutic sword. They recognize that the frequent repetition of hypnotic procedures not infrequently leads to insanity. There is little doubt in the author's mind that some of the methods of treatment carried on in connection with the Emmanuel Movement are either conscious or unconscious forms of hypnotism, at least the operators certainly put their patients frequently into the hypnoidal state. This is the one unfortunate thing connected with the Emmanuel Movement. And this is to be regretted, since it is wholly unnecessary that the originators of this movement should have chosen to use procedures which are so close akin to the practice of hypnotism. In the end their entire system would have been more efficacious, had these practices been eliminated.

We feel impelled especially to condemn the public exhibitions carried on by professional hypnotists. The authorities should speedily bring these demonstrations to an end. They are highly debasing and demoralizing.

CHRISTIAN SCIENCE

Christian Science is the most notable of all the modern cults, in which a single idea has been effectively organized into a religious propaganda. Mrs. Eddy in her teachings made doubly sure that her followers were delivered from the realms of imaginary disease, by denying the existence and reality of all diseases. We have explained in former chapters the psychology and physiology upon which this system of teaching, in common with all similar methods of healing, operates. Thousands of people believe in so-called Christian Science, not because they understand it or accept all its teachings, but because, in the absence of any better teaching, they were literally driven to it in an effort to find the peace and happiness which come as a result of deliverance from fear. Christian Science and its philosophy are certainly not upheld by the conclusions of modern science; and as far as the author has been able to discern, Christ never on any occasion required His followers to dethrone their reason and believe in His formulas and teachings in a blind and unreasoning manner.

Christian Science seems to be the emphasis of the denial element in psychotherapy. They deny the existence of those influences which they are desirous of evading or avoiding. Christian Scientists think of health and happiness as the natural heritage of man, and, believing this to be true, they lay hold of these influences as their normal mode of life, and have probably experienced them more than any other body of professed Christians in the world.

It is certainly a sad commentary upon the orthodox teachings of professed Christians, who claim to follow the teachings of

Jesus, to contrast the downcast and discouraged attitude of most church members with the good cheer and happiness which the average Christian Scientist enjoys, in spite of the confusing teachings of their system. It is certainly greatly to the credit of Christian Scientists that they have got what health and happiness they have out of the truth at their disposal, and their success certainly constitutes a stunning rebuke to the modern teachers and exponents of Christianity.

We present the following summary of the methods of operation whereby Christian Science and other popular systems of mind cure effect their apparently wonderful healings and create their large, enthusiastic following: .

1. They are a powerful popular protest against modern materialism and rationalism.

2. These psychic systems of healing are an unconscious protest against wholesale drug-medication and other unnatural and irrational methods of treating disease.

3. Christian Science and kindred cults are easy to believe: they involve but little self-sacrifice or personal humiliation.

4. These new psychic cults are pleasant to the natural man, in that they deny or ignore the orthodox doctrines of sin, and exalt erring man to the place of a god.

5. Christian Science and allied cults are new and therefore entertaining; they are more or less mysterious and therefore fascinating; and this latter property they will undoubtedly ever retain. Their teachings are unquestionably unfathomable — they will always be surrounded by the aroma of mystery.

6. All their psychic teachings afford immediate deliverance from an accusing conscience.

7. Christian Science prospers because it eliminates worry, notwithstanding the fact that its philosophy is unscientific.

8. These occult teachings chloroform the judgment and reason. They are systems of blind belief, and involve the unconditional surrender of the mind to the thing believed.

9. Christian Science represents the uplifting power of faith and strong resolution. This only goes to show the powerful influence of the mind over the body when thoroughly dedicated to a single idea, even though that idea be essentially wrong.

PSYCHIC FADS AND FAKES

10. It is a species of mental deception which the believer can be taught to practise upon himself; and the very deceptiveness of it constitutes both its charm and its compelling power over those who surrender to it.

11. Last, but not least, many of these systems of healing, including Christian Science, have gone on in the world in spite of their error, because they do contain a grain of truth not generally recognized by either scientists or religionists, and that is — the influence of mind over matter.

REASON *versus* SOPHISTRY

Having in the last few chapters systematically discussed the methods of modern psychotherapy, we desire here to lay special emphasis upon the wisdom of dealing honestly and squarely with all persons suffering from psychic disorders. We believe that the future of psychotherapy lies along the line of appealing to the patient's reason (true and honest suggestion), of strengthening the patient's will-power (consistent reëducation), as well as in the direction of psycho-analysis — the laying of the full facts before the patient and, having secured his co-operation, sympathetically assisting him to fight his battle out to a successful issue; standing by him until he has achieved the victory and is master of himself.

SUMMARY OF THE CHAPTER

1. All through the ages sharp and unscrupulous persons have deceived and imposed upon the credulous and unsuspecting. It is to be deplored that in the twentieth century people are still devoted to charms, relics, and shrines.

2. Quack doctors and famous patent medicines owe their reputation and popularity either to alcohol and other deceptive habit-forming drugs, or to the power and possibilities of suggestion.

3. Astrology, palmistry, and phrenology are psychic fakes and therapeutic deceptions. Phrenology tells very little about what you have been or what you are capable of being; its answer is necessarily in the rough.

4. Clairvoyance and fortune-telling are ingenious psychic fads. Clairvoyance, when not pure fakery, is a prostitution of that wonderful gift of discerning spirits — character-reading. Fortune-telling is pure humbuggery.

5. Crystal-gazing and shell-hearing represent a species of self-deception which certain nervous persons practise upon themselves. These phenomena are due to the outward projection of images and sounds.

6. In trances and the cataleptic state, consciousness seems to be pushed far out toward the periphery. It is at a dead level of intensity all over the field. Trance mediums always see visions in harmony with their own theological views. Many victims of trance visions come sincerely to believe that their experiences are divine revelations.

7. Automatic writing and speaking are due to psychic reversion. Touch and motor sensations are the suggesting causes. These are projected outward as in the other cases auditory and visual sensations are. They do not, however, enter into the focus of attention; that is, into the central consciousness, and so appear as messages from another world, or as an unknown tongue.

8. Strictly speaking, the reality of telepathic power is an unfounded assumption. The so-called facts of telepathy may be explained by analogy with familiar modes of communication. on the ground of coincidence, or in harmony with the general belief in the existence of a Universal Mind.

9. Spiritualism is nine-tenths trickery. Only rarely are its phenomena genuine. Spiritualism cannot be adjudged in the experimental laboratory; it must be referred to the theological courts. The practice of seeking information from the dead is condemned in the Scriptures.

10. Dowieism and similar so-called faith cures are based on the assumption that sin and sickness are analogous; sin is cured by prayer — why not sickness? Sin is a cause; sickness an effect; causes may be cured by prayer; effects usually demand material coöperation for their removal.

11. So-called New Thought and Mental Science, as far as suggestion is concerned, are as old as the hills. Why should the psychic truths and comforting possibilities of Christ's teachings be torn from His Gospel and set up as a new religion — as a "New Thought" or some other cult or ism?

12. Hypnotism is an unnatural, abnormal, and exceedingly

dangerous procedure. No good can ordinarily be accomplished by hypnosis which cannot be more beneficially effected by other methods. Hypnotic sleep is not a natural sleep. Hypnosis is produced by a dissociation between the central and marginal consciousnesses.

13. Christian Science emphasizes the denial element of psychotherapy. In order to be rid of false disease, it denies the real as well. The success of Christian Science constitutes a stunning rebuke to the modern teachers and exponents of Christianity.

14. True psychotherapy involves the employment of reason in the place of sophistry, and the use of honest suggestion and sympathetic reëducation, instead of deception and dishonesty.

CHAPTER XXXIX

PRAYER THE MASTER MIND CURE

THE PSYCHOLOGY OF PRAYER.— THE PHYSIOLOGY OF PRAYER.— THE THERAPEUTICS OF PRAYER.— THE PRAYER CURE.— THE PROSTITUTION OF PRAYER.— PRAYER AN INSPIRATION TO WORK.— CHRISTIANITY THE HIGHEST PSYCHOTHERAPY.— RELIGIOUS WORRY AND SPIRITUAL GRIEF.— THE NEW MIND IN THE OLD BODY.— THE GOSPEL OF RECKONING.— PHYSICAL RIGHTEOUSNESS AN AID TO SPIRITUAL LIVING.— SUMMARY OF THE CHAPTER.

NO discussion of applied psychotherapy would be complete without the consideration of prayer. A careful study of the province of prayer in health and disease has convinced the author that this time-honored practice is second to no other in its power to influence favorably the mental state and to liberate the soul from its bondage of fear, doubt, and despondency.

THE PSYCHOLOGY OF PRAYER

True prayer is a sort of spiritual communion between man and his Maker, a sympathetic communication between the soul and its Saviour. We do not look upon prayer as a means of changing God's will. The *Divine* Mind does not need to be changed; He is ever beneficent and kindly disposed toward mankind. While prayer does not change God, it certainly does change the one who prays, and this change in the mind of the praying soul is sometimes immediate, profound, and often wholly inexplicable.

True prayer, then, is found to be a practice consisting of powerful mental, moral, and spiritual factors. The *mental factor* in genuine prayer is that of suggestion and self-surrender. Sincere prayer is the most powerful method and the most legitimate manner in which suggestion can be made to the human mind. Not only is the suggestion of prayer autosuggestion — the ideal form of suggestion — but this suggestion is made to the mind when it is in a state of surrender, unconditional surrender to the mind of God and not to the mind of man. Psychology and psychotherapy are unable to portray such an ideal state of the human mind for the favorable reception of suggestion, neither can they point out such powerful and wholesome means of administering this suggestion as by the simple childlike practice of old-fashioned prayer. (See Fig. 42.)

The *moral element* of prayer is that it keeps the mind focussed upon high ideals, upon things which are ennobling and elevating. Prayer, in an unusual manner, imparts moral courage and wholesome confidence to the suppliant. Prayer is a direct preventive of many of those reprehensible social and moral practices which inevitably breed worry, remorse, and sorrow of heart. Prayer strengthens the will, in contradistinction to hypnotism, which usually weakens it.

The *spiritual factor* in prayer is strong; no other phase of human experience is fraught with such extraordinary possibilities for spiritual strength and development. Prayer actually generates moral energy and creates spiritual courage. The prayer life is the life of spiritual power and moral victory.

THE PHYSIOLOGY OF PRAYER

The domain of prayer is not limited alone to the spiritual, moral, and mental realms; it concerns and influences even the physical body. The praying soul usually is found upon bended knees and with bowed head. This bending of the physical knee reflexly aids in bending the will and the mind of the one who prays. There is a close interrelationship between the attitude of body and the attitude of mind.

We recently examined a nervous, excited patient with a rapid heart, irregular pulse, abnormal breathing, extreme pallor of the face, and with blood-pressure of 160 mm. After explaining to the patient that she was suffering from no real or organic disease, we requested her to retire into a quiet, darkened near-by office and engage in prayer for ten minutes; she was asked earnestly and sincerely to pray to God that He might help her and deliver her from her state of nervous agitation.

In fifteen minutes, when the patient returned, her pulse was normal; the voice had acquired a new tone of confidence; the strength and expression of the eye — yes, of the whole face — had completely changed: in place of anxiety and dissatisfaction, there now appeared an expression of rest, courage, and happiness; and a triumphant smile was upon the face, indicative of the assurance of victory. The blood-pressure was 150 mm., and within thirty minutes it descended to 140 mm.

Prayer is able, directly, immediately, most powerfully, and most favorably to influence the physical functions of the body; that is, genuine prayer, the prayer of faith, exerts its beneficent influence upon the body, while other kinds of prayer may be highly injurious to the physical health, as will be noted presently. True praying assists the petitioner in gaining control over various physical propensities and animal passions. Prayer is a means of bringing the body into subjection to the mind, and the mind into obedience to the spiritual faculties and to the *D*ivine Mind.

It is impossible to restrict the province and possibilities of prayer as regards its influence upon the human mind and body. We would here again remind the reader that man is not a mere material machine. We are forced to recognize that the human mind and body are regulated by certain laws which we are unable fully to explain on the material grounds of physics and chemistry.

THE THERAPEUTICS OF PRAYER

Any practice that can wield such a mighty influence over mind and body as that exerted by prayer must indeed possess tremendous therapeutic possibilities. In discussing prayer as a therapeutic agent, we in no way aim to belittle its influence as a religious practice or a spiritual force. We freely concede that its power is almost unlimited in these realms. In his "Varieties of Religious Experience," Professor James says: "As regards prayer for the sick, if any medical fact can be considered to stand firm, it is that in certain environments, prayer may contribute to recovery, and should be encouraged as a therapeutic measure."

Another scientific authority, *D*r. Hyslop, Superintendent of

FIG. 42. THE PRACTICE OF OLD-FASHIONED PRAYER.

the Bethlehem Royal Hospital, London, in speaking of prayer as a therapeutic agent, says: "As an alienist and one whose life has been concerned with the sufferings of the mind, I would state that of all hygienic measures to counteract disturbed sleep, depressed spirits, and all the miserable sequels of a distressed mind, I would undoubtedly give the first place to the simple habit of prayer. Let there but be a habit of nightly communion, not as a mendicant or repeater of words more adapted to the tongue of a sage, but as a humble individual who submerges or asserts his individuality as an integral part of a greater whole. Such a habit does more to calm the spirit and strengthen the soul to overcome incidental emotionalism than any other therapeutic agent known to me."

There can be little doubt that the psychological and therapeutic value of prayer has been greatly underestimated by modern reformers and psychotherapists. A number of years ago we saw a desolate, forlorn, and downcast woman, the most pitiable creature we ever looked upon, kneel down in a gospel mission in the slums of Chicago, and after sobbing out: "God be merciful to me a sinner," arise from her knees. From that day to the day of her death, some five years afterwards, this regenerated woman led a consistent, pure, and wholesome life. Now, we freely grant that spiritual forces were at work in this woman's soul. Such an experience as hers must indeed be what the theologians describe as the "new birth," for the practical changes in her life did clearly show that she had literally been "born again." The things she once loved she now hated, and the things she formerly hated she now loved. The transformation of character seemed to be absolute and complete.

The author has seen scores of cases, and our readers have no doubt experienced it in their own lives, where prayer, in a moment of time, has wrought just such marvellous physical and spiritual changes in the life. All physicians who have largely to do with mental disorders and nervous diseases are coming to appreciate more and more the therapeutic value of simple and earnest prayer.

In the case of those who are so distracted and so nervous that they cannot formulate their prayer into words, who are unable to express their prayerful desires, it is often necessary that their mental minister should place in their hands some inspiring and uplifting form of short prayer, which may guide them into the praying habit until such a time as their soul can come to express itself spontaneously.

THE PRAYER CURE

Recently, in the clinic, we have most thoroughly tested the therapeutic value of prayer. For certain nervous patients, the victims of worry and fear, we have often prescribed regular and systematic prayer. We have been astonished to discover the wide range of functional disorders, physical disturbances, and psychic difficulties, which have been wholly cured or greatly helped by this simple procedure; and to our utter amazement, some of the most remarkable cures were effected in the case of patients who frankly told us, at the time we prescribed prayer, that they did not believe in praying, that they did not have faith in God. To such we would explain that a dose of salts or an ounce of castor oil would be likely to produce certain effects upon them quite regardless of their belief; therefore, that if they would only follow our directions in regard to prayer, they would probably experience certain desirable effects independent of their belief.

Among many patients treated by the therapeutics of prayer, the following case is cited as a typical instance: Mrs. B—, a widow with three children, had been coming to the clinic for several weeks, and had been helped but little by our physical ministrations. One morning she said she was thoroughly discouraged; that she really thought she was going to lose her mind; that it would be useless to take more treatment. After listening again to her story, we talked to her for half an hour, telling her what a wonderful improvement she would make if she could get over the idea that her case was incurable, or that she was going crazy. We then ventured the opinion that we had a cure that would work in her case if she would only consent to try it. After thoroughly arousing her curiosity as to what this cure might be, and after securing a written promise from her that she would take our cure without question, absolutely and unquestioningly follow our directions in every detail, we proceeded to write out a prescription as follows: "Three times a day, regularly, at hours you may select, go into the front room; pull down the blinds; place a chair in the middle of the room; kneel down in front of this chair; close the eyes and pray from ten to fifteen minutes. Form your prayer into words; speak softly, but distinctly. Pray about anything or for anybody you choose, except yourself. Under no circumstances must you mention yourself or pray for yourself; that is, you must not pray about your disease or your mental difficulties. You may pray for yourself in the sense of asking for spiritual help, but in no case must your nervous disorders be mentioned in your prayers. You are to do this for three weeks, and then report to this clinic."

On receiving this prescription, the patient began at once to explain that she had lost all faith in God, and that she did not believe in prayer; whereupon we exhibited her written promise to follow our directions, and she immediately stopped all objection, giving us her word that she would do as we had prescribed. At the end of three weeks this patient appeared and reported that she had gained a complete victory over all her mental difficulties; that she had also gained five pounds in weight, was sleeping well, and that her neighbors were beginning to speak of her rapid improvement. This patient reported that after the third day she entered heartily into her prayers, and that each day she was more and more strengthened, refreshed, and invigorated. This entire chapter could be filled with the experience related by this one patient. The physicians in attendance at the clinic on this particular morning were profoundly impressed with the therapeutic power and possibilities of simple prayer — with its psychic value, independent of its spiritual province. One physician, with a tearful eye, said to the author at the close of the clinic: "I did not know we had such a tremendous healing force lying about unused."

THE PROSTITUTION OF PRAYER

In this connection we desire to utter a warning against morbid methods of prayer. No procedure is capable of great good without at the same time being susceptible of perversion and great harm. Another case will illustrate the harm of prayer, when it consists of a meaningless recital of one's difficulties, serving as a source of adverse auto-suggestion to the mind. Such methods of prayer tend to weaken and debilitate the mental and moral powers. About a year ago we had a patient, a young man, twenty-two years of age, who was fighting a great moral battle. He became very much discouraged; broke off his marriage engagement; severed his connection with the church; and at the time we met him, seriously contemplated suicide. Having tried numerous methods of giving him help and relief, we finally made bold to advise that he was in need of moral strength — spiritual power — and suggested that he would find great help in systematic prayer. To this he replied: "Why, doctor, I have prayed about my troubles until two o'clock in the morning, and then after my great struggle with God, I would soon fall again into my sin. The more I pray, the worse I get; nothing will do me any good. It is either the insane asylum or the grave for me." After listening to this recital of his experience, it occurred to us that in his case, prayer was being prostituted into a form of adverse and unwholesome suggestion; that he had prayed about his moral perversity so much that this very praying had become a direct aid in keeping the wicked idea everlastingly before his mind. Instead of making a helpful and uplifting suggestion out of prayer, he was making it harmful and debasing. And so we made bold to suggest the following procedure in his case: We asked him to reunite with the church; to see his *fiancée* and set a new wedding-day; to begin to lay plans for securing a flat, and actively engage in selecting the furnishings. We asked him to let his mind freely dwell upon the happy home he would have and the splendid children who would come to bless it. We had him sign a written agreement not to think, talk, or pray about his troubles for two weeks. We explained to him as best we could, that when he had asked his Heavenly Father to help him in a matter of this kind, that it was not necessary to ask more than once; that further prayer should be devoted to thanking God for the help that was to come and in expressing gratitude for the help that even now had already come.

We are glad to report that in this case, after his method of praying had been turned from one of constant adverse suggestion into one of thanksgiving and gratitude, he was highly successful. From that day on, this young man became an absolute victor over his besetting sin. And so it is apparent that prayer can be so perverted as to become a means of great harm as a therapeutic procedure. The author's highest conception of prayer is that silent and spiritual communion between the spirit of the creature and the Spirit of his Maker. In the early stages of therapeutic praying it is very necessary that the prayer should be calmly and distinctly uttered in words, that the petitioner may hear his own prayer, for this greatly increases the influence and suggestive power of the procedure.

It is our opinion that in the case of the patient first mentioned, the mere silent kneeling before the chair in the middle of the room possessed not a little therapeutic power. Many a nervous patient would soon cure himself, if he would perfectly relax and silently rest for fifteen minutes three times a day. There is good therapeutic advice in that old Scripture: "Be still, and know that I am God."

PRAYER AN INSPIRATION TO WORK

Prayer is not only a means whereby the mind of man and the divine forces are brought into coöperation, but if it is uttered in faith, it usually leads the one who prays to put forth every effort to bring about the answer of his prayers. Genuine prayer is an expression of courage and confidence combined with faith and good works.

Although prayer is a powerful therapeutic agent, we must fully recognize that neither belief in our prayers, nor suggestion, nor reëducation will take the place of proper physical ministrations and the scientific care of the diseased or disordered body. Prayer may be the breath of the soul; prayer may be the avenue whereby the diseased mind is eliminated and the Divine Mind brought in to replace it; prayer is the great channel by which man can harmonize his mind with that of his Maker; nevertheless, good food, pure water, fresh air, and deep breathing, together with mental and physical exercise, are absolutely essential to the recovery of most nervous and psychic disorders.

The proper regulation of the diet, the hygiene of the bowels, the breathing of pure air, and the drinking of pure water, have much to do with the cure of nervous semi-invalids. Prayer must not be used merely as a means of giving relief to hysterical feelings, or as an excuse for repeatedly telling the Almighty how much you have done for Him, and how little He has done for you. If the spirit of faith and optimism, of thanksgiving and joy, is not found in prayer, it may become an unconscious means of further debilitating and depressing the neurasthenic and nervous patient. It is not only wise to prescribe prayer, but it is also necessary to teach people how to pray. Jesus must have recognized that the world knew little about how to pray, for the only form He left on record was that wonderful prayer, commonly known as the Lord's Prayer, which He gave to the disciples in answer to their request: " Lord, teach us to pray."

We do not teach that prayer should not be used as a safety-valve for the soul. It is far better when the feelings, the emotions, and the internal pressure have arisen almost to the bursting point — it is far better for the Christian to pour out his soul to God in prayer, than to participate in an outburst of anger or to indulge in a fit of bad temper. If it is absolutely necessary that the one should have a vent of some sort to relieve himself, prayer will be found to be a successful and satisfactory mode of obtaining such relief. Even when prayer is accompanied by more or less weeping and wailing, it is certainly preferable to a hysterical outbreak or to a verbal explosion of raving and ranting.

CHRISTIANITY THE HIGHEST PSYCHOTHERAPY

We are forced to recognize the therapeutic value of prayer, no matter with what system of belief or religion it may be associated; but we have spoken of prayer in this text with the thought of its being a part of practical Christianity. *The author regards prayer as the master mind cure, and Christianity as the highest and truest form of psychotherapy.* There can be no question that the Christian religion, when properly understood and truly experienced, possesses power both to prevent and cure numerous mental maladies, moral difficulties, and physical diseases. This entire book has been devoted to the psychology and physiology of faith and fear, and it must be evident to the reader that fear and doubt are disease-producing, while faith and hope are health-giving; and in the author's opinion, the highest possibilities of faith and the greatest power of hope are expressed in the Christian religion; the teachings of Christ are the greatest known destroyers of doubt and despair.

No one can appreciate so fully as a doctor the amazingly large percentage of human diseases and sufferings which are directly traceable to immorality, dissipation, and ignorance — to unwholesome thinking and unclean living. The sincere acceptance of the principles and teachings of Christ with respect to the life of mental peace and joy, the life of unselfish thought and clean living, would at once remove more than one-half the difficulties, diseases, and sorrows of the human race. In other words, more than one-half of the present afflictions of mankind could be prevented by the tremendous prophylactic power of the Christian religion.

Christianity applied to our modern civilization — understandingly *applied,* not merely believed or accepted — would so purify, uplift, and vitalize us that the human race would immediately stand out as a new order of beings, possessing superior mental power and increased physical force. Irrespective of the future rewards of the Christian religion, laying aside all discussion of future life, it would pay any man or woman to live the Christ life just for the mental and physical rewards which it affords here in this present world. Some day the world may awake to the point where it will recognize that the teachings of Christ are potent and powerful in the work of preventing and curing disease. Some day our wonderful boasted scientific developments, as regards mental and moral improvement, may indeed catch up with the teachings of the Christian religion.

RELIGIOUS WORRY AND SPIRITUAL GRIEF

Repeatedly we have called attention to the fact that the body does its best work when the mind is kept entirely off the physical functions. The physical body is most healthy when least thought of. To concentrate the mind on any internal organ will sooner or later result in deranging its functions and aid in producing physical disease. Introspection is destructive of health and encourages disease; and this truth holds equally good in the spiritual and moral realms. The less one thinks about one's spiritual life, the more healthy and wholesome it becomes. And we are reminded in this connection of the statement once made by that great evangelist, Mr. Dwight L. Moody. One day on meeting a friend he had not seen for many years, he was asked, "Well, Mr. Moody, how is your soul?" To this question Mr. Moody replied: "Well, I am sure I don't know. I have been so busy working for other people that I haven't had time to think anything about my soul; I guess it is all right." And we would suggest that Mr. Moody probably never experienced a holier and more truly spiritual moment in his life than he did at that very time, at that moment when he was utterly unmindful of the immediate state and workings of his own soul. When the praying Christian has committed his soul to the keeping of his Maker; when he is walking in the light of life as he discerns it; what worry about his soul should find a place in his mind?

It is only when the body is sick that we are reminded that we have one; it is only when the stomach is sick that we are aware of its presence. And so we are persuaded that it is only when the soul is diseased — sin-sick — that we are ever reminded that we have one. When all is well, when one is living the faith life, when the soul is at peace with God and with its fellows, we are inclined to believe that the spiritual life is much like that described by Mr. Moody. We are so busy and so happy with our unselfish efforts to help our fellow man, that we have not time to stop and think of our own soul. And why should we? Having accepted the peace and fellowship extended by our Maker, why should we not pass on with joy and rejoicing, directing our greatest efforts to the reconciliation of the heart-broken, sorrow-stricken, and downtrodden members of the race, who have not yet discovered the beauties of this life of faith — this life of man's oneness with God?

THE NEW MIND IN THE OLD BODY

The great battle of life consists in an incessant struggle between mind and matter. "For the flesh lusteth against the Spirit, and the Spirit against the flesh; and these are contrary the one to the other; so that ye cannot do the things that ye would." (Gal. V:17.)

The Apostle Paul was the great philosopher of the Christian religion. His portrayals of the warfare between the carnal and spiritual natures, between mind and body, are vivid and classic. Paul recognized that while religion was able to change the mind, it did not necessarily change the body; and so he wrote: "I keep under my body, and bring it into subjection; lest that by any means, when I have preached to others, I myself should be a castaway." (I Cor. IX:27.) Paul certainly recognized the great truth of Christian psychology — that while we may secure a new mind, we are in no wise delivered from the old body.

The spiritual nature expresses itself in the choice of mind, whereas the carnal nature manifests itself through the desires and passions of the flesh. The regeneration of the mind is entirely possible. Spiritually, a man can be "born again," start out afresh with new and heaven-born desires; and this wonderful process can be wrought in an instant, in a moment of time, by the simple choosing of the "mind of Christ" in the place of the mind of self; by the simple surrender of the human will to the *Divine* Will.

But it is not so with the body, with its hereditary taints, its passions, and its perverted appetites and craving desires. These attributes of the flesh stubbornly and constantly dispute the rule and reign of the higher powers of the mind. The spiritual nature is, as it were, engaged in combat with a vicious animal that ever seeks to encompass its overthrow and effect its destruction. The body must be subdued — tamed; it must be constantly watched; the flesh cannot be trusted; the soul must be safeguarded against the waywardness of the body, as expressed by Paul: "Put ye on the Lord Jesus Christ, and make not provision for the flesh, to fulfil the lusts thereof." (Rom. XIII:14.)

But can we do nothing for the body, to make easier this contest with the world, the flesh, and the devil? Yes, much can be done to disarm the flesh. While the body does not experience conversion in the same manner as does the spiritual nature, it may be slowly improved by proper attention to habits of diet, exercise, etc., and in this way the internal warfare between the spirit and the flesh may be greatly lessened.

The *new mind* is compelled to take up its residence in the *old body*. It is only reasonable that we should do everything possible to render the old body a fit habitation for the new mind. We are certainly under obligation to clean up the old fleshly house, to put into it only those food materials which are clean and pure, and capable of improving the bodily structure by replacing broken down material with superior matter. Likewise, the habits of eating and drinking should be carefully studied to see that no deteriorating substance is taken into the body which will irritate the nerves, poison the brain, weaken the resistance, and thus make the flesh a prey to the thousand and one agencies of destruction which abound on every side.

In a few words, it is our Christian duty to keep the body in a sound and healthy condition, to keep it unirritated; to eschew those things which fire the animal nature and strengthen vicious tendencies; and which, thereby, weaken the power of mind over matter, and in the end bring their victims into hopeless subjection and slavery to the carnal vices and whims of the flesh. Concerning this the apostle writes: "What? Know ye not that your body is the temple of the Holy Ghost which is in you, which ye have of God, and ye are not your own? For ye are bought with a price; therefore glorify God in your body, and in your spirit, which are God's." "Whether therefore ye eat, or drink, or whatsoever ye do, do all to the glory of God." (I Cor. VI:19, 20; X:31.)

THE GOSPEL OF RECKONING

According to Paul's teaching, the fundamental law of the Christian life is based on *reckoning*. The apostle teaches that by divine grace the believer in Christ actually becomes just what he (the believer) by faith reckons himself to be. Christianity enjoins that one must *think* life before attaining the spiritual resurrection. Paul said: "Likewise, reckon ye also yourselves to be dead indeed unto sin, but alive unto God through Jesus Christ our Lord." (Rom. VI:11).

Concerning his own struggle in the contest between mind and matter — spirit and body — and the final victorious outcome, Paul wrote: "I find then a law, that, when I would do good, evil is present with me. For I delight in the law of God after the inward man: but I see another law in my members, warring against the law of my mind, and bringing me into captivity to the law of sin which is in my members. O wretched man that I am! who shall deliver me from the body of this death? I thank God through Jesus Christ our Lord. So then with the mind I myself serve the law of God; but with the flesh the law of sin. There is therefore now no condemnation to them which are in Christ Jesus, who walk not after the flesh, but after the spirit." (Rom. VII:21 — VIII:1.)

It will not always appear to Christian believers that the body of sin is dead, but it is their privilege, by faith, to reckon that they are dead indeed unto sin. And standing upon this platform of faith, it is the Christian's privilege to experience. Romans VI, verses 12-14. "Let not sin therefore reign in your mortal body, that ye should obey it in the lusts thereof; Neither yield ye your members as instruments of unrighteousness unto sin; but yield yourselves unto God, as those that are alive from the dead, and your members as instruments of righteousness unto God. For sin shall not have dominion over you."

But what shall we do with the flesh after we recognize that it is not yet dead unto sin? The answer is: "Mortify therefore your members which are upon the earth; fornication, uncleanness, inordinate affection, evil concupiscence, and covetousness, which is idolatry." (Col. III:5.) How shall we mortify the flesh? By simply reckoning it to be dead, and then leaving it alone. Mortification is a process of nature which spontaneously takes place when things die. Don't seek to embalm, to excuse, to embellish, to compromise, with the deeds of the flesh.

That this victory of the spirit over the flesh is entirely dependent on the psychic state and attitude is shown by Eph. IV:22-24, which says: "That ye put off concerning the former conversation the old man, which is corrupt according to the deceitful lusts; and be renewed in the spirit of your mind; and that ye put on the new man, which after God is created in righteousness and true holiness."

PHYSICAL RIGHTEOUSNESS AN AID TO SPIRITUAL LIVING

Obedience to the laws of health is an effectual means of disarming the flesh — as it were, of removing the weights tied about the sinking soul — which will enable the mind to survive and the spirit to rule. While it is true that we cannot eat and drink ourselves into the Kingdom of God, it is equally true that many are eating and drinking themselves out of both the Kingdom of Heaven and the kingdom of health.

Every act of obedience to the laws of life, and every effort to "cleanse ourselves from all filthiness of the flesh and spirit" (II Cor. VII:1), are powerful helps to the mind in its battle to control matter. They are direct aids to the spirit in its struggle to master the body. Likewise, every transgression of physical law which results in weakening, irritating, and sickening the body, serves as an additional weight about the neck of the soul to hold it down in its efforts to rise above the polluted waters of the physical and material realm.

Good physical health — a nervous system in perfect equilibrium, sound digestion, a pure blood stream, an active and well-regulated eliminative system — these are all physical means of grace to the spiritual nature. They represent the "old man" cleaned up and disarmed to the fullest possible extent. In such a condition it is infinitely easier for the new mind to manage the old body.

SUMMARY OF THE CHAPTER

1. Prayer is a sort of spiritual communion between man and his Maker. It is second to no other practice, in its power to influence the mind and liberate the soul.

2. While prayer may not change God, it certainly does change the one who prays; and this mental transformation is sometimes immediate, profound, and wholly inexplicable.

3 The mental factor in true prayer is that of suggestion and self-surrender — self-surrender of the human will to the Divine Mind. There is tremendous psychotherapeutic power in simple old-fashioned prayer.

4. The moral element of prayer consists in keeping the mind focussed on high ideals. Prayer strengthens the will, in contradistinction to hypnotism which usually weakens it.

5. The spiritual factor in prayer is found in its ability to generate moral energy, and its power to create spiritual courage. Prayer is the secret of spiritual victory.

6. The practice of prayer very markedly influences the performance of many physical functions. Prayer influences the body favorably or unfavorably according as it is dominated by faith or fear.

7. The psychological and therapeutic value of prayer has been greatly underestimated by modern reformers and psychotherapists. The prayer of faith is the gateway to the new birth — the new mind.

8. The prayer cure is the treatment *par excellence* for numerous nervous, worried, and hysterical patients. Prayer possesses a positive value as a therapeutic agent, even in the experience of those who doubt its efficacy and who have little faith in a prayer-hearing God.

9. The prayer of faith is a source of favorable and powerful auto-suggestion to the mind of the one who prays; while the prayer of doubt and fear may become highly injurious because of its power of adverse suggestion.

10. Prayer may be so prostituted as to become a source of moral weakness and spiritual defeat. It is sometimes necessary to forbid patients praying about their peculiar or particular obsessions and other harassing difficulties.

11. Genuine prayer inspires the one who prays to put forth every intelligent effort to bring about the answer to his prayers.

12. Although prayer is a potent therapeutic agency, it cannot take the place of proper physical ministration and the scientific care of the diseased or disordered body.

13. The practice of prayer constitutes a safety-valve for

mind and soul. A season of praying will often prevent an outburst of anger or a fit of bad temper.

14. Prayer is the master mind cure. Christianity is the highest and truest form of psychotherapy. The highest possibilities of faith and the greatest power of hope are expressed in the teachings of Christ.

15. If Christianity were practically applied to our modern civilization, it would so purify and vitalize the race that more than one-half of our sorrow and sickness would immediately disappear.

16. The less one thinks of one's spiritual life, the more healthy and wholesome it becomes. The soul, like the body, never reminds us of its presence, unless something has gone wrong.

17. While both theology and psychology teach the possibility of man's securing a new mind, physiology demonstrates the impossibility of our getting a new body, in the same sense. The new mind must take up its habitation and fight its battles in the same old body.

18. While the body cannot experience conversion as does the spiritual nature; nevertheless, it can be slowly improved and effectively disarmed, by proper attention to the habits of diet and exercise.

19. It is a Christian duty to keep the body in a sound and healthy condition; to keep it unirritated; to eschew those practices which fire the animal nature and inflame the vicious passions.

20. Both psychologic and Christian philosophy teach that what the human soul reckons itself by faith to be — eventually, that is, just what it will become. The thought of life in the mind, precedes the spiritual resurrection.

21. Physical righteousness is a great aid to spiritual living. Obedience to the laws of health is an effectual means of disarming the flesh in its incessant warfare against the spirit.

CHAPTER XL

THE EMANCIPATED LIFE

THE BONDAGE OF CIVILIZATION.—PHYSICAL EMANCIPATION, THE SIMPLE LIFE FOR THE BODY.—MENTAL EMANCIPATION, THE SIMPLE LIFE FOR THE MIND.—SOCIAL EMANCIPATION, THE SIMPLE LIFE FOR THE COMMUNITY.—DOMESTIC EMANCIPATION, THE SIMPLE LIFE FOR THE HOME.—MORAL EMANCIPATION, THE SIMPLE LIFE FOR THE SOUL.

THE civilized races are at present suffering the blight of numerous unnecessary physical maladies, while the mind of man is fettered with fear, and the human soul is well-nigh crushed with worry and sorrow; all of which is largely, if not wholly, preventable. Much of the unhappiness of mankind is due to physical transgression, mental worry, moral delinqueney, and the exacting demands of conventional society.

THE BONDAGE OF CIVILIZATION

Man is a sovereign being with soul freedom, mental independence, and moral option; but to-day our complex civilization and highly developed commerce are rapidly turning men and women into highly specialized intellectual and industrial machines. This is well illustrated by the case of the young woman from the tenement district, who went to work in a box factory, to make paper boxes. She was paid for her services at so much a hundred boxes. She reported that she enjoyed the work, and she was very sociable with the other young girls who worked with her, some of whom were younger than she. After the first few weeks she ceased to talk with her fellow-workers, and her sociability at home was noticeably decreased. When asked for an explanation for this change in temperamental behavior, she replied: "I have learned that I cannot make so many boxes when I talk, therefore I cannot earn so much money."

After a year of work in this paper-box factory, the entire expression on this young woman's face had become more or less changed. She went to work in the morning, came home at night, and after doing her washing and ironing or other necessary work, went to bed. Up again in the morning, and off at work all day — just like a machine. In answer to further questions at this time with respect to her once buoyant and joyful temperament, she said: "No, I don't think any more. I have learned that when I think about anything while at work, I cannot make so many boxes, and then I cannot earn so much money."

One would naturally think that the sacredness of the sovereign individuality which has been given to man would naturally protect us against the slavery of imitation, but this is not so. The power of suggestion, the dread of adverse criticism, and the fear of ridicule, make of otherwise intelligent men and women, abject slaves to the prevailing fashions. Man has largely lost sight of the fact that diversity of character and expression is the law of creation. No two leaves, even on the same tree, are exactly alike. The race is losing sight of the fact that the supreme duty of man is to live at his best — ascertain the conditions essential thereto, and faithfully adjust his life to them.

The human race is drifting into bondage to the conventionalities of commerce and civilized society. The emancipated life is the efficient life, the simple life. History abundantly proves that vice, intemperance, indolence, and the complexity of civilization, are the chief factors in the decay, the ruin, and the downfall of nations. Many of our modern diseases are practically limited to the civilized races. Culture and education, instead of delivering the race from fear, in many cases serve but to multiply our fears and increase our anxieties.

By far the majority of the diseases of savagery are caused by microbes, and are therefore subject to control and elimination by quarantine and sanitation; while the mental diseases, the moral maladies, and the bad-habit disorders of the civilized races can be eradicated only by bringing about the mental, moral, and physical emancipation of the people.

FIG 43. RIGHT AND WRONG SOCIAL TENDENCIES.

The national supremacy and the military triumphs of the simple-life peoples, from the Medes to the Japs, constitute a strong indictment against the unwholesomeness of the modern tendency to multiply false and material needs, to overindulge the physical appetites and passions, and consequently to overburden the mind with fear and worry. The modern highly complex methods of civilized living resemble an engine with the throttle wide open: there exists no reserve power.

PHYSICAL EMANCIPATION — THE SIMPLE LIFE FOR THE BODY

As we increase the complexity of modern living, it becomes necessary that very simple and hygienic habits should be generally adopted. It is highly essential that men and women of the twentieth century should give daily study and intelligent thought to the cultivation and preservation of health. The integrity of the civilized races is dependent upon getting away from the house — from the sedentary life. Man is in every sense an outdoor animal, and sunshine and fresh air are indispensable to his health and happiness. Many of our modern maladies, such as bronchitis, pneumonia, catarrh, and tuberculosis are purely and simply house diseases.

Many a man could deliver himself from mental bondage and moral depression by merely learning how to breathe, how to breathe deeply and naturally. Thousands of people are habitually suffering from semi-suffocation, due to their insufficient and unnatural methods of breathing.

Free and regular water-drinking in connection with systematic bathing, together with the proper regulation of the diet — eating the right amount of good food at right times — would set many a chronic dyspeptic free from the bondage and terrors of his digestive disturbances.

Daily exercise in healthful and properly adjusted clothing, together with regular rest, sound sleep, and wholesome reereation, would emancipate many a soul, now held securely by the fetters of chronic disease and mental depression. Let the civilized nations open their eyes to the fact that plain living and high thinking go together.

MENTAL EMANCIPATION — THE SIMPLE LIFE FOR THE MIND

Civilized people have not yet reached the place where they

are willing to break away from that debilitating and fear-ridden practice of constantly worrying about what other people think of them. We are more or less victims of blind and unreasoning prejudices — and prejudice is a sort of mental cork, which prevents good ideas from entering the mind, and sometimes also prevents splendid thoughts escaping therefrom.

Most people constantly practise mental repression — that is, they do not cultivate original habits of thought, and do not encourage the mind honestly and fearlessly to express itself. This sort of psychic slavery is one of the curses of the conventionality which ever attaches itself to a state of civilization. Many a great mind has been dwarfed and crippled by the paralyzing influence of this social hypocrisy.

An uncontrolled and explosive temper is like dynamite to happiness. A single fit of anger is able to destroy the tranquillity of the mind for days and even weeks. The serpent of suspicion is a mind poison, a thing to be greatly feared and constantly shunned; while despondency is inhuman and unnatural; every intelligent man and woman should maintain perpetual quarantine against it.

The inordinate itching for publicity, the unnatural and unwholesome desire for notoriety, makes slaves out of otherwise intelligent people. The desire to be regarded as "somebody," and the unnatural tendency to climb to the "top of the heap," must be blamed for a great deal of our present-day unhappiness, heartache, and sorrow.

Simplicity brings the joy and satisfaction that belong to the emancipated mind. Joy and satisfaction are not to be found in things or in riches, but in the soul.

Let simplicity and sincerity of speech displace our modern methods of "counterfeit talk." The little boy was not far from right, when he wrote, in his essay on words, "Speech is made to cover up our thoughts." Let sanctified common sense displace the universal desire for excitement and the ever-present tendency to exaggerate, to overdraw, to overstate, to distort, to magnify, and to create a sensation.

Let the mind be carefully nourished, wisely supplied with diversified mental food. Let the mind be properly fed, not merely fascinated. An exclusive diet of novels is not good for the development and upbuilding of the intellect. Wholesome fiction may have its place as a sort of mental recreation; but it is certainly unwise, especially in the case of young people, to permit the mental nourishment to be composed exclusively of novels.

Self-control is the great secret and source of human health and happiness. Study how properly to work both mind and body, but also study the divine law of mental rest. Studiously shun cankering care and that life of perpetual anxiety and suspense to which so many are unfortunately addicted. Avoid fear thought and worry and all their mental cousins; and remember it is time to take a vacation, to call a halt, when you find you are dreaming at night about your work.

There can be little doubt that our modern strenuous methods of living have much to do with increasing the mental instability of the race. Insanity is increasing by leaps and bounds — out of all proportion to the normal growth of population. The author believes that the unwholesome complexity, the unnecessary multiplication of false demands and fictitious duties on the part of modern civilization, is indirectly concerned in undermining the mental stamina of the race; and the same evil work is accomplished by the direct influence of mental worry and other unhygienic practices.

SOCIAL EMANCIPATION — THE SIMPLE LIFE FOR THE
COMMUNITY

Thousands of women are rendered exceedingly nervous and held in social bondage by their foolish endeavors to shine in society. Thousands of both men and women labor under the lash of debts and mortgages for no reason other than that they may enjoy the delusions of luxury. The idea that one must have fine clothes, diamonds, or automobiles, in order to maintain this place in society, has wrought the ruin and compassed the downfall of many otherwise intelligent and happy families.

Modern society is suppressing and deforming the individuality of its devotees. Social usages and conventionalities are producing the " social stereotype." The rising generation are taught to uphold and ape the customs, habits, and mannerisms of the preceding generation. Genius, talent, and personality are choked and strangled by this insane desire to run the rising generation into our standard social moulds.

The civilized nations are rapidly creating false and arbitrary standards of taste. Our methods of living are becoming increasingly extravagant, and all this results in producing dissatisfaction and discontent on the part of the lower classes of society, when they are unable to secure these material possessions, which they are being taught to regard as essential to happiness and good living.

There is altogether too great a tendency to classify modern society according to dollars. We are becoming, as a nation, afflicted with a false pride of wealth and power. The mind is ever filled with thoughts of discontent because we do not possess the wealth and the artificial prestige and power which are supposed to accompany riches. To those who really know the inner lives and experiences of the wealthy classes and the high social sets, it becomes readily apparent how unhappy and dissatisfied are the majority of these multi-millionaires and social butterflies. The rising generation should be fully taught respecting the follies of fashion and the emptiness of wealth, as well as the vulgarity of the wanton waste of it, and the ostentatious display of those things which money is able to buy.

There can be no doubt that much mental sorrow, and often downright dishonesty, is born of the tendency of the civilized races to have too many supposed social needs. Young men and women come to regard their happiness as dependent upon the possession of certain material blessings, or on the ability to indulge in certain expensive forms of amusement and recreation. The civilized races are in danger of becoming veritable bondservants to the threatened domination of the sovereignty of fictitious needs.

The social functions, banquets, and other lavish entertainments of modern society constitute an appalling waste both of time and money. The energy and means foolishly and often harmfully squandered by one-half of the world, would, in a short time, result in educating and delivering the other half from its intellectual slavery and industrial bondage. (See Fig. 43.)

The unnatural mental tension and high blood-pressure ever associated with social conquest and fashionable entertainments, are rapidly undermining the nervous strength and the vital resistance, especially of the women in the higher circles of society. There is little doubt in the author's mind that these unnecessary social strains upon the nervous system are largely responsible for the alarmingly increasing tendency on the part of women in the higher social sets to resort to the regular use of narcotics and drugs. It soon develops that tea and coffee, or even cigarettes, are unable to afford the desired relief, so there is an ever-present tendency to resort to morphine, opium, or cocaine. It should be remembered that the drug fiends are not all found among the destitute and unfortunate of the slums; they are likewise to be found in large numbers in the mansions on the boulevards.

DOMESTIC EMANCIPATION — THE SIMPLE LIFE FOR THE HOME

The life of the average housewife and mother is too often made one of unnecessary drudgery and useless anxiety. In the modern home life there is altogether too much of a tendency to confuse the tasks which are secondary in importance with those duties which are essential and vital. Housekeeping is made burdensome by the necessity of giving attention to a hundred trifles, the utter neglect of which would in no wise interfere with the happiness and usefulness of the home life. Remember that the house is not the home — the home is made by the character and spirit of the people who live in the house. Do not forget the value of the porch, the yard, the garden — and the children.

Let us not make the mistake of keeping the younger members of the family in a state of constant worry by our incessantly nagging them because of their peculiarities of character and individuality of dress, or their particular way of making their toilet or combing their hair. Let the mothers also exhibit their independence and individuality in the matter of house decoration, and in the arrangement of the furnishings. Why should we dress our persons or arrange our house without regard to our personal tastes and desires, simply because it is the current fashion? It is certainly time that the spirit of independence should begin to characterize the domestic life of the civilized races.

Too often business necessity and social demands are permitted to crush out the family life. We have time for business engagements and social entertainments, but no time for husband and wife to devote to each other or to their children. Too often the home life is only a half-way house in the social struggle for recognition and preëminence. Parents not infrequently become strangers to each other; and in our great cities, among the social set, children (in families where they are to be found) become veritable strangers to their parents.

How long before otherwise intelligent men and women will dare to recognize the folly of false etiquette and the uselessness of the extreme demands of modern civilized society? Instead of running our children into the stereotyped social mould of life, why not encourage the development of the individuality and temperament of each child? And it is in this connection that our modern stereotyped methods of education become apparent. Why should children be compelled to pass through a routine system of education, and allowed to exercise their talents only in certain specified lines? Let us hope that the educational systems of the future will make provision for the individual growth and development of the child.

MORAL EMANCIPATION — THE SIMPLE LIFE FOR THE SOUL

The author's purpose in writing this book has been to afford a scientific foundation for the cultivation of faith and the elimination of fear It has been our aim to furnish a rational basis for the encouragement of faith and hope. We deplore every false and untrue method of generating faith; nevertheless we are bound to recognize that the average man would prefer a wild and baseless hope to the most scientific and approved form of "rational despair." After looking at the question from every possible standpoint, we are bound to conclude that man is incurably religious — his mental, moral, and spiritual life demands the consolation, the inspiration, and the restraint of religious faith. In our worthy efforts to satisfy this natural spiritual craving, the time has certainly come when we should begin to emancipate ourselves from slavery to the groundless beliefs and superstitious vagaries of past generations.

Modern civilization is cursed with the blight of selfishness. It stands in imminent danger of that social decay which inevitably follows upon the heels of self-seeking and industrial oppression.

We need to recognize the necessity for nourishing the moral nature and exercising the soul: the spiritual nutrition must not be neglected. Further, we are forced to recognize that the health of the soul is tremendously influenced by the bodily state, and *vice versa*.

Let us recognize that real moral freedom and genuine spiritual liberty in no wise lead to infidelity or atheism. Let us have a conscience void of offence toward God and toward man; and the author's advice to his every reader is — if you do not have a good religion, get one. If you have a religion and it has not so changed you as to effect your emancipation from fear and worry, then we would advise that you change your religion and get one that will.

APPENDIX

APPENDIX A

ANATOMY AND PHYSIOLOGY OF THE BRAIN AND NERVOUS SYSTEM

IT is highly essential in the study of mental hygiene, that one should have a practical knowledge of the form and function of the brain and nervous system.

THE HUMAN BRAIN

The human brain consists of three parts: The cerebrum or fore brain, the cerebellum or hind brain, and the medulla oblongata. The brain substance consists of the cell bodies of untold thousands of little nerve cells with their numerous nerve processes or fibres.

The brain is covered by three membranes known as meninges. One is a fibrous substance lining the interior of the skull and extending down and around the spinal cord. Inside of this is a loose meshwork of delicate fibres, the spiderweb membrane or arachnoid. The third or inner membrane consists of a thin delicate structure resting directly upon the brain substance. There is found a meshwork of small blood vessels within the inner membrane.

The weight of the adult brain is about fifty ounces. That is the weight of the male brain; the female brain weighs about six ounces less. The cerebrum or higher brain is divided into two hemispheres, each of which is further divided into numerous lobes. Each lobe is the seat of some special intellectual process, or the headquarters of some particular bodily function.

The brain is richly supplied with blood vessels and also contains many lymph channels. At the base of the brain, these blood vessels form a perfect circle, which allows of the free and even distribution of the blood and the equalization of its pressure.

The *cerebrum* is composed of gray matter and white matter.

The gray matter is found in two groups. That of the cortex or outside of the brain, and that found in the basal ganglia. The white matter of the brain consists of nerve fibres, while the gray matter is largely composed of nerve cells.

The *basal ganglia* are small collections of nerve matter at the base of the brain, which have to do with the regulation of many special functions. There are three great principal groups of basal ganglia. Three great groups of nerve fibres are also found in the cerebrum, which carry the messages to and from that important higher centre of the mind.

These basal ganglia serve as sort of middlemen, or private secretaries, to the brain centres. When certain physical acts, such as walking or writing, are frequently performed, the basal ganglia acquire the ability of carrying on these habitual movements without taxing the higher brain centres, it being only necessary to start the process by orders from the special mind centres. This accounts for the formation of many habits, both good and bad, and also explains why it is so difficult to break oneself of a habit when once it is formed.

The *pons varolii* is the bridge of brain matter which unites the various other parts of the brain, connecting the cerebrum with the cerebellum and the medulla oblongata.

The *cerebellum* is also composed of gray and white matter. It lies at the back part of the base of the skull, while the *medulla oblongata,* the lowest division of the brain, is in reality the top of the spinal cord. It forms the union of the spinal cord and the brain. The medulla is very properly placed at the top of the spine, for it is indeed the head and ruler of all the magnificent and marvellously adapted mechanism of the spinal nervous system. Any injury to this important centre would prove more surely fatal than to any other portion of the brain. The medulla literally holds the reins of life; it also acts in the role of intermediary between the brain centres above, and the spinal centres below.

FUNCTIONS OF THE BRAIN

The various centres of feeling and voluntary action are found on the outside and superficial portions of the brain. The centres of thought action are located over to the front,

APPENDIX

while the centres controlling muscular action are located toward the middle of the brain. The brain centres for the eye, ear, and nose are rather to the back and lower part.

The reader should not get the idea that there are certain minute circumscribed portions of the brain which are known to be connected with certain mental powers or physical movements. We possess no such exact knowledge respecting the brain centres; but physiologists do know in a general way the particular portions of the brain which are concerned in many definite mental and physical actions, such as writing, seeing, hearing, walking, talking, and word-remembering (See Fig. 1), and so it often occurs that in brain tumors and certain forms of epilepsy, the part of the body first to engage in the muscular contractions which immediately precede the convulsions, often indicates quite accurately the location of the tumor or other disturbance in the brain.

The nerves passing from the brain or going to it through the *spinal column*, are either sensory or motor nerves. The sensory nerves carry impressions from the skin, the muscles, the special organs of sense, and from various other parts of the body to the brain centres; while the motor nerves carry motor impulses from the brain to the muscles and various other organs.

THE SPINAL CORD

From the medulla oblongata, the spinal cord continues downward in the spinal canal of the backbone. It is about eighteen inches long, and is composed of gray matter and white matter, the gray matter being inside of the cord instead of on the outside as in the case of the brain. The spinal cord has three protecting membranes, the same as the brain, inflammation of which is known as spinal meningitis.

The white fibres of the spinal cord are gathered together into six clearly defined bundles on either side, each of which carries on a special work in the transmission of nerve impulses to and from the brain. The spinal nerves come out from the cord on each side and form thirty-one pairs. Each nerve arises from two roots, an anterior or motor root, and a posterior or sensory root, the latter having associated with it a special nerve mass or body called the *spinal ganglion*. In addition to these thirty-one pairs of nerves branching out from the spinal cord, it should be remembered that we have twelve pairs or sets of *cranial nerves* which originate in the brain. The special function of each, according to number, is as follows:

1. Olfactory — the nerve of smell.
2. Optic — the nerve of sight.
3. Motor Oculi — moves the eyeball.
4. Patheticus — moves the eyeball.
5. Tri-facial — the nerve of facial sensation and motion, sending branches to the tear duct and muscles of expression.
6. Abducens — moves the eyeball.
7. Facial nerve — the motor nerve of the face. It has a branch which is concerned in the sense of taste.
8. Auditory — the nerve of hearing.
9. Glossopharyngeal — associated largely with the sense of taste.
10. The pneumogastric — contains both motor and sensory fibres. Its branches are distributed to the coverings of the brain, to the ear, the pharynx, the voice-box, the heart, the lungs, the gullet, the stomach, and the liver. This nerve is also known as the vagus.
11. Spinal accessory — acts on the soft palate and certain muscles.
12. Hypoglossal — this nerve is notable in that it moves the tongue: it is the talking-nerve.

REFLEX ACTION

The nerves passing back and forth across the spinal column, connecting the various incoming and outgoing nerve-tracts, serve the purpose of creating a short-cut for the passage of nerve impulses. For instance, if one touches a hot stove unawares, the impressions of burning and danger do not have to pass to the higher centres in order to secure the instantaneous withdrawal of the hand. The sensation of pain in the finger is immediately flashed over the sensory nerves to the spinal cord, and here, by means of this cross-nervous connection, reflex action takes place. That is, the nerves passing to the muscles controlling the hand are immediately excited, and at once despatch the necessary orders to the proper muscles to withdraw the hand from danger. This constitutes reflex action, and practically all the muscles of the body have their reflex centres in the spinal column. (See Fig. 2.)

This explains how we can close the eye without thinking, when danger threatens. It is also by this reflex action that we cough to remove the mucus from the throat, sneeze to throw irritating substances out of the nose, and vomit to empty the stomach when nauseated.

Nerve impressions from the skin or other organs of special sensation may excite a muscle or group of muscles to action in different ways. The sensory impulses may pass up the spinal cord to the conscious sensory centres of the cerebrum over the *long circuit* and excite to action the conscious motor centres of the upper brain. (See Fig. 2.)

The majority of common and habitual nerve impressions do not travel this long circuit; they go by the automatic or *short circuit* to the basal ganglia where they are received, and where they set in motion the motor nerves going down from the brain to the muscles, just as effectually as if the inpulses had been carried to the conscious brain centres. (See Fig. 2.)

Again, we possess certain *natural reflexes,* reflexes associated with breathing and the circulation, whose sensory impulses are transferred to the motor nerves in the medulla. The cerebellum contains reflex centres which regulate posture and equilibrium.

Lastly, we have the involuntary spinal reflex centres previously mentioned. A study of the diagram (Fig. 2.) will make these various nerve paths perfectly plain.

Every muscle of the body is controlled by these lowly centres of the spine. Not a single muscle is directly controlled by the lofty motor cells of the upper brain. The spinal cord can truly say to the brain, "If you wish to move a hand or a foot, you must ask me to do it for you." "All right," answer the higher centres of the brain. "We recognize our dependence upon you, but see to it that you don't move hand or foot unless we tell you to." And so the orders come from the brain, while action proceeds from the spine.

THE NERVES

The nervous system is in reality a continuation or extension of the brain and spinal cord. Each pair of nerves branching out from the spinal cord is divided into an anterior and a posterior root, branches of which eventually encircle the entire body, extending out to the arms and hands, and down to the legs and feet. (See Fig. 3.) The entire nervous system — brain, spinal cord, and nerve branches — are all composed of certain little individual cells or nerve-units called neurons.

The *neuron* consists of a cell body and its processes or branches. Every neuron possesses one branch for transmitting outgoing impulses. This branch is called the axone, neuraxone, or neurite. Most neurons possess one or more branches which bring afferent impulses toward the cell body. These afferent branches are called dendrites. Sensory impressions received by the sensory nerve-endings in the skin are transmitted over afferent fibres to the cells in the posterior root ganglion of the spinal cord. Thence by way of the axonic branch into the spinal cord where they may be transmitted either to a spinal motor neuron to form the reflex arc, or transmitted through sensory tracts to the sensory centres of the brain. (See Fig. 3.)

It would thus appear that the nerve paths from any part of the body to the brain are not continuous. From no part of the body can nerve impressions passing through the spinal cord reach the brain over a continuous tract. Nerve impulses must ordinarily pass over from one to three different nerves in reaching the brain centres.

Nerve impressions are received and originated by the gray matter of the brain and spinal cord. All ganglia contain this gray matter, the cell-bodies of nerves, or neurons. These nerve cells have nuclei, and are held together by a sort of connective tissue which serves as a groundwork or bed, and is called *neuroglia*. In certain nervous diseases and toxic states of the blood this neuroglia tissue is irritated, whereupon it begins to contract down like scar tissue and squeezes the very life out of the nervous system, resulting in various nervous diseases, such as spinal sclerosis.

The white nerve fibres consist of two kinds. Those which are covered by a sheath, which serves as a sort of insulation, and which may be compared to the rubber or gutta-percha insulation of electric wires; and other fibres which are not thus insulated. All nerves are supplied with special blood vessels.

All up and down the spinal column, nerve branches cross back and forth between the various nerve tracts, while the great majority of all the nerve fibres cross from one side to the other as they are leaving the spinal column and entering the brain. This explains why a blood clot on the right side of the brain produces paralysis on the left side of the body.

Nerve impulses are carried back and forth, to and from the nerve centres, by currents of *neuricity*, a mysterious energy, which, in many respects, resembles electricity, and which can be measured and studied much the same as electrical currents. It probably is a form of electricity.

TRANSMISSION OF NERVE IMPULSES

Physiologists have devised ingenious instruments for measuring the rate of transmission of nerve impulses. Going up a sensory nerve to the brain, nerve impulses move about 180 feet a second, while coming down a motor nerve from the brain, the impulses travel only about 160 feet a second. While neuricity in many ways resembles electricity, they are very different in their rates of transmission, for in the time neuricity is moving less than 200 feet, an electrical current traverses a copper wire 180,000 miles.

This difference in the rate of transmission of what are thought to be identical forces, is partly explained by the fact that the electricity is travelling over an inanimate copper wire, while the neuricity or nerve impulse is travelling over a *live* thinking wire. That this is the case is clearly shown by the fact that when an incoming nerve impulse reaches a nerve centre, a marked and measurable delay occurs before the outgoing impulse is despatched from the centre. A physiologist has explained it thus:

"The advent of an afferent impression by the afferent nerve is a busy time for the centre, during which many processes, of which we have very little exact knowledge, are being carried on in it. It takes some time to deliberate what it will do. The shortest period of a reflex act has also been measured in a few simple reflex arcs, only to show that the delay at the centre exceeds in time both afferent inflow and efferent outflow. Hence, when several nerve centres have to adjust themselves to know what they are all to do about some afferent excitation, one centre sometimes inhibiting the others during the process, the final outcome may seem to be a very deliberate affair. Without knowing it, therefore, a man may have good physiology in his exclamation, 'If only I had stopped to think!'"

ENERGY GRANULES

When the healthy nerve is rested, as in the morning after a good night's sleep, the cell-body, under the microscope, is found filled with large numbers of small sand-like granules (Nisel's granules). These granules are believed to represent the energy accumulated during rest and sleep. As the nerve begins its day's work, and as the day wears on, these granules gradually disappear, until at night, when the body is fatigued and the brain is sleepy, the nerve cells are found to be practically free from these little granules, all their energy having been used up. (See Fig. 4.)

It would seem that the nerve cells during rest and sleep actually accumulate energy, and these little sand-like granules might fittingly be compared to a minute storage battery or to a chemical powder, the explosion of which generates waves of nerve or electrical energy, which flash over its branches, carrying the messages which the thinking part of the cell originates; for each little cell-body must be regarded as a small brain.

The fibril network of the cell is thought to be the cell's nervous system. (See Fig. 5.) The larger brain of the skull, and the great solar plexus of the abdomen, are merely vast collections of untold millions of these tiny nerve cells or brain bodies. The collecting together of their long branches and their arrangement in bundles or cables, creates the spinal cord, containing numerous separate bundles of nerves, part of which go up to the brain and part of which come down.

UNIV. OF
CALIFORNIA

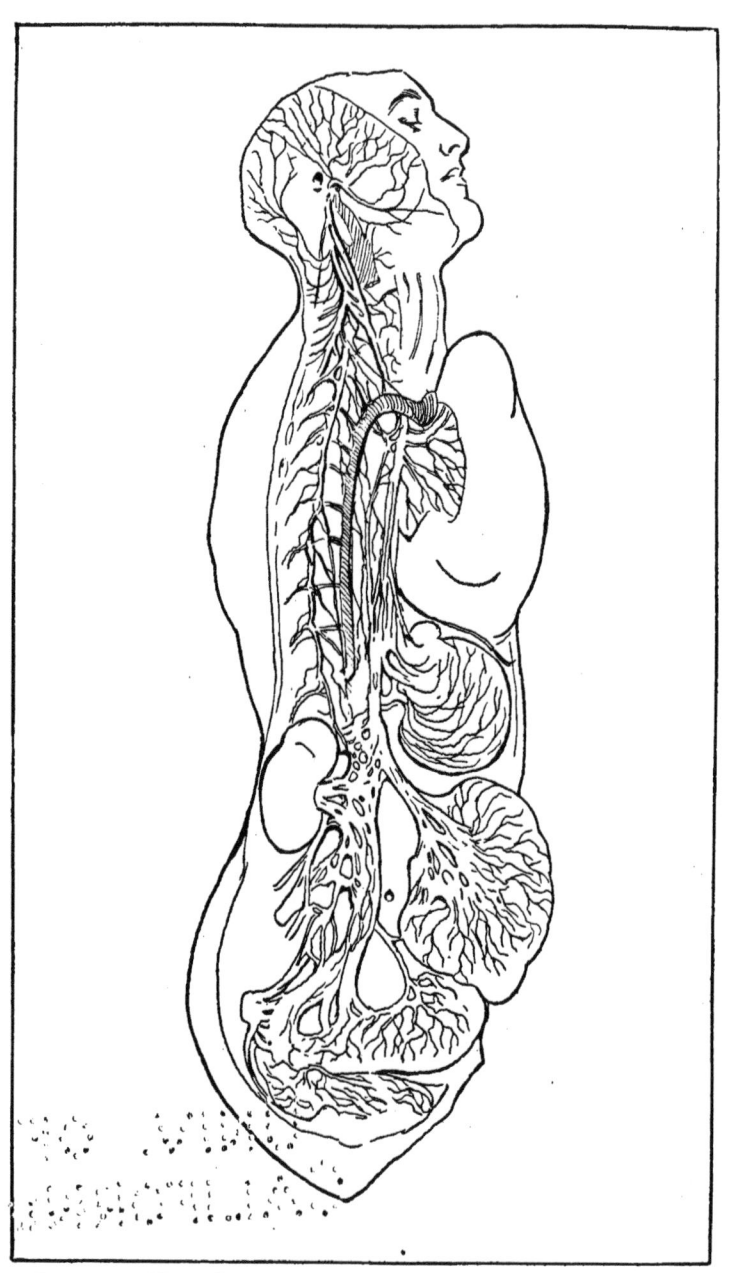

FIG. 6.— *The Sympathetic Nervous System.*

APPENDIX

THE SYMPATHETIC NERVOUS SYSTEM

While the nerves coming from the brain and spinal cord are more largely concerned with the body's sensations, muscular movements, and voluntary acts; all the vital processes of the body including breathing, the circulation of the blood, digestion, and elimination, are very largely regulated by the involuntary or sympathetic nervous system. This special system of nerves is formed by a double chain of nerve masses or ganglia which are connected together by intervening cords, and extend down on either side of the spinal column from a small point of origin near the base of the skull to near the end of the spine.

Branches from this system are found in all the ganglia connected with the voluntary or central nervous system.

Special collections of sympathetic nerve matter are found in various parts of the body, especially in the chest and pelvis and more notably in the abdomen, where is found the solar plexus, or abdominal brain. Similar nerve masses or ganglia of the sympathetic system are also found in the walls of all the internal organs.

The *solar plexus* is the greatest collection of nerve matter to be found in the body outside of the skull. It consists of a great network of nerves and ganglia and is found deep-seated in the abdomen in the region of the lower border of the stomach. It receives branches from the pneumogastric of the voluntary nervous system in addition to the sympathetic nerves, and distributes many fibres to all the vital organs of the abdomen. (See Fig. 6.)

These chains of sympathetic nerve ganglia on either side of the spine, and which extend down into the cavities of the chest and abdomen, are connected by cross branches, while throughout the body, the two nervous systems make numerous contacts, often by means of certain special relay stations, previously described under the term *ganglia*.

FUNCTION OF THE SYMPATHETIC SYSTEM

The sympathetic nervous system has its headquarters in the abdomen — in the "abdominal brain." The sympathetic nerves spread to every part of the body, especially to the so-called vital organs, which have to do with the maintenance and regulation of life. They control the heart, blood vessels, lungs, stomach, liver, kidneys, and bowels.

It is apparent that man has two brains — two nervous systems. He has two sources from which come orders to regulate and control the body; and it is well that this is so, for such an arrangement makes it quite impossible for human beings rashly to commit suicide by stopping the heart or ceasing to breathe.

You can stop breathing for a few seconds, but as soon as enough carbonic acid gas (CO_2) collects in the blood, the respiratory centres are excited, imperative orders to breathe are sent to the lungs, and you can no longer hold your breath. You may give orders to the heart to stop beating, but it will not obey. About seventy times a minute it receives the command of the cardiac nerve centres to beat, and in faithfulness it responds. Only within certain limits can you increase or decrease its beat, and then, as a rule, only by increasing or decreasing the necessity therefor.

The further wisdom of this dual nervous system is shown by the fact that the mind and muscle of man wear out from the day's work. Sleep is absolutely necessary to muscular recuperation, mental rest, and to enable the nerve cells to reassemble their disappearing energy granules. But while the man is asleep, the functions of heart and lungs, as well as the work of digestion and nutrition, must of necessity go on without interruption, and this is made possible by the fact that these organs of life and nutrition are largely under the control of the sympathetic nervous system, which neither slumbers nor sleeps from the cradle to the grave.

So a man may take his required rest and slumber on in unconscious sleep, but all the while the ever-watchful sentinels of the sympathetic nerve centres carry on the vital functions of the body without interruption — never the loss of a single heart-beat or the lapse of one respiratory cycle.

FUNCTION OF THE SPECIAL SENSES

The special functions of the body are carried on and regulated by the organs of special sense, special nervous mechanisms, such as those of the eye, ear, tongue, nose, and the sense of touch.

1. SIGHT. The camera, by the action of sunlight on silver salts, takes pictures in black, or shadow. The construction of the eye is somewhat after the fashion of the camera, except that the pictures of the eye appear in white, and every color of the object observed is actually reproduced. The pigment or paint for the coloring of objects on the retina of the eye is similar to that found in the bodies of the dead red blood corpuscles in the liver.

As the form and color of objects seen through the eye change, the pictures painted upon the retina must also be changed. It requires time for the invisible artist constantly painting these pictures, to change the outlines, and this explains why the projecting spokes of the rapidly revolving wheel present a solid appearance, and also why a bright object, when viewed for some time, can be seen for a moment after turning away from it. It takes time to efface the pictures upon the retina and produce others in their place.

By means of the nerves passing from the retina of the eye to the sight centre of the brain, all pictures appearing in the eye are reproduced in the brain. Modern science has achieved the wonderful feat of communicating a photograph by electricity over a wire for hundreds of miles, but this wonderful accomplishment has existed in the normal eye and mind since the dawn of creation. Another mystery about sight is that the objects seen actually appear on the retina of the eye upside down, and, yet, when transmitted to the sight centres of the brain, everything is suddenly and wonderfully reversed and appears right side up.

2. HEARING. The ear is a sort of trumpet-like expansion designed to collect sound waves. Immediately connected with the drum are found several little bones so arranged as to magnify the sound, somewhat after the fashion of the transmitting devices of the modern telephone. There is also a provision for decreasing the intensity of sound when too loud. The most wonderful part of the ear is the organ of Corti, which reproduces the sound for the recognition of the hearing centres. This wonderful little organ acts after the manner of the membrane in the transmitter of a telephone whose vibrations reproduce tones of varying intensity and complexity.

While asleep, the eyes of necessity are closed, but the ears are never closed. When sound asleep, the hearing is in function, but the hearing centres have been so trained that they will not respond to ordinary sounds that are heard during sleep. They are aroused only by the extraordinary or unusual. This fact probably explains the curious interweaving of certain sounds heard at night into the dreams.

3. SMELLING. The sense of smell has its end organs in the nose, and special centres in the brain. It is one of the most remarkable of the special senses. It is highly developed in many of the lower animals (as in the dog), but poorly developed in modern man. The nose seems to be able to recognize an almost unlimited number of odors; but while light waves, sound waves, and substances tasted, have been carefully classified, strange to say, no one has ever been able to classify odors. We usually describe what we smell by comparing it with something else. If the sense of smell were normal and the person smelling were healthy, in connection with the sense of taste, this special sense would probably serve as a fairly reliable guide to the selection of proper and wholesome food, and the avoidance of poisons and other dangers. The sense of smell is greatly injured by the use of snuff, by tobacco-smoking, and by constantly living in polluted atmospheres, or by the inhalation of air containing poisonous and irritating gases.

4. TASTE. The sense of taste is connected with the mouth and tongue, more largely the latter. We really have but four tastes: bitter, sweet, sour, and salty. Apparently we enjoy other tastes, but in reality we smell many of the substances which we think we taste. The enjoyment connected with the sense of taste, therefore, is largely dependent upon the sense of smell. For instance, when one eats an onion, he apparently tastes many flavors; but if one will hold his nose while eating the onion, or eat it when suffering from a very bad cold, it will be found to be almost tasteless. The sense of taste, inasmuch as it indirectly regulates digestion and nutrition, is one of the most important of all the special senses.

5. THE SENSE OF TOUCH. The sense of touch is located throughout the skin and is commonly made to include

the special senses of temperature, weight, and location. It consists of a vast network of nerves which end in the skin, and which are reflexly connected with the spinal centres which control the muscles. This sense is also connected with certain higher centres of recognition in the brain.

The function of the special senses connected with touch is constantly to report to the higher nerve centres the condition of the substance touched, with respect to temperature, danger, contact, and station.

APPENDIX B

A CASE OF CHRONOLOGICAL MEMORY

AT the time the following observations were made, the subject, Mr. C., was about thirty years of age. His general health was apparently good, and he had never passed through any severe illness. Four years before these observations Mr. C. had engaged in a scuffle with an armed man and was dealt a severe blow on the head with a gunstock. A short time after this accident he developed a typical case of Jacksonian epilepsy. Immediately after each attack the patient seemed to be in more or less of a dazed condition, during which time he would often engage in unusual and extraordinary escapades, even to the extent of going out on the streets at night and holding up pedestrians at the point of a revolver. As time passed these attacks of post-epileptic insanity grew more and more severe, and lasted for a longer period of time.

During these periods of mental aberration following his epileptic attacks, the patient would wander away from home, sometimes being absent from one to three days. It was during one of these periods, when he was aimlessly wandering about town, that he was picked up and brought to the institution, where the author was permitted to make the observations here recorded. The patient was at this time also under the observation of Dr. W. B. Holden.

Shortly after being placed in his bed and under guard, the patient began to talk in an apparently rational and chronological manner. His eyes seldom moved, his stare was fixed and concentrated straight ahead. It was soon apparent that he was relating a section of his life-experience in chronological order, day by day and hour by hour. All went well until he came down to the time in his life marked by the fight in which he was hit over the head with the gunstock, whereupon he was immediately seized with a paroxysm of convulsions of extraordinary strength and duration. It required four men to hold him in the bed at this time, or rather on the bed, for mattress and all were quickly precipitated to the floor. On recovering from this attack, Mr. C. was given employment in the institution. He held this position for almost two years, during which time he had a number of these attacks or seizures, and the author was present at no less than six distinct attacks, each lasting from two to three hours up to thirty-six hours. We will not undertake to report in detail all the observations made upon this remarkable case, but will give a few general conclusions respecting the chronological accuracy and relative infallibility of memory.

Immediately after a paroxysm of convulsions, this patient would begin to talk in a moderate tone of voice — somewhat of a monotone — concerning his life experience, his general thoughts and acts. He would begin with some Monday morning, by stretching his arms as on awakening in bed. He spoke very distinctly when expressing his leading thoughts, while he would quickly slur over numerous unimportant matters. At one time when under observation, it required him only twenty minutes to pass through a day's experience; and during this brief time he repeated aloud his chief thoughts and described or illustrated in abbreviated pantomine, his chief acts. He would sometimes move his hands during these narratives, but never undertook to leave the bed, lying quietly on his back and talking continuously. He would pass through a day's experience in from ten minutes to half an hour, apparently grow sleepy, and with but a few seconds of silence, which corresponded to the night's sleep, would awaken, yawn, stretch his arms upward, yawn again, and then would immediately begin the narration of another day's thoughts and actions.

There were certain exciting periods or experiences in his life, which, whenever he approached them in his chronological narration, would invariably precipitate a series of violent convulsions, during which he demonstrated very extraordinary physical prowess. After he had a number of these attacks in the institution, where he had become known to both nurses and physicians, great interest came to be manifested in this phenomenon of speech and thought reproduction, especially when the reproducer of his memory would accidentally strike his brain record at a point covered by his sojourn in the institution. It was at such times that he would repeat experiences that could be checked up by witnesses present. For instance, one day, when in a spell of this kind, he very accurately described going to the author's office, described a prolonged conversation with Dr. Holden, one of his medical attendants, as well as various experiences with nurses and others about the institution. In this way we were able very accurately to determine that his recital was truthful and chronological.

During one of his longer recitals he passed through three years and a half of his life, apparently relating all the leading thoughts and chief events. At another time he passed over a period of eleven days which were very thoroughly known to his attendants and observers, and his recital included every known conversation of this period, each of which was very fully, accurately, and chronologically repeated.

I remember of one day when he was about to describe an experience with me. I told this experience as best I could in advance of his narrative. In fifteen or twenty minutes he reached the experience I had just anticipated, and gave it just as accurately, filling in a number of details that had slipped my mind; but wherein the details of his story were different from those of mine, I was compelled to recognize that in each and every case he was right and I was wrong; and thus it was demonstrated that his memory in the trance state was far more reliable than my normal memory.

In another instance he related an experience where he had conducted some sort of religious service in which he had publicly read the fourteenth chapter of the Gospel of John. This chapter, verse by verse, was read from the vacant palm of his open hand which he held before his distant gaze. A Bible was quickly secured and it was found that he was following the text, making only those mistakes which might commonly be made — which he did in all probability make during the original reading. This public meeting, which he was now re-

APPENDIX 521

hearsing, had been held some six weeks previously. The author verified all these facts by finding that the meeting had been held, and that this was the very chapter he had read from the Bible. After he came out of this trance-like state, repeated tests and observations showed that he did not know a single verse of this chapter by heart. He could not repeat a single line of the chapter accurately. On numerous occasions he made quotations of poetry and bits of prose, which we afterwards discovered he had never committed to memory.

Not only would he be seized with a series of violent convulsive paroxysms when approaching certain peculiar events in his life's experience, but when these chronological recitals of his life history would extend down to the time of his last epileptic seizure, they would unfailingly precipitate another attack. His narrative would move along smoothly until it approached within a few minutes of the time represented by his last epileptic fit, whereupon he would begin to grow uneasy, talk in an indistinct and jumbled manner, saying that he was afraid he was going to have another "spell," and almost immediately he would pass into a series of convulsive seizures. This was so marked that his nurses came quite thoroughly to know just when these intercurrent seizures or fits would take place; knowing they would usually occur during the relation of certain experiences, and invariably so when his chronological recital was allowed to progress on to a point where it was brought to date — up to the time of the beginning of a given attack.

The more recent the experience which he recited, the more fully and completely were the details of thought and conversation reproduced. When describing his experience of fifteen years previous, it would sometimes require but three or four minutes to pass through a day of his life. It was very plain that he translated into words only those experiences of that day which stood out prominently — his leading thoughts and chief acts. Whereas, when this peculiar mechanism of memory would happen to strike a memory record of more recent times, it was found to be far more complete in detail, and on one occasion it required him one hour and a half to describe his thoughts and conversations of a single day; but irrespective of the detail of his narrations, they were invariably found to be *chronological.* As far as it was possible to check up his narrations, he was never observed to describe a thing out of its chronological order, either with reference to the occurrences of a single day or in narrating the experiences of a longer period of time, day by day.

In passing through an experience of this sort, ranging from a few hours to two days, he never slept, but talked incessantly. He would take no nourishment during this time, but would sit up in bed and drink from one to three glasses of water, his mouth becoming very dry. He would stop his talking only long enough to drink this water. The expression of his face was usually quite fixed, except on certain occasions, when his face would grow pale and an angry look would come across it; at other times his countenance would light up while he was describing some ridiculous experience or relating some humorous episode. After experiencing anywhere from two or three to twelve or fourteen of these intercurrent attacks of convulsions, he would come out of the entire attack in a sort of semi-conscious state, begin to look around the room, recognize persons present, and complain of a great sense of physical weariness and mental fatigue. He would usually go immediately to sleep, sleeping from eight to fifteen hours. On awakening he would dress himself, eat sparingly, and be non-communicative for from twenty-four to forty-eight hours, having a great desire to be by himself.

Careful inquiry showed that he possessed absolutely no memory of anything that had happened since the time of his seizure. He could always recall that his mind was feeling "queerly," as he described it, and that he was afraid he was going to have another "spell." None of his various depredations (in one of these conversations he described holding up six men in one evening, and four strange purses were found on his person) could be recalled to his mind. He was blissfully ignorant of all he had done and everything he had said. He knew of these things only by quizzing his nurses.

It was during one of these post-epileptic chronological recitals of his life experience that we secured the information that led us to suspect that it was the blow over the head with the gunstock that was responsible for his Jacksonian epilepsy. This led to the operation performed upon his skull at a point where the scar was found — the removal of a thickened piece of the bone-plate. Immediately after this operation his attacks became less frequent and less violent. After a thorough reformation of his habits of living — discarding tobacco, tea, and coffee, taking but little animal food — he entirely recovered from these attacks. One year after his operation he ceased to have them altogether, and now a number of years have passed and he has had no subsequent attacks. He holds a responsible position in a prominent business establishment. He has since married and has three healthy and normal children.

The observation and study of this case was enough thoroughly to satisfy the author with respect to a number of propositions in modern psychology. First, that the memory retains well-nigh everything which has passed through the state of consciousness; while the recollection or the power of recalling facts and experiences may be very imperfect and incomplete, all the incidents exist in the subconscious or marginal state, relatively perfect and complete. Second, that the mind possesses an inherent chronological sense; that its memories are grouped and stored in chronological order; that the marginal consciousness (subconscious mind) is in possession of all the memory-data of the mind and is able to recall and reproduce the same in logical and chronological order.

Careful study of this case could not but impress the observer that the human brain-memory is somewhat analogous to a phonograph cylinder, while the mind performs in the capacity of that power which operates, utilizes, reproduces, and otherwise manipulates those things recorded on the brain through the sensory receiving apparatus of the body.

APPENDIX C

MULTIPLE PERSONALITY

IN further explanation of the question of multiple personality mentioned in Chapter XXXV, the following case is abstracted from that remarkable work, "Multiple Personality," by Drs. Sidis and Goodhart.

The formation of many personalities, their dramatic play, their dissociation, new associations, interrelations, and sense of familiarity can possibly be best brought home to the reader by a concrete example from the vast domain of abnormal psychology. The following remarkable case, studied by Dr. Morton Prince of Boston for a number of years, will probably best illustrate the meaning of multiple personality.

"When Miss Beauchamp first came under observation she was a neurasthenic of a very severe type. She was a student in one of our colleges, and there received a very good education. But in consequence of her neurasthenic condition it was simply impossible for her to go on with her work. She was a wreck. In temperament she is a person of extreme idealism, with a very morbid New England conscientiousness, and a great deal of pride and reserve, so that she is very unwilling to expose herself or her life to anybody's scrutiny. She is a person of absolute honesty of thought and speech. I feel sure we can rely upon and trust her absolutely and completely. I have never known her, nor has any one, I believe, known her — as herself, or the person whom we call herself — in any way to indulge in any deception; nevertheless, every safeguard has been employed to guarantee the *bona-fide* character of the phenomena.

"Now she came to see me in this neurasthenic state, but I found treatment was of almost no use. The usual methods were employed, with no result, and it seemed as if her case was hopeless. Under treatment she went easily into the somnambulistic state. This somnambulistic state came later to be known as 'B. II.,' while the first personality with whom I became acquainted, Miss Beauchamp herself, was known as 'B. I.' Now I used to notice that as B. II. she was continually rubbing her eyes; her hands were in constant motion, always trying to get at her eyes. Still I paid very little attention to it, or placed very little significance in this fact, merely attributing it to nervousness.

"One day when I referred to something that she had said or done in a previous state, when I supposed she was B. II., she denied all knowledge of it and said it was not so. This surprised me, and I attributed the denial at first to an attempt at deception. The next time, she denied what she had previously admitted, and so it went on, denying and then admitting, until it dawned upon me that I was each time dealing with an entirely different personality; and this proved to be the case. It turned out that when she went into the state of which she later denied the facts, she was an entirely distinct and separate person. This third personality, which then developed, came to be known as 'B. III.' We had then three mental states — B. I., B. II., and B. III.

"B. I. knew nothing of the others. B. II. knew B. I., but no more. B. III. knew both B. I. and B. II.

"Now B. III. has proved to be one of the most interesting of all the personalities that have developed in the case. In one respect it is one of the most remarkable personalities, I think, that has ever been exhibited in any of the cases of multiple personality. B. III., like B. II., was constantly rubbing her eyes, so that I was frequently compelled to hold her hands by force to prevent her from doing so. When asked why she did this, she said she wished to get her eyes open, and it turned out afterwards that it was she who was rubbing the eyes of B. II. in the earlier times. At this time I prevented B. III. from opening her eyes for the reason that I feared that, if she got her eyes open and was thereby able to add the visual images of her surroundings to her mental state as B. III., these same images of her surroundings which she would also have, of course, when she was B. I., would by force of the association awaken all her mental associations as B. III., and that, in consequence, B. III. would be constantly coming into existence of her own accord.

"This afterward proved to be the case. B. III. always insisted upon having her eyes opened, complaining that she wished to see, and had a 'right to see.' One day, sometime after this, while she was at home, owing to some nervous excitement, she was thrown into the condition of B. III., and then, as I was not there to prevent it, she rubbed her eyes until she got them open, and from that time to this, she (B. III.) has had a spontaneous and independent existence.

"This personality dates her whole independent existence from this day, and she always refers to events as being 'before' or 'after' she got her eyes open Now this personality came afterward to be known as Sally Beauchamp. She took the name for fun one day, and by that name she has been known ever since. In character she differs very remarkably from B. I. B. I. is a very serious-minded person, fond of books and study, of a religious turn of mind, and possesses a very morbid conscientiousness; she has a great sense of responsibility in life. Sally, on the other hand, is full of fun, does not worry about anything; all life is one great joke to her; she hates books, loves fun and amusement, does not like serious things, hates church — in fact, is thoroughly childlike in every way. She is a child of nature. She is not as well educated as is Miss Beauchamp, although she reads and writes English well; yet she complains constantly that she cannot express herself easily in writing.

"She cannot read French or any of the foreign languages which Miss Beauchamp knows, and she cannot write shorthand; in short, she lacks a great many of the educational accomplishments which the other character possesses. She insists, although of this I have no absolute proof, that she never sleeps, and that she is always awake while Miss Beauchamp is asleep. I believe it to be true. Then Miss B. is a neurasthenic; Sally is perfectly well. She is never fatigued and never suffers pain.

"During the first year Sally and Miss Beauchamp used to come and go, alternating with one another. At first whenever B. I. became fatigued or upset from any cause, Sally was likely to come, the periods during which the latter was in existence lasting from a few minutes to several hours. Later, these periods became prolonged to several days. It must not be forgotten that though Miss Beauchamp knows nothing of Sally, Sally, when not in the flesh, is conscious of all Miss Beauchamp's thoughts and doings, and the latter could hide nothing from her.

"Curiously enough Sally took an intense dislike to B. I. She actually hated her. She used to say to me, 'Why, I hate her, Dr. Prince!' and there was no length to which Sally would not go to cause her annoyance. She would play every kind of prank upon her to make her miserable. She tormented her to a degree almost incredible. While Sally would never do anything to make any one else unhappy, she was absolutely remorseless in the way she tormented Miss Beauchamp by practical jokes and by playing upon her sensibilities. I will give a few illustrations: If there is one thing which Miss Beauchamp has a perfect horror of, it is snakes and spiders. They throw her into a condition of terror. One day Sally went out into the country and collected some snakes and spiders and put them into a little box. She brought them home and did them up in a little package, and addressed them to Miss Beauchamp, and when B. I. opened the package, they ran out and about the room and nearly sent her into fits. In order to get rid of them she had to handle them, which added to her terror. Another joke was to take Miss Beauchamp out into the country when she was very tired, and in an unfit condition to walk; that is, Sally would take a car and go out six or seven miles into the country to some retired place, and there wake up Miss Beauchamp, who would find herself far out in the country with no means of getting home, no money in her pocket, and nothing for it but to walk. She had to beg rides when she could from passing wagons, and came back tired, worn out, used up for a week.

"A great friend of Miss Beauchamp, to whom she was

under strong obligations, had asked her to knit a baby's blanket. She worked on that blanket for nearly a year; as soon as it would be near completion, Sally would unravel it, and she would have to begin the task again, only to have Sally pull the whole thing to pieces again. Finally, she came to herself one day and found herself standing in the middle of the room tied up in a perfect network and snarl of worsted yarn; the yarn was wound round the pictures and then round and round the furniture, the bed, the chairs, obliging her to cut it to get out of the snarl. Another favorite joke of Sally's was to make Miss Beauchamp lie. She had the power when she pleased, of producing aboulia, and also of making B. I. say and do things against her will; for after a fashion she can get control of her arms and legs, and also of her tongue.

"Sally made her tell most frightful fibs. For instance, when asked who lived in a small squalid little house at the edge of the road, she said 'Mrs. J. G.,' a very prominent lady in society, and very wealthy. 'Why, I thought she was rich!' 'Oh, yes, but she has lost all her money now.' Miss Beauchamp would be mortified at hearing herself tell these astounding barefaced fibs, which her listener must know were fibs, but she could not help it. Again, for a time at least, Sally put B. I. on an allowance of five cents a day. She would find the money waiting for her in the morning on the table with a note saying that it was her allowance for the day and she could not spend more. Sally took away her postage-stamps, and if Miss Beauchamp wrote a letter it had first to be exhibited to Sally, and if Sally approved it, it was posted; if not, it did not go, and that was the end of it.

"Miss Beauchamp is a person with a great sense of dignity, and dislikes anything that smacks of a lack of decorum or of familiarity. Sally had a way of punishing her by making her sit on a chair with her feet upon the mantelpiece. B. I. could not take her feet down, and was mortified to think she had to sit that way. Sally carries on a correspondence with Miss Beauchamp, writes letters to her pointing out all the weak points of her character, dwelling on all the little slips and foibles of her mind, telling her all the reckless acts and secret thoughts, indeed, everything she has done that would not bear criticism. In fact, when she has a chance to stick a pin into her, she does it. When Miss Beauchamp wakes in the morning, she may find pinned on the wall of the room verses containing all sorts of personal allusions, letters calling her names, telling fictitious things that people have said about her, in short, doing everything imaginable to make her life miserable. Nevertheless, at times when she has gone too far, Sally has got frightened, and then she would write me a letter and ask for help, saying that she 'could not do anything with Miss Beauchamp,' and I really must help her.

"Although B. I. knows nothing of Sally, Sally not only is conscious of Miss Beauchamp's thoughts at the moment they arise, but she is capable, as I have said, of controlling her thoughts and her arms and legs and tongue to a certain extent. Sally can produce positive and negative hallucinations in B. I. and frequently does so for a practical joke. During the times when Sally is in existence, B. I. is, as Sally puts it, 'dead,' and these times represent complete gaps in Miss Beauchamp's memory, so that she has no knowledge of them whatever. 'What becomes of her?' Sally frequently asks. Sally is never 'dead.' Her memory is continuous; there are no gaps in it. She not only knows — simultaneously, as I said — all of B. I.'s thoughts and emotions and sensations, but more than that, Sally's thoughts are entirely distinct from and independent of B. I.'s thoughts, with which they are coexistent, but not identical. B. I.'s thoughts are not Sally's thoughts. Sally's thoughts coexist alongside of and simultaneously with B. I.'s; but Sally's mental life is made up of entirely different and separate thoughts and feelings from B. I.'s, so that Sally will have a train of thought and at the same time with B. I., of an entirely different nature. All this is also true of the relation of Sally's mind to the personality B. IV., who came later, excepting that Sally does not know B. IV.'s thoughts. While either B. I. or IV. is thinking and feeling one thing — is depressed and self-reproachful, for example — Sally is feeling gay and indifferent and enjoying Miss B.'s discomfiture and perhaps planning some amusement distasteful to her."

APPENDIX D

MENTAL *DIAGNOSIS* BY THE REACTION METHOD

THE following experiments, designed to point out the influence of the mental states upon conduct in speech, were conducted by Henke and Eddy, under the direction of the *D*epartment of Psychology in Northwestern University, and are here reported at the author's request, for the purpose of further explaining and demonstrating the methods of psychoanalysis, and mental diagnosis by association of ideas, and the reaction method, mentioned in Chapter XXXV. (The complete report of this work is published in the "Psychological Review," of March, 1910.)

EXPERIMENT I

Material: a dark room, in one corner are a child's desk, upon which is a volume of "Christmas Carols," a bottle of red ink, pen, paper, and Jastrow's volume on "The Subconscious." A hammer is tied to a gas fixture over the desk. In the opposite corner of the room is a table on which is a crushed hat covered with cobwebs. There are two subjects in the experiment. (Typewritten instructions are supplied to these subjects.)

The method of carrying out the experiment was as follows:

1. Only one of the two subjects is to enter the room. He is given the typewritten instructions. He is to sit at the desk and read certain pages from the child's book.

2. He is to write the first page of "The night before Christmas."

3. He is to pick up the other book, Jastrow's book, note the author, title, etc.

4. He is to untie the hammer from the gas fixture and examine it carefully.

5. He reads from the typewritten page: "This is the oldest

building on the campus. It is constructed entirely of wood; in the basement is a carpenter shop, well-filled with lumber, shavings, oil, etc. It is a veritable fire-trap. The building is heavily insured because of the danger from fire. The upper floor has been practically abandoned. Fire might break out at any moment. Employ the next five minutes in devising a scheme for escape from this building, in case of fire. At the end of five minutes a signal will be given.

6. " Behind you is a door. Near this is a rope fifty feet long — long enough, in other words, to reach from the window to the ground.

7. " When you go from this room, do not talk to any one about these directions or the contents of the room."

8. One of the two men is now taken to the lecture room and tested before a class of forty students, by the Association Reaction Method. A list of thirty-eight words has been prepared. Fourteen of these words are irrelevant, twenty-four are relevant; that is, they suggest the contents of the room, etc. One of the fourteen irrelevant words first named is suggested to the student and he is asked to utter the first word which is suggested by it as quickly as possible. The time which passes between the uttering of the word and the subject's respouse is measured. The remainder of the first fourteen words are employed in like manner. The average of the first fourteen intervals gives the subject's normal association time. We then proceed to utter to him the remaining words in turn. The association time is measured as in the other case. This subject is dismissed from the room and the other of the two first named is brought in. He is tested likewise.

At the end of this test the association times, as measured from the first student, are compared with the association times as measured in the case of the second student. The entire class, after this comparison, was unanimous in the belief that the first student tested had been in the room described above, and that he was making an attempt to conceal his having been there; that the other student had been there also but that he was making no attempt to conceal it. The basis of their judgment was the length of his association time. In all of these cases in which the subject was confronted with a relevant word, his association time was long, if he was trying to conceal his having been in the room. Otherwise, it was the normal time as determined by the first fourteen reactions.

EXPERIMENT II

There are three subjects in this experiment. The two subjects of the previous experiment are excluded. The room, as described above, is also employed in this experiment. Its purpose is to determine who of the three subjects had been in the room, and was trying to conceal his having been there; who had been there, but was not trying to conceal it; and who had not been there at all, and did not know anything at all about the room or its contents. These subjects were brought before the same class in turn, and tested by use of the same set of words described in connection with the first experiment; and the class before whom the test was made, was called upon to decide the questions indicated above. The conclusion of the class was not unanimously in accordance with the facts; but the majority hit upon the fellow who had been there and the one who had not been there.

EXPERIMENT III

In this experiment two subjects were employed. The room and its contents have nothing to do with the situation. The following was substituted therefor:

In a drawer of a table in the laboratory there were placed three bottles of ink — one red, one green, one violet; two pieces of glass — one red and one blue; a one-pound iron weight, one handkerchief scented with asafœtida, a copy of "The Psychology of Advertising," and a copy of "The Native Tribes of Central Australia." The instructions contained in the drawer of the table were as follows:

1. "Take up the book 'Psychology of Advertising.' Who is its author? Read the advertisement on page 34.

2. "There are three bottles of ink in this drawer. Notice their colors. Are the bottles full or empty?

3. "Take up the book on 'The Native Tribes of Central Australia.' How many pages are in this book? Turn to page 33, and notice the picture of the old man, also notice the picture of the winsome lass on page 47."

a. Both of the subjects of this experiment might enter the room and perform the series of acts according to the instructions.

b. Either might do so.

c. Neither might do so.

4. After deciding upon *a*, *b*, or *c*, and following the directions, they were allowed to conceal or not to conceal their having examined the contents of the drawer. A new list of words was prepared, the first fourteen successive words being irrelevant, the remainder being relevant.

Next, the association time of these subjects was determined as in the other experiments; and again, the judgment of the class was correct. Both had been in the room and had followed the directions contained in the table drawer. One had tried to conceal it, the other had not tried to conceal it. As a general conclusion of these tests, it may be said that the situation might easily be made so complex as to make a correct judgment, upon the question raised in the experiment, impossible. It should also be said that in the last experiment the class was not unanimous in its judgment, but a substantial majority made a correct report.

NOTE: Another series of experiments of the same kind, in which the situation was more simple than that in any of the cases described, were performed at Vassar College. Out of fifty-three cases there were fifty-two correct judgments made by a class of thirty or forty students.

INDEX

A

"Abdominal brain" (see solar plexus).
Abrams, *Dr.*, on the "blues," 383.
Absent-mindedness, theory of, 411.
"Absent treatment" and telepathy, 463.
Abstraction, a part of conception, 44, 53.
Accidents, to the brain, 17; in relation to psychotheraphy, 307; in relation to worry, 367.
Acidity of the blood and the mind, 27.
Acromegaly, 184.
Act of breathing, the, 190.
Actions, ancestors of habit, 51; voluntary and involuntary, 51; defined, 54; and reflection, 451.
Acute, disorders and the mind, 12; infections and mental disturbances, 31; diseases and the mind, 149, 306; disease, defined, 293.
Adenoids, influence on the mind, 32.
Adrenalin, 183.

Adulterated foods and adulterated thoughts, 29.
Affections, as influenced by faith and fear, 99; the, and blood-pressure, 136; effect on nutrition, 177.
Affirmation, the crowning act of thought, 50; defined, 54.
Affliction, source of, 323.
"After images," experiments regarding, 245.
Age, in relation to brain centres, 17; a factor in worry, 364.
Air, fresh, and the intellect, 22.
Alarm, in relation to fear, 108.
Alcohol, and brain action, 17; effects of, on mind, 28; effects on blood-pressure, 29, 133, 136, 282; and the vital resistance, 147; in relation to worry, 351.
Alcoholism and mind-cure, 307.
Alexander the Great and magicians, 79.
Allbutt, *Dr.*, on granular kidney, 159.
Almanacs, ancient, 85.
Altruistic work, hygienic value of, 437.

Anæmia, effects on the mind, 28; relative, 145; cured by the mind, 145; result of disappointment, 182; psychic prevention of, 269.

Anatomy of the brain, xi, 505; of the nervous system, xiii; of the neuron, xiii; of the sympathetic nerves, xiv.

Ancient error and superstition, 5; views of the mind, 15; health delusions, 79; medical superstitions, examples, 80; physician-priests, 311.

Angels, as healers, 81.

Anger, in relation to metabolism, 30; and the fear life, 109; effects of, on blood-pressure, 134; produces body poisons, 146; effect on secretions, 146; cause of biliousness, 157; effects on digestion, 166; the curse of, 326; acute, 390; physiology of, 391; augmented by gesticulation, 447; results of, 496.

Angina pectoris and the emotions, 117.

Angioneurotic œdema and the mental state, 127, 215.

Animal, heat, influence of mind on, 273; passions, influenced by prayer, 478.

Animals, why free from dyspepsia, 27; reasoning of, 49; psychology of, 350; why they do not worry, 351; relaxation of, 398.

Anti-bodies and antitoxins, 147;

Antitoxin, 147; in diphtheria, 267.

Apollo, the god of healing, 79.

Apoplexy and blood-pressure, 128, 132; and heart failure, 141, 268; and brain diseases, 227.

Appendicitis and fear, 129; mistaken suggestion of, 435.

Appetite, as concerned in gastric secretion, 9; a factor in digestion, 162; juice, the, 165; in nutrition, 179.

Army, health of, and the mental state, 150.

Art of living easy, the, 379.

Arterial tension, significance of, 132.

Arteriosclerosis, effects on mind, 32; and the mental state, 123; and cheerfulness, 268.

Ascites, caused by fear, 126.

Assimilation in relation to mental action, 29; crippled by the mental state, 176; process of, 176.

Association of ideas, 47, 53; as influenced by faith and fear, 98; in mental diagnosis, 417; by suggestion, 429.

Associative memories, in relation to worry, 409.

Assurance and the faith life, 108; of faith, the, 328.

Asthma and hay fever, 194; cured by suggestion, 195;

mechanism of, 196; psychic prevention of, 272.
Astrology in health and disease, 84, 86; examples of, 85; and healing, 101; a superstition, 458.
Astronomy and medicine, 84.
Atmospheric purity and temperature, 23.
Attention, state of, 40; defined, 40, 52; a factor in worry, 357; and the physical functions, 382.
Auditory nerve, deceptive excitation of, 244.
Autointoxication and the mind, 27; and mental sluggishness, 29.
Automatic nerve reflexes, xii; writing and talking, 462.
Automatism, purposes of, 412, 413.
Auto-suggestion and health books, 296; hygienic, 301; Paul on, 328; or positive thinking, 372; a factor in prayer, 477; adverse in prayer, 482.

B

Baby, the, a cure for worry, 379.
Babylonians, views of the intellect, 15; and astrology, 84.
Backache, from nervous tension, 393.
Baldness, from nerve strain, 214, 234.

Balzac, walking mania, 285.
Baptisms, freedom from colds, 150.
Barbers, as surgeons, 89.
Barker, Dr., on reëducation, 445.
Basal ganglia, functions of, xi, 506.
Baths, influence on the mind, 30; reaction influenced by the mind, 124; in connection with psychotherapy, 263; in the treatment of worry, 383.
Beggar, blind, healing of, 324.
Belief, contrasted with faith, 316.
Bernheim, Dr., on psychic cure of aphonia, 272.
Bible, the, on faith and fear, 321; on anger and anxiety, 326; on worry, 327; on suggestion, 327; on psychic and physical treatment, 331; on spiritualism, 467.
Bile, regulation of flow, 7.
Biliousness, 9; and the brain, 27; caused by anger, 157.
Biologic instinct, 71.
Birthmarks, psychic element in, 278; and the mother's fear, 279.
Bismuth, in X-ray experiments, 167.
Bladder, mental factor in action of, 159; memory action of, 410.
Blindness, hysteric, cured by faith, 245.

Blisters, psychic origin of, 215.
Blood, state of, in relation to the mind, 27; the, and the brain, 28; letting, a discarded practice, 89; movement of, 125; cells, and the mental state, 143; cells, white, 144; poisons, 145; supply, local, and the mind, 211; cells, psychic conservation of, 269.
Blood-pressure, in relation to sleep, xv; and the chemical messengers, 8; and brain action, 28; effects of faith and fear on, 122; modified by psychic influences, 131, 268; determination of, 131; significance of, 132; case of ex-convict, 133; and the emotions, 134; and nervous prostration, 134; and the affections, 136; and religion, 137; an indication of sincerity, 138; psychic regulation of, 138; mechanism of, 140; and adrenalin, 183; a factor in intemperance, 282; influenced by prayer, 477.
"Blues," the, and shadow breathing, 24, 186; the cause of, 383.
Blushing, psychic element in, 128; mechanism of, 212.
Bodily functions and mental control, 12; state, influence of, on the mind, 21; exercise, and the mental state, 25; disease, and the mind, 31; weight, and the mental state, 31; states and the emotions, 41; defences, how influenced, 144; weight, mental factors in, 180; carriage, and the mind, 200.
Body, the, as a controlling force, 10; the, and the will, 59; and the marginal consciousness, 68; as influenced by faith and fear, 99; stamped with the tone of the mind, 148; temperature, thermo-electric, 217; influence of prayer on, 478; in relation to the soul, 488; the simple life for, 495.
Boils, caused by worry, 214.
Bondage of ignorance, the 5; imaginary chains of, 360; of civilization, 493.
Bones, in relation to blood-making, 329.
Bouchard, on body poisons, 145.
Bowels, inactivity of, and mental depression, 9; as the seat of emotions, 15; action of on mind, 169; muscular movements of, 205.
Brain, the, represents highest bodily development, xi; citadel of will, xi; home of spiritual emotions, xi; the human, xi, 505; anatomical divisions, xi; anatomy of, xi; centres, xi, 507; storm, how prevented, xiv; as re-

lated to thought, xv; in relation mind, 4; the organ of mind, 4; seat of mind's authority, 11; only recently associated with mind, 15; mind, and personality, 15; does not secrete thought, 16; action, compared to stomach action, 16; relation to personality, 16; does not originate speech, 16; centres, for talking, 16; functions of the two hemispheres, 16; purpose of inactive half, 16; centres, in relation to age, 17; servant of mind, 17; does not think, 17; and mind, 17; size of, 18; of man and monkey compared, 18; changed by education, 18; action, retarded by foul air, 22; action, and breathing, 24; and biliousness, 27; and the blood, 28; internal bath of, 29; starvation in anæmia, 30; action and elimination, 30; disorders and bodily diseases, 31; as controlled by the will, 58; effects of mental state on, 220; circulation of, 220; rest, determined by psychic state, 222; fatigue, and the mind, 223; fag, caused by worry, 224; storm, caused by fear, 224; energy, increased by optimism, 224; strength in relation to mental state, 225; endurance, increased by joy, 226; diseases, and apoplexy, 227; psychic element in health of, 273; storms, theory of, 412; fag, fatigue of, 419; physiology of, 505; functions of, 506.
Brains, the two, 16.
Breathing and brain action, 23, 24; and the "blues," 24; and endurance, 24; muscular work of, 59; influence of, on oxidation, 178; influence of mind on, 186; deep and shallow, 186; deep, a dyspepsia cure, 187; the act of, 190; tracings of, 196; nervous mechanism of, 196; in relation to the mind, 271; in the treatment of worry, 383; and moral depression, 495.
Bright's disease and blood-pressure, 132.
Bromides, effect on blood-pressure, 133.
Bronchitis and the mental state, 123, 126.
Bunions, influence on mind, 25.
Business, psychic element, in, 283.

C

Cancer, ancient cures for, 87; death from fear of, 148; in relation to fear, 182.
Capacity for work, 204.
Capillary contraction and the mental state, 123, 126.
Carbon dioxid, a respiratory regulator, 186; output, effect of mind on, 188.

Cardiac rhythm, the, 115; nutrition, and the emotions, 117; endurance, 117; nerve-centres, 118; psychic response, 119; nervous mechanism, 120; action, psychic influence on, 268; disorders, functional and organic, 291; disorders, in relation to psychotherapy, 302.
Care, destructive influence of, 359.
Carnal nature, warfare with spiritual, 487.
Carriage, physical, and the mind, 200.
Cat, digestion experiments on, 166; experiments on bowel action, 171; mental state of, and digestion, 205; -mewing mania, 317.
Catalepsy, psychology of, 461.
Catarrh, in relation to the mental state, 123.
Cathartic, action modified by suggestion, 171.
Cells, man a community of, 6; chemical interrelationship of, 7; intercommunication by nerves, 8; their nerve supply, 19, 174; intelligence of, 71; nutrition of, 173; oxidation in, 178.
Central consciousness, the, 65; defined, 67; compared with the marginal, 73.
Centres, of the brain, xi; of speech and word-memory, 18.

Cerebellum, the, xi, 506.
Cerebrum, the, xi, 505.
Certainty, and the faith life, 108.
Chaldeans and astrology, 84.
"Change of life," false notions of, 397.
Character, modified by habits, 18; defined, 54, 60; and conscience, 60; development and fear, 99; development and the mind, 280; transformation of, 281; transformation by prayer, 479.
Charms, in relation to healing, 100; deception of, 457.
Cheerfulness and sunshine, 22; and the faith life, 108; resists disease, 149; effects on nutrition, 174; effects on expression, 203; a beautifier, 209; and heart action, 268; a fatigue preventer, 269; and deep breathing, 272; prevents stoop-shoulders, 272; normalizes the feelings, 273; a therapeutic agent, 328.
"Cheering up," effects on patient, 181; a cure for worry, 378.
Chemical, messengers of the blood, 7; juice, the, 165.
Chemistry, an illustration of healing laws, 106.
Chest development and the mind, 24; the, 188.
Child culture and fear, 99; psychology of, 276; the pre-

INDEX

natal psychic influence on, 278.

Children, stunted by foul air, 22; confusion of imagination in, 42; effects of fear on, 99, 276; fear of darkness, 277; fear of noises, 277; suggestion in early life, 279; habit formation in, 341; worries of, 364; a cause of worry, 366; fear of storms, 376; a cure of worry, 379; suggestibility of, 427; suggestive cure of "bumps," 430; suggestible when asleep, 432; nagging of, 499; stereotyped training of, 500.

Chills, produced by fear, 124; psychic influence on, 216.

Choice, the final act of thinking, 50; effects of faith and fear on, 98.

Choking, from fright, 206.

Cholera, imaginary, 149, 170; pseudo, from fright, 206.

Chorea, psychic causes of, 203.

Christ, as a healer, 322; teaching of, regarding fear, 324; faith teachings of, 324; teachings on worry, 327; healings of, limited by faith, 330; our grief-bearer, 333; heals the infirm woman, 360.

Christian experience, why unsatisfactory, 316.

Christian Science, and healing, 103: cure, of habit-cough, 193; mission of, 256, 257; attitude toward, 257; sectarian aspect of, 262; secret of success, 300; views of trouble, 401; theory of disease, 430; philosophy of, 471; how it works, 472.

Christianity, in relation to blood-pressure, 139; and mental cures, 284; a transcendent psychic force, 316; versus theology, 317; a system of reckoning, 334; a worry cure, 380; and mental science, 468; the highest psychotherapy, 484; prophylactic value of, 485.

Chronic disease and the mind, 12, 149; defined, 293.

"Church sleep," of the early Christians, 81.

Cigarettes and social strain, 499.

Circulation, the, as a unifying influence, 7; and deep breathing, 24; and the emotions, 41; influence of mind on, 122; and skin reaction, 124; equilibrium, experiments on, 127; and the skin, 210; psychic element in, 268; diseases of, functional and organic, 291; disorders of, in relation to psychotherapy, 302; effects on the emotions, 447.

Civilization, fear a factor in, 401; the bondage of, 493; in relation to anxiety and worry, 494.

Clairvoyance and healing, 102; a psychic fake, 459.

Classification, a part of conception, 44, 53.

Climate in relation to psychotherapy, 263.

Clothing, fashionable, effects on mind, 25.

Cloudiness and the mental state, 22.

Cocaine and blood-pressure, 29; and capillary contraction, 123; and social strain, 499.

Co-conscious mind, (see marginal consciousness.)

Coffee, effects on the nerves, 28; and capillary contraction, 123.

Cold hands and feet, psychic causes, 126; sensation of, and the mind, 216.

Colds, and the mental state, 123; following funerals, 150; psychic prevention of, 216.

Comets, a cause of worry, 354.

Community, the, simple life for, 497.

Comparative summary of the Bible on faith and fear, 335.

Comparison, a part of conception, 44, 53; of central and marginal consciousnesses, 73.

"Complex formation," theory of, 409; psychic results of, 410.

Complexes, independent action of, 415; conserved in the marginal consciousness, 428.

Conception, process of, 44; defined, 44, 53; effects of fear on, 96.

Concepts, defined, 45, 53.

Conclusion of the whole matter, 248.

Condiments, effects of, 28.

Confessional, psychic value of, 315.

Confidence, and the faith life, 108.

Congestion and the mind, 123, 125, 128; local, mental factor in, 126; experiment illustrating, 127; prevented by cheerfulness, 268.

Conjurors and mumblers, 84.

Conscience, defined, 54, 61; and character, 60; voice of, 64, 65, 69; in relation to health, 318; clear, a worry cure, 380.

Conscientiousness and the faith life, 109.

Conscious mind, the, 66; compared with the subconscious, 74.

Consciousness, motor discharge of, 19; the state of attention, 40; defined, 40, 52; the central, 65; the marginal, 66; marginal in health and disease, 67; the three phases of, 69; the spiritual, 69, 70; the intellectual, 70; the physical, 71; in automatic writing, 462.

Constipation, effects of, on the mind, 29, 30; and the mental state, 169, 170; and nutrition, 176; induced by the mental state, 205.
Consumption, and chest-development, 189.
Contagious diseases and the mind, 148; in relation to psychotherapy, 306.
Contentment, value of, 379.
Conventionality, slavery to, 494.
Conversion, religious, 417; an apparent case of, 479.
Convulsions and epilepsy, 236.
"Cool-headedness," need of, 345.
Coöperation of cells, 7.
Coördination, muscular and nervous, 395.
Cough habit, 192; psychic prevention of, 272.
Coughing, psychic, 191; suggestive, experiments in, 191; nervous, 344.
Counting, obsession, the, 343.
Courage, and the faith life, 109; effects on muscular action, 198.
Cowardice and the fear life, 109.
Cowards, nervous, 454.
Cretin, illustration of body's power over mind, 32.
Cretinism, 183.
Crime, in relation to hypnotism, 421; in relation to metabolism, 30.

Crowd, psychology of, 286.
Crystal-gazing, psychology of, 460.
Cure of worry, 371.
Cures, the work and study, 421.
Cutaneous action and the mind, 211; sensation, and eruptions, 215.

D

Daily sweat, value of, 25.
Darkness, child's fear of, 277.
D'Arsonval galvanometer, experiments on, 201.
Darwin, on plant feeling, 71.
Dawn of scientific healing, 253.
Daydreaming, use and abuse of, 451.
Dead bodies, overcoming fear of, 374.
Death, caused by fright, 119; caused by worry, 148; rate, the, 151; rate, psychic factor in, 270; the fear of, 428.
Deep breathing and brain action, 24; and shallow, 186, 271; in cure of invalidism, 204.
Defeat, effects on health, 150.
Delusions, 39; ancient health, 79; origin of, 95; result of fear, 226; in relation to sight, 244.
Demonology and temple sleep, 81; in relation to healing, 101.
Dendrites, the, xiii.

*D*epression, relieved by exercise, 25.
De Quincey, on opium, 445.
*D*espair, religious cure of, 485.
*D*espondency, due to toxins, 8; from defective elimination, 9; and sunlight, 22; and shallow breathing, 24; and metabolism, 29.; and the fear life, 108; effects on nutrition, 174; cured by prayer, 181; cured by deep breathing, 187; perverted prayer in, 482.
*D*etermination, and the faith life, 109.
*D*evil-chasing mania, 317.
*D*iagnosis, in relation to pathology, 260; mental, by reaction method, 530.
*D*iagram of psychology, key to, 52.
*D*iarrhœa, caused by fear, 170, 171; caused by fright, 205.
*D*iet and mental efficiency, 27; in relation to intemperance, 28; in relation to psychotherapy, 263; newspaper influence on, 365; in relation to spirituality, 488.
*D*ifficulties, minimizing, 376.
*D*igestion, an illustration of thinking, 4; influence upon the mind, 26; and sleep, 26; mental factors in, 161; strength of, 162; improved by diversion, 163; slow, 167; worry, or nervous dyspepsia, 167; and nutrition, 175; psychic influence on, 270; disorders, functional and organic, 291; disorders, in relation to psychotherapy, 303.
*D*ilatation of the heart, psychic, 119.
*D*ipsomania, moral mastery of, 319.
*D*iscounting fear and sensation, 375.
*D*isease, determined by fixed laws, 6; due to mental causes, 12; and the mind, 31; caused by unhealthy emotions, 42; in relation to marginal consciousness, 67; and superstitution, 78; in relation to demons, 81; and Providence, 84; faith and fear in, 99, 148, 249; the soil of, 149; prevention of, 258; methods of investigating, 259; resistance of, the mind in, 269; psychology of, 289; acute and chronic, 291; acute and chronic, defined, 293; philosophy of, 294; defined, 294; the language of, 244; psychic element in, 300; cause and cure of, 300; the denial of, 300; a result of sin, 318; as a cause of sin, 318; the Bible on, 321; mental origin of, 364; influenced by dreams and imagination, 408; in relation to " complex formation," 410; morbid contemplation of, 432.

INDEX 545

Diseased mind and false difficulties, 43; imagination, dangers of, 43; imagination, defined, 96.

Diseases, how they influence the mind, 21; imaginary, 43, 47, 50; functional and organic, 289; functional and organic, compared, 291; miscellaneous, 293; curable by psychic influences, 301, 302; of the circulation in relation to the mind, 302; incurable by psychic influences, 303; partially curable by psychic influences, 303; mental and nervous, in relation to the mind, 304; respiratory, and the mind, 305; metabolic, and the mind, 305; miscellaneous, and the mind, 305; contagious and infectious, in relation to the mind, 306; of civilization and savagery, 494.

Dislocation of ideas, 407.

Disposition, influenced by digestion, 26.

Dissatisfaction and the fear life, 108; versus discontent, 285.

Dissociation of ideas, 411; in nervous shock, 419; of ideas, by suggestion, 429; in mediums, 466.

Divine healing, sectarian aspects of, 262; sustenance, 331; healing, a field for fakers, 457; mind, and telepathy, 465.

Divorces, psychology of, 282.

Doctors, neglect of mental medicine, 313; relation to healing movements, 315.

Dogs, Pawlow's, 165, 167.

Domestic trouble and blood-pressure, 136; emancipation, 499.

Double function of one mind, 72.

Doubts, damnation of, 333; disease-producing, 485.

Dowieism and demonology, 467.

Dowie's method of healing, 106; philosophy of disease and healing, 432.

Dreams, suggestive, 408; a cause of psychic disturbances, 408; "fixed," theory of, 412; books, a superstition, 460.

Drink, in relation to blood-pressure, 136; cures, fraudulent, 319.

Drinking at meals and worry, 156.

Dropsy, caused by fear, 126, 147.

Drowsiness, explanation of, xv.

Drugs, effects on blood-pressure, 133; in medical practice, 254; future use of, 259; habits, psychic factor in, 281; habits, the mind in overcoming, 282; a delusion in

Drugs — *continued*
worry, 381; effects on consciousness, 445.
Drunkenness and psychotherapy, 307, 319.
Dual nature of one mind, 66.
Dubois, on false hydrophobia, 202; on reëducation of the will, 419.
Ductless glands, the, 182, 271.
Dynamometer tests, modified by the mind, 199.
Dyspepsia and mental vigor, 30; mental origin of, 162; cured by sociability, 163; quick lunch, 163; psychic, 163; nervous, 167; cured by psychic fads, 176; cured by deep breathing, 187; mental prevention of, 270; made worse by contemplation, 448.
Dyspeptic grouch, the, 26.

E

Eating, in relation to thinking, 26, 27; between meals, why harmful, 28.
Economy of habit, the, 340.
Eddy, Mrs., her spiritistic revolt, 257; philosophy of disease and healing, 430.
Education, of inactive brain centres, 17; results in physical brain changes, 18; and the judgment, 49; evils of stereotyped, 500.
Effect of the mind on the brain, 220; of mind on the nervous system, 229; of the emotions on the nerves, 229.
Electrical belts, cures due to suggestion, 431.
Electrical-reaction area, 213.
Electricity and suggestion in insomnia, 438.
Electropaths, mission of, 255.
Electrotherapy, in connection with psychotherapy, 263.
Elephant, illustration of imaginary bondage, 360.
Elimination and brain action, 30; skin, and the mind, 211.
Emancipated life, the, 493.
Emancipation of medical practice, 253.
Emmanuel movement, dangers of, 314; in relation to hypnotism, 470.
Emotional response of the heart, 118; energy, 413; "trauma," 414.
Emotions, as influenced by drugs, 17; and images, 40; defined, 41, 53; physical origin of, 41; distorted, a cause of disease, 42; as influenced by faith and fear, 95; effect on the heart, 113; effect on blood-pressure, 134; poisons of, 146; effect on urinary flow, 159; effect on digestion, 161; effect on intestines, 166; effect on the nervous system, 229; fearful, effects of, 267; a factor in suggestion, 317; necessity of control, 375; revival of,

407; form psychological ruts, 414; religious power of, 414, 422; distinguished from ideas, 445; dangers from strong, 446; conventional, 446; the control of, 446; physical reactions of, 446; result of uncontrolled, 447.

Empiricism in medicine, 253.

Endurance, effect of mind on, 198.

Energy, granules of the neuron, xiii, 512; relation to sleep, xv; restored by rest, 30; discharged by fear, 223; leakage, 344.

Enteroptosis, in relation to the mind, 207; prevented by cheerfulness, 272.

Enthusiasm and the faith life, 109.

Environment, in relation to consciousness, 75; psychic element in, 276; effects on character, 280; harmonizing with, 400.

Enzymes, action of, 167.

Epidemics, psychology of, 296.

Epilepsy, ancient cure of, 80; psychic origin of, 236; a case of, demonstrating memory, 409, 518.

Equilibrium, centre of, xiii.

Errors, ancient, and mental healing, 5; of vision, 38; effects on mental action, 41; defined, 52.

Eruptions, skin, psychic origin of, 215.

Evolution, 10; of modern psychology, 25; of psychic into physical diseases, 295.

Examples of ancient medical superstition, 80; of astrology, 85.

Excitement and the blood-pressure, 134; needless, 395.

Excretions, as chemical messengers, 7.

Exercise and mental activity, 25; and mental depression, 495.

Exhaustion, psychic cure of, 273.

Expression, muscles of, 203; psychic element in, 247.

Extravagant tension, 393.

Eye, as related to sight, 17; strain, effects on mind, 33; inaccuracies of function, 38; diseases, ancient cure for, 80; strain, from nervous tension, 393.

F

Fads, therapeutic message of, 255; health, a cause of worry, 365; psychic value of, 383; psychic, 457.

Faith, psychology of, 92; defined, 92; influence on the mind, 93; modifies sensations, 93, 95; in relation to mental mastication, 95; action on imagination, 96; action on phantasy, 96; effects on mental digestion, 96; in relation to idea-association,

Faith — *continued*
98; effect on higher mental powers, 98; in relation to character, 99; in health and disease, 99; a health promoter, 99, 106; healing, as a cure, 102; the master key to mental healing, 106, 107; healing, principles of, 107; life, factors in, 107; effects on heart action, 114; effects on the circulation, 122, 268; effects on blood-pressure, 131; psychologic and theologic, 140; effects on vital resistance, 143; effects on antitoxins, 147; resists infection, 148, 150; effects on healing, 149; on secreting glands, 153; on digestion, 161; on bowels, 170; on metabolism, 173; secret of healing, 176; effects on assimilation, 177; on the ductless glands, 183; on respiration, 186; on muscular action, 198; on strength, 199; on skin action, 209; on heat regulation, 209; on elimination, 211; on sensation, 215; on brain, 220; on nervous system, 229; on special senses, 241; a beautifier, 248; summary of effects, 249; delivers from hereditary bondage, 281; an aid to temperance, 282; in the family life, 283; an antitoxin for fear, 286; a vital energy, 315; greater definition of, 316; the Bible on, 321; the liberty of, 324; the essential of life, 324; assurance of, 328; reward of, 329; essential to psychic healing, 330; material aids to, 331; the philosophy of Christianity, 334; Biblical comparison with fear, 335; false, compared to morphine, 382; essential to suggestion, 427.

Fakes, psychic, 457.

False sympathy and selfishness, 394.

Family trouble and blood-pressure, 136; and intemperance, 282; life, psychology of, 282; life, crushed by society, 500.

Fanaticism, religious, 363.

Fashion, the fear of, 342; slavery to, 494.

Fatigue, due to toxins, 8; in relation to mind and body, 9; in relation to the will, 59; muscular, and fear, 199; decreased by faith, 200; museular, of psychic origin, 201; produced by fear, 223; of fear, the, 296; psychology of, 297; of work and worry, 297; state, the, 392; suggestive, 392; treated by indifference, 392; and the emotions, 414; states, treatment of, 418; physiological, theory of, 418; psychic, theory of, 418; psychic-pathological, theory of, 419; of neurasthenia, 419.

Fear, Mosso on its bodily reactions, 19; psychology of, 92; defined, 92; influence on the mind 93; modifies sensations, 93, 95; in relation to mental mastication, 95; effects on imagination, 96; on phantasy 96; on mental digestion, 96; on memory, 97; on idea-association, 98; on higher mental powers, 98; a mental plight, 98; in relation to character, 99; action on children, 99; a universal mental disease, 99; in health and disease, 99; a disease producer, 106; life, factors in, 107; a vital depressant, 114; effects on heart action, 114; on circulation, 122, 268; on blood-pressure, 131; in an ex-convict, 133; effects on vital resistance, 143; produces subtle poisons, 146; effects on antibodies, 147; on infection, 148; on healing, 149; on the secretory glands, 153; on digestion, 161; on the bowels, 170; on metabolism, 173; on assimilation, 177; on ductless glands, 183; on respiration, 186; on muscular action, 198; on strength, 199; acute, diverse effects of, 205; effects on skin action, 209; on heat regulation, 209; on elimination, 211; on sensation, 215; on brain, 220; on nervous system, 229; on special senses, 241; a beauty destroyer, 248; summary of effects, 249; psychic deliverance from, 261; effects on body, 267; a factor in plague mortality, 270; influence on children, 276, 279; of darkness, by children, 277; deliverance from, in infancy, 277; in relation to birthmarks, 279; condemns to hereditary bondage, 281; disguised as forethought, 281; in the family life, 283; a psychic disease, 286; a psychic contagion, 295, 296; the fatigue of, 296; the casting-out of, 297; conquered by faith, 298; the Bible on, 321; the bondage of, 323; the reward of, 329; the torment of, 330; the spirit of, 332; the sword of, 333; the blight of, 333; a factor in worry, 357; replace with faith, 373; the ancestor of worry, 374; discounting, 375; of insanity, 297; as a religion, 401; a factor in civilization, 401; associative memories of, 407; in relation to dreams, 408; Prof. Mosso on, 433.

Feelings, as influenced by drugs, 17; defined, 39, 52; psychic nature of, 94; indicated on galvanometer, 201;

psychic element of, 245; "tone," accompanying ideas, 413.
Fetishes, 104.
Fevers and brain disorders, 31; wrong treatment of, 89; influenced by emotions, 217; psychic factor in, 273.
Fibril network of nerve cells, xiv.
Fictitious sensations, 39; troubles, 43; worries, 361.
Fidgety state, the, 389.
Fiery foods and fiery thoughts, 28.
"Fits," psychic origin of, 236.
Flat chest and frail minds, 24.
Flaubert, on imaginary taste, 242.
Flesh, mortification of, 489.
Fogs, depressing effects of, 22.
Food, digestion of, illustration of thinking, 16; combination and the mind, 28; effects of irritating, 28.
Forethought, in contrast with fear thought, 350.
Forgetfulness, theory of, 411.
Fortune-telling, a psychic fraud, 459.
Fractures and mind cures, 308.
Frend, Prof., on psycho-neuroses, 415.
Fresh air and the intellect, 22.
Fretting, destructive influence of, 359.
Fright, nervous exhaustion of, 419; illustration of physical effects, 433.

Function of brain hemispheres, 16; of special senses, 514.
Functional diseases, from mental causes, 12; defined, 289; the special field of psychotherapy, 290, 301; compared with organic, 291; evolution into organic, 295; in relation to "complex formation," 410; helped by prayer, 480.

G

Gait, physical, and the mind, 200.
Galvanometer, fatigue experiments on, 201.
Games, in treatment of worry, 383.
Ganglia, the spinal, xii, 508; of the sympathetic, xiv; basal, work of, 506.
Gastric juice, and the emotions, 161; quality of, 162.
Gault, Prof., on optical suggestion, 245.
Germs, in relation to faith and fear, 149.
"Getting on the nerves," 393.
Giantism, 184.
Gift of tongues, the, 463.
Gladstone, on worry, 381.
Glands, secretory, and the mind, 153; the ductless, 182.
Glandular secretion and the mind, 11.
God as a healer, 321; sustenance of, 331.
Goethe, on psycho-prophylaxis, 269.

INDEX

Goitre, exopthalmic, and anxiety, 116; effects of mental state on, 183.
Golden rule, the life of, 383.
Good-Samaritan work, 383; a cure of despondency, 436.
Gormandizing and mental action, 29.
Gospel of relaxation, the, 397; of reckoning, 488.
Gout, ancient cure for, 80.
Grant, Gen., headache cured by Lee's surrender, 435.
Grave's disease and anxiety, 116.
Gray hair, produced by fear, 214; Metchnikoff's theory of, 234.
Greeks, healing delusions of, 81.
Grief, and the fear life, 108; and the circulation, 123; and blood-pressure, 138; effect on nutrition, 174, 175; paralyzing effects of, 182; spiritual, 485.

H

"Habit sensation," origin of, 95; cough, 192; the chronic kicking, 354; bondage, power of, 361; fatigue, in neurasthenia, 389; the happiness, 401.
Habits, in relation to the nerves, 18; how formed, 51; power of, 51; defined, 54, 340; and the subconscious mind, 66, 68; effect on galvanometer tests, 202; our master, 280; physiology and psychology of, 338; nervous mechanism of, 338; formation of, 339; of thinking, how formed, 340; sensory factors in, 340; economy and tyranny of, 340; in children, 341; automatic, in cure of nervous, 345; nervous rhythm of, 346; can they be changed? 347; how they master us, 413; basal ganglia, as concerned in, 506.
Hair, destroyed by worry, 148; discolored by fear, 214.
Hallucinations, 39; origin of, 95; result of fear, 226; in relation to hearing, 244.
"Hand-squeeze" power, lessened by fear, 199.
Happiness and the faith life, 108; promotes nervous economy, 223; psychology of, 285; hunger for, a cause of worry, 351; the habit of, 401.
Hardening of the arteries, effect on the mind, 32.
Harmonizing with environment, 400.
Harp, compared to the brain, 16.
Hate, conquered by love, 298.
Hatred, and the fear life, 108.
Hay-fever and asthma, 194; cured by suggestion, 195; excited by a wax rose, 411.
Headache, from deficient elimination, 9; from the stom-

Headache — *continued*
ach, 26; from intestinal disorders, 29; from disorders of the nose and eye, 32; ancient cure for, 80; and blood-pressure, 132; powders, 133; suggestive cure of, 434.

Healing, in relation to relics, 82; not an evidence of divinity, 90; faith, principles of, 107; not an evidence of righteousness, 107; power, the, 149; dependent on faith, 176; dawn of scientific, 253; promoted by cheerfulness, 269; movements, in relation to doctor and minister, 314; the Bible on, 322; faith essential to, 330; cults, suggestion in, 430; methods of non-drug, 440; cults, rapid spread of, 441; fakes and frauds, 457; magnetic, a fraud, 463.

Health, determined by fixed laws, 6; safeguarded by mind, 11; and disease, in relation to the mind, 21; promoted by sunlight, 22; ideas, conflict with disease thoughts, 48; and faulty judgment, 49; in relation to the marginal consciousness, 67; in relation to superstition, 78; delusions, ancient, 79; delusions, later, 87; faith and fear in, 99, 249; defined, 294; the affirmation of, 300; and disease, the Bible on, 321; divine source of, 322; in relation to worry, 364; fads, a cause of worry, 365; improvements, cures worry, 382; influenced by dreams and imagination, 408; influenced by emotions, 414; in relation to suggestion, 432; in relation to righteousness, 490.

Hearing, how aroused, 37; an illustration of psychic operations, 66; psychic element in, 243; sense of, 515.

Heart, supposed seat of soul, 15; diseases, and the mind, 31; how affected by emotions, 113, 115, 116; strength, and the emotions, 114; failure, and suggestion, 114; rate, 115; rest, 116; nutrition of, 117; endurance of, 117; failure, prevented by faith, 118; diseases, and worry, 118; emotional response of, 118; psychic response of, 119; psychic dilatation of, 119; nervous mechanism of, 120; sensations referred to, 120; as concerned in blood-pressure, 141; failure, and apoplexy, 141; failure, psychic prevention of, 268; diseases functional and organic, 291; diseases, in relation to psychotherapy, 302.

Heat, regulation, influence of mind on, 209; stroke, and the

mental state, 213; sense of, and the mind, 216; regulation, process of, 216; psychic control of, 273; stroke, conditions in, 308.
Heaviness, physical effects of, 329.
Hebrew priests and sanitation, 312.
Hemispheres of brain, function of, 16.
Hemorrhages and the mind, 308.
Hereditary knowledge, 47.
Heredity, in relation to consciousness, 75; psychic element in, 276, 277; influence of mother's mind on, 278; laws of, 280.
Hiccoughing and yawning, 193; control of, 195.
High living, in relation to intemperance and morals, 28; blood-pressure, significance of, 132; pressure living, 268.
Higher mental powers, in relation to faith and fear, 98.
Hindoo magician, performance photographed, 458.
Hobgoblins, effect on children, 276.
Hodge, Dr., on fatigue, 296.
Holiday, half, beneficial to the mind, 31; improves metabolism, 180; a worry cure, 380.
Holy Spirit, the, and telepathy, 465.
Home, the simple life for, 499.

Homeopathy, mission of, 254; sectarian role of, 262.
Honey-bees, fatigue experiments on, 296.
Hoodoos, a form of worry, 359.
Hope, health-giving, 485.
Hopefulness and the faith life, 108.
"Hormones," defined, 7; role of, 158; modified by fear, 146; a factor in nutrition, 173.
Horses, experiments on telepathy, 463.
Household, cares and worry, 366; diseases, 495; keeping, useless burdens of, 499.
How the mind is influenced by bodily states, 21; we think, psychology, 35.
Howard, Major, on suggestion and pain, 434.
Human brain, the, xi.
Hunger, significance of, 19; a factor in digestion, 161.
Hurry, needless, 395; chronic habit of, 346.
Hydropaths, mission of, 255.
Hydrophobia, imaginary, 149, 202, 227.
Hydrotherapy, mission of, 255; in connection with psychotherapy, 263.
Hygiene and psychotherapy, psychic dangers of, 296; in relation to prayer, 484.
Hypnotism, relation to consciousness, 69, 74, 75; and

Hypnotism —*continued*
  healing, 101; suggestion in, not ideal, 373; a false worry cure, 381, 382; a failure in nervousness, 402; recall of lost memories in, 412; value of, in psychoanalysis, 416; a failure in reëducation, 420, 451; erroneous ideas concerning, 421; unnecessary to suggestion, 430; in relation to crystal-gazing, 460; its place in psychotherapy, 469; the morals of, 470; the psychology of, 470; compared with mesmerism, 470; suppression of public exhibitions, 471; weakens the will, 477.
Hypochondria, a state of mind, 226; caused by worry, 362.
Hypochondriac, the, 389.
Hyslop, Dr., on therapeutics of prayer, 478.
Hysteria, theory of, 235, 411; and the marginal consciousness, 235; caused by worry, 362; deformities of, from dissociation, 412.
Hysteric, the, 389.
Hysterical contractures, case of, 203.

I

Ice bag, in weak heart, 117.
Idea association, by suggestion, 429.
Idea discrimination, 48; defined, 54.
Ideas, how originated, xv; illegitimate, 45; association of, 47; defined, 48, 54; false, deception by, 406; dislocation of, 407; dissociation of, 411; conserved in the marginal consciousness, 428; and emotions, control of, 445.
Identity, how maintained, 15.
Ignorance, the bondage of, 5; and ancient medicine, 35; diseases of, 485.
Illusions, optical, 38; origin of, 95.
Images, and emotions, 40; true and false, 41; defined, 52.
Imaginary diseases, and difficulties, 43, 47, 50; and faulty judgment, 49; reality of, 231; cures, status of, 283; bondage, chains of, 360.
Imagination, and opium, 17; and phantasy, 42; functions of, 42; defined, 53; action of faith and fear on, 96; diseased, defined, 96; in relation to disease, 269; the climate of the soul, 285; and suggestion, 408.
Immorality, and high living, 28; a cause of worry, 362; diseases of, 485.
Impress of mind upon matter, 19.
Impression, a factor in memory, 46, 53.

INDEX

Inaccuracies of thinking, the, 38.

Indigestion, and mental rigor, 30; mental origin of, 163; and the mental state, 176; psychic prevention of, 270.

Individual, the unity of, 6.

Industrial causes of worry, 367.

Infancy, the habit-forming period, 339.

Infections, acute, and brain disorders, 31; and fever, 148, 149; diseases, in relation to psychotherapy, 307.

Infirmity, the spirit of, 360.

Inflammations and the mental state, 123, 128.

Influence, the physical diseases in the mind, 21; of faith and fear on the mind, 93; of mind on the circulation, 122; on vital resistance, 143; on respiration, 186; on skin and heat regulation, 209; on special senses, 241.

Insane, ignorant treatment of, 6; treatment of, 88.

Insanity, and superstition, 88; and heart disorders, 118; and blood-pressure, 132; physical improvement in, 182; in relation to consciousness, 235; resulting from psychic shock, 408; increase of, 497.

Insomnia, from deficient elimination, 9; and blood-pressure, 132; suggestion in, 372, 438; relieved by relaxation, 398; a cause of neurastheia, 440.

Insomniac, the, 389.

Instinct, significance of, 19; animal, 47; voice of, 71.

Intellect, seat of, 15; relation to brain and personality, 16; and right-handedness, 16; builder of personality, 17; and disease, 21; and fresh air, 22; destroyed by dyspepsia, 30.

Intellectual, centres of brain, xi; operations, in relation to consciousness, 68; consciousness, the, 70; consciousness, and the nerves, 72.

Intelligence, relation to brain, size, 18; universal, and telepathy, 464.

Intemperance, and diet, 28; psychic factor in, 281; and blood-pressure, 282.

Internal glands, secretions of, 32.

Intestinal fermentation and the mind, 26; and mental sluggishness, 29; action on the emotions, 166; effects on mind, 169.

Intestines, muscular movements of, 205.

Intoxication, relation to psychotherapy, 307.

Introspection, a cause of disease, 486.

Intuition, defined, 47, 54; relation to consciousness, 75.

Invalidism, cured by deep breathing, 204; chronic, 355.
Investigating disease, methods of, 259.
Involuntary spinal reflexes, xiii.
Irregular practitioners of medicine, 440.
Isaiah, on mind and health, 322; on poultices, 331.
Itching, psychic origin of, 215.
Itch-mite and mind cure, 308.

J

Jacksonian epilepsy, demonstrating memory, 409, 518.
Jacob, experiments of, on suggestion, 328.
James, on faith, 324.
James, Prof., on impress of mind on matter, 19; on cure of worry, 383; on therapeutics of prayer, 478.
Jaundice, 9; caused by fright, 157.
Jews, health practices of, 312.
Job, sufferings of, 323; his psychology, 330.
John, on faith, 324.
Johnson, Samuel, obsession of, 285.
Joy, and heart action, 114; effect on expression, 203; on the mind, 226; the secret of, 496.
Judgment and reason, 49; defined, 49, 54; as influenced by faith and fear, 98.

K

Key to diagram of psychology, 52.
Kicking, habit, chronic, 354; posts, an obsession, 342.
Kidney, inaction and depression, 9; action, and the mind, 30; mental factor in secretion of, 159; granular, caused by anxiety, 159.
Kidneys, as the abode of the intellect, 15.
"Kings' evil" (see scrofula).

L

Labor, difficulties, and worry, 367.
Laboratory, modern psychological, 35; in the study of disease, 260.
Lacethin of urine, influenced by mind, 240.
Lachrymal gland and the emotions, 154.
Language of disease, the, 294.
Laughter, a worry cure, 379.
Lee, Annie, spasms of, 285.
Legal regulation of psychic frauds, 457.
Lehmann's experiments on telepathy, 463.
Lencocytosis, and the mental state, 144.
Liberty of faith, the, 324.
Life, not controlled by physical laws, only, 10; failures, from indigestion, 26; the emancipated, 493.

INDEX

Light, recognition of, 65; an illustration of psychic operations, 65.
Lighting of schools and work rooms, 23.
Lincoln, on trouble, 376; melancholia of, 285.
Linement, reputation depending on suggestion, 435.
Liquor cures, fraudulent, 319.
Liver, regulation of secretions, 7; as the seat of the intellect, 15; congestion of, and the "blues," 24; a poison destroyer, 27; action, and the mind, 30; and the pancreas, 157.
Living, easy, the art of, 379.
Local congestion, and the mind, 126; blood supply, and the mind, 211.
Lockjaw, imaginary, 149; false, 202, 206.
Loss of memory, from indigestion, 27; theory of, 412; and fear of insanity, 447; of sleep, worry over, 448.
Lourdes water and suggestion, 439.
Love, and the faith life, 108; influence on nutrition, 177; the gospel of, 401.
Low blood-pressure and nervous prostration, 134.
Lunacy, delusion of, 108.
Lung disorders and the mind, 31; effects on the mind, 188; strength and capacity, 189.
Luxury, effects of, 497.
Lymph stream, the, 146.
Lymphacytosis, influenced by mental state, 147.

M

Macrophages, perverted action of, 144.
Magicians, as healers, 79.
Magnetic healing, 102; a fraud, 463.
Magnetism, personal, and suggestion, 430.
Malaria, and brain disorders, 31.
Malicious animal magnetism and telepathy, 463.
Malnutrition, cured by psychic fads, 176.
Mammary secretion, the, 158; psychic influence on, 271.
Man, a community of cells, 6; made in God's image, 10; mind of, compared to monkey, 18; why he cannot eat like animals, 27; a three-fold being, 41, 71; a reasoning animal, 49; defined, 52; a religious animal, 69; the worry animal, 351; a suggestible animal, 417; an outdoor animal, 495; incurably religious, 500.
Manias, forms of, 431.
Marginal consciousness, the, 66; defined, 66; in health and disease, 67; preferred to subconscious mind, 67; and

Marginal consciousness — *con.* the body, 68; compared with the central consciousness, 73; and hysteria, 235; latent ideas in, 416; tyranny of, 428; a creature of suggestion, 429; in relation to happiness, 429; unused energy of, 432; effects of drugs on, 445; in trances and catalepsy, 461.; and mediums, 466.

Massotherapy in connection with psychotherapy, 263.

Mastication, an aid to the mind, 29.

Materia medica, in relation to psychotherapy, 264.

Material aids to faith, 331.

Materialism, recent reaction against, 21, 257.

Matter, as influenced by mind, 4; as impressed by mind, 19.

Maudsley, *Dr.*, on effects of fear, 148.

Mediæval medical schools, 83.

Medical superstition, ancient, 79, 80; schools, mediæval, 83; errors, 88; superstition, modern, 90; student, experiment on, 129; practice, emancipation of, 253; authority, decline of, 254; students, suggestive diseases of, 365.

Medicinal therapy and the doctor, 259.

Medicine, ancient, 35; men, 100; schools of, and suggestion, 430.

Mediums, controlled by personal beliefs, 461; honest and dishonest, 466; and dissociation of complexes, 466.

Medulla oblongata, the, xi, 506; relation to vital work, 60.

Melancholia, caused by indoor living, 23; and astrology, 86.

Memory, affected by dyspepsia poisons, 27; loss of, from autointoxication, 29; child confuses with imagination, 43; powers of, 45; defined, 46, 53; in relation to false diseases, 47; demoralized by fear, 97; theory of the loss of, 145; associative, in relation to worry, 350, 409; sometimes a mischief-maker, 407; demonstrated in a case of epilepsy, 409; physiological, and complex formation, 410; failure of, from dissociation, 412; loss of, and fear of insanity, 447; a case of chronological, 518.

Menopause, false notions of, 397.

Mental, panic, safeguards against, xiv; laziness and toxins, 8, 27; messages, between the cells, 8; messages, and stomach secretion, 9; causes of functional disorders, 12; safety brake, the, 12; dulness, and foul air, 23;

INDEX 559

vigor, lessened by overwork, 26; efficiency and diet, 27; perversity and metabolism, 30; conclusions, necessity for checking up, 38; errors, due to inaccuracies of sensation, 39; mastication, 40, 95; dyspepsia, 96; digestion, 96; malnutrition, 97; powers, effects of faith and fear on, 98; telepathy and healing, 101, 463; agitation and heart action, 119; depression and disease, 149; endurance, and the psychic state, 224; origin of nervous disorders, 231; energy and the psychic state, 273; obsessions, 341; uneasiness, results of, 346; concentration, a cause of worry, 349; work and worry, 358; drugs, or false teaching, 382; emancipation, 495.

Mental action, and motor reaction, 19, 271; retarded by fogs, 22; and muscular exercise, 25; governed by the will, 58; and metabolism, 29, 173; inaccuracies of, 38; in vital resistance, 269; and prayer, 476.

Mental diagnosis or psychoanalysis, 414; hypnotism in, 416; method of, 449; by the reaction method, 530.

Mental disorders, functional and organic, 292; in relation to psychotherapy, 304.

Mental healing, and religious superstition, 5.

Mental hygiene or psychoprophylaxis, 266.

Mental medicine, faith the master key to, 106; and moral hygiene, 311; separation from medicine and religion, 313.

Mental science and Christianity, 468.

Mental state, the, as influenced by acute and chronic disease, 31; in relation to consciousness, 68; and heart strength, 116; influence on blood-pressure, 131; on vital resistance, 143, 147; in relation to antitoxins, 147; and digestion, 161; and intestinal action, 169; and oxidation, 178; effect on muscles, 198; effects on brain, 220; and nutrition, 271.

Mental therapeutics, theory of, 68; in the cure of worry, 371.

Merriness, a therapeutic agent, 29, 325.

Merry heart, physical effects of, 329.

Mesmerism, (see hypnotism).

Messengers, chemical, of the blood, 7; the vital, 9.

Metabolic poisons, and the intellect, 27; disorders, functional and organic, 292; relation to psychotherapy, 304.

Metabolism, and the mind, 29; psychic factor in, 173; favored by deep breathing, 187; mental influence on, 271.

Metchnikoff, on gray hair, 234.

Method of practising reëducation, 448.

Microbes, intestinal, and mind, 29; in relation to faith and fear, 149.

Microscope, the emancipator of medicine, 35; in the study of disease, 260.

Midnight suppers, effects of, 26.

Migraine, in relation to the psychic state, 435.

Milk secretion, altered by anger, 146; mental factor in, 154, 159.

Milton, considered crazy, 285.

Mind, and matter, 3; differentiated, 3; what is it? 3; as related to the brain, 4, 17; how expressed, 4; the mother of thought, 4; power over matter, 4; holds balance of power, 10; supremacy of, 10; the monitor of health, 11; defined, 12; ancient views of, 15; relation to brain and personality, 16; the designer of personality, 17; brain, servant of, 17; as influenced by opium and alcohol, 17; compared to musician, 17; and brain size, 18; of man and monkey, 18; dominated by the will, 18; impress of, upon matter, 19; as influenced by bodily states, 21; and sunlight, 22; and the weather, 22; influenced by the stomach, 26; and biliousness, 27; and condiments, 28; and elimination, 30; as influenced by rest, 30; possibilities of deception, 45; and the will, 57, 58; dual nature of, 66, 73; the conscious, 66; process of "making up," 67; connects morals and matter, 73; comparison of conscious and subconscious, 73; as influenced by faith and fear, 73; and the circulation, 122; stamps its tone on the body, 148; and the secretory glands, 153; influence on respiration, 186; in asthma and hayfever, 194; and skin action, 209; and heat regulation, 209; and electric body reaction, 213; restored by determination, 222; and the nervous system, 229; and special senses, 241; in preventing disease, 266; in preventing indigestion, 270; and the muscles, 272; influence on animal heat, 273; in character development, 280; in functional and organic diseases, 290; in relation to contagions, 306; influenced by dreams, 408; the "new," 417; influenced by sugges-

INDEX

tion, 428; organization of, 444; in telepathy, 464; new, in old body, 487; and matter, struggle between, 487; simple life for, 495.
Mind cure, distorted by ignorance, 5; false, how avoided, 36; in imaginary diseases, 44; and reason, 50; fraudulent, compared to drugs, 381; modern, principles of, 405; prayer, the master, 476, 484.
Mind, the subconscious, 66; defined, 67; compared to the conscious, 74.
Ministers, relation to Christian science, 257; cooperation with physicians, 314.
Miracle workers, ancient, 83.
Miscellaneous diseases, functional and organic, 292.
Misconceptions, results of, 45.
Mission of pain, the, 294.
Mock worries, 383.
Modern psychotherapy, 35; evolution of, 255; therapeutics, scope of, 257; methods of investigating disease, 259; psychotherapeutic principles, 405.
Mohammed, convulsions of, 285.
Money, mania for getting, 431.
Monkey, brain of, 18.
Monks, as healers, 83.
Moods, changing, and complex formation, 410.
Moody, Mr., on welfare of the soul, 486.

Moon, and agriculture, 86.
Moral, despair from deficient elimination, 9; depression and sunshine, 22; nature and bad breathing, 25; freedom, of man, 50; plane, the, 69; suggestion, in nervous disorders, 233; therapeutics, necessity for, 257, 422; therapy, in relation to doctors, 258; hygiene, and mental medicine, 311; mastery, the, 311; causes of worry, 362; nutrition, the, 380; element in prayer, 477; emancipation, 500.
Morality, influenced by faith and fear, 99.
Morals, as influenced by disease, 21.
Moroseness, and the fear life, 109.
Morphine, and blood-pressure, 29, 133, 282; used by society, 499.
Morphinism, 307.
Mortification of the flesh, 489.
Moses, sanitary laws of, 312.
Mosso, Prof., on bodily reactions to fear, 19; on fear and fever, 433.
Mother, psychic influence on the unborn, 278; crushing care of, 366.
Motor, centres of brain, xi; reaction of consciousness, 19; "discharge," the path of, 339.

Mouth digestion, importance of, 155.
Mozart, obsessions of, 285.
Multiple personality, theory of, 411; a case of, 524.
Muscle, fatigue and the mind, 9; affected by the mental state, 198; reading, theory of, 206.
Muscles, of expression, 203; of mastication, 271; contraction of, in bed, 398.
Muscular exercise and mental action, 25; work, and the will, 59; movements of stomach, 166, 205; strength and endurance, 198; increased by confidence, 199; fatigue, and fear, 199; fatigue, psychic, 201; spasms, 202; relaxation, 202; sensation, 206; system, and the mind, 272.
Music, effects on digestion, 167; psychic factor in its enjoyment, 243; psychic influence of, 422; stimulating and depressing, 423.
Musical instrument, illustration of the brain, 17.

N

Narcotics, used by society, 499; periodical use of, 346.
Nations, factors in downfall, 494.
Natural reflexes, xiii, 509.
Nature, liberal provisions of, 17; of man, three-fold, 71; of sensations, psychic, 94; trust of, a worry cure, 377; does her best when unmolested, 396.
Nausea, psychic, 9.
Nero and the magi, 79.
Nerve, impressions, route to brain, xii; habits, how formed, 18; supply of active cells, 19; impulses, in relation to consciousness, 19; supply of the cell, 174; energy, conserved by joy, 223; centres, aroused by psychic power, 267; strain, finding cause of, 396; impulses, transmission of, 511.
Nerve cells, energy granules of, xiii; in brain and cord, 8; appearance in fatigue, 296.
Nerves, the cranial, xii, 508; living telegraph wires, 4; irritated by toxins, 8; the trophic, 234; conserved in mind cure, 301; "getting on," 393; anatomy and physiology of, 510.
Nervous, reflexes, the, xii; fatigue, from overwork, 9; control of heart, 116; dyspepsia, 167; control, and the mind, 230; strength, increased by optimism, 231; energy, and the mind, 233; equilibrium, 235, 399; paralysis, 236; tension, chronic, 346; rhythm of habit, 346; energy, excitable waste of,

INDEX

390; temper, 390; tension, extravagant, 393; control, the practice of, 396; shock, from fright, 419; patients treatment of, 450; cowardice, 454.

Nervous diseases, effect on mind, 33; psychic prevention of, 273; functional and organic, 292; in relation to psychotherapy, 304; increase of, 387; and suggestion, 435; caused by selfishness, 436.

Nervous mechanism, of the heart, 120; in blood-pressure, 140; of salivary secretion, 154; of pancreatic secretion, 158; of constipation, 170; of diarrhoea, 171; of breathing, 186, 196; of blushing, 212; of habit, 338.

Nervous prostration, blood-pressure in, 134; and worry, 362; defined, 388; purpose of, 392.

Nervous system, function of, xi; the voluntary, xiii; the sympathetic, xiv, 513; a means of cell communication, 8; gateway to the mind, 41; in relation to mind, 72, 229; effects of mind on, 229, 273; effects of emotions on, 229; physiology of, 505.

Nervousness, in relation to the mind, 239; a form of energy leakage, 344; and relaxation, 387; defined, 387; psychology of, 391; a short-circuit of sensation, 391; and selfishness, 394; not an actual disease, 397; royal remedy for, 401; methods of treatment, 401; hygienic management of, 402; influenced by prayer, 477.

Neuralgia, psychic cure of, 226.

Neurasthenia, and blood-pressure, 132, 134; cured by religion, 225; by socialism, 225; psychic cause of, 230, 231, 232; cured by a fire, 231; caused by worry, 297, 362; in relation to habit-sensation, 340; causes of, 388; of the change of life, 397; as related to dreams, 408; and complex formation, 410; and dissociation of ideas, 411; fatigue of, 419; work and rest cure in, 419; treatment by reëducation, 420; work and study cure, 421; caused by sleep-worry, 448; prayer in, 448.

Neurasthenic, the, 389.

Neuraxone, the, xiii.

Neuricity, xiii, 511.

Neuroglia, the, 510.

Neuron, anatomy of, xiii, 510; number of, 8; recuperated by rest, 30.

Neuroses, origin of, 447.

New birth of theology, 281; a case of, 479.

New remedies, as cure-alls, 260.

New thought, sectarian aspects of, 262; and mental science, 468.
Nightmare, subconscious, 412.
Nisel's granules, 512.
Noises, child's fear of, 277.
Non-drug healing, methods of, 440.
Notoriety, itching for, 496.
Novels, as mental diet, 497.
Nutrition, and the mental state, 29; psychic factors in, 173, 271; of the cell, 173; and digestion, 175; influenced by the affections, 177; appetite in, 179; of the skin, 214; nerves of, 234; disorders of, 292; the moral, 380.

O

Obsessions, the slavery of, 341; psychic, 341; the psychology of, 341; selfish factors in, 342; motor, 342; counting and walking, 343; and complex formation, 409.
Odors, fictitious, 242.
Oedema, caused by fear, 126; angioneurotic, and the mind, 127, 215.
Old age, worries of, 365; influenced by mind, 123.
Operations, fake, in nervous disorders, 437.
Opium, and brain action, 17; action modified by suggestion, 171, 206; effect on consciousness, 445; used by society, 499.

Optical illusions, 38.
Optimism, a factor in the faith life, 107; and vital resistance, 143; an energy conservator, 223; psychic capital stock, 224; a cure for hypochondria, 227.
Optimistic life, the, 93.
Order, a remedy for nervousness, 345; as an obsession, 345.
Orderliness, the craze for, 454.
Organic diseases, defined, 289; the mind in, 290; compared with functional, 291; evolved from functional, 295.
Organization of the mind, 444.
Origin of thought, the, 37; of sensation, psychic, 94; of the neuroses, 447.
Osler, Dr., on mind cure, 301; on faith, 315; on worry, 376.
Osteopaths, mission of, 225.
Osteopathy, sectarian role of, 262.
Outdoor living promotes mental health, 23.
Overcoming evil with good, 416.
Overeating, lessens mental energy, 27; and under thinking, 28.
Overwork, in relation to the mind, 9; reaction of, on mind and morals, 25.
Oxidase, 178.
Oxidation in the cell, 178; increased by faith, 271.

Oxygen, the vital fuel, 187; intake, effects on mind, 188.

P

Pagan ideas of healing, 79.
Pain, effects on mind, 32; origin of, 37; fictitious, 39, 45; increased by fear, 94; habitual, origin of, 95; inhibition of, 276, 239; psychic element in, 238; deceptive cure of, 239; not wholly psychic, 239; lessened by psychic control, 274; mission of, 294; lessened by relaxation, 399; suggestive treatment of, 434; of childbirth and suggestion, 434.
Pale skin and the mental state, 126; psychic causes of, 212.
Pallor, mechanism of, 212.
Palmistry, a fraud, 458.
Pancreas, the, 157.
Pancreatic juice, regulation of secretion, 7; nervous element in, 236.
Panics, psychology of, 283; suggestive, 286, 431.
Papules, psychic origin of, 215.
Paraesthesias, origin of, 95.
Paralysis, cured by suggestion, 237.
Parasites, and mind cure, 308.
Passion, emotional, 447; influenced by prayer, 478.
Patent medicine cures 103; deception of, 458.

Pathology, in diagnosis, 260.
Patience, and the faith life, 109.
Paul, a good psychologist, 285; teaching of, on faith and fear, 324; on auto-suggestion, 328; on mind and matter, 487-489.
Pawlow, work on digestion, 161, 162, 165; dogs, and physiological memory, 410.
Payot, on reflection and action, 452.
Pellagra, and mental diseases, 31.
Pepsin, action of, 167.
Perception, defined, 40, 52.
Percepts, as mental food, 39; defined, 52.
Periodic swelling, and the mind, 127.
Periodicity, in nervous rhythm, 346.
Peristalsis, and the mental state, 170.
Pernicious anaemia, and the psychic state, 144.
Personal magnetism, really suggestion, 430.
Personality, how maintained, 15; relation of, to the brain and mind, 16; designed by mind, 17; modified by habit, 18; multiple, theory of, 411; deformed by society, 498; multiple, a case of, 524.
Perspiration, psychic influence on, 213.
Perverted prayer, 482.

Pessimism, a factor in the fear life, 107.
Pessimist, a social barnacle, 224.
Phagocytosis, and the mind, 145.
Phantasy, defined, 42, 53; action of faith and fear on, 96.
Phases of consciousness, 64.
"Phobias," special, 359.
Phosphates of urine, influenced by mental state, 240.
Phototherapy, in connection with psychotherapy, 263.
Phrenic nerves, depressed by fear, 196.
Phrenology and healing, 103; scientific status of, 459.
Physical basis of thought, xv, 37, 39; endurance and respiration, 24; development and mental vigor, 25; senses, inaccuracies of, 38; origin of emotions, 41; consciousness, the, 71, 72; carriage, the, 200; causes of worry, 364, 366; health, and worry, 382; reaction to anger, 391; functions, influenced by prayer, 478; remedies, in relation to prayer, 483; emancipation, 495.
Physical diseases, and the mind, 21; and brain disorders, 31.
Physical righteousness and spirituality, 490.
Physical therapy, and the doctor, 258; in connection with psychotherapy, 263.
Physicians, neglect of psychotherapy, 251, 313; highest work of, 258; -priests, ancient, 311; coöperation with ministers, 314; relation to psychotherapy, 315; responsibility for the healing cults, 441.
Physiologic section, the, 111; therapeutics, progress of, 258.
Physiological unity of man, 6; coördination, 7; memory, theory of, 416; fatigue, theory of, 418; reaction, of emotion, 446.
Physiologist's, view of man, 10.
Physiology, of sympathetic nervous system, xiv; of habit, 338; of anger, 391; of prayer, 477; of brain and nervous system, 505.
Pituitary body, influence of secretion, 32; the, 184.
Placebos, a form of suggestion, 103.
Plague, fear element in, 270; the psychology of, 296.
Planes of consciousness, the, 69.
Plants, feeling of, 71.
Play, spirit of, lessens fatigue, 200.
Plethysmographic cure, the, 196.
Poisoning, in relation to psychotherapy, 307.

Poisons, acid, as a cause of sleep, xv; metabolic, and the mental state, 27; psychic, blood, 145; emotional, 146.
Pons varoli, the, 506.
"Poor circulation," psychic causes of, 210.
Portal congestion and the "blues," 24.
Positive thinking, auto-suggestion, 372.
Poverty, in relation to worry, 367.
Power of mind over matter, 4; of memory, 45.
Practice of nervous control, the, 396.
Prayer, healing, rise of, 83; as a healing influence, 101; in faith healing, 107; cure for despondency, 181; cure for nervous disorders, 233; in paralysis, 237; as a worry cure, 380; psychology of, 476; the master mind cure, 476, 484; mental factor in, 476; moral element in, 477; strengthens the will, 477; spiritual factor in, 477; physiology of, 477; effects on blood-pressure, 477; therapeutics of, 478; transforms the character, 479; cure, the, 480; method of prescribing, 481; prostitution of, 481; relaxation of, 483; inspiration of, 483; and physical remedies, 483; a psychic safety-valve, 484.

Preachers, neglect of mental medicine, 313.
Prejudice, working of, 496.
Prenatal influences, psychic elements of, 277.
Prevention of disease, 258.
Priests, ancient physician, 311.
Prince, Dr., on multiple personality, 524.
Principles of psychotherapy, 405.
Process of heat regulation, 216.
Prolapsus, visceral, and the mental state, 207.
Prophets, professed, origin of, 461.
Prophylaxis, the doctor's great work, 258.
Prostitution of prayer, 481.
Protein diet, high, effects on mind, 29.
Proverbs, perverted, a cause of worry, 355.
Providence in relation to disease, 84, 323.
Psalmist, the, on fear, 323.
Psychasthenic, the, 389.
Psychic, influence over gastric secretion, 9; origin of sensation, 94; response of the heart, 119; modification of blood-pressure, 131, 138; state, as influenced by religion, 140; blood poisons, 145; influence on antitoxins, 147; over secretions, 153; dyspepsia, 163; "juice," the, 165, 270; factor, in nutri-

Psychic — *continued*
tion, 173; fads and dyspepsia, 176; control of appetite, 179; coughing, 191; control of muscles, 198; fatigue, 201; control of electric reactions, 214; state, effects on brain, 220; cure of paralytics, 237; disorders, neglect of, 255; cults, mission of, 256; therapy, in relation to physicians, 258; teaching, the new, 260; prisoners, 261; powers, limitations of, 267; element, in the circulation, 268; influence on sensation, 274; element in heredity and environment, 276; factor in intemperance, 281; disorders, evolution into physical, 295; element in disease, 300; obsessions, 341; deceptions, 381; shocks, and insanity, 408; insurrection, 412, 413; fatigue, theory of, 418; influence of music, 422; desperadoes, 447; fads and fakes, 467; difficulties and prayer, 480; element in moral victory, 490; slavery of conventionality, 496.

Psycho-analysis, or mental diagnosis, 414; method of applying, 415, 416; in relation to reëducation, 448.

Psychologic section, the, 3.

Psychologist's, view of man, 10.

Psychology, how we think, 35; modern, 35; new and old, 36; diagram of, 52; defined, 55; of faith and fear, 92; evolution of, 255; basis of, 261; of child-culture, 276; of the family life, 282; of business, 283; of panics, 283; of the crowd, 286; of disease, the, 289; of epidemics, 296; of health literature, 296; of fatigue, 297; of love and hate, 298; of habit, 338, 339; of worry, 350; of animal tricks, 350; of emotion, 414; of suggestion, 428; of shell-hearing and crystal-gazing, 460; of automatic writing and talking, 462; of telepathy, 463; of hypnotism, 470; of Christian Science, 471; of prayer, 476.

Psycho-neuroses, 415.

Psychopath, the, mission of, 256.

Psycho-pathological fatigue, theory of, 418.

Psycho-prophylaxis, or mental hygiene, 266.

Psychotherapy, retarded by superstition, 5; fanatical transition stage, 256; dawn of, 260; laboratory basis of, 261; prostituted by theology, 262; and hygiene, 262; not an exclusive system, 262; in functional diseases, 290; in various disorders, 302; in heart disorders, 302; in cir-

culatory disorders, 302; in digestive disturbances, 303; in mental and nervous diseases, 304; in respiratory disorders, 305; in metabolic disorders, 305; in miscellaneous diseases, 305; in contagious and infectious diseases, 306; in accidents and poisoning, 307; in intoxications, 307; and parasites, 308; of the ancient priests, 312; the Bible on, 321; principles of, 405; defined, 405; the field of, 406; in relation to prayer, 477; Christianity, the highest, 484.
Pulse, intermittent, and fear, 115; the, 129; tracings of faith and fear, 129.
Pure air and the intellect, 22; food and pure thoughts, 27.

Q

Quack doctors and healing, 103.
Quackery, psychic element in, 458.
Quick lunch dyspepsia, 163.
Quinine, in malaria, 259, 267.

R

Rabies, false, 227.
Rationalisms, reaction from, 257.
"Reaction method" in mental diagnosis, 530.

Reason, and judgment, 49; defined, 49, 54; inaccuracies of, 50; attorney general of the mind, 57; voice of, 65, 70; and consciousnes, 74; in relation to faith and fear, 98; and sophistry, 473.
Reckoning, the gospel of, 488.
Recollection, doorkeeper of memory, 46, 53.
Recreation and the mind, 30; psychic value of, 383.
Red blood corpuscles and the mind, 143.
Reëducation, of brain centres, 17; and habit, 338; of the will, in nervousness, 401; and suggestion, 417; the goal of psychotherapy, 418; by direct conversation, 419; of the will, 443; defined, 444; Dr. Barker on, 445; methods of, 448; range, 450; in relation to hypnotism and suggestion, 451; system in, 453.
Reflection, a part of conception, 44, 53; and action, 45.
Reflex action, defined, xii, 508.
Reflexes, the nervous, xii; automatic, xii, 509; natural, xiii, 509; spinal, xiii, 509.
Reform, obsession of, 342.
Relative anæmias, 145.
Relaxation, muscular, 202; a cure for chorea, 230; and nervousness, 387; gospel of, 397; in bed, 398; insomnia remedy, 398; versus resis-

Relaxation — *continued*
tance, 399; a factor in prayer, 483.

Relics, a health delusion, 82; worship of, 100; psychic frauds, 457.

Religion, a mind cure, 44; a natural instinct, 61; in relation to faith, 100; and blood-pressure, 137, 139; a dyspepsia cure, 176; effects on healing, 176; cure for despondency, 181; a cure for neurasthenia, 225; Christian, and mind cure, 284; psychotherapeutic value of, 315, 383; as a drink cure, 319; in relation to worry, 362, 380; "going crazy over," 365; the, of fear, 401; the, of love, 401; Christian, the highest psychotherapy, 484; as influenced by health, 490; value of, 501.

Religious, worry and blood-pressure, 135; emotion, power of, 204, 414, 422; life, the, 316; suggestions, power of, 317; fanaticism and worry, 363; conversions, 417; revivals, suggestion in, 430; movements, built on trances, 461; worry, 485.

Remorse, and the fear life, 109.

Reptiles, overcoming fear of, 374.

Resistance, vital, and the mind, 147; muscular, replaced by relaxation, 399.

Respiration, effects on mind and body, 24; influence on oxidation, 178; psychic influences on, 186; centres of, 196.

Respiratory, poisons, effects of, 23; curve, the, 195; disorders, functional and organic, 292; in relation to psychotherapy, 305.

Responsibility, a cause of worry, 353.

Rest, in relation to mind, 30; essential to mind, 31; cure, the, in chronic fatigue, 419.

Resurrection, the spiritual, 489.

Retention, a power of memory, 46, 53.

Revivals, suggestion in, 430.

Rhythm, nervous, of habit, 346.

Richardson, Dr., on diabetes, 159.

Riches, false source of happiness, 352; delusion of, 498.

Rickets, influence on mind, 32.

Ridicule, in the cure of worry, 374.

Right-handedness, and the brain, 16.

Righteousness, physical and spiritual, 490.

Rush, useless, 395.

S.

Sabbath rest, psychic value of, 31.

Saints, the, as healers, 82.
Saliva, modified by mental state, 154, 155; secretory mechanism of, 154; a metabolic factor, 155; digestive powers of, 156; memory secretion of, 410.
Salivary secretion and the mind, 154; flow, retarded by fear, 156.
Sample Stomach of Pawlow, 165.
Sanitation, in relation to psychotherapy, 264.
Schiller, on psycho-prophylaxis, 269; obsession of, 285.
Schools of medicine, suggestion in, 430.
Schopenhauer, shaving obsession of, 285.
Science of suggestion, the, 427.
Scientific healing, dawn of, 253.
Scope of modern therapeutics, 251.
Scrofula and the king's touch, 87.
"Secretin," 7; role of, 158.
Secretions, as chemical messengers, 7; modified by fear, 146; mental factor in, 153, 270; in general, 153; effects of music on, 167.
Secretory glands and the mind, 153; disturbances, functional and organic, 291; in relation to psychotherapy, 303; physiological memory of, glands, 410.
Sedentary life, the, and despondency, 22.
Self-consciousness, a cause of worry, 358.
Self-control, need of, 345, 373; a remedy for nervousness, 401; and the emotions, 447; and the health, 497.
Selfishness, duty to combat, 378; and false sympathy, 394; a cause of nervous disorders, 436.
Self-mastery, 452.
Self-mutilation, 413.
Sensations, of sight, 37; of hearing, 37; of taste, 37; of pain, origin, 37, 239; defined, 37, 52; inaccuracies of, 38; fictitious, 39, 94, 406; route through the mind, 42; modified by faith and fear, 93, 216; psychic origin of, 94, 246; referred to the heart, 120; psychic deception of, 125; muscular, 206; skin, and the mind, 215; of heat and cold, 216; experiments respecting, 246; in habit formation, 340; a factor in worry, 358; necessity for discounting, 375; double origin of, 432.
Sense of smell, how stimulated, 37; impressions, necessity for checking up, 38.
Sensitiveness, a cause of worry, 353.

Sensory impressions, how transmitted, xiii.
Sexual glands, secretion of, 32.
Shakespear, on man's mental vision, 350.
Shallow breathing, and shallow thinking, 24, 186.
"Sham feeding" of Pawlow, 165.
Shell-hearing, psychology of, 460.
Shrines, and healing, 83; worship, 102; psychic frauds, 457.
Sickness, influenced by the mind, 21; in general, 150; a result of sin, 318; the Bible on, 321; in relation to worry, 364.
Sighing, from mental depression, 194.
Sight, how aroused, 37; inaccuracies of, 38; psychic element in, 244; deceptive stimulation of, 407; function of, 515.
Significance of high blood-pressure, 132.
Simple life, the, for the mind, 495; for the body, 495; for the community, 497; for the home, 499; for the soul, 500.
Simplicity, the joy of life, 496.
Sin, as a cause of sickness, 318; a happiness destroyer, 318.
Size of brain in relation to intellect, 18.

Skin, inactivity, and depression, 9; action, and the mind, 30, 211; circulation and worry, 124; reaction, 124; influence of mind on, 209; area of, 209; circulation, 210, 211; nutrition of, 214; sensation and eruptions, 215.
Slavery of obsessions, 34; psychic, 496.
Sleep, how caused, xv; and digestion, 26; and stomach motility, 27; in relation to consciousness, 74; walkers, 207; antidote for work, 223; relaxation during, 398; relation to dissociation, 412; and suggestion, 438; false notions of necessity, 448; relation to hearing, 516.
Sleepiness, theory of, xv; from deficient elimination, 9.
Sleeping rooms, ventilation of, 23.
Sleeplessness, from autointoxication, 29; cured by indifference concerning, 378.
Slow digestion, 167.
Slums, relation of physical and moral conditions, 22.
Smell, in relation to digestion. 9; arousal of, 37; psychic element in, 242; experimental tests of, 243; suggestive experiments on, 438; sense of, 516.
Smelling, sense of, 516.
Snakes, overcoming fear of, 374.

Sneezing, and the psychic state, 193.
Social life, early, and suggestion, 279; cause of worry, 366; emancipation, 497.
Socialism, as a neurasthenic cure, 225.
Society, effects on health, 497; in relation to narcotics, 499.
Socrates, fits of, 284.
Soil of disease, the, 149.
Solar plexus, the, xiv, 513.
Solomon, on faith and fear, 325.
Sorrow, effects on nutrition, 174, 175; a cause of infirmity, 360.
Soul, the, 40; unconsciousness of, when all is well, 486; simple life for, 500.
Sound, recognition of, 65; illustration of psychic operations, 65; fictitious, 244.
Sovereign will, the, 56.
Spasms, ancient cures for, 87; muscular, 202.
Special senses, influence of mind on, 241; and suggestion, 438; functions of, 514.
Speech, not originated by brain, 16; and work memory centres, 16; centres, accidents to, 17; psychic element in, 247, 274.
Spinal nerves, xii; ganglion, xii, 507; cord, anatomy of, xii, 507; reflexes, xiii.
Spirit, the, defined, 55; of fear, the, 332; of infirmity, 360; the universal, and telepathy, 465.
Spiritistic deluge, the, 256.
Spiritual factor in mind, 61; mind, the, 64, 69; consciousness, 70, 72; therapeutics, and physicians, 258; causes of worry, 362; nutrition, and worry, 380; factor in prayer, 477; grief, 485; nature, war with the carnal, 487; resurrection, the, 489; living, and physical righteousness, 490.
Spiritualism, and healing, 103; genuine and false, 466; scientific view of, 467; a theological proposition, 467; Biblical view of, 467.
Steps, obsession of counting, 344.
Stimulants, periodic use of, 347.
Stomach, and the psychic state, 9; action, and brain action, compared, 16; influence upon mind, 26; action, and sleep, 27; effects of mind on, 162, 166; muscular movements of, 166, 205; disorders, in relation to psychotherapy, 303.
" Stomach-ache in the head," 26; ancient cures for, 80.
"Stoop shoulders," and the mental state, 189, 190, 201.
Storms, unreasoning fear of, 395.
Strain, needless, 395.

Strength, decreased by fear, 199; and suggestion, 432; dependent on nerve impressions, 433.

Strength test, modified by the mental state, 199.

Study cure, the, in nervous disorders, 421.

St. Benedict, as a surgeon, 82; Martin, a reputed healer, 82.

St. Vitus's dance, and the mental state, 230.

Subconscious mind, the, 66; defined, 67; compared with the conscious, 74; and latent ideas, 416; tyranny of, 428; a creature of suggestion, 429; unused energy of, 432; effect of drugs on, 455; in trances and catalepsy, 461 and mediums, 466; memory, a case of, 523.

Subconscious nightmare, 412.

Substitute cure, the, for worry, 373.

Sugar, pills, power to cure, 104; in urine, increased by fear, 157; variation of, in diabetes, 179.

Suggestion, in relation to consciousness, 75; in diabetes, 158; effects on mammary secretion, 159; in dyspepsia, 164; in constipation, 171; and sneezing, 193; and yawning, 194; in asthma and hay-fever, 194; and valvanometer experiments, 201; in skin disorders, 215; in nervous disorders, 233, 435; in paralysis, 237; in the cure of pain, 239, 434; in relation to vision, 245; in early social life, 279; in habit formation, 280; in the family life, 282; intensified by numbers, 286; and health literature, 296; religious, power of, 317; the Bible on, 327; in the case of Job, 330; a cause of disease, 365; in medical books, 366; in the treatment of worry, 371; true and false, 372; at retiring time, 378; fatigue, 392; and the menopause, 397; in hysteria, 412; a factor in physical remedies, 418; in the healing cults, 418; and patent medicines, 418, 458; in the cure of fictitious fatigue, 419; the science of, 427; direct and indirect, 427; in children, 427; and faith, 427; psychology of, 428; in relation to death, 428; and the marginal consciousness, 429; by direct challenge, 429; idea-association by, 429; the universality of, 429; best made in the working state, 429; hypnotism unnecessary to, 430; in the child's bumps, 430; in professional life, 430; in revivals, 430; and personal magnetism, 430; should be physiological and psychological, 430; in different

INDEX

schools of healing, 430; a mental contagion, 431; in electric belts, 431; in sleeping children, 432; the path to new energy, 432; in relation to health, 432; and the temperature sense, 433; in headache, 434; a factor in medicines, 435; and sleep, 438; and the special senses, 438; in obscure diseases, 439; in relation to reëducation, 451; in charms and relics, 457; in quackery, 458; in astrology and palmistry, 458; in phrenology, 459; in clairvoyance and fortune-telling, 459; in telepathy, 463; in magnetic healing, 465; and spiritualistic mediums, 466; in so-called Divine healing, 467; a factor in prayer, 477; adverse, in prayer, 482.

Suggestion, auto, hygienic value, 301.

Suggestive therapeutics, theory of, 68, 102, 103; imaginations and dreams, 408; reeducation, 417; panic, 431.

Suicide, mental, how prevented, 12.

Summary of faith and fear, on the heart, 121; on the circulation, 129; on blood-pressure, 142; on vital resistance, 151; on secretion, 160; on digestion, 171; on metabolism, 185; on breathing, 197; on muscles, 207; on skin and heat regulation, 218; on the brain, 228; on the nervous system, 240; on the special senses, 248; on the whole man, 249; Biblical, 335.

Sunlight, and the mind, 22.

Sunstroke, psychic element in, 227.

Supernatural elements of faith, 140.

Superstition, and ancient errors, 5; regarding diseases, 35; as related to health, 78; examples of ancient medical, 80; and insanity, 88; medical, 88, 90.

Supra consciousness, or the spiritual mind, 64, 65; analysis of, 72.

Suprarenal gland, secretion of, 32; bodies, the, 183.

Supremacy of mind, the, 10.

Supreme, court of the mind, 56; Being, faith in, a worry cure, 371, 381.

Surgical operations and the mental state, 149; diseases, and mind cure, 308.

Suspicion and the fear life, 108.

Sweat, altered by the mind, 154; glands, 213.

Sweating, psychic influence on, 213.

"Swellings," caused by fear, 126.

Sympathetic nervous system, the, xiv, 513; functions of,

Sympathetic — *continued*
xiv, 513; nature's safety-brake, 12; and fatigue, 59; in relation to the mind, 72; and heart control, 120.
"Sympathetic power" cures, 87
Sympathy, false, and selfishness, 394.
Syphilis and brain disorders, 31.
System and order, 345; in thought and work, 453.

T

Talent, in relation to consciousness, 75.
Talking, automatic, psychology of, 462.
Taste, in relation to stomach secretion, 9; sense of, how aroused, 37; metabolic regulator, 156; buds, and digestion, 156; psychic factors in, 241; sense of, 516.
Tea, effects on nerves, 28; and capillary contraction, 123.
Tear gland and the emotions, 154.
Telegraph, an illustration of mental operations, 16.
Telepathy, and healing, 102; theory of, 463; the physics of, 463; compared to gravitation, 464.
Temper, as influenced by fogs, 22; effect on bowels, 170; the Bible on, 326; nervous, 390.
Temperament, in relation to exercise, 25; effected by faith and fear, 99; peculiarities of, worry over, 352.
Temperamental shortcomings, 283.
Temperature, and atmospheric purity, 23; sense, deception of, 125; local, influenced by mental concentration, 126; sense, the, 216; modified by will power, 218; influenced by suggestion, 433.
Temple sleep, 81; and healing, 101.
Temptation, defined, 54, 61.
Tension, chronic, nervous, 346; extravagant, nervous, 393.
Theatre-going and nervous disorders, 421.
Theological prostitution of psychotherapy, 262.
Theology, separation from therapeutics, 312; differentiated from Christianity, 317.
Therapeutics, suggestive, theory of, 68; section, 251; evolution of, 254; fads in, mission of, 255; scope of, 257; physiologic, progress of, 258; divorcement from theology, 312; moral, 422; music in, 422; of prayer, 478.
Thermal sense, experiments on, 247.

INDEX

Thermo-electric body temperature, 217; -therapy, in connection with psychotherapy, 263.

Thinking, the process of, xv; compared to digestion, 4; as related to the brain, 17; in relation to eating, 26, 27; inaccuracies of, 38; increased on retiring, 398.

Thirst, significance of, 19.

"Thorns in the flesh," mission of, 284.

Thought, physical basis of, xv, 37, 39; not secreted by the brain, 16; dominated by the will, 18; crowning act of, 50; the mechanism of, 340; weak habits of, 401; system in, 453.

Thoughts, responsibility for, 57; relation to consciousness, 68; replace diseased with healthy, 377.

Three-fold, consciousness, the, 69; nature of man, 71.

Throat, fear-paralysis of, 206.

Thymis gland, secretion of, 32.

Thyroid gland, secretion, 32; the, 183.

Timidity, a cause of worry, 352.

Tobacco and blood-pressure, 29; and capillary contraction, 123; effects on smell, 516.

Tolstoi, effects at flying, 285; on faith, 315.

Tongue, coated, causes of, 156.

Tongues, the gift of, 463.

Toothache, ancient cure for, 87; psychic cure of, 226.

Torpid liver and brain action, 27.

Touch, sense of, 516.

Townshend, Col., and heart control, 118.

Toxins, 8; effects on mental action, 29; in constipation, 123; effect on white blood-cells, 144; a cause of nervousness, 388.

Train riding, without resistance, 400.

Trances, physiology and psychology of, 461.

Treatment, modern, of disease, 258; of worry, the physical, 383; of nervousness, 401; of fatigue states, 418.

Trifles, magnification of, 354.

Trophic nerves, the, 234.

Trouble, imaginary, 367; passing nature of, 376; practice of sleeping over, 380; really non-existent, 401.

Tuberculosis and chest development, 189.

Tumors, ancient cures of, 87.

Typhoid fever and brain disorders, 31.

Tyranny of habit, the, 340.

U

Ulcers, caused by suggestion, 235.

Unconscious mind, the (see marginal consciousness,).
Unity of the individual, 6.
Universal intelligence and telepathy, 464.
Universality of suggestion, 429.
Unreal sensations and disease, 45.
Unselfishness, a cure for worry, 378.
Urine, altered by the mental state, 154, 159; in diabetes, modified by mind, 157; secretion influenced by mental action, 159.

V

Vacation, essential to good work, 31; good effects of, on digestion, 163; improves metabolism, 180; value of, 380; a necessity when dreaming of your work, 497.
Vacillation, and the fear life, 109.
Vagus nerves and pancreatic secretion, 159.
Varicose veins and suggestion, 128.
Vasoconstrictor nerves, function of, 125, 212.
Vasodilator nerves, action of, 212.
Ventilation, influence on mind and body, 22; of schoolrooms, 23.
Vibrotherapy in connection with psychotherapy, 263.

Vice, a cause of sickness, 318.
Victory, effects on health, 150; spiritual, psychic element in, 490.
Visceral circulation and the emotions, 41; displacements and the mental state, 207.
Vision, errors of, 38; an illustration of psychic operations, 66; functions of, 515.
Visions, the psychology of, 461.
Vital messengers, the, 9; work, and the will, 60; energy, 150; resistance and the mind, 143, 147, 269; energies, conserved by faith, 223; seepage, 344.
Voice, of conscience, the, 69; of reason, the, 70.
Voluntary nervous system, the, xiii; in relation to mind, 72.
Vomiting centres and the mind, 169.

W

Wagner, considered insane, 285.
Warts, ancient cures for, 80; in relation to mind cure, 215.
Water, drinking and the mental state, 29; 30; in the treatment of disease, 255.
Watermelons, superstition regarding, 168.
Weapon ointment cure, 87.
Weariness and the mental state, 204.

INDEX

Weather, effects on mind and morals, 22; worry regarding, 353.
Weight, bodily, and the mind, 180.
Wetting the bed, and suggestion, 160.
White blood cells, the, 144.
Whooping cough and fear, 193.
Wild oats, mental harvest of, 33.
Will, the, dominates the intellect, 18, 67; defined, 55, 57, 76; sovereign, 56; sensory motor, 56; idea-motor, 56; spontaneous impulse, 56; deliberate, 56; functions of, 57; and the mind, 57; and personality, 57; ranking officer of intellect, 58; and the body, 59; and vital work, 60; a psychic stimulant, 267; in character development, 280; reëducation of, in nervousness, 401; reëducation, the goal of psychotherapy, 418; reëducation of, 443; overridden by strong emotions, 446; in relation to prayer, 477; method of reëducation, 449.
Will power, and thinking, 18; forms of, 56; and self control, 57; in the cure of invalidism, 204.
Witchcraft, 6, 317; ancient cure for, 80; and telepathy, 463.
Women, nervous and excitable, 390; nervous tension of, 393; as professional invalids, 394; talking propensity of, 396; and insanity, 397; and the use of narcotics, 499.
Word-memory centres, 16; how arranged, 18.
Words, not created by brain, 16; not essential to expression, 41.
Work, improves metabolism, 180; capacity for, 204; cure, in neurasthenia, 419; in nervous disorders, 421; in relation to prayer, 483; system in, 453.
Worms and mind cure, 308.
Worries, necessity for pinning down, 376.
Worry, caused by bad breathing, 24; caused by the physical state, 33; in relation to consciousness, 74; and the fear life, 108; a cause of heart disease, 118; and the circulation, 123; and blood-pressure, 135; in missionary work, 135; a cause of drinking, 137; a cause of anæmia, 145; a hair destroyer, 148; a cause of death, 148; effects on digestive secretions, 156, 161, 166, 205; and dyspepsia, 167; and nutrition, 174; effects on goitre, 183; paralyzing to muscles, 198, 202; a beauty killer, 209; and heat prostration, 213;

INDEX

Worry — *continued*
a cause of boils, 214; and gray hair, 214; and the skin, 215; and brain circulation, 221; and brain rest, 222; not neutralized by sleep, 223; a cause of brain-fag, 224; a cause of neurasthenia, 231, 362; and nerve starvation, 234; and baldness, 234; and paralysis, 237; a mind destroyer, 266; disguised as discretion, 281; a cause of high blood-pressure, 282; the fatigue of, 297; a happiness destroyer, 318; the Bible on, 327; among Christians, 332; nature and cause of, 349; defined, 349; a form of fear, 350; psychology of, 350; general causes of, 351; and alcohol, 351; due to happiness-hunger, 351; over temperamental peculiarities, 352; natural causes of, 354; over trifles, 354; the growth of, 355; enjoyed by some, 355; over perverted proverbs 355; circle, the, 357; and self-consciousness, 358; and mental work, 358; a cause of infirmity, 360; fictitious, 361, 376; and hypochondria, 362; moral causes of, 362; and religious fanaticism, 363; physical causes of, 364; dependent on age, 364; and health fads, 365; social causes of, 366; industrial causes of, 367; the cure of, 371; overcoming, 373; cured by self-control, 373; fear, the ancestor of, 374; not cured by resistance, 375; cured by trusting nature, 377; by combating selfishness, 378; cured by children, 379; religion and prayer in the cure of 380, 383; delusion of drugs in, 381; cured by improving health, 382; physical treatment of, 383; and fads, 383; removed by mental surrender, 399; and dreams, 408; in relation to associative memories, 409; and complex formation, 409; over insomnia, 448; prevented by prayer, 477; religious, 485.

Wounds, healing, and the mind, 150.

Writing, automatic, psychology of, 462.

X

X-ray, observation of digestive movements, 166, 167; of bowel action, 171, 205; and psychotherapy, 263.

Y

Yawning, and hiccoughing, 193; and suggestion, 194.

Z

Zeal, misguided, results of, 363.

Zodiac, signs of, in disease, 86.